Stan Armington

Stan has been organising and leading treks in Nepal since 1971. A graduate engineer, he has also worked for the US National Park Service in the Yellowstone and Olympic parks, as well as serving as a guide on Mt Hood in Oregon. Stan is a fellow of the Royal Geographical Society, and a member of the American Alpine Club, the Explorers Club, and the Alpine Stomach Club. He lives in Kathmandu where he spends his time opening new bars and trekking companies.

From the Author

A word of thanks to the many people who encouraged and assisted me with writing this book. Sushil Upadhyay, Shanan Miller, Bob Pierce, Chuck McDougal, Yangdu Gombu, Bruce Klepinger, Gil Roberts, Erica Stone, Dana Keil, Harka Gurung, Elizabeth Hawley, Jim Williams, Lila Bishop, Richard Irvin, Ann Sainsbury, Sergio Fitch Watkins, Brian Weirum, Daniel Tamang, Alison Stone and Jungly John were all a great help. They provided me with information about recent changes, places I had not been, or things I did not understand, and they checked my version of facts for accuracy. Hundreds of trekkers have helped me by asking questions that I would never have thought of otherwise.

This book could never have been written without the help of the many sherpas who led me up and down hills and patiently answered my questions about what we were seeing. Passang Geljen, Dawa Lama, Pemba, Ang Mingma, Passang Temba, Bhakta Raj, Phorba Sonam and Nawang Chuldim helped with this edition.

David Shlim's medical chapter gives a first-class analysis of the medical problems of a trek, and Lewis Underwood wrote the many Flora & Fauna sections throughout the book.

Many people provided assistance and information about the Mustang trek. Broughton Coburn accompanied the one-week dash to Lo Manthang when permits cost $500 per week, or part thereof. Thomas Laird provided hospitality, introductions and a bottle of scotch in Lo Manthang. Professor

Trilok Chandra Majupuria assisted with research and mapping. The Lo raja, his secretary, Chandra Bahadur Thakali, and our horseman, Tashi Wangel, were particularly helpful and patient with all my queries.

During the exploratory trip to Tibet, Karchung of Ngari Travels and Sangey Tenzing of Purang Guest House kept us moving and fed, as did our guide, Kelsang. Choying Dorje, better known as 'Kailas Dorje', assisted in Darchan and later helped correct the information about Ngari. During that trip our sirdar, Bhakta Gurung, managed to keep us moving and our cook, Babu Ram Bhattarai, prepared outstanding meals under some truly appalling conditions. Our Humli guide, Kunga Dorje, provided extraordinary insight and assistance.

Once again, thanks to Tony and Maureen Wheeler, who pushed me to tackle this project and continue to provide suggestions on how to improve it. Tony also is responsible for the tipping guidelines for group trekkers.

Thanks to Cambridge University Press for permission to quote four lines from *Nepal Himalaya* by H W Tilma, and to Barry Bishop from *National Geographic* and Art

Lange from Trimble Navigation who helped me understand the complications of the Global Positioning System.

Thanks also to *Himal* magazine for allowing me to use an article on the Arun Power Project, and the 1991 Cambridge & Southampton Joint Universities Himalayan Research Expedition for supplying the Ghandruk village map.

Brown (Aus), Kate Morris (UK), J Nield (HK).

Many other readers' contributions are acknowledged in Lonely Planet's *Nepal – a travel survival kit*.

Aus – Australia, Can – Canada, CH – Switzerland, HK – Hong Kong, NL – Netherlands, UK – United Kindom, US – United States of America.

From the Publisher

This edition of *Trekking in the Nepal Himalaya* was edited by Miriam Cannell. Glenn Beanland was responsible for the design, layout and mapping, and Jane Hart designed the cover. Thanks to Diana Saad for proofreading, Rachel Black for help with layout and Chris Lee Ack for help with mapping. Thanks also to Rob Flynn for computer troubleshooting.

Thanks to the following trekkers who have written to us with new information and helpful suggestions: Serge Abramowski (CH) & Friederike Tschampa (CH), Rachel Rosen (Can), James Earl (Aus), Iztok Turel (Slovenija), Sharon Kinsman (US), Frank van der Gun (NL), Martin Charlton, David

Warning & Request

Things change, prices go up, schedules change, trails disappear, good places go bad and bad ones go bankrupt – nothing stays the same. So, if you find things better or worse, recently opened or long since closed, please tell us. Write to Lonely Planet, or to the author, c/o Malla Treks, PO Box 5227, Kathmandu, Nepal.

Between editions, when it is possible, we'll publish the most interesting letters and important information in a Stop Press section at the back of the book. All information is greatly appreciated, and the best letters will receive a free copy of the next edition. We give away lots of books, but unfortunately not every letter/postcard receives one.

Contents

Map Legend

BOUNDARIES

...............International Boundary
...............Internal Boundary
...............Disputed Boundary

ROUTES

...............Freeway
...............Highway
...............Major Road
...............Unsealed Road or Track
...............City Road
...............City Street
...............Railway
...............Walking Track
...............Cross-Country Route
...............Ferry Route
...............Cable Car or Chairlift

AREA FEATURES

...............Park, Gardens
...............National Park
...............Built-Up Area
...............Pedestrian Mall
...............Market
...............Cemetery
...............Glacier
...............Beach or Desert
...............Rocks

HYDROGRAPHIC FEATURES

...............Coastline
...............River, Creek
...............Intermittent River or Creek
...............Lake, Intermittent Lake
...............Canal
...............Swamp

SYMBOLS

✪ **CAPITAL**		...............National Capital
◉ **Capital**		...............State Capital
⊘ **CITY**		...............Major City
● **CITY**		...............City
● Town		...............Town
● Village		...............Village
■		....Hotel, Pension (Place to Stay)
▼		...........Restaurant (Place to Eat)
☻		...........Pub, Bar (Place to Drink)
✉	☎	...............Post Office, Telephone
❶	❸	...........Tourist Information, Bank
⊖	℗	...............Transport, Parking
⏛	⛺	...............Museum, Youth Hostel
⊞	⛺	Caravan Park, Camping Ground
†	⊡ †	...............Church, Cathedral
☪	✡	...............Mosque, Synagogue
⊥	⛩	...............Temple, Stupa

✈		...............Airport or Airfield
✛	★	...............Hospital, Police Station
◩	✿	...........Swimming Pool, Gardens
❖	🐘	...............Shopping Centre, Zoo
⚲	⌐	...Winery or Vineyard, Picnic Site
←	A25	One Way Street, Route Number
∴		.......Archaeological Site or Ruins
⏠	⚑	...........Stately Home, Monument
⚎	⊡	...............Castle, Tomb
⌢	⌂	...................Cave, Hut or Chalet
△	※	...........Mountain or Hill, Lookout
⚓	⚓	...............Lighthouse, Shipwreck
)(	⚭	...............Pass, Spring
		...............Ridge
		...............Rapids, Waterfalls
		.......Cliff or Escarpment, Tunnel
		...............Railway Station

Note: not all symbols displayed above appear in this book

Preface

To travel in the remote areas of Nepal today offers much more than superb mountain scenery. It provides an opportunity to step back in time and meet people who, like our ancestors many centuries ago, lived free of complications, social, economic and political, which beset the developed countries. To the Nepal peasant, his life revolves around his homestead, his fields and, above all, his family and neighbours in the little village perched high on a Himalayan mountainside. Here we can see the meaning of community, free of the drive of competition. We see human happiness despite – or because of – the absence of amenities furnished by our modern civilisation.

Change will come to the Nepalese way of life, but it behoves travellers from the modernised countries to understand and respect the values and virtues of life today in rural Nepal. They have much to teach us about how to live.

John Hunt

Lord Hunt was the leader of the 1953 Mt Everest expedition when Sir Edmund Hillary and Tenzing Norgay Sherpa scaled the peak for the first time.

Introduction

The Himalaya, the 'abode of snows', extends from Assam in eastern India west to Afghanistan. It is a chain of the highest and youngest mountains on earth and it encompasses a region of deep religious and cultural traditions and an amazing diversity of people. Nowhere is this diversity more apparent and the culture more varied and complex than in Nepal. This book concentrates on trekking in Nepal – not quite the same experience as trekking in the Himalaya of India, Pakistan and China, even though the traditions may be similar.

A trek in Nepal is a special and rewarding mountain holiday. Do not lose sight of this as you read about the problems you may encounter and the formalities you must cope with to arrange a trek. These sound worse than they really are.

If you trek on your own, remember that you will be far from civilisation as you know it (including medical care, communication facilities and transport), no matter how many local hotels or other facilities may exist. It is only prudent to take the same precautions during a trek in Nepal as you would take on a major hiking or climbing trip at home, and carry a basic medical kit. There will often be nobody but your own companions to help you if you are sick or injured. Dr Shlim's excellent Health & Safety chapter will help you prepare for many possible problems.

Tourism is a major source of foreign exchange in Nepal and important for the country's continued economic development. The government encourages tourists to visit Nepal because they spend money. The people in the hills expect to gain a bit of

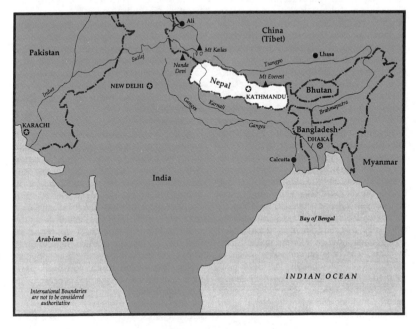

International Boundaries are not to be considered authoritative

income from every traveller. Even the poorest porter in the hills buys an occasional cup of tea from local inns and purchases rice from villagers. I have made a few suggestions on how to arrange a trek in a manner that is economically beneficial to both you and Nepal, with a minimum of hassle.

The information here is based on my experiences in leading and organising treks and living in Nepal since 1970. A lot of my opinions have crept in, especially relating to trekking equipment and cultural interaction. If you've done a lot of hiking, you will certainly have developed preferences for the gear you need to be comfortable. Read my suggestions about equipment, then make your own decisions.

People of various means and temperaments read and use this book. Be aware that there are many ways to approach a trek. If you have booked a group trek, it may amaze you that there is any need to discuss the relative merits of carrying a sleeping bag. However, a budget trekker may find this discussion useful, yet consider it preposterous that anyone would pay US$75 per day or more to trek. There is room for both attitudes (and a lot in between) in Nepal and you will certainly meet 'the other half' during your trek. This book is your introduction to these diverse opinions and styles.

I have tried to avoid preaching about how to behave on a trek. Obviously, you should pay for what you eat and drink, bury your faeces, minimise the amount of firewood that you use, respect local customs and attitudes and try to interact gently with Nepal. Some trekkers do not do this, and it is unlikely that anything I write will change that. In rare cases, an innkeeper might overcharge you, abuse you, refuse food or accommodation or insult you. Filthy hotels, campsites and latrines may disgust you along some popular trekking routes. If this happens, it is because someone (probably the person who stayed there last night) contributed to the problem. You have the choice of continuing to escalate the mess or doing your own small part to make Nepal more pleasant for those who follow.

Why Trek in Nepal?

Just as New York is not representative of the USA, so Kathmandu is not representative of Nepal. If you have the time and energy to trek, don't miss the opportunity to leave Kathmandu and see the spectacular beauty and the unique culture of Nepal. Fortunately for the visitor, there are still only a few roads extending deeply into the hills, so the only way to truly visit the remote regions of the kingdom is in the slowest and most intimate manner – walking. It requires more time and effort, but the rewards are also greater. Instead of zipping down a freeway, racing to the next 'point of interest', each step provides new and intriguing viewpoints. You will perceive your day as an entity rather than a few highlights strung together by a ribbon of concrete. For the romanticist, each step follows the footsteps of Hillary, Tenzing, Herzog and other Himalayan explorers. If you have neither the patience nor the physical stamina to visit the hills of Nepal on foot, a helicopter flight provides an expensive and unsatisfactory substitute.

Trekking in Nepal will take you through a country that has captured the imagination of mountaineers and explorers for more than 100 years. You will meet people in remote mountain villages whose lifestyle has not changed in generations. Most people trust foreigners. Nepal is one of only a handful of countries that has never been ruled by a foreign power.

Many of the values associated with a hiking trip at home do not have the same importance during a trek in Nepal. Isolation is traditionally a crucial element of any wilderness experience but in Nepal it is impossible to get completely away from people, except for short times or at extremely high elevations. Environmental concerns must include the effects of conservation measures on rural people and the economic effects of tourism on indigenous populations. Even traditional national park management must be adapted because there are significant population centres within Sagarmatha (Mt Everest) and Langtang national parks.

Trekking does not mean mountain climbing. While the ascent of a Himalayan peak may be an attraction for some, you need not have such a goal to enjoy a trek. Throughout this book, trekking always refers to walking on trails.

While trekking you will see the great diversity of Nepal. Villages embrace many ethnic groups and cultures. The terrain changes from tropical jungle to high glaciated peaks in only 150 km. From the start, the towering peaks of the Himalaya provide one of the highlights of a trek. As your plane approaches Kathmandu these peaks appear to be small clouds on the horizon. The mountains become more definable and seem to reach impossible heights as you get closer and finally land at Kathmandu's Tribhuvan Airport.

During a trek, the Himalaya disappears behind Nepal's continual hills, but dominates the northern skyline at each pass. Annapurna, Manaslu, Langtang, Gauri Shankar and Everest will become familiar names. Finally, after weeks of walking, you will arrive at the foot of the mountains themselves – astonishing heights from which gigantic avalanches tumble earthwards in apparent slow motion, dwarfed by their surroundings. Your conception of the Himalaya alters as you turn from peaks famed only for their height to gaze on far more picturesque summits that you may never have heard of – Kantega, Ama Dablam, Machhapuchhare and Khumbakarna.

The beauty and attraction of the Nepal Himalaya emanates not only from the mountains themselves, but also from their surroundings. Nepal is a country of friendly people, picturesque villages and a great variety of cultures and traditions that seem to exemplify many of the attributes we have lost in our headlong rush for development and progress in the West.

Facts about the Country

HISTORY

What is now Nepal was once a collection of feudal principalities sandwiched between Moghul India and Tibet. You can see the palaces of these ancient rulers as you trek through Nepal at places such as Sinja near Jumla, Besi Sahar (Lamjung) near Dumre, Lo Manthang, Gorkha and, of course, the Kathmandu Valley. Many of these small kingdoms had little or no contact with Kathmandu. The early history of the Kathmandu Valley, with its Licchavi Dynasty from the 3rd to 13th centuries and the Malla reign from the 13th to 18th centuries, had little effect on the remote hill regions.

In 1769, Prithvi Narayan Shah, the ruler of the House of Gorkha, succeeded in unifying these diverse kingdoms and established the general shape of the present borders of Nepal. He also founded the Shah Dynasty. The present king of Nepal, King Birendra Bir Bikram Shah Dev, is a direct descendant of Prithvi Narayan Shah.

Rana Prime Ministers

In 1846, the prime minister, Jung Bahadur Rana, conspired with the queen regent to gain control of the country. He invited all the top political and military leaders to a party and ambushed them in what is known in Nepalese history as the Kot Massacre. The site of the massacre, the Kot, still stands near Hanuman Dhoka in Durbar Square. Following the massacre, Jung Bahadur decreed that the post of prime minister was to be hereditary, taking the precaution to ensure that the title passed to a younger brother if the ruler had no qualified son. The Ranas adopted the title Maharaja and ruled the country for 104 years. Jung Bahadur visited England and France and was received with all the honours due a head of state.

Despite Jung Bahadur's refusal to adopt European practices which conflicted with his Hindu beliefs, he was fascinated with European architecture. The profusion of white stucco neoclassical palaces in Kathmandu was inspired by this journey.

The Ranas kept Nepal isolated and allowed almost no foreign visitors. After losing a fierce war with imperial India, they conceded most of their territory, which now comprises the northern areas of the Indian states of Kashmir, Himachal Pradesh, West Bengal, Bihar and Uttar Pradesh. They also agreed to allow a British 'resident' in Nepal, but he was not permitted to leave the Kathmandu Valley.

Re-Emergence of the Monarchy

In 1950, King Tribhuvan, assisted by the Indian embassy in Kathmandu, fled to India. The rule of the Shah kings was reinstated through an armed people's revolution led by the Nepali Congress Party. King Tribhuvan instituted political reforms and, until the 1990 revolution, was credited with being the father of democracy in Nepal.

During a period of political squabbling, the number of political parties in Nepal grew to more than 60. In 1960 Tribhuvan's son, King Mahendra, engineered a bloodless palace coup, declared a new constitution, jailed all the leaders of the then government and announced a ban on political parties. He established a partyless *panchayat* ('five councils') system that was answerable only to the monarch.

The political system was described as 'partyless panchayat democracy' and allowed direct election of local leaders and representatives to the Rastrya Panchayat, the National Assembly. Although the council of ministers was made up of members of the Rastrya Panchayat, the king retained the right to appoint a quota of legislators, effectively retaining control.

King Birendra succeeded to the throne in 1971. After a period of political unrest, he declared that a national referendum would decide whether the country would adopt a multiparty system or retain the panchayat system 'with suitable reforms'. The 1980 referendum endorsed the panchayat system by a narrow margin and was thereafter cited as the will of the people.

The 1990 Revolution

Being a landlocked country, Nepal depends on its neighbour, India, for most of its manufactured goods and for access to the sea. In March 1989, the Trade & Transit Treaty between Nepal and India expired. Pride and protocol prevented the two countries from reaching any agreement on an extension. The issue was further complicated by Nepal's recent purchase of hundreds of truckloads of military supplies from China. India reduced the number of entry points into Nepal to the minimum required by international law, raised tariffs on Nepalese goods and severely limited the supply of petroleum products. Nepal's economy and quality of life declined and there was considerable popular unrest with the government's inability to resolve the issue.

This unrest reached a crescendo in the spring of 1990 when the 'illegal, banned' political parties began to severely criticise the panchayat system for corruption, human rights violations and incompetence. The various opposition factions coalesced into a united force, bent on the restoration of democracy in Nepal under the leadership of Nepal's new 'father of democracy', Ganesh Man Singh. The government replied with a show of force that escalated from arrests to public beatings and shootings. After the resignation of several ministers forced the issue, the king reconstituted the cabinet and promised that grievances would be reviewed and appropriate changes made.

But the people were not mollified. In a spectacular display of unity, more than 200,000 people took to the streets of Kathmandu on 6 April 1990, chanting pro-democracy slogans. After exercising restraint throughout most of the day, the police attacked the demonstrators, first with bamboo staves and then with guns. Hundreds of people were killed or wounded. The army took control of the city. During a tense weekend curfew, the king negotiated with opposition leaders, then late in the evening of 8 April proclaimed that the ban on political parties was lifted.

The next day the country erupted in an outpouring of joy. If you happen to be in Kathmandu on this anniversary, you will probably witness ceremonies honouring those martyrs killed during the revolution.

The interim council of ministers appointed in the aftermath of the revolution included leaders of various parties, many of whom had spent time in jail as political prisoners. The reforms are far from complete and there are signs of stress within the system. Most Nepalese, however, are generally optimistic about the future.

One of the major accomplishments of the new government was the restoration of better relations with India. Hopes increased that imports of Indian goods, especially fuel, and the export of Nepalese goods to India would aid Nepal's economic recovery.

The 1991 Elections

Elections were held in 1991 in which the Nepali Congress Party gained a majority and formed a government. The mood of the public was upbeat for a while, but the inexperience, sometimes coupled with sheer incompetence, of the elected government demoralised the average Nepalese. The various communist parties banded together to organise several crippling strikes and demonstrations against the ruling Nepali Congress Party. The government cracked down on the communists with brutal force in which dozens of agitators were killed by the police. A political understanding was finally reached between the warring parties, and Nepal moved towards the path of political stability.

In late 1993 the Nepali Congress politicians and leaders took to squabbling amongst themselves. With the political honeymoon between the voters and the communist parties being virtually over, the

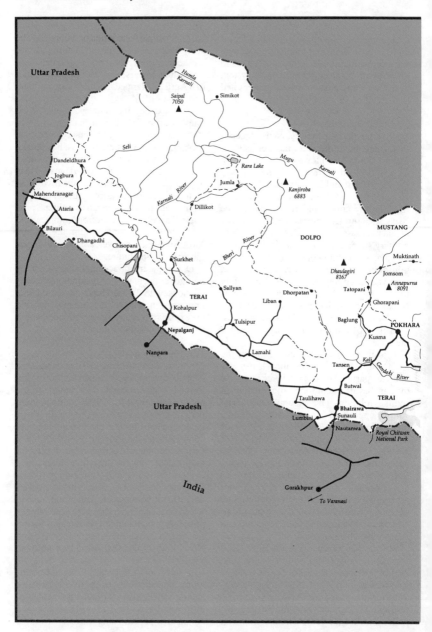

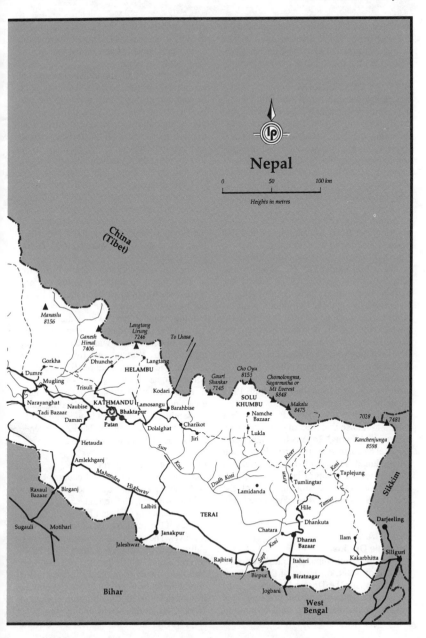

Nepal

0   50   100 km

Heights in metres

resurgent royalist parties of the panchayat era were being looked upon as saviours. The next set of national elections, due in 1995, will reflect the mood of the general public.

HISTORY OF TREKKING

The first trekker in Nepal was Bill Tilman, who somehow wrangled permission from the maharaja in 1949 to make several treks, including the Kali Gandaki, Helambu and Everest. His exploits are described in *Nepal Himalaya*, reprinted by the Seattle Mountaineers as part of a Tilman collection. Another early visitor was Maurice Herzog, who led a French expedition to Annapurna in 1950.

During King Tribhuvan's visits to India, the king met Boris Lissannivich, a Russian ballet dancer who was running a club in Calcutta. Boris convinced the king that people would like to visit Nepal and would actually pay for the experience. Soon a few well-heeled ladies flew from Patna to Kathmandu's Gaucher ('cowfield') Airport in an Indian Airlines Dakota. Boris accommodated them in his new establishment, the Royal Hotel. The women were charmed by Boris and the exotic kingdom of Nepal. Thus Nepalese tourism was born. The Royal Hotel and its Yak & Yeti bar became the meeting place for climbers from the 1950s until 1971 when the Royal hotel was closed.

Colonel James O M Roberts was the first person to realise that trekking would appeal to tourists. 'Jimmy' Roberts had spent years in Nepal attached to the British residency and accompanied Tilman on his first trek. In 1965 he took a group of ladies up the Kali Gandaki and founded Mountain Travel, the first of the adventure travel companies now burgeoning worldwide.

GEOGRAPHY
Geologic Origins

Imagine the space Nepal occupies as an open expanse of water, once part of the Mediterranean Sea, and the Tibetan Plateau, or 'roof of the world', as a beachfront property. This was the prehistoric setting until 60 million years ago, prior to the Indo-Australian

plate's collision with the Eurasian continent. As the former was pushed under Eurasia, the earth's crust buckled and folded and mountain-building began.

The upheaval of mountains caused the temporary obstruction of rivers that once flowed unimpeded from Eurasia to the sea. However, on the southern slopes of the young mountains, new rivers formed as trapped, moist winds off the tropical sea rose and precipitated. As the mountains continued to rise and the gradient became steeper, these rivers cut deeply into the terrain.

The continual crunching of the two plates, augmented by phases of crustal uplifting, created yet new mountain ranges and once again the rivers' courses were interrupted. If the forces of erosion eventually prevailed, long east-west valleys were formed. If not, lakes resulted.

The colossal outcome was the formation of four major mountain systems running north-west by south-east and incised by the north-south gorges of, not only new rivers, but the original ones with watersheds in Tibet that are older than the mountains themselves. In conjunction with the innumerable rogue ridges that jut out from the main ranges, the terrain can be likened to a complex maze of ceilingless rooms.

The mountain-building process continues today, not only displacing material laterally, but sending the ranges yet higher and resulting in natural erosion, landslides, silt-laden rivers, rock faults and earthquakes.

Physiographic Regions

Nepal is a small landlocked country that is 800 km long and 200 km wide. In the longitudinal 200 km, the terrain changes from glaciers along the Tibetan border to the flat jungles of the Terai, barely 150 metres above sea level. The country does not ascend gradually from the plains. Rather, it rises in several chains of hills that lie in an east-west direction, finally terminating in the highest hills in the world – the Himalaya. Beyond the Himalaya is the 5000-metre-high plateau of Tibet. Despite the height of the Himalaya, they are not a continental divide. Several rivers flow from Tibet through the mountains and hills of Nepal to join the Ganges in India. Many other rivers flow southward from the glaciers of the Nepal Himalaya. These rivers have scarred the country with great gorges in both north-south and east-west directions. This action has created a continual series of hills, some of which are incredibly steep.

From east to west, the geographic division of the kingdom is less clearly defined, though there are clear political divisions. Nepal is divided into 14 zones, several of which extend across the country from the Terai to the Tibetan border.

The primary difference between eastern and western Nepal is that the influence of the monsoon is less in the west. In the east the climate is damp and ideal for tea growing, the conditions being similar to Darjeeling in India. In the far west the climate is quite dry, even during the monsoon season.

Another influence on the east-west division is the large rivers that flow southward in deep canyons. These rivers often limit east-west travel as they wash away bridges during the monsoon. For this reason the major trade routes are south to north, from Indian border towns to Nepalese hill villages.

Despite the steepness of the country, there is extensive farming on thousands of ancient terraces carved into the hills. Pressure from the increasing population is forcing people to bring even the most marginal land into cultivation. This has resulted in erosion, flooding and landslides. Extensive systems of trenches and canals provide the irrigation necessary for food production. Houses are near family fields and a typical Nepalese village extends over a large area. The hilly terrain often creates an elevation differential of several hundred metres or more between the highest and lowest homes.

Geographers divide the country into three main physiographic regions or natural zones: the Terai, the Middle Hills and the Himalaya.

The Terai The Terai is the southernmost region of Nepal and is an extension of the Gangetic plains of India. Until 1950 this was a malarial jungle inhabited primarily by rhinoceros, tiger, leopard, wild boar and deer. Now, with malaria controlled, farming and industrial communities cover the Terai. The region holds about 47% of Nepal's population and the majority of the country's cultivable land. The Terai includes the big cities of Nepalgunj, Birganj, Janakpur and Biratnagar, but most of the region is dotted with small villages – clusters of 40 or 50 houses in the centre of a large area of cultivated fields.

Just north of the Terai is the first major east-west chain of hills, the Siwalik (or Churia) Hills and then the Mahabharat Range. In some parts of Nepal only farmers live in these hills, but in other parts they are the sites of large and well-developed villages such as Ilam, Dhankuta and Surkhet.

The Middle Hills The Middle Hills, a band only 60 km wide, are home to about 45% of the population. This is the home of the ancient Nepalese people. Kathmandu, Patan, Bhadgaon, Pokhara, Gorkha and Jumla are all in the Middle Hills. Kathmandu lies in the largest valley of the kingdom and according to legend the valley was once a huge lake. Other than the Kathmandu and Pokhara valleys, the Middle Hills are hilly and steep.

The Himalaya The Himalaya and its foothills make up only a small portion of the kingdom along the northern border. This inhospitable region is the least inhabited part of Nepal. Less than 8% of the population live here. Most of the villages sit between 3000 and 4000 metres elevation, although there are summer settlements as high as 5000 metres. Winters are cold, but the warm sun makes most days comfortable. Because of the short growing season, crops are few and usually small, consisting mostly of potatoes, barley and a few vegetables. The primary means of support is trading and the herding of sheep, cattle and yaks. Part of this region, Solu Khumbu, is the home of the Sherpas. Mountaineering expeditions and trekking have a large influence on the economy of this area.

In the west the Himalayan region is an area of Tibetan influence and parts of this region are behind the main Himalayan range.

North of the Himalaya is the high desert region or trans-Himalaya, similar to the Tibetan Plateau. This area encompasses the arid valleys of Mustang, Manang and Dolpo, as well as the Tibetan marginals (the fourth range of mountains that sweep from central to north-western Nepal, averaging below 6000 metres in height). The trans-Himalaya is in the rain-shadow area and receives significantly less precipitation than the southern slopes. Uneroded crags, spires, and formations like crumbling fortresses are typical of this stark landscape.

CLIMATE

Nepal has four distinct seasons. Spring, from March to May, is warm and dusty with rain showers. Summer, from June to August, is the monsoon season when the hills turn lush and green. Autumn, from September to November, is cool with clear skies, and is the most popular trekking season. In winter, from December to February, it is cold at night and can be foggy in the early morning, but afternoons are usually clear and pleasant,

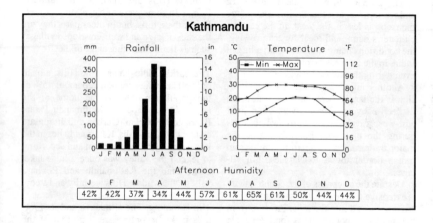

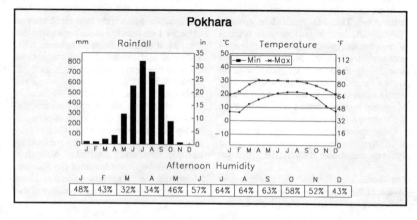

though there is occasional snow in the mountains.

Because Nepal is quite far south (at the same latitude as Miami and Cairo) the weather is warmer and winter is much milder at lower elevations, including Kathmandu at 1400 metres. It rarely snows below 2000 metres.

The monsoon in the Bay of Bengal governs the weather pattern. The monsoon creates a rainy season from the middle of June to the middle of September. It is hot during the monsoon and it rains almost every day, but it is a considerate rain, limiting itself mostly to the night. During this season, trekking in most of Nepal is difficult and uncomfortable. Clouds usually hide the mountains and the trails are muddy and infested with leeches.

It usually does not rain for more than one or two days during the entire autumn season from mid-October to mid-December. During winter and spring there may be a week or so of rainy evenings and occasional thunderstorms blanket the hills with snow. The Himalaya makes its own localised weather, which varies significantly over a distance of a few km. Despite the sanguine assurances of Radio Nepal that the weather will be '...mainly fair throughout the kingdom', always expect clouds in the afternoon and be prepared for occasional rain.

Most of the precipitation in the Himalaya occurs during the summer monsoon. There is less snow on the mountains and on many of the high trails during winter. Everest itself is black rock during the trekking season, becoming snow-covered only during summer. There are always exceptions to this weather pattern, so be prepared for extremes. Winter snowstorms in December and January may make an early spring pass crossing difficult and can present an avalanche danger, especially on the approach to the Annapurna Sanctuary.

In Kathmandu, spring and autumn days are comfortable and the evenings are cool, usually requiring a light jacket or pullover. Winter in Kathmandu brings cold foggy mornings and clear evenings, but pleasant day temperatures with brilliant sunshine most days after the morning fog has lifted. It never snows in Kathmandu, though there is frost on cold nights in January and February. The hottest month is May, just before the rains start.

FLORA

There are 6500 known species of trees, shrubs and wildflowers in Nepal. In the temperate areas the flowers emerge as winter recedes and the rivers swell with snow melt, while in the subtropics, the bloom is triggered by warmer temperatures and spring showers. Americans and Europeans will recognise many of the species in the temperate areas, and residents of South-East Asia will recognise many of the subtropical species.

The height of floral glory can be witnessed in March and April when rhododendrons burst into colour. The huge magnolias of the east with their showy white flowers borne on bare branches are also spectacular, as are the orchids (there are over 300 varieties in Nepal). Not far behind is the blossoming of a variety of shrubs, while on the ground, blue irises and lavender primulas appear. The succession of flowers continues higher up as the monsoon approaches.

Unless one is content and able to identify wildflowers by their leaves or dried seed capsules, it is necessary to visit the temperate and alpine areas during the monsoon season. In order to do this, one must be prepared to sacrifice comfort and views. However, this is the time to see the true colours of the Himalaya. The southern slopes and the inner valleys are particularly lush at this time. Mints, scrophs, buttercups, cinquefoils, polygonums and composites abound in these areas, while in the alpine areas, dwarf rhododendrons, junipers, ephedras, cotoneasters, saxifrages and primulas paint the bleak landscape.

Western Nepal, particularly the Dolpo area, is reminiscent of Kashmir in its rich variety of flora. Being in the rain-shadow area, monsoon conditions are more amenable for visitors – the region is drier and free of leeches. In order to witness the full regalia,

Vegetation Zones
In western Nepal, forests usually extend to higher elevations than elsewhere in the country due to drier conditions and a more northerly latitude. Above the cultivation zone the forests are less disrupted, although they do come under pressure from summer herders and wood-gatherers.

Tropical Zone (Up to 300 metres) Sal, a broad-leafed, semideciduous hardwood, dominates here. The leaves are used for 'disposable' plates, and the wood is used for construction. It varies little from east to west and is a climax species.

There is also a deciduous moist forest in this zone, of acacia and rosewood, as well as open areas of tall elephant grass. The grass areas are burned off in winter, which helps preserve them – otherwise they would be succeeded by a moist forest. These two habitats are known as seral communities, because if they are left undisturbed, they would both be replaced by the sal climax forest.

The silky cotton tree with its thorny trunks when young, and smooth-buttressed trunk bases when older, has leafless limbs that burst into bright red flowers in early spring. It is also a part of the moist forest. The cotton or 'kapok' from these trees is used for stuffing cushions and mattresses.

These forest types are typical of the Churia Hills and Inner Terai, though sal and silky cotton are also found in the subtropical zone.

Subtropical Zone (1000 to 2000 metres) The dominant species east of the Kali Gandaki are the true chestnuts and a member of the tea family, schima. The spiky flower clusters of the chestnuts appear in the fall, while the fragrant white flowers of the schima bloom in late spring. Due to chestnut wood's popularity as a source of fuel, it is often depleted.

In the west, the chir pine is found on all aspects. The species has long needles in bundles of three and is also found in the east, but confined to drier southern slopes.

Lower Temperate Zone (1700 to 2700 metres) Evergreen oaks are indigenous to this zone. In the east, the oaks of the wet forests are festooned with moss and epiphytes and have dense understoreys. In the west, another oak preferring dry conditions is present, as well as on the sunny slopes of the east.

A common wet forest that occurs mostly on north and west faces in western Nepal is comprised of horse chestnut, maple and walnut. Alder and birch are prevalent along watercourses.

the time to visit is July and August. From Jumla east one may recognise ground orchids, edelweiss, corydalis, campanulas, anemones, forget-me-nots, impatiens and roses. Higher up in the alpine areas, the larkspurs, geraniums, poppies, sedums and saxifrages proliferate.

In the trans-Himalaya, common vegetation is primarily from the legume family, such as the spiny caragana and astragalus, as well as from the honeysuckle family (eg lonerica).

In the post-monsoon season, when most people choose to visit, the flowers of summer are all but gone, save for some straggler blooms and those not palatable to grazing animals. However, in the subtropical and lower temperate areas, some wildflowers are fortunate and survive environmental degradation, such as the pink luculia, mauve osbeckia and yellow St John's wort. The flowering cherry trees also add colour to the autumn village scenes as do the blue gentians in the temperate areas. Otherwise, one can enjoy the autumn yellows of withering maples and ginger, and the reds of barberry shrubs. When the dark temperate forests are back lit, the moss appears luminescent, and the epiphytic ferns and orchids shine like tiny paper lanterns.

In the Kathmandu Valley, Australians will find the familiar silky oak with its spring golden inflorescence, and bottlebrush and eucalyptus. Though fast-growing timber species in their native country, in the valley these trees are planted as ornamentals along

Homogeneous blue-pine forests occur extensively in the west, mostly on south faces, and range to the tree line. This species is hardy and fire resistant, thriving well in habitats modified by humans. It is also found throughout the east, but to a lesser extent. The blue pine is distinguished from the only other pine in Nepal, the chir pine, by its shorter needles in bundles of five, and long, pendulous cones. Both species are used for carpentry and roofing, while the resin is converted to turpentine.

Upper Temperate Zone (2400 to 4000 metres) Another evergreen oak widespread throughout the dry forests of the west exhibits two types of leaves, the young ones spiny, while older leaves have smooth edges. In the east, this species is confined to southern slopes, but is heavily cut for fodder and fuel.

The spectacular wet rhododendron forests are interspersed with hemlock and fir. *Rhododendron arboreum*, the national flower, reaches heights of 18 metres and ranges in colour from red to white. There are more than 30 species of rhododendron in Nepal, but these are found more extensively in the east than the west. Unfortunately, this tree is felled for fuel or turned into charcoal.

There is also a high conifer forest where blue pine is found in pure stands. In the west it occurs with fir and spruce, in the east, firs, hemlocks and yews associate with blue pine. Firewood and roofing shingles are the common usages for these species. A mixed broad-leafed forest of maple and laurel is also typical of this zone.

Subalpine Zone (3000 to 4000 metres) Silver fir mixed with oak and birch extend to the tree line in the west. East of the Kali Gandaki, only birch is found to the tree line, though under wetter conditions, dwarf bamboo and shrub rhododendron may replace it. In dry areas, juniper species occur to the tree line.

Alpine Zone (4000 metres to Snow Line) In this realm above the tree line, vegetation must cope with extremes in ground temperatures, and moisture gradients that range from nothing in winter to profuse in summer. Only the most tenacious of wildflowers thrive here, generally by being hirsute or having thick underground stems (rhizomes). A successful example is stellara, common above 5500 metres.

In the trans-Himalaya, the vegetation is restricted to the arid-adapted species of the Tibetan Plateau. ■

with cherry, poplar and jacaranda. The latter, with its lavender blossoms, is from South America, as is bougainvillaea and the giant pointsettias. Historically, the Nepalese have been avid gardeners of such exotics as hibiscus, camellia, cosmos, salvia and marigold.

FAUNA
Birds

More than 800 species are known in Nepal, more birds than in Canada and the USA combined, or nearly 10% of the world's species! Resident bird numbers are augmented by migratory species, as well as winter and summer visitors.

Eight species of stork, some as high as 150 cm, have been identified along the water courses of the Terai. Cranes are similar in appearance, but not as well represented save for the demoiselle cranes that fly down the Kali Gandaki and Dudh Kosi for the winter before returning in spring to their Tibetan nesting grounds. Herons and egrets are quite common in the tropics and subtropics, and distinguished in flight by their curved-neck posture, as opposed to the outstretched necks of storks and cranes.

Most of the waterfowl are migratory. Many can be seen at the Kosi Barrage in the eastern Terai and in the Chitwan and Bardia areas. The swift-flying bar-headed goose has been observed flying at altitudes near 8000 metres.

Raptors or birds of prey are found in all sizes in the Himalaya, and are especially prevalent with the onset of winter. One of the first raptors to leave is the small Eurasian kestrel that must flap its wings at regular intervals, or rapidly when hovering. By comparison, the Himalayan griffon is a heavy bird that must wait for thermal updraught to allow its soaring, gliding flight. The griffon and the lammergeier, with wingspans of nearly three metres, are carrion eaters, though often mistaken for eagles. There are, however, true eagles, including the resident golden eagle common in the Khumbu, as well as other species that are known to migrate in large numbers in the Kali Gandaki region. Many medium-sized raptors have highly variable plumages and are difficult to identify in the sky.

There are six species of pheasant in Nepal, including the national bird, the impeyan pheasant, the male of which has a plumage of iridescent colours. These birds are known as downhill fliers, as they do not fly, per se, and must walk uphill! When flushed they will cant and swerve downhill to evade enemies such as the golden eagle. The cheer and koklas pheasants are only found west of the Kali Gandaki, while the kalij pheasant is common throughout, but with different colour phases.

Nepal hosts 17 species of cuckoo which are characterised by their distinctive calls. Arriving in March, they herald the coming of spring. The Indian cuckoo has a recognisable *kaphal pakyo* call, Nepali for announcing that the fruit of the box myrtle is ripe. The common hawk cuckoo has a repetitious call that sounds like 'brain fever', which rises in a crescendo – aptly described by British sahibs as they lay sweating with malarial fevers. Most cuckoos are social parasites, meaning they lay their eggs in the nests of other species.

One of the most colourful, varied and vocal families is the timalids, or babblers and laughing thrushes, common from the tropical Terai to the upper temperate forest. They are from eight to 33 cm in size and live in both terrestrial and arboreal habitats. They are found individually or in large, foraging parties, and can often be identified by their raucous calls. The black-capped sibia with its constant prattle and ringing song is an integral part of the wet temperate forests. The spiny babbler is Nepal's only endemic species.

There are three pairs of species amongst the crow family; their appearance and behaviour are virtually identical, but each species occupies a different altitudinal range. The red-billed blue magpies are residents of the subtropical zone, while the yellow-billed species are found in the temperates. The Indian tree pie prefers the tropics while the Himalayan species lives in the subtropics and temperates. Above the tree line, two species of chough, congregating in large flocks in winter, are prevalent. Though they often overlap in range, the yellow-billed chough is found higher and is known to enter mountaineers' tents high on Everest. Another of the crow family, also bold and conspicuous in the trans-Himalayan region, is the large raven.

Besides such families as kingfishers, bee-eaters, drongos, minivets, parakeets and sunbirds, there are a host of other passerines, or perching birds throughout Nepal. These include 30 species of flycatchers and nearly 60 species of thrushes and warblers. Many smaller species congregate in heterogeneous flocks, not only for feeding purposes but also for protection.

In the Kathmandu Valley, the sparrows and pigeons demonstrate adaptability to urban centres by their sheer numbers. Dark kites, hawk-like birds with forked tails, are common over the city. At sunset, loose groups of crows, mynas, egrets and kites fly to their respective roosts. After dark, the noisy ruckus of the spotted owlets substitutes for the cacophony of car horns. The robin dayal, with its cocked tail, is the common songster of early mornings. Pulchowki, Nagarjun and Shivapuri are excellent areas for finding birds of subtropical and temperate habitats, while the Gokarna Safari Park offers a cross section of species typical of the valley floor.

In the Pokhara region, the Indian roller is conspicuous when it takes flight and flashes the iridescent turquoise on its wings. Other-

A	B
C	
D	E	F

People of Nepal

A Gurung (SA) D Rai (SA)
B Tibetan (RI'A) E Sherpa (SA)
C Limbu (SA) F Brahmin (SA)

Flora & Fauna of Nepal
A Himalayan tahr (DA)   D Rhododendrons (RE)
B Poincettias (SA)   E Yak (SA)
C Snow leopard (JS)

Top: Girl in wheat field (RI'A)
Bottom: Hill bazaar (SA)

Top: Mt Everest from Kala Pattar (SA)
Middle: Sunset on Mt Cho Oyu (RI'A)
Bottom: Machhapuchhare (SB)

wise, while perched, it appears as a plain brown bird. Local superstition has it that if someone about to embark on a journey sees a roller going their way it is a good omen. If they see a crow, however, it is a bad omen and the trip is aborted. Many trips must be destined for delay thanks to the presence of the common crow!

Mammals

As one might expect, due to habitat degeneration from both natural and human causes, opportunities for seeing wildlife are usually restricted to national parks, reserves and western Nepal, where population is sparse. Wildlife numbers have also been thinned due to poaching for pelts or other parts that are considered to be delicacies or medicinally valuable. In addition, animals are hunted because of the damage they inflict on crops and domestic animals.

At the top of the food chain is the royal Bengal tiger, the most magnificent cat, which is solitary and territorial. Males have territorial ranges that encompass those of two or three females and may span as much as 100 sq km. The Chitwan National Park of the Inner Terai and the Royal Bardia National Park in the western Terai protect sufficient habitat to sustain viable breeding populations.

The spotted leopard is an avid tree climber and in general more elusive than the tiger. These nocturnal creatures, like tigers, have been known to become human-eaters when they have grown old or been maimed. Humans are not only easy prey, but once the taste is acquired, they lose interest in their natural prey. Local people have likened them to evil spirits because of their success at evading hunters.

The snow leopard is often protected from hunters, not only by national parks, but also by inhabiting inhospitable domains above the tree line as well as sensitive border regions. Its territory depends upon the ranges of ungulate herds, its prey species, as well as breeding females. Packs of wolves compete directly and when territories overlap, the solitary snow leopard will be displaced.

The one-horned rhinoceros is the largest of the three Asian species of rhino and is a totally different genus from the two-horned African varieties. It has poor eyesight and though weighing up to two tonnes, is amazingly quick. Anyone who encounters a mother with its calf is likely to be charged, a disconcerting experience, even if you are atop an elephant. The rhino is a denizen of the grasslands of the Inner Terai, specifically the Chitwan Valley, although it has also been reintroduced to the Royal Bardia National Park.

The Indian elephant, like the one-horned rhino, is starkly different from its African relative, belonging to a separate genus. The only wild elephants known to exist in Nepal are in the western part of the Terai and Churia Hills, though individuals often range across the border from India. Elephants are known to maintain matriarchal societies, and females up to 60 years of age bear calves. Though able to reach 80 years of age, elephants' life spans are determined by dentition. Molars are replaced as they wear down, but only up to six times. When the final set is worn, the individual dies of starvation.

Periodically, male and occasionally female elephants, enter a 'musth' condition that makes them excitable and highly aggressive. While in this agitated state they have been known to trample villages. When a herd goes on the rampage outsiders, or non-Hindus, are often summoned as the elephant is considered a holy animal because of the much-loved Ganesh, the elephant-headed god of the Hindu pantheon.

There are several species of deer, but most of them are confined to the lowlands. The spotted deer is probably the most beautiful, while the sambar is the largest. The *muntjak*, or barking deer, which usually makes its presence known by its sharp, one-note alarm call, is found up to 2400 metres, while the unusual musk deer, with antelope-like features and only 50 cm high at the shoulder, ranges even higher.

There are two primates: the rhesus macaque and the common langur. The rhesus are earth-coloured with short tails and travel on the ground in large, structured troops, unafraid of humans. The langur are arboreal, with black faces, grey fur, long limbs and tails. Because of Hanuman, the monkey god in the Hindu epic the *Ramayana*, both species are considered holy and are well protected. The rhesus ranges from the Terai up to 2400 metres, while the langur goes higher, up to 3600 metres.

In the Kathmandu Valley, rhesus macaques at the Swayambhunath and Pashupatinath temples take advantage of their holy status and relieve worshippers of their picnic lunches and consecrated food.

Two even-toed hoofed mammals are found in the alpine regions. They are the Himalayan tahr, a near-true goat, and the blue sheep, which is genetically stranded somewhere between goats and sheep. The male tahr poses majestically in its flowing manes on the grassy slopes of inner valleys, while the blue sheep turns a bluish-grey in winter and is found in the trans-Himalayan biotope.

The Himalayan black bear is omnivorous and a bane to corn crops in the temperate forests. Though it rarely attacks humans, its poor eyesight may lead it to interpret a standing person as making a threatening gesture and to attack. If so, the best defence is not to run, but to lie face down on the ground – particularly effective when one is wearing a backpack. Nepal's bears are known to roam in winter instead of hibernating.

There are some prominent canines, though behaviourally they are fairly shy. The jackal, with its eerie howling that sets village dogs barking at night, ranges from the Terai to alpine regions. It is both a hunter and scavenger, and will take chickens and raid crops.

The pika, or mouse-hare, is the common guinea pig-like mammal of the inner valleys, often seen scurrying nervously between rocks. The marmot of western Nepal is a large rodent, but with a mustelid-like appearance; it commonly dwells in the trans-Himalayan zone. The marmot is also found in Sikkim and Bhutan, but not eastern Nepal

– such gaps in speciation are not uncommon across the Himalaya.

Noisy colonies of flying foxes or fruit bats have chosen the trees near the old Royal Palace in Kathmandu and the chir pines at the entrance to Bhaktapur as their haunts. They are known to fly great distances at night to raid orchards, before returning at dawn. They have adequate eyesight for their feeding habits and do not require the sonar system of insectivorous bats.

Pulchowki, Nagarjun and Shivapuri are good areas for possible sightings of small mammals. The Gokarna Safari Park contains introduced deer species.

Reptiles
There are two indigenous species of crocodile: the gharial and marsh mugger. The gharial inhabits rivers and is a prehistoric-looking fish-eating creature with bulging eyes and a long, narrow snout. The marsh mugger prefers stagnant water and is omnivorous, feeding on anything within reach. Due to the value of its hide and eggs, the gharial was hunted to the brink of extinction, but has increased in numbers since the establishment of a hatchery and rearing centre in Chitwan. Both crocodiles inhabit the Terai.

Though venomous snakes such as cobras, vipers and kraits are present, the chance of encountering one is small, not only because of their usual evasive tactics, but also because they are indiscriminantly slaughtered. The majority of species are found on the Terai, though the mountain pit viper is known higher up, along with a few other nonvenomous species.

ECOLOGY
Except for a few manufacturing centres, agriculture dominates the economy. In the hill regions people have cultivated every possible piece of land except where the hillsides are too steep or rocky to carve out even the smallest terrace. Much of the land between the Himalaya and the Terai has been worked and sculpted over the centuries to provide space for crops, animals and houses. Because of this, forests lying within the

inhabited zone, especially on the southern slopes, have been lopped, cut and cleared.

Plant Use

The Terai is considered the rice bowl of Nepal, though rice is usually grown up to 2000 metres, or higher in the west. It is usually planted before the advent of the monsoon, transplanted soon after and harvested in the autumn. The rich vibrant greens of the rice plant during the monsoon contrast with the subtle, diffused tones as it ripens.

If possible, wheat is planted in the cleared rice fields and harvested in spring. Fields of yellow-flowering mustard are planted for making cooking oil. Corn is planted in spring, especially on the hillsides, while millet is grown above the rice zone. Barley is sowed in the higher altitudes, as well as buckwheat with its pink and white flower cluster. The Sherpas grow potatoes up to 4000 metres, and have been doing so since the crop was introduced, probably from Darjeeling in the middle of the last century. Besides providing an important food staple, the prosperity attained from trading potatoes allowed Sherpas to begin building their *gompas* (temples) and for their culture to flourish.

Amongst the crops, on the berms dividing the plots, various other food crops are grown, including soya beans, lentils, sesame, and chilli peppers. The bright red and yellow plants with clustered seed heads seen amidst the shades of greens are *Amaranthus*, once an important food and medicinal grain for the Aztecs and Incas.

To keep animals out of crops, the Nepalese use assorted spiny or unpalatable exotics as natural barriers. Besides prickly pear cactus and agave, there are several euphorbias used, such as the red-flowering crown of thorns, spurge and physic nut.

There are numerous trees planted around villages and fields, all for some kind of purpose, be it for shade, fruit, fodder or medicine. Bananas, mangoes, papaya, citrus fruits, peaches and apples have all brought new income to the remote hill areas.

Fodder such as rice stalks and corn sheaves are often dried and stored in trees, while seed corn is stored under the eaves of houses. A variety of fig trees provide shade for pilgrims and travellers. The magnificent mushrooming canopies of banyan and pipal tress are unmistakable, usually found together atop a stone dais (platform) designed for accommodating porters' loads. The banyan has hanging aerial roots and leathery elliptical leaves, while the pipal has a heart-shaped leaf with a long spur. The Buddha is believed to have received enlightenment under a pipal tree, and Hindus revere the banyan as an embodiment of Lakshmi, the goddess of wealth, and the pipal as an embodiment of Narayan (Vishnu).

Bamboo grows under a variety of conditions and is found throughout Nepal. Giant bamboo is common in the tropics and dwarf bamboo in the temperates. This grass species is used for basketry and, where forests are depleted, particularly in the east, for building. The Rais work bamboo into everything from water vessels to entire houses.

Kitchen gardens are common features in villages and are comprised of greens, beans, turnips, radishes, pumpkins, cucumbers, taro and squash. Bauhinia, with its distinctive camel-hoof leaves and orchid-like flowers, is grown near houses; the leaves are used for fodder and the flowers cooked or pickled. In the west, tobacco is a commonly seen plot in villages, as are fields of cannabis grown for hemp. In addition, stinging nettles are picked with thongs, anaesthetised by boiling and eaten as greens. Eupatorium is a redstemmed daisy with heart-shaped leaves called *ban mara* ('death of forest') by the Nepalese. A native of Latin America introduced into the Himalaya during the last century, it invades subtropical and temperate zones, and is widespread. Covering deforested hillsides, it is unpalatable, even for sheep and goats, and is a prime indicator of environmental degradation.

Animal Husbandry

Bovines play an important role in rural and urban Nepal. Cows are sacred and are not slaughtered, nor used as beasts of burden –

they bear calves, and provide milk and, of course, multipurpose dung. The beasts of burden on the lowlands are usually castrated bulls, or oxen. In the Kathmandu Valley, the cows wandering and sleeping in the streets have been let loose by pious Hindus. Because the bull is Shiva's steed, and Pashupatinath is a major Shaivite temple, bulls are also considered holy and generally are not used to pull ploughs in the valley.

Water buffaloes belong to a different genus, but are still lumped with the bovines. These animals lose their body hair as they mature and must wallow to dissipate heat and for sun protection. The males are used as beasts of burden and are butchered. The females produce a creamy milk, which is also converted into yoghurt. These animals tend to be skittish, a trait probably inherited from their wild ancestors, and those at the Koshi Tappu Reserve in the eastern Terai are considered aggressive and dangerous.

The long-haired yaks, no longer found in the wilds of Nepal, are also very temperamental and are mostly used for stud service. What one generally sees are hybrids, which have confusing names. First of all, the female yak is called a *nak*. The nak or yak can be crossbred with cattle, which produces a more docile creature suitable for carrying loads. Locally, the male is called a *zopkiok* or *dzopkyo* and the female a *zhum* or *dzum*. The dzum lactates well and produces a better quality milk than the nak. The second generation of these hybrids is sterile.

In the Kali Gandaki and more recently on the southern approaches to the Everest region, donkeys and mules are being used as pack animals. These beasts are often adorned with headgear of dyed plumes and mirrors, and collars of bells. Also, in autumn, during the prime festival season, herds of goats and sheep are driven down from Tibet to be sold for ritual slaughter and the subsequent feasts.

Conservation

As long as the Nepalese marry early, feel uncertain about infant survival and desire sons to look after them in their old age and perform funeral rites, the population of Nepal will continue to burgeon. With population tension, the forests will continue to be depleted, erosion caused by humans will compound that which is natural, water supplies will dry up and floods will inundate the lowlands.

The visitor should not, however, adopt the role of the vociferous critic. Nepal is making positive changes, but traditional societies require long lead times for change. Amongst others, there are various alternative energy schemes underway, probably the most successful being the hydroelectric project of Solu and the soon-to-be-augmented unit above Namche Bazaar. The Annapurna Conservation Area Project (ACAP) is also an innovative approach, incorporating not only other alternative-energy developments, forest conservation and environmental education, but an effective strategy of getting the Nepalese people directly involved in determining their own destiny.

Conservation is typically a concept of affluent countries with land and resources to spare, a luxury unknown in the Third World. With dwindling space and forests, it is difficult for a farmer to grasp why land should be set aside for tigers and rhino, especially when they ravage crops, take domestic animals, and generally make a hard life even harder.

Visitors should ensure that they minimise their impact on the environment. Trekking groups or individuals staying in lodges should insist that kerosene, as opposed to firewood, is used for cooking meals and heating water. One should also minimise the use of non-biodegradable products (especially plastic and batteries) as there are no facilities for their disposal. One potential nightmare is the trend to sell water in plastic bottles, which are expensive and completely unnecessary if you carry your own water bottle and iodine. See the Facts for the Trekker chapter for more information on minimising your impact on the environment. Also, see the Books section in that chapter for a list of supplementary reading on flora, fauna and national parks.

POPULATION

Nepal's population of more than 19 million is growing at an alarming rate. The majority live in the Terai or in small hill villages, and only 800,000 people live in the Kathmandu Valley.

Trekking in Nepal is not a wilderness experience. Most people live in the tiny villages that blanket the hills. Even in the high mountains, small settlements of stone houses and yak pastures dot every possible flat space. Much of the fascination of a trek is the opportunity to observe and participate in the life of these villages. People truly live off the land, using only a few manufactured items such as soap, kerosene, paper and matches, all of which are imported in bamboo baskets carried by barefoot porters.

It is difficult for most Westerners to comprehend this aspect of Nepal until they actually visit the kingdom. Our preconception of a roadless area is strongly influenced by the places we backpack or hike to at home – true wilderness, usually protected as a national park or forest. In the roadless areas of Nepal there is little wilderness up to an elevation of 4000 metres. The average population density in Nepal is more than 122 people per sq km. Only about 17% of the country is classified as cultivable land. If we alter this statistic to eliminate all the mountainous places, the average rises to an incredible 709 or more people per sq km of cultivated land. The size and type of rural settlements varies widely, but most villages have from 15 to 75 houses, a population of 200 to 1000 and cover an area of several sq km.

Rather than detracting from the enjoyment of a trek, the hill people, particularly their traditional hospitality and fascinating culture, make a trek in Nepal a special kind of mountain holiday unlike any other in the world.

PEOPLE

Anthropologists divide the people of Nepal into about 50 'ethnic groups'. This is a convenient term to encompass the various categories of tribe, clan, caste and race. Each ethnic group has its own culture and traditions. Everyone is proud of their heritage and there is no need for embarrassment when asking someone about their ethnicity (*jaat* or *thar* in Nepali). Often it's not even necessary to ask, as many people use the name of their ethnic group, caste or clan as a surname.

While some groups are found only in specific regions, many groups are spread throughout the country. Nepal has historically been a nation of traders, acting as intermediaries for transactions between India and Tibet, so there is a history of extensive travel and resettlement.

The caste system has many 'occupational castes' and these groups have also spread throughout the country. Potters (Kuhmale), butchers (Kasain), blacksmiths (Kami), tailors (Damai), cobblers (Sarki), goldsmiths (Sunar), clothes washers (Dhobi) and others have travelled throughout Nepal to ply their trade.

Many ethnic groups have their own language, but almost everyone speaks Nepali – the *lingua franca* or trade language of the country – as a second language.

As the hill population has increased, many hill and even Himalayan people have migrated to lower elevations and the Terai in order to improve their lot. The following regional classification is, therefore, a bit artificial, but it does represent the traditional environment of each group.

Throughout Nepal

Brahmins The Brahmins (Bahuns in Nepali) are the traditional Hindu priest caste and speak Nepali as their first language. They are distributed throughout the country in both the Terai and Middle Hills. Many Brahmins are influential businesspeople, landowners, moneylenders and government workers. They are very conscious of the concept of *jutho*, or ritual pollution, of their home and food. Always ask permission before entering a Brahmin house and never enter a Brahmin kitchen. Brahmins traditionally do not drink alcohol.

Chhetris The other major Hindu caste is

Chhetri. In villages they are farmers, but they are also known for being outstanding soldiers. The Chhetri clans include the Ranas and the ruling family of Nepal, the Shahs. Thakuris are a group of Chhetris descended from the Rajputs in India and have the highest social, political and ritual status.

Newars The original inhabitants of the Kathmandu Valley are the Newars. To this day they remain concentrated in the valley in the cities of Kathmandu, Patan, Bhaktapur, Kirtipur and in smaller towns. Newars have a rich cultural heritage and are skilled artisans; a lot of the traditional art of Nepal is Newar crafted. There are both Buddhist and Hindu Newars. In the hills you are likely to meet Newars as government officers and merchants.

Musalman Nepal's Muslim population is known as Musalman. They live in the Kathmandu Valley, the eastern Terai and throughout the western hills. They migrated to Nepal from India, predominantly from Kashmir and Ladakh. Musalman are traditionally traders and dominate Kathmandu's trade in handicrafts, souvenirs, shoes and bangles.

Tibetans Tibetans are found mostly in Kathmandu at Boudhanath and Jawalakhel and in the Himalayan border regions. Often called Bhotia, this group includes both recent migrants and Tibetans who settled here long ago. The Sherpas, Dolpo people and other groups were originally from Tibet, but settled in Nepal so long ago that they have built up their own traditions and culture. There are significant Tibetan settlements in the hills at Solu Khumbu, Jumla, Dolpo, Hile and Pokhara.

Middle Hills

Tamangs You will encounter Tamangs, one of the most important groups in the hills, on almost every major trek. Tamangs believe they originally came from Tibet and speak a Tibeto-Burman language among themselves. They practise a form of Tibetan

Buddhism and there are Buddhist temples in many Tamang villages, though they have no monks, nuns or monasteries. Tamang priests are usually married and participate in regular day-to-day activities. Most Tamangs are farmers and live at slightly higher elevations than their Hindu neighbours, but there is a lot of overlap. The women wear gold decorations in their noses and the men traditionally wear a *bokkhu*, a sleeveless woollen jacket. The rough black-and-white blankets that you see in homes in the hills and in Kathmandu shops are a Tamang speciality.

Ta-mang literally means, 'horse soldier'. Tamang legend says they migrated to Nepal at the time of Genghis Khan as cavalry troops. Though they are primarily hill people, many Tamangs have moved to Kathmandu where they are employed as weavers of Tibetan rugs and as painters of high-quality *thangkas*. They also work as rickshaw drivers and porters; the 'sherpa' on your trek is more likely to be Tamang than Sherpa.

Rais Like the Tamangs and Sherpas, Rais speak a Tibeto-Burman language of their own and have a very unusual culture. They practise an indigenous religion that is neither Buddhist nor Hindu, though it has a fair amount of Hindu influence. Rais have very characteristic Mongoloid features which make them easy to recognise.

Some Rai villages are extremely large and boast 200 to 300 households. Typically, Rai villages are spread out over the hillside with trails leading in every direction. Finding the right route in these villages is always a challenge.

Rai people are very independent and individualistic. The 200,000 or so Rais in the eastern hills speak at least 15 different languages which, although seemingly closely related, are mutually unintelligible. When Rais of different areas meet they must converse in Nepali.

Rais (along with Limbus, Magars and Gurungs) are one of the ethnic groups which supply a large proportion of the recruits for

Rai woman

Tibetan and Assamese warlords. The Kirantis only joined the Gurkhali kingdom in 1774.

Many Limbus have adopted Subba as a surname and many men serve either in Gurkha regiments or in the Nepalese army. Limbus are the inventors of *tongba*, a tasty, but very potent, millet beer that is sipped through a bamboo straw. Their religion is a mixture of Buddhism and shamanism and they have their own dhamis. Most Limbu people live in the region east of the Arun River. You will be in Limbu country during the entire Kanchenjunga trek.

Gurungs Gurungs often serve in the Nepalese army and the Nepalese police, as well as in the Gurkha regiments of both the British and Indian armies. It is not unusual to meet ex-soldiers on the trail who have served in Malaysia, Singapore, Hong Kong and the UK. The stories of their exploits, told in excellent British-accented English, provide fascinating trailside conversation. An important source of income in most Gurung villages is the salaries and pensions of those in military service. The remaining income is from herding, particularly sheep, and agriculture – rice, wheat, corn, millet and potatoes. Access to many high pastures, including the Annapurna Sanctuary, is possible because of trails built by Gurung sheep herders.

Gurungs are Mongoloid in feature. It is easy to identify the men by their traditional clothing of a short blouse tied across the front and a short skirt of white cotton material, or often a towel, wrapped around their waist and held by a wide belt. In the Ghandruk area near the Annapurna Sanctuary, Gurung men fashion a backpack out of a piece of coarse cotton looped across the shoulders.

The Gurung funeral traditions and dance performances (the latter staged at the slightest excuse) are particularly exotic, and it is often possible to witness such aspects of Gurung life during a trek in this region. You will find Gurungs throughout the Annapurna region as well as at major settlements in the east, including Rumjatar, south of Jiri.

the well-known Gurkha regiments of the British and Indian armies.

An unusual sight, to Western eyes, in regions of Rai influence is the *dhami*, shamans who are diviners, spirit mediums and medicine men. Occasionally you will see them in villages, but more often you will encounter them on remote trails, dressed in elegant regalia and headdresses of pheasant feathers. The rhythmic sound of the drums that a dhami continually beats while walking echoes throughout the hills. Most Rais live between the Dudh Kosi and Arun valleys. You will meet them on the Everest trek and the trek from Khumbu to Dharan.

Limbus The Rais and Limbus are known collectively as the Kiranti. The Kiranti are the earliest known population of Nepal's eastern hills where they have lived for at least 2000 years. Early Hindu epics such as the *Mahabharata* refer to the warlike Kirantis of the eastern Himalaya. From the 7th century CE (the Common Era or AD), the Arun Valley was the site of fierce fighting between

Magars You will find Magars throughout Nepal, generally living south of their Gurung neighbours. Traditionally they are farmers and stonemasons, but many Magars serve as soldiers in Gurkha regiments and in the Nepalese army. Magars can be either Hindu or Buddhist. Hindu Magars practise the same religion as the Brahmins and Chhetris and employ Brahmins as priests. Magar women often wear necklaces of Indian silver coins. You will encounter Magars on most treks in Nepal. They are often integrated into villages dominated by other groups.

Sunwars One of the dominant groups in the region east of Kathmandu is the Sunwar, particularly in the villages of Ramechhap, Charikot and Okhaldunga. The women wear gold ornaments in their nose and ears and the men often join the Nepalese army. They live in whitewashed stone houses with black window frames. They worship their own gods, but employ Brahmins as priests. You will be in Sunwar country on the Everest trek during the drive from Lamosangu to Jiri.

Jirels A small subgroup of the Sunwars that live in and near Jiri are known as Jirels. Unlike the Sunwars, they use Buddhist lamas as their priests.

Thakalis The Thakalis originally came from the Kali Gandaki (Thak Khola) Valley, but they have migrated wherever business opportunities have led. They are traditionally excellent businesspeople and hoteliers and have created hotels, inns and other businesses throughout Nepal. Their religion is a mixture of Buddhism, Hinduism and ancient shamanistic and animistic cults, but they claim to be more Hindu than Buddhist. Despite their history of trade with Tibet, the Thakalis are not of Tibetan ancestry. They are related to the Tamangs, Gurungs and Magars.

Himalaya
Sherpas The most famous of Nepal's ethnic groups is the Sherpas, even though they form only a tiny part of the total population and live in a small and inhospitable region of the kingdom. Sherpas first came into prominence when the 1921 Mt Everest reconnaissance team hired them. The expedition started from Darjeeling in India and travelled into Tibet. Because many Sherpas lived in Darjeeling, it was not necessary to travel into 'forbidden' Nepal to hire them.

The Sherpa economy has become highly dependent on tourism and many Sherpas have developed Western tastes and values. This Western influence has made wages and other costs higher and non-negotiable in areas of Sherpa influence. It has given Sherpas the reputation among many independent trekkers for being rather grasping and difficult to deal with. Once fees and conditions are agreed to, or a trekking agent or shop is negotiating for you, you will probably find them charming and helpful. Sherpa-run hotels usually have fixed prices and do not entertain bargaining.

Though the most famous Sherpa settlements are in Khumbu, near Everest, Sherpas are found throughout the eastern part of Nepal. There are Sherpa villages from Helambu, north of Kathmandu, all the way to the Indian border. There are also large Sherpa populations in both Darjeeling and Sikkim in India. Most Sherpa villages are at elevations above 2500 or 3000 metres.

Sherpas frequently name their children after the day of the week on which they were born. Sunday is Nima and the following days are Dawa, Mingma, Lakpa, Phurba, Passang and Pemba. They often add the prefix 'Ang' to the name (similar to the English suffix 'son' or abbreviation 'Jr'). You would call Ang Nima 'Nima' for short, but never 'Ang'.

Manangis Manang, the region north of Annapurna, is the home of the Manangis. A decree by King Rana Bahadur Shah in 1784 gave them special trading privileges which they continue to enjoy. These privileges originally included passport and import and export concessions not available to the general population of Nepal. Beginning long ago with the export of live dogs, goat and sheepskins, yaks' tails, herbs and musk, the

Elderly man, Kathmandu valley (RI'A)

Top: Small village near Pokhara (GB)
Middle: Magar home, Sikha (RI'A)
Bottom: Small village near Pokhara (TW)

trade has now expanded into the large-scale import of electronic goods, cameras, watches, silk, clothing, gems and other high-value items in exchange for gold, silver, turquoise and other resources available in Manang.

The trade network of the Manang people extends throughout South-East Asia and as far away as Korea. It is not uncommon to see large groups of Manang people jetting to Bangkok, Singapore and Hong Kong. Manangis call themselves Nye-shang, but many Manang people adopt the surname Gurung on passports and travel documents, though they are more closely related to Tibetans than to Gurungs.

Dolpo People The isolation of the Dolpo people in the remote region north of Dhaulagiri has made them one of the most undeveloped, traditional groups in the kingdom. They are traders, specializing in the exchange of sheep, yaks and salt between Nepal and Tibet. You will meet them in Dolpo, especially in Tarap and Ringmo villages. Dolpo people have a reputation for staying continuously occupied, particularly with spinning wool by hand as they walk.

Loba The people of Lo live in the fabled and once forbidden region of Mustang. They compete with the Thakalis for trade in salt and wool, keep yaks, donkeys, mules and herds of sheep, and have close ties with Tibet. The region was once ruled by the raja of Mustang, but since 1952 his position has been only honorary. He has the rank of lieutenant colonel in the Nepalese army.

Baragaunle The upper Kali Gandaki, including Kagbeni and Muktinath, is the traditional home of the Baragaunle – the people of '12 villages'. They are of Tibetan ancestry and practise a kind of Tibetan Buddhism that has been influenced by ancient animistic and pre-Buddhist Bon-po rituals. The elegantly dressed women you will see near Muktinath are from this group.

Terai

Tharus The largest and probably the oldest group in the Terai is the Tharu. Now mostly peasant farmers, they once lived in small settlements of single-storey thatched huts within the jungle, which gained them the reputation for being immune to malaria. They have their own tribal religion based on Hinduism. Tharu women have a special dignity, and play a large role in their society. You will meet Tharus in Biratnagar, Nepalgunj and in Royal Chitwan National Park.

Dhanwar, Majhi & Darai These three related groups live along the Terai's river valleys and are among the poorest and least educated of Nepal's ethnic groups. Majhi traditionally live by fishing and operate dugout canoe ferries throughout the country.

Other Groups The Satar, Dhangar, Rajbansi, Koche and Tajpuri are other Terai groups. You are not likely to meet these people during a trek.

Nonethnic Groups

Sherpa Guides Since the first expedition to Mt Everest in 1921, Sherpas have been employed on treks and mountaineering expeditions. Their performance at high altitude and their selfless devotion to their jobs impressed members of early expeditions. Later expeditions continued the tradition of hiring Sherpas as high altitude porters. Most of the hiring was done in Darjeeling or by messages sent through friends and relatives into the Solu Khumbu region of Nepal (where most Sherpas live).

The practice continues to the present day, with trekking organisations hiring Sherpas either as permanent employees or on a per-trek basis. The emphasis shifted from Darjeeling to Kathmandu and to the Solu Khumbu region itself as these areas became accessible to foreigners.

It is confusing to discuss the role of Sherpas on an expedition or a trek as 'sherpa' can refer both to an ethnic group and to a function or job on a trek. Sherpa with a capital 'S' refers to members of that ethnic group, while on a trek or expedition a sherpa (lower-case 's') usually fulfils the role of trek guide or mountaineer. Traditionally, sherpas are Sherpas, but there are many exceptions. In this book, 'Sherpa' always refers to members of that ethnic group. I have also used the words sherpa and guide interchangeably.

Generally a sherpa is reasonably experienced in dealing and communicating with Westerners and can speak some English. The job of sherpa comprises several roles: *sirdar* (leader), cook, kitchen boy, guide or high altitude porter. The head sherpa on a trek or expedition is the sirdar and he is responsible for all purchases and for hiring porters. In the lowlands, a sherpa acts as a trekking guide, asking directions from the locals, if necessary, to find the best trail to a destination. Cooks and kitchen boys can produce amazing trailside meals. The term 'kitchen boy' is used for an assistant cook or kitchen hand, but women and men of all ages can fill the position.

The term 'sherpa' does not imply a high degree of technical mountaineering skill. Although they live near the high Himalayan peaks, Sherpas usually did not set foot on them, except to cross high passes on trade routes. This changed when the British introduced them to the sport of mountaineering. Many trekking sherpas have served as high altitude porters on mountaineering expeditions, carrying loads along routes already set up by technically proficient mountaineers. The Nepal Mountaineering Association school in Manang now provides mountaineering training to Nepalese guides. If you need an experienced mountaineering sherpa, be sure that he has attended this course.

Sherpas are not the only high altitude climbers. Sambhu Tamang reached the summit of Everest with the Italian expedition in 1973, becoming the first non-Sherpa Nepalese to reach the summit of a major Himalayan peak. Numerous other Nepalese of various ethnic groups have now climbed peaks throughout the country.

Porters carry loads, and their job finishes once that load reaches camp. Once the group is in camp, the job of the sherpa begins. A porter may be a member of any ethnic group. Many Rais, Tamangs and Magars spend almost their entire lives on the trails serving as porters. They carry loads, not only for trekkers, but also to bring supplies to remote hill villages. Expeditions use either the term 'high altitude porter' or 'sherpa' to denote those who carry loads to high camps on the mountain.

Gurkhas Nepalese who enlisted in the British and Indian armies became known as Gurkhas. The name is derived from the ancient town of Gorkha which was the home of Prithvi Narayan Shah, the founder king of Nepal. The British army applied the name Gurkha to all Nepalese and coined the name Gurkhali for the Nepali language.

In the old British army there were 10 Gurkha rifle regiments, but when India gained independence in 1947 it took six of the regiments and the UK retained four. The UK still maintains Gurkha recruiting centres at Pokhara and near Jawalakhel in Kathmandu. Most Gurkhas are Rais, Limbus, Gurungs and Magars in roughly equal number, though the Gurkha regiments also accept recruits from other ethnic groups. The Nepalese word for Gurkha soldier is *Lahure*.

Sahibs Nepalese in the hills tend to call Western (or Japanese) men *sahib* (pronounced like 'sob'). A Western woman is a *memsahib* and a porter is a *coolie*. These terms no longer hold the derogatory implications that they did during the British Raj. In a peculiar turnabout, the locals call a lone trekker a 'tourist' and someone with a trekking group a 'member'.

CULTURE

Nepal represents a culture far older and in many ways more sophisticated than Western culture, but you are not visiting a museum. Rather, you are visiting a country that is vibrantly alive, where many people live more comfortably and, in many cases, more happily than in the West. The more you listen and observe, the more you will learn and the more people will accept you. If you must try to teach Nepalese hill people something, try teaching them English. English is a key to upward mobility for employment in, or the running of, any business that deals with foreigners. This is the one element of Western culture that everyone desires – the English language. Spending your time conversing with a sherpa or porter in English as you stroll the trail together will be a good start towards a lasting friendship.

When trekking you will have a chance to meet and become acquainted with Sherpas and members of other Nepalese ethnic groups. The background of these people is completely different from what you are familiar with in the West. Treks are a fascinating cultural experience, but are most rewarding when you make some concessions to the customs and habits of Nepal.

Avoiding Offence

Nepalese are traditionally warm and friendly and treat foreigners with a mixture of curiosity and respect. *'Namaste'* ('Hello, how are you?') is a universal greeting. Most Nepalese speak at least some English, though smiles and gestures work well where language is a barrier.

Always double-check when asking for information or directions. As Nepalese hate to say 'no', they will give you their individual versions whether they know the answer or not. Their intention is not to mislead you; it is only to make you happy that you received an answer. You can often circumvent this problem by asking questions in a way that require a choice of alternatives rather than yes or no answers.

The following section offers some more suggestions and considerations that will make your trek more enriching. (See also Social & Environmental Considerations in the Facts for the Trekker chapter.)

Visiting a Temple Nepal is a Hindu country, although the Sherpas and most other high mountain people are Buddhists. In Kathmandu, you will be refused entry to a Hindu temple if you are wearing leather shoes or a leather belt. There are other temples that you will not be allowed to visit at all. Buddhist temples (gompas) are less restrictive, but you should still ask permission to enter and remove your shoes when you do – and definitely ask permission before photographing religious festivals, cremation grounds and the inside of temples.

If you meet the head lama inside a Buddhist gompa it is appropriate to present him with a white silk scarf called a *kata*. It is traditional to include a donation to the gompa inside the folded kata. The lama will remove the money and either keep the kata or place it around your neck as a blessing. Place the kata you are offering on the table or in the hands of the lama; do not place it around his neck. Monetary offerings should be in odd numbers like Rs 101; a donation of an even amount like Rs 100 is inauspicious.

Photographing People During a trek you will have many opportunities to photograph local people. Some people, however, will not want you to photograph them. Always ask before photographing women. There are always cases of shyness that you can overcome with a smile, a joke or using a telephoto lens, but don't pay people for taking their picture. Some people are afraid that a camera might 'steal their soul', but more often they are concerned about how photographs will eventually be used. Many photographs of hill people in Nepal, especially Sherpas, have been printed in books, magazines and brochures. The Sherpas, in particular the women, are afraid that a photo of them will be reproduced in quantity and eventually burned, thrown away or even used as toilet paper. This is a major reason that many local people will refuse photographs, and it should be respected.

Environmental Considerations There are a number of things the visitor can do to prevent pollution and other forms of environmental degradation. (See also the Facts for the Trekker chapter, and 'A Request from ACAP' in the Annapurna chapter.)

- Pick up papers, film wrappers and other junk.
- Use locally made toilets *(charpi)* whenever available, no matter how revolting they might be.
- Burn all your toilet paper and bury your faeces.
- Don't make campfires, as wood is scarce in Nepal.

Dress & Behaviour These are also important considerations for the trekker, and include the following points:

- Nudity is completely unacceptable and brief shorts are not appreciated. Men should always wear a shirt.
- Public displays of affection are frowned upon.
- Don't pass out balloons, candy and money to village children as it encourages them to beg. Trekkers are responsible for the continual cries of children for *mithai* (candy), *paisa* (money) and 'boom boom' (balloon). Well-intentioned trekkers thought they were doing a service by passing out pens for use in school, so clever kids now ask for pens.
- Don't tempt people into thievery by leaving cameras, watches and other valuable items around a hotel or trekking camp. Keep all your personal belongings in your hotel room or tent. This also means that you should not leave laundry hanging outside at night.

Food & Etiquette Most Nepalese eat with their hands. In many places you will not be offered a spoon, but one is often available if you ask. The Nepalese use only their right hand for eating and will expect you to do the same. If you eat with your hand, manners dictate that you wash it before and after eating. A jug of water is always available in restaurants for this purpose.

- Don't touch food or eating utensils that local people will use. Any food that a (non-Hindu) foreigner has touched becomes jutho ('polluted') and cannot be eaten by a Hindu. This problem does not apply to Sherpas, however.
- Do not put more food on your plate than you can eat. Once it has been placed on your plate, food is considered polluted.
- Don't throw anything into the fire in any house – Buddhist or Hindu. In most cultures the household gods live in the hearth.
- When you hand something to a Nepalese, whether it is food, money or anything else, use your right hand.
- Nepalese will not step over your feet or legs. If your outstretched legs are across a doorway or path, pull them in when someone wants to pass. Similarly, do not step over the legs of a Nepalese.
- The place of honour in a Sherpa home is the seat closest to the fire. Do not sit in this seat unless you are specifically invited to do so.

Life in the Hills

Most rural Nepalese families are self-sufficient in their food supply, raising all of it themselves and selling any excess in the few places, such as Kathmandu and Pokhara, that do not have a strictly agricultural economy. In return, the villagers buy mostly nonfood items that they cannot raise or produce themselves. These include sugar, soap, cigarettes, tea, salt, cloth and jewellery.

Throughout Nepal this exchange of goods creates a significant amount of traffic between remote villages and larger population and manufacturing centres. In the roadless hill areas, porters transport goods in bamboo baskets which are carried with a tumpline across their foreheads. During the many days they travel, porters either camp alongside the trail and eat food that they have brought from home or purchase food and shelter from homes along the trail. There are occasional tea shops, called *bhattis*, but porters rarely patronise them for more than an occasional cup of tea. Prices in bhattis are much higher than sharing an already prepared meal with a family. Often porters travel in groups and take turns cooking food that they carry themselves.

Second in importance to the transportation of goods is the flow of people between the colder Himalayan regions and the warmer climates of the Terai. Some of the movement is caused by seasonal migrations, but many people move permanently because of the pressures of increasing population in the hills. People also travel extensively in connection with weddings, funerals, festivals, school and government or military business.

Several of the hundreds of festivals that occur annually in Nepal require people to visit the homes of their relatives. Of particular importance is the Dasain festival in October, during which time thousands of people from a wide variety of economic and social backgrounds travel from urban centres to hill villages in a style that befits their standing. Their mode of travel may range from trailside camps, similar to those of porters, to service by an entire household staff. It is certainly rare, but still possible, to see porters carrying a woman in a sedan chair or basket.

Men who were born in hill villages and served in a Gurkha regiment in the British or Indian army return home to their villages on leave or upon retirement. They often have a huge retinue of porters to carry items they have collected during their assignments in Singapore, Hong Kong, Brunei or the UK.

Therefore, a wide variety of modes of travel exists on the trails of Nepal. Whatever their means of travel and whatever their economic status, travellers make a direct contribution to the economy of most villages through which they pass. In some cases, it is through the purchase of food; in others it is the buying of necessary goods or services; and in yet others it is the hiring of local people to serve as porters for a few days. The inhabitants of villages along major trails have come to expect and depend on this economic contribution – in much the same way as our cafes, roadhouses, motels and petrol stations rely on highway travellers of all sorts to provide their income.

Another phenomenon in the hills is that people come into continual personal contact with others. There are no trail signs, few hotel signs and no maps available locally. So no matter how shy a person may be, travellers must continually ask for directions or help in finding food and other items. They must also ask for information about places to stay, how far it is to the next village, etc. Many Westerners seem to have lost this ability, and rely on the isolation of a car to insulate them from strangers. They rarely need to ask directions because of the abundance of road signs and maps. The passing scene becomes merely another picture, framed by a car window.

Because Nepalese are constantly talking and exchanging important information, conversation often develops into long exchanges of pure chitchat or useless information. When trekking, you will hear the most commonly learned English phrases: 'What time is it?' and 'Where are you going?'. A traveller may spend an hour or two discussing trail conditions, where they have been, politics, the weather, crop conditions, the price of rice in a neighbouring village, who has just married (and who isn't, but should be), who died recently or hundreds of other topics – all with a complete stranger whom they may never meet again. This is an important part of life in the hills as there are no telephones, newspapers, TVs and few radios. Most news comes from travellers. It certainly is more stimulating to hear first-hand experiences than a radio news broadcast. Once a family has planted the crops for the season, there isn't much to do beyond the day-to-day activities of house cleaning, cooking and taking care of children, until harvest time. Besides their economic importance, travellers offer a valuable diversion, a source of information and a glimpse into a new and different world.

FESTIVALS

It is said that there are more festivals in Nepal than there are days in the year. Most Nepalese festivals are celebrated in homes and there is often little to see or photograph. Festivals complicate treks because government offices close, so you cannot get a trekking permit, and porters disappear home, occasionally leaving you at the side of the trail with your baggage.

Festivals are scheduled in accordance with the Nepalese calendar and the phase of the moon and can vary over a period of almost a month with respect to the Gregorian (Western) calendar. Nepalese months overlap Western months. The annual festival cycle through the Nepalese year is:

Baisakh – April to May
Naya Barsa & Bisket Jatra The Nepalese New Year always falls in mid-April. The

Nepalese Folk Songs

You are almost certain to hear folk songs in the hills. If you are travelling with sherpas and porters your own crew will probably entertain themselves – and you – with songs and dances to the accompaniment of a two-headed drum called a *madal*. If you are staying in hotels the entertainers may be villagers, a trekking groups' porters or the children of the hotel owner.

Most songs consist of an endless series of verses and a chorus. One or two people who know the words to verses usually take the lead and everyone joins in the chorus. Here are two of the most popular songs and a rough translation of the lyrics.

Resham Pheeree Ree

Resham pheeree ree, Resham pheeree ree
Udeyra jaunkee dandaa ma bhanjyang
Resham pheeree ree
*The silk cloth is fluttering, the silk cloth is
fluttering
Should I fly to the hilltops and the ridges
The silk cloth is fluttering*

Ek naley bunduk, dui naley bunduk, mriga lai takey ko
Mriga lai mailey takey ko hoeina, maya lai dankey ko
*One-barreled gun, twin-barreled gun targeted at the deer
It's not the deer that I am aiming at, but at my dear*

Chorus:
Resham pheeree ree, Resham pheeree ree
Udeyra jaunkee dandaa ma bhanjyang
Resham pheeree ree
*The silk cloth is fluttering, the silk cloth is fluttering
Should I fly to the hilltops and the ridges
The silk cloth is fluttering*

Kukur lai kutti kutti, biralo lai suri
Timro hamro maya priti dobato ma kuri
*To the dog it's puppy, puppy, to the cat it's meow meow
Our love is waiting at the crossroads*

Repeat chorus

people of Bhaktapur celebrate the Bisket Jatra (Death of the Snake Demons Festival) on this day. Two chariots are drawn pell-mell through the narrow alleyways of the town and a mighty tug of war ensues. The winners draw the chariots to their locale. A huge lingam pole is erected in the middle of the town by drunken revellers.

Mata Tirtha Aunsi Mother's Day is the day when children offer gifts, money and sweets to their mother and literally look at their mother's face. Those whose mother is dead make a ritual pilgrimage to Mata Tirtha Aunsi near Thankot.

Rato Machhendranath Jatra The Red (Rato) Machhendra festival, also known as Bhota Jatra or the Festival of the Vest, is held annually in Patan just before the monsoon on a date decided by astrologers. Both Hindus and Buddhists celebrate the festival. The idol of Machhendra is brought from Bungmati village to Pulchowk and paraded on a huge tottering chariot through the alleys of Patan to Jawalakhel. On an auspicious day, the

Saano ma sano gaiko bachho bhirai ma, Ram Ram
Chodreh jana sakena mailey, baru maya sanghai jaun
Tiny little baby calf is in danger at the precipice
I couldn't leave it there, let's go together, love

Repeat chorus

Paan Ko Paat
Paan ko paat
Maya timi lai samjhanchhu deen ko raat
Marsyangdi sa la la
Beetle leaf
Sweetheart, I keep you in mind for days and nights
Like the flow of the Marsyangdi

Timro hamro bhet bhako deena, bhet bhako deena
Saanglo paani dhamilo mun keena, paan ko paat
On the day we met, the day we met
The water was clear, why then was the heart so murky

Chorus:
Maya timi lai samjhanchhu deen ko raat
Marsyangdi sa la la
Beetle leaf
Sweetheart, I keep you in mind for days and nights
Like the flow of the Marsyangdi

Maya bhaye auw aggi sarey ra, auw aggi sarey ra
Chhaina maya jau maya marey ra, paan ko paat
If you love me, come forward, come forward
If you don't love me, dismiss it and go

Repeat chorus

Phewa tal ma sanglo chha paani, sanglo chha paani
Yo ramailo chhodera kahan janey, paan ko paat
The water in lake Phewa is clear, the water is clear
Where would you want to go and abandon this delight ∎

king and queen of Nepal, along with top government officials and thousands of devotees, descend upon Jawalakhel to catch a glimpse of the jewel-encrusted *bhoto* (vest) that Machhendra has been safeguarding for centuries.

Buddha Jayanti The main festival celebrating the full moon of Buddha's birth is held in Lumbini, the birthplace of Buddha. Similar festivals are held at Swayambhunath and Boudhanath. Processions carry the Buddha's image and all through the night,

glowing butter lamps and blazing electric lights celebrate Buddha's birth.

Shrawan – July to August
Ghanta Karna or Ghatemangal On the Night of the Witch, street urchins set up barricades all over the city and solicit donations from motorists, bikers and even pedestrians. A mock funeral procession is held later in the day, followed by a feast. Effigies of the devil, made of bamboo poles and leaves, are erected on every crossroad of the city.

Nag Panchami On the Day of the Snake God, Brahmin priests are hired by all households to cleanse their houses by pasting a picture of the *naga* (snake) over their doorways. *Pujas* (prayers) are performed and offerings of milk and honey are left for the snake gods. The nagas are pacified through prayers and their protection and blessings are sought.

Gokarna Aunsi Father's Day is similar to Mother's Day. People offer sweets, money and gifts to their fathers and look at their father's face. Those without fathers go to the Bagmati River at Gokarna to bathe and have their father's soul blessed.

Janai Purnima The Festival of the Sacred Thread is also known as Raksha Bhandhan and is celebrated on the full moon day of August. Higher caste Hindu men change the sacred thread they wear around their chests. In the hills of Nepal, devotees descend upon Shiva temples with a *jhankri* (medicine man) leading the throngs from each village.

Gai Jatra During the Festival of the Sacred Cows, children and adults dressed as cows pass through the city streets to honour the souls of their relatives who have recently died. It is also the day on which newspapers are legally allowed to defame and slander any and all persons.

Bhadra – August to September
Krishna Jayanti Krishna's birthday is celebrated with a huge festival at the stone temple of Krishna in Patan Durbar Square. Hymns and religious songs are sung all night by devotees. The king and queen of Nepal pay their respects to Krishna at the Krishna Mandir.

Teej Brata On the day of fasting for wives, all Nepalese wives fast from sunup to midnight of that day to ensure that their husbands have good fortune and a long life. Heavily bejewelled women wearing red saris descend upon Pashupatinath to dance and sing the day away. Colourfully attired hill

women trek down to Kathmandu for this festival.

Indra Jatra The Festival of the King of Gods is an eight-day festival at Kathmandu Durbar Square. The purpose of the festival is to ask Indra for post-monsoon showers for the harvest of the rice crop. This is the day the Living Goddess, or Kumari, of Kathmandu presides over a colourful ceremony attended by the king and queen, government officials and foreign diplomats.

Kartik – October to November
Dasain (Durga Puja) The 10-day festival of Dasain, celebrating Durga's triumph over evil, is the biggest festival in Nepal. All creeds and castes participate. People visit their families all over the country to rejoice over the goddess Durga's triumph. Banks and government offices are closed and most of the country comes to a standstill for the

Dasain Ferris wheel

duration of this festival. It is difficult to start a trek during Dasain because buses and planes are jammed and porters are totally unavailable.

Tihar (Diwali) The 'festival of lights' is the second most important festival in Nepal during which people pay homage to Laxmi, the goddess of wealth. Houses are given new coats of paint, hundreds of oil lamps and candles are lit, firecrackers are recklessly tossed into the streets and most households are packed with men gambling the night away. The goddess blesses gamblers who have made her happy.

Poush – December to January
Seto Machhendranath Snan The Seto (White) Machhendra is Kathmandu's version of Patan's Rato (Red) Machhendra. The chariot of Machhendra is built on Durbar Marg and dragged to Ratna Park. On the day deemed auspicious by astrologers, the Living Goddess presides over a function where Machhendra is bathed by priests.

Magh – January to February
Maghey Sankranti The first day of the Nepalese month of Magh, marking the end of winter, is an important festival all over the country. The Sankhamul Ghat in Patan is alive with devotees taking ritual baths in the Bagmati River, even though this is one of the coldest days of the year!

Falgun – February to March
Losar A two-week festival of drunken revelry commemorates the Tibetan New Year in February. Though strictly a Buddhist affair, Hindus (like Tamangs) who believe in both religions, also participate. The Sherpas are likely to be in a drunken stupor for two weeks, so treks tend to be difficult to arrange at this time.

Shiva Ratri On the sacred night dedicated to Shiva, thousands of Hindu pilgrims descend upon Pashupatinath, the holiest Hindu temple in the world – the abode of Shiva. Bonfires burn throughout the night to seek Shiva's blessings. All wood that is not nailed down is stolen by urchins who then spend all night basking in Shiva's glorious bonfires.

Holi Nepal's water-throwing festival is a merry affair during which people douse each other with buckets of scarlet liquid and daub red powder on their faces. The youngsters nowadays use acrylic paint and sewer water to enjoy themselves. Hashish cakes and *bhaang* (a cannabis flavoured drink) are legally sold on this day.

Chaitra – March to April
Ghora Jatra The Nepal army takes over the Tundikhel parade ground in Kathmandu on horse racing day to display its skills in warfare, acrobatics, motorcycle stunts and horse racing. Legend has it that the horses are raced to trample devils who may rise out of the ground to create havoc.

Balaju Jatra Thousands of pilgrims keep an all night vigil at the Swayambhunath Temple. The following day they trek to the 22 waterspouts at Balaju for a ritual bath.

RELIGION
In Nepal, Hinduism and Buddhism are mingled into a complex blend which is often impossible to separate. The Buddha was actually born in Nepal but the Buddhist religion first arrived in the country around 250 BCE (Before Common Era or BC), introduced, so it is said, by the great Indian Buddhist emperor Ashoka himself. Later Buddhism gave way to Hinduism, but from around the 8th century CE, the Tantric form of Buddhism practised in Tibet also began to make its way across the Himalaya into Nepal. Today Buddhism is mainly practised by the people of the high Himalaya, like the Sherpas, and also by Tibetans who have settled in Nepal. Several ethnic groups, like the Tamangs and Gurungs in the Middle Hills and the Newars in the Kathmandu Valley, practise both Buddhism and Hinduism.

Officially Nepal is a Hindu country, but in practice the religion is a strange blend of

Hindu and Tantric Buddhist beliefs, with a pantheon of Tantric deities tagged onto the list of Hindu gods or, in many cases, inextricably blended with them. Thus Avalokitesvara, the prime Bodhisattva of this Buddhist era, becomes Lokesvara, a manifestation of the Hindu god Shiva, and then appears as Machhendranath, one of the most popular gods of the Kathmandu Valley. Is he Hindu or Buddhist? Nobody can tell.

The vast majority of the population is Hindu, and Buddhists make up most of the balance. There are also small groups of Muslims and a few Christians. The Muslims are mainly found close to the border with India, and in the odd isolated village. Some ethnic groups, such as the Tharus and the Rais, have their own form of religion and worship the sun, moon and trees, though their practices retain many Buddhist and Hindu influences.

Hinduism

India, the Indonesian island of Bali, the Indian Ocean island of Mauritius, and possi-

Shiva

Brahma

bly Fiji, are the only places apart from Nepal where Hindus predominate, but it is the largest religion in Asia in terms of the number of adherents. Hinduism is one of the oldest extant religions, with firm roots extending back to before 1000 BCE.

The Indus Valley civilisation developed a religion which shows a close relationship to Hinduism in many ways. Later, it further developed on the subcontinent through the combined religious practices of the Dravidians and the Aryan invaders who arrived in the north of India around 1500 BCE. Around 1000 BCE, the Vedic scriptures were introduced and gave the first loose framework to the religion.

Hinduism today has a number of holy books, the most important being the four Vedas, or Divine Knowledge, which are the foundation of Hindu philosophy. The

Vishnu

Mahabharata where Krishna relates his philosophies to Arjuna.

Hinduism postulates that we will all go through a series of rebirths, or reincarnations, that eventually lead to *moksha*, the spiritual salvation which frees one from the cycle of rebirths. With each rebirth you can move closer to or farther from eventual moksha; the deciding factor is your karma, which is literally a law of cause and effect. Bad actions during your life result in bad karma, which ends in a lower reincarnation. Conversely, if your deeds and actions have been good you will reincarnate on a higher level and be a step closer to eventual freedom from rebirth.

Dharma is the natural law that defines the total social, ethical and spiritual harmony of your life. There are three categories of dharma, the first being the eternal harmony which involves the whole universe. The second category is the dharma that controls castes and the relations between castes. The third dharma is the moral code which an individual should follow.

Upanishads are contained within the Vedas and delve into the metaphysical nature of the universe and soul. The *Mahabharata* is an epic poem describing in over 220,000 lines the battles between the Kauravas and Pandavas. It contains the story of Rama, and it is probable that the most famous Hindu epic, the *Ramayana*, was based on this. The Bhagavad Gita is a famous episode of the

The Hindu religion has three basic practices. They are puja (worship), the cremation of the dead, and the rules and regulations of the caste system. There are four main castes: the Brahmin, or priest caste; the Chhetris, or soldiers and governors; the Vaisyas, or tradespeople and farmers; and the Sudras, or menial workers and craftspeople. These

---

Gurus & Sadhus

A guru is not so much a teacher as a spiritual guide, somebody who by example or simply by their presence indicates what path you should follow. In a spiritual search one always needs a guru. A sadhu is an individual on a spiritual search. They're an easily recognised group, usually wandering around half-naked, smeared in dust with their hair and beard matted. Sadhus most often follow Shiva and generally carry his symbol, the trident or *trisul*.

Sadhus are often people who have decided that their business and family life have reached their natural conclusions and that it is time to throw everything aside and go out on a spiritual search. They may previously have been the village postal worker, or a businessperson. Sadhus perform various feats of self-mutilation, and wander all over the subcontinent, occasionally coming together in great pilgrimages and other religious gatherings. Important pilgrimage sites for sadhus are Pashupatinath in Kathmandu, and the sacred sites of Gosainkund and Muktinath. Many sadhus are, of course, simply beggars following a more sophisticated approach to gathering in the paisa, but others are completely genuine in their search. ∎

Important Figures of Tibetan Buddhism

The following is a brief guide to some of the gods and goddesses of the Tibetan Buddhist pantheon. It is neither exhaustive nor scholarly, but it may help you to recognise a few of the statues you encounter in gompas during a trek.

Padmasambhava – the 'lotus-born' Buddha – assisted in establishing Buddhism in Tibet in the 8th century. He is regarded by followers of Nyingmapa Buddhism as the second Buddha. He is also known as Guru Rimpoche.

Avalokitesvara – 'glorious gentle one' – one of the three great saviours or Bodhisattvas. He is the Bodhisattva of compassion and is often pictured with 11 heads and several pairs of arms. His Tibetan name is Chenresig and the Sherpas call him Pawa Cherenzig.

Manjushree – the 'princely lord of wisdom' – is regarded as the first divine teacher of Buddhist doctrine. He is also known as Jambyang. Manjushree is said to have made the cleft in the mountains that drained the lake that once flooded the Kathmandu Valley.

Vajrapani – 'thunderbolt in hand' – is one of the three great saviours or Bodhisattvas. He is also known as Channadorje. The thunderbolt represents power and is a fundamental symbol of Tantric faith; it is called a *dorje* in Tibetan and *vajra* in Sanskrit.

basic castes are then subdivided, although this is not taken to the same extent in Nepal as in India. Beneath all the castes are the Harijans, or untouchables, the lowest, caste-less class for whom all the most menial and degrading tasks are reserved. Westerners and other non-Hindus are outside the caste system, and are therefore unclean. West-

Sakyamuni – the 'historical Buddha' – born in Lumbini in southern Nepal in the 5th century BCE, he attained enlightenment under a pipal (Bo) tree and his teachings set in motion the Buddhist faith. In Tibetan-style representations he is always pictured sitting cross-legged on a lotus flower throne.

Maitreya – the 'Buddha of the future'. He is passing the life of a Bodhisattva and will return to earth in human form 4000 years after the disappearance of Buddha (Sakyamuni).

Milarepa – was a great Tibetan magician and poet who is believed to have attained the supreme enlightenment of Buddhahood in the course of one life. He lived in the 11th century and travelled extensively throughout the Himalayan border lands, including Kailas, Shey Gompa, Nupri and Nelam near Kodari on the road from Kathmandu to Lhasa. Most images of Milarepa picture him smiling, holding his hand to his ear as he sings.

Tara – 'the saviouress' – has 21 different manifestations or aspects. She symbolises fertility and is believed to be able to fulfil wishes. Statues of Tara usually represent Green Tara, who is associated with night, or White Tara, who is associated with day. ■

erners are not allowed to enter Hindu temples. Any food that is touched by a Westerner, or put on their plate, becomes 'polluted' and must be discarded.

Westerners have trouble understanding Hinduism principally because of its vast pantheon of gods. In fact you can look upon all these different gods simply as pictorial representations of the many attributes of a god. The one omnipresent god usually has three physical representations. Brahma is the creator, Vishnu is the preserver and Shiva is the destroyer and reproducer. All three gods are usually shown with four arms, but Brahma has the added advantage of four heads.

Each god has an associated animal known as the 'vehicle' on which they ride, as well as a consort with certain attributes and abilities. Generally each god also holds symbols; you can often pick out which god is represented by the vehicle or symbols. Most temples are dedicated to one or other of the gods, but most Hindus profess to be either Vaishnavites (followers of Vishnu) or Shaivites (followers of Shiva). A variety of lesser gods and goddesses also crowd the scene. The cow is, of course, the holy animal of Hinduism.

Hinduism is not a proselytising religion since you cannot be converted. You're either born a Hindu or you are not; you can never become one. Similarly, once you are a Hindu you cannot change your caste – you're born into it and are stuck with it for the rest of that lifetime. Nevertheless Hinduism has a great attraction for many Westerners and India's 'export gurus' are numerous and successful. Because proselytising and conversion are not part of Hindu tradition, Nepalese law prohibits these practices, so Nepal has been spared the influence of missionaries and evangelists.

Buddhism

Strictly speaking Buddhism is not a religion, since it is not centred on a god, but a system of philosophy and a code of morality. Buddhism was founded in northern India about 500 BCE when Siddhartha Gautama, born a prince, achieved enlightenment. Gautama Buddha was not the first Buddha but the fourth, and is not expected to be the last 'enlightened one'. Buddhists believe that the achievement of enlightenment is the goal of every being so eventually we will all reach Buddhahood.

The Buddha never wrote down his dharma

or teachings, and a schism later developed so that today there are two major Buddhist schools. The Theravada or Hinayana, 'doctrine of the elders' or 'small vehicle', holds that the path to nirvana, the eventual aim of all Buddhists, is an individual pursuit. In contrast, the Mahayana, or 'large vehicle', school holds that the combined belief of its followers will eventually be great enough to encompass all of humanity and bear it to salvation. To some, the less austere and ascetic Mahayana school is a 'soft option'. Today it is chiefly practised in Vietnam, Japan and China, while the Hinayana school is followed in Sri Lanka, Burma (Myanmar) and Thailand, and by the Buddhist Newars in the Kathmandu Valley. There are other, sometimes more esoteric, divisions of Buddhism including the Tantric Buddhism of Tibet which is the version found in the Himalayan regions of Nepal. Tibetan Buddhism was influenced by the ancient animistic Bon-po tradition, and there are a few pockets of Bon-po remaining in Nepal, especially in Dolpo.

The Buddha renounced his material life to search for enlightenment but, unlike other prophets, found that starvation did not lead to discovery. Therefore he developed his rule of the 'middle way', moderation in everything. The Buddha taught that all life is suffering, but that suffering comes from our sensual desires and the illusion that they are important. By following the 'eight-fold path' these desires will be extinguished and a state of nirvana, where they are extinct and we are free from their delusions, will be reached. Following this process requires going through a series of rebirths until the goal is eventually reached and no more rebirths into the world of suffering are necessary. The path that takes you through this cycle of births is karma, but this is not simply fate. Karma is a law of cause and effect; your actions in one life determine the role you will play and what you will have to go through in your next life.

In India Buddhism developed rapidly when it was embraced by the great emperor Ashoka. As his empire extended over much of the subcontinent, so Buddhism was carried forth. Later, however, Buddhism began to contract in India because it had never really taken a hold on the great mass of people. As Hinduism revived, Buddhism in India was gradually reabsorbed into the older religion.

Buddhism is more tolerant of outsiders than is Hinduism; you will be welcome at most Buddhist temples and ceremonies. In Kathmandu and in the hills there are Buddhist monasteries that are willing to provide spiritual training and advice to Westerners.

Buddhism prohibits any form of killing, a contrast to Hinduism in which some forms of the religion require animal sacrifices to appease the goddess Kali.

LANGUAGE

Nepali is the working tongue of Nepal and is understood by almost everyone in the country. Newars, Tamangs, Rais, Sherpas and many other ethnic groups have their own language which they speak among themselves, but they use Nepali outside their own region. Nepali is the first language of the Brahmins, Chhetris and Thakuris – the highest castes in Nepal. It belongs to the Indo-Aryan family of languages, derived from Sanskrit. Its nearest relative today is Kumaoni, spoken in a region of north-west India. Nepali has much in common with Hindi, the official language of India, which has the same origins. It has also taken many words from Persian, through Hindi.

It's not difficult to learn a bit of the language, and it can add greatly to your enjoyment of trekking. Nepalese aren't fussy about the language and will appreciate an effort to learn it. You'll find a little Nepali can go a long way.

Since Nepali, like Hindi, uses the Devanagari script, for English speakers it must be transliterated to Roman script. There are many systems of transliteration, but the one used here is from Meerendonk's *Basic Gurkhali* dictionary. To make it easier to see the difference in pronunciation, I have used 'aa' where he uses 'ā'.

Lonely Planet's *Nepal Phrasebook* also provides a handy introduction to the language.

Pronunciation

a	as in	*u*p
aa	as in	f*a*ther
e	as in	caf*e*
i	as in	r*i*m
o	as in	g*o*
u	as in	f*u*ll
ai	as in	*ai*sle

A big key to the correct pronunciation of Nepali is the 'a' and 'aa' sound. The sound represented here by a single 'a' is like the 'u' sound in 'up' and the sound of 'aa' is a true 'a' sound as in 'car' or 'far'. For example, *chhang* is pronounced like 'bung' or 'rung', not like 'clang' or 'bang'.

Another difficulty is the 'h' sound. In Nepali the 'h' almost vanishes in pronunciation, particularly when it follows a consonant. Ask a Nepali to pronounce *dhungaa* (stone) and *dungaa* (boat); they will probably sound the same to you, as will *ghari* (wristwatch) and *gaari* (automobile). To a Westerner, *mahango* (expensive) sounds like 'mungo', but a Nepali would include (and hear) the 'h' sound. In the transliteration used here, 'ch' is pronounced as in the English 'chin', while 'chh' sounds like a combination of 'ch' plus 'h'. The letter 'r' is rolled and is pronounced almost like 'dr'; some transliteration systems replace the 'r' with a 'd' or combine them as 'dr'.

Why isn't the language written as it sounds? Each of these sounds is a different letter or character in the Devanagari script used to write Nepali, and in Nepali they are distinct letters and sounds – even if they sound the same to Westerners. Nepali has more vowels than English, so English letters must be combined to represent these sounds.

In Nepali, the verb is placed at the end of a sentence. Grammatically, questions are identical to statements. The differentiation is made by the intonation pattern of the voice. For example, *thik chha* (with a rising tone) means 'Are you OK?'. While *thik chha!* answers 'Yes, I'm OK!'.

Greetings & Civilities

Hello/Goodbye.
namaste
Thank you.
dhanyabaad (not commonly used)
Where are you going?
tapain kahan jaane?
What is your name?
tapainko naam ke ho?
My name is...
mero naam...ho
How are you?
tapailai kasto chha?
I am well.
sanchai chha
What is this?
yo ke ho?
It is cold today.
aaja jaaro chha
It is raining.
paani parchha
That's OK.
thik chha
I know.
thaahaa chha
I don't know.
thaahaa chhaina

Trekking Words & Phrases

house	*ghar*
shop	*pasal*
latrine	*charpi*
steep uphill	*ukaalo*
steep downhill	*oraalo*
left	*baayaan*
right	*daahine*
straight ahead	*sidha*
tired	*thaakyo*
cold (weather)	*jaaro*
warm (weather)	*garam*

This river is cold.
yo kholaa chiso chha
Which trail goes to...?
kun baato...jaanchha?
Is the trail steep?
baato ukaalo chha?

Where is my tent?
mero tent kahaan chha?
What is the name of this village?
yo gaaunko naam ke ho?
Where is a shop?
pasal kahaan chha?

Food Words & Phrases

local inn	*bhatti*
beer (local)	*chhang* or *jaanr*
whisky (local)	*rakshi*
tea	*chiyaa*
water	*paani*
hot water	*taato paani*
cold water	*chiso paani*
boiled water	*umaleko paani*
meat	*maasu*
chicken (meat)	*kukhoroko maasu*
bread	*roti*
egg	*phul*
food	*khaanaa*
vegetable	*saag*
cooked vegetable	*tarkaari*
cabbage	*banda kobi*
cauliflower	*kauli* or *phul kobi*
chilli	*khorsaani*
corn	*makai*
lentils	*daal* or *kodo*
mustard	*tori*
potatoes	*aalu*
radish	*mula*
rice (cooked); also food in general	*bhaat*
spinach	*saag*
soybeans	*baatamaas*
turnips	*gyante mula*
yams	*sutaani*
hot	*taato*
hot (spicy)	*piro*
tasty	*mitho*

Please give me a cup of tea.
ek cup chiyaa dinuhos
Do you have food (rice) now?
aile bhaat chha?
It is enough.
pugchha
Is the food good?
khaana mitho chha?

Other Useful Words

happy	*khushi*
enough	*pugyo*
yes (it is...)	*ho*
no (it is not...)	*hoina*
this	*yo*
that	*tyo*
mine	*mero*
yours	*timro*
his, hers	*unko*
expensive	*mahango*
cheap	*sasto*
big	*thulo*
small	*sano*
good	*ramro*
not good	*naraamro*
maybe	*hola*
clean	*saaph* or *saphaa*
dirty	*mailo*
heavy	*gahrungo*
here	*yahaan*
there	*tyahaan*
where	*kahaan*
which	*kun*

Family

mother	*aamaa*
father	*baabu*
son	*chhoro*
daughter	*chhori*
elder brother	*daai*
younger brother	*bhaai*
elder sister	*didi*
younger sister	*bahini*
friend	*saathi*

Animals & Crops

cow	*gaai*
dog	*kukur*
horse	*ghoraa*
pig	*sungur*
bird	*charo*
chicken	*kukhoro*
water buffalo	*bhainsi*
male yak	*yak*
female yak	*nak*
barley	*jau*
buckwheat	*paapad*
millet	*kodo*

field rice	*dhaan*
husked rice	*chaamal*
tobacco	*surti*
wheat	*gahun*

Places

hill/mountain	*daanda*
snowy mountains	*himal*
hills	*lek*
the plains	*terai*
landing place, ferry	*ghat*
alpine pasture	*kharka*
alpine hut	*goth*
river	*kholaa*
major river	*kosi*
small stream	*naalaa*
stream (in Hindi)	*nadi*
lake	*kund, pokhari, taal*
trail	*baato*
mountain pass:	
Nepalese	*bhanjyang*
Tibetan	*la*
western Nepal	*laagna*
village	*gaon*
resting place	*chautaara*
Buddhist monument	*chorten*
arch-shaped chorten	*kani*
Tibetan Buddhist temple	*gompa*
Hindu temple	*mandir*
wall or stone carved with prayers	*maani*

Time & Dates

day	*din*
morning	*bihaana*
night	*raat*
today	*aaja*
yesterday	*hijo*
tomorrow	*bholi*
day after tomorrow	*parsi*
sometime	*bholi-parsi*

What time is it (now)?
    (aile) kati bajyo?
Five o'clock.
    paanch bajyo

Numbers

1	*ek*	16	*sohra*
2	*dui*	17	*satra*
3	*tin*	18	*athaara*
4	*chaar*	19	*unnaais*
5	*paanch*	20	*bis*
6	*chha* (some say *chhe*)	25	*pachchis*
7	*saat*	30	*tis*
8	*aath*	40	*chaalis*
9	*nau*	50	*pachaas*
10	*das*	60	*saathi*
11	*eghaara*	70	*sattari*
12	*baahra*	80	*ashi*
13	*tehra*	90	*nabbe*
14	*chaudha*	100	*ek say*
15	*pandhra*	1000	*ek hajaar*

Facts for the Trekker

General Information

VISAS & EMBASSIES

Nepal's immigration rules are complex, cumbersome and, above all, expensive. All foreigners, except Indians, must have a visa. Visas are issued by Nepalese consulates overseas or they can be issued when you arrive in Nepal, either at the Kathmandu airport or at a road border with India or Tibet. If you stay in Nepal for more than one month, you will require a visa extension. To trek, you must obtain a trekking permit from the immigration office specifying the time and route of your trek.

A 30-day visa is available when you arrive in Kathmandu. You must fill in an application form and theoretically you should have a photograph, though this requirement is overlooked if you don't have one. A Nepalese visa costs US$40 whether issued in Nepal or overseas. At Kathmandu airport the fee is payable in US cash dollars only. In 1993, those who did not have US dollars were required to stand in the currency exchange queue to change money into US dollars to pay for the visa.

Now the rules become even more complicated. There should be a minimum 30 days gap between your last departure and your next arrival unless you have a re-entry permit or double-entry visa. Re-entry permits are issued only in Kathmandu and cost US$40 for one entry, US$70 for two entries or US$200 for multiple entries. Double-entry visas are available only from overseas embassies and consulates and cost US$80. If you do arrive within the 30-day period you can still return to Nepal, but must pay a visa fee that depends on the total length of time you have been in Nepal within the last year. If you have been in Nepal one month or less the cost is US$50, two months it is US$60 and three months or more it is US$70.

Visa extensions cost US$2 per day for the second and third month. If you get a fourth month extension it costs US$3 per day. You can stay in Nepal for a maximum of 120 days per year on a tourist visa. After that you should stay out of Nepal for a year. The costs of visa extensions are quoted in US dollars, but are payable in Nepalese rupees at the prevailing rate on that particular day.

Don't overstay a visa. Airport officials often refuse to allow passengers to board a departing flight if their visa has expired, even for a single day, though it may be possible to pay a fine if the current rules allow this. There is a 200% fine plus the regular visa fee for not getting a visa extension on time.

Nepalese embassies and consulates abroad issue one-month visas. The cost is usually the local equivalent of US$40. In many countries, Nepal has appointed honorary consuls who are not employees of the Nepalese government. When honorary consuls issue visas they often levy a service charge to cover the expense of maintaining a visa office on behalf of the Nepalese government. The list of embassies and consulates that follows identifies the honorary consuls.

There is no advantage to having a visa in advance except for the time you save at the airport when you arrive. If you are arriving by road it might save some hassle and delay if you already have a visa, but you can get a visa at any road border, even the funky Kodari checkpost on the road to Tibet. A Nepalese visa is valid for entry for three months from the date of issue. Do not apply too soon or it will not be valid when you arrive in Kathmandu.

Nepalese Embassies & Consulates

Australia
  Christine Gee, Honorary Consul, 48 Mitchell St, McMahons Point, Sydney, NSW 2060 (☎ 02-956-8815, fax 02-956-8767)
  W A Johns, Honorary Consul, Suite 23, 18-20

Bank Place, Melbourne, Vic 3000 (☎ 03-602-1271, fax 03-670-6480)
Lillian Roberts, Honorary Consul, Suite 2, 16 Robinson St, Nedlands, WA 6009 (☎ 09-386-2102, fax 09-386-3087)

Bangladesh
United Nations Rd, Road R 2, Baridhara Diplomatic Enclave, Dhaka (☎ 601890, 602091)

Belgium
Rodolphe Wiedmann, Honorary Consul, 149 Lamorinierstraat, B-2018, Antwerp, Belgium (☎ 03-230-8800)

Canada
William H Baxter, Honorary Consul, 310 Duport St, Toronto, Canada M5R 1V9 (☎ 416-968-7252)

China
No 1, Sanlitun Xiliujie, Beijing (☎ 532-1795)
Norbulingka Rd 13, Lhasa, Tibet Autonomous Region (☎ 36890, 22881)

Denmark
Ole Janus Larsen, Honorary Consul, 2 Teglgaardstraede, 1452 Copenhagen K (☎ 33-133165)

Finland
Gustav Mattson, Honorary Consul, Erottaja 11 A 14, 00130 Helsinki (☎ 680-2225)

France
45, bis Rue des Acacias, Paris 75017 (☎ 4622-4867)

Germany
Im Hag 15, D-5300 Bonn 2 (☎ 0228-343097/9)

India
1 Barakhamba Rd, New Delhi 110001 (☎ 332-9969, 332-7361)
19 Woodlands, Sterndale Rd, Alipore, Calcutta 700027 (☎ 711124/03)

Italy
Anselmo Previdi, Honorary Consul, Piazzale Medaglie d'Oro 20, Rome 00136 (☎ 348176)

Japan
14-9 Tokoroki 7-chome, Setagaya-ku, Tokyo 158 (☎ 3705-5558)

Myanmar (Burma)
16 Natmauk Yeiktha, Yangon (☎ 533168)

Netherlands
Jurgen Herbert Kurras, Honorary Consul, Prinsengracht 687, Gelderland Building, 1017 JV Amsterdam (☎ 020-250388)

Pakistan
House No 506, Street No 84, Attaturk Ave, Ramna G-6/4, Islamabad (☎ 210642, 212754)

Philippines
Nicola O Katigbak, Honorary Consul, 1136-38 United Nations Ave, Paco 2803, Manila (☎ 589393)

Spain
Lluis Belvis, Honorary Consul, Mallorca 194 Pral 2A, 08036 Barcelona (☎ 03-323-1323)

Sweden
Claes-Olof Livijn, Honorary Consul, Eriksbergsgatan 1A, S-114 30 Stockholm (☎ 08-679-8039)

Switzerland
1, rue Frederic-Amiel, 1203 Geneva (☎ 022-344-4441)
Dr Hans Ulrich Vetsch, Honorary Consul, Asylstrasse 81, 8030 Zurich (☎ 01-475993)

Thailand
189 Soi 71 Sukhumvit, Bangkok (☎ 391-7240, 390-2280)

UK
12A Kensington Palace Gardens, London W8 4QU (☎ 071-229-6231/1594)

USA
2131 Leroy Place NW, Washington, DC 20008 (☎ 202-667-1551)
820 Second Ave, Suite 202, New York, NY 10017 (☎ 212-370-4188)
Mary B Sethness, Honorary Consul, 1500 Lake Shore Drive, Chicago, Illinois 60610 (☎ 312-787-9199)
William C Cassell, Honorary Consul, Heideberg College, Tiffin, Ohio 44883 (☎ 419-448-2202)
Richard Blum, Honorary Consul, Suite 400, 909 Montgomery St, San Francisco, California 94133 (☎ 415-434-1111)
Lucille G Murchison, Honorary Consul, 16250 Dallas Parkway, Suite 110, Dallas, Texas 75248 (☎ 214-931-1212)
Josephine Crawford Robinson, Honorary Consul, 212 15th St NE, Atlanta, GA 30309 (☎ 404-892-8152)

Visa Extensions & Trekking Permits

To get a visa extension or trekking permit, go to the central immigration office (☎ 418573) in Kathmandu, near the Royal Palace on Tridevi Marg at the entrance to Thamel. The office accepts applications Sunday to Thursday from 10.30 am to 2 pm and on Friday from 10.30 am to noon. The office is closed on Saturdays and holidays. Visa extensions and trekking permits are sometimes available the same day, but during the busy season you should allow up to three working days for an extension to be processed. At peak times the queues are long and the formalities are tedious.

A large sign at the entrance to the immigration office details the latest rules and regulations. Trekking and travel agencies can assist with the visa extension process and can usually save you the time and tedium of queuing.

Every visa extension or trekking permit requires your passport, money, photos and an application form. Collect all these documents before you start waiting in the queue. There are several instant photo shops near the immigration office, but Polaroid photos are expensive. If you plan ahead, there are many photographers who will provide passport photos within a day. Kathmandu is a good, inexpensive place to stock up on extra photos of yourself for future travels. Prior to October 1993 you were required to produce bank receipts to prove you had changed US$20 per day for every day of visa extension. This requirement has been dropped and replaced by a US$2 per day fee for visa extensions. You can extend your visa up to a total stay of three months without undue formality; the fourth month of extension not only costs more (US$3 per day for the month), but requires a special application. Theoretically, you are allowed to stay in Nepal for a maximum of four months per year on a tourist visa.

For more details about trekking permits, see the Trekking Information section later in this chapter.

One-week visa extensions and two-week trekking permits are also available in Pokhara.

Re-Entry Permits

If you are travelling from Nepal to India or Tibet and returning to Kathmandu within 30 days you should get a re-entry permit before you leave Nepal. This is an easy process at the immigration office. Don't overlook it or you will be obliged to pay excessive visa fees on your return.

CUSTOMS
Arrival

Nepal's customs formalities are among the most thorough in the world. Customs officials at Kathmandu airport open most bags and inspect them. If you arouse suspicion, you may even be subjected to a body search.

The duty-free allowance includes 200 cigarettes, 20 cigars and one bottle of liquor. There is a duty-free shop in the arrival hall of Kathmandu airport. Personal effects, including trekking equipment, are permitted free entry. Excessive amounts of film, 16 mm movie equipment, firearms or food and gear for mountaineering expeditions are subject to special restrictions.

Nepal prohibits the import and export of gold and a substantial part of the efforts of customs inspectors is to detect smuggled gold. Some items of obvious use to tourists, such as video cameras and laptop computers, are allowed, but customs officials write the details of the equipment in your passport to ensure that you take it out of the country when you leave. Other so-called luxuries, such as video players and televisions, require an import licence. If you are carrying such items they will be impounded and kept in customs bond until you depart. Things often get lost or broken in the customs bond facility; avoid bringing anything to Nepal that might end up there.

You may not import Nepalese currency and only Nepalese and Indian nationals may import Indian currency. There is no restriction on bringing in either cash or travellers' cheques, but the amount taken out at departure should not exceed the amount brought in. The rules say that you should declare cash or travellers' cheques in excess of US$5000.

Departure

Baggage is also inspected when you leave the country. Nepal prohibits the export of antiques. Items that look old should have a certificate from the Department of Archaeology. Other prohibited exports are gold, silver, precious stones, wild animals and their skins and horns and all nonprescription drugs, whether processed or in their natural state. You will be hassled if you carry out a fancy statue without a certificate stating that it is not an antique.

Warning

There is considerable money to be made by smuggling gold, drugs and foreign currency into or out of Nepal. Nepalese may approach you in Kathmandu or Hong Kong offering you money, free air tickets or other incentives to carry goods for them. The penalties are severe, informants are everywhere and the jails in Nepal are dreary. Forget it!

TRAVEL INSURANCE

Trekking and travel agents can offer a travellers' insurance policy. Coverage varies from policy to policy, but will probably include loss of baggage, sickness and accidental injury or death. Most policies also cover the reimbursement of cancellation fees and other costs if you must cancel your trip because of accident or illness, or the illness or death of a family member. It's probably worth purchasing this inexpensive protection, especially if you are travelling on nonrefundable advance purchase plane tickets.

Be sure that the policy does not exclude mountaineering or alpinism or you may have a difficult time settling a claim. Although you will not engage in such activities, you may never be able to convince a flatland insurance company of this fact. It would also be prudent to check the policy to be sure that it specifically covers helicopter evacuation.

If you purchase insurance and have a loss, you must submit proof of this loss when you make an insurance claim. If you have a medical problem, you should save all your bills and get a physician's certificate stating that you were sick. If you lose something covered by insurance, you must file a police report, no matter how remote the location. No insurance company considers a claim without such documentation. Police checkposts in Nepal will provide a police report if there is a major theft. They are all familiar with this bit of bureaucracy.

Currently, there is no rescue insurance available in Nepal. In 1994, the Himalayan General Insurance Company in Kathmandu was working to prepare a scheme that would cover helicopter rescue. This might be in place by the time you arrive in Nepal. To be certain of being covered, you should organise your rescue insurance before you leave your home country.

Helicopter Evacuation

If you are injured and unable to travel, you can ask for a rescue helicopter or charter flight from a remote airstrip only if you have some definite proof that you can pay for it. It costs more than US$1500 for a helicopter evacuation from 4000 metres near Mt Everest. Helicopters have saved the lives of several people who left Nepal without paying the bill for the rescue flight. The Royal Nepal Army, which operates the service, now refuses to send a chopper unless they have cash in hand. All trek organisers have an agreement in Kathmandu that guarantees payment for helicopter evacuations, though they will bill you later for the service. Some embassies will also guarantee helicopter payments. If you are going on an extended trek, register with your embassy and ask about their policy on rescues.

MONEY

The Nepal Rastra Bank (the national bank of Nepal) determines the value of the Nepal rupee (Rs) against a 'basket of currencies' and fixes exchange rates against several currencies. Radio Nepal, Nepal Television, Nepalese and English newspapers all announce the rates every morning. In March 1994 the exchange rates were:

US$1	=	Rs 49
A$1	=	Rs 35
UK£1	=	Rs 73
DM1	=	Rs 29
FF 1	=	Rs 8.6
Indian Rs 1	=	Rs 1.6

There are 100 paisa (p) in a rupee. In the hills, shopkeepers often do their calculations in units of 50 paisa, called a *mohar* – Rs 1.50 equals three mohar. In Kathmandu, virtually everything is rounded to the next higher rupee.

You can change money officially at banks and exchange counters authorised by the Nepal Rastra Bank. Hotels in Kathmandu and Pokhara are also licensed to change foreign currency; rates are almost the same as the bank. When you change money, be sure to get a receipt with the stamp of the bank or hotel. They don't always volunteer to give you this, but if you plan to exchange any money back when you leave Nepal you must have a bank receipt. You can reconvert only 15% of the total amount supported by exchange receipts back to foreign exchange. You can do this only at the airport when you depart from Nepal.

You can carry either cash or travellers' cheques for your expenses in Nepal. Both American Express and Visa have refund facilities in Kathmandu. US dollars are the most acceptable, though banks are also happy with pounds sterling, Australian dollars and most European currencies. (Note that Scandinavian money is sometimes difficult to change.) US cash dollars are the primary medium of exchange for hotels, airlines and the government. You must have US dollars for a visa and will have less hassle everywhere if you carry greenbacks, though US$100 notes are subject to special scrutiny and confirmation by the bank because of a rash of counterfeit bills.

Credit cards are slowly gaining acceptance in Kathmandu, but are worthless in the hills. If you are an American Express cardholder, you can get US dollar travellers' cheques with a personal cheque at the American Express office. Nepal Grindlays Bank can provide a cash advance in Nepalese rupees or US dollar travellers' cheques against a Visa card.

Prices for hotel accommodation and airline tickets are quoted in US dollars and you are required to pay for these in foreign currency. You must pay for tickets on domestic flights in foreign cash or travellers' cheques; Royal Nepal Airlines does not accept credit cards. If you plan to fly back from Lukla, Pokhara or Jomsom at the end of a trek, be sure you have enough foreign currency, preferably in US dollars, to purchase a plane ticket (if you did not buy a ticket in advance). You should carry enough cash on a trek to buy a plane ticket in case you need one in an emergency.

If you will be trekking on your own, you should carry enough money in rupees to cover all your expenses on the trek. It is often difficult to change foreign currency or travellers' cheques except in Kathmandu or Pokhara.

Black Market
Because of Nepal's foreign exchange restrictions, the black market is so sophisticated that rates can change hourly depending on conditions in Hong Kong and the Middle East. The government makes occasional efforts to curb this trade, which is centred around Thamel in Kathmandu. Rates and availability can change rapidly, though you can sometimes obtain a 10 to 15% premium over the official rate. It's illegal, of course, and the money is often used in the drug trade.

Costs
If you stay in hotels as you trek, estimate your costs at Rs 200 to Rs 300 per day for food and from Rs 25 to Rs 50 per day for dormitory lodging. Add 50 or 60% to these costs when you trek above 3500 metres. Estimate US$20 to US$40 per day per person if you plan to hire porters, sherpas and all the trappings yourself. Local trekking companies charge US$30 to US$75 per day for an organised trek. If you book a trek overseas it will cost you US$100 or more per day, including the services of a Western leader.

The money you take on the trek should be in notes ranging from Rs 1 to Rs 100. There are banknotes of Rs 500 and Rs 1000, but it may be difficult to find change for these in the hills, though hotels in Namche and Jomsom can usually handle them. If you have big notes, you can get change at banks in Namche, Chame, Jomsom and Pokhara. If you are going to a particularly remote area such as the Arun River or far west Nepal, you should carry stacks of Rs 1, Rs 5 and Rs 10 notes, but this is not necessary on the more popular routes. Consider yourself lucky that paper money is now accepted throughout Nepal. The 1953 Everest expedition had to carry all its money in coins. The money alone took 30 porter loads!

Tipping

Waiters in Kathmandu expect tips of Rs 5 to Rs 10 in smaller restaurants and from 5 to 10% in hotels. Bellhops and maids are happy to receive about Rs 10. Trek and travel guides expect substantially more. Taxi drivers don't expect tips, but it is OK to leave them loose change.

Trekking lodges, generally being owner-operated, do not solicit tips, but they certainly do not refuse them. Sherpas and porters on group treks expect a generous tip, called baksheesh, at the conclusion of a trek. It is difficult to offer prudent guidelines about such tipping, but a tip of between 10 and 40% of the total wage is the norm.

Bargaining

Before bargaining, try to establish a fair price by talking to locals and other travellers. Paying too much feeds inflation, while paying too little denies the locals a reasonable return for their efforts and investments. Not everything is subject to bargaining: respect standard food, accommodation and entry charges, and follow the going rate for services.

Bargaining should never be treated as a matter of life and death importance – it's usually regarded as an integral part of a transaction and is, ideally, an enjoyable social exchange. Nepalese do not ever appreciate aggressive behaviour. A good deal is when both parties are happy. Try to remember that Rs 10 might make quite a difference to the seller, but in hard currency it amounts to 20 US cents.

WHEN TO GO

There are two major factors to weigh as you

Tips for a Trekking Crew

If there is one thing that seems certain to cause endless confusion for trekkers, particularly those on an organised trek, it's the question of tipping. Tipping, or more correctly baksheeshing, the trekking crew has become an expected custom but doing it right is far from easy. If you're trekking by yourself it's not a problem of course. If you've just got a single guide or porter it's also quite easy – you simply tip about 10% of the amount you pay, or about one day's pay for every week you walk.

The real confusion comes when you have a big group with lots of trekkers and, therefore, an even bigger team with sirdar, sherpas, cooks, kitchen crew and porters. Apart from the sheer number of people involved there will also be all sorts of questions of rank and pay scales. In this situation it's going to be virtually impossible for each individual trekker to tip each individual member of the trekking crew so the best system is to pool the money and pay each person individually but as a single tip from the entire group.

Try to tip about one day's pay for each week of the walk. Starting with porters, this means about Rs 150 for a seven-day trek. The kitchen crew should then get about Rs 400, the sherpas or guides about Rs 500, and the cook and the sirdar about Rs 800. That may seem reasonably straightforward but the bigger the trekking party the more complicated the sub-rankings and the more delicate the nuances of privilege and importance. The cook may have an assistant cook, the sherpas may be junior and senior, there may be an assistant sirdar and the fifth kitchen 'boy' may not be a kitchen boy at all but a porter whose brother happens to be in the kitchen crew. Also the numbers can vary; just when you've worked out there are 10 porters two of them may be dropped off because you've eaten all the food they've been carrying. Or another porter may be added along the way.

It's best to have all this worked out at least approximately before the trek starts. If there are 10 porters to tip Rs 150 each you need to have 10 Rs 100 notes and 10 Rs 50 notes to hand when the time for the final pay out rolls round. And be ready to baksheesh 12 porters if you discover at the last moment there were 12 not 10. It's also a good idea to conduct the final operation with military efficiency. Don't try and hand out money to a milling mob, line those porters up and get them to step forward one at a time otherwise you'll certainly be getting the third kitchen boy and fifth porter confused! Don't worry about it too much, you've been providing solid, reliable employment and though your trekking crew may work hard you're unlikely to see anything but smiling faces when the trek is over. ■

decide when to go to Nepal: crowds and weather. As a general rule, the better the weather, the more people come to Nepal to go trekking. During the high tourist season in October and November, flights and hotels are fully booked and hotels and trails in the hills can be horrendously busy.

During autumn the nights are cold in the mountains, but the bright sun makes for pleasant day temperatures – in the high 20s°C, falling to 5°C at night, between 1000 metres and 3500 metres. At higher altitudes temperatures range from about 20°C down to -10°C. Mornings are usually clear with clouds building up during the afternoon, disappearing at night to reveal spectacular starry skies. During winter it is about 10 degrees colder.

Early December usually has a lull, but this is also a good trekking season. The Christmas period is cold, but this is the holiday season in Japan and Australia and these nationalities dominate flights and hotels. High passes, especially Thorung La on the Around Annapurna trek and Laurabina Pass on the Gosainkund trek are usually closed from late November to March. February is still cold, though less so as the spring trekking season of March and April approaches. The Middle Hills, especially around Pokhara, are full of dust and haze in April and May, but the high country is usually clear. Trekking tapers off in the heat of May except at high elevations.

The monsoon is a good time to visit Kathmandu, but there are few trekkers among those who come. A monsoon trek is possible if you are willing to put up with the rain, leeches, slippery trails and lousy mountain views. Flights operate throughout the monsoon to Lukla, Jumla and Jomsom, so it is possible to fly in and trek above the leech line.

Many of the new treks to recently opened restricted areas are good summer treks. Mustang and Simikot are partially in the Himalayan rain shadow, so trekking conditions are good throughout the monsoon season. Most of the restricted area treks are impossible during the winter season.

WHAT TO BRING

I place considerable emphasis on the selection of equipment for a trek, but in fact you can get by with a minimal kit if you can handle rough conditions and do not plan to go above 4000 metres. The task of selecting proper gear can almost overpower some people, but it is not a complex or difficult undertaking. Preparing for a trek is no more complicated than equipping yourself for a weekend backpacking trip. In some ways it is simpler. There is no food to worry about and no eating utensils or cooking pots to organise. There are no tents to stow and less overall concern with weight and bulk.

I've seen people trekking with almost nothing – a jumper (sweater) and a hash pipe. When the weather is good, when hotels are not full and you have no health problems, this arrangement can work, though innkeepers and police frown on the hash pipe. But the mountains are not always kind and you may not find warm bedding or space in a hotel. If you do head out totally unprepared, you will be on your own. Few people, either locals or other trekkers, will give up their own clothing or sleeping bag to help you when you run into trouble.

You probably already have most of the equipment needed for the trek if you hike much in cold weather. A trek is a good place to destroy clothing that is outdated or nearly worn out. A long trek, five weeks or so, is just about the maximum useful life for some clothing items. If your clothing wears out during the trek, you can have repairs done at village tailor shops – they use hand-operated sewing machines.

If you follow my suggestions for equipment, you can have many happy hours – planning the trek, sorting gear, packing and repacking. It is a fine way to spend boring evenings. If you don't have lots of time, you can probably gather most of the items you need in a single visit to an outdoor equipment shop. See the Equipment Checklist appendix for detailed information on clothing and other gear to take.

What you carry in addition to your own clothing will depend on the style of trekking you choose and, if you have arranged a trek through an agency, what they provide. It is helpful to have all your gear – particularly shoes and socks – before you leave home, but some very good new and used equipment is available in Nepal (particularly useful if you're in the middle of a longer trip through Asia). Most of it is at lower prices than elsewhere. You cannot depend on getting the proper size of boots and running shoes, and socks are hard to find, but otherwise you can fully outfit yourself if you have two or three days.

If you plan to carry food and kitchen gear on a trek, you should also plan to buy this in Kathmandu. The section on planning a trek later in this chapter provides more details of what kind of food and equipment you can expect to find in Nepal.

If you are on a prearranged trek, it is better to have your entire kit organised in advance, otherwise you might spend the night before the trek scouring all over Kathmandu for a particular item.

If you come straight to Nepal, you can bring all your trekking clothes and equipment with you from home, but if you're in the middle of a longer trip through Asia, you might need to buy or hire some trekking equipment in Kathmandu.

BUSINESS HOURS & HOLIDAYS

Saturday is the weekly holiday. The working week is Sunday to Friday, though many offices work only a half day on Fridays. Most offices open at 10 am and close at 5 pm (4 pm in winter when the days are short). Shops are usually open from 9.30 am to 7.30 or 8 pm. Banks, offices and most shopping areas are closed on Saturdays and most festival days and religious holidays. See the Festivals section in the Facts about the Country chapter for a list of Nepal's major cultural events and festivals.

Punctuality is not a Nepalese habit, but if you are dealing with a government office or a diplomatic functionary you should try to arrive within five to 10 minutes of the appointed time.

POST & TELECOMMUNICATIONS

The GPO is at Sundhara (The Golden Tap) in Kathmandu. It is open Sunday to Friday from 10 am to 5 pm.

The Foreign Post Office sends and receives parcels and is next to the GPO. Parcels sent to Nepal must be cleared through customs. This can be a tedious, complicated and disappointing process. Do not allow anyone to send a package to you in Nepal and think twice before sending any Nepalese a package larger than an envelope.

There is a postal service throughout the hills of Nepal. You will find post offices and letter boxes in many remote villages. It can be fun to mail postcards and letters from these facilities, but don't be frustrated if they don't reach their destination.

Sending Mail

As with all mail in Asia, you should personally take outgoing letters to the post office and watch the postal clerk cancel the stamps. The post office can be chaotic. Unless you are collecting letters from poste restante, it's better to employ someone to mail letters for you. Most hotels will mail letters for you, and Pilgrims Bookshop in Thamel offers a mailing service for a reasonable fee.

The only practical way to send letters to Nepal is by airmail. Surface mail (by sea via Calcutta) takes months. The mail service to and from Nepal is not particularly reliable, so send important letters by registered mail. Never send cheques through the mail. If someone is sending you money, it should be done through a bank.

Receiving Mail

Poste restante at the GPO will want to see your passport when you collect letters. A more reliable way to collect mail is to arrange to have it sent to a company that has a post office box. Many embassies will receive mail on your behalf. American Express has an office in Kathmandu that handles client mail.

Telephone, Fax, Telex & Telegraph

International telephone calls, telex and telegrams are coordinated through the Central Telegraph Office, about two blocks south of the GPO. The international telephone and telegraph counter is open around the clock. Hotels will book overseas calls and send telexes for a service charge.

Sabha-Doot, in an upstairs office near KC's restaurant in the Thamel area of Kathmandu, is run by the owners of the Kathmandu Guest House and offers a full range of telex, fax, mail, photocopy and telephone services around the clock. Similar establishments have sprung up throughout both Kathmandu and Pokhara.

Nepal has a sophisticated new international communications system and is within easy reach of almost any place on the international direct dialling system. Nepal's IDD code is 977 and its telex code is 891. For outgoing IDD calls the international access number is 00 followed by the country code.

Fax has virtually replaced telex in Nepal for both domestic and international communications. Most hotels, travel agencies and trekking companies have fax facilities.

There are few public telephone booths, but most small shops will allow you to use their phone for a rupee or two.

There is a direct dial service within Nepal to Pokhara and most cities in the Terai. In the hills a few villages now have telephone service. The entire trekking community in Kathmandu was flabbergasted in October 1993 when a single telephone was installed in Lukla, once one of the most difficult locales in the country to communicate with. Where telephone service does not exist you can send domestic telegrams, but they are sent in Nepali, so there is a good chance of confusion by the time it has been translated.

Domestic STD Codes

The following list is mostly a curiosity, but includes many trailheads and does show how many remote places now have telephone service:

Baglung	068
Besi Sahar	066
Bhairahawa	071
Biratnagar	021
Birgung	051
Charikot	049
Dhading	010
Dhankuta	026
Dumre	065
Gorkha	064
Hile	026
Kusma	067
Lukla	038
Nepalgunj	081
Pokhara	061

TIME

Nepal has one time zone which is five hours and 45 minutes ahead of GMT/UTC. When it is noon in Kathmandu, standard time is 6.15 am in London, 4.15 pm in Sydney, 1.15 am in New York and 10.15 pm the previous night in San Francisco. The 15-minute difference is said to be a reflection of the exact time at the summit of Gauri Shankar.

If you drive or fly to Tibet, the time change can be fun. Tibet is on Beijing time, so when you cross the border at Kodari, set your watch ahead two hours and 15 minutes.

During winter the days are short – first light is about 6 am and it gets dark about 6 pm. Nepal has no summer time, but by March the days are about two hours longer, so you could trek from 5 am to 7 pm if you wished.

ELECTRICITY

Nepal's electricity is nominally 220 V, 50 cycles, but fluctuations are severe and unpredictable. You must use a voltage stabiliser to protect all sensitive electronic equipment.

There is a power shortage in Nepal, so there is both scheduled and unscheduled load shedding. Until new generating capacity is provided, the lights will probably be off for two hours a night. If you want to read in the evening or, heaven forbid, use a portable computer, check whether your hotel has a generator.

There are many kinds of plugs used in Nepal, mostly the Indian round pin variety that tend to burn out. Rather than carry a collection of plugs, stop in at a local electric shop in Kathmandu and have them make up an adaptor that connects whatever plug you have to whatever socket your hotel has. It should cost less than Rs 50 for a custom-made connector.

There is locally generated electricity in a surprising number of villages throughout the hills. It is mostly in the 220 V range, but it's unstable and usually on only at night. You might be able to charge batteries (although a solar charger would be a more versatile solution) but you should not plan to rely on anything that needs electricity when trekking.

WEIGHTS & MEASURES

Nepal has adopted the metric system, though in the hills shopkeepers often use an ancient system of weights and measures. In the hill system there are eight *maanas* to a *paathi*, a unit of volume equivalent to about 4½ litres. The old unit of weight is the *dharni*, about 2.4 kg, which is divided into 12 *pau*. Often, however, the unit of measurement is whatever container is most convenient. Kerosene and cooking oil is usually sold by the bottle – a 650 ml beer bottle. A 'tin' usually refers to a 19 litre mustard oil tin, but I have seen sherpas flummoxed by a shopkeeper who used a fruit tin that held only about five potatoes.

While counting and talking figures, the words *lakh* (100,000) and *crore* (10 million) are commonly used. You may often see figures written using this system: 1,02,00,000 equals one crore and two lakhs.

BOOKS

There are hundreds of books about Nepal, Tibet and the Himalaya, some dating back to the 1800s. A trip to your local library will provide you with an armload of fascinating books. The following list includes publications that are historically important and describe important aspects of trekking in Nepal. Most are recent enough to be available in large libraries. You can buy many of these books and others not available in the West in Kathmandu.

Another good source of material about Nepal is the (American) *National Geographic* magazine. Over the years, about 10 issues have had some material on Nepal and the Himalaya. Also look for copies of the *Himalayan Journal*, an annual publication of the Himalayan Club in Bombay, India.

Kathmandu has some of the best and least expensive bookshops in Asia. In addition to a huge variety of books about Nepal and Tibet, there are thousands of new and used paperbacks available at moderate prices. A paperback book is very useful on a trek, both to relieve boredom while waiting for meals, buses and planes, and as a source of emergency toilet paper.

Two good shops for books about Nepal are Pilgrims in Thamel and Himalayan Booksellers, which has branches in Thamel and on Durbar Marg near the clocktower. New and used paperbacks are available from bookshops everywhere. Kailas Bookshop near the Yak & Yeti hotel is affiliated with Pilgrims and has a huge stock of books about Nepal, Tibet and Eastern religions. By special arrangement you can visit the 3rd floor which houses a fascinating rare-book section. Here you can probably find any out-of-print book on the Himalaya, though the price will be highly inflated.

The following list includes general books about trekking and Nepal. Books that specifically relate to individual treks or regions of Nepal are listed in the appropriate chapters.

Geography

Nepal – the Kingdom in the Himalayas (Kummerly & Frey, Bern, 1980), by Toni Hagen, is still the definitive documentation of the geology and people of Nepal, with many fine photos.

Mount Everest, the Formation, Population & Exploration of the Everest Region (Oxford University Press, London, 1963), by Toni Hagen, G O Dyhrenfurth, C Von Fürer Haimendorf & Erwin Schneider, is a shortened version of material in Hagen's book, combined with other works describing the Solu Khumbu region in detail. The maps are good.

People & Society

Himalayan Traders (John Murray, London, 1975), by C Von Fürer Haimendorf, studies the change in trading patterns and culture among Himalayan peoples throughout Nepal.

People of Nepal (Ratna Pustak Bhandar, Kathmandu, 1967), by Dor Bahadur Bista, gives an excellent overview of the various ethnic groups in Nepal. Bista is Nepal's foremost anthropologist.

The *Festivals of Nepal* (George Allen & Unwin, London, 1971), by Mary M Anderson, describes the important festivals of Nepal and provides a lot of background information on the Hindu religion.

Vignettes of Nepal (Sajha Prakashan, Kathmandu, 1980), by Harka Bahadur Gurung, provides personal accounts of treks throughout Nepal. The book includes good historical and geological background information and many maps.

Himalayan Pilgrimage (Shambhala Publications, Boston, 1981), by David L Snellgrove, is an account of a Tibetan scholar's explorations of Nepal. It contains lots of information about Dolpo, Mustang and Nupri.

Escape from Kathmandu by Kim Stanley Robinson is an off-the-wall romp around Nepal. There's an effort to free a captured yeti, an illegal ascent of Everest with a reincarnate lama and an encounter with Jimmy Carter.

Travels in Nepal (Aurum Press, London, 1988), by Charlie Pye-Smith, is a travel account and an interesting study of the impacts and benefits of foreign aid to Nepal.

Fatalism & Development – Nepal's Struggle for Modernization (Orient Longman, Hyderabad, 1991), by Dor Bahadur Bista, is a controversial analysis of Nepalese society and the dynamics that operate within it. There is a very good historical introduction, and the author looks especially critically at the role of the caste system. It provides very useful background if you expect to have extensive dealings with Nepalese businesspeople or government officials.

Nepali Aama – Portrait of a Nepalese Hill Woman (Moon Publications, Chico, California, 1991), by Broughton Coburn, is an account of a US Peace Corps volunteer's encounters with an elderly Gurung woman.

Natural History

Birds of Nepal (Kathmandu, 1976), by Robert L Fleming Sr, Robert L Fleming Jr & Lain Bangdel, is the definitive work on the hundreds of species of birds in Nepal. It contains many outstanding colour paintings.

Discovering Trees in Nepal (Sahayogi Press, Kathmandu, 1984), by Adrian & Jimmie Storrs, gives good information about the trees of Nepal, including their economic and cultural significance.

Flowers of the Himalaya (Oxford University Press, London, 1984), by Oleg Polunin & Adam Stainton, is highly technical and very detailed and is the recognised reference book for Nepal's flowers.

Himalayan Flowers & Trees (Sahayogi Press, Kathmandu, 1978), by Dorothy Mierow & Tirtha Bahadur Shrestha, is the recognised field guide to the plants of Nepal.

A Guide to the Birds of Nepal (Tanager Books, Dover, New Hampshire, 1985), by Carol & Tim Inskipp, is too large to be used as a field guide but is an excellent reference book.

Mountaineering

Nepal Himalaya (Cambridge University Press, London, 1952), by H W Tilman, is one of my favourites. It's a delightful book filled with Tilman's dry wit and describes the first treks in Nepal in 1949 and 1950. The book is out of print and hard to find, but it is part of a Tilman anthology published by the Seattle Mountaineers.

Americans on Everest (J B Lippincott, Philadelphia, 1964), by James Ramsey Ullman, is the official account of the 1963 US expedition.

The Ascent of Rum Doodle (Dark Peak, Sheffield, 1979), by W E Bowman, is the classic spoof of mountaineering books. It's a good diversion after reading a few expedition accounts that take themselves too seriously.

Language

Nepal Phrasebook (Lonely Planet, Melbourne, 1992) is a handy phrasebook with a good section on trekking.

Basic Gurkhali Grammar (Singapore, 1964), by M Meerendonk, is a good introductory text on Nepali, which the British army calls Gurkhali. It was written for the army, so it teaches a slightly 'weird' military vocabulary.

Basic Gurkhali Dictionary (Singapore, 1960), by M Meerendonk, is a pocket-sized dictionary of the Nepali language. It is quite useful once you understand the rudiments of the grammar.

Trekkers Pocket Pal (Avalok, Kathmandu, 1977), compiled by the Summer Institute of Linguistics, is yet another phrasebook for trekkers.

Sherpa Nepali English (Nepal Lithographing, Kathmandu, 1989), by Phinjo Sherpa, is the first Sherpa phrasebook.

Tibet

Tibet by Thubten Jigme Norbu & Colin Turnbull contains an excellent account of the culture and religion of Tibet by the brother of the Dalai Lama.

The Secret War in Tibet by Michel Peissel is a one-sided description of the resistance of Khampa warriors against the Chinese in Tibet. It was published in England as *Cavaliers of Kham*.

Seven Years in Tibet by Heinrich Harrer is a best-selling book describing Harrer's adventures in Tibet before the Chinese occupation. It also contains commentary on Harrer's discussions with the Dalai Lama.

Trekking & Travel Guides

Nepal – a travel survival kit (Lonely Planet, Melbourne, 1993), by Tony Wheeler & Richard Everist, is a complete guidebook to Nepal.

Nepal Namaste (Sahayogi Press, Kathmandu, 1987), by Robert Rieffel, is a good general guidebook written by a long-term resident of Kathmandu.

A Guide to Trekking in Nepal (The Mountaineers, Seattle, 1985), by Stephen Bezruchka, has detailed information about how to organise a backpacking or teahouse trek. There are many route descriptions.

Trekking in Nepal, West Tibet & Bhutan (San Francisco, Sierra Club Books, 1989), by Hugh Swift, has route descriptions that are not as detailed, but it covers a larger area than other books.

Treks on the Kathmandu Valley Rim (Sahayogi Press, Kathmandu, 1982), by Alton C Byers III, describes one-day and overnight treks near Kathmandu.

Trekking in the Himalayas (Allied Publishers, Bombay, 1980), by Tomoya Iozawa, is a well-illustrated trekking guidebook with lots of hand-drawn maps and sketches.

Nepal Trekking (Bergverlag Rudolf Rother, Munich, 1975), by Christian Kleinert, is a set of route descriptions in a fancy plastic cover that you can carry while trekking. The book suggests some very ambitious routes and schedules.

Trekking in Nepal (Allied Publishers, New Delhi, India, 1985), by Toru Nakano, has descriptions, maps and photographs of many remote treks that Nakano made when he travelled with mountaineering expeditions.

The Trekking Peaks of Nepal (Crowood Press, Wiltshire, England, 1989), by Bill O'Connor, is an excellent reference for anyone thinking about doing any climbing in Nepal.

Health

Medicine for Mountaineering (The Mountaineers, Seattle, 1992), by James A Wilkerson, is an outstanding reference book for the layperson. It describes many of the medical problems typically encountered in Nepal. One copy of this book should accompany every trekking party.

Mountain Medicine (Crosby, Lockwood, Staples, London, 1975), by Michael Ward, is good background reading on the subject of cold and high altitude problems.

Where There is No Doctor (The Hesperian Foundation, Palo Alto, California, 1977), by David Werner, is also a good layperson's medical guide with lots of application to Nepal.

Altitude Sickness (American Alpine Club, New York, 1979), by Peter Hackett, is required reading for anyone who treks above 4000 metres.

MAPS

The best series of maps of Nepal is the 1:50,000 series produced by Erwin Schneider for Research Scheme Nepal Himalaya and printed in Vienna. They cover the Everest region from Jiri to the Hongu Valley, Kathmandu Valley and Langtang. They're available from many map shops overseas and at many bookshops in Kathmandu. The fantastically coloured maps are also fantastically expensive – about US$8 a sheet, but if you are doing any serious trekking they are worth it. If you are planning a climb, they are absolutely necessary.

The excellent Survey of India series (an inch equals a mile) are restricted and hard to obtain because in India maps are secret documents. The US Army Map Service produced a set of maps in the 1950s (Series U502 at 1:250,000) based on the Survey of India maps. Though they are outdated, the topography is quite accurate except in north-western Nepal. Stamfords bookshop in London has reprinted the entire series.

Other maps are available as blueprints of traced maps produced in Nepal. They aren't really very accurate, but they will give you some idea of where you are going. Two series of quite good printed maps are produced in Kathmandu; one is published by Mandala Maps and another by Nepa Maps.

Both the Royal Geographical Society and the National Geographic Society have made special maps of the Everest region. The Police Adventure Foundation has also produced a series of maps. The Nepal Mountaineering Association has produced a map that shows the location of, and routes to, all the peaks open for climbing.

All of these maps are available at bookshops in Kathmandu.

MEDIA
Newspapers & Magazines
The *Rising Nepal* is the daily English-language newspaper. There are numerous other daily and weekly papers in both English and Nepali. Since the 1990 revolution, the prime minister has emphasised total freedom of the press. Consequently, these publications now actually carry some news. The *Kathmandu Post*, a private English-language daily, and the weekly *Independent* offer nongovernmental viewpoints.

Nepal Traveller is a monthly magazine that is distributed free to all passengers on arrival at the airport. It has an excellent Kathmandu city map, a description of the current festivals and usually contains good advice about trekking.

Radio & TV
Radio Nepal broadcasts from 6 am until 11 pm and uses short wave frequencies to reach the remote hill areas. Frequencies are 5005, 7165 and 792 kHz in Kathmandu and 684 kHz in Pokhara. It broadcasts the news in English at 8 am and 8 pm. During the climbing season a special mountaineering weather report follows the English news.

Even without a radio, you should have no problem listening to Radio Nepal in the hills. As a gesture of generosity, most Nepalese people try to entertain the entire village by playing the radio at high volume.

Nepal Television broadcasts in Kathmandu, Pokhara and several Terai towns. In 1985 Nepal became one of the last countries in the world to begin television broadcasts. The news is broadcast in English at 10.15 pm. STAR TV (Satellite Television for the Asia Region) broadcasts from Hong Kong with a satellite footprint that covers from Korea to the Middle East. Many hotels in Kathmandu have dishes, so you can watch BBC news, sports and MTV day and night. Some hotels also broadcast CNN, but to do so requires two dishes because it is on a different satellite from the more popular STAR TV.

FILM, VIDEO & PHOTOGRAPHY
Film is available in Kathmandu, but it is a bit more expensive than overseas and it may have been through an airport x-ray machine

before reaching Nepal. One of the large photo labs or a supermarket can probably supply any kind and quantity of film that you need. Colour print film may be available in the hills, but it is probably what another trekker sold when he ran out of money. Make certain you take enough film on a trek. On a two or three week trek, 20 rolls of 36 exposure film is not too much.

Nepal has regulations governing commercial filming. If you plan to make a 16 mm movie, you will certainly need the help of a trekking agent in Nepal, although 8 mm movies and videos are not subject to any special restrictions except in national parks where you are charged US$100 for even a tiny video 8.

There are many colour print processing facilities in Kathmandu. Das Photo (☎ 213-621), Nepal Colour Lab (☎ 211290) and Photo Concern (☎ 223275) are fairly reliable and can handle colour prints and E-6 or Ektachrome slides. Colour enlargements are produced in Kathmandu at reasonable prices. Ganesh Photo Lab (☎ 216898), in an alley behind Hanuman Dhoka, is the place to go for B&W processing.

Photo Concern on New Rd is the best place to go for batteries, accessories and camera repairs. You can also buy a second-hand camera from many photo shops. Some surprisingly high quality cameras show up on their shelves at bargain prices (read the later section on theft if you are wondering where they come from).

You can buy blank VHS video cassettes at supermarkets and shops on New Rd, but it is hard to find blank tapes in other formats. It's almost impossible to rent video cameras in Nepal.

Remember to allow for the exceptional intensity of mountain light when setting exposures at high altitude. At the other extreme it's surprising how often in Nepal you find the light is insufficient. Early in the morning, in deep valleys on trek, or in gloomy temples and narrow streets you may often find yourself wishing you had high-speed film.

A flash is often necessary for shots inside

temples or to fill in shots of sculptures and reliefs.

Most Nepalese in Kathmandu are content to have their photograph taken but you should always get permission first. People in the hills can be very camera shy. Also, bear in mind that if someone poses for you (especially those saintly sadhus), they may insist on being given some baksheesh for doing so.

Respect people's privacy and bear in mind that most Nepalese are extremely modest. Although people carry out many activities in public (they have no choice), it does not follow that passers-by have the right to watch or take photographs. Riverbanks and village wells, for example, are often used as bathrooms, but the users expect as much consideration and privacy as you would in your own house.

Religious ceremonies are also often private affairs, so first ask yourself whether it would be acceptable for a tourist to intrude and to take photographs at a corresponding ceremony in your home country, and then get explicit permission from the senior participants. The behaviour of many would-be *National Geographic* photographers at places like Pashupatinath (the most holy cremation site in Nepal) is horrendous. Imagine the outrage a bus load of scantily clad, camera toting tourists would create if they invaded a family funeral in the west.

DANGERS & ANNOYANCES
Personal Safety & Theft
In 1974 I wrote '...there is virtually nothing to fear in Nepal from thieves, hijackings or the other horrors of our urban civilisation'. Unfortunately, this has changed and it pays to be cautious about your companions – whether fellow trekkers or porters – and your belongings, especially when you camp. There are frequent reports of items being stolen from the tents and hotel rooms of trekkers, even in the most remote villages. There have even been incidents of violent crime, something previously unheard of in Nepal.

There is at least one roving gang of thieves

Top: Group porter (RI'A)
Left: River crossing (SA)
Right: Steep trail (SA)

   Top: Mani Rimdu festival, Tengpoche (SA)
Middle: Sleeping Vishnu (TW)
Bottom: Sadhu (RE)

who watch trekkers and go after those who display valuable items or who have large amounts of cash. Most thefts have been from those who had things we would recognise as worth stealing – with the possible exception of boots. Boots are high on the list of desirable items (along with money and cameras). Don't leave your boots near the door of your tent or outside a hotel room. The most frequent thefts occur in Naudanda, Ghandruk, Dhampus and Hyangja on the Annapurna Trek. Another danger spot is the Chisopani/Seopuri area at the beginning of the Helambu Trek, but it pays to be cautious everywhere. Always be especially cautious within two or three days of a road on which buses might offer a quick getaway. If you are camping, be warned that thieves often cut tents in the night and reach inside to grab whatever is handy.

The US Embassy in Kathmandu makes the following suggestions:

While Nepalese are generally friendly and present no threat to trekkers, the number of violent incidents in recent years against trekkers has unfortunately increased. Crime, while still low by Western standards, does exist on the trails. Westerners have been the victims of murder and violent assaults. All the victims have been travelling alone or as a couple. The general motive seems to have been robbery, even though the possessions of some of the victims were insignificant by American standards. To help you enjoy your trek and to minimise the risk of unpleasant incidents, the embassy recommends that you take the following precautions:

- Register with the consular section, giving the trek itinerary and dates of the trek.
- Do not travel alone. Join up with other Westerners going along the same trail if you are alone in Nepal.
- Do take a porter or guide. Backpacking by yourself may seem the noble thing to do but it is dangerous. You will also be doing a disservice to Nepal by not contributing to the local economy.
- Arrange for porters and guides through a reputable trekking agency, friends or the embassy so that they can be traced if you have trouble. Do not just pick up a porter or guide off the street, no matter how friendly he may appear.
- Do not make ostentatious displays of your cash or possessions. Store all valuable items in Kathmandu at your hotel or lodge. Be sure to obtain a detailed receipt of your items from the hotel or lodge.
- If possible, camp at night near other trekkers. Do not walk along trails after dark.
- Don't leave your passport as collateral for renting trekking equipment. You may need it in an emergency.
- Be sure to register at all the police and immigration posts along the trail and go only on the route prescribed in your trekking permit.
- If you encounter problems along the trail, report them to the nearest police or immigration post. When you return to Kathmandu, report any unresolved problems to the appropriate trekking agency or hotel as well as the police and the Ministry of Tourism.

The embassy recommends that you do not take night buses in Nepal. There have been serious problems recently with bandits holding up these buses.

Despite this caution, you will find most Nepalese to be friendly, helpful and honest. It is, however, essential that you travel with a well-chosen companion – either another Westerner or a guide – for your own safety. The chance of theft is still remote, but a sprained ankle, debilitating illness or other misfortune can occur at any time. It is only common sense, applicable to a hiking trip anywhere, that you should not travel alone in the mountains.

Strikes & Demonstrations

Nepal's political process now involves communist-style demonstrations and strikes. They are generally peaceful, but any large gathering of people can cause problems. Often there are processions in the street and meetings in Tundikhel, the parade ground in the centre of Kathmandu. If you come across a large group of slogan-chanting youths, it's best to avoid them in case you end up on the downstream side of a police *lathi* charge (a team of police wielding bamboo staves) or worse. A normal procession or demonstration is a *julus*. If things escalate there may be a *chakka jam* ('jam the wheels') in which all vehicles stay off the street, or a *bandh* in which not only do vehicles not ply the roads, but all shops, schools and offices are closed.

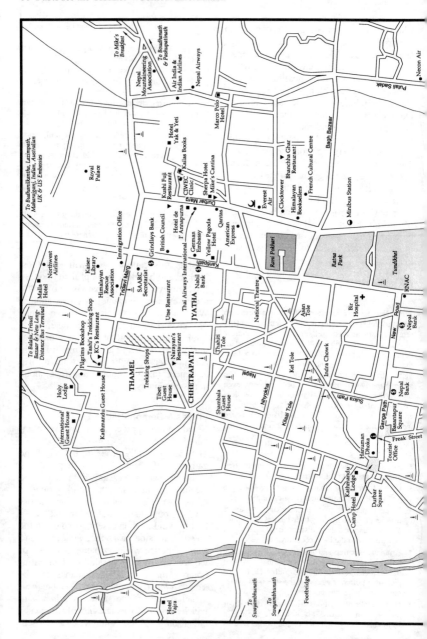

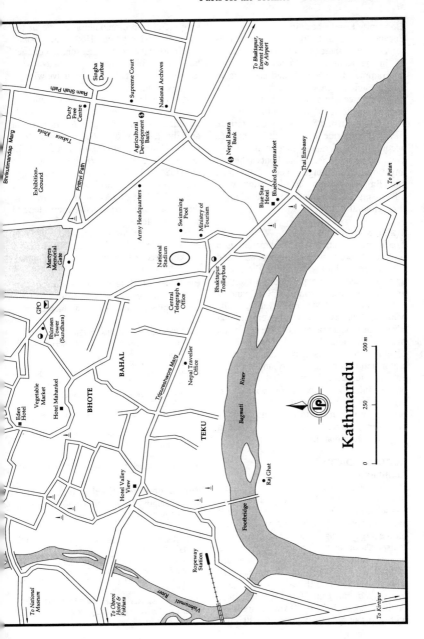

Kathmandu

To Bhaktapur, Everest Hotel & Airport

Singha Durbar

Supreme Court

National Archives

Ram Shah Path

Duty Free Centre

Agricultural Development Bank

Nepal Rastra Bank

Thai Embassy

Bhrikutimandap Marg

Tukucha Khola

Prithvi Path

Exhibition-Ground

Army Headquarters

Swimming Pool

Ministry of Tourism

Blue Star Hotel

Bluebird Supermarket

To Patan

Martyrs Memorial Gate

National Stadium

Bhaktapur Trolleybus

GPO

Central Telegraph Office

Bhimsen Tower (Sundhara)

BAHAL

BHOTE

Tripureshwora Marg

Nepal Traveller Office

Vegetable Market

Hotel Mahankel

Eden Hotel

TEKU

Bagmati River

Hotel Valley View

Raj Chat

Footbridge

To National Museum

To Oberoi Hotel & Pokhara

Ropeway Station

Vishnumati River

To Kirtipur

0   250   500 m

Electricity Load Shedding

Because of various factors (everyone blames someone else) there is a shortage of electricity in the Kathmandu Valley. There is a programme of scheduled load shedding in which each neighbourhood has a power outage for two hours a night. The times vary; at one time the schedule called for lights out from 6 to 8 pm and 8 to 10 pm on alternate days. In practice the schedule changes according to a seemingly random pattern, so you may be subjected to blackouts at almost any time. One strange aspect of the load shedding programme is that brightly lit advertising signs continue to blaze all night throughout the city.

Traffic & Pollution

Traffic on the streets of Kathmandu is a rumpus of pollution-belching two, three and four-wheel vehicles wending their way around a mass of people and a variety of animals. Doomsters compare Kathmandu's pollution to that of Mexico City. Sergio, the Mexican trek leader, assures everyone that it's nowhere near that bad. But the collection of ancient vehicles, low-quality fuel and lack of emission controls makes the streets of Kathmandu particularly dirty and unpleasant. Traffic rules do exist, but are rarely enforced; be especially careful when crossing streets or riding a bicycle. Consider bringing a face mask to filter out dust and emission particles if you plan to ride a bicycle in Kathmandu.

ACCOMMODATION
Kathmandu

Hotels in Kathmandu range from the luxurious to downright depressing. The Hotel Association of Nepal has a reservation desk at the airport and touts from small hotels meet every arriving flight, often offering free transportation to their hotel. Except at the budget end, Kathmandu hotel rates are expensive for what you get. Government tax adds considerably to the cost; it is charged on a sliding scale from 10 to 15% depending on the rating of the hotel. If you are trekking with an organised group, your trek will prob-ably include accommodation at one of the more expensive hotels. Hotels are booked solid during the trekking season, so you may have to do a bit of shopping, or take advantage of the airport touts, if you arrive without a reservation.

Kathmandu's budget accommodation is centred around the Thamel area. Hotels include the famous *Kathmandu Guest House* and the lesser known but adequate *Tibet Guest House, Star, Garuda,* and *Shakti* hotels and *Potala Guest House*. Costs are in the US$5 to US$10 per night range. When you choose a hotel, check the room for street noise. Nepalese drivers use their horn more than their brakes, so streetside rooms tend to be intolerable.

Ecotel Nepal (☎ 414432, fax (977) 1-229380, telex 2766 ECOTEL NP) offers a booking service for budget hotels in Thamel.

Bottom-End Hotels Hotels and guest-houses in this category range from US$10 to US$30 plus 10 or 12% tax and include:

Hotel Blue Diamond, Jyatha (☎ 226320, fax 226392)
Hotel Gauri Shanker, Sallaghari, Thamel (☎ 411605, 417181)
Hotel Manaslu, Lazimpat (☎ 413470, fax 416516)
Hotel Shree Tibet, Thamel (☎ 419902, 211092, fax (977) 1-419361)
Kathmandu Guest House, Thamel (☎ 418733, 413632, fax 417133)
Pilgrims Hotel, Thamel (☎ 416910, fax 22983, telex 2765 TWARI NP)
Potala Guest House, Thamel (☎ 226566, 220467)
Tibet Guest House, Chetrapati (☎ 414383, 214951, fax 226945)
Utse Hotel, Thamel (☎ 226946, 228952, fax 226946)

Mid-Range Hotels Hotels and guesthouses in this category range from US$30 to US$80 plus 12 or 13% tax and include:

Hotel Ambassador, Lazimpat (☎ 414432, 410432, fax 413641)
Hotel Blue Star, Tripureshwore (☎ 211472/3, fax 226820, telex 2322 BLUSTR NP)
Hotel Marsyangdi, Thamel (☎ 412129, 414105, fax 410008)
Hotel Vajra, Swayambhunath (☎ 272719, 271545)
Hotel Woodlands, Durbar Marg (☎ 222683, 220123, fax 225650)

Hotel Yellow Pagoda, Kantipath (☎ 220337/8, fax 228914, telex 2268 PAGODA NP)
Manang Hotel, Thamel (☎ 410993, 419924, fax 415821)
Marco Polo Business Hotel, Kamal Pokhari (☎ 415984/432, fax 413641)

Top-End Hotels Hotels in this category range from US$80 to US$125 plus 14% tax, and include the following:

Hotel Malla, Lekhnath Marg (☎ 418385, fax 418382, telex 2238 MALLA)
Hotel Narayani, Pulchowk (☎ 521442/711, fax 521291, telex 2262 NARANI NP)
Hotel Shangri La, Lazimpat (☎ 412999, fax 414184, telex 2276 HOSANG NP)
Hotel Shanker, Lazimpat (☎ 410151/2, fax 412961, telex 2230 SANKER NP)
Hotel Sherpa, Durbar Marg (☎ 228898, 222585, fax 222026, telex 2223 NEPCOM NP)
Kathmandu Hotel, Maharajganj (☎ 418984, 410786, fax 414091, telex 2256 HOKAT NP)

Over-the-Top Hotels Hotels in this bracket range from US$125 and up, plus 15% tax:

Hotel de l'Annapurna, Durbar Marg (☎ 221711, fax 225236, telex 2205 AAPU NP)
Hotel Everest International, Naya Baneshwore (☎ 220614/567, fax 226088, telex 2260 HOTEVS NP)
Hotel Soaltee Oberoi Tahachal (☎ 211211, fax 272205, telex 2203 SOALTE NP)
Hotel Yak & Yeti Durbar Marg (☎ 413999, fax 227782, telex 2237 YKNYTI NP)

Hotels in the Hills

Local inns or *bhattis* have existed for centuries in the hills. A bhatti is usually a wooden or maybe even a bamboo structure close to the trail, with the large house of the owners situated some distance away. It usually has a simple mud stove with a pot of milk and another pot of hot water to make tea. There is usually a jug or two of *chhang* or *rakshi* in the back room to provide a bit of alcoholic diversion for the village elders and the few overnight guests who happen along. Where trekking has not developed, these reasonably primitive establishments are still the only hotel facilities available.

As trekking increased and as Nepalese travellers began to have a bit more money,

facilities improved and the tiny inns have expanded into the extensive system of hotels that now serves major trekking routes. Most hotels in the hills are family-run affairs that started in the living room. Some have separate quarters for guests, but most are still living room affairs at which the family that operates the inn eats and sleeps in the same building, and often the same room, that they offer to guests.

Only since the mid-1970s have trekkers become an important source of income in the hills, so most of the hotels that cater to trekkers opened after 1979 or 1980. Some of these have obtained government loans and have become quite grand. Several inns on the Jomsom trek even have sidewalk cafes where you can enjoy a meal in the sun. These establishments are popular with trekkers and have English-language signboards. Some hotels offer private rooms, but many have only dormitory accommodation or the communal living space available.

Often the husband of the house is away trading or working as a porter or trekking guide. Usually the wife manages things, but sometimes hotels are left in the care of children. Some pretty weird meals and service can result when a six or eight-year-old tries to deal with customers. In remote areas that trekkers do not frequent, the 'hotel' may exist only in the mind of the proprietor and will consist of sharing the eating and living accommodation with a family.

The primary incentive for operating a hotel in the hills is to turn locally produced food, labour and firewood into cash. The hills of Nepal are increasingly becoming a cash-oriented society. There are few ways to earn this cash, other than operating a hotel, that allow people to remain at home and tend to the house, children, livestock and crops. The prices at most hotels in the hills are artificially cheap for this reason. Intense competition and the lack of an alternative way to secure cash keeps prices ridiculously low. It certainly is not profitable to sell a cup of tea with sugar for Rs 1 (about two US cents) when sugar is Rs 16 per kg, tea is Rs 38 per 250 gram packet and it takes a full day to fetch a load of firewood. There is a movement in the major trekking areas to standardise rates for food and accommodation, so that most hotels in a particular village charge the same.

FOOD
Nepalese Food
The most common meal in Nepal is *dal bhat* – rice (bhat) with a soup made of lentils (dal) poured over it. Hill people subsist on dal bhat and a thick paste called *dhindo*. This is coarse ground corn or millet, often mixed with a few hot chillies. In the northern regions people call this dish *tsampa* and make it from roasted and ground barley. Sherpas and other Himalayan people often mix tsampa with buttered and salted Tibetan tea.

The local diet rarely includes meat or eggs, so dal provides the primary source of protein. *Roti* (unleavened bread) or *chappati* is another frequent addition to a meal and often substitutes for rice. Other items may supplement a meal, usually a curry made from potatoes or whatever vegetables are available locally.

Trekking Food
Although some hotels in the hills can conjure up fantastic meals, the standard hotel diet is dal bhat, or at higher elevations, potatoes. Dal bhat twice a day for a month presents a boring prospect to the Western palate. On major trek routes, restaurants vary in standard from primitive to luxurious, and beer, Coke and other soft drinks are available at high prices. The menus are often attractive and extensive, but too often the menu represents the innkeeper's fantasy of what they would like to serve, not what's available. No matter what the hotel advertises, the choice almost always comes back to rice, dal, potatoes, pancakes and instant noodles.

Thirty years ago, Tilman observed that a person can live off the country in a sombre fashion, but Nepal was no place in which to make a gastronomic tour. It hasn't changed. In Kathmandu, a city of half a million people, it takes a lot of imagination to provide the variety in diet that Westerners expect. In remote regions, it is almost impossible to provide this variety, unless you bring the food with you. Most people can adapt to a Nepalese diet, but try it for a few days at home so you know what to expect. Boiled rice with a thick split pea soup poured over it is the closest approximation to dal bhat. This experiment might help convince you to fill the remote corners of your backpack with spices, trail snacks and other goodies.

Kathmandu Restaurants
Trekkers attach great importance to their stomachs. Kathmandu's restaurants have responded by offering some of the most varied menus in Asia. In Thamel, try *KC's*, the original budget travellers' restaurant, *La Dolce Vita* for Italian food and *Himthai* for Thai food. There are many other restaurants and pie shops, particularly in Thamel, that serve meals in the Rs 50 to Rs 100 range. Old stand-bys in Thamel include the *Pumpernickel Bakery*, *Le Bistro*, *G's Terrace*, *Utse*, *Old Vienna* and *Narayan's Restaurant*. On Durbar Marg try *Hot Breads* for cakes and snacks and *Mike's Cantina* for Mexican food. You can find dal bhat at street-corner restaurants, but for safety, stick to the *Thyabhu*, *Bhanchha Ghar* or the *Nanglo Pub* if you want Nepalese food.

For a big splurge, head for the hotels for good Indian, Chinese and continental food. Indian food at the *Ghar E Kabab* in the Hotel Annapurna and at the *Far Pavilions* in the Everest International is expensive. The *Kabab Corner* in the Hotel Gautam is cheaper. *Mountain City* in the Malla has Sichuan food and the *Chimney Room* in the Hotel Yak & Yeti is the last incarnation of Boris' legendary restaurant.

DRINKS
Soft Drinks & Bottled Water
Nepal has all the international brands of soft drinks. All are sold in bottles, not cans. The bottle deposits are more than the cost of the drink, so leave the bottle behind when you quaff a Coke at a trailside stall. Locally produced fruit drinks are sold in cardboard cartons and many of these have made their

way into the hills, offering a refreshing thirst quencher. Look for mango *frooty* and apple *appy*.

So-called mineral water is available throughout Nepal and the plastic bottles make emergency trekking water bottles. The plastic bottles are not recyclable and there are mounds of empty mineral water bottles throughout the hills. You can help reduce this aspect of litter by passing up the mineral water and drinking water you have treated with iodine. This may, in fact, be a safer solution than mineral water. Even in Britain there was a scandal about tap water being sold in bottles – imagine what happens in Nepal, where controls and testing are nonexistent.

Alcohol

For a small country, Nepal has a thriving beer industry. The local brands, Star, Golden Eagle, Iceberg and Cheers come in 650 ml bottles. Tuborg and San Miguel also brew in Nepal and distribute in cans if you want to carry them on your trek.

Despite the traditional Brahmin abstinence, a lot of alcohol is consumed in Nepal. The local potions are chhang and rakshi, which can be quite tasty and potent, but there are also numerous Western-style liquors available. The notorious Kukhri Rum makes a fine after-trek drink on cold nights. Snow Lands Gin advertises its roots in London, Glasgow and Kathmandu.

Trekking Drinks

Don't drink tap water or stream water anywhere. Instead, stick to soft drinks, bottled water, beer, or water you have purified yourself. It can be difficult to get boiled water on a trek. Ask an innkeeper if the water is boiled and they will assure you that it is, even if it has just been taken from the river. This response illustrates several unusual facets of Nepalese culture and personality. Most hill people do not understand germs. They accept good naturedly the desire of Westerners that their drinking water be boiled, but few people understand why. They often believe that Westerners like only hot water. Another consideration is that Nepalese like to please others and dislike answering any question negatively. So, you get a 'yes' answer to almost every question, particularly 'Is this water boiled?'. Hotels also do not like to prepare boiled water because it uses fuel and takes up space on the stove – and they can't charge for the service.

There are two easy solutions that ensure that you have safe drinking water: good tea must be made from boiling water, so a cup of tea will always be made with boiled water; and treating water with iodine solves the boiled water problem in a way that does not consume scarce fuel. See the discussion of this technique in the Health & Safety chapter.

If you decide to sample chhang and rakshi, remember that chhang is made from water straight from the river, not boiled water.

Throughout Nepal a cup of tea is served with a large dollop of milk and presweetened with sugar. To avoid this, order 'black tea'.

THINGS TO BUY

Bring enough money to buy whatever souvenirs, incredible bargains or art objects you may find. In Kathmandu there are Tibetan carpets (US$90 to US$150), woollen jumpers and jackets (US$5 to US$25). Some genuine Tibetan art pieces (US$20 plus) and semiprecious stones (US$15 to US$25) are also available. On the trek you may find objects from Tibet (prayer wheels, thangka paintings, butter lamps and bells) or Sherpa household articles (chhang bottles, boots, aprons, carpets and cups) at prices from US$1 to more than US$100.

Most Tibetan jewellery, statues and handicrafts were historically and traditionally made by Newar craftspeople in Nepal. You can often buy modern reproductions of Tibetan antiques that are as authentic as antiques smuggled in from Tibet.

If you plan to make a major purchase in Nepal, first visit an importer at home and find out what is available at what price. Especially note the quality, so that you will have a basis for comparison in Nepal. Many pieces exported from India and Nepal may be available in your locale at prices lower

Tibetan prayer wheel

than in retail shops in Kathmandu because of large-volume discounts. Tibetan carpets made in Nepal are for sale in San Francisco, for example, for less than it would cost to buy one in Nepal and ship it home.

Other bargains in Kathmandu include extra visa photos, trekking and climbing gear, woollen socks and cotton clothing. You can also buy embroidered T-shirts in a variety of standard patterns or with your own special design.

Trekking Information

TYPES OF TREK
In Nepal there are numerous ways to arrange a trek because of two major factors. Firstly, inexpensive (by Western standards) professional and nonprofessional labour is available to carry loads and to work as guides

and camp staff. Secondly, you can almost always find supplies and accommodation locally because there are people living in even the most remote trekking areas.

I have classified the many possible ways of trekking into four approaches: backpacking, teahouse treks, self-arranged treks and treks with a trekking company. There is a lot of overlap among these, because many aspects of each trekking style spill over into the next. A backpacking trek that stays a few nights in hotels has many of the attributes of a teahouse trek. A teahouse trek with porters starts to become a self-arranged trek. A self-arranged trek that uses the services of a trekking agency in Nepal is similar to the trekking company approach.

Backpacking
The backpacking approach of a light pack, stove, freeze-dried food and a tent really is not an appropriate way to trek in Nepal. So much food is available in hill villages that it doesn't make much sense to try to be totally self-sufficient while trekking. This is true throughout Nepal except in the high mountains above 4500 metres. Backpackers violate two cardinal rules for travellers in Nepal. Because they are self-sufficient, they do not contribute to the village economy. Also, they must do so many camp chores that they do not have the time or energy to entertain the villagers that will gather to watch them.

At higher altitudes, however, the backpacking approach works. Depending on the terrain and local weather conditions, villages are found up to 4000 metres, but above this there isn't much accommodation available except in tourist areas such as Annapurna Sanctuary and Everest. It is also difficult to arrange to hire porters who have the proper clothing and footwear for travelling in cold and snow. If you plan to visit these regions, you may wish to alter your trekking style and utilise a backpacking or mountaineering approach to reach high passes or the foot of remote glaciers.

A good solution is to leave much of your gear behind at a temporary 'base camp' in the care of a hotel or trustworthy sherpa. You can then spend a few days carrying a reduced load of food and equipment on your own. This will provide you with the best of both worlds: an enriching cultural experience that conforms to the standards and traditions of the country in the lowlands, and a wilderness or mountaineering experience in the high mountains.

Teahouse Treks

The Nepali word bhatti translates well as 'teahouse'. It is a bit pretentious to call some of these village establishments a hotel, but the Nepalese use of English translates restaurant or eating place as 'hotel'. Since the word hotel has, therefore, been pre-empted, Nepalese use the word 'lodge' for sleeping place or hotel. Thus, in the hills of Nepal a 'hotel' has food, but may not provide a place to sleep, while a 'lodge' always offers accommodation. Many innkeepers specify the services they provide by calling their establishments 'Hotel & Lodge'. To avoid all this semantic confusion, I have used hotel, lodge and teahouse interchangeably. In reality you can almost always find both accommodation and food at any trailside establishment.

The most popular way to trek in Nepal for both Nepalese and Westerners is to travel from teahouse to teahouse. Hotel accommodation is most readily available in the Khumbu (Everest) region, the Langtang area and the entire Annapurna region. In these areas you can operate with a bare minimum of equipment and rely on teahouses for food and shelter. In this manner, it will cost from US$3 to US$10 a day, depending on where you are and how simply you can live and eat. It becomes much more expensive at high altitudes and in very remote areas.

Most Thakali inns (found along the Pokhara to Jomsom Trek) have bedding available – usually a cotton-filled quilt. Sometimes the bedding has the added attraction of lice and other bed companions. Bring along your own sheet or sleeping bag to provide some protection against these bugs. During the busy trekking seasons in October to November and March to April, it may be difficult to find bedding every night on the Jomsom Trek. Bedding is not usually available at hotels on the Everest trek or around Annapurna, so on these treks you should carry your own sleeping bag.

Although many hotels in the hills are reasonably comfortable, the accommodation in some places may be a dirty, often smoky, home. Chimneys are rare, so a room on the 2nd floor of a house can turn into an intolerable smokehouse as soon as someone lights the cooking fire in the kitchen below. Often it is possible to sleep on porches of houses, but your gear is then less secure. The most common complaint among trekkers who rely on local facilities is about smoky accommodation.

By arranging your food and accommodation locally, you can move at your own pace and set your own schedule. You can move faster or slower than others and make side trips not possible with a large group. You can spend a day photographing mountains, flowers or people – or you can simply lie around for a day. Hotels provide a special meeting place for trekkers from throughout the world. You are free (within the limits imposed by your trekking permit) to alter your route and change your plans to visit other out-of-the-way places as you learn about them. You will have a good opportunity to see how the people in the hills of Nepal live, work and eat and will probably develop at least a rudimentary knowledge of the Nepali language.

You are, however, dependent on facilities in villages or in heavily trekked regions. Therefore you must trek in inhabited areas and on the better known routes. You may need to alter your schedule to reach a certain hotel for lunch or dinner. You can miss a meal if there is no hotel when you need one or if the hotel you are counting on is closed. A few packets of biscuits in your backpack are good insurance against these rough spots. Most of the major routes are well documented, but they are also well travelled. A hotel can be out of food if there are many other trekkers or if you arrive late. You may have to change your planned destination for the day when you discover that the lunch you ordered at an inn will take a very long time to prepare. You will usually make this discovery only after you have already waited an hour or so. It is wise to be aware of these kinds of problems and to prepare yourself to deal with them.

If you deviate from popular routes, be prepared to fend for yourself at times. If, however, you carry food, cooking pots and a tent to use even one night, you have already escalated beyond the teahouse approach into a more complex form of trekking with different problems.

Self-Arranged Treks

A third style of trekking is to gather sherpas, porters, food and equipment and take off on a trek with all the comforts and facilities of an organised trek. On such a trek you camp in tents, porters carry your gear, sherpas set up camp and cook and serve meals. You carry a backpack with only a water bottle, camera and jacket.

Trekkers who opt for this approach, particularly with a small group of friends, often have a rewarding, enriching and enjoyable trip. You can use a trekking company in Nepal to make some or all of the arrangements, though you may have to shop for an agency that suits you. Some Nepalese trekking companies offer equipment for hire, some will arrange a single sherpa or porter and some will undertake only the entire arrangements for a trek.

If you want to have everything organised in advance, you can contact a Nepalese trekking company by mail or fax and ask them to make arrangements for your trek. There are more than 150 trekking companies in Kathmandu that will organise treks for a fee and provide all sherpas, porters and, if necessary, equipment. Unless you have a good idea of what you want, it will require a huge volume of correspondence to provide you with the information you require, to determine your specific needs, to define your precise route and itinerary and to negotiate a price that both parties understand. Mail takes

up to three weeks each way to and from Australia, the Americas or Europe. It's better to use a telex or fax machine. Be specific in your communications and be sure that the trekking company understands exactly who will provide what equipment. It is most embarrassing to discover on the first night that someone forgot the sleeping bags.

One solution is to go to Nepal and simply sort out the details in an hour or two of face to face negotiations with a trekking company. You should be prepared to spend a week or so (less, if you are lucky) in Kathmandu settling these details. An alternative to endless correspondence with Nepal is to use the services of the overseas agent of a Nepalese trekking company. These agents should have someone who can give you the information you require, and they should have a regular system of communication with Nepal. Dealing with an agent usually involves paying them a fee to make all the arrangements. This then becomes the 'trekking company' approach.

Trekking with a Trekking Company

Companies specializing in trekking can organise both individual and group treks from the USA, Germany, UK, Japan, Switzerland, France, Australia, New Zealand and Scandinavia. Each overseas trekking agent works through a particular trekking company in Nepal. Some agents have agreements for the exclusive representation of a Nepalese company in their own country. I have listed the names and addresses of some of the major trekking agencies in the Getting There & Away chapter.

A usual condition of an arranged trek is that the group must stick to its prearranged route and, within limits, must meet a specific schedule. This means that you may have to forego an appealing side trip or festival and, if you are sick, you will probably have to keep moving with the rest of the group. You also may not agree with a leader's decisions if the schedule must be adjusted because of weather, health, political or logistical considerations.

You will be trekking with people you have

not met before. Although some strong friendships may develop, there may also be some in the party you would much rather not have met. For some people, this prospect alone rules out their participation in a group trek. The major drawback, however, will probably be the cost. Organised treks usually start at US$100 per person per day of the trek. One of the major expenses is the services of a Western leader who acts as guide, cultural interpreter and social director. On the positive side, by fixing the destination and schedule in advance, all members of the group will have prepared themselves for the trip and should have proper equipment and a clear understanding of the schedule and terrain. Read the brochures and other material prepared by the agent to see if it is likely to attract the type of people you'd get along with.

Most prearranged treks cater for people to whom time is more important (within limits) than money. For many, the most difficult part of planning a trek is having the time to do so. These people are willing to pay more to avoid wasting a week of their limited vacation sitting around in Kathmandu making arrangements or waiting along the way for a spare seat on a plane. A trekking agent usually tries to cram as many days in the hills as is possible into a given time span. Trekking agents make reservations for hotels and domestic flights well in advance. Thus theoretically, these hassles are also eliminated.

Because the group carries its own food for the entire trek, a variety of meals is possible. This may include canned goods from Kathmandu and imported food bought from expeditions or other exotic sources. A skilled cook can prepare an abundant variety of tasty Western-style food. The meals a good sherpa cook can prepare in an hour over a kerosene stove would put many Western cafes to shame.

A group trek carries tents for the trekkers. This convenience gives you a place to spread out your gear without fear that someone will pick it up, and probably means that you will have a quiet night. In addition, a tent also gives you the freedom to go to bed when you choose. You can retire immediately after dinner to read or sleep, or sit up and watch the moon rise as you discuss the day's outing.

Money and staff hassles rarely surface on an arranged trek. The sirdar is responsible for making minor purchases along the way and ensures a full complement of porters every day. Unless you are particularly interested, or quite watchful, you may never be aware that these negotiations are taking place.

A group trek follows a tradition and routine that trekkers and mountaineers have developed and refined for more than 50 years. You can travel in much the same manner as the approach marches described in *The Ascent of Everest*, *Annapurna* and *Americans on Everest*, a feature not possible with other styles. If your interest in the Himalaya was kindled through such books, you still have the opportunity to experience this delightful way to travel. There are many reasons why these expeditions went to all the trouble and expense to travel as they did.

It is an altogether refreshing experience to have all the camp and logistics problems removed from your responsibility so you are free to enjoy fully the land and the people which have attracted mountaineers for a century.

APPROACH TO TREKKING
A Trek is Not a Climbing Trip
Whether you begin your trek at a roadhead or fly into a remote mountain airstrip, a large part of your trek will be in the Middle Hills region at elevations between 500 and 3000 metres. In this region, there are always well-developed trails through villages and across mountain passes. Even at high altitudes there are intermittent settlements used during summer by shepherds, so the trails, though often indistinct, are always there. You can easily travel on any trail without the aid of ropes or mountaineering skills. There are rare occasions when there is snow on the trail, and on some high passes it might be necessary to place a safety line for your companions or porters if there is deep snow. Still, alpine techniques are almost never used on a traditional trek. Anyone who has walked

extensively in the mountains has all the skills necessary for an extended trek in Nepal.

Though some treks venture near glaciers, and even cross the foot of them, most treks do not allow the fulfilment of any Himalayan mountaineering ambitions. Nepal's mountaineering regulations allow trekkers to climb 18 specified peaks with a minimum of formality, but you must still make a few advance arrangements for such climbs. Many agents offer so-called climbing treks which include the ascent of one of these peaks as a feature of the trek. There are a few peaks that, under ideal conditions, are within the resources of individual trekkers. A climb can be arranged in Kathmandu if conditions are right, but a climb of one of the more difficult peaks should be planned well in advance. The section on climbing, in the last chapter of this book, describes these processes in more detail.

A Trek Requires Physical Effort

A trek is physically demanding because of its length and the almost unbelievable changes in elevation. During the 300-km trek from Jiri to Everest base camp and return, for example, the trail gains and loses more than 9000 metres of elevation during many steep ascents and descents. On most treks, the daily gain is less than 800 metres in about 15 km, though ascents of as much as 1200 metres are typical of some days. You can always take plenty of time during the day to cover this distance, so the physical exertion, though quite strenuous at times, is not sustained. You can always take plenty of time for rest.

Probably the only physical problem that may make a trek impossible is a history of knee problems on descents. In Nepal the descents are long, steep and unrelenting. There is hardly a level stretch of trail in the entire country. If you are an experienced walker and often hike 15 km a day with a pack, a trek should prove no difficulty. You will be pleasantly surprised at how easy the hiking can be if you only carry a light backpack and do not have to worry about meal preparation.

Previous experience in hiking and living outdoors is, however, helpful as you make plans for your trek. The first night of a month-long trip is too late to discover that you do not like to sleep in a sleeping bag. Mountaineering experience is not necessary, but you must enjoy walking.

PERMITS & FORMALITIES
Trekking Permits

A Nepalese visa is valid only for the Kathmandu Valley, Pokhara and Chitwan National Park in the Terai. To travel outside these regions you need a trekking permit. The permit specifies the places you may visit and the duration of your trek. Long ago, trekking permits cost Rs 1 and were basically a translation of your passport into Nepali. Now the fees have increased, there is no Nepali at all on the permit and the issuance of trekking permits has become a large-scale industry. Theoretically you can leave your passport in a hotel safe during a trek, because a trekking permit is sufficient documentation to travel throughout Nepal.

Trekking permits are issued by the immigration office. The procedure is similar to getting a visa extension and involves a lot of queuing and waiting. There are preprinted trekking permit application forms, each a different colour, so you only need to state 'Everest', 'Annapurna', 'Kanchenjunga' or 'Langtang' on the application if you are headed to one of these areas. Be sure you fill in the right application form, otherwise you will wait in a long queue, only to be sent back for another form if the colour is incorrect. Once you have filled in the application, waited in a queue, presented all the necessary documents and paid the fee, you will be told to come back after 5 pm and queue again to pick up the completed document.

The preprinted forms allow all the possible routes in each region. For less common destinations, you should include on the application an extensive list of village or district names. If you are headed for an unusual locale, check that the immigration office writes these destinations correctly on your trekking permit. Only the immigration offices in Kathmandu or Pokhara can alter the permit.

It is not necessary, as it once was, to have a trekking company arrange a trekking permit for you, although a trekking company can usually get a permit faster than you can. Permits for restricted areas and for Kanchenjunga are issued only to organised groups arranged by a trekking company; other areas are open to individual trekkers.

You *must* have a trekking permit. Police checkposts are abundant on every trekking route and you will be endlessly hassled if you do not have proper documentation. Rangers at entrance stations to national parks and the Annapurna Conservation Area Project (ACAP) checkpost at Chhomrong also conscientiously check permits and collect park fees.

A normal trekking permit costs US$5 per week for the first four weeks of trekking and US$10 per week thereafter. Permits for Dolpo and Kanchenjunga treks cost US$10 per week for the first four weeks and US$20 per week thereafter. The exorbitant fees for restricted-area trekking permits are detailed in the chapter on restricted areas. You must have a valid visa extension for the full period of trekking before you can apply for a trekking permit.

National Park & Conservation Fees

If you trek in the Annapurna region, you will enter the ACAP area and must pay a conservation fee of Rs 650. This is collected at the same time you pay for the trekking permit and a special stamp is stuck on your permit as a receipt.

The national park fee of Rs 650 is also collected at the time your trekking permit is issued if your trek enters a national park.

Restricted Areas

There are many parts of Nepal into which the entry of foreigners is strictly controlled. Many treks that may be suggested on a map are in restricted areas and you either cannot get a trekking permit for those regions or must travel with a liaison officer and pay for a special permit. Some areas specifically closed to foreigners are: Walunchung Gola,

Rolwaling and the route to Nangpa La in Khumbu. When planning your trek, assume that these areas will remain closed. Don't count on a last-minute change in the rules. Police checkposts are numerous in the hills and police will turn you back if you try to trek into a restricted area.

Officially there are no longer any restricted areas in Nepal. The immigration office rules now state that 'trekkers are not allowed to trek in the notified areas previously known as restricted'. Rather than get involved in all this semantic complication, I will continue to use 'restricted' to refer to places that are closed to trekkers, or open to trekkers only when accompanied by a policeman (a liaison or 'environmental' officer).

There are many reasons why the restricted areas exist. In most cases, it is a hangover from a time when the border with China was more sensitive than it is now. Environmental groups, particularly the Nepal Nature Conservation Society, are pressuring the government to keep some places closed for ecological reasons to avoid both cultural and environmental degradation. Because trekkers require assistance when something goes wrong (accident, illness or theft), the government restricts some areas because it doubts that it could provide the security that trekkers need. There are also political reasons for some restrictions. In the 1970s, for example, the Jomsom trek was closed because a major foreign-aided military operation had been mounted there in support of the Khampas in Tibet.

There are many influences on the decision to open or close certain parts of Nepal to foreigners. Recent changes have liberalised both trekking and climbing, and there is considerable pressure to open more areas to trekkers. You should check with a trekking agency or the central immigration office before planning an unusual trek.

INFORMATION SOURCES
Trekking Companies

In addition to normal travel agencies, Nepal has a special group of travel agencies that are licensed as trekking companies. In theory, a trekking company arranges treks and does not handle air tickets and transportation, while a travel agency does handle transportation but does not arrange for sherpas, porters and food for treks. In practice, either kind of company manages to furnish all the facilities that are needed for any aspect of travel and trekking.

There are more than 150 trekking agencies in Nepal, ranging from large companies that operate in cooperation with major overseas agencies to small operations that support a single family. The following is an arbitrary list of agencies which have a reliable history and are likely to reply to correspondence and faxes from overseas. The list includes the biggest and best trekking companies, those that have office staff and can deal with correspondence and a few small ones that have made a name for themselves.

A complete list of trekking companies is available from the Department of Tourism or from the Trekking Agents Association of Nepal (TAAN).

A walk through the bazaars of Kathmandu will uncover many trekking company offices that are not on this list or even the list prepared by TAAN. Many of these are reliable and easy to deal with in person once you arrive in Nepal, and some can handle inquiries by mail or fax. Most companies price their treks using a complicated formula based on the number of days, number of people and the destination.

You can get a lot of advice from trekking companies, but remember that they are trying to sell you their services. You will be more welcome and get more comprehensive information if you choose one company and work with them to plan your trek and then buy your air tickets and rent equipment through them.

Adventure Nepal Trekking
   Tridevi Marg, Thamel, PO Box 915, Kathmandu
   (☎ 412508, fax (977) 1-222026)
Ama Dablam Trekking
   Lazimpat, PO Box 3035, Kathmandu
   (☎ 415372/3, fax (977) 1-416029, telex 2460
   WELCOM NP)

Annapurna Mountaineering & Trekking
   Durbar Marg, PO Box 795, Kathmandu
   (☎ 222999, fax (977) 1-226153, telex 2648
   YETI)
Asian Trekking
   Tridevi Marg, Thamel, PO Box 3022,
   Kathmandu (☎ 413732, 415506, fax (977) 1-
   411878, telex 2802 ASTREK)
Bhrikuti Himalayan Treks
   Nag Pokhari, PO Box 2267, Kathmandu (☎/fax
   (977) 1-413612)
Crystal Mountain Treks
   Naxal, Nag Pokhari, PO Box 5437, Kathmandu
   (☎ 412656, fax (977) 1-412647)
Himalayan Hill Treks & River Tours
   Baluwatar, PO Box 1066, Kathmandu
   (☎ 410740, fax (977) 1-471630, 411277)
Journeys Mountaineering & Trekking
   Kantipath, PO Box 2034, Kathmandu
   (☎ 225969, 229261, fax (977) 1-229262, telex
   2375 PEACE)
Lama Excursions
   Durbar Marg, PO Box 2485, Kathmandu
   (☎ 220186, 226706, fax (977) 1-227292, telex
   2659 LAMEX)
Lamjung Trekking & Expeditions
   Patan, PO Box 1436, Kathmandu (☎ 521607,
   522964, 521057, fax (977) 1-226820)
Malla Treks
   Lekhnath Marg, PO Box 787, Kathmandu
   (☎ 410089, 418387/9, fax (977) 1-418382, telex
   2238 MALLA NP)
Mountain Travel Nepal
   PO Box 170, Kathmandu (☎ 414508, 413019,
   fax (977) 1-414075, telex 2216 TIGTOP)
Nepal Himal Treks
   Baluwatar, PO Box 4528, Kathmandu
   (☎ 413305)
Nepal Treks & Natural History Expeditions
   Gangapath, PO Box 459, Kathmandu
   (☎ 471577, 472556, fax (977) 1-225131, telex
   2239 KTT)
Sherpa Co-operative Trekking
   Durbar Marg, PO Box 1338, Kathmandu
   (☎ 224068, fax (977) 1-227983, telex 2558
   NEPEX)
Sherpa Society
   Chabahil, Chuchepati, PO Box 1566,
   Kathmandu (☎ 470361, fax (977) 1-470153)
Sherpa Trekking Service
   Kamaladi, PO Box 500, Kathmandu (☎ 220423,
   222489, fax (977) 1-227243, telex 2419 STS)
Treks & Expedition Services
   Kamal Pokhari, PO Box 3057, Kathmandu
   (☎ 418347, 410895, fax (977) 1-410488)
Venture Treks & Expeditions
   Kantipath, PO Box 3968, Kathmandu
   (☎ 221585, 225780, fax (977) 1-220178, telex
   2637 TEMTIG)

Yeti Mountaineering & Trekking
  Ramshah Path, PO Box 1034, Kathmandu
  (☎ 410899, fax (977) 1-410899, telex 2268
  PAGODA)

Other Information Sources

Kathmandu Environmental Education Project (KEEP) This internationally recognised project operates an information centre, reading room and coffee shop on the 2nd storey of the Tilicho Hotel, about 100 metres west of the immigration office, and is the best source of advice and information about trekking (☎ 418755, fax (977) 1-227628).

Himalayan Rescue Association (HRA) The HRA (☎ 418755) has an office next door to KEEP in the Tilicho Hotel. The office maintains a logbook with recent information about trekking conditions and provides information on equipment and health considerations for trekkers. It's open Sunday to Friday from 11 am to 5 pm.

The HRA was founded in 1973 and operates aid posts staffed with volunteer doctors in Pheriche on the Everest trek and Manang on the trek around Annapurna. The aid posts charge for medical services to cover their operating costs and the salaries of Nepalese staff, but otherwise the entire organisation is operated by volunteers. The HRA survives because of donations, memberships and the sale of T-shirts and emblems. The organisation deserves your support.

Nepal Mountaineering Association (NMA) This office (☎ 411525, 416278) is in Hatisar behind the Hotel Yak & Yeti, near the Krishna Bread Factory. It issues all permits for trekking peaks and collects reports from expeditions when they return.

Department of National Parks & Wildlife Conservation The national parks office (☎ 220912/850, 227926, fax 227675) in Kathmandu is located at Babar Mahal on the road to the airport. They have material available about the Nepal's eight national parks, three wildlife reserves and can provide information about current conservation efforts.

Trekking Agents Association of Nepal (TAAN) The TAAN office (☎ 225875, 223352), PO Box 3612, is on Kantipath, next to the Hotel Yellow Pagoda. It can provide an up-to-date list of trekking companies in Nepal and may be able to give you information about new or changed trekking regulations.

Department of Tourism The tourist information office on New Rd near Basantapur has government publications and an information counter. Most Nepalese who have lived all their lives in Kathmandu are not well informed about life in the hills, so you will probably not get much sophisticated trekking information from the people who staff the counter.

FOOD & EQUIPMENT

It is possible to rely entirely on hotels for meals during your trek and not carry any food at all. Most trekking hotels have supplies of tinned food, chocolate bars, biscuits, toilet paper and other essentials, but you may want to carry a small supply of goodies to use for emergencies or to relieve the boredom of dal bhat.

In Kathmandu, numerous food shops in Thamel and Asan Tole carry a large range of staples. The Bluebird Supermarket has branches in the Blue Star Hotel and Lazimpat. Nanglo Bazaar and Fresh House near Joche Tole (near Freak St) both have open shelves where you can wander about and choose from a wide variety of Indian and imported foods, tinned meat and fish, spices and sweets. Nanglo and Bluebird also carry a few imported medical supplies and useful chemicals such as potassium permanganate to sterilise vegetables and Lugol's solution to purify drinking water. You can often find drink powders, such as Tang, which make iodine-treated water more palatable. Check prices as you fill your shopping basket in these shops. They carry expensive imported food alongside Indian and Nepalese equivalents that are much less expensive.

There are several Nepalese-produced packaged foods that can add variety to meals. Two brands of muesli and granola are available, and several companies produce a large variety of biscuits. Yak cheese is available in Thamel shops and at the dairy near the Hotel Malla. The Pumpernickel Bakery in Thamel can provide natural grain bread that will last for many days on the trail. Pilgrims Bookshop carries a variety of herbal teas that offer a respite from caffeine-based tea and coffee. Nepalese natural peanut butter will appeal to Americans, but be careful how you carry it because the oil tends to leak into your backpack.

If you are arranging a fully organised trek with a cook and porters, you will make major food purchases of canned goods, rice and other staples. All good trekking cooks can estimate how much you need for a trek, depending on the number of people, the destination and duration. There are food wholesalers that operate out of tiny shops in Asan Tole and Lazimpat that can provide amazing quantities of food in a few hours.

Kitchen Equipment
If you have hired a full crew, you will need a portable kitchen. Pots and pans, plates and eating utensils are available throughout the Kathmandu bazaar. If you do buy this equipment, beware that your cook does not buy lots of extra items that catch his eye. A kerosene pressure lantern is a useful but troublesome addition to the kitchen gear. It helps to extend the day by allowing you to prepare breakfast early and end your dinner late.

Stoves & Fuel
The national park rules prohibit the use of firewood in all mountain national parks. If you have a cook and are trekking in a national park, arrange for a stove. Indian kerosene stoves are expensive and delicate, so if you plan for only a short stay in a national park you might consider having

meals in hotels. Theoretically, the entrance station personnel will check to see that you have a stove and kerosene if you enter the park with a group.

The use of kerosene is also required in the Annapurna Sanctuary. Kerosene is for sale at Chhomrong at the entrance to the Annapurna Sanctuary and stoves and jerry cans are available for rent.

Trekking Equipment Shops
The best trekking equipment shops are in Thamel and Basantapur (Freak St). These specialize in equipment rental, but will also sell almost anything in the shop. Nepal's import policies do not allow the large-scale import of trekking and climbing equipment. Most gear that is available in Kathmandu was brought into the country by mountaineering expeditions so almost everything available in shops is second-hand. Any new gear is equipment that an expedition imported and never used. The other source of equipment for trekking shops is trekkers who sell off their sleeping bags and other cold-weather gear before they head off to the warmer climate of South-East Asia.

Because equipment is imported in such a haphazard way, the trekking gear available in Kathmandu tends to be either high-tech mountaineering equipment or low-quality, travel-worn castoffs. For trekking, you want a middle ground. A down parka suitable for the top of Everest isn't very practical for a trek to Tatopani, and a sleeping bag that has spent a month on the beaches of Goa isn't going to do the job at Everest base camp. There is neither a reliable stock of any particular item nor a complete range of clothing sizes. In order to find what you need, you will have to spend time going from shop to shop looking for the right size, quality and price.

In addition to hand-me-downs there is a wide range of locally produced trekking and climbing gear. Nepalese tailors are producing tents, sleeping bags, down jackets, rucksacks, camera cases, gaiters and ponchos. Much of this is reasonably good quality and will probably be suitable for a trek. However, the nylon fabric, thread and fittings might not stand up to the beating of a mountaineering expedition. The largest local manufacturer of rucksacks and jackets sells them under the brand name Climber. Many items are copies of high-tech brand name equipment, right down to the label. Many of the Lowe Pro and Karrimor packs and camera cases in Kathmandu trekking shops are pirate copies. The prices are right, but don't be fooled into thinking you are getting a bargain on brand-name equipment. Some items, such as ponchos for Rs 350 and small day packs for Rs 700, are such bargains that you can almost afford to use them once and throw them away.

Hiring Equipment

It is possible to hire everything that you need for a trek – from clothing to sleeping bags, tents and cooking pots. Large sizes of shoes are often difficult to find as are gas cartridges, freeze-dried food (sometimes) and good socks. Otherwise, you can arrange everything you need in Kathmandu, though it will probably take a day or two of shopping.

If you plan to rent gear, remember that all shops require a deposit to ensure that you return the equipment in good condition. This can cause complications if you don't want to change money to pay the deposit. You might leave signed travellers' cheques or a passport with the shop, but neither of these is a good idea. Cash dollars can solve the problem, so carry some if you plan to rent equipment. A guide that the shopkeeper knows can occasionally make a personal guarantee that you will return the gear, thus saving the hassle of a deposit. Be sure to check the bill and receipt carefully before you leave the rental shop.

Some trekking companies will also rent tents, sleeping bags, mattresses and cooking pots. If you hire a guide from the same company, he can certainly serve as a guarantee and avoid the deposit problem. If you are hiring a cook, it may be worth making a deal with a trekking company to rent kitchen equipment. New kitchen equipment can cost upwards of Rs 300 per trekker and is difficult to sell at the end of the trek.

A limited supply of equipment is available for sale and rent in Pokhara, Lukla, Namche Bazaar and a few private homes in the Everest region. Namche Bazaar has fantastic trekking equipment shops because many expeditions jettison their gear here. If you are trekking around Annapurna, you need high altitude equipment only for the two or three days it takes to cross the pass. There is a need for equipment in Manang and Muktinath so it is likely that some enterprising person will arrange to have gear available on both sides of the Thorung La before too long. Other than these places, you probably won't find any gear for rent or sale in the hills except by blind luck (a mountaineering expedition returning home, for example).

The following table of costs applied for the hire or purchase of trekking equipment during autumn 1993. Expect to pay more during the high season. In the off season, especially during the monsoon, you can probably do better than the costs I have here. Note that the lower prices for parkas, sleeping bags, duffel bags and rucksacks are for items made in Nepal; the higher costs are for imported items.

	Rs per day	Rs to buy
woollen mittens	NA	150-350
ski gloves	NA	600-900
sleeping bag		
down-filled	20-30	3600-6000
fibre-filled	10-15	3000-5000
parka		
down-filled	20-25	3000-6000
fibre-filled	5-10	1600-3000
duffel bag	NA	300-500
daypack	10-15	300-800
large rucksack	20-25	1400-2500
water bottle	NA	150-250
torch (flashlight)	NA	50-100 (new)
trekking boots	10-25	1500-2500
light trekking shoes	NA	1700-2000 (new)
hat, with brim	NA	100-175
hat, woollen	NA	150-250
sunglasses or goggles	NA	150-300
socks (thick woollen)	NA	150-185
jumper	NA	100-250
rainwear (poncho)	NA	350-500
umbrella	NA	150-200

NA – these items are usually not available for rent

GUIDES & PORTERS
Guides
On the Everest, Langtang and Annapurna treks the routes are so well known by everyone that you do not need a guide to help you find the way. Still, a good guide will be useful in making your trek easier (and often cheaper) by negotiating on your behalf for food and accommodation during the trek. Also, a guide will hopefully show you places of interest and short cuts that you might have otherwise overlooked. There are, of course, poor guides who will do nothing but complicate everything throughout the trek and make considerable money at your expense. If you travel with a sherpa to Khumbu there is the additional benefit of an invitation (almost always) to the house of your guide where you can become familiar with the Sherpa culture. Part of this introduction will probably include you and your guide getting drunk as a result of Sherpa hospitality. In remote regions there are fewer signs that say 'Hotel', so a traveller must find accommodation and food by asking from house to house. A guide can be indispensable in such situations.

Nepal has a very structured society – a hangover from the caste system. This structure leads to people having very definite ideas, ingrained since birth, about what jobs they will or will not do. If someone considers themselves a trekking guide, they will be reluctant to carry a porter load. Porters are often reluctant to do camp chores or other duties unless they have hopes of moving up in the pecking order. If a porter agrees to do extra work, guides may discourage or even prevent the porter from doing this to maintain their own status. The ideal guide/porter combination is a rare phenomenon, though a few do exist. If you are lucky enough to find one of these people, you can probably get away with a single employee for a trek.

Porters
Hiring only a single porter or hiring several porters without a guide sounds like a good idea and is usually easy to arrange, but it is not always easy to control this sort of situa-

tion on the trail. While most porters are reliable, they usually have little education in the Western sense. They tend to be superstitious and are, of course, subject to fear, fatigue, uncertainty and ill health. Porters may decide that they have gone far enough and want to return home, in which case they may just vanish. If you have a sherpa who has hired the porters for your trek, it is the sherpa's responsibility to assure their performance. Thus, if a porter vanishes your sherpa may be embarrassed enough to carry the load until another porter can be found. Sherpa guides are not at all happy about carrying a load, so you can be sure that they will find a new porter in a hurry. If you have hired the porter yourself, you must either sit alongside the trail until a replacement comes along, or carry your own heavy baggage.

Trying to manage your own team of porters without a guide is complicated because you must constantly be aware of where each porter is in order to protect your possessions. Unless, of course, you have somehow managed to secure the services of people who have already proven their reliability. Even this isn't foolproof. I've had a porter, who had already been on two treks, disappear on the third trek with two duffel bags of gear. On group treks the sirdar hires a porter leader, or *naike*, who chases up and down the trail keeping track of porters and coaxing them on to the day's destination.

Where to Hire Guides & Porters
You can hire guides through trekking companies, trekking equipment shops or referrals from other trekkers. Trekking shops are more willing to help you if you offer a fee for their advice or hire equipment from them. Many restaurants and hotels, particularly in the Thamel area of Kathmandu and in Pokhara, have bulletin boards. These often have messages from trekkers who are looking for trekking companions or are recommending a reliable guide. Also check at the KEEP and HRA offices for guide, porter and companion referrals.

You can often find out-of-work sherpas outside the immigration office or in tiny restaurants in Asan Tole specializing in local dishes and rakshi. Hiring a guide directly is a hit or miss situation. You might find someone brilliant or you might have endless problems. They will convince you of their ability by producing certificates and letters from past (always satisfied) customers. It is not likely that you will hit upon someone whose sole purpose was to steal from you, but such people do exist and are offering their services as guides. All embassies in Nepal suggest that you either go through a known intermediary, or check references carefully before you employ a guide.

October, November, March and April are very busy trekking months. Any sherpa who does not have a job during these months may be of questionable reliability. At other times, it is often possible to find excellent staff.

You can sometimes hire sherpas and porters in Lukla and Pokhara. Except during October and early November you will probably be successful if you fly to Lukla and try to arrange a trek without any advance preparations. However, there are no sherpas or porters available at Jomsom or Langtang.

A good trekking guide can arrange porters. Things will work much better if you tell the guide where you wish to trek and how much you are prepared to pay, after which you go off for a cup of tea to let him do all the negotiations on your behalf. On a long trek, an experienced guide will lay off porters as the party eats through porter-loads of food. He will also replace porters when they get nervous because they are too far from their homes.

Wages

It is becoming difficult to suggest specific rates for porters' and guides' wages. Political and social pressures in Nepal have resulted in occasional exorbitant demands for wages and benefits. Union organisers are working to improve the lot of trekking workers and are trying to establish minimum wages and other facilities. Many guides and porters, however, are operating at a subsistence level and will work for considerably less than the union scale.

Consult the HRA, TAAN or a trekking company for the latest guidelines.

Wages for porters will probably be between Rs 125 and Rs 150 per day for trekking, but demand from other trekkers and expeditions can drive prices higher. Road-building in the hills also pushes up porter wages while the construction passes through a village. Porters expect to buy their own food out of their wages, so you do not ordinarily have to carry food for them. However, unless you do provide food and shelter for porters, you will always have to camp near a village where they can buy food.

Tradition dictates that guides receive a lower salary than porters, usually Rs 100 to Rs 150 a day (in 1993), but they also receive accommodation and food. If you are staying at inns, it will amaze you how much your guide can eat and drink. Set a limit on the guide's food bill before you set out or pay him a daily food allowance, though this must increase at higher elevations where food is more expensive. If you are really watching your pennies you could always carry a small amount of food and cook it yourself if you have a guide. This leads, however, to hiring a porter to carry the food and cooking pots because tradition also dictates that a guide does not carry a load. Suddenly your trek transmogrifies into a 'do it yourself' trek with all its attendant bureaucratic hassles.

Clothing & Equipment

One important point to consider when you employ porters is the provision of warm clothing and equipment for cold and snow. If you are going into snow, you must provide goggles, shoes, shelter and clothing – porters are not expendable. Also provide plastic sheets (available in Kathmandu) so that porters can protect themselves and your baggage from rain.

In Khumbu, clothing is usually not a problem because you will probably hire Sherpas who have their own shoes and warm clothing – ask them to be sure. The place where most problems occur with porters is crossing Thorung La, the pass between Manang and Muktinath on the trek around

Annapurna. From whatever direction you approach the pass, the route starts in low tropical country and any porters that you hire will probably be from these lowland regions. When you reach the snow, the unequipped lowland porters either quit and turn back or continue foolishly without proper clothing or footwear, often resulting in frostbite, snow blindness or even death. Porters are not usually available in Manang or Muktinath, so it is really worth the extra planning and expense to buy porter equipment in Kathmandu (though occasionally such items are available in Manang) if you plan to use porters on this pass. You should also have some sort of shelter for them for the one or two nights that shelter is scarce.

When you do provide equipment for porters, be sure to make it clear whether it is a loan or a gift. In reality it will be very hard to get back equipment that you have loaned unless you are very determined and thick-skinned. The porters and sherpas have special techniques to make you feel guilty and petty when you ask for the return of equipment.

Porter Insurance

Trekking rules require that trekkers insure all their sherpas and porters for Rs 100,000 (about US$2000) against accidental death. So few trekkers do this that you would surprise an insurance company if you asked them to arrange insurance. There is no system for checking on whether you actually purchase insurance, though you will certainly have a major row if there is an accident and you cannot produce an insurance certificate. If you are planning to climb one of the trekking peaks, you must insure any Nepalese who go beyond base camp. There is a system for checking on insurance in this situation.

Trekking companies have a blanket policy that covers all their staff. Oriental Insurance Co and Rashtriya Bima Sansthan in Kathmandu can provide the required coverage for a fee of about US$8 per person. These companies can also provide, at a higher cost, the mandatory insurance for sherpas if you are climbing a trekking peak.

Stoves for Porters

The rules for restricted areas prohibit the use of firewood for cooking, even by porters. This policy is encouraged by environmental groups in Nepal and by ACAP. To implement this, you will need to arrange stoves for the porters. This usually includes providing a cook to prepare porter food unless someone in the party is prepared to take on the role of permanent stove mechanic. As you plan the trek with your sirdar, pay special attention to how the preparation of porter food will be handled. Certain ethnic groups cannot eat food prepared by others and many porters can be unhappy about eating certain kinds of food or food prepared in a particular way.

Other Considerations

An important consideration when you decide to trek with a guide or porters is that you place yourself in the role of an employer. This means that you may have to deal with personnel problems including medical care, insurance, strikes, requests for time off, salary increases and all the other aspects of being a boss. Be as thorough as you can when hiring people and make it clear from the beginning what the requirements and limitations are. After that, prepare yourself for some haggling – it's almost impossible to protect against it.

ON THE TRAIL
Staying in a Hotel

When you arrive at a hotel for the night, reach an agreement with the innkeeper on the cost for sleeping. Look around and see what facilities the hotel provides and determine the cost of meals. Some inns waive the sleeping charge if you eat meals there. In other inns the sleeping charge can be as little as Rs 5, though most charge Rs 10; it's up to Rs 20 or Rs 50 per person in more sophisticated lodges.

There are a few special hotels in the hills, particularly those that obtained government loans, and a few special facilities in Lukla and Jomsom that cater to people who are tired of trekking. These all charge US$20 or more. During times of heavy demand, such as during a flight back-up at Lukla or when snow on the pass has caused a backlog of trekkers at Manang or Muktinath, innkeepers charge what the traffic will bear. Accommodation becomes expensive and difficult to find. Most times, however, accommodation will cost from Rs 10 to Rs 20 and will be found without too much trouble.

Hotels at high elevations rarely have private rooms. Instead, their dormitories have several huge beds that sleep 10 or 20 people, often in two tiers. High altitude can make people uncomfortable, sleepless, crabby and strange. In hotels there can be a lot of thrashing about and opening and closing of doors throughout the night. Ear plugs are a good investment. If you value sleep and privacy, reconsider the advantages of bringing your own tent.

Since a hotel also doubles as a home, whether it has a sign that says 'Hotel' or not, you may have a difficult time sleeping until the entire household has retired. Trekkers who walk and exert themselves all day require more sleep than they normally do at home, often as much as 10 or 11 hours each night. Village people who are not exerting themselves during the day can get by with six to eight hours. This presents an immediate conflict in lifestyle and sleep requirements. The conflict escalates when the inevitable booze and card party erupts in the next room or, worse yet, in your bedroom. Another universal deterrent to sleep is the ubiquitous Radio Nepal which does not stop broadcasting until 11 pm.

During the trekking season there is a daily rush for hotels. It's quite mad to spend your holiday in competition with other trekkers racing to get a good space or a private room at the best hotel in the next village. In the Everest region, in particular, this can be dangerous because of the elevation gain and the chance of altitude sickness. If you find yourself travelling on the same schedule as a gaggle of other trekkers, relax for half a day and try to operate a half-day behind them. Traditional lunch spots are often deserted in the evening and hotels that are crowded at night can be empty at lunch time.

Meals Usually the innkeeper keeps an account of all the food and drink that you consume and collects payment for everything in the morning. It's worth keeping track yourself because other trekkers' food often makes its way onto your account when the hotel gets busy. Many hotels have menus that show all their prices, including the charges for sleeping. There is rarely any bargaining and the menu really does represent a fixed, and usually fair, price. Check the prices before you order to avoid later hassles. Strangely, the places most prone to bargaining are the fancy hotels – the US$10 per night and up variety – that have lost a lot of their business to smaller and cheaper facilities.

Meals typically take an hour or two to prepare unless there is stew or dal bhat already cooked, so soon after arriving you should order your meal and establish a time to eat. There are some pretty sophisticated short-order kitchens that operate in the hills, the best being at Namche, Lukla and along the Kali Gandaki. If you patronise one of these, you may get an exotic Western-style meal. More often the choice is between dal bhat with vegetables *(tarkari)* at Rs 20 to Rs 40 or dal bhat with meat *(maasu)* for Rs 20 to Rs 30 extra. Eggs *(phul* or *andaa)*, when available, cost Rs 2 to Rs 6 each.

Most hotels offer an extensive choice of bottled soft drinks, beer and bottled water. Tea or coffee will be made with milk and laden with sugar. If you want black tea or coffee, be sure to order it that way. Many hotels can also concoct exotic drinks with rum, local rakshi and fruit.

At high altitudes, hotels become more expensive. Tea costs Rs 2 in the lowlands, Rs 3 in places more than three or four days from the nearest road, and Rs 10 or Rs 20 in high places such as Lobuje and Annapurna base camp. When food and drink is expensive it is tempting to economise and eat and drink less. You must resist this temptation because a large liquid intake is one of the important aids for the prevention of altitude sickness.

A low food intake can leave you weak and subject to hypothermia.

Daily Routines Most Nepalese do not eat breakfast and have only milk tea when they arise. They have a heavy brunch of rice and vegetables around 10 am. When staying in a local inn, you will find it faster to operate in the same manner. If you order a large breakfast early in the morning, you will probably have a late start. Sophisticated inns are usually able to deal with short orders in the morning, though it is still better to organise this the evening before. You can also save time in the morning by carrying some cereal or muesli for breakfast. *Chiuraa* (beaten rice), available locally, makes a less tasty but satisfactory substitute. You should be able to move for a few hours on tea and biscuits, arriving at 9 or 10 am at a place that has dal bhat prepared.

If you want to have lunch at noon or 1 pm you will almost certainly have to wait an hour or two while the hotel keeper cooks rice specially for you. Depending on your mood and fitness this may or may not be an attractive break in the day. If you find yourself with a long wait, accept it and use the time for a good rest rather than agitate to try to get things moving faster in the kitchen. A hotel can become chaotic when 20 people order 20 different things in a dozen diverse languages. This confuses even a Western cook who uses order slips and has a complete stock of goods. In a small hotel where the innkeeper cooks everything over a single wood fire or kerosene stove with a limited supply of pots, it can get crazy. If you can adjust to the local schedule of tea for breakfast and a 10 am brunch, you will avoid a lot of waiting in kitchens. If you cannot adjust, you can still save yourself a lot of time and hunger by talking to other trekkers and combining your orders into two or three dishes. In addition to saving time, this is also the environmentally sound way to conserve scarce fuel.

Food for Your Guide Dealing with an inn when you have a guide is another matter. Theoretically a guide is more sophisticated than a porter and should have the ability to organise an inexpensive and trouble-free trek. This sophistication also may be a mastery of ways to make money with a minimum of work. If you have a responsible guide, the easiest approach is to have your guide arrange everything and then pay the bill yourself in the morning. Sometimes the guide will leave you with a bill for several glasses of chhang, extra food and the losses at last night's card party. In such cases, one solution is to agree on a daily rate for his subsistence. Each of you can then pay for your own food and accommodation separately. It should cost from Rs 80 to Rs 150 per day for a guide to live on a trek. If you add another Rs 50 for drinks and cigarettes you are providing a generous allowance.

Cultural Considerations At inns along the main trekking routes you can behave just as you would in any small hotel anywhere. In remote regions where the hotels cater mainly to locals, you should take special care to follow the customs of the people. Staying out of the kitchen goes a long way towards this. Nepalese traditionally eat rice with their right hand and always wash their hands before and after eating. Many small hotels will serve you a meal without providing eating utensils, but most can find a spoon if you ask.

Staying in a Nepalese Home
If you are in a particularly remote region where there are no hotels, you can often arrange food and accommodation in private homes. You could also end up in a home if your guide has friends in a particular village, if someone is just opening a new lodge or in an emergency when you cannot make it to the next hotel. Though it may appear that you are a guest, the householder always expects that you will pay for your food and lodging. Prices are flexible in such a situation, but usually the owner of the house will quote a fair price in the morning when you depart – but they will be shy and you will have to ask how much.

In a private home, you will probably have to wait until everyone else decides to go to sleep before you can roll out your sleeping bag. Be sure to find out where the toilet facilities are, if they exist. Don't dispose of garbage of any kind in the cooking fire. If there is a religious statue or altar, arrange your bed so your feet do not point in that direction when you sleep. (See also the Culture section in the Facts about the Country for more details about avoiding offence.)

Beware of low doorways when you enter a house. It is said that a low doorway teaches you humility, but more often it can result in a nasty bang on the head.

Coping with Guides & Porters

If you are on an organised trek, the sherpa sirdar's resources will include only the food, equipment, money and instructions that either you or the trekking company provide. No matter how scrupulous the arrangements

and how experienced your sherpa staff, there will be some complications. A trek is organised according to a prearranged itinerary and the sherpas expect to arrive at certain points on schedule. If you are sick or slow, and do not tell this to the sherpas, you may discover that camp and dinner are waiting for you far ahead. Be sure to communicate such problems and other desires to the staff.

Most trekking sherpas are true professionals. They will make a lot of effort to accommodate you if they understand what you want. If you do not wish to follow their daily routine, you must decide this early in the trek. A routine, once established with the sherpas, is difficult to change later.

You may buy or bring some special food 'goodies' that you are saving for high altitudes or an important occasion. If you hand these over to a cook at the outset of the trek, you are likely to find them (despite instructions to the contrary) cooked during the first few days of the trek or, worse yet, served to

---

A Typical Day in a Trekking Group

A group trekker begins the day at 6 am with a call of 'tea sir'. A cup of tea or coffee soon appears through the tent flap. After you drink your tea or, as I do, spill it all over the tent, you pack your gear and emerge to a light breakfast of Darjeeling tea, coffee, porridge and eggs or pancakes. While you are eating, the sherpas take down the tents and pack up loads for the porters. The entire group is usually on the way by 7 am. The early start takes advantage of the cool morning to accomplish most of the day's hike. Even on a group trek, many trekkers find an opportunity to hike alone for much of the day. The porters are slower and the sherpas, especially the cook crew, race on ahead to have lunch waiting when you arrive.

There are many diversions on the trail. It is not unusual to find sherpas and fellow trekkers in shops or bhattis. Sometimes the entire group may stop to watch a festival or some other special event along the way. At a suitable spot, usually about 11 am, there is a stop of an hour or two for lunch. The noon meal includes the inevitable tea, a plate of rice, potatoes or noodles, some canned or fresh meat and whatever vegetables are in season.

The afternoon trek is shorter, ending about 3 pm when you round a bend to (hopefully) discover your tents already set up in a field near a village. The kitchen crew again prepares tea and coffee soon after arrival in camp. There is then an hour or two to nurse blisters, read, unpack and sort gear, wash or explore the surrounding area before dinner.

Trekking groups usually have Western food with chicken, goat, mutton or buffalo meat frequently, though not daily. The cow is sacred in regions of Hindu influence, so beef is unavailable. The cook varies the rice diet by substituting potatoes, noodles and other items. The food is tasty and plentiful, but will probably be pretty boring after two weeks or so. Even so, the meals will be taxing the imagination of the cooks, who will be providing a variety of foods which they never experience in their own meals. Most trekkers feel healthy and fit on this diet as the food is fresh and organic, with no preservatives.

The sun sets early during the trekking season, so it is dark by 6 pm. There is time to read by candlelight in tents or to sit around talking in the dark. To conserve firewood, there is never a campfire. Most trekkers are asleep by 8 or 9 pm. ■

Leeches

Leeches are more of an annoyance than a health hazard, but they do make a mess and leave an uncomfortable itching sore once they have drunk their fill of your blood. During the monsoon, leeches are everywhere; hanging from twigs and leaves waving in the air trying to find a warm body to attach to. They do not thrive above about 3000 metres and vanish surprisingly quickly as soon as the rains stop. They also can appear equally quickly in the spring after a spell of several days of rain. If you trek on a major trekking route during the normal trekking season from October to May you will probably not encounter a leech.

Leeches usually stay close to the ground and gain entry to your body over the top, or through the eyelets, of your boots. Once inside, they can easily bore through the fabric of your socks. You often do not notice them until your shoes start squishing with bloated leeches and blood-soaked socks. Be especially careful if you make a toilet stop in the bushes during leech season.

Leeches secrete a novocaine-like substance so that you do not notice when they poke a hole in you. They then fill themselves with blood and, once satiated, drop off to digest their dinner.

There are numerous folk remedies for leeches, all designed to prevent them from attaching themselves to you. Salt, lemon juice, mosquito repellent and kerosene may all be rubbed into the ankles or socks. Whether the mess that these repellents cause is worse than the occasional leech is open to question. If a leech has just arrived on your shoe, it is often possible to just flick it off with your finger or, if you are squeamish, a stick. Once a leech has attached itself to you it may be pulled off, or made to drop off by torturing it with a pinch of salt or a burning cigarette. Leeches are not like ticks; they do not leave any part of themselves behind, so it is perfectly safe to simply pull them off. ■

---

the sherpas. You should keep any special food in your luggage to prevent such mistakes.

If have organised your own trek and are travelling with porters, their ability to cover the required distance each day will limit your progress. Porters carrying 30 kg up and down hills cannot move as fast as a trekker carrying a light backpack. Other factors such as weather, steepness of the trail, sickness and festivals can turn a schedule upside down. Beware especially of the Dasain festival in October when porters are almost impossible to find and tend to vanish without warning.

You will rarely experience a strike, but you may find that the evening discussion of the next day's destination has turned into a delicate negotiating session. On major trails there are certain stopping places that all the porters are familiar with, and it is difficult to alter them. I once congratulated myself on having covered three 'porter days' of walking by lunch time the third day. I looked forward to covering a good distance after lunch. An embarrassed sirdar then informed me that our lunch spot would also be our

camp for the night. He explained that by definition it took three full days to reach where we were and whether it had taken us that long or not was immaterial. Nothing I could say (or pay) would entice the porters to go further until the following day when we were able to start trekking early in the morning, on schedule.

Route Finding

It isn't easy to get totally lost in the hills, but finding the trail you want, particularly through a large village, can sometimes be a challenge. If you are on a major trekking route, most local people know where you are going. If you see children yelling and pointing, you probably have taken a wrong turn. Watch for the lug sole footprints of other trekkers and for arrows carved into the trail by guides with trekking parties. It is always worthwhile to talk to local people and ask them about the trail to your next destination and discover what facilities you can expect to find on the way.

If you are in a less frequented area, you must ask people. Be sure to phrase the question in a way that forces them to point the way. *Kun baato Namche Bazaar jaanchha?* (Which trail goes to Namche Bazaar?) will usually do the job. If you point to a trail and ask if it goes where you want to go, most Nepalese will say yes, because they like to please you. When asking directions, ask the name of the next village. People near Jiri probably have no idea where Namche Bazaar is, but they know the trail to Shivalaya, the next village.

In particularly remote areas, be ready for confusion about destinations and times. I've seen situations where asking directions has developed into a massive argument involving 10 people, each having an opinion on the best route and the time involved.

Police Checkposts

There are police posts throughout the country. While the trekking rules do not specifically state that you should seek out and visit every police post along a trekking route, some police officers seem to believe this to be the case. As a general rule, if there is a sign, barrier, or a cop standing on the trail, it would be prudent to pay a call on the local constabulary. Formalities are usually as simple as writing your name in a register, but in some places they can become cumbersome with forms to fill in and endorsements on your trekking permit. In national parks, what looks like a police checkpost is usually an army post where your national park entrance receipt will be examined to make sure you've paid the park fee.

TREKKING ROUTES

The following quotation is one of the Tibetan 'elegant sayings' attributed either to Nagarjuna, the Indian mystic who lived in the 2nd century CE, or to the head lama of the Sakya Monastery in Tibet in 1270 CE:

The teacher can but point the Way,
The means to reach the Goal
Must vary with each Pilgrim.

In this book I have described most of the well-known trekking routes in Nepal. These descriptions will give you some insight into the type of country and culture that you may encounter on specific treks. They should also help you to choose the area you wish to visit, because they give an indication of the difficulty of each trek and the number of days it will take to follow a particular route.

I've tried to include a general explanation of the lay of the land and cultural background, but these are not self-guiding trail descriptions. If you are not travelling with a Nepalese companion, you must continually ask hoteliers or other trekkers about the correct path. If you are with a guide, he or she will be asking questions as you travel. What to us may be a major trekking route is likely to be, for the people of a village, only a path from Ram's house to Bir Bahadur's house to Dawa's house. In our minds we string all these sections of trail together to form a major route to some place that village people may never go.

Many trekking routes either travel in an east-west direction or go to high mountain regions. Local people do not often follow these routes because most trade routes are south to north and avoid high elevations. There is nothing more frustrating than wandering around the hills of Nepal looking for the correct trail. It is impossible, no matter how detailed the route description, to document every important trail junction. Also, trails change for a multitude of reasons. The descriptions that follow portray what you may expect if you follow the shortest available routes, but it will be all too easy to get lost if you try to walk through Nepal using only this as a guide. Develop the habit of talking to people and asking questions.

Just as it is impossible to document every trail junction, it is also impossible to describe every possible trek. What follows is a description of the major routes, a few optional side trips and some alternative routes that avoid backtracking. You should seriously consider backtracking, however. Often the second time over a particular trail provides insights and views that you did not see or appreciate the first time.

If you're making your first trek in Nepal, it is likely that you will choose one of these routes. They are not only the best known, but are also the most attractive. There is good reason for the fame of the Everest trek, the Jomsom trek and other well known routes. Most of the treks I've described, except those in the restricted areas, have hotels of some sort available every night, and reasonably well-defined trails. The exceptions are western Nepal, the Khumbu to Hile route, the Lamidanda trek and Barahbise to Jiri.

You may be tempted to go to some other region where there won't be so many tourists because of stories and articles you may have read about the 'freeway' to Everest. When you listen to these discussions you should place them in their proper perspective. Even in 1993, the 'overcrowded' conditions in the Everest region consisted of 12,000 trekkers over a period of a year. More people would stay in a typical US national park camp ground on a single weekend night.

No matter where you trek there will be local people living and moving through the area. Getting to remote and unexplored areas has little meaning in Nepal unless you are prepared to tackle a Himalayan peak.

Route Descriptions

The following is a list of the main trekking routes described in this book:

Mt Everest Region
Jiri to Namche Bazaar
Lukla to Everest Base Camp
Namche Bazaar to Gokyo
Namche Bazaar to Thami
Lukla to Lamidanda
Barahbise to Jiri

Annapurna Region
Annapurna Circuit
Jomsom Trek
Baglung to Tatopani
Annapurna Sanctuary
Around Annapurna
The Royal Trek

Langtang & Helambu
Langtang Trek
Across Ganja La
Helambu Circuit
Gosainkund
Jugal Himal

Eastern Nepal
Solu Khumbu to Hile
Basantpur to Kanchenjunga North
Taplejung to Kanchenjunga South
Kanchenjunga North Side to South Side
Makalu Base Camp

Western Nepal
Jumla to Rara Lake
Jumla to Dolpo
Across the Kagmara La
Dunai to Phoksumdo Lake
Do & Tarap
Pokhara to Dunai

Restricted Areas
Mustang Trek
Around Manaslu
Shey Gompa
Humla to Mt Kailas

Other Destinations
Kathmandu to Pokhara
Ganesh Himal
Rolwaling
Tilicho Lake
Mugu
Nar & Phu

In each section there is a brief introduction outlining some of the many other options possible in that region. There are many routes in Nepal that proceed over high passes, but I have described only three of these: Ganja La, Thorung La and Kagmara La. These pass crossings have the dangers of rockfall, avalanches and high altitude. All members of the party, including the sherpas and porters, must have good equipment before you attempt these routes. The chance of snow increases from December to April and snow on a pass may force you to turn back.

Daily Stages

I have separated the route descriptions into daily stages. This helps to make them readable and gives a quick estimate of the number of days required for each trek. The suggested night stops are the ones most trekkers use. In all cases, wood, water, food for porters (and usually chhang for sherpas) and a place large enough to pitch four or five tents are available at each night stop. Accommodation and

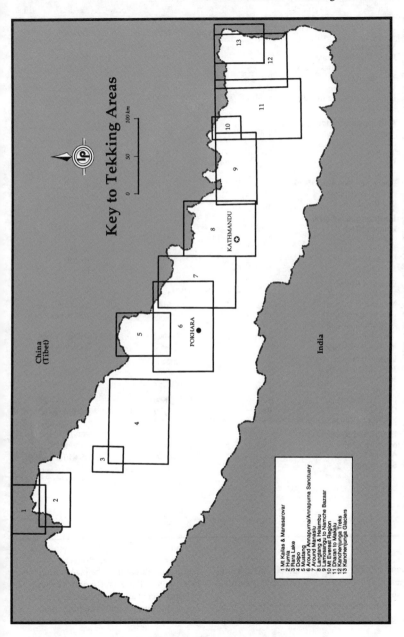

Key to Tekking Areas

China (Tibet)

India

KATHMANDU

POKHARA

0   50   100 km

1 Mt Kailas & Manasarovar
2 Humla
3 Rara Lake
4 Dolpo
5 Mustang
6 Around Annapurna/Annapurna Sanctuary
7 Around Manaslu
8 Langtang & Helambu
9 Lamosangu to Namche Bazaar
10 Mt Everest Region
11 Dharan to Makalu
12 Kanchenjunga Treks
13 Kanchenjunga Glaciers

	Days	Difficulty	Max Elevation	Costs
Mt Everest Region				
Jiri to Namche Bazaar	9	***	3500	Rs 650
Lukla to Everest Base Camp	15	****	5545	Rs 650
Namche to Gokyo	9	****	5318	Rs 650
Namche to Thami	2	***		
Lamidanda Escape Route	5	***	2800	
Barahbise to Jiri	6	***	2300	
Annapurna Region				
Annapurna Panorama	7-8	**	3800	Rs 650
Ghandruk Loop	3-4	**	3800	Rs 650
Tatopani Loop	7-8	**	3800	Rs 650
Jomsom Trek	9	***	3800	Rs 650
Baglung to Tatopani	2	**	1180	Rs 650
Annapurna Sanctuary	15	***	2470	Rs 650
Around Annapurna	18	****	5416	Rs 650
The Royal Trek	4	*	1730	Rs 650
Langtang & Helambu				
Langtang Trek	10	***	4300	Rs 650
Across Ganja La	7	*****	5200	Rs 650
Helambu Circuit	7	**	3490	Rs 650
Gosainkund	7	***	4610	Rs 650
Jugal Himal	10	***	3800	Rs 650
Eastern Nepal				
Solu Khumbu to Hile	12	****	3349	
Kanchenjunga North	22	****	5140	US$10 per wk
Kanchenjunga South	16	***	4620	US$10 per wk
Kanchenjunga North Side to South Side	2-4	*****	4663	US$10 per wk
Makalu Base Camp	20	****	5000	Rs 650
Western Nepal				
Jumla to Rara Lake	6-9	***	3050	Rs 650
Jumla to Dolpo	6-12	***	3820	US$10 per wk
Across Kagmara La	4	****	5115	US$10 per wk
Dunai to Phoksumdo Lake	6	***	3660	US$10 per wk
Do & Tarap	10-14	****	5190	US $10 per wk
Pokhara to Dunai	13	****	3970	
Restricted Areas				
Mustang Trek	9-14	****	3970	US$700
Around Manaslu	20	****	5100	US $70 per wk
Shey Gompa	5-6	***		US$700
Humla to Mt Kailas	20-25	****	5630	US$90 per wk

N/A = foreigners not allowed to use hotels, * = easy, ***** = hard

food are also usually available at each suggested stop for those who are relying on local inns.

When you trek these routes, either with an organised group or alone, you may find that you are not stopping at the places listed here. Don't panic. This is not a tour itinerary that requires you to be in Namche Bazaar on Tuesday. Your actual stopping place will depend on your fitness, whether you or

Season	Hotels	Other Information
Oct-May	good	lots of up and down; allow 23 days to visit base camp
Oct-Dec	excellent	potential altitude problems & flight hassles in Lukla
Oct-Dec, Feb-May	good	altitude problems (easy to get too high too fast)
Oct-May	good	side trip from Namche; good for acclimatisation
Oct-Apr	minimal	interesting country with few trekkers; very hot in May
Oct-May	minimal	alternative to long bus ride to Jiri
Oct-Apr	excellent	outstanding views from Poon Hill
Oct-Apr	excellent	good introduction to trekking; scenic Gurung villages
Oct-Apr	good	Gurung villages; apple pie & hot spring
Oct-May	excellent	follows deep Kali Gandaki Gorge to Muktinath
Oct-May	good	easy route that avoids climb over Ghorapani hill
Oct-Nov, Mar-Apr	very good	spectacular mountains; danger of avalanches
Oct-Nov, Mar-Apr	mostly good	varied scenery; one high pass; probable snow
Oct-Apr	minimal	easy introductory trek but few facilities, so few trekkers
Oct-May	very good	high mountains & glaciers close to Kathmandu
Oct-Nov, Mar-May	none	may require technical mountaineering skills when snow
Oct-Apr	very good	transport from Kathmandu cheap & easy
Oct-Nov, Mar-Apr	acceptable	dangerous when snow
Oct-Nov, Mar-Apr	none	fewer trekkers than most destinations
Oct-Apr	minimal	hot in Arun Valley; alternate exit or approach to Khumbu
Oct-May	minimal & basic	long hot approach; remote base camp
Oct-May	minimal & basic	flights to/from Taplejung; excellent mountain scenery
Oct-May	none	glacier crossing; possible snow
Oct-May	none	steep climb to Barun Valley; snow likely
Mar-Oct	poor	complicated logistics, but an outstanding trek
Mar-Oct	minimal	deep forests; interesting villages
Mar-Oct	none	high, remote and potentially dangerous
May-Oct	none	steep, exposed trails
May-Oct	none	steep, exposed trails when bridges washed out
May-Oct	none	long walk with few villages; great views of Dhaulagiri
May-Oct	N/A	walled city; Tibetan culture & scenery
Oct-May	N/A	long trek on steep trails; great views of Manaslu north face
May-Oct	N/A	lots of mystique surrounding 'Crystal Mountain'
Jul-Oct	N/A	very remote; extra expense to travel in China

someone in your party is sick on a particular day, the weather, trail conditions, arrangements with the porters and whether you find some place more interesting or attractive than the village I have described. Porters can severely influence the speed at which you travel, as their heavy loads make them slow. Your trek should allow you the freedom and opportunity to move as fast or as slowly as you wish. It's a vacation, so don't take schedules and timetables too seriously where they are not necessary.

It is easy to alter the number of days suggested here. Perhaps you can cut a day or two off the time if you walk from first light to sunset each day, but since a trek is a continual experience, not simply progress to a particular destination, there is little point in rushing the trip only to get to some place that may not be as engrossing as where you are now. At high altitudes you should proceed no faster than the ascent times recommended here in order to avoid altitude sickness. You can lengthen any trek to almost any degree by side trips, rest days and further exploration of inviting looking villages

Readers continually point out that they trekked either slower or faster than the 'schedules' in this book. That is the way it should be. Nobody gets a prize for completing a trek in fewer days than the route descriptions in this book, nor is there any punishment for taking longer. Breaking the description into days is simply a way to give you some guidelines to help you select and plan a trek and to help you understand what distances porters will agree to carry their loads each day.

Times & Distance
The route descriptions do not list approximate walking times. Any moderately fit trekker can accomplish the suggested daily stages in a single day. The stages do, however, tend to become more difficult in the later days of each trek, because fitness improves as the trek progresses. Porters also can accomplish each stage in a single day and will almost always agree to the stages listed here.

I did try to record walking times but it is boring trying to keep track of when you stop, when you walk and when you rest. When I compared the times on a particular trip with the times for that same trek the last time I travelled it, I found unbelievable variations. This must have depended on other factors that I did not record, such as my mood, physical condition, the condition of the trail, the number of other people and cattle on the

trail, how many photographs I took, and the weather. Because of these wide variations in walking times, I have not attempted to project approximate times for anyone else. Most days require from five to eight hours of walking.

If you really need to know times, you can ask people on the trail. Nepalese hill people use a unit of distance called a *kos*, the distance that a person can walk in one hour. *Namche Bazaar kati kos laagchha?* should elicit a reply that approximates the number of hours to Namche Bazaar (as should *Namche Bazaar kati gantaa laagchha* or 'How many hours to Namche Bazaar?'). It is more fun and rewarding to try to talk to people instead of continually looking at a book and checking it against your watch.

Another statistic that is difficult to determine is distance. It is easy to judge distances from a map, but a printed map is two-dimensional. With the many gains and losses of altitude – and all the turns and twists of the trail – a map measurement of the routes becomes virtually meaningless. In researching a guidebook to Glacier National Park in the USA, a friend pushed a bicycle wheel odometer over every trail in the park to get accurate distance measurements. I have neither the ambition nor the patience for such a project and, besides, it would take most of the fun out of a trek. You gain a different perspective of travelling by discussing how many days to a particular destination rather than how many km. Most of the days listed here are 10 to 20 km of trekking, depending on the altitude and steepness of the terrain.

Maps
The maps included in this book are based on the best available maps of each region. As with everything else, they are reasonably accurate but not perfect. To make them legible, I have deleted most villages and landmarks not mentioned in the route descriptions. In some cases, even major villages and mountains have vanished from the maps. The maps do not show elevations, as these are detailed in the route descriptions.

Instead of contour lines, the maps depict

only ridge lines. This is the line of the highest point on a ridge. If the trail crosses one of these brown lines, you must walk uphill. If the trail leads from a ridge line to a river, you must walk downhill. In the lowlands where the hills are gentle, the location of ridge lines can be more arbitrary than when they cross the top of a high peak.

The maps show mountain peaks in their true position, but villages may not always be located accurately. The problem occurs because of the size of villages. Where does the dot go for a village that is three km from end to end and which has no real centre or town square? The trails and roads follow the general direction indicated on the maps, but a map this size obviously cannot show small switchbacks and twists in the trail.

Trek Profiles

These profiles indicate the altitude changes for the major treks. They are reasonably to scale, in that the horizontal axis relates to days on the trek and thus gives an indication of the steepness of the trail. Most high and low points are marked for each day, therefore when there are many ups and downs in a single day, the scale becomes a bit distorted. When you compare treks looking at these profiles, look at the number of climbs, not the height of them; the vertical scale is the

same on each chart. The most frightening of these profiles is the Rara Lake loop in western Nepal because it crosses several ridges each day, but all the profiles look like saw teeth because treks in Nepal go from ridgetops to river valleys and back to ridgetops.

Altitude Measurements

The elevations shown in the route descriptions are composites, based on my measurements with an altimeter and the best available maps. Most elevations correlate with the Survey of India maps of the 1960s except where these are obviously wrong, a frequent occurrence in western Nepal. The Schneider map series that covers Everest and Langtang used the Survey of India maps as a starting point but refined most elevations, so I have used these elevations in the areas covered by these maps. Except for specific elevations shown on the Schneider maps, I have rounded all elevations to the nearest 10 metres. The elevations of peaks are those shown on the official mountaineering regulations of Nepal, except for peaks in the Everest region where I have used the elevations as shown on the 1978 edition of the Schneider Khumbu map.

This uncertainty over precise elevations will cause no problems during a trek. The

---

Altimeters

If you carry a properly calibrated altimeter on a trek you will find that it agrees with the elevations here up to an elevation of about 3500 metres. At higher elevations your altimeter will read lower than the elevations listed here and those shown on maps. To understand the reason for this, you will have to think back and recall a bit of high school physics.

Altimeters calculate barometric pressure by measuring the change in the volume of air in a tiny sealed container called an aneroid drum. This volume changes according to pressure – and temperature. Altimeters are calibrated to compensate for temperature change according to a standard formula. Most altimeters follow the Comit International de Navigation Arienne (CINA) standards in which the temperature is assumed to drop 0.65˚C for every 100 metres of altitude. Using this formula, the assumed temperature at 4000 metres is -11˚C and at 5000 metres is -17.5˚C. On a typical day in Nepal during the trekking season the temperature is likely to be closer to +15˚C, a difference of 26˚C at 4000 metres and 32.5˚C at 5000 metres. This causes the altimeter to read 416 metres low at 4000 metres and 650 metres low at 5000 metres. To be accurate you must record the temperature and make the necessary conversion to obtain the correct altitude. Read the book that came with your altimeter for more details. There are some new altimeters on the market that have built-in thermometers, but most of these still assume that temperature varies according to the CINA specifications and do not make the temperature correction automatically. ∎

Global Positioning System

A recent development in mapping is the Global Positioning System (GPS) developed by the US military. This involves 24 satellites operating in six orbital planes at an altitude of 20,200 km. These birds put out coded signals that may be received by small units on earth. With the magic of computer chips that can solve the several sets of simultaneous equations the readings produce, these instruments can determine their absolute location with surprising precision.

This all sounded wonderful, so I rushed out and bought a Sony hand-held GPS from a shop in Hong Kong. It worked, but I discovered several things that were not advertised. Firstly, there are two signals. The precise positioning service (PPS) signal is coded so that it is available only to the US military. The standard positioning service (SPS) code is available to the public – and so far the US government has not figured out a way to charge users for this. Secondly, the US department of defence has the ability to degrade the public signal by broadcasting slightly erroneous clock and orbital data for 'security purposes'. The intentional 'noise' they put into the signals is called 'selective availability'. Thirdly, there are the normal errors that you would expect such as electronic noise, satellite clock errors and atmospheric errors. What this all means is that the GPS produces a reading every second or so and these readings can vary by several hundred metres.

This is all fine for establishing a location; an error of 100 metres or so makes no difference on the scale of the maps in this book or even for plane or ship navigation. However, this is not satisfactory for elevation measurements. If I told you that the climb from the river to the ridge was 100 metres, give or take 500 metres, this book would probably end up in the river. To further complicate matters, because of the geometry of the satellite positions, elevation is the least accurate of the GPS readings; the error in vertical position is two to five times worse than the accuracy of the horizontal position.

To overcome the selective availability problem, surveyors use a system called a 'differential GPS'. This involves two GPS units, one at a fixed, known location and the other in the field, operating at precisely the same time and using either a computer or a two-way radio to coordinate the readings. This is obviously not a practical system to employ while trekking hundreds of km away from a base station.

One way to eliminate some of the random errors without using a differential GPS system is to average the readings. If you are lucky, this can help to improve accuracy since the selective availability 'noise' varies and seldom stays the same for a particular satellite for more than a few seconds. I tried this with the Sony, sitting for five minutes writing down readings as fast as I could. I then upgraded to another GPS, a Garmin GPS-100, three times the price of the Sony, that has a built-in averaging system.

I have now hauled the Garmin GPS around on several treks and established elevations and location using the averaging system which theoretically produces measurements of horizontal position accurate to within five to 15 metres. Vertical measurements are still subject to greater error, though the manufacturer does not specify an estimate of the accuracy. Significant errors can still occur, even with averaging, but they seem to minimised. Most of the readings obtained have either agreed with maps or shown mapping errors, particularly on the old Survey of India maps. To obtain averaged GPS readings, the unit must sit outside for five to 10 minutes (though it takes about 24 hours of averaging to get an accuracy of 10 metres). A GPS naturally attracts village children, and occasionally the police, who wonder what this machine is – with all its lights, buttons and beeps. I have had to learn to be a bit surreptitious therefore, though not as secretive as the *pundits*, the explorer spies of the Survey of India. These were Indians who travelled through Nepal and Tibet in the 1860s disguised as traders or pilgrims who paced off the country counting their steps on rosary beads, determining elevation by measuring the temperature of boiling water, and concealing their notes inside prayer wheels. With all this, we can understand how a few errors crept into their maps.

If you want to play with one of these toys and plan to use it in the mountains, I suggest you investigate the higher end models. The smallest hand-held units are designed for navigation at sea and usually do not have either the averaging feature or the ability to download data into a personal computer, which is essential if you want to use two units together in a differential GPS situation. With only a single unit and without averaging, the elevation readings are not accurate enough for serious mountaineering or trekking use. The system is quite new and there is a dearth of published information about it, though I suspect that its use by mountaineers – and even trekkers – will become far more prevalent in the future. ■

primary reason that you need to know the elevation is to learn whether the trail ahead goes uphill or downhill and whether it is a long ascent (or descent) or a short one. The elevations shown here fulfil that purpose. The idea of precise elevations becomes even more complicated because villages cover such large areas. What is the 'correct' elevation of a village such as Bung, which extends almost 500 vertical metres up a hillside?

Changes

In the 1980s, major new roads were opened to Jiri, Gorkha, Hile and along the Narayani River from Mugling to Narayanghat. Construction of the Dumre to Besi Sahar road (at the start of the trek around Annapurna) is still proceeding slowly, and there are plans to extend this road as far as Chame. The Trisuli Bazaar to Dhunche road now takes several days off the Langtang trek and the new extension to Somdang opens up a major portion of Ganesh Himal. The trek to Jomsom now starts with a drive that bypasses the old trekking haunts of Hyangja, Suikhet and Naudanda. The road leaves the Jomsom trail near Birethanti and heads south and west to Baglung, offering an alternative approach to Jomsom. There is also a major road planned up the Arun River valley to provide support for the construction of a hydroelectric project. The road up the Indrawati Valley towards Helambu is finally being repaired and put back into service.

Roads also change the relative importance of villages. Lamosangu, for example, was a major road head from 1970 to 1981. It lost its importance and many of its facilities when Jiri became the roadhead. The same will probably happen to Dumre when a sensible bus service begins up the Marsyangdi. Roads also bring about an increase in theft. Before a road reaches a village, travel must always be on foot and nobody complains. No self-respecting Nepalese will walk when a bus is available, but the bus fares on the new roads are expensive – creating a new demand for cash. For many, the only source of easy cash is theft, and the road offers a quick getaway.

Be especially watchful of your possessions within a few days' walk of any road.

Trail and bridge construction is also proceeding at a furious pace in the hills. Local governments and foreign aid programmes have reconstructed or widened many trails. On the Everest trek, a new trail has changed the route significantly, bypassing some places and visiting villages that the old expedition route did not reach before. The Swiss are planning an extensive new series of bridges in the hills. Landslides and flood damage is becoming more frequent as villagers remove the forest cover and topsoil washes away. These phenomena can alter trek routes drastically as whole villages can disappear and trails can require extensive detours to cross slide areas.

The construction of small trekker hotels and the conversion of private homes into hotel facilities is proceeding at an even more frantic pace. New hotels spring up every week on the major trek routes. They also vanish when the innkeepers get bored or discover that the costs are higher than the potential returns. The competition for trekker rupees is intense, so innkeepers lower their prices to attract customers, and it becomes hard to make a hotel pay its way. There are pressures for hotels to improve the way they deal with fuel usage and sanitation, particularly toilet facilities, so this may change the number and location of hotels before long.

I have mentioned many hotels by name. When you look for these places, you may find a hotel with a different name. There is a funny system in Nepal that allows a hotelier to avoid tax by changing the name of his company. Often the *Namaste Hotel* becomes the *New Namaste Hotel*, but sometimes the new name is quite different.

A trek route changes because of the season. The routes described here work during the trekking season from October to May, though some high passes, particularly in Dolpo, are open only in October and November and again in May. If you trek during the monsoon, the trails may not bear any resemblance to what I have described in this book. Bridges can be washed away and trails become flooded during this season. In early October, and again in April and May, rice is growing in many of the terraces along most trek routes. Many campsites that are excellent in November and December are under water in the rice-growing season. Hotels in high places, particularly Gorak Shep, Annapurna Sanctuary and along the Ghorapani to Ghandruk route, often close in the coldest part of winter (December to February) and during the monsoon.

Place Names & Terminology

The route descriptions list many places that do not correlate with names in other descriptions of the same route or with names on maps. The diversity occurs because there is no universally accepted form of transliterating Nepali and Tibetan names into English. Different authorities will spell the same place name in different ways. To make matters more complicated, a particular place may have several different names. Mt Everest, for example, is also known as Sagarmatha (Nepali), Chomolungma (Sherpa) and Qomolangma Feng (Chinese). The same applies for many village names.

In 1984 the Nepalese government set up a committee to assign new Nepalese names to 31 peaks and three tourist places that had been known before only by English names. I have mentioned the new names in the text, but I have also used the old English names to avoid confusion.

Many maps produced before 1960 had very little ground control and village names had little resemblance to reality. This is particularly true of the maps prepared by the US Army Map Service that Nepalese mappers have traced and distributed as trekking maps in Kathmandu.

Throughout the text I refer to 'trekking peaks'. These are the 18 peaks that can be legally climbed by trekkers with a simple application and fee to the Nepal Mountaineering Association.

Proper geographical usage defines the left side of a river or glacier as that which is on the left when you face downhill in the direc-

tion of flow. This terminology often confuses me when following a river uphill – the 'left side' of the river is on your right. Fortunately, most Himalayan rivers travel either north-south or east-west, so I have tried to avoid the 'proper' usage by referring to riverbanks by points of the compass, but in some cases it has been necessary to refer to the 'true right' bank.

In the route reports that follow I have translated many names and descriptions, but to avoid a lot of repetition I have used several Nepali and Tibetan words throughout the text. These include names of the ethnic groups that populate Nepal's hills: Tamang, Chhetri, Brahmin, Rai, Sherpa, Gurung, Limbu, Newar and Magar.

You will see several Buddhist monuments during a trek. A *maani* is a single stone or stone wall carved with the Tibetan Buddhist prayer *om mani padme hum*. A *chorten* is a round stone monument; a *kaani* is an arch over a trail, usually decorated with paintings on the inside; and a Tibetan Buddhist temple or monastery is called a *gompa*. A *chautaara* is a stone resting place under a tree and usually has a shelf for porter loads.

Rivers are called, in decreasing order of size: *kosi, khola, naalaa* and sometimes *nadi* and *gaad*. A mountain pass is called *la* in Tibetan and Sherpa and *bhanjyang* or *laagna* in Nepali. Lakes are *taal, kund* or *pokhari* and a ridge is a *daanda, lek* or *deorali*. A high pasture is a *yarsa* or *kharka*; during summer, herders live in a kharka in a temporary shelter called a *goth* (pronounced like 'goat'). The flat plains of Nepal, near the Indian border are called the Terai, and the local booze is chhang and rakshi.

All those 'aa' words look strange, so I have lexiconically misspelt several frequently used words including *tal*, *danda*, *mani*, *kani*, *nala*, *lagna*, *dal* and *bhat*.

Social & Environmental Considerations

A Nepalese View of Foreigners

Although Nepal has been accessible to foreigners only since 1950, there are few places in the kingdom that either trekkers, photographers, expeditions or foreign aid representatives have not visited. Foreigners, particularly light-skinned Westerners, stand out readily in Nepal. The Nepalese view foreigners according to the stereotype created by those who have preceded them. They, too, will contribute to the image of the next Westerners who happen to come along.

Unfortunately, the image which has predominated is one of great wealth and a superior culture which Westerners wish to share with the Nepalese. Such traditions as passing out balloons, sweets and pens to kids are part of this, but it is on a far grander level that the real image has developed.

Mountaineering expeditions have spent seemingly limitless sums of money for porters, sherpas and equipment, including a lot of fine gear for the high altitude sherpas. At the conclusion of an expedition, excess food and gear is usually given away rather than being repacked and shipped home. This type of extravagance, even though it is often supported by foundations and other large organisations and not by the expedition members themselves, leads many Nepalese to believe, with some justification, that Westerners have a tremendous amount of money and will simply pass it out to whoever makes the most noise.

An interesting by-product of this phenomenon is that a variety of used mountaineering gear was once for sale in Kathmandu at ridiculously low prices. This was possible because nobody in Nepal ever had to pay for it. A Nepalese received it as a gift or bought it for a very cheap price, then sold it for whatever they could get. Now, however, prices are the same or higher than they are in the West. Astute shopkeepers have seen equipment catalogues and charge according to the retail prices for new items.

The sherpas and other Nepalese who deal with trekkers and expeditions are aware of the cost of an air ticket to Nepal from the USA, Europe or Australia. For people in a country with an annual per capita income of US$170, US$1500 for a plane ticket is an astronomical amount of money. No matter how small a trekker's budget may be, they were still able to get to Nepal. The Nepalese know this and are unwilling to accept a plea of poverty from someone who, according to their standards, has already spent the equivalent of about three years' wages, or enough money to build two large houses. It is impossible to explain the difference in our relative economic positions to a Nepalese in the hills.

Many trekkers and expedition members in the past have given substantial tips to sherpas. Reports of US$100 tips are not unheard of. Compare a tip of US$40 for a six-day trek to a sherpa's total salary of US$10. This type of extravagance forces wages up, resulting in higher demands on the next trekker or expedition. It also contributes to an unhealthy view of Westerners as rich, lavish and foolish. This image makes it difficult for individuals on a tight budget to convince a Nepalese person that they cannot afford outrageous salaries, tips or huge amounts of food during a trek.

Well-intentioned trekkers often overreact to the needs of porters and sherpas on treks and provide an exorbitant amount of free equipment to their staff. This is certainly kind and generous, and porters do need to be equipped with warm shoes, clothing and goggles when they are travelling into the mountains. Many trekkers overdo this, however, and it is becoming increasingly common for porters to demand fancy new equipment. They then pack it away to keep it in pristine condition to sell later. On the trek they often use their own old blankets to keep warm. Porters need protection and attention, but many trekkers have gone far beyond what is necessary. This overgenerous behaviour has created unreasonable expectations in the minds of many porters and makes it difficult and expensive to hire them, especially in the Annapurna region.

Foreign aid projects have built schools, hospitals, roads, and electricity and water projects in Nepal. These facilities are largely supported by contributions from Western organisations, although there is usually an effort to require contributions of local labour and money. Nepal needs these projects and they perform a great service, but this method of financing does help sustain the preconception of Westerners as people with a lot of money from which they can readily be parted if they are approached with enough cleverness.

Many trekkers feel a strong affinity for villagers or sherpas they have met. Many have supported the education of local children or even provided free overseas trips for them. This practice is certainly worthwhile and kind, but it does encourage Nepalese people to seek such favours in their dealings with Westerners. The US Embassy has published a paper, titled *So You Want to Take Your Sherpa to America*, that points out some of the procedures and pitfalls of this process.

The problem is not confined to the hills and the efforts of some thoughtless individuals. Many nations are eager to gain a foothold in what they feel is a strategic part of the world. They spend vast sums of money on aid programmes in Nepal to strengthen their position. Such programmes might not contribute further to an unhealthy view of Westerners (and would undoubtedly do more good) if they did not also support the Westerners who work for them in lavish style. Many foreigners live in Kathmandu and other places in Nepal in conditions similar to their Western homes. They eat food flown from home at their own government's expense and are served by more servants than they could conceive of at home.

Most foreigners carry with them an astonishing array of camera gear, tape recorders and other gadgetry. It's obvious that these things are expensive, even by Western standards. Yet many people are careless and do not protect this wealth. A surprising number of trekkers leave cameras behind on rocks or give their watches away at the end of a trek. The Nepalese see that not only can Westerners afford to buy such expensive things, but they don't even take care of them. Compare this attitude to that of the porter carrying a double load of 60 kg to make more money or the sherpa kitchen boy with patched and repatched jeans, shoes and backpack.

The government seems to assume that foreigners have an endless supply of money and will continue to pay for the privilege of visiting, trekking and climbing in Nepal. The vast array of visa, trekking, rafting, climbing, filming, entry, re-entry, import, export, hunting, liaison officer and departure fees all appear to be aimed at collecting as much money as possible from tourists under any pretence. The US$50,000 fee of climbing Everest and the 1993 fine of US$100,000 for violating expedition rules seem to indicate a lack of appreciation, not only for 'the freedom of the hills', but also an unrealistic evaluation of the amount of money that typically impoverished Western mountaineers have at their disposal.

This is the Westerner with whom the Nepalese is familiar. They may also recognise the qualities of sincerity, happiness or fun, but the primary quality they see is wealth. Many Nepalese consider it their personal obligation to separate Westerners from a share of their money. They may do this by appealing to a sense of fair play, through trickery or blackmail (a porter's strike in a remote location), through shrewdness, or even by outright thievery. Westerners retain this image, no matter what they do personally to dispel it, and an appreciation of this is very helpful in developing an understanding of local attitudes during a trek in Nepal.

Environmental Considerations
The Problem The population of Nepal is

growing at a furious rate. In the 19 years since this book was first published the population has increased from 12 to more than 20 million. Development is moving ahead at an even faster pace. During the 15 years from 1978 to 1993, the number of vehicles in the country increased from fewer than 7500 to more than 70,000, the majority of which are in the Kathmandu Valley. There are now real traffic jams in Kathmandu and the unnecessary noise and pollution caused by these vehicles is immediately noticeable. There are now few days with clear mountain views, yet 15 years ago the towering white mountains and clear blue skies framed the Kathmandu Valley. Now you can see the smog from your plane as it approaches Kathmandu.

In the hills, this growth is manifested in many ways. There was a furore 20 years ago about garbage left by trekkers and expeditions along the Everest route. This was not an important issue compared to the current problems of sanitation, overgrazing, deforestation, landslides and uncontrolled development of hotels for trekkers.

There is no systematic waste disposal system in the hills, and many hill people are acquiring more and more manufactured items from Kathmandu. A look at the stream of worn-out shoes and broken toys in the streets of Namche will show that litter is not only a trekking problem. The piles of garbage and human waste at Ghorapani and on the route to Annapurna Sanctuary and the relentless clearing of rhododendron forests between Ghorapani and Ghandruk to allow even more hotel construction are, however, related to trekkers. Yet the protection afforded by a national park can lead to greater pressures. It takes a staff of more than 100 army personnel to manage and enforce the regulations of Sagarmatha National Park, which has a local population of less than 2500 people.

It is naive to think of maintaining the ecological balance of the Himalaya in a pristine state. There are simply too many people living in the hills. To accomplish this goal it would be necessary to relocate entire villages, as was done in both Lake Rara and Royal Chitwan national parks.

The primary reason for the destruction of forests throughout the Himalayan hill region is the pressure of a population that requires natural vegetation for food, fodder, fuel and even shelter. The lack of roads and other development, combined with the lack of any local deposits of fossil fuels, allows no easy alternative. About 70% of Nepal's total domestic energy consumption is wood. The inevitable result of the destruction of forests is an increase in erosion and extensive loss of topsoil.

The most dramatic result of deforestation is huge landslides that carry away fields,

---

Don't Drink Mineral Water on a Trek

A recent phenomenon in the hills is the large-scale use of bottled mineral water by trekkers. So-called mineral water is produced in both India and Nepal and is always packaged in sealed plastic bottles. Assuming you get a genuine bottle, what you are usually getting is tap water that has been filtered and passed by an ultraviolet light – a process that is supposed to purify the water. What you really get could be anything.

What happens to the bottle when you drink this litre of water? It is not recyclable, it is of no use to anyone, it does not biodegrade (ever), and it is bulky. Empty mineral water bottles have surpassed pink Chinese toilet paper as the eyesore of the Nepal Himalaya.

There are many ways to obtain safe drinking water. All these are described in detail in the Health & Safety chapter of this book. If you don't like the taste of iodine, bring flavouring. Vitamin C tablets are also said to kill the iodine taste, but be sure you let the iodine do its work before you add the vitamin C or flavouring. You can also purchase bottled soft drinks wherever you find mineral water. These come in glass bottles that are valuable enough that trash collectors wander the hills collecting bottles to carry back to Kathmandu for refilling. ∎

houses and occasionally entire villages. As you fly or trek in Nepal you can easily spot many examples of these landslides. One solution would be a massive tree planting campaign, but to hill people this is expensive and unrewarding because they must fence off the plantations to protect them from cattle and goats. Fencing is expensive and the financial returns are a long way off.

Tourists, particularly trekkers, contribute to the mess. A typical hotel burns from three to eight loads (about 25 kg each) of firewood per day and a large trekking party can consume from three to five loads a day. Regulations that ban the use of firewood in national parks and restricted areas do not apply to those who use hotels, except in parts of the Annapurna region where ACAP has ensured that firewood is forbidden to everyone. This hotel loophole exempts individual trekkers and the porters of trekking parties from any limit on fuel consumption. During 1992, 12,325 trekking permits were issued for the Everest region, 27,661 for the Annapurna region and 8558 for Langtang. The number of individual trekkers, as opposed to group trekkers, is an indication of how many people used trekking lodges. In Langtang the majority of the trekkers (63%) trekked on their own; in Everest 47% were individuals and in Annapurna 45% trekked without using a trekking company.

What You Can Do to Help Everyone should agree that the hill people have a right not only to live in their traditional home sites but also to try to improve their standard of living. Their lifestyle may appear picturesque, but it is a meagre subsistence-level lifestyle that could be improved in numerous ways by many forms of development. Trekkers can contribute to this development, not only through their cash but through their example. Solutions to the energy problem, such as hydroelectric plants, biogas generators, solar energy units and the wholesale import of fossil fuels, all take time and cost money.

As solutions are developed and implemented, they will change the trekking experience – and certainly increase costs.

When attempts are made in this direction, it is reasonable to support them, even when the result is a more expensive trek. It will cost more to eat at a hotel that has a new energy-efficient wood stove or a kerosene stove and a proper latrine, and it will cost more to trek with a group that uses no firewood. It is through this sort of direct economic encouragement that you can help and teach hill people. If you are on an organised trek, be sure the toilet pits are dug deeply and are filled in completely when you leave a campsite. If your trek staff is not digging the pits deeply enough, or not filling them in properly, the time to solve that problem is on the spot. It does no good to go home and write a letter complaining about something that could have been easily solved by some simple assistance and instructions from you.

Hoteliers have become aware that clean hotels and toilets and solar heating attract more customers. Trekkers should encourage hotels that adhere to environmentally sound practises so that hoteliers will find the means to continue their attempts. The hotel system in the hills should become something that not only turns firewood into cash, but also serves as a demonstration for all villagers of the need for, and advantages of, limiting their dependence on the forests.

One good start is to spurn the offers of hot showers unless they are solar-heated. You can talk to other trekkers and try to order the same food at the same time so a hotel can do all the cooking at once instead of keeping a fire roaring throughout the day. You can purify your water with iodine instead of ordering boiled water. The process of conserving energy will take time and effort, as old habits and traditions are hard to change.

Even in Kathmandu and Pokhara, where alternatives are readily available, many homes, hotels and restaurants rely on firewood for cooking. Hundreds, perhaps thousands of loads of wood are carried into the cities, not only by porters but also by huge Mercedes trucks.

Conditions admittedly are bad, but the situation is not totally bleak. Trekking companies and many hotels in the hills now use alternative fuel as a matter of course. Trekking sherpas dispose of trash properly and are far more concerned about their country than they were when I first started trekking. Most Nepalese now understand the magnitude of the problem. While some bureaucrats are simply waiting for a foreign aid project to provide answers, some government officials and Nepalese entrepreneurs are making efforts to develop Nepal-style solutions.

One project that fascinates me is the project developed by the Global Resources Institute to produce electric vehicles in Kathmandu. In the Kathmandu Valley the distances are short and speeds low, so it is an ideal place for electric-powered vehicles. Changing even a small fraction of petrol or diesel vehicles to electric power could make a dramatic difference in air quality in the Kathmandu Valley. For more information about this innovative project contact the Global Resources Institute, PO Box 7057, Kathmandu (☎ 410656) or PO Box 11752, Eugene, OR USA (☎ 503-344-2204).

If you are interested in current events in Nepal's efforts towards environmental protection, subscribe to *Himal*, a bi-monthly magazine published in Kathmandu. An annual subscription costs US$25 and is available from:

Himal
    PO Box 42, Lalitpur, Nepal (fax 977-1-521013)
Barbara Bella & Associates
    500 Sansome St, Suite 101, San Francisco, CA 94111 USA
Indra Ban
    12 Norfolk St, Paddington 2021, Australia

Kathmandu Environmental Education Project (KEEP) also publishes a newsletter. You can become a friend of KEEP for UK£12 or US$20 per year. Write to them at PO Box 4944, Tridevi Marg, Kathmandu, or 72 Newhaven Road, Edinburgh EH6 5QG, UK (☎ 031-554-9977).

Health & Safety

This chapter was written by Dr David R Shlim, Medical Director of the CIWEC Clinic, Kathmandu, and medical adviser to the Himalayan Rescue Association.

Adventure travel puts you into situations where there is inherent uncertainty, isolation and risk. People who contemplate an adventurous holiday, such as a trek in Nepal, often worry about a number of things that could go wrong, including flight delays, bad weather, equipment failure and unstable political situations. Yet fear of illness is perhaps the most common – and the most reasonable – concern of travellers to Nepal. Fortunately, the CIWEC Clinic, a nonprofit community clinic dedicated to the welfare of foreigners in Nepal, has published a large number of papers in medical journals on the medical problems of tourists in Nepal.

The following chapter is an attempt to share with trekkers and tourists to Nepal the specific knowledge the clinic has gained over the past 10 years. I hope it will help you to diagnose and treat your own illnesses when you are away from medical care, and to seek help appropriately when medical care is available to you.

Preparation for a Trek

MEDICAL EXAM & PRESCRIPTIONS
Most trekking agencies supply an examination form for your doctor which outlines some of the potential problems of a trek. It's important that your doctor views the examination as more than a routine life-insurance exam, and that any abnormalities, chronic problems or special medicines are listed on the form. If you are trekking alone, it's a good idea to carry a brief outline of your medical history and notes on any special problems or allergies. This will help in case you do have an accident or illness in a remote

region. It is also worthwhile investigating little nagging problems or any unexplained recurrent symptoms before you go, because problems have a way of escalating under the stresses of travel.

A thorough dental examination is highly recommended because reliable dental care is difficult to obtain in Nepal. People who wear contact lenses can have trouble with grit and dust both in Kathmandu and in the mountains. Make sure you have back-up prescription glasses and sunglasses in case you can't wear your lenses at some point. Bring all the contact lens washing solution that you will need. People with a history of asthma tend to have trouble in Kathmandu, but are generally OK in the mountains. Make sure that you bring a supply of appropriate asthma medication in case you experience difficulties away from medical care.

PHYSICAL CONDITIONING
People over age 45 often worry about altitude and potential heart problems. There is no evidence that altitude is likely to bring on previously undiagnosed heart disease. However, having your first heart symptoms in a remote village at 4200 metres and two weeks' walk from a hospital increases anxiety and the difficulty of obtaining treatment. If an older person runs or hikes regularly on difficult terrain, there is no reason at present to think that altitude will be an increased risk for that person. If you would like reassurance because you are not very active in your daily life, a stress electrocardiogram obtained near the time of your trip will bring you to your maximal heart rate and exertion under a controlled situation and detect any heart strain.

Physical training, particularly walking up and down hills, is the best method of preparing for trekking in Nepal. Jogging helps, but does not really prepare you for the hills unless you run on hills. Weight training can help build leg strength for the relentless 2000-metre climbs that occur on some treks. It is not just aerobic conditioning that is important, but you must try to condition your joints, particularly the knees, to continual uphill and downhill travel. The only way to do this is to take walks up and down hills. Cycling builds thigh strength but doesn't condition the legs to the pounding they can take. Other forms of aerobic conditioning, such as stairmasters, rowing machines and Nordic tracks, can have benefit before a trek. But walking up and down hills is still the best preparation. Adequate physical conditioning before your trek does not guarantee success, but it certainly can make any trip much more enjoyable.

IMMUNISATIONS & PROPHYLAXIS

Nepal has no official vaccination requirements for entry. However, you should make an effort to protect yourself from some of the serious infectious diseases that can be prevented by vaccine or prophylactic (preventive) measures.

It is often said that you should consult a doctor regarding immunisation advice before travelling to Asia. In all fairness to your doctor, it is very difficult to have current or accurate information about travelling in Asia unless you have a special interest in that area. By not wanting to seem unhelpful or unknowledgeable, your doctor may give off-hand advice based on old data or inaccurate memory or lack of awareness of the real problems. If you consult your doctor, give them a chance to tell you whether they actually know anything about travel in Asia. If not, see if you can be referred to a travel clinic that has some particular interest in the problem. The goal is to receive all of the immunisations and prophylaxis that are important, without receiving any that you don't need. I have seen trips ruined by adverse reactions to malaria drugs that were not needed in the first place. A list of possible vaccinations follows. (See also the Medical Problems & Treatment section for more information about the illnesses.)

- *Hepatitis A* Hepatitis A is a miserable disease that can be fatal on rare occasions. It almost always ends one's trip to Asia, and can lead to months of recuperation. As a protection against hepatitis A, gamma globulin (immune serum globulin) may be useful for people who must travel at the last minute, or who do not plan to travel repeatedly to the developing world. However, for long-term protection, the new hepatitis A vaccine is a better option.

  Gamma globulin is not a vaccine, but a collection of antibodies purified from the blood of people who are immune to hepatitis A. (Note that there is no risk of acquiring the HIV virus (AIDS) from gamma globulin, since the process of manufacturing the product is completely lethal to all viruses.) The 'borrowed' antibodies offer a high degree of short-term protection for someone who might be at risk of contracting hepatitis A. The regimen is one cc for every month of travel, plus one extra. Thus, the dose would be two cc for one month, three cc for two months, four cc for three months, and a maximum of five cc for four months of travel. One should seek another dose of gamma globulin after four months of travel.

  For long-term travellers and expatriates the hepatitis A vaccine should become the method of choice for avoiding hepatitis A. It has been approved in some European countries and is gradually being approved around the world. Various regimens are still being tried, but they all seem to be effective at preventing hepatitis A for perhaps five to 10 years. For a one-time traveller going on a trip of less than a few months, gamma globulin may prove less expensive and easier to obtain, since it is given as a single injection close to the time you leave.

- *Hepatitis B* Hepatitis B can be a much worse infection than hepatitis A, leading to chronic liver disease, cirrhosis and death in some cases. It is acquired through contact with blood or through sexual contact. Thus, there is little chance of casually acquiring this infection without exposure to contaminated needles, receiving a transfusion, or having unprotected sex. We have monitored hepatitis in foreigners in Nepal for 10 years and have found no casually acquired hepatitis B infections. For long-term travellers to many countries, or for expatriates who plan to be abroad for several years, the hepatitis B vaccine is safe and effective with few side effects. The regimen for hepatitis B immunisation is a series of three shots over a six-month period.

- *Typhoid* This disease is prevalent in Nepal. There are three types of vaccines to consider. The original killed whole-cell vaccine offers a very high level of protection, but the shot itself can make people feel mild to moderately ill for 24 to 48 hours. A new oral typhoid vaccine (Berne Ty 21a) has become popular due to its lack of side effects, but it may not be as protective as the injectable vaccine. It is available in capsule form (one pill taken every other day for three or four doses), though a new liquid form of the vaccine may prove to be more effective than pills. A third vaccine, called the capsular polysaccharide typhoid vaccine, is marketed by Merieux. It has good efficacy and very few side effects. A potential drawback is that it does not offer protection against paratyphoid fever, which is also very common in Nepal. Since typhoid or paratyphoid fever is almost never fatal in foreigners, and is treatable by an oral antibiotic, the choice of vaccine may not be critical. You should feel reasonably safe using any of these products.

* *Meningococcal Meningitis* An epidemic of meningococcal meningitis occurred in the Kathmandu Valley in 1983 and during the next two years, six foreigners contracted the disease and two died. In March 1985, the US Center for Disease Control issued an alert to travellers to be vaccinated against meningococcal meningitis before travelling to Nepal. Since then there have still been sporadic cases of meningitis in travellers to Nepal, and the advice to be vaccinated still holds. The vaccine is free of serious side effects, is not painful, and good protection lasts for three years or more from a single injection. Unlike most of the other vaccine-preventable diseases, meningococcal meningitis can be rapidly fatal if it occurs away from medical care.

* *Polio* The current generation is no longer afraid of polio because vaccination has made it rare in the West. However, no such eradication has taken place in Asia, and a booster for people who have been previously immunised is recommended before travelling to Nepal. One's childhood polio immunisations wear off over time, because there is no boosting effect from wild polio virus any more. If you have been immunised in childhood, one booster as an adult (either oral or injectable) should be obtained before travelling to Asia. If you somehow grew up without getting immunised, you should have the injectable vaccine before heading out to Asia. Do not use the oral polio vaccine as an adult if you have never had polio vaccine in any form. You can use the oral vaccine as a booster if you have been previously immunised by either method.

* *Rabies* Modern rabies vaccine is now a highly purified substance with high effectiveness and few side effects. The drawback is that it is relatively expensive. Rabies is a severe brain infection caused by a virus transmitted by animal bites, mainly dogs and occasionally monkeys in Nepal. The disease is uniformly fatal once the symptoms have manifested. Therefore, all efforts must be made to avoid getting the disease once you have been exposed.

There are two strategies employed with the rabies vaccine. One is called pre-exposure immunisation and consists of three shots spaced over one month. These injections prime your immune system against rabies, and if you are bitten by a suspicious animal, you just need two more shots, three days apart, as a booster. If you don't take the pre-exposure immunisation, and you are bitten by a potentially rabid animal, you will need the full immunoprophylaxis which consists of five injections spaced over one month, and a single injection of rabies antibodies called rabies immune globulin. The rabies immune globulin is often very hard to obtain (in Nepal it is available only at CIWEC Clinic) and is very expensive (from US$350 to US$650 for the injection depending on your body weight).

A recent study that we conducted in Nepal calculated that only one out of 6000 visitors is bitten by a suspicious animal. If you are planning to come to Nepal for only one or two months, I think that the pre-exposure series is not necessary. If you are planning to travel in Asia for three months or more, and are going to remote areas where the rabies vaccine is going to be hard to obtain (and rabies immune globulin impossible to obtain), then you should consider having the pre-exposure series. Once you have the series, a booster should be obtained every two or three years.

* *Tetanus & Diphtheria* The vast majority of people from Western countries receive these vaccines in childhood. The tetanus and diphtheria germs are worldwide, and overseas travel is a good chance to catch up on your immunity. You should take a booster if it has been longer than 10 years since your last one. It is especially important to ask for a tetanus booster if you are over 50 years old, as studies have shown that this population is more likely to have let their tetanus boosters lapse.

* *Cholera* Although cholera vaccination is no longer required to enter any country in Asia, the recent spread of cholera to South America, and the emergence of new strains in Asia have kept that disease in the public limelight. Although the disease can be devastating to local populations at times, the risk of acquiring cholera as a traveller to Asia is negligible. Therefore, the current injectable cholera vaccine is not recommended for any traveller to Nepal.

• *Malaria* There is currently no vaccine against malaria. Travellers to areas where malaria is a risk must rely on trying to prevent mosquito bites and taking prophylactic medication to try to avoid malaria infections. In Nepal, malaria transmission is limited to the lowland area adjoining India (the Terai). There is no risk of malaria in Kathmandu, Pokhara, or any of the main trekking areas. I have never seen anyone acquire malaria while trekking in Nepal, but I have seen several treks ruined by adverse reactions to antimalarial drugs which were not needed in the first place.

The risk in the Terai is very low, and travellers traversing the area for one or two days (on the way to a trekking destination) probably do not need malaria prophylaxis. Travellers who visit a jungle lodge in Nepal are at theoretical risk, but there have been only two cases of malaria acquired by foreigners in the Terai in the past 10 years.

Although resistance of falciparum malaria to chloroquine has been documented in Nepal, most of the malaria is the more sensitive vivax strain. Thus, chloroquine phosphate (Aralen) or chloroquine sulfate (Nivaquine) as a single weekly dose (500 mg) would probably be adequate in the Terai. For the mild chloroquine-resistant strains found in Nepal and on the Indian subcontinent, chloroquine plus proguanil (Paludrine) 200 mg per day is recommended. US authorities recommend mefloquine for all of these areas, but the potential for adverse effects may be slightly higher with this drug.

Hygiene on the Trek

WATER PURIFICATION
As repugnant as it sounds to put it this way, the germs that cause diarrhoea, typhoid fever and hepatitis are acquired mainly from eating someone else's stool. One of the major medical advances of Western countries was to develop a sure way of keeping stool out of the water supply. This problem has not been solved in Nepal, and all water must be viewed as being potentially contaminated. While there is no consensus on the best method of purifying water in all circumstances, the following section examines some of the considerations.

Boiling
All of the stool pathogens (disease producers) are killed by boiling water. Although the length of time that many sources dictate that water must be boiled varies from five to 20 minutes, a consensus paper by the Wilderness Medical Society in the USA has confirmed that just bringing water to the boil is sufficient to kill all potential disease-causing organisms, even at high altitude.

Iodine
As an alternative to boiling, chemicals can be added to water to kill the pathogens. Iodine preparations and chlorine preparations are equally effective in killing the germs, but iodine is a bit more reliable in the field. There are three practical ways to carry iodine on a trek: as tetraglycine hydroperiodide tablets, lugol's solution and iodine crystals.

Tetraglycine hydroperiodide tablets are not available in Nepal, and can deteriorate in as little as six months in their original containers. If you can find a fresh bottle of these tablets, they are convenient to use and not messy to carry. One bottle contains 50 tablets, enough to purify 50 litres of water.

Lugol's solution is a water-based iodine concentrate; eight drops per litre of water is sufficient to purify reasonably clean, cool water. It is available in Kathmandu at supermarkets and many pharmacies, especially the larger ones on New Rd.

To use iodine crystals, place four or five grams of crystals in a 30-ml glass bottle. The iodine is available from some pharmacies in Kathmandu and this amount will treat an almost limitless amount of water. Fill the bottle with water and wait 30 minutes. The resulting solution, minus the crystals, may be added to your water bottle to purify the water for drinking. Add 15 to 30 cc of the solution to your one-litre water bottle and wait for 30 minutes before drinking. Refill the glass bottle at the same time, and after 30 minutes it will be ready to use again as well. Be particularly careful not to ingest an iodine crystal as this can be fatal. If you are adding flavouring like Tang or Gatoraid to the water, do not add it until after the iodine has had time to work.

In general, with any of the purification

methods, the cleaner the water appears and the warmer it is, the less iodine that is necessary. If you find you don't like the iodine taste, use a smaller amount of iodine and allow the bottle to sit for longer before drinking it. It will be just as safe and will taste better. A rough rule is to double the waiting time if you cut the iodine amount in half. No evidence has been presented that using iodine to purify water, even for long periods of time, causes any harm.

Water Filters

Filtering devices for field use have become popular in recent years. There is debate as to whether the filters can eliminate viruses that cause diarrhoea or hepatitis (some say the viruses stick to larger particles and can be filtered that way; the viruses are in fact hundreds of times smaller than the smallest holes in all commercial filters). The filters can be expensive (up to US$180 or more). A 0.1 micron filter is necessary to filter harmful bacteria (a filter this size would also trap amoeba and *Giardia* cysts, which are much larger). Filtering can eliminate suspended particles that might hamper the effects of iodine, allowing you to use a smaller dose. Some filters incorporate a pentaiodine resin which iodinates the water as it filters it. This would seem to be an adequate method, but if you are going to add iodine, perhaps you don't need the bulky filter at all. For the most part, water in Nepal appears clear and has good taste, so filtering for sediment and taste is not usually necessary.

FOOD PREPARATION

Unfortunately, just treating your water carefully will not eliminate the chances of eating someone else's stool. Throughout Nepal there is very little use of sewers to dispose of human waste. Thus, stool is found throughout the environment, and finds its way into your food. In the spring trekking season, flies are abundant and can be a major factor in spreading stool contamination into restaurants and trekking kitchens. Lapses in kitchen hygiene, such as preparing raw meat on the same counters as other foods, not

washing kitchen surfaces regularly, and cooks not washing their hands after going to the toilet contribute to the risk of gastrointestinal illness in Nepal. Vegetables and fruits can also be contaminated from the soil they are grown in, or from handling along the way. The general rule is to not eat any vegetables that cannot be peeled or freshly cooked unless you are certain of the methods that have been used to soak them. Many restaurants in Kathmandu now soak their vegetables in an acceptable manner to make them safe, but if you are not sure, don't eat them. The locally brewed chhang, a fermented brew made from corn, rice or millet, is reconstituted with untreated water and is a frequent source of infection for unwary travellers. However, since the drinking of chhang is so tied up in social custom, many travellers are forced to put aside their judgment so as not to offend generous hosts. Also, try to avoid eating foods that are cooked once early in the day, and then reheated (perhaps inadequately) when you place your order. These types of foods can incubate bacterial growth throughout the day.

PERSONAL HYGIENE

Making a point of washing your own hands frequently can also help prevent illness. The tiny amounts of water that might cling to dishes and glasses washed in untreated water are not likely to make you sick, and drying the dishes can eliminate this problem. In general, the likelihood of getting sick is related to the amount of contamination you ingest. You should always do your best to avoid known sources of contamination, but don't worry excessively about those areas in which you have no control.

One area you can control is the disposal of toilet paper. The trails of pink and white toilet paper in popular trekking areas are disgusting, and growing every year. To successfully burn toilet paper after use, pull it open before lighting (put matches or a cigarette lighter in with your toilet paper). Urine-soaked paper is harder to burn. Carry a little plastic shovel (now available in many backpacking stores) to bury it, or carry it in a plastic bag for later disposal. There is no excuse for leaving toilet paper exposed along the trail!

Medical Problems & Treatment

DIARRHOEA

Diarrhoea is the most common illness acquired by travellers in Nepal. Travellers' diarrhoea is often dismissed in travel books as a mild, self-limiting disorder, for which no specific treatment is required. When antibiotic treatment is discussed, the hazards of the treatment are often emphasised out of proportion: lack of efficacy, prolongation of the carrier state, breeding of resistant strains, and adverse reactions to the drugs. No one stresses how miserable one can be with diarrhoea, or how severely it can interrupt carefully made travel plans, or even jeopardise the success of an expedition that has been planned for years.

Travellers' diarrhoea is simply infectious diarrhoea, acquired while travelling, usually because standards of public health and hygiene in developing countries are minimal to nonexistent. The organisms that cause diarrhoea are passed in stool, and are acquired from eating or drinking contaminated food or water. See the earlier hygiene section for a discussion on how to purify water and avoid contaminated food.

Causes of Diarrhoea

Diarrhoea in travellers can be caused by toxins, viruses, bacteria or protozoa. The toxins are waste products of certain bacteria that can grow on food and, once ingested, can cause severe intestinal symptoms, such as vomiting and diarrhoea, for six to 12 hours. This is what is known as food poisoning; no infection takes place in the intestine and treatment can only be supportive. Viruses can cause vomiting and diarrhoea, or either one alone, but account for less than 5% of diarrhoea cases at CIWEC. Once again

treatment can only be supportive. Bacteria are the major cause of diarrhoea in travellers in Nepal, accounting for about 85% of cases clinically, and include *E. Coli, Shigella, Campylobacter*, and *Salmonella*, in decreasing order of frequency. There are several other organisms, known collectively as protozoa, that can also cause diarrhoeal disease. The major protozoa are *Giardia* (accounting for about 12% of cases) and *E. histolytica* (1%). Other protozoa are *Cyclospora* (which occurs only from May to September), *Dientamoeba fragilis* and *Cryptosporidium*. Altogether, about 95% of the diarrhoea cases we see in our clinic are treatable with an antibiotic.

Bacterial diarrhoea is characterised by the sudden onset of relatively uncomfortable diarrhoea. Protozoal diarrhoea is characterised by the gradual onset of tolerable diarrhoea. Although these two syndromes can overlap to some extent, this method of looking at the problem has proven extremely useful. Sudden onset means that you can usually recall the precise time of day your illness began. Patients will also report that the diarrhoea and associated symptoms were quite bothersome right from the start. In contrast, protozoal diarrhoea usually begins with just a few loose stools, making people wonder if they are getting sick. The symptoms might be two to five loose stools per day, with mild cramping and urgency as the usual accompanying symptoms. People often wait one to two weeks before seeking treatment, whereas those with bacterial diarrhoea will seek help within one to two days.

Bacterial Diarrhoea

The sudden onset of relatively uncomfortable diarrhoea is the minimum description of bacterial diarrhoea. Additional specific symptoms can only add to the certainty of the diagnosis. Fever, vomiting, or blood in the stool can all be present, and are much more often associated with bacterial diarrhoea than protozoal diarrhoea.

Food poisoning (caused by toxins that can be produced by bacteria growing on contaminated food) can present exactly like bacterial diarrhoea. However, the difference is that by the time the person who has food poisoning is able to seek help (that is, strong enough to leave their rooms or the immediate vicinity of a toilet), they are usually on the way to recovering rapidly. People with bacterial diarrhoea may have vomiting and fever in the first 12 hours of their illness, but these symptoms usually subside spontaneously, leaving diarrhoea and cramps as the only persistent symptoms. The distinction between food poisoning with vomiting and bacterial diarrhoea with vomiting is not critical to make in the first 12 hours, since the patients can't take an antibiotic until the vomiting has stopped anyway. If all symptoms go away rapidly, no therapy is needed; if diarrhoea persists, it is likely to be a form of bacterial diarrhoea.

Viral gastroenteritis has essentially the same symptoms as bacterial diarrhoea. However, since we know in Nepal that viruses are uncommon in comparison to pathogenic bacteria, we usually treat patients as if they presented with bacterial diarrhoea.

Bacterial diarrhoea is almost always self-limiting, but the length of time can vary from a few hours to over two weeks. However, now that effective treatment exists, it doesn't make sense to wait from two to 10 days to see if you are going to get better on your own. Currently all pathogenic bacteria that can cause diarrhoea are susceptible to a group of antibiotics known as fluoroquinolones. The two most commonly used are norfloxacin or ciprofloxacin. Therefore, it is not necessary to know exactly which bacteria you have in order to recommend treatment.

Antibiotic treatment with a quinolone antibiotic can shorten the illness to one day and side effects are extremely rare. Antibiotic resistance will inevitably come, but as long as the use of the antibiotic is limited to travellers, resistance will be almost impossible to induce against a background of hundreds of millions of local people who are not using the drug.

The treatment for all bacterial diarrhoea is either norfloxacin (400 mg) twice a day for three days, or ciprofloxacin (500 mg) twice a day for three days. Longer treatment is clearly not indicated, and shorter treatment is currently under study. There is little reason to choose between norfloxacin and ciprofloxacin; we prefer norfloxacin since it works very well, is less expensive, and may have slightly fewer side effects than ciprofloxacin.

Other antibiotics, such as sulfamethoxasole-trimethoprim (Bactrim), ampicillin, tetracycline, or doxycycline do not have much usefulness against bacterial diarrhoea in Nepal. Bacterial resistance to these antibiotics ranges from 30 to 95%.

Protozoal Diarrhoea

Protozoa are single-celled animals which inhabit the upper intestine, just beyond the stomach. They are oval shaped and propel themselves around with a tail when they are in the host. When they decide it's time to move to another host, they secrete a sturdy shell and become a nonactive cyst. These cysts are strong enough to survive in mountain streams, in dust, and to pass through the intense stomach acid of a new host. They can be killed in water by boiling or by adding iodine.

Giardiasis An infection with the *Giardia lamblia* parasite is characterised by the gradual onset of rumbly diarrhoea and increased gas. Stools are often urgent, but not necessarily crampy. Upper abdominal pain can occur, but vomiting is rare. There is often a daily pattern of several loose stools in the morning, followed by a relatively normal day except for the occasional urgent bowel movement. This organism is thought by tourists to be the most common cause of diarrhoea in Nepal, but this is not true. It is present in about 12% of our patients.

Once *Giardia* protozoa have been ingested they begin causing symptoms after one or two weeks (not the next day after a suspect meal). Upper abdominal discomfort, 'churning intestines', foul-smelling burps and farts, and on and off diarrhoea are the main characteristics of *Giardia* infections. Often people have symptoms for a week to a month or more before deciding to seek treatment because it is not very severe each day, and they hope it will go away.

The best treatment for giardiasis is quinacrine (100 mg) three times a day for five to seven days. This drug is well tolerated, works rapidly, and failure to cure is very rare. However, this drug is becoming difficult to obtain in many countries. Tinidazole is used in most of the world (with the exception of the USA) to treat both giardiasis and *E. histolytica*. It is usually given as a single two-gram dose daily. However, a growing number of treatment failures has led us to recommend tinidazole (two grams per day for two consecutive days) to treat giardiasis.

In the USA, an alternative is metronidazole (Flagyl) which is similar to Tinidazole but has a much shorter biological half-life. Dosage is 250 mg three times a day for seven days. Tinidazole and metronidazole have similar side effects, which consist of mild nausea, fatigue, and a metallic taste in one's mouth. Neither drug can be taken with alcohol.

E. histolytica infection is treated easily in Nepal with two grams of tinidazole per day for three consecutive days, followed by diloxanide furoate (furamide) (500 mg) three times a day for 10 days. This regimen is highly effective and well tolerated. In the USA metronidazole is used in large doses, 750 mg three times a day for 10 days.

Amoebiasis The term amoebiasis refers to an infection with a specific type of amoeba known as *Entamoeba histolytica* and accounts for only 1% of diarrhoea in our patient population in Nepal. This is an important figure to remember, since the local laboratories diagnose amoebiasis in almost everyone who submits a sample. The reasons for over-diagnosis of *E. histolytica* infection seems to be firstly that the labs mistake macrophages for amoebas (macrophages are large white blood cells commonly seen in severe bacterial infections), and secondly that they call any amoeba *E. histolytica* (a number of other non-pathogenic amoebas

are commonly encountered in stool exams). If you have had diarrhoea for only a few days, be very sceptical of a local laboratory that reports that you have amoebas, especially if they also report the presence of white blood cells. A person presenting with amoebiasis will commonly have several weeks of low-grade diarrhoea, alternating every few days with either normal stool or constipation. Very rarely, a person with *E. histolytica* will present with classic amoebic dysentery: frequent passage of small amounts of bloody, mucoid stool, associated with cramps and painful bowel movements. This classic form of amoebiasis is so rare in travellers in Nepal that we see about one case per year at most.

Cyclospora This organism infects the upper intestine, causing diarrhoea, fatigue and loss of appetite. The illness lasts from two to 12 weeks, averaging six weeks. There is currently no treatment, but research is underway to find a cure. Fortunately, the illness is a risk in Nepal only from May to September, which is outside the trekking season, so most trekkers are not at risk. It has been shown to be waterborne, and though iodine may not be sufficient to kill it, it is easily killed by boiling.

Cryptosporidium This is another parasite of the upper intestine which causes a prolonged, low-grade diarrhoea. It is rare in Nepal, accounting for only a handful of cases per year. It is self-limited, and no treatment is available at present.

Dientamoeba fragilis Because this parasite resembles an amoeba, and has no cyst form, diagnosis is difficult. It can cause low-grade symptoms for a number of weeks. When diagnosed, it can be treated with tetracycline (250 mg) four times a day for 10 days, with excellent results.

Other Causes of Diarrhoea
Tropical Sprue Tropical sprue is a syndrome of fatigue, weight loss and chronic

diarrhoea. Sometimes patients can date the onset of this illness to an acute bout of diarrhoea that never quite cleared up. The cause of tropical sprue is thought to be an infection with some type of intestinal organism, but the exact cause has not been discovered. The diarrhoea is often not prominent after a while, and people present to the doctor with fatigue and weight loss. We usually look at the stools a few times to try to find a protozoan parasite, and often treat people for suspected *Giardia* or *E. histolytica* infections. If we fail to find a cause for their diarrhoea, or the treatment fails to improve their symptoms, we perform a d-xylose absorption test. This test can determine whether the upper intestine is able to absorb food normally. This test is always abnormal in the presence of tropical sprue. If the d-xylose test shows poor absorption, we treat for tropical sprue, with tetracycline (500 mg) twice a day for six weeks, along with folic acid, five mg per day. Improvement is dramatic within a few days of the start of treatment.

Symptomatic Treatment
Drugs & Antibiotics For many years travellers have relied on antimotility drugs, such as diphenoxylate hydrochloride (Lomotil) or loperamide (Imodium), to control the symptoms of diarrhoea until the self-limited infection runs its course. These days, loperamide seems to be favoured over diphenoxylate, but both drugs are used with more caution. Prolongation of symptoms in people who have invasive bacterial diarrhoea seems to be the major risk. We see people getting distended bowel, and increased discomfort in some cases, and prolonged constipation is also common. Effective antibiotic treatment of bacterial diarrhoea can make people asymptomatic within a day, whereas untreated bacterial infections can last from several days to two weeks. I recommend that diarrhoea severe enough to make you think about an antimotility agent should be treated with an antibiotic. Loperamide should be used when travel is required before the antibiotic can

bring the infection under control. What else can you do when you wake up at 5 am with severe diarrhoea, and have to ride a bus for the next 12 hours?

Supportive Care Diarrhoea can result in the loss of a great deal of fluid from the body, and much of the ill feeling associated with diarrhoea (weakness, dizziness) is just from dehydration. People with diarrhoea are often reluctant to drink fluids because they feel nauseated, or the fluids cause cramping when they reach the stomach. The best approach to rehydration is to take frequent small sips of fluid (a friend can often encourage the sick person to drink). Oral rehydration solution (a mixture of sugars and salt that is easily absorbed by the intestines) is much more important for infants and children than adults, but tastes terrible if unflavoured.

Much has been written about specific dietary approaches to diarrhoea, but there is no scientific evidence to support any one view. Some people believe that not eating for a while will improve diarrhoea, while others suggest specific foods such as bananas, dry toast or yoghurt. However, none of these ideas has been tested. I would suggest that if you are not hungry don't force yourself to eat, but continue to drink fluids. If you're hungry, it is OK to eat foods that appeal to you as long as you initially avoid greasy or spicy foods.

When you have diarrhoea there is an exaggeration of the gastro-colic reflex, which means that when you put food in your stomach, it immediately causes your intestines to contract, resulting in cramps and more diarrhoea. This reflex is not harmful, nor will it make whatever caused your diarrhoea worse. Once the initial cramps or diarrhoeal episode pass, it is often possible to finish eating your meal.

VOMITING
Vomiting associated with bacterial diarrhoea is a potentially serious problem, since it adds to dehydration and prevents any efforts at rehydration. We have never seen severe

dehydration in adults who had diarrhoea but not vomiting. Vomiting almost always occurs at the beginning of bacterial diarrhoea, usually lasting six to 12 hours. Rarely, vomiting and diarrhoea persist together for four or five days, resulting in individuals who are quite dehydrated and miserable. They often have to be helicoptered out of the Himalaya in this condition.

Vomiting also prevents taking an oral antibiotic to shorten the infection. There are currently no injectable drugs known to shorten the course of bacterial diarrhoea. The only option is to try treatment with an anti-vomiting drug until the person can retain the oral antibiotic, such as norfloxacin. However, in our experience it is almost impossible to stop the vomiting associated with bacterial diarrhoea by injecting an anti-vomiting agent. Anti-vomiting therapy appears to work most effectively if given just as the repeated, spontaneous vomiting is stopping. An injection of promethazine, or prochlorperazine, or a suppository of either drug, can eliminate the threat of further vomiting, allowing norfloxacin to be taken, which will then shorten the diarrhoeal illness dramatically. One can also try an oral anti-vomiting agent at this point, but it could come up again.

WORMS

These intestinal parasites are never the cause of diarrhoea and rarely the cause of any symptoms. They can occasionally be associated with vague mild abdominal discomfort. It takes seven weeks or so for a worm egg, once ingested, to grow into an adult worm and to start to lay eggs, which can be seen in the stool exam. Studies have shown that approximately 95% of Nepalese have worm eggs in their stool. Despite these overwhelming figures, worm infestation in foreigners is relatively rare. Even among US Peace Corps volunteers living for two years in remote villages, the rate of worm infestation was less than five per cent.

Whether it is important to take worm medicine at the end of an Asian trip is hard to say. However, the medicine is quite free from side effects, and thus it is not a major decision if you want to be sure you are not carrying worms home. The medicine is mebendazole (Wormin in Nepal): one pill twice a day for six days.

The most common worms, *Trichuris* and *Ascaris*, are acquired by eating the eggs. Hookworms are acquired by walking barefoot through areas where people defecate. The larva burrow through the skin and make their way to the intestine through the blood stream. Very rarely, travellers acquire tapeworms from eating undercooked meat. All of these worms have a limited life span and cannot reproduce within the intestines, so infections in travellers tend to be extremely light and would all end within two years without treatment. The only exception is the rare infection with *Strongyloides stercoralis*. The eggs of this worm can hatch in the intestine, and the larva can burrow back into the intestine, causing a gradually increasing infection.

UPPER RESPIRATORY INFECTION (COLDS)

Upper respiratory infection almost always begins as a virus (the common cold). The symptoms consist of some combination of runny nose, congestion, sore throat and cough. The viruses can be picked up on airplanes, crowded buses and trains, in restaurants, or any place where you might encounter people with colds. Under normal circumstances the cold should last three to seven days and go away by itself. However, under the stress of travel, and particularly trekking, colds can be complicated by bacterial infection. The viruses break down the defensive barriers in the lining of your nose, throat and lungs, allowing the normal bacteria that are living there to become invasive. This can result in ear infections, sinus infections, or bronchitis (chest infection). Twenty per cent of the patient visits at the CIWEC Clinic are for complications of colds; the actual rate of colds that don't require medical treatment might be a lot higher. Severe colds can result in missed treks and missed goals on a trek. Knowing how to recognise and treat the complications of a cold appropriately can save you many days of misery, and help preserve your long-established trekking plans.

Sinus Infection (Sinusitis)

Sinus infection is the most common complication of a cold. The sinuses are hollow spaces in the bones of the face that connect to little holes in the back of the nose. Viruses can travel from the nose to the sinuses, causing inflammation which can allow bacteria to invade. Once the bacteria invade, you might feel pressure or pain in a particular portion of your face, and the mucus running from your nose might turn thick and yellow or green in colour. Finding small amounts of blood when you blow your nose is also common. As the infection goes on, you may lose your appetite and feel much more tired than usual.

There may be no clear-cut division between your initial cold symptoms and the sinus infection. Many people come to us with a 'cold' that simply hasn't gone away after two or three weeks. This is how sinus infections most commonly present. Any cold that is either not getting better, or getting worse after seven to 10 days should be considered a possible sinus infection and you should think about taking an appropriate antibiotic. Some of these prolonged infections will eventually clear up on their own, but an antibiotic will make them better within days. The antibiotic of choice is amoxicillin, if you are not allergic to penicillin. If you are allergic to penicillin, you can try erythromycin, but it is not as sure a cure. There is a new generation of erythromycin-based antibiotics, such as azithromycin, which are taken once a day, and have a much broader spectrum. The problem is that they are quite expensive at present. However, if you are allergic to penicillin, you should ask your doctor about these new antibiotics.

Bronchitis

Bronchitis is the second most common complication of a cold. Bronchitis is an infection of the breathing tubes in the lungs. The symptoms are a progressively worse cough, accompanied by the production of greenish or yellowish mucus when you cough. Bronchitis is similar to sinusitis in that there may not be a clear point in time at which your viral cold becomes a bacterial bronchitis. Seven to 10 days is long enough to wait before thinking of treating a cough that is not getting any better on its own. The same drugs recommended for sinusitis are good treatment for bronchitis as well, and the two infections are often present at the same time.

A deep cough accompanied by high fever may represent a deeper infection called pneumonia (an infection of the lung tissue itself). The same antibiotics can be used, but you may be quite sick with a pneumonia and wish to seek professional medical attention.

Inner Ear Infection

The third common complication of a cold is an inner ear infection (otitis media). This type of infection is very common in small children because their eustachian tubes (which allow the inner ear to equalise air pressure with the outside) are small and can get blocked easily. The infection is uncommon in adults, but seems to be more common in adult travellers. A cold is almost always present for several days, and then one gets the sudden onset of fever and severe ear pain, usually in only one ear. A doctor can make the diagnosis by looking at the ear drum through an otoscope, but if this is not available, you can treat yourself with any of the antibiotics used to treat sinusitis or bronchitis.

FEVER

Fever means an elevation in body temperature above normal, which is usually 37°C (98.6°F). Fever almost always means that you have acquired some kind of infectious disease. By itself, it does not tell you the cause, but by evaluating the associated symptoms and the travel history, one can often make a good guess, even while trekking in a remote area. Some fever-related illnesses go away without treatment (the flu), while others will require treatment (typhoid fever). The purpose of trying to guess the cause of a fever is to determine whether specific treatment will be of benefit, and whether the trek should be abandoned.

If specific symptoms are associated with a fever, the cause can usually be determined. If one has the onset of severe diarrhoea and fever, a bacterial dysentery can be suspected. If one has a thick or colourful nasal discharge and sinus pain and a fever, sinusitis may be present. Fever with a severe cough may be bronchitis or pneumonia. A large abscess in the skin also can cause a fever.

Sometimes a fever occurs with only a vague feeling of being unwell, such as headache, fatigue, loss of appetite, or nausea. In the first few days of such an illness it is difficult to determine the cause of the fever. We have found, however, that there are five main diseases which account for almost all the presentations of fever and headache and malaise in Nepal. By taking a careful history and noticing key aspects of the fever and headache, a presumptive diagnosis can often be made. The five diseases are as follows:

Viral Syndromes

The circumstances of travel means exposure to many more viruses than one would encounter at home. The influenza viruses and others can be passed through respiratory droplets, which means they can be inhaled in airplanes, buses, and crowded restaurants. The disease usually has an abrupt onset of fever, often very high (40°C) on the first day. A headache is often present, and is typically very motion sensitive, which means it hurts to turn the head suddenly or to step down hard. The illness usually lasts two to four days and goes away without specific treatment. It usually ends abruptly, the fever and headache staying about the same for the duration of the illness. The key hints that you may have a virus are the abrupt onset, the characteristic motion-sensitive headache, and the fact that it goes away just about the time that you are getting worried that it might not.

Enteric Fever (Typhoid)

Enteric fever is an infection with one of two specific bacteria, *Salmonella typhi* (typhoid fever) or *Salmonella paratyphi* (paratyphoid fever). The two illnesses are identical, which is why it is convenient to refer to them as enteric fever. The bacteria are passed in the stools of infected persons, and Nepal has a very high rate of enteric fever in the local population. The same precautions that one follows to prevent diarrhoea will help to prevent enteric fever. A vaccine exists to help prevent the disease and was shown to be 90% effective in preventing enteric fever of both types in travellers in Nepal (the study was done in the CIWEC Clinic).

The illness begins with the gradual onset of fever and headache and fatigue. On the first few days the fever is often low, and it is hard to tell if you are really getting sick or not. After three or four days, the fever rises to 40°C or more, and fatigue begins to be profound, although some people have milder cases. The headache is typically dull and not motion sensitive. Loss of appetite, nausea, and even vomiting can develop as well as poor concentration. Overall, after four or five days, the patient feels very weak, moves slowly, and doesn't want to eat. The disease can be distinguished from the viral illnesses by its gradual onset, the dull character of the headache, and the fact that the person is getting worse at a time when the viral patient should be getting better.

Enteric fever is one of the treatable causes of prolonged fever. If suspected, treatment should be started while trekking, since the person will remain sick for up to a month without treatment, and complications can result. The treatment for adults is ciprofloxacin (500 mg) every 12 hours for 10 days. An alternative is chloramphenicol (500 mg) four times a day for 10 days, although this potentially has more side effects. Sulfamethoxasole-trimethoprim (Bactrim) can be effective, but was erratic when we used it at CIWEC. In children under 18, the drug of choice is high doses of amoxicillin, 50 mg per kg per day in three divided doses. For a 40-kg child, this would be 50 x 40 = 2000 mg per day divided by three, or 667 mg every eight hours. This can be safely rounded down to 500 mg every eight hours.

The response to treatment is slow but steady, with the fever persisting for another two to five days. You can tell that the treatment is working because the patient starts to feel better, and the height of the fever is a little bit lower each day until it is gone. The infected person is only contagious through his or her stool, and does not need to be isolated from the group. Since the disease produces such profound fatigue and malaise, the person almost always has to abandon his or her trek.

Hepatitis A

Hepatitis A is a viral infection of the liver which is acquired by eating something contaminated with stool from an infected person. There are three main viruses which can cause hepatitis in Nepal: hepatitis A, hepatitis B, and enterically transmitted nonA-nonB (now known as hepatitis E). Hepatitis A can be almost completely prevented by taking immune serum globulin (gamma globulin) every four months while travelling, or having a hepatitis A vaccination (see the earlier immunisations section). If you have taken gamma globulin appropriately and you get sick with a fever and headache and nausea, you can practically rule out hepatitis as the cause.

The incubation period of hepatitis is usually four weeks. Shorter periods have been noticed, but they are unusual. So if you have just come to Nepal within the past two weeks, you can't have hepatitis. If you have travelled for a few months, and have not taken gamma globulin, then you are eligible to have hepatitis A. Hepatitis A starts with the relatively gradual onset of fever, headache, nausea and loss of appetite. The nausea and loss of appetite are often more pronounced than in the other illnesses. The headache is slightly motion sensitive, but is usually dull. These symptoms go on for four or five days. At that point the urine turns a dark tea colour, and the whites of the eyes appear yellow (this colour change is called

jaundice). The fever ends at this point; nausea, fatigue and loss of appetite are now the main symptoms and can go on for two weeks to a month. There is no specific treatment to shorten the illness, and the trek is finished at this point (and usually the whole vacation). The person should be encouraged to drink to prevent dehydration, and to eat and drink whatever he or she can stomach (except alcohol) to avoid profound weight loss. The bright side is that illness with hepatitis A does confer life-long immunity to that disease.

The main clues to hepatitis A infection are at least a month of travel in Asia, no history of taking gamma globulin, relatively gradual onset of fever and nausea and loss of appetite, and the abrupt end of fever when the jaundice becomes apparent.

Malaria

Malaria is a protozoan parasite which is transmitted between humans by a certain species of mosquito. There are four types of malaria, but two types, falciparum malaria and vivax malaria account for 90% of all cases worldwide. In the Indian subcontinent, vivax malaria is the most common. Falciparum malaria is the only type which has become resistant to chloroquine and other drugs. Malaria can be prevented in most cases by taking certain prophylactic drugs (see the Immunisations & Prophylaxis section).

The clues to a malaria infection are travel in an endemic area without taking prophylaxis (or in a falciparum area that might be resistant), fever, headache, muscle aches, and chills that go away for a day or so, leaving the person feeling remarkably well between episodes, and then a return of the symptoms. Steady fever can be a presentation, and a blood test might eventually be necessary to make the diagnosis. If you are ill where a blood test is available, by all means have the test before starting self-treatment.

The southern portion of Nepal (the Terai) has vivax malaria, but it is very rare for travellers to get infected there. Overall, there are only about a half dozen cases of malaria diagnosed in travellers in Nepal per year. The incubation period is usually a minimum of two weeks, but it can stretch to several months or a year or more in the case of vivax malaria, so if someone presents with malarial symptoms, check their travel history: they may have visited Africa a year before, or India or Thailand on their way to Nepal.

The treatment of vivax malaria is chloroquine phosphate or chloroquine sulfate as follows: 1000 mg of the salt (the larger number on the bottle) to begin, then 500 mg six hours later, 500 mg 24 hours later, and 500 mg 48 hours later. Improvement is almost immediate, and the trek could be continued if the fever goes away and stays away. If you treat presumptively with chloroquine, and it seems to work, the treatment should be followed, when you reach medical care, with a two-week course of the drug primaquine to completely rid the liver of the vivax parasites.

Dengue Fever
Dengue fever is caused by a virus carried by a mosquito which tends to favour urban environments. It is endemic in northern India, particularly in the Delhi-Agra-Jaipur triangle. It is also endemic in Thailand. The fall seems to be the higher risk time of year. The disease is not present in Nepal, and thus all the cases that we see in Nepal are imported from India or Thailand.

The disease has a very predictable incubation period, from five to 10 days. Thus, if the person has not been in an endemic area within the past 10 days, the disease is not possible. Exposure in transit in Delhi or Bangkok, however, can be a risk for the disease.

The disease has a very typical presentation which can allow the diagnosis to be made presumptively in most cases. The onset is very abrupt, with high fever on the first day. Headache is almost always present, centred mainly behind the eyes, with movement of the eyes exacerbating the pain. Muscle aches and backaches are more prominent than in

the other diseases discussed here. The nickname for the disease is 'breakbone fever'. Nausea and vomiting can be present. A characteristic rash is almost always present, but is not seen unless looked for. The rash is a continuous faint reddening of the skin on the trunk, which resembles a light sunburn. If you press your hand flat against the stomach or back for a few seconds, and then remove it, the skin will blanch white from the pressure and preserve the imprint of the hand for a few seconds. This blanching effect lasts only a half second or so on normal skin.

There is no treatment for the disease, but making the diagnosis allows you to not start treatment for some other disease, or to panic. The fever lasts from three to six days, then goes away suddenly, along with all the other symptoms. The person feels weak for an additional one to two weeks, but some people recover quite quickly.

MOUNTAIN SICKNESS
The Himalayan Rescue Association (HRA) has a saying that 'the Himalaya begins where other mountain ranges leave off'. This refers to the fact that even if you trek to a height of 5500 metres, you are still only at the base of most mountains. Exposure to these altitudes requires some adjustment by your body, a process called acclimatisation. If you move up in altitude too quickly, a syndrome known as acute mountain sickness (AMS) can develop.

In the early 1970s, when trekking was just becoming popular in Nepal, many groups had the shock of watching someone become ill with what seemed like the flu or a chest infection and then die within a day or two. As many as five to 10 people a year died in the Everest region alone out of a total of only 500 trekkers to the area in those few years. In the past 10 years there have been only one or two altitude-sickness deaths per year in tourists, an average of one AMS death for every 30,000 trekkers.

However, every mountain-sickness death in trekkers is preventable. In the fall of 1989, two Japanese trekkers died of AMS in the same trekking group in the Gokyo Valley on two consecutive days. Many of the new trekkers in Nepal are not experienced mountain hikers, and are unaware of the hazards of going to a remote area and high altitude. At a time when everything is known about prevention of AMS, it is terribly tragic to still see mountain-sickness deaths among trekkers in Nepal. If you follow the simple advice outlined in this chapter, you won't have to worry about dying from mountain sickness.

Acclimatisation is the term we use to describe the process by which your body adapts to altitude. We can think of acclimatisation in two ways: as sufficient acclimatisation to avoid getting altitude sickness; or as additional acclimatisation to allow your performance to be at its peak at a given altitude. The first form of acclimatisation takes place within a day or two at each new altitude, if you have not moved up more quickly than your body can adjust. The second form of acclimatisation can take anywhere from two to four weeks. In this chapter we are mainly concerned about the first form of acclimatisation.

Your body adjusts to altitude by increasing

A Series of Errors

Diagnosing and responding to AMS involves making a number of key decisions. To outline how this process can take place, and to give some hints about the subtlety of AMS at times, I will go step-by-step through an actual case of AMS and point out some of the decisions that could have changed the outcome.

A 41-year-old man who was fit and an experienced trekker set off with his wife and a group of friends to trek from Kirantichhap to Kala Pattar. He had some dizzy spells at lower altitudes, but this had occurred occasionally throughout his life and did not raise concern. The group approached altitude gradually, and took a rest day at Namche (3440 metres). They then ascended to Tengpoche Monastery at 3870 metres. The next morning he noted a headache, but continued on to Pheriche.

Note One Any headache that develops at altitude should be considered an early sign of AMS and the person should not ascend. People occasionally get headaches for other reasons at altitude, but since there is no way to distinguish these from AMS headaches they should be treated the same. In my three seasons working at the HRA Aid Post in Pheriche I found that any symptom of AMS invariably became worse with ascent.

The group spent the night at Pheriche and walked up the neighbouring Imja Khola Valley the next day, returning to Pheriche to sleep. The headache persisted, but his appetite was apparently all right. He visited the HRA doctor at the aid post.

Note Two The persistence of the headache only helps confirm its relationship to altitude. Often early AMS is accompanied by loss of appetite, but the absence of a specific symptom does not rule out AMS. This is why I don't stress a list of symptoms, but just a general sense of not doing well. However, headache is a symptom that must never be ignored. The man did in fact visit with the HRA doctor, but spoke with him only in general terms and did not confess having a headache. If he had, he would have been told not to ascend the next day.

The man moved up to Lobuje (4930 metres) the next morning. Along the way he began to have trouble with his balance, but remained apparently in good spirits. He decided that the balance trouble was either his old dizziness returning, or a reaction to some medication he had taken for his headache. He spent the night at Lobuje.

Note Three Difficulty with balance, or ataxia in medical terms, is an ominous sign of AMS and demonstrates increasing brain swelling. Because of his previous problem with balance, and the possible obscuring effect of taking medication, he chose to believe that there was an alternative explanation for his symptoms other than AMS. However, two of the explanations are harmless if the rate and depth of breathing. This is the earliest, and probably the most important, adjustment. Studies have shown that people who adapt well to altitude automatically increase their breathing more than individuals who get altitude sickness easily. This sensitivity to a change in altitude appears to be genetic. Other adaptations include an increase in heart rate, and a slow increase in red blood cells. Once you are acclimatised to a given height for a few days, you are very unlikely to get mountain sickness at that height, but you can still get ill when you travel higher.

AMS occurs as the result of failure to adapt to higher altitudes. Fluid accumulates in between the cells in the body and eventually collects where, unfortunately, it can do the most harm: in the lungs and brain. As fluid collects in the lungs, you become breathless more easily while walking, and eventually more breathless at rest. A cough begins, initially dry and irritative, but progressing to the production of pink, frothy sputum in its most severe form. The person ultimately drowns in this fluid if he or she doesn't descend. This syndrome is referred to as high altitude pulmonary edema

---

ignored, one can be fatal. Which explanation would you want to believe at this point? In addition, most people suffering from AMS begin to become irritable and antisocial after a while. The man's good spirits unfortunately helped obscure the growing seriousness of the problem.

They set out early the next morning for the planned round trip to Kala Pattar (5545 metres). He found he was too weak to make it even to the base of Kala Pattar, and eventually had to be helped back to Lobuje, arriving there at 4.30 in the afternoon. Because it was late in the day (they were trekking in December), they decided to have him rest overnight at Lobuje and descend the next day.

Note Four As we have already decided that he should not have ascended to either Pheriche or Lobuje, his decision to try to reach Kala Pattar in light of a headache, difficulty in balance, and increasing weakness can only be seen as tragic.

By now the group was suspecting AMS and considered descent, but were worried about the difficulties of following the trail in the dark and the cold. The man went straight to bed at 4.30 pm and had no interest in dinner. At 7.30 pm he was checked and found to be able to answer questions. At 1.30 am his wife could not awaken him. He was examined and found to be deeply comatose and unresponsive to any stimulation. In the next 20 minutes, while he was still being examined, his pulse suddenly stopped, and although cardiopulmonary resuscitation was tried for two hours, the man was dead.

Note Five Once the diagnosis of AMS is considered, and a person's condition is deteriorating at altitude, it is never too late in the day or night to descend. Sherpas are phenomenal at carrying people on their backs, and it's often possible to find yaks that can be ridden. It is quite likely that if the victim had begun descending at 4.30 in the afternoon and kept going until there was some sign of improvement (often just 500 metres or less), he would have lived.

This true story demonstrates the subtlety of AMS at times, and the danger of guessing that symptoms might be due to something else. Trekking at altitude should be a very safe activity. It will be if you pay attention to your body and to the behaviour of your friends and allow time to adjust to the extreme altitudes that seem deceptively low because of the height of the surrounding peaks. The fact that 5000 tourists a year rather than 500 now trek to Kala Pattar has not lowered its altitude. ■

(HAPE). When fluid collects in the brain, you develop a headache, loss of appetite, nausea, and sometimes vomiting. You become increasingly tired and want to lay down and do nothing. As you progress, you develop a problem with your balance and coordination (ataxia). Eventually you lay down and slip into coma, and death is inevitable if you don't descend. This syndrome is called high altitude cerebral edema (HACE). HAPE and HACE can occur singly or in combination.

Prevention of AMS

Awareness of these syndromes has caused some trekkers to be unnecessarily anxious as they trek. The progression of symptoms is usually steady, but quite slow if symptoms are ignored, taking 24 to 48 hours or more.

The onset of early symptoms, particularly headache or breathlessness, should be a warning that you have reached your limit of acclimatisation for now and not to ascend further until the symptoms have cleared, which they usually do in one or two days. If you continue climbing with symptoms, they will inevitably become worse. If symptoms don't clear up within 24 to 48 hours, or you are steadily getting worse, then you should descend at least to the last altitude at which you felt well. When you feel fit and well it is safe to continue. However, if you have become quite ill before you descend, requiring someone else to help you down, you should not try to re-ascend on that particular trek.

AMS has been reported at any altitude over 1800 metres, although it occurs more commonly and more severely at higher altitudes. In general you should not ascend more than 300 metres per day above 3000 to 4000 metres. Instead of walking for short distances, most people spend an extra day at, for example, 3700 metres before moving up to 4300 metres, thus averaging 300 metres per day. But no schedule will guarantee the individual trekker that he or she will not have symptoms.

Over the past 10 years, 80% of altitude sickness deaths occurred in organised trekking groups, even though only 40% of people trekked in an organised group. It is ironic that people who would seem to be in the safer situation of having an experienced group leader and plenty of logistical support are significantly more likely to die of altitude sickness than trekkers who are travelling on their own from teahouse to teahouse. The reasons for this apparent disparity are that people who elect to trek with organised groups have the problem of sticking to a group schedule. If they fail to acclimatise on a given day they often have to be left behind. Since people don't want to be left behind on a 'trip of a lifetime', they will often hide or minimise their symptoms. Even if their symptoms become apparent, an inexperienced trek leader may choose to minimise the importance of the symptoms to avoid the logistical complications of having to split up the group. Trekkers arranging their own treks have the luxury of being able to take an extra day at will if they don't feel well. This luxury of extra time in the schedule can be life saving.

Trekkers tend to be very goal oriented, and ambition can lead them to want to deny their symptoms. Over the years people have come to me with AMS symptoms which they explain away as being due to the sun, dehydration, hitting their head on a low doorway, sleeping in smoky teahouses, medicine they have taken, bronchitis, the flu, in fact anything except mountain sickness. None of these substitute conditions can be fatal; ignored AMS can be consistently so.

If you feel ill at altitude and you are not sure why, assume it is AMS and respond accordingly. Guessing wrong can have serious consequences. The HRA aid posts in Pheriche and Manang can give you helpful advice, but if you are on your own, be cautious. All of the fatalities in recent years have been in people who persisted in ascending despite symptoms that should have been recognised as AMS. By all means relax and enjoy your trek if you are feeling well, but be prepared to rest an extra day or so if you are not.

I have condensed all of the teachings about altitude sickness into three rules:

1. Learn the early symptoms of mountain sickness, and recognise when you have them.
2. Never ascend to sleep at a new altitude with *any* symptoms of AMS.
3. Descend if your symptoms are getting worse while resting at the same altitude.

Treatment of AMS

The treatment of AMS is first to not ascend with symptoms, and if symptoms are more severe, to descend. Descent will always bring improvement and should not be delayed in order to try some other form of therapy in serious cases. In rare cases where descent is difficult or impossible, a portable pressure chamber (Gamow bag) is effective.

The Gamow bag is the newest form of treatment for altitude sickness but is, in a sense, the oldest: descent. The bag has been in use at the HRA aid posts in Pheriche and Manang since 1988. It seems that one hour's treatment in the bag is very effective at improving the mild to moderate symptoms of acute mountain sickness, and this improvement may persist, even after coming out of the bag. Severe cases of mountain sickness (HACE and HAPE) are improved in the bag, but this improvement tends to deteriorate after coming out of the bag, requiring repeat or prolonged (four to six hours) treatment in the bag. It is possible to rent a Gamow bag in Kathmandu or the USA, and should be considered if you are travelling into a remote high-altitude area where descent is difficult.

Three medications have been proven useful as an adjunct to treating acute mountain sickness.

Acetazolamide (Diamox) Diamox can prevent mild symptoms of AMS if taken prior to ascent. However, the HRA does not recommend its routine use in the Himalaya since treks often last for a month, and the majority of people will not need any drug. It is useful in treating the headache and nausea associated with mild AMS, and it also can improve your sleep at altitude if you are being disturbed by the irregular breathing and breathlessness that can occur normally in sleeping people at altitude. My recommendation regarding Diamox is to carry it with you, use it to treat mild symptoms, and use it prophylactically only if you have had experience before with AMS on a certain schedule. The usual dose is 250 mg every 12 hours as needed. Recent evidence has shown that 125 mg (half a tablet) every 12 hours may be just as effective, with fewer side effects. Mild tingling of hands and feet is common after taking Diamox and is not an indication to stop its use. Some people fear that Diamox can somehow 'mask' the symptoms of AMS, but there is no basis for this fear. If you take Diamox and improve, you have improved. If you don't improve, consider descent. People with a known allergy to sulfa drugs should not take Diamox, although allergic reactions to Diamox itself are extremely rare.

Dexamethasone (Decadron) Dexamethasone is a potent steroid drug which improves the symptoms of HACE through an unknown mechanism, apparently without improving acclimatisation. It is an important drug to carry for emergency use, but it should never be taken prophylactically to prevent AMS. People with severe headache and loss of balance can be improved enough with this drug to allow them to avoid a night-time descent, or to convert them from a stretcher case to being able to walk. The improvement with dexamethasone is occasionally so dramatic that people might be tempted to continue upward while still taking the drug. However, since adaptation to altitude has not been improved, this could be dangerous. Once the drug is started, the person should refrain from going to a higher altitude while still taking it. If you are able to go off the drug for 24 hours and have no further symptoms, you may continue your ascent.

Nifedipine Nifedipine is a drug that is ordinarily used to treat heart problems and high blood pressure. However, it has been shown to reduce pressure in lung blood vessels, dramatically improving severe HAPE. For this reason, nifedipine should be included in trekking first-aid kits. The initial dose is 10 mg every eight hours. Further ascent should not be made while taking the drug.

FROSTBITE

Frostbite is not a major concern on most trekking trails on most days. However, from October to April, storms can occur that dump a metre or more of snow on the high passes. The two most popular treks, to Kala Pattar and around Annapurna, take people above an altitude of 5000 metres. The combination of high altitude and snow can produce frostbite very easily in unwary or unprepared trekkers.

On the Annapurna circuit, most of the walking is at low to moderate altitude on easy trails. Therefore, the temptation is great to wear either running shoes or lightweight cloth-and-leather hiking boots. The heavy boots that would be necessary to cross the Thorung La in snow seem like too great a burden to carry for the one or two days they might be needed. If snow catches trekkers at the pass, they try to push on in their light shoes, and frostbite can result. High altitude plays a deceptive role in inducing frostbite, making tissue more susceptible to cold injury due to lack of oxygen to protect the skin cells. Several frostbitten people have told me that they were very surprised to see that they were frostbitten because they had felt colder in other settings without getting any cold injury.

What is frostbite? Frostbite is the injury resulting from frozen skin tissue. The circulation of warm blood to the extremities ordinarily can prevent them from freezing in cold weather if the extremities are protected enough from the environment. When hands or feet get cold they first feel cold, then numb, and then they begin to freeze. In extreme cold, touching a piece of metal or spilling petrol on your hands can induce instant freezing of skin, but in the Himalaya one almost always goes through the progression of cold to numb to frozen.

The key to prevention is to notice when your feet or hands have gone numb and to stop *immediately* to warm them up. Once they have gone numb, you have no control over whether they are starting to freeze, since you can't feel it. To warm up numb feet you must stop walking, get out of the wind, avoid sitting directly on the snow if possible, take off your boots, and place your feet against someone's abdomen or under their arms. The return of feeling is often painful for a short time. Put on dry socks if your socks have gotten wet. Be prepared to stop and warm your feet every time they get numb. If your whole body is cold, it's important to increase your clothing layers, add a hat, get out of the wind, and drink hot drinks where possible.

If you are not vigilant enough, you may notice that the skin on your toes or fingers has frozen. The digits will be numb and feel hard and waxy, with a whitish appearance. The one acceptable way to warm up frozen extremities is by a process of rapid rewarming, which may be hard to perform if you are not carrying stoves and large pots. The technique is to heat enough water to submerge the frozen extremity. The water should be at a temperature of around 34 to 37°C (91 to 97°F). The extremity is placed in the water until it rewarms and a red flush of circulation returns. This process can be very painful. Blisters may form, and the foot will then have to be protected from further trauma.

Most of the time (every case that I have observed in trekkers) the frostbite is not noticed until the person reaches their next destination, and the foot has already re-warmed during the descent. The people take off their shoes and notice that blisters have formed. If a disaster has occurred, such as getting lost on a pass and spending one or two nights out, the toes may appear blackened and shrivelled, without the formation of blisters. This is a sign of freezing and thawing and re-freezing, and means that deeper damage has taken place.

There is no treatment for frostbite once it has occurred. There is a growing feeling that non-steroidal anti-inflammatory drugs might be useful in limiting the damage after freezing has occurred, and these should be started. However, the main aspect of treatment is to prevent further trauma, and to prevent infection. It is not necessary to start taking antibiotics. If there are blisters or open skin, the involved area should be washed in a sterile fashion, and a sterile dressing applied. If there are only deep blisters, with hard skin over them, or blackened skin, dressings may not be necessary. Walking should be abandoned or kept to a minimum. Evacuation by horse, yak, or helicopter may be necessary depending on the degree of injury.

There are only a handful of people who get frostbite injuries each year, but like altitude sickness, these injuries are all preventable. Even relatively minor frostbite ends the trip and forces a return to one's home country, since healing can take several months. If you are going above 4000 metres, be prepared for walking in snow.

TRAUMATIC INJURIES

Trauma is the most common cause of death among trekkers in Nepal, and a major cause of evacuation. Trauma results most often from falling off a trail, or having something fall on you while trekking. Nepal features a wide variety of trails, ranging from smooth valley bottoms to heart-in-mouth exposed rock traverses. Many accidents take place during a momentary lapse in judgment: scrambling up or down for a photo, not paying attention to your feet, trying to climb between trails on steep terrain after taking a wrong turn. Ironically, one activity associated with serious trauma among trekkers is getting up at night to go to the toilet. I have seen a dislocated hip, badly broken arms, legs and ribs from misjudging where the toilet was, or simply walking off a wall or cliff in the dark. Plan your night-time toilet route before going to bed.

We found in our studies of trekking accidents that sometimes it was the more experienced trekkers who got hurt. This seemed to be due to the fact that they were going into harder terrain on less-travelled routes. It is important to concentrate when

you are walking, and to concentrate even harder towards the end of the day when your legs and mind are both tired. We tend to see more ankle injuries towards the end of the day, when people are tired and can't control their foot placement as well. It is also important to look up and try to assess the risk of rock or snowfall from above. Some gullies are obvious chutes for rockfall or avalanche. Look for signs of recent rockfall or icefall, and don't linger in these areas. If you are crossing an obvious landslide or large rockfall area, rest before you start across, and then don't stop in the middle. This simple advice once saved my life in the Everest region, when I forced myself to push on across an unstable area near a river even though I was out of breath at 4200 metres. Thirty seconds later the area where I had wanted to rest was swept by a huge rockfall.

Initial Assessment

Trauma usually occurs in a very sudden and unexpected manner, leaving bystanders momentarily stunned. Scrambling to reach someone who has fallen, you may forget some basic rules of safety. Make sure that other members of the group are out of danger, and then be careful to take a route to the victim that doesn't expose that person to further rockfall. If the situation is still very unstable, with continued rock or icefall, you may have to move the person out of danger before a complete assessment.

When you and the victim are in a safe spot, you have to make an initial assessment of his or her condition. This can be done quite quickly, and the process of doing this helps you to organise your thoughts and begin to come up with a plan. It is important to approach the person with a set of priorities in mind, rather than be forced to react emotionally as each injury is uncovered. The rule of ABC has been proven to be very useful to help a rescuer move from an overall emotional reaction to a plan of action. ABC stands for 'Airway, Breathing, and Circulation'. If the person is conscious and talking, then obviously the airway and breathing are all right. However, if the person is unconscious it is necessary to immediately check to see if their breathing is obstructed, and if not, whether they are breathing at all. You can then check for signs of circulation by feeling for a pulse. In a traumatic fall, if the victim has no respiration or pulse when you reach them, they are dead. Cardiopulmonary resuscitation (CPR) is futile in this situation.

If the person is still alive, but not conscious, or is confused and combative, then they have a head injury. Make note of that, but keep on with your initial assessment. Inspect the head, look for signs of scalp laceration (feel the back of the head), and then feel all the rest of the bones in the body briefly, looking for swelling or deformity that might indicate a fracture. If the person is awake, they can generally tell you where they hurt, but do a complete assessment anyway; the person may be unaware of a large cut on their back, for example. Once you have done an initial assessment, you will be aware of their level of consciousness, any large cuts or bruises, and any signs of broken bones. The next step is to begin to stabilise all these injuries.

Bleeding

Most cuts will stop bleeding on their own, but relatively large arteries may keep pumping blood for a long time, particularly scalp wounds. Put direct pressure with a cloth or dressing over the area that is bleeding, and press relatively hard. Don't keep pulling off the dressing and looking to see if the bleeding has stopped. Apply pressure for five full minutes before you look to see if the bleeding has stopped. You can then tie a dressing over the wound and hopefully move on to assessing other injuries. If you move the patient around, you may restart the bleeding, so make sure you check the dressing as needed. Large wounds may benefit from cleaning and suturing, even in the field, but this can wait until all other aspects of the situation have been stabilised. It is not necessary to elevate a limb to stop bleeding, and it is almost never necessary to use a tourniquet on a limb to stop bleeding. Large lacerations can be cleaned and sutured even

several days later, so don't feel a great urgency to do a repair unless you are trained to do so and have the appropriate equipment. If you do know how to repair lacerations, I recommend doing so, since the infection rate in my experience has been very low, and the comfort and ease of caring for a wound that has been closed makes it worthwhile to take the risk of closing a wound in a field situation.

Fractures

Broken bones hurt. A conscious person can usually direct your attention to an area of concern. If things look out of place, then a fracture may be obvious. A non-displaced fracture may just hurt a lot. There is relatively little urgency to trying to fix a broken bone, since healing will take many weeks at best. Suspected non-displaced fractures should be splinted to protect them from further injury. Obviously displaced fractures should be splinted after some attempt is made to straighten out the deformity by pulling gently in a straight line on the hand or foot until the arm or leg straightens out. Have someone else stabilise the joint just above the fracture so you have something to pull against. This will work well on the arm and lower leg, but it will be impossible to hold a broken thigh bone (femur) straight without a special splint. In the case of a broken femur, try to straighten the leg gently, and then tie the injured leg to the good leg to try to hold it in place. A good splint will keep the broken bone ends from moving around inside, will decrease internal bleeding, and will make the patient much more comfortable. Pad the inside of the splint to protect the skin, and check frequently to make sure that the splint is not cutting off circulation to the hand or foot.

If the broken bone is associated with a laceration of the skin, the fracture is said to be 'compound', which means that the normal problems of the fracture have been 'compounded' by the risk of infection due to the exposure to the outside environment. Compound fractures require much more urgency than non-compound ('simple') fractures, as the bone ends should be thoroughly cleansed in an operating room as soon as possible. Put a sterile dressing soaked in Betadine or other disinfectant over the wound, and splint as usual. If you have antibiotics, you should start them immediately. The best choice would be cephalexin (500 mg) four times per day.

Internal Injuries

Bleeding from the skin is obvious and can be controlled by direct pressure. Internal bleeding may not be obvious at first, and there is no way to stop this bleeding in the field. You can suspect internal bleeding if the person shows signs of a rapid pulse and pale, cool skin after you have otherwise stabilised them. A tender or gradually distending abdomen can mean internal bleeding in the abdomen, usually from the spleen or liver. Bleeding in the chest can be from major arteries, and there is little that you can do to stop it. 'Shock' is a very specific medical term that is often misused by the general public. It refers specifically to the inability of a person to maintain an adequate circulating blood volume. It does not refer to the emotional reaction to an injury. If a person is truly in shock, then evacuation to a hospital is your only hope. Since evacuation in Nepal can take 24 hours, some people will die before they can be rescued.

Head Injury

The terms 'unconscious' and 'coma' are vague generalisations. These two terms can describe a wide range of reactions, ranging from temporary amnesia following a blow to the head, to complete unresponsiveness to deep pain. An altered mental state following a blow to the head is due to direct trauma to the brain. Most often this is just a bruise, and the person will improve steadily. However, if a blood vessel is actually torn, blood may accumulate in the closed space of the skull, gradually squishing the brain. Thus, it is important to note whether a head-injured person is getting better or worse with time.

Most cases of brief unconsciousness of less than a minute are not associated with any serious internal injury to the brain. The person may be confused, initially combative, and have trouble remembering what is happening to them, but they improve steadily over a number of hours. The medical term for this condition is 'concussion', which simply means a blow to the brain severe enough to cause a brief change in consciousness. A more seriously injured person may not respond to spoken commands, but might be making spontaneous movements, or push your hand away when you touch them. The most seriously injured person will not respond in any way to your touching them or talking to them. Try to note just how an unconscious person is responding when you first seem them, and then keep track whether they appear to be getting worse or better. If they are slowly getting better, you usually can be reassured that they will recover. If they are getting worse, there is very little you can do except to try to get them to advanced medical care, and to be sure that they are in a position that allows them to breathe freely.

OTHER MEDICAL PROBLEMS
Animal Bites (Rabies)

All mammals are thought to be capable of carrying and passing on rabies. Dogs are the most common transmitter of rabies virus to humans, but the virus has been passed by cats, monkeys, cows, horses, raccoons, foxes, bats and skunks among others. Although rodents are generally thought not to become rabid, it is not certain that they cannot transmit rabies. Nepal is considered to be highly endemic for rabies, mainly in the street dog population. There are numerous monkeys around certain temples in Kathmandu, and since they have constant contact with the dogs, they are thought to be capable of transmitting rabies. Tourists are occasionally bitten by rodents while staying in local houses. Although rodent bites are thought to be low risk, we recommend rabies treatment for rodent bites acquired in Nepal.

Dogs infected with rabies may not show any signs of illness at the time you are bitten. However, all infected dogs who had rabies virus in their saliva at the time they bit you will go on to show signs of brain infections within seven to 10 days. The bottom line is that if you receive a bite or a scratch from an animal in Nepal, and the animal is not a closely observable pet, you will need to seek post-exposure rabies immunoprophylaxis. One should try to obtain these shots as soon as possible after the incident, but it is not necessary to try to find a doctor in the middle of the night. In practice, tourists in Nepal were able to get to a doctor within three days, and people who were trekking got back to medical care within five days. This figure compares favourably to the average delay in treatment in the USA, which is five days.

We have noted, over the years, that we have never treated anyone twice for a possible rabies exposure. This suggests that either it is rare to get bitten (which it is), or that people who have been bitten modify their behaviour towards animals such that they avoid future incidents. It is sensible to be aware of animals around you in the street. Don't step around blind corners, or step into courtyards without looking first to see if you will surprise a sleeping dog, or a dog with puppies. Be aware that the monkeys around temples are extremely aggressive, and are used to humans being a source of food in their packs. Don't walk around eating, and don't try to feed the monkeys. A little awareness can save you hundreds of dollars in treatment, many hours of worry, and weeks of not having to try to arrange a series of rabies shots.

Conjunctivitis

Conjunctivitis is a bacterial or viral infection of the pink lining around the eye (the conjunctivae). One often awakens with a slightly swollen eye with increased redness in the pink areas, and occasionally some redness in the white part of the eye. Usually there is some sticky material around the eye that you can wash away in the morning. Although it can be painful, it is more of a nuisance than anything else. Antibiotic eye drops can clear up bacterial infections within a day or so. Viral infections will clear themselves in a

few days as well. Most of the infections seem to be bacterial, so using antibiotic eye drops makes sense. The infection almost always starts in one eye, but can spread to the other eye. Use the drops frequently on the first day, every two to three hours. As the infection improves, you can use the drops less often, and then stop as soon as the eye seems normal (usually two to three days).

If the eye is severely painful, or the white part of the eye is very red, or your vision is impaired, seek medical help from an eye specialist. There are a few eye conditions which travellers occasionally get that require specialized diagnosis and treatment, such as uveitis, or herpes virus infections of the cornea.

Gastritis

The stomach and upper intestine are usually quite resistant to the normal stomach acid that aids in digestion. However, raw areas in the stomach lining or intestinal lining can develop, and these raw areas are very sensitive to acid, much as an abrasion on your skin would be more sensitive to acid than your intact skin would be. If these raw areas are in your stomach, we call the illness 'gastritis'. If the raw area is in the intestine beyond the stomach we more often call it an 'ulcer'. The main symptoms of gastritis or an ulcer are burning pain in the upper part of the stomach. In the beginning it can be intermittent, either when your stomach is quite empty, or sometimes right after you eat. If you develop a consistent pattern of burning upper abdominal pain while trekking, you can treat it either with antacid pills or liquid, which soak up the acid in your stomach, or more effectively, with an acid-blocking mechanism which stops the stomach from making acid. The two most commonly used acid-blocking medications are cimetidine and ranitidine. If you have any history of ulcer or gastritis in the past, it would be a good idea to carry some of these medicines with you on a trek, just in case your symptoms are stirred up by the combination of new organisms, stress and diet.

Medical Problems & Medications

Diarrhoea & Vomiting
  norfloxacin
  tinidazole
  Imodium or Lomotil
  rehydration salts
  metoclopramide
  promethazine suppositories
Colds
  throat lozenges
  Actifed
  codeine phosphate
  amoxicillin
  erythromycin
Blisters & Skin Infection
  antiseptic (eg Betadine)
  cephalexin
  erythromycin
Rashes & Insect Bites
  diphenhydramine
  miconazole cream
  hydrocortisone 1% cream
Traumatic Injuries
  Ibuprofen
  codeine
Altitude Sickness
  acetazolamide
  dexamethasone
  nifedipine
Other Medical Problems
  gastritis – antacids
  constipation – dulcolax pills
  urinary tract infection – norfloxacin
  vaginitis – mycostatin vaginal tabs
  conjunctivitis – sodium sulamyd
   eye drops
  internal ear infection – amoxicillin,
   cephalexin, erythromycin or azithromycin ∎

Haemorrhoids

The veins of the lower intestine form loops around the anus. Under conditions of strain (either constipation or diarrhoea), a loop of vein can become distended and form a blood clot, which is initially quite painful. The veins are called the haemorrhoidal vessels, and a clotted, distended vein is called a haemorrhoid. If the swollen, tender vein is on the outside of the anus, it is called an 'external haemorrhoid', and if the vein is on the inside, popping out occasionally, it is called an 'internal haemorrhoid'. External haemorrhoids can occasionally be cut open

and the pain relieved, but this procedure is fairly painful, even with a local anaesthetic, and difficult to perform in the field. Soaking the haemorrhoid in hot water will quickly reduce inflammation and swelling, and within a few days the crisis will have passed. Internal haemorrhoids require special treatment from a physician. However, external haemorrhoids are much more common among trekkers. The various creams that exist to treat haemorrhoids offer marginal benefit at best.

Kidney Stone

Over a period of time, chemicals from the urine can begin to harden and form small stones in the collecting system of the kidney. Occasionally these stones dislodge and become wedged in the narrow channel of the ureter (the tube from the kidney to the bladder). The pain associated with a stone in the ureter is excruciating. The pain usually starts rather abruptly in the back under the lowest ribs and spreads around to the groin in front. The pain is always on one side or the other, not both. Victims usually are very restless, unable to find a comfortable position, often pacing around, or leaning over a table or chair. Severe abdominal pain from some other cause usually causes people to want to lay still, so someone with severe pain on one side who wants to keep moving around probably has a kidney stone. The person may vomit from the severe pain. Blood is usually not visible in the urine, but can be found on microscopic examination.

Fortunately, 95% of kidney stones eventually work their way down the ureter into the bladder, at which point the pain is completely relieved. The stone is later urinated out without further difficulty. All one can do is try to control the pain, with injectable narcotics, if available, or whatever is at hand. Most of the time we allow three days or so for the stone to pass on its own, as long as there is no fever. The presence of a kidney stone and a fever may mean that the kidney is infected, and this is a medical emergency since the infection cannot be cleared until the stone is removed. Evacuation is usually nec-

Description of Medications & Their Use

Modern medicines have great value in fighting disease and relieving suffering. However, all medications are potentially harmful. Some have very rare but serious side effects (penicillin), while others have very common but not serious side effects (tinidazole). Every decision to use a medication must weigh the risks (usually small) against the benefits (usually great). The medications mentioned in this chapter and listed in the first aid kit at the end are generally safe to use if you have no history of allergy to the particular medication.

In general, there are two reasons for using medications: to relieve the ill-effects of a disease without treating the cause (symptomatic), or to treat the underlying cause of the disease and thereby relieve the symptoms (therapeutic).

Symptomatic Medications

Name	Description	Potential Side Effects	Dose
acetamenophen (paracetamol)	for relief of mild pain & to help reduce high fever	none	2 tablets every 4 hrs
Actifed*	decongestant for relief of discomfort due to colds, sinus infection, or internal ear infection	jitteriness, sedation	1 tablet every 8 hrs
antacid tablets	chewable tablets for relief of heartburn or burning stomach pain	mild diarrhoea	1 or 2 tablets every hr or so until relief
codeine phosphate	narcotic pain reliever; also a cough suppressant (to allow sleep), a constipating agent (to permit bus travel) & for relief of intestinal cramps	nausea, vomiting, stomach pain, rash	1 or 2 tablets every 4 hrs for coughs or diarrhoea; up to 4 tablets every 4 hrs for severe pain
dexamethasone (Decadron*)	potent corticosteroid for rapid improvement of AMS (HACE)† symptoms; does not help acclimatisation; use only in emergencies	euphoria, acute psychosis (rare)	4 mg every 6 hrs
diphenhydramine (Benadryl*)	antihistamine for relief of severe itching due to insect bites or allergic reactions; can be used as a mild sedative for sleeping	sedation	1 tablet every 6 hrs as needed
hydrocortisone 1% cream	steroid skin cream for relief of itching insect bites, allergic rashes	none (if used for less than a month)	apply to lesions every 2-4 hrs as needed
Ibuprofen*	anti-inflammatory drug with pain-relief properties; can be used for 'Sahib's Knee' & other muscular pain	stomach pain; ulcer; allergy (for people allergic to aspirin)	1 tablet every 6 hrs; must be taken with food; stop taking if stomach pain develops
Imodium* or Lomotil*	closely related drugs derived from narcotics which paralyse the bowel for relief of diarrhoea; should not be used casually, but is useful for urgent bus or plane travel. Warning: paralysing the bowel can worsen or prolong infection.	constipation	2 tablets to start then 1 after each loose stool until relief, then 1 every 6 hrs; do not exceed 8 in 24 hrs, or take when fever/bloody stools present unless appropriate antibiotic is also taken
metoclopramide	relief of nausea & vomiting	uncontrolled muscle contractions of face & neck (rare)	1 tablet every 6 hrs as needed

| promethazine suppositories | anti-nausea medication for relief of nausea & vomiting | sedation | 1 inserted in rectum every 8 hrs |
| rehydration salts | mixed with a litre of boiled water, replaces chemicals & fluid lost through vomiting & diarrhoea | none | should be encouraged if dehydration is suspected |

Therapeutic Medications

Name	Description	Potential Side Effects	Dose
acetazolamide (Diamox*)	prevention & treatment of mild altitude sickness; not to be taken by people allergic to sulfa drugs	tingling of fingers & toes	½ a tablet twice on the day before ascent (prevention); 1 tablet twice daily for treatment
amoxicillin	antibiotic treatment for inner ear & sinus infection, urinary tract infection, bronchitis & pneumonia; not to be taken by penicillin-allergic people	rash, diarrhoea, yeast vaginitis	1 tablet every 8 hrs for 7-10 days (7 days for bronchitis, 10 for all other infections)
azithromycin	antibiotic for treatment of upper-respiratory infection; can be substituted for amoxicillin in penicillin-allergic people	diarrhoea, nausea	1 tablet morning & afternoon on first day; then 1 pill every morning for 4 more days
cephalexin	antibiotic treatment for abscesses & other skin infections; can also be substituted for amoxicillin; must not be used by penicillin-allergic people	none	1 tablet every 6 hours for 10 days
ciprofloxacin	potent antibiotic for treatment of bacterial diarrhoea & typhoid fever; also good for urinary tract infection	nausea, vomiting	500 mg every 12 hrs (3 days for diarrhoea, 7 for urinary tract infection; 10 for typhoid)
miconazole cream (Daktarin*)	for suspected fungal infections	possible local allergic reaction	apply 3-4 times per day until rash has gone
mycostatin vaginal tablets	for treatment of yeast vaginitis	none	insert 1 tablet morning & night for 7 days
nifedipine	is usually used to treat heart disease, but also improves severe AMS symptoms (HAPE) †	dizziness, weakness	10-20 mg every 8 hrs
norfloxacin	limits symptoms & duration of bacterial dysentery; also treats urinary tract infection. Warning: cannot be used in children aged under 18 years	nausea	1 tablet every 12 hrs for 2-3 days to treat dysentery or for 7 days to treat a urinary tract infection
sodium sulamyd eye drops	antibiotic solution for treatment of eye infections	possible local allergy	1-2 drops every 3 hrs for 3 days
tinidazole	antibiotic effective against *Giardia* & amoebas;	fatigue, queasiness metallic taste in mouth	4 x 500-mg tablets all at once for 2 days (for giardiasis) or 3 days (amoebic infection); don' take with alcohol

* indicates a brand name
† see earlier Mountain Sickness section for explanation

essary for a kidney stone that doesn't pass within one day, as the person cannot proceed on foot. If the pain subsides and stays away for 12 hours or so, the stone has probably passed, and the trek can continue.

Skin Diseases

Skin problems are common in travellers. Travellers generally are bothered by one of four major problems: allergic reactions, bacterial skin infections, fungal infections and skin mites.

A generalised rash due to an allergic reaction can consist of fixed spots in a variety of locations which are usually symmetrical (equal on both sides of the body), or of raised, red spots with itches that move from one spot to another (urticaria). Either rash is usually caused by either a new medicine, a new vaccine, or a new food. Travellers are often taking new medications for the first time and may discover that they have an allergy to one of these new drugs. Try to figure out what you might have taken internally that might have triggered the reaction. The rash can be treated with antihistamines in mild cases, or corticosteroids in more severe cases.

A painful, red swelling that keeps getting worse over the hours is probably a bacterial skin infection. Staphylococcal infections that cause boils are common in travellers and account for about two-thirds of the skin problems in our clinic. If the boil is tense and painful, it may need to be opened and drained by a physician. Antibiotics are necessary to get rid of the infection. Cephalexin is the best choice (if you are not allergic to penicillin).

A round red patch, clearing in the centre and advancing at its edges, is usually a fungus and can be treated with an anti-fungal cream. These lesions can also occur in the groin and in the armpits. They are not painful, and do not cause swelling of the skin around the lesion.

Small very itchy red spots, usually seen in clusters or in small straight lines suggest an infestation with a tiny skin mite, causing a disease called 'scabies'. This is relatively common in travellers, and is treated by a skin cream rubbed onto the whole body and left on for one day.

Many other skin conditions can arise, but we can't list them all here. Just remember that skin conditions (such as psoriasis, eczema and allergic dermatitis), that could have occurred at home, can coincidentally occur while travelling. You need to consider, when you have a new skin problem, whether it is a travel-related or not.

Snow Blindness

Snow blindness is a temporary painful condition resulting from a sunburn of the clear surface of the eye (the cornea). It results from heavy exposure to ultraviolet radiation, almost exclusively in situations where someone is walking on snow without sunglasses. Snow blindness is almost unheard of where there is no snow on the ground to reflect additional light rays into your eyes. In Nepal it can affect people who don't carry sunglasses, someone who has an accident on snow and loses their sunglasses, and porters, who generally don't own sunglasses, or sell the ones they have been given. If you are in a party of trekkers trying to cross a high pass that is covered with snow, try to make sure that everyone has something to protect their eyes as they go.

The treatment is simply to try to relieve the pain. Cold cloths held against the outside of the eyelids help relieve the pain and swelling. Antibiotic eye drops are not necessary, and anaesthetic drops should be avoided as they slow down the healing and make the eyes vulnerable to other injuries. The cornea will be completely repaired within a few days. There are no long-term consequences to this injury.

Trekker's Knee

Trekking in Nepal invariably involves multiple long ascents and descents. If one's legs have not been gradually accustomed to walking uphill and downhill through training, there is a chance that you will develop some degree of sore knees after making a long descent. The pain generally comes from mild trauma repeated thousands of times on the descent. The two areas that are most involved are the outer side of the knee, and the area under the kneecap. The pain can make it difficult to walk, and you may have to rest for a few days before continuing. Anti-inflammatory pills are helpful, as are ski poles or a walking stick. The pain can take several weeks to go away completely, but there are no long-term consequences.

Blisters

Blisters on the feet result from repeated rubbing of the skin against a hard surface (the inside of your shoe or boot). The superficial surface of the skin eventually gets lifted off its base, and fluid collects in the resulting bubble. Blisters can usually be avoided by conscientious attention to your feet as you hike. Any sore spot on your foot while walking should be investigated immediately, and some form of additional protection should be put over the area that is being rubbed. There are many commercial products on the market to protect the feet from blisters in specific areas. Moleskin is the most popular item, but adhesive tape can also work well. Newer products, utilising soft gels, have recently been added to the mix of products. Using a thin inner sock inside a thicker sock can provide a sliding layer that can reduce the friction on the foot. Try not to begin a trek in brand new shoes or boots.

Blisters are not infected when they first form, but after the bubble breaks, bacterial infection can develop. Try to wash the area and keep it clean. If swelling and redness develop, you will need to take oral antibiotics.

Stress

Even when things are going well, travel is stress. Stress can make your body more susceptible to illness, particularly the new strains of viruses that you will be encountering for the first time. The crossing of time zones, all-night train, plane and bus rides, tropical heat, Himalayan cold, noise, dust

and culture shock all combine to occasionally bring the most hardened traveller to his or her knees. Most illnesses acquired in this manner are short-lived and minor, and in the course of a long trip are barely remembered, although they seem devastating while they are happening. On shorter trips they can interfere with tight schedules, but other than being aware of stress and taking what steps you can to reduce it, there is little you can do to prevent occasional illness while travelling.

SEXUALLY TRANSMITTED DISEASES

Most of the STDs that we used to worry about have become minor concerns in the face of the very real threat of acquiring HIV infections (AIDS) from casual sexual contact.

Travellers often behave as if the time that they spend travelling is not part of their 'real' life. Those looking for adventure may be looser with their sexual behaviour than when they are at home. They may be lonely after prolonged travel, or just in search of new thrills. The new sexual partner might be another traveller, a local man or woman, or a prostitute. Any of these people could be a source of an STD. I have seen several cases of women who contracted genital herpes from one or two nights spent with a casual partner (another traveller) who failed to warn them that they had this disease. Male travellers may have recently been with prostitutes (especially in Thailand), and could also be harbouring gonorrhoea or syphilis, or HIV. Apart from abstinence, the only sure way of minimising the chances of contracting STDs is to use condoms.

AIDS can also be spread by infected needles and by blood transfusion. Try to insist on brand new disposable needles and syringes for injections. These can be purchased from local pharmacies. Blood screening for AIDS is being introduced in many Asian countries, but can't always be done in an emergency. Try to avoid a blood transfusion unless it seems certain that you will die without it.

Women's Health

Gynaecological Problems

It is not clear whether the risk of vaginitis is increased in women travelling in Asia or not. However, it can be most uncomfortable, and even frightening, it you have not had it before, or are not carrying any treatment, especially in a remote area. Yeast vaginitis is by far the most common. The symptoms are vaginal itching which progresses to burning and more severe discomfort. There is often an increased vaginal discharge. A number of non-medical douches and other treatments have been successful for some women, but the definitive treatment is with an antifungal tablet, such as miconazole, inserted morning and night for seven days. Yeast infection can often be triggered by recent use of some oral antibiotics. If the symptoms don't clear up promptly, you may have acquired another vaginal infection, and you should try to see a doctor if you can.

Some women travellers note that their periods stop for a while, or become irregular. We are not sure why travel can interfere with the menstrual cycle, but it does not appear to be associated with any reason for concern.

Urinary Tract Infection

The urinary tract is usually free from bacteria. In women, the short tube from the bladder to the outside (the urethra) can allow bacteria to invade from the vagina. An infection called 'cystitis' (inflammation of the bladder) can result. The symptoms are burning on urination and having to urinate frequently and urgently. Blood can sometimes be seen in the urine. Fever is usually not present unless the infection has spread to the kidneys. Sexual activity with a new partner, or with an old partner who has been away for a while can trigger an infection, probably from the trauma of sexual intercourse. Symptoms of cystitis should be treated with an antibiotic because a simple infection can spread up the ureters to the kidneys, causing a more severe illness. The best choice of antibiotic is norfloxacin (400 mg) twice a day for seven days. Ciprofloxacin (500 mg) twice a day for seven days is also a good choice. Commonly used antibiotics for urinary infections, such as Bactrim and Amoxicillin, are not as effective in Nepal due to wide-spread resistance to these two antibiotics. However, if they are all you have, certainly try them.

Pregnancy

The decision to go trekking in Nepal (or to travel around Asia) while pregnant should not be taken lightly. Although little is known about the possible adverse effects of altitude on a developing foetus, almost all authorities recommend not travelling above 3650 metres while pregnant. In addition to altitude, there is the constant risk of getting ill, and not being free to take most medications to relieve either the symptoms or the disease. There is no evidence that travel increases the risk of miscarriage, but one in five pregnancies ends in miscarriage in any case, sometimes accompanied by profound bleeding which might require an emergency dilatation and curettage, or put you at risk for requiring a blood transfusion.

Even normal pregnancies can make a woman feel nauseated and tired for the first three months, and have food repulsions or cravings that can't be satisfied by dal-bhat in Nepal. During the second trimester, the general feelings improve, but fatigue can still be a constant factor. In the third trimester, the size of the baby can make walking difficult or uncomfortable.

Most vaccinations can be given safely during pregnancy, but the actual effects of all immunisations during pregnancy are not known. Chloroquine can be taken safely during pregnancy, but mefloquine definitely cannot.

One can certainly find examples of successful travel while pregnant. But since the outcome of pregnancy is always in doubt, one should be careful about exposures to altitude, infectious diseases or trauma while pregnant. Travelling to Asia while pregnant should not be undertaken lightly, and if you are uncertain about how you will feel, it might be better to be on a beach in Bali than trekking to Tatopani.

Rescue

If you walk into the mountains for two weeks from Kathmandu, you are two weeks' walk from Kathmandu. This fact often does not impress itself on trekkers until they become sick or injured on the trail and need to return to Kathmandu. Radios are few and far between in Nepal, and roads are just beginning to extend into the hills. The HRA provides medical clinics and doctors in Pheriche near Mt Everest, and in Manang, on the Annapurna circuit, and there are a few other health posts. In general, however, once you head into the hills, it will be up to you to get yourself out. Here are some hints for accomplishing this.

First of all, don't panic. If someone falls, take some time to assess the situation; suspected broken bones may only be bruises, a dazed person may wake up and be quite all right in an hour or two. If the problem is severe diarrhoea, try to follow the guidelines in the diarrhoea section. If it is severe mountain sickness, descend with the victim; do not wait for help. If the illness is severe, but not diagnosable, evaluate your options. In most areas of Nepal, some kind of animal will be available to help transport a sick or injured trekker. In western Nepal, ponies are common; in the mountains, yaks are usually available. As extraordinary as it may seem, many Nepalese are both willing and capable of carrying Westerners on their backs for long distances. An Australian woman who broke her leg by slipping on some ice on Poon Hill above Ghorapani was carried for three days by a series of porters and later became tearful as she recalled how kind and thoughtful they had been, demonstrating concern for her comfort while they were struggling under a 60-kg load.

Sometimes either the seriousness of the injuries or the urgency of getting care will make land evacuation impractical. If you happen to be near one of the airfields in the hills, you may be able to arrange a seat on a scheduled flight. By negotiation, space can usually be found for a seriously injured or ill trekker, or a charter flight might be arranged, but the airport officials are quite unsympathetic to trekkers who are merely demoralised by the unexpected hardships of trail life and hope to jump the queue to get out sooner. If there is no nearby airfield, or if you know the flights are only once a week and just went yesterday, then the only alternative is to request a helicopter rescue flight.

Helicopter Rescue

The helicopters that are used for rescue are operated through the VVIP section at Kathmandu's Tribhuvan Airport (☎ 414-670). When these helicopters are not available, the Nepal army will supply them. There are six small Alouette choppers and three large Pumas. The Alouettes are used for most rescues and cost the victim US$600 per hour of flight time. A typical rescue flight will cost between US$1500 and US$2000. Once a request is sent, and a helicopter actually leaves Kathmandu, you must pay for it, whether in fact you still need or want rescue or whether the helicopter is unable to find you. The helicopter will not leave Kathmandu until someone in Kathmandu has either paid a cash deposit or guaranteed the cost of the flight in writing. In practice this is usually a trekking agency (if the victim has been trekking with an agency), or the victim's embassy. Depending on the rules of the embassy, sometimes the victim's parents or family must be contacted in their home country to guarantee payment before the embassy will front the money. Registering with your embassy on arrival in Kathmandu can greatly expedite the rescue process.

Arranging a rescue usually takes one day, although if the weather permits, helicopters can sometimes leave the same day the message is received. Most of the time, if the message arrives in Kathmandu in the afternoon, the helicopter will leave early the next morning. Given that it usually takes at least a day to have someone hike to a radio post or send a message out of an airstrip, it can take one or two days for a helicopter to arrive once a decision has been made that it is necessary. Rarely, a helicopter will not be available at all due to mechanical troubles or prior commitments, or the message cannot be passed due to a religious festival.

Flying on rescue flights has made me familiar with some of the difficulties involved. One of the most important pitfalls is the rescue request itself. Give *details*! Try to assess the patient's condition and give the degree of urgency. If they have frostbite injuries and can't walk, but are otherwise stable, say this. If they are unconscious and have an apparent broken hip, send this in the message. On the basis of your rescue request alone, the pilots and the doctors involved will have to decide whether to take a chance and fly through bad weather, or wait for the usually better weather in the morning. The army pilots do not receive extra pay for rescue flights, and are often forced to take unusual chances while trying to perform rescues. Don't risk other lives needlessly with unnecessary flights or inadequate information.

Place names in Nepal are often confusing, and rescue requests sometimes mistakenly give the name of a district rather than a village, forcing rescuers to comb large tracts in sometimes unsuccessful efforts to find someone. Once a request is sent, stay put for at least two days, or make it clear in the message where and how you will be travelling. If you see the helicopter, make elaborate efforts to signal it. It is very difficult to pick out people on the ground from a helicopter moving at 145 km/h, especially if you are unsure where to look. Try to locate a field large enough to land a helicopter safely, but do not mark the centre of the field with cloth, as this can fly up and wreck the rotors on landing. If you are a trekker who has not sent for a helicopter, *do not wave at a low-flying helicopter!* We have made a number of unnecessary and occasionally dangerous landings only to find that the people had nothing to do with a victim and were just waving!

When I was working at the Pheriche aid post near Mt Everest and an emergency situation arose, the sight of a rescue helicopter was the sweetest thing I can ever remember seeing. If you are ever rescued in Nepal, make a point of thanking the pilots and doctors who often risk their lives to help you out of a tight spot. If there are alternatives for getting out of that tight spot, don't ask others to risk their lives for you. In the last few years there has been a disturbing trend for tired and disillusioned trekkers to try to charter helicopters out of the mountains. Don't contribute to this unfortunate practice, which sometimes makes helicopters unavailable for real rescues.

While helicopters can fly as high as 6000 metres, they are unable to land and take off above 5500 metres as the air is too thin to give the rotors sufficient lift. Therefore, there is currently no way to expect to be rescued from trekking or mountaineering peaks.

Insurance which specifically covers rescue is available at low cost in your home country, but not in Nepal. It is highly recommended. (See Travel Insurance in the Facts for the Trekker chapter for more information.)

Treating Nepalese

Almost every trekker will encounter a situation where they are asked to give some kind of medical treatment to a sick Nepalese in the hills. The potential patient may just have a headache, or may be covered with severe burns from which he or she will most likely die. The moral dilemma that the trekker is occasionally faced with can remain with them for long after the trek. There is no simple answer, but I will offer some guidelines to help you think about the problem before you encounter it.

The Nepalese government is attempting to establish and maintain health posts in remote areas. So far, this has not brought medical care to the majority of the people. The local people often have their own healers, beliefs and practices regarding health. When these prove ineffective, or out of growing curiosity, the local people may consult passing trekkers, whether they are doctors or not. In many areas there is no understanding at all of the basis of Western medical practice. Ideas that we take for granted, such as the relationship of germs to infection, have no meaning to these villagers. A pill can be seen as a form of magic, the shape, size, and colour often having more meaning than an attempted explanation that the medicine will kill the germs.

Thus, some of the medical interactions are based on villagers' desire to get closer to a form of Western magic. This has created a form of medical 'begging', whereby it is not clear whether the person is indeed ill at the time of the encounter. It is fair and advisable under these circumstances to say that you have no medicine. Otherwise the pills are indiscriminately given out at later times, possibly doing someone some harm.

A Nepalese person who is clearly suffering from a problem presents another level of dilemma. If you can clearly recognise the problem and know that your treatment will be effective, and have a way of explaining this to the people involved, there is no reason to withhold this treatment from someone who can clearly benefit. If you do not know what is going on, or are not sure of the right treatment, don't try to give medical treatment due to misguided compassion. You may do more harm than good, or the treatment failure may lead the villagers away from seeking appropriate Western medical care at a health post in the future.

The fact that you are trekking through at that moment does not mean that you suddenly have to take on the continuing insoluble problems of remote village life. The feelings of compassion and wanting to help are natural, but if you see that you truly can't offer anything that is likely to improve the situation, don't feel obligated to 'do something'. The fact that there are large populations in the world that can't call an ambulance and be rushed to a hospital with serious illness is a reality that catches the Western trekker emotionally unprepared. The discovery of these feelings and the processing of your reactions are part of the reason for trekking.

In summary, the problem remains a difficult one. Try to be aware of, and refer to, local health posts whenever possible (the Khunde Hospital in the Khumbu is a good example). If this is not possible, determine whether you can definitively help someone and then do so if your resources allow. If you are not sure what to do, you can express your concern but admit that you don't have anything to offer. The Nepalese can usually accept this gracefully.

First Aid Kit

The following is a suggested list of supplies and medications that would be useful for a group of four persons travelling for two weeks or more on trek in Nepal. It is based on the experience of what happens most often to people on a trek. The list should be modified to adjust for individual preferences and allergies, and for the remoteness and difficulty of travel. (See the earlier table of medications and their use in the Medical Problems & Treatment section of this chapter for more information on the medicines in this list.)

Supplies
thermometer (low reading preferred)
scissors
tweezers
roll of tape (two cm adhesive or paper)
sewing needle
10 gauze pads (10-cm square)
large sterile dressing
rolled cotton bandages (two x 10 cm, one x 7.5 cm))
Band-aids (plasters)
moleskin
muslin triangular bandage (for sling)
Betadine antiseptic
elastic bandage (10 cm)
Steri-strips

For people with medical training, consider adding materials for suturing in the field and for administering injectable medications:

syringes
needles
anaesthetic
needle holders
forceps
suture material

Medications

The following is a list of possible medications with suggested quantities in brackets:

acetamenophen (paracetamol) 500 mg (x 20)
Actifed (x 20)
amoxicillin* 500 mg (x 30)
antacid tablets (x 20)
Bisacodyl pills (x 10)
cephalexin* 500 mg (x 40)
ciprofloxacin 500 mg (x 20)
codeine phosphate 15 mg (x 60)
diphenhydramine 50 mg (x 15)
hydrocortisone 1% cream (one tube)

ibuprofen 400 mg (x 40)
loperamide (Imodium) or Lomotil (x 20)
metoclopramide 10 mg (x 10)
miconazole cream (one tube)
mycostatin vaginal tablets (x 14)
norfloxacin 400 mg (x 24)
promethazine suppositories 50 mg (x 4)
rehydration salts (six packets)
sodium sulamide 10% eye drops (one bottle)
throat lozenges (eg Strepsils)
tinidazole 500 mg (x 16)

For people with medical training, consider adding:

meperidine injectable 100mg/ml (5 to 10 ml bottle)
promethazine injectable 50mg/ml (5 to 10 ml bottle)
dexamethasone injectable 4mg/ml (5 ml bottle)
haloperidol 5mg/ml (5 to 10 ml bottle)

*Note: penicillin-allergic people should not take amoxicillin or cephalexin. Substitute erythromycin 500 mg (28 tablets) for both medications, or use azithromycin 250 mg (10 tablets).

Getting There & Away

AIR
To/From Asia
The most reasonable connections to Kathmandu are via Bangkok, Hong Kong and Singapore. There are reduced inclusive tour (IT) fares on all these sectors. Bangkok flights are heavily booked in October, November, April and early May, but it's sometimes worth hanging around the airport looking for a stand-by seat to Kathmandu. A one-way fare from Bangkok costs from US$180 to US$190.

From India the fares are high, flights are fully booked – usually by Indian tourists – and reservation procedures are chaotic. The only concessional fares are for students. There are flights to Kathmandu from Delhi, Calcutta, Patna and Varanasi. The one-hour Delhi to Kathmandu flight costs around US$145.

Kathmandu has some other interesting airline connections. China Southwest Airlines, part of the Civil Aviation Administration of China (CAAC) group, operates a flight from Lhasa to Kathmandu on Saturdays. This spectacular one-hour flight costs US$190 and is supposed to operate from April to December. You can also fly from Paro in Bhutan on Druk Air, or from Yangon (formerly Rangoon, Burma) and Dhaka (Bangladesh).

To/From Europe & the Middle East
Royal Nepal Airlines Corporation (RNAC) operates two flights per week to London and one from Paris via Dubai. Contact its agency in London for cheap excursion fares. All of RNAC's European flights operate via Frankfurt.

Lufthansa also operates direct Frankfurt-Kathmandu flights with weekly service throughout the year and more frequent flights during the high season. A return ticket costs around US$825. German bucket shops can produce special deals on these.

Pakistan International and Bangladesh Biman both have a one-airline service from Europe to Kathmandu, though both require a connection in either Karachi or Dhaka. Also try charter companies; LTU operates a weekly flight from Germany to Kathmandu during winter.

To/From North America
North America is halfway around the world from Nepal, so you have a choice of crossing either the Atlantic or Pacific oceans. If you are flying via the Atlantic, you will probably be happier connecting with a direct flight to Kathmandu from London or Frankfurt. Avoid flights via India as the Delhi to Kathmandu fare is high and transit facilities at Delhi airport are tedious. Pacific routes usually require an overnight stay in Bangkok or Hong Kong, but there are frequent flights and most airlines have APEX fares of about US$600 one way from the west coast to Kathmandu.

To/From Australia
Look for routes via Singapore, Hong Kong or Bangkok. Typical fares are around A$1600 return. Kathmandu is not on any airline routes for 'round-the-world' (RTW) tickets, and is usually charged as an extra segment on the Australia to London route. If you are travelling to the UK, you might find a cheap fare on RNAC from either Bangkok or Singapore, via Kathmandu, to London.

ORGANISED TREKS
If you arrange a trek through an overseas trekking company, they should be able to either recommend a group flight or arrange air transportation, hopefully at a reasonable rate, on space that they have prebooked. In October, early November and late December these may be the only seats available to Nepal.

Trekking Agents

I have used the term 'trekking agent' to describe the company, travel agent or individual that is organising the trek. If you are trekking on your own, you are the trekking agent. If you are arranging the trip yourself, you can skip many advance preparations because you can only deal with the trekking agent after you arrive in Kathmandu.

If you are trekking through a trekking agent, be aware that various organisers of treks provide different equipment and facilities. Be sure to read the material provided by your trekking agent. They may provide some of the equipment or services that I have suggested you arrange yourself. Similarly, be sure that they do not expect you to bring something that I have not suggested.

It becomes difficult to prepare an up-to-date list of all trekking agents throughout the world because new agents spring up (and disappear) every season. The following list includes a number of established agents who have specialized in Nepalese trekking for many years. It makes no pretence of being a complete list of every trekking agent in the world.

The huge number of agents now selling trekking trips makes it difficult to make any judgement about the quality of service you may expect. From each agent you should be able to get any additional information you need about Nepal and trekking; most have staff who have trekked in Nepal. All these agents offer a variety of treks and several choices of dates. Most of them can also arrange your plane tickets to and from Nepal if you wish. Most will also allow you to book your trek and flights through your own travel agency.

Australia & New Zealand

Ausventure
    Suite 1, 860 Military Rd, Mosman, NSW 2088 (fax 02-969-1463)
Peregrine Adventures
    258 Lonsdale St, Melbourne, Vic 3000 (☎ 03-663-8611, fax 03-663-8618)
Venture Treks
    71 Evwlyn Rd, Howick, Auckland, New Zealand (☎ 09-799855)

World Expeditions
    3rd floor, 441 Kent St, Sydney, NSW 2000 (☎ 264-3366, 008-803-688, fax 02-261-1974)

USA & Canada

Adventure Center
    1311 63rd St, Suite 200, Emeryville, CA 94608 (☎ 800-227-8747, fax 510-654-4200)
Himalayan Travel
    112 Prospect St, Stamford, CT 06901 (☎ 800-225-2380, fax 203-622-0084)
Ibex Expeditions
    2657 West 28th Ave, Eugene, OR 97405 (☎ 503-345-1289, fax 503-343-9002)
Inner Asia
    2627 Lombard St, San Francisco, CA 94123 (fax 415-346-5535)
Journeys International
    4011 Jackson Rd, Ann Arbor, MI 48103 (fax 313-665-2945)
Mountain Travel Sobek
    6420 Fairmount Ave, El Cerrito, CA 94530 (☎ 800-227-2384, fax 510-525-7710)
Mountain Travel Canada
    101-511 West 14th Ave, Vancouver, BC V5Z 1P5 (fax 604-876-4354)
Nature Expeditions International
    PO Box 11496, Eugene, OR 97440 (fax 503-345-3286)
Wilderness Travel
    801 Allston Way, Berkeley, CA 94710 (fax 415-548-0347)

UK

Exodus Expeditions
    9 Weir Rd, London SW12-OLT (☎ 081-673-0859)
ExplorAsia
    Blenheim House, Burnsall St, London SW3 5XS
Explore Worldwide
    1 Frederick St, Aldershot, Hants GU11 1LQ (fax 0252-343170)
Sherpa Expeditions
    131A Heston Rd, Hounslow, Middlesex, TW5 0RD (fax 081-572-9788)
WEXAS International
    45 Brompton Rd, Knightsbridge, London SW3 1DE (fax 071-589-8418)

France

Explorator
    16 Place de la Madeleine, 75008 Paris (fax 42-66-53-89)

Germany
Dav Berg-und-Skischule
   Am Perlacher Forst 186, D 8000 München 90
   (☎ 098-651-0720)
Hauser Exkursionen
   Neuhauserstrasse 1, 8000 München 2
Sporthaus Schuster
   Rosenstrasse, 8000 München 2

Other European Countries
Arca Tour
   Bahnhofstrasse 23, CH-6300 Zug, Switzerland
   (fax 042-23-18-23)
ARTOU
   8 Rue de Rive, CH-1204 Genève, Switzerland
   (☎ 022-311-84-08, fax 781-2058)
Intertrek
   Nollisweid 16, CH-9050 Apenzell, Switzerland
   (fax 071-872-423)
Trekking International
   Via Giafrancesco Re, 78-10146 Torino, Italy

Asia
Alpine Tour Service
   7F Kawashima Building, 2-2-2 Shimbashi,
   Minato-ku, Tokyo 105 (fax 03-508-2529)
Himalaya Kanko Kaihatsu
   5F Kaikei Building, 3-26-3, Shimbashi, Minato-
   ku, Tokyo
Mera Travel
   Suite 1030, 10/F Star House, 3 Salisbury Rd,
   Tsimshatsui, Hong Kong (fax 735-5873)

LEAVING NEPAL
Reconfirming Reservations
Airline reservations out of Kathmandu are
difficult to get at any time, but are particularly hard to obtain during the trekking
season in Nepal. You must always reconfirm
reservations or the airline will cancel them.
This is not an idle threat, as it often happens.
Take the time before your trek to reconfirm
your flight out of Nepal. A bit of planning
can save a last-minute drama at the airport.
All airlines have fully booked their flights
out of Kathmandu from mid-October to the
end of November, and during January and
April. If you don't have a reservation, make
a booking before you start your trek. By
booking three to five weeks ahead, you may
get a seat. If you wait until you finish your
trek to book a seat, you will certainly have
to wait a week or two for a flight. Be sure to
allow a four or five-day buffer if you are
flying out of Lukla or Jomsom.

Airport Tax
The airport tax on departure is Rs 600 to
nearby countries that are members of
SAARC (see Glossary), Rs 700 to other destinations. Other airport taxes in the region
are:

From	Tax
Bangkok, Thailand	200 baht
Dhaka, Bangladesh	Tk 300
Hong Kong	HK$150
India	I Rs 150 to Nepal, I Rs 300 to places outside the Indian subcontinent
Karachi, Pakistan	Rs 200
Lhasa, Tibet	yuan 60
Singapore	S$15

Getting Around

AIR

Nepal's domestic network includes some of the most remote and spectacular airstrips in the world. The approaches to these airstrips are difficult. Many are on mountainsides surrounded by high peaks. Therefore, if there are clouds or high winds, the pilot cannot land. The classic remark by one pilot explains the picture perfectly: 'We don't fly through clouds because in Nepal the clouds have rocks in them'. Domestic service in Nepal is famous for delayed or cancelled flights to remote regions because of bad weather.

If your trek involves a flight in or out of a remote airstrip, you will probably experience a delay of several hours or, more often, several days. Delays are the price you pay for the timesaving and convenience of flights in Nepal. Pack a good book into your hand luggage to make the inevitable waiting at airports a little more tolerable.

There are now a number of private companies operating alongside the long-running, government-owned Royal Nepal Airlines Corporation (RNAC). The new companies have the same prices as RNAC, although RNAC offers a 25% discount to students under 26 with valid ID.

Airlines

RNAC Royal Nepal Airlines still operates the most comprehensive range of scheduled flights around the country. The aircraft used are Hawker Siddeley 748s (AVROs) on the major routes and short take-off and landing (STOL) Twin Otters to the smaller places. It serves all domestic airports in Nepal except Shyangboche. Destinations of interest to trekkers that are served by RNAC include Bajura, Bhojpur, Biratnagar, Chaurjhari, Dolpa, Jomsom, Jumla, Lamidanda, Lukla, Manang, Nepalgunj, Phaphlu, Pokhara, Rumjatar, Simikot, Surkhet, Taplejung and Tumlingtar. RNAC offices are at the corner of Kantipath and New Rd (☎ 226574, 220757).

Everest Air Everest Air flies two German Dornier 228 planes, with air-con cabins, comfortable seats and good-sized windows. It has scheduled flights to Bhairawa, Bharatpur, Biratnagar, Jomsom, Jumla, Lamidanda, Phaphlu, Pokhara, Ramechhap and Rumjatar. The airport in Lukla is too rough for the Dorniers, so Everest Air will not operate flights to Lukla until the rocks are removed from the runway. Everest Air offices are on Durbar Marg, opposite Rani Pokhari (☎ 228392, 222290, fax (977) 1-226795).

Nepal Airways Nepal Airways has three Yak-12s, Chinese made Twin Otter-type aircraft, and one Avro. It operates flights to Bhairawa, Bharatpur, Biratnagar, Jomsom, Jumla, Lukla, Nepalgunj, Pokhara and Tumlingtar. Nepal Airways' office is in Kamaladi (☎ 415191, 418494, fax (977) 1-416754).

Necon Air Necon Air has three Avro aircraft and flies to Bhairawa, Bharatpur, Biratnagar, Nepalgunj, Pokhara, Simra and Tumlingtar. Necon's offices are on Ram Shah Path (☎ 418608/809, fax (977) 1-416754).

Dynasty Aviation Dynasty is basically a charter operator and operates two helicopters. Helicopter charter service is available up to an altitude of 4875 metres (16,000 feet) at a cost of US$1000 per flying hour. Dynasty Aviation is in Naya Baneshwore, on the airport road (☎ 225602, fax (977) 1-522958).

Asian Airlines Helicopter Asian Airlines operates charter and scheduled helicopter service using 26-passenger Russian MI-17 helicopters. The helicopter schedule includes flights to the trekking destinations of Lukla, Shyangboche, Jomsom, Manang, Taplejung, Phaphlu and Tumlingtar. Its office is in Bhatbhateni near the Chinese Embassy, PO Box 4695 (☎ 417753, 410086 fax (977) 1-414594).

Reservations

It may seem a bit silly to describe how to buy an air ticket, but RNAC has so many complicated and strange rules and regulations that it's worth some discussion.

It is advisable to book domestic flights two weeks in advance for Lukla, and a week in advance for other destinations. Just as for flights out of Nepal the most important rule is to reconfirm and reconfirm again. Names can easily 'fall off' the passenger list, particularly where there is pressure for seats.

In Kathmandu It is best to book domestic flights in person because the airline will confirm seats only after you pay the fare and it has actually issued the ticket. You must pay for tickets in foreign currency. RNAC doesn't take credit cards, so bring cash or travellers' cheques – and exact change, if possible. If you are using a trekking company or travel agency, they can make the flight booking for you and expedite the payment process. Local people pay a lower fare than foreigners on most flights.

There are many obstacles to booking a seat on a domestic flight, but the most common problem is 'no seats'. Agents book seats to Lukla, Jomsom and Pokhara up to two years in advance for their groups. There is a lot of seat swapping among local agencies in Kathmandu, so when the airlines have no seats you may still find one by checking with a few travel or trekking agencies. Seats can also mysteriously become available at the last minute, so it's always worth a trip to the RNAC office to ask for a reservation. It's more complicated now with so many domestic airlines; this is where a resourceful trekking company or travel agent can be helpful.

In the Hills There are no airline computers or telexes in the hills. Each airline operates a manual system with handwritten reservation lists for outlying stations. The Kathmandu office cannot confirm a flight back to Kathmandu after the reservations list is sent to the remote airstrip. Once the list leaves Kathmandu, only the outlying station can confirm a seat. The Kathmandu office usually sends the list a week ahead of the flight, but the time varies for each destination.

If you are planning to fly out from Lukla, it would be prudent to confirm your flight back to Kathmandu before starting the trek. The trouble is that you must then buy a ticket. If your flight does not operate and you decide to walk out, you can only obtain a refund for the ticket in Kathmandu. Having a ticket can be useful, however. Sometimes there is such a crowd in Lukla that the airline just stops selling tickets.

Another Lukla peculiarity is that when a passenger backlog occurs, RNAC often enforces the rule that they will only accept tickets with confirmed reservations. They can declare 'open' and 'request' tickets void, and require you to walk to Kathmandu or to buy a new ticket.

Reservation Cancellations On domestic flights there is always a cancellation charge. If you do not fly, be sure to cancel your reservation on time and have it recorded on your ticket as proof. If you cancel a reservation more than 24 hours before the flight there is a 10% cancellation charge. If you cancel less than 24 hours before the flight, the charge is 33% of the ticket cost. For 'no shows' there is no refund at all. An interesting loophole is that if a flight is delayed by more than one hour, there is no cancellation charge if you decide not to fly.

Flight Check-in

Once you have a ticket and a confirmed seat, the fun is just beginning. If you are lucky, your flight will exist when you get to the airport, your name will still be on the seating chart, your baggage will be accepted, the flight will depart and it will land at the destination. This sometimes happens, but often something goes wrong. Bad weather or other complications frequently force the delay or cancellation of flights.

Check-in for domestic flights begins an hour before the flight. It is wise to be in line when the counter opens in case of some snag. In the morning, there are often Sherpa businesspeople at the airport trying to send cargo to Lukla and other remote destinations. These people often offer to assist you with checking in so that they can use your unused baggage allowance. It's usually safe to accept their offer and also let them try to solve any glitches that occur.

If you have a lot of trekking gear, try to have someone with you who can send it later if it is off-loaded from the flight. The allowance on Lukla flights is nominally 25 kg, but sometimes this limit is arbitrarily reduced. On other domestic flights the limit is 15 kg. Sometimes space is at such a premium that extra baggage cannot be accommodated, even if you agree to pay the excess charge.

Both checked luggage and hand luggage are subject to a security check. Be sure you put your pocket knife in your checked baggage so that airport security does not confiscate it. Theoretically you will get the knife back on arrival, but it's one more delay.

Flight Cancellations

When this happens, start again. Having a confirmed seat on a flight that did not operate usually does not gain you any priority for the next flight. In Lukla you will go from having a boarding pass in hand to the bottom of the waiting list. If you are lucky, and your plane does come, you will go ahead of those who may have been waiting a week or more. In Kathmandu there is no such system, but RNAC operates a complex programme of 'delayed schedule', 'nonscheduled' and 'charter' flights. You can often find a seat if you are willing to spend some time at the RNAC office, but it's almost like starting from the beginning again. An agent can be helpful in such situations.

BUS

The public bus service in Nepal is very much

designed to accommodate the Nepalese. The buses are slow, tremendously crowded and noisy; the seats are narrow and closely spaced. Tickets are written only in Nepali script and departure announcements are made only in Nepali. If you are going to Pokhara or to Chitwan, there are more comfortable tourist buses which operate more like a Western bus service. If you are headed to more remote destinations, you have a choice between flying, hiring a private vehicle or taking a tiring, uncomfortable bus journey.

In 1993, a new bus terminal opened on the Ring Rd about five km north of the Kathmandu city centre. All buses (except the tourist buses) for destinations outside the Kathmandu Valley depart from this facility. Tickets are sold from a row of counters, each labelled (in Nepali only) with a number and a destination. Several companies operate on each route so tickets are sold on a rotating system. For this reason, it's fairly arbitrary which company's bus you will travel on, though this probably doesn't make much difference. Seats are assigned when you purchase a ticket; if possible try to get a front seat, or a seat near the door, as these have a bit of legroom.

Tickets go on sale the day before departure, so if you make two trips out to the bus station, you might have a choice of seats. Otherwise it's fairly safe to assume that you can arrive a few hours before departure and get a seat on one of the many buses that operate to each destination. A notable exception to this is during the Dasain holiday in the autumn, when bus seats are at a premium.

There is a long row of ticket windows. When tickets go on sale for a particular route, a temporary sign with a number and destination, both in Nepali, is hung above the window. The numbers are not necessarily in numerical order. To make matters more confusing, the numbers on the ticket windows do not correpsond to the entirely separate set of numbers that are used to label the departure bays.

There is an inquiries counter at the bus terminal, and many Nepalese speak enough

English to point you in the right direction. As you wait, watch your fellow passengers for sudden movement. One common announcement interspersed with the blaring music on the loudspeaker is something like 'Bus number 2153 is broken, so please come to the window and exchange your tickets for seats on bus 1535'.

To help get you started, see the table showing ticket window numbers for some important trekking and tourist destinations

One way to minimise the crowd conditions is to take a night bus. These operate on many long-distance routes and are usually more comfortable than express buses. Most night buses have '2x2 folding seats'. These are almost Western-sized reclining seats and, theoretically, only as many seats are sold as are available, and there are no stops en route to take on extra passengers. If you visit the bus terminal at about 6 pm, you can see the difference between the day and night buses.

When budgeting your expenses, include the extra charges for luggage. Large pieces of baggage go on the roof. You must either drag it up the ladder on the back of the bus or pay a rupee or two to have someone do it for you. The baggage charge is often negotiable with the conductor and is higher for the so-called express and deluxe services. If you have a lot of gear, the baggage costs can add up to more than the cost of the bus seat.

An 'express' bus is anything but express,

but it certainly beats a local bus. Local buses can take twice (or more) as long as an express. An express bus, in turn, takes about twice as long as a private vehicle.

Pokhara is served by many companies. In addition to the express buses designed for local people, there are several companies that run express buses for foreigners. Student Travels, Memoire Travels, Arun Travels and the famous Swiss Bus all provide more comfortable seats than their competitors at a cost of Rs 200. The other advantage of the tourist buses is that they are allowed to depart from downtown Kathmandu. This saves an early-morning taxi ride to the bus terminal, and endless delays as the driver looks for extra passengers along the Ring Rd as the bus winds its way out of the valley.

Unlike aeroplanes, which depart with a minimum of ceremony, buses in Nepal make a great drama out of their departure. Honking horns, racing engines, last-minute baggage loading, and an attempt to cram a few extra passengers, chickens and goats on board make for a huge production that can often delay departures. Bring a book to read.

Occasionally it is possible to sit on the roof of the bus after it leaves Kathmandu. This is often an attractive spot if the weather is warm and it gets you out of the smoke-filled bus. The roof is either a more or a less dangerous place to be in case of an accident, depending on the circumstances. Buses have a nasty

Window Number	Destination	Travellers' Information
1, 2	Kakarbhitta	Darjeeling, India
3	Ilam	far eastern Nepal
5	Dharan, Hile & Dhankuta	Eastern Nepal treks
6	Biratnagar & Ilam	far eastern Nepal
10	Janakpur,	Terai
13	Nepalgunj, Mahendranagar, Surkhet, Dhangadi, Hetauda, Tadi Bazaar (Chitwan), Narayanghat, Birganj & Janakpur	
14	Trisuli & Dhunche	Langtang treks
15, 16	Birganj	Indian border
17	Pokhara	
18	Gorkha, Besi Sahar & Pokhara	
23, 24	government buses (Sajha Yatayat) to Palpa, Bhairawa, Nepalgunj, Tadi Bazaar, Bharatpur, Rajbiraj, Dang, Surkhet, Birganj, Pokhara & Trisuli	

habit of rolling over, driving off steep embankments or colliding head-on. One place on the bus is probably as safe as another.

Buses stop for a multitude of reasons – breakdowns (mostly), police checkposts, road tolls, tea breaks, meal stops and chats with the drivers of other buses.

Mugling, the lunch stop on the Pokhara road, is a well-organised fast-food operation serving dal bhat with a curried vegetable or meat side dish. Other meal stops patronised by buses can be a bit rough. The bus driver gets a free meal by stopping at a particular restaurant, so look up and down the road for a place that is less crowded and might have better food than the one that the driver chose. In any case, get your meal organised before you do any wandering around; once the driver decides it's time to go, everyone immediately piles into the bus.

CAR & 4WD
Rental
It's expensive to hire a car or Land Rover to get to the start of a trek, but it's much more comfortable and can save a lot of time compared to public transport.

You can rent a car in Nepal, but even Hertz and Avis usually supply a driver – free. Traffic can be chaotic and an accident puts the driver in jail until the situation is resolved, so it's not a good idea to drive in Nepal unless you are familiar with the country and are used to dodging the cows, chickens, kids, bicycles and rickshaws that pop up out of nowhere. Traffic is supposed to stay on the left side of the road, though this is not obvious when you watch vehicle movements.

Land Rovers that will undertake either long or short-distance trips can be found in front of the Mt Makalu Hotel, near New Rd. Rates are negotiable.

TAXI
Most travel agencies can arrange cars or you can negotiate with one of the private taxis that hang out in a lane just off Durbar Marg behind the Hotel Sherpa.

HITCHING
Hitching is unheard of in Nepal. Even the poorest Nepalese pays for a ride in a bus or truck, so you will almost certainly be expected to pay for any ride you get unless you get picked up by a kindly expatriate.

Road Building
From Kathmandu, narrow mountain roads run north to China and south to India to connect the valley to the outside world. However, Nepal is undertaking a major road-building programme and extensive construction is under way everywhere. An east-west highway that runs near the Indian border is nearing completion and many roads now wind their way a long distance into the hills.

Roads planned for the 1990s include a road from Surkhet to Jumla in west Nepal and on to Mugu and Humla. If this road is built, these presently inaccessible regions will become more popular trekking destinations.

Another road on the drawing boards is a major east-west road in the Middle Hills, connecting Dipayal and Silgadi in the far west to Jajakot and Musikot, then to Beni and Pokhara. The eastern part of the route leaves the Jiri road and heads south to Ramechhap, then heads east to Okhaldunga with a spur to Salleri near Phaplu, then continues east to Bhojpur and Taplejung. The new trekking opportunities that this road presents are endless.

When trekking in the Annapurna region, you will cross the new road, presently under construction, from Pokhara to the Kali Gandaki Valley. The master plan is for this Chinese-financed road to extend all the way to Lo Manthang in Mustang and on to Tibet. Depending on your outlook, this may either enhance or destroy the trek to Jomsom.

The oldest road into Kathmandu, the Tribhuvan Rajmarg, is almost redundant. Most vehicles coming to Kathmandu use the east-west Mahendra Rajmarg and a road along the Narayani River from Mugling to Narayanghat. Once the roads end, all travel is on a system of trails that climb the steep hills of Nepal as no road possibly can. ■

LOCAL TRANSPORT
To/From the Airport

Taxis are usually available at the airport, but fares vary according to demand. Drivers should use a meter, but often do not. There is a limousine service with a booking counter inside the airport where you can arrange a private car for Rs 200. Taxis usually charge the same as the limousine service. When taxis are in short supply, drivers cover their meters with a dirty rag and prices double or triple. There are blue public buses that operate on a fixed route to several hotels, including those at Thamel, for Rs 15.

Bus

Blue Isuzu and Mitsubishi buses and private minibuses cover the entire valley on various routes. During rush hours they resemble sardine cans, but at other times Rs 1 or Rs 2 gets you around in relative comfort.

Taxi

Metered taxis are inexpensive and abundant during the day. However, they are hard to find after 8 pm, and those that are available will quote you their own 'take it or leave it' rates. If you are stuck out late without a taxi, try a large hotel or call the night-taxi service

on ☎ 224374. Three-wheeled scooters are also metered and are slightly cheaper than taxis, but a ride in one of these is a bone-rattling adventure.

Rickshaw

Rickshaws are available in some parts of the city. They can be fun, but be sure to negotiate the price beforehand.

Motorbike & Bicycle

It costs Rs 40 per day to rent a Chinese or Indian single-speed bicycle. Mountain bikes are available in Thamel for Rs 100 to Rs 125 per day. Be careful of cars when you are on a bicycle, especially vehicles making nonstop left turns at red lights.

With a driving licence, you can rent motorbikes for Rs 60 per hour or Rs 300 per day.

Tempo

There is a system of jitneys that operates on fixed routes throughout Kathmandu using tiny Indian scooters called tempos. These are not for Western foreigners, who generally are too big and heavy to fit inside the vehicles.

Mt Everest Region

The Everest or Solu Khumbu region is the second most popular trekking area in Nepal. It would probably be the most popular destination, but it is more difficult to get to Solu Khumbu than to the Annapurna area. To get near Everest, you must either walk for 10 days or fly to Lukla, a remote mountain airstrip where flights are notoriously unreliable.

Solu Khumbu is justifiably famous, not only for its proximity to the world's highest mountain (8848 metres), but also for its Sherpa villages and monasteries. The primary goal of an Everest trek is the Everest base camp at an elevation of about 5340 metres. But you cannot see Everest from the base camp, so most trekkers climb Kala Pattar, an unassuming 5545-metre bump on the southern flank of Pumori (7145 metres).

Other than the problem of access, the other major complication to an Everest trek is the high likelihood of Acute Mountain Sickness (AMS). This potentially deadly disease, commonly known as altitude sickness, is caused by climbing too quickly to a high elevation. Be sure to read the section on mountain sickness in the Health & First Aid chapter if you are planning an Everest trek. If you suffer symptoms of altitude sickness and cannot go to base camp, you can still make a worthwhile trek to less ambitious destinations such as Namche Bazaar, the administrative headquarters of the Khumbu region; Khumjung or Thami, more typical Sherpa villages; or Tengpoche Monastery. From Tengpoche you will have an excellent view of Everest and its more spectacular neighbour Ama Dablam (6856 metres).

INFORMATION
Books

There is almost too much information available about Everest. In addition to the books I have listed, there are at least 100 more books and thousands of magazine articles about the Sherpas and Mt Everest. Whether your interest is in mountaineering, Buddhism, anthropology, natural history or environmental preservation, you can probably find literature about the Everest region that you can relate to.

Sagarmatha, Mother of the Universe (Cobb/Horwood Publications, Auckland, 1985), by Margaret Jefferies, is a detailed description of the Mt Everest National Park.

The Sherpas of Nepal (John Murray, London, 1964), by C Von Fürer Haimendorf, is a rather dry anthropological study of the Sherpas of the Solu Khumbu region. The sequel is titled *The Sherpas Transformed*.

Sherpas – Reflections on Change in Himalayan Nepal (Oxford University Press, Oxford, 1990), by James F Fisher, is an account of changes in Sherpa culture and practices as a result of schools and tourism. Some of the conclusions are so controversial that it was the target of a Sherpa book-burning in Namche Bazaar.

High in the Thin Cold Air (Doubleday, New York, 1962), by Edmund Hillary & Desmond Doig, describes many of the projects undertaken by the Himalayan Trust. It also contains the story of the scientific examination of the Khumjung yeti skull.

Schoolhouse in the Clouds (Penguin, London, 1968), by Edmund Hillary, describes the construction of Khumjung school and other projects in Khumbu. This provides good background information on where all those bridges, hospitals and schools came from.

Mani Rimdu, Nepal (Toppan Co, Singapore, 1976), by Mario Fantini, contains colour photos and descriptions of the dances of the Mani Rimdu festival at Tengpoche Monastery.

Forerunners to Everest (Harper & Row, York, 1954), by Rene Dittert, Gabriel Chevalley & Raymond Lambert, translated by Malcolm Barnes, is a description of the two Swiss expeditions to Everest in 1952. It includes a fine description of the old expedition approach march.

Faces of Everest (Vikas, New Delhi, 1977), by Major H P S Ahluwalia, is an illustrated history of Everest by a summiter of the 1965 Indian expedition.

Everest (Allen Lane, London, 1981), by Walt Unsworth, gives a detailed history of mountaineering on Everest.

Maps

The Everest area has been mapped to death; there are more detailed maps of this area than any other part of Nepal. The entire region is covered in detail by the Schneider maps. These map titles are: *Khumbu Himal* (which covers Namche Bazaar to Mt Everest); *Shorong/Hinku* (Solu and the Hongu Valley); *Dudh Kosi* (Lamidanda to Lukla); *Tamba Kosi/Likhu Khola* (Jiri to Junbesi); *Rolwaling Himal* (Rolwaling and Gauri Shankar); and *Lepchi Kang* (Barahbise and Kodari).

A map titled the *Mount Everest Region*, published in the UK, covers about the same region as the map of the same name in this book in the section on the Everest trek. The UK map is available by mail from the Royal Geographical Society, 1 Kensington Gore, London SW7, at a cost of UK£5 per copy.

The November 1988 issue of *National Geographic* contained a 1:50,000 computer-enhanced topographic map of the Everest area. This map does not cover much of the trekking route, but is a fascinating document to study. Copies are available in Kathmandu bookshops.

The US Army Map Service sheet, 45-2 *Mount Everest*, isn't worth carrying because there are so many better maps of the region. Many locally produced maps are available in Kathmandu. The *Nepal-Khumbu* map produced by Nepa Maps is available in Kathmandu, as are numerous blueprinted maps that vary in detail and quality. For fun, there's also available a reprint of the map that was produced by the 1920 Everest expedition.

Place Names

Maps and route descriptions for the Everest

trek become confusing because of conflicting names for the same place. There are both Sherpa names and Nepali names for many villages. I have used the Nepali names here because these are on all official maps and records. The Sherpa names for villages along the route appear in parenthesis after the more common Nepali name.

FESTIVALS

In addition to the February celebration of the Tibetan New Year, or Losar, there are two uniquely Sherpa festivals that you may encounter in Solu Khumbu, Mani Rimdu and Dumje.

Mani Rimdu

This festival is celebrated at the monasteries of Tengpoche, Thami and Chiwang. The monks wear elaborate masks and costumes and through a series of ritualistic dances, dramatise the triumph of Buddhism over Bon, the ancient animistic religion of Tibet. The first day of Mani Rimdu involves prayers by the lamas in the monastery courtyard. The second day is the colourful lama dancing, when lamas wear brocade gowns and wonderfully painted papier-mâché masks. Hundreds of Sherpas from throughout Khumbu attend the performance; it is an important social occasion as well as an entertaining spectacle. Along with the serious and intricate dances the lamas also dramatise two absurd comic sequences that make the entire performance a grand and amusing event. On the final evening of Mani Rimdu the villagers join in an all-night Sherpa dance.

The Tengpoche celebration of Mani Rimdu is usually the November-December full moon. Large crowds of Westerners attend this ceremony and hotel accommodation is at a premium. Even tent space is hard to come by. Prices creep up in accordance with the capitalist tradition of charging what the traffic will bear. The monastery charges for entrance tickets, with a hefty surcharge for movie cameras.

A spring celebration of the Mani Rimdu festival is held on the day of the full moon closest to the middle of May each year in

Thami. Mani Rimdu at Thami tends to be a little more spirited (literally) than the festival in autumn at Tengpoche, because the weather is warmer in spring and the *rimpoche*, or reincarnate lama, at Thami is more liberal than the Tengpoche lama.

Mani Rimdu is also held in autumn at Chiwang Gompa in the Solu region, usually on the same day as Tengpoche's Mani Rimdu. This monastery is set high on a ridge overlooking Phaphlu and Salleri.

Dumje

Dumje is a celebration of the birth of Guru Rimpoche. It is a six-day celebration that takes place in June when few tourists are in the Khumbu. Eight families sponsor the event each year. It is a heavy financial burden, so this responsibility is rotated in turn among the villagers. Separate celebrations take place in the villages of Namche Bazaar, Khumjung and Thami.

ACCOMMODATION

There are hotels of varying degrees of sophistication all the way from Jiri to Everest base camp, but there is not the profusion of hotels and bhattis (tea shops) that there is in the Annapurna area. Many times on the walk from Jiri you will hike for two or three hours without finding any facilities, and for several days you will have to schedule your night stop according to the available accommodation.

In Lukla and beyond the competition among hotels is intense. Some hotels are outstanding and almost all have both private rooms and dormitory accommodation. There is a lot of variety in price and facilities, so you can walk on to the next place if you cannot find something that suits you.

Above Namche Bazaar most hotels have only dormitory facilities consisting of huge bunks that sleep eight to 10 people. One common phenomenon at high altitude is very strange dreams and even nightmares. These occurrences lend a bit of entertainment to a night in a crowded lodge on the way to Everest.

During the trekking season the hotels fill up quickly. You will probably get involved in a daily race with other trekkers to get the best, and sometimes only, accommodation. This can be dangerous at high elevations because altitude sickness is encouraged by overexertion and a fast ascent. At Pheriche and Lobuje, particularly, you must be a bit aggressive in dealing with the crowds.

The Hotel Everest View, above Namche Bazaar, is a Japanese project that caters to the blue-rinse set. The hotel was closed from 1982 until 1989, but it has recently been renovated and is now open – and expensive. All 12 rooms have private bathrooms with Western toilets. Rates start at US$135 per person per night; meals are extra. The hotel operates the flights to Shyangboche airstrip and offers charter flights in Pilatus Porter aircraft for US$740 per hour. Book through its Kathmandu office on Durbar Marg (☎ 224854/271, 223871, fax 227289).

Sherpa Guide Lodges is a chain of lodges based on the European mountain hut system. A chain of 11 lodges covers every night stop from Jiri to Namche Bazaar. You can book a fully guided trip with prearranged accommodation in private rooms, or just book yourself into the lodge system with confirmed accommodation every night. The lodges must be prebooked as they do not accept walk-in customers, so don't be put off when you are turned away at one of their facilities. Book through the USA office (☎ 916-994-3613, fax 916-994-3475) or in Nepal at PO Box 3776 (☎ 415841, fax (977) 1-416047).

Hotel Sagarmatha in Lukla offers package deals with flights, hotel accommodation and short treks. Prebook with its Kathmandu office, PO Box 500, Kathmandu (☎ 220423, 222489, fax 227243).

Electricity

There has been a proliferation of local hydroelectric projects in the Everest region since 1989. Many villages have public or privately supplied electricity of varying standard that usually operates during the evening hours only. Electricity is expensive, so many private homes cannot afford it, however, most lodges have electricity for lighting. Most electric schemes do not have enough capacity for cooking, so lodges still rely on firewood or kerosene. Among the villages on the Everest trek that already have electricity are Jiri, Kenja, Junbesi, Salari, Manidingma, Khari Khola, Lukla, Namche Bazaar and Tengpoche. The next evolutionary steps are discos, videos and satellite dishes, all of which are already appearing along this route.

GETTING THERE & AWAY
You can either fly or walk to the Everest region. Those who fly to Lukla miss out on the historic and culturally fascinating route followed by the Everest expeditions of the '50s and '60s, although the trek has changed a lot in the past 40 years.

Trailheads
Jiri This is the starting point for 'walk to Everest' treks. You should plan on a 10-day trek from the roadhead at Jiri, 188 km from Kathmandu. If you take the time to walk from Jiri, the hike will help to acclimatise and condition you to visit Everest base camp or climb Kala Pattar. You can then either fly out from Lukla or walk back by an alternative route to Kathmandu. Direct buses to Jiri depart from the new bus terminal north of Kathmandu. There are at least two buses daily at 6 am and tickets cost Rs 108. The buses that serve Jiri are dilapidated, crowded and slow, so if you have the wherewithal and a group of five or six people, you might consider hiring a Land Rover.

Barahbise Five km beyond Lamosangu and 85 km from Kathmandu is the starting point of an extended Everest walk-in trek. There is no express bus service to Barahbise, so you must take a funky local bus which takes five to six hours, but it's cheap – only Rs 45. You can make the trip by private car or taxi in about 2½ hours.

Lamosangu Lamosangu was the starting point for Everest treks before the road to Jiri was completed. It is still shown on many trekking maps, but it is now simply a transit point for buses headed to Barahbise and Jiri.

Dharan & Dhankuta These villages in south-east Nepal can be used as starting or ending points for an Everest trek. See the details of how to get to these villages in the Eastern Nepal chapter.

Mountain Airports
When flying to one of the mountain airstrips near Everest, do not attempt a quick visit to the base camp because you won't have had time to acclimatise. Allow at least eight or nine days to reach the base camp region if you fly to Lukla. You can return from the base camp to Lukla in as few as four or five days, so it takes an absolute minimum of two weeks for a safe trek to the base camp. Precise scheduling is complicated because flights to Lukla often do not take off as planned. Allow a few spare days for both the flight in and the flight out.

Lukla At 2800 metres, this airstrip is served by 19-passenger Twin Otter and Yak-12 aircraft that carry (due to the high elevation) only 14 or 15 passengers to and from Lukla. If you truly have a limited amount of time, you can fly to Lukla and spend as little as six days to visit Namche Bazaar and Tengpoche, but beware of flight delays. Only RNAC and Nepal Airways (known locally as 'Airways') operate flights to Lukla. The runway is too rocky for Everest Air's low-slung Dornier aircraft.

Lukla is unique. A Hillary team built Lukla airstrip as part of the Khunde Hospital project in 1965, envisioning it as a makeshift strip to handle emergencies at the hospital. RNAC expanded the strip in 1977 and the Department of Civil Aviation added a control tower in 1983. It is now the second-busiest airport in Nepal. The flight approach path is totally visual; there are no instruments or navigational aids of any kind. If there are clouds, no planes arrive, which occasionally occurs for days at a time during periods of extended bad weather. Flight planning is complicated because while only 60% of trekkers to the Everest region fly to Lukla, 96% of them fly out of Lukla.

Situated on the side of a mountain, the grass strip is built on a slant so that there is an elevation difference of about 60 metres between the ends of the runway. This slope slows planes and helps them stop before they run into the mountain peak that rises from the eastern end of the 450-metre-long runway.

RNAC often enforces a rule at Lukla that they will honour only tickets with confirmed reservations. At such times they totally reject 'open' or 'request' tickets. If you are planning to fly out of Lukla, you should select a date, get a confirmed reservation and have the ticket issued in Kathmandu.

Shyangboche This tiny airstrip is served by a six-passenger, single-engine Pilatus Porter aircraft and sometimes by scheduled Asian Airways helicopter flights. Shyangboche is above Namche Bazaar at an elevation of 3565 metres. It is used by guests at the Hotel Everest View and for occasional charter flights.

RNAC has contracted the operation of Shyangboche flights to the Hotel Everest View. To buy a Shyangboche seat, go to the Trans Himalayan Tour/Hotel Everest View office on Durbar Marg (☎ 224854, 223871) or to the Hotel Everest View itself above Khumjung. The cost is US$160 one way and US$290 return, with a five-kg baggage allowance. Excess baggage is US$2 per kg.

Phaphlu It's a four-day walk from Lukla and six days from Namche Bazaar to Phaphlu (2364 metres). If you have an extra few days this may be a viable alternative for flights both to and from the Everest region. Phaphlu airstrip was extended in 1986 to accommodate Twin Otter (19-passenger) aircraft. Few tourist groups use the airstrip, so you might find a seat at the last minute. RNAC operates four flights a week and Everest Air serves Phaphlu with two flights weekly.

Lamidanda This airport is about five days' walk south of Lukla. It is a largely unknown

alternative as either an approach to or exit from the Everest region. From Lamidanda there are RNAC and Everest Air flights to Kathmandu. RNAC also flies to Biratnagar where you can take a bus or plane to Kathmandu.

Biratnagar This city is in the Terai, southeast of Lukla. RNAC operates an eastern Nepal hub from Biratnagar that serves the airports of Bhojpur, Lamidanda, Phaphlu, Rumjatar, Tumlingtar and Taplejung. Because there is no morning fog in Biratnagar, early-morning flights operate more regularly than in Kathmandu. RNAC experimented with a Biratnagar to Lukla flight, but has discontinued it for the 1993 season. There is a night bus service between Biratnagar and Kathmandu, so you could use this to save money if you travel via Biratnagar.

Airfares
The following table shows one-way fares between the main mountain airstrips and Kathmandu airport:

Kathmandu-Lukla	US$83
Kathmandu-Phaphlu	US$77
Biratnagar-Phaphlu	US$66
Kathmandu-Biratnagar	US$77
Kathmandu-Lamidanda	US$66
Biratnagar-Lamidanda	US$50
Kathmandu-Shyangboche (charter flight)	US$160

Flight Delays
Both RNAC and Nepal Airways schedule three or four flights a day to Lukla. In reality there are usually either more or less than four flights because of cancellations, extra flights, charters or delayed flights.

When flights are cancelled, those who have planned to fly to Kathmandu must wait. Soon a backlog of people builds up, each person convinced that he or she must fly on the next available aircraft. The situation often becomes ludicrous, but provides a great opportunity to develop patience and to become acquainted with trekkers from all over the world as you wait together. The stories of overcrowding in the Everest area now become real. In the past, 350 or more people have waited here – especially in late October and early November each year. The problem usually solves itself within a week, but it's important to prepare yourself for a long delay for any flight to or from Lukla. It's also possible to depart from Lukla exactly on schedule.

See the description of the trek to Lamidanda for a few horror stories and Lukla jokes, as well as some suggestions on what you can do if you find yourself stranded here.

Shyangboche flights are expensive but provide an emergency exit from Khumbu. Hotel guests receive priority on flights, so it's sometimes possible (but expensive) to check in at the Hotel Everest View for a night and move to the head of the Shyangboche waiting list.

SPECIAL RULES
Fees & Permits
All the treks described in this chapter require the payment of the Rs 650 entrance fee to Sagarmatha National Park. If you take a video camera into the national park you are also subject to a US$100 fee for a filming permit. There are no other specific fees for treks in the Everest region, but donations are expected at all monasteries and gompas that you visit.

The Everest trekking permit does not allow you to go north of Thami towards the Nangpa La leading to Tibet.

Fuel
The use of kerosene as a fuel is required in the Sagarmatha National Park and is encouraged elsewhere. The Lukla Himalayan Club has convinced villagers not to sell firewood to trekking groups.

Jiri to Namche Bazaar

This section details the first nine days of a 21-day trek from Jiri to the Everest base camp. This is the best way to do an Everest trek, but I have broken it into two sections because most people fly to Lukla and only trek the high altitude portion of the route. This means that the portion of the trek from Jiri to Lukla is often uncrowded, and therefore much better trekking country. From Namche you can follow the Lukla to Everest base camp route and then fly out from Lukla. You can also make an excellent 32-day trek by walking on to Hile instead of flying from Lukla. The description of this route is in the Eastern Nepal chapter.

The Everest trek involves a tremendous amount of up-and-down walking. A glance at the map will show the reason why. All the rivers in this part of Nepal flow south from Himalayan glaciers, but the trek route proceeds east. Therefore the trail must climb to the ridge that separates two rivers, descend to the river itself and ascend the next ridge. Even though the trek begins at an elevation of 1860 metres, on the sixth day it crosses the Dudh Kosi at only 1500 metres – after considerable uphill walking. If you total all the uphill climbing, it will come to almost 9000 metres of elevation gain from Jiri to the Everest base camp. The Jiri road saves almost 4000 metres of uphill walking over the old approach from Lamosangu.

Day 1: Kathmandu to Jiri
The first part of the drive is via the Arniko Rajmarg, the Chinese-constructed Kodari Highway that links Nepal with Tibet. The road follows the Chinese trolley bus route to Bhaktapur, then passes smoke-belching brick factories, finally leaving the Kathmandu Valley and passing by the old Newar towns of Banepa and Dhulikhel. If it is clear as you pass Dhulikhel, you should have an excellent panoramic view of the eastern Himalaya, including Ganesh Himal, Langtang Lirung and Dorje Lakpa.

The road descends to Panchkal, the starting point for Helambu treks, then follows the Indrawati River downstream to its confluence with the Sun Kosi at Dolalghat, crossing the river on a large bridge 57 km from Kathmandu. The Sun Kosi ('gold

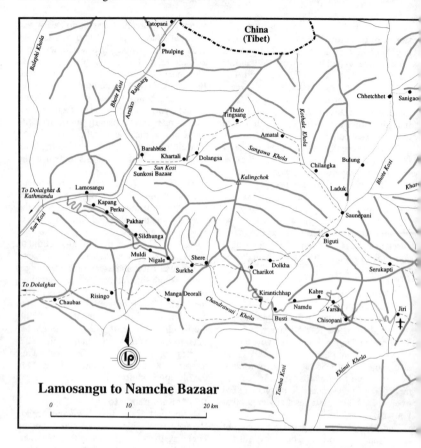

China
(Tibet)

Balephi Khola

Tatopani

Phulping

Bhote Kosi

Amiko Rajmarg

Thulo
Tingsang

Amatal

Kohale Kholu

Chhetchhet   Sanigao

Barahbise
Khartali   Dolangsa

Sangawa Khola

Chilangka   Bulung

Sun Kosi
Sunkosi Bazaar

Kalingchok

Bhote Kosi

Laduk   Khar

To Dolalghat &
Kathmandu

Lamosangu

Kapang
Perku

Saunepani

Sun Kosi

Pakhar

Biguti

Sildhunga

Muldi   Shere
Nigale
Surkhe

Dolkha
Charikot

Serukapti

To Dolalghat

Risingo

Manga Deorali

Chaubas

Chandrawati   Khola

Kirantichhap   Kabre

Namdu   Yarsa   Jiri

Busti   Chisopani

Lamosangu to Namche Bazaar

Tamba Kosi

Khimti Khola

0   10   20 km

river') is one of Nepal's major rivers; it is possible to make a week-long rafting expedition from Dolalghat all the way to the Terai. The road climbs over a ridge behind Dolalghat, passing the junction of the road to Chautaara and the trek to Jugal Himal (see the Langtang & Helambu chapter). The road descends from the ridge and follows the Sun Kosi north to Lamosangu, a bustling bazaar about 50 km south of the Tibetan border. Just north of Lamosangu is a hydroelectric power plant built with Chinese aid.

At Lamosangu the bus crosses the Sun Kosi and joins the Swiss road, climbing

towards the top of the 2500-metre ridge that forms the watershed between the Sun Kosi drainage to the west and the Tamba Kosi drainage to the east. The villages in this area are of mixed ethnic and caste composition. Most of the population is either Chhetri or Brahmin (who speak Nepali as their first tongue) or Tamangs.

A new series of Km posts start here. The bridge is Km 0 and Jiri is Km 110. After some initial switchbacks as the road leaves the Sun Kosi Valley, the road turns east and heads up a canyon towards the top of the first ridge. The first large settlement along the road is

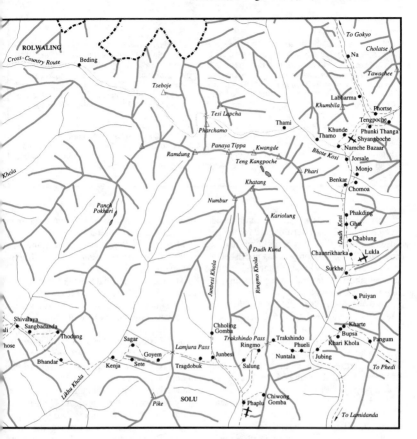

Pakhar (1980 metres). This is a predominantly Tamang village, and is the site of a Swiss vehicle and road maintenance centre. There is little mineral wealth in Nepal, but near Pakhar there is an economically viable source of magnesite, a mineral that refractories use. Nepal Orind Magnesite Corporation has a mine here and plans to export magnesite to India and other countries using a cable ropeway that stretches from here to Lamosangu. From Pakhar the road climbs along the top of a ridge towards the pass. Buses often stop at **Muldi** (3540 metres) for tea or lunch at one of several bhattis.

After crossing the pass at 2440 metres the road makes a long sweep around the head of the valley, finally reaching **Charikot** at the road junction for **Dolkha** at Km 53.

Dolkha is a large and diverse bazaar a few km to the north. This is the departure point for treks to Rolwaling (see the Other Trekking Areas). There are several hotels here and it might be prudent to grab a snack if the wait is particularly long, as the police often decide to check trekking permits and record all comings and goings of vehicles and foreigners. Though buses are often late because of breakdowns, road problems or an excess

---

The Road to Jiri

By bus it takes a full day to cover the 188 km from Kathmandu to Jiri. The development of roads has been a characteristic of this trek since the first Everest expedition in Nepal. In 1953 the British Everest expedition started from Bhadgaon in the Kathmandu Valley. By 1963 the US expedition could begin from Banepa, saving a day of walking over the British. The Kodari road allowed the trek to begin from Dolalghat in 1967 and from Lamosangu in 1970. The Jiri road reached Kirantichhap in 1980 and by 1984 it was finally possible to drive all the way to Jiri. There is talk of continuing the road further, perhaps to Phaphlu or even to Namche Bazaar, but this is still only a dream and no firm plans exist.

The Swiss Association for Technical Assistance (SATA) built the Jiri road as part of the Integrated Hill Development Project, a large programme of agricultural development in this region. It employed labourers to build the road instead of using machines. This was intended to have a beneficial economic impact by employing hundreds of workers. A direct effect of this approach to road building is that it raises porter wages and creates a porter shortage. ■

---

of bureaucratic formalities, you rarely need to spend a night in a hotel along the road. The buses continue their trip at night, no matter how late. The Swiss project has published a pamphlet, titled *Dolkha*, that describes several short treks and excursions in the region near Charikot.

The road descends from Charikot through a region of heavy settlement to Kirantichhap at 1300 metres, 64 km from Lamosangu. It then makes a circuitous descent from Kirantichhap into the Tamba Kosi Valley. This is a fertile area, containing a good deal of terraced land for irrigated paddy cultivation. The population is mainly Brahmin and Chhetri, but there are also Tamangs and a few Newars. Crossing the river on a large steel bridge at 800 metres, the road makes a steep ascent to Namdu. The only part of Namdu that you can see from the road is the large school. Namdu and its neighbouring village, Kabre, are large and spread out. Reafforestation and agricultural projects, part of the Swiss development scheme, are operating in both villages.

The road climbs above Namdu and past **Mina Pokhari**, one of the road project stations. This settlement is a good example of a phenomenon that takes place as road construction continues. Mina Pokhari hardly existed before SATA conceived the road. For several years the road ended here and Mina Pokhari became a boom town. When the road finally reached Jiri, Mina Pokhari lost

its importance. Many villages have suffered just such a rise and fall – Dumre on the Pokhara road, Betrawati on the Langtang road and Lamosangu, Pakhar and Kirantichhap on the road to Jiri.

The road finally reaches the top of a forested ridge at 2500 metres. It remains high and contours around the head of the valley in forests above the village of Thulo Chaur. The road descends along the top of a ridge above Jiri to Jiri Bazaar (2100 metres), where there are a few hotels and a weekly Saturday market. It is a short descent to the main village of Jiri (1860 metres) where the road ends at a cluster of hotels near the Swiss dairy and agricultural project. The *Sherpa Guide Lodge,* the *Cherdung Lodge* and the *Sagarmatha Hotel* are all along the road which attracts a collection of smoke-belching, horn-blowing buses much too early in the morning.

The people of Jiri and the surrounding area are Jirels, a subgroup of Sunwars whose language is related to that of the Sherpas.

You have a few choices to make as you plan your first few days of trekking. On your own, you can reach Thodung or Bhandar on the first day – it is a long hard day – and Sete on the second day, in accordance with the schedule here. If you have porters, or are not in good shape, you may have trouble reaching Bhandar the first day. You will probably have to settle for Shivalaya on the first day and Bhandar on the second day. Whichever

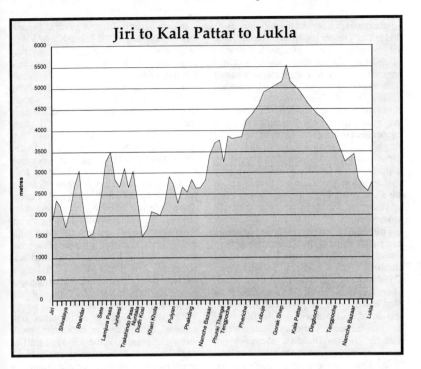

Jiri to Kala Pattar to Lukla

way you schedule it, plan on spending a night at either Sete or Sagar to break the long climb to Lamjura Pass into two stages. The elevation gain from the river to the pass is almost 2000 metres – a fairly difficult climb to make in a single day unless you are in outstanding condition.

Day 2: Jiri to Bhandar

The walking starts at the end of Jiri's main street. Climb past some houses, then turn right, climbing diagonally towards the top of the ridge. The first part of the hike is in deep forests then fields, passing the tiny settlements of Bharkur and Ratmati and finally reaching pasture as it nears the top of the ridge. There is a bhatti at Chitre, a short distance below the pass.

Crossing the ridge at 2400 metres, the trail begins to descend into the Khimti Khola

Valley. From Mali, a sparsely populated Sherpa settlement at 2240 metres, the trail descends alongside a stream, crossing it on a small wooden bridge, then emerges into the main valley where a suspension bridge leads to **Shivalaya**, a small bazaar and police checkpost at 1750 metres. Food and accommodation here is mediocre; it is close enough to Jiri that few people stay here. At night you may hear the howls of jackals *(shyaal)* that roam the nearby hills.

The old trail went via **Those** (pronounced 'toe-say') and provides an alternative to the newer direct route. To reach Those (Maksin) from Jiri, follow a trail downstream along the eastern side of the Jiri Khola. The trail climbs a bit in forests, then drops to join the old route from Lamosangu. The trail descends past Kattike to the Khimti Khola then follows the river upstream to Those at 1750 metres. A good camp is just beyond the iron suspension bridge that crosses the Khimti Khola. There are several hotels in the village itself. Beware of 2nd-floor rooms above smoky kitchens here. The village is a large pleasant bazaar with a cobblestone street and whitewashed houses. Once the largest market on the trail between Lamosangu and Namche Bazaar, its importance has greatly diminished now that the Jiri road is complete. Many of the Newar shopkeepers here have closed or abandoned shops and hotels. It's possible to buy items manufactured locally from the nearby sources of low-grade iron ore. Rooster lamps are a speciality. From Those, the trail leads upstream to Shivalaya where it joins the route from Jiri.

From Shivalaya the route crosses a stream and passes some houses, then starts a steep ascent towards the next pass. It's a 350-metre climb to a schoolhouse at **Sangbadanda** (2150 metres), where there is a small bhatti. There are several hotels between here and the pass, and more on the pass itself. Along this section of trail you will see the first *mani* walls on the route. These are stones covered with the Tibetan Buddhist inscription *om mani padme hum*, usually translated as 'hail to the jewel in the lotus', though its true translation is much more complex and mysterious. You should walk to the left side of these walls as the Buddhists do.

Leaving Sangbadanda, the trail climbs less steeply past several isolated but large and prosperous houses. Just above a large house with blue windows is a mani wall that has some unique and well-preserved stones on its southern side. To find it, peek around each wall after you pass it on the left. There is a small tea shop at Kosaribas (2500 metres), then the trail becomes reasonably level, and even descends a bit, as it goes towards the head of the canyon.

Crossing a stream on a wooden bridge, the trail ascends steeply in forests to another tea shop, crosses another stream, this time on two logs, then makes a final climb through forests. On the top of the pass at 2705 metres is an impressive array of long mani walls, signifying that the trek is now entering an area dominated by Tibetan culture. There is a sweeping view of the Likhu Khola Valley and the village of Bhandar (Chyangma), a large Sherpa settlement, far below in a hanging valley.

You can make a side trip to **Thodung** either by climbing north for about 1¼ hours from the pass or by detouring from the main trail just beyond Sangbadanda. Thodung (3090 metres) is the site of Nepal's first cheese factory built by the Swiss in the 1950s. The Dairy Development Corporation now operates it. Your reward for the long hard climb to the factory is a feast of cheese, yoghurt and yak (actually nak) milk. Cheese is available year-round but other fresh dairy products are available only during autumn. From Thodung you can trek down the ridge and rejoin the main trail at the top of the pass, then descend to Bhandar. Good food and accommodation is available in Thodung if you have the courage to seek out the manager in the presence of several huge Tibetan mastiff dogs.

Just below the pass is an important trail junction. After a one or two-minute walk below the pass, take the left-hand trail to reach Bhandar. By continuing straight you would stay high on the ridge and eventually end up crossing a pass south of Lamjura in the Solu region. Few foreigners ever use this route.

After an initially steep descent on stone steps, the trail reaches the outskirts of the large village of Bhandar and descends gradually through fields and pastures to a gompa and two imposing *chortens* at 2200 metres. A chorten is literally a receptacle for offerings and often holds religious relics. Each of its elements has a symbolic meaning. The square or rectangular base symbolises the solid earth. On the base is a half-spherical dome, symbolising water. On top of the dome is a rectangular tower, the four sides of which are painted with a pair of eyes, the all-seeing eyes of Buddha. What appears to be a nose is actually the Sanskrit character for the number one, symbolising the absoluteness of Buddha. Above the rectangular tower is a conical or pyramidal spire (symbolising fire) with 13 step-like segments, symbolising the 13 steps leading to Buddhahood. On top of the 13 steps is an ornament shaped like a crescent moon symbolising air, and a vertical spike symbolising ether or the sacred light of Buddha. The two chortens at Bhandar are painted frequently and are well preserved. One has a pyramidal spire and the other has a circular conical spire. A large chorten is called a *stupa*; there are stupas at Boudhanath and Swayambhunath in Kathmandu

There are some hotels just below the gompa and there's an excellent camping spot in a large meadow about a 15-minute walk below the village. Several hotels surround the village square in Bhandar and several others are just below these; try the *Dawa Lodge* or the *Buddha Lodge*. The *Shobha Hotel* has a radio and watch-repair shop on the premises. Stop at the Medical Hall Health Centre for any last-minute medical supplies.

Day 3: Bhandar to Sagar
From the hotels at Bhandar the trail descends through the lower fields of the village, then follows a small stream. It crosses the stream on a covered wooden bridge, then descends through deep forests for a while. Leaving the forests, the trail drops into a steep canyon, passing the settlement of Baranda, then finally meets the same stream, crossing it on another covered bridge at Tharo Khola. There is a hotel here, but food is also available in Kenja, about 1½ hours away. The route turns north, following the Likhu Khola, crossing the river on a suspension bridge at 1510 metres. This bridge replaces an ancient chain-link bridge that collapsed under a load of 12 porters during the approach march for the US Everest expedition in 1963. You can see the remains of the abutments for the old bridge just downstream of the high suspension bridge.

As you follow the trail up the east bank of the river to Kenja, watch for grey langur monkeys in the forests. Continue along the east bank of the river, climbing over a spur, through the settlement of Namang Gaon, before crossing a small suspension bridge at

Kenja (1580 metres), a small village inhabited by Newars and Magars. When I first came here in 1969, Kenja was a single dingy shop. Now there are 15 shops, restaurants and at least 10 hotels operated by Sherpas who have migrated from the village of Kyama, several km to the north. The large *Sherpa Guest House* has accommodation for more than 40 people; the *New Everest Hotel* is so large that its dining room is in a separate building across the trail. There is a weekly market in Kenja on Sunday. One speciality here is instant tailoring performed on hand-operated sewing machines.

Leaving Kenja, the ascent towards the high Lamjura ridge begins. The first part of the ascent is very steep, then it becomes less severe as you gain elevation. After about two hours of climbing, a large house appears. This is not a hotel, but food and accommodation is sometimes available. There is also a welcome supply of water.

The house marks a trail junction. The left fork leads to the north and climbs around the hillside to the Sherpa settlement of Sagar (Chandra) at 2440 metres, a large village with two-storey stone houses and an ancient village gompa. It is possible to camp in the yard of the school, one of the projects of the Himalayan Trust (headed by Sir Edmund Hillary). There are no true hotels in Sagar, but this is a Sherpa village, so many people are willing to take guests into their homes. The trek is now completely in Sherpa country. With the exception of Jubing, all the remaining villages up to Namche Bazaar are inhabited by Sherpas.

If you are trekking on your own, take the right-hand fork. This is the trail to **Sete** (2575 metres), a small defunct monastery where there are three small hotels and a camp ground. There is a water shortage in Sete, especially during spring.

Day 4: Sagar to Junbesi
From Sagar or Sete it is a long, but fairly gradual, climb – although in spots it gets steep – to the top of the 3530-metre Lamjura Pass. The way is scenic and varied and it is one of the few parts of the trek that has no

villages. The trek gets into moist mountain forest, with huge, gnarled, moss-covered rhododendron, magnolia, maple and birch trees. There is often snow on the trail and the mornings are usually frosty throughout the trekking season. On very rare occasions snow blocks the pass for a few days, but the crossing usually presents no difficulties.

In spring the ridge is alive with blooming rhododendrons – the white, pink and red blossoms cover the entire hillside. The flowering occurs in a band of a few hundred metres that moves up the hill along with the spring weather. The first blooms start at lower elevations in mid-February and finally reach the pass in mid to late April. This day is also a delight for the bird lover. Nepal has more than 800 species of birds and some of the most colourful ones are found in this zone – sunbirds, minavets, flycatchers, tits, laughing thrushes and many others.

The trail from Sagar joins the Sete trail at **Dagcho**, a small settlement of several simple lodges near two small ponds. The forest changes from pines to rhododendrons and the trail continues to climb to **Goyem** – five hotels at 3300 metres. Although Goyem is only about two hours from either Sagar or Sete, it's best to have lunch here because the next hotel of any consequence is in Tragdobuk, at least three hours away, although there is a small bhatti about 30 minutes below the pass on the other side. The trail climbs steeply up the ridge, finally reaching a mani wall. Here the trail leaves the ridge and begins to contour northward towards the pass on a trail that is always muddy and often covered with snow or ice.

Deep in a forest of large silver birches, the trail passes three kharkas (communal grazing areas) each consisting of a goth or two and a mani wall. Herders use these in spring and summer and leave them empty from October to June, though sometimes they masquerade as teahouses during the trekking season. The houses have no roofs, so they cannot be used as shelter. Since you will probably be crossing the pass about noon or early afternoon, it will be cloudy, cold and windy. There is no view of Hima-

layan peaks from the pass, though there are glimpses of the top of some snow peaks on the way up. If you're here in the early morning, you will undoubtedly see planes crossing the pass en route to Lukla. The deforestation on the upper portion of this route is shocking; it has all happened in the past 10 years.

The pass is the highest point on the trek between Jiri and Namche Bazaar and is marked by a tangle of stones, twigs and prayer flags erected by devout travellers. On the eastern side of the pass the route descends steeply for about 400 metres through fragrant fir and hemlock forests to a stream and a small hotel. The trail then enters open grassy country and descends gently through fields and pastures to the small settlement of **Tragdobuk** (2860 metres). There are hotels here, but they usually close on Saturdays when the owners go to the market in Salleri, about three hours' walk to the south. The trail climbs from Tragdobuk to a huge rock at the head of the valley, then climbs over the ridge to a vantage point overlooking Junbesi (Jun), a splendid Sherpa village amidst beautiful surroundings at 2675 metres. Numbur (6959 metres), known in Sherpa as Shorong Yul Lha ('god of the Solu'), towers over the large green valley above Junbesi.

Junbesi is the northern end of the Sherpa region known as Solu (Shorong in Sherpa). On the whole, the Sherpas of Solu are economically better off than their cousins in Khumbu because the fertile valley here is at a lower elevation, so they can grow a wide variety of crops. In recent years employment with expeditions and trekking parties has done much to improve the lot of both the Solu and Khumbu Sherpas.

A short distance below the ridge is a trail junction marked by a sign:

The big building in front of you is a monastery called Serlo. All are welcome to drop in. We speak some English and (real!) fruit juice are available. You might enjoy seeing the statues, taking some pictures, or asking some questions about the things we do here. We can offer food and lodging also.

If you do not visit the monastery, stay on the main trail and descend on the gently sloping trail to Junbesi, keeping to the left of a huge mani stone, and enter the village near a small hotel. There is an abundance of hotels in Junbesi so it is worth doing a bit of investigation before settling in. Several lodges offer hot showers and other enticements. The *Ang Domi Lodge* is on the left as you enter the village, and the large *Junbesi Guest House* and *Ang Chopa Lodge* dominate the village square. Trekking groups camp either behind the *Everest Trekkers Lodge* or below the village on the banks of the river because the schoolmaster does not allow camping in the school yard. The Junbesi school is one of the largest and most active of the Hillary schools with more than 300 pupils attending classes from primary through to high school.

The region near Junbesi is well worth exploring, and a day spent here can offer a variety of alternatives. To the north of Junbesi, about two hours away, is the village of **Phugmochhe** (3100 metres), where there's a Traditional Sherpa Art Centre. En route to Phugmochhe, a short diversion will allow a visit to **Thubten Chhuling**, a huge Tibetan Buddhist monastery about 1¼ hours' walk from Junbesi.

The trail to Thubten Chhuling starts in front of the Junbesi village gompa and follows the Junbesi Khola upstream, crossing it on a bridge, then makes the final climb to the monastery at 3000 metres. The central gompa is large and impressive and often has more than 450 monks chanting both inside and outside. The monastery expects an offering from any visitor, whether foreign or Sherpa. There is no accommodation or food available here. There are small cells all over the hillside that are the residences of monks and nuns. You probably won't be welcome at these because many of the inhabitants are on extended meditation programmes. The monastery was founded in the late 1960s by Tushi Rimpoche, who travelled to Nepal with many monks from Rongbuk Monastery in Tibet. It is a large, active and impressive religious community.

To rejoin the main trail without returning to Junbesi, follow a yak trail that climbs from Thubten Chhuling to the Lapcha La (3475 metres), a pass marked by a large chorten and many prayer flags. The Schneider map does not show this trail, but it shows Thubten Chhuling as Mopung. The trail is steep, tiring and confusing, so a guide is almost essential. From the monastery, continue up the hill, cross a stream and angle steeply up the side of the ridge. As you near the ridge there is a maze of trails but you should proceed generally south-east and always up. The trail down from the Lapcha La is a herders' trail that drops steeply to the Ringmo Khola, passing through the yards and fields of several houses. It requires about three hours of tough walking to reach Ringmo from Thubten Chhuling.

Day 5: Junbesi to Nuntala
Below Junbesi the trail crosses the Junbesi Khola on a wooden bridge at 2640 metres. Just beyond the bridge there is a trail junction. The right-hand or downhill trail leads to Phaphlu, the site of an airstrip and also a hospital that is operated by the Himalayan Trust. South of Phaphlu is Salleri, the administrative centre for the Solu Khumbu district. The route to Khumbu follows the left-hand trail that leads uphill. After it has climbed high on the ridge, to nearly 3080 metres, there is an excellent view of Everest, Chamlang (7317 metres) and Makalu (8475 metres). This is the first view of Everest on the trek and the peak seems dwarfed by its neighbours. The *Everest View Sherpa Lodge* can provide you with a cup of tea and a comfortable place to contemplate the scene.

The trail turns north, descending through **Salung** (2980 metres), where there are four simple lodges, to the Ringmo Khola at 2650 metres. This is one of the last opportunities to wash clothes and bathe in a large river, as the next river, the Dudh Kosi, is too cold for all but the most determined.

From the river the trail ascends to **Ringmo** where Dorje Passang, an enterprising (and very patient) Sherpa has succeeded in raising a large orchard of apples, peaches and apricots. The fruit has become so abundant that many fruit products – including delicious apple rakshi, apple cider, dried apples and even apple pickles – are available at reasonable prices from the Apple House. At Ringmo the trail joins the 'road' from Okhaldunga to Namche Bazaar rebuilt by several aid programmes between 1980 and 1984. From here to Namche, labourers widened and levelled the trail and rebuilt many bridges. The aid programmes paid for the work with food instead of cash. The result will probably never be a motorable road, but you can now walk side by side with your friends on the wide trail and the route avoids many steep ascents and descents that had characterised the old expedition route.

Just beyond Ringmo the trail passes two mani walls. The second wall hides another unexpected opportunity to get lost. Go to the left of the mani wall, make a U-turn and head uphill. The straight trail heads north through unpopulated country (not even a single house), eventually reaching Ghat in the Khumbu Valley after five days. It is not a practical trekking route; several porters perished on this trail during the approach march for the 1952 Swiss Everest expedition.

Assuming you are on the correct trail, it is a short ascent from Ringmo to **Trakshindo Pass** (3071 metres), marked by a large white chorten. A little above Ringmo is a sign advertising a 15-minute walk to the Trakshindo cheese factory. It is worth a visit. Cheese is available year-round (at the time of research, the price was Rs 75 per kg), but fresh dairy products such as yoghurt *(dahi)* and milk *(dudh)* are available only in summer and early autumn. Food and accommodation is available at the cheese factory and also at the pass itself in three tiny hotels.

A few minutes below the pass, on the eastern side, the trail passes the isolated monastery of Trakshindo, a superb example of Sherpa monastic architecture. The monastery is certainly the most imposing building seen so far on the trek. Two hotels are outside the monastery grounds. The trail then descends through a conifer and rhododendron forest alive with birds. There are a few

shepherds' huts alongside the trail, but the route is mostly in dense forest. The trail crosses several picturesque streams on wooden bridges just before it reaches Nuntala (Manidingma) at 2320 metres. Here there are stone-walled compounds enclosing numerous hotels ranging in quality from mediocre to crummy. There is also one small shop. The largest hotel in Nuntala is the *Sherpa Guide Lodge,* which sometimes does not accept walk-in guests; if so, try the *Danfay, Mountain Trekkers* or the *Reasonable Lodge.*

Day 6: Nuntala to Khari Khola

From Nuntala the descent continues to the Dudh Kosi ('milk river') – the largest river en route since the Sun Kosi. Most of the trail is well graded, though it sometimes passes through terraced fields and the yards of houses, then descends steeply through forests to a chautaara (resting place) overlooking the river. From here it becomes rough and rocky and drops about 100 metres to a suspension bridge across the Dudh Kosi at 1500 metres. The trail now concludes its trip eastward and turns north up the Dudh Kosi Valley. The trail on the eastern side of the river is rough as it crosses debris left by a flood that destroyed a previous incarnation of this bridge in 1985. Beware of stinging nettles *(sisnu)* from here to Chaunrikharka. Local people use nettles as cattle fodder, as a vegetable (they pick them with bamboo tongs) and to make rough cloth. The nettles inflict a painful rash the instant you touch them. At the end of the bridge, turn left and climb through fields of barley, wheat and corn to the sprawling village of **Jubing** (Dorakbuk) at 1680 metres. The people of this village are Rais. Look for signs of Rai culture in this area – the garlands of marigolds that decorate the Dudh Kosi bridge and the traditional bamboo pipes instead of plastic hose for the village water supply.

The trail stays below the village, climbing past the *Amar Hotel* and the post office at its northern edge at an elevation of 1800 metres. Beyond Jubing there is a short climb across a side valley, then a steep climb over a spur.

Everest Region
A Lukla airstrip (SA)
B Khumjung village & Khumbila peak (SA)
C Sherpa (the late Dawa Tenzing) (SA)
D Kala Pattar (SA)
E Namche Bazaar (RI'A)

Everest Region
Top: Mt Everest (SA)
Middle: View above Gokyo (RI'A)
Bottom: Sete monastery (SA)

From this ridge you can see Khari Khola (Khati Thenga) below you and the peak of Khumbila at the northern end of the Dudh Kosi Valley. Khari Khola is predominantly a Sherpa village, though it also has a small Magar community. Descend a bit on a sandy trail, then it's a pleasant walk into the main Khari Khola Bazaar at 2070 metres. There are several hotels here, many of which have recently changed their name. The *Trekkers Inn* and the *Namaste Lodge* are at the western end of town as you enter. In the noisy and congested centre of town are the *Star Lodge*, the *Panorama* and *Nuru Lodge*. No camping is allowed in the school yard, but there is a campsite (for a fee) beyond the village, and another just across the bridge.

You can save a day on the trek by continuing to Bupsa on the same day, then Ghat the following day and Namche the day after that. This is possible because the new trail has eliminated several steep climbs. If you have porters, however, you may have trouble convincing them to change the schedule because tradition dictates that the camping places should be the ones described here.

Day 7: Khari Khola to Puiyan

From Khari Khola you can see a white chorten on the ridge in Bupsa. The trail descends from Khari Khola village and crosses a stream with the same name on a suspension bridge near some water-driven mills at 2010 metres, then makes a steep climb to **Bupsa** (Bumshing) at 2300 metres. There is a hotel halfway up the ridge, a big hotel complex on the ridge and two others, including the *Gauri Shanker Lodge,* about 10 to 15 minutes up the trail. The Bupsa Gompa has been renovated and a lama is usually on hand if you want to visit it.

The trail then climbs steadily, but gently, through forests inhabited by monkeys. The Dudh Kosi canyon is extremely steep here and in many places you can see all the way to the river, 1000 metres below. Climb past *The Knock Lodge* and up to a cleft in the rock, then into another canyon before reaching a ridge at 2900 metres overlooking Puiyan (Chitok), a Sherpa settlement of about 10 houses completely surrounded by forests at 2730 metres. Much of the forest near this village was cut down in the '70s to make charcoal which many hotels and villagers used for fuel in the Khumbu region before kerosene became easily available.

From the ridge, the trail turns almost due east as it descends into the deep canyon of the Puiyan Khola. This portion of the trail was built during the 1984 renovation; in many places it is narrow and exposed, especially where it was blasted out of a vertical rock wall. At one point there is a collection of logs and shrubbery, to give you a false sense of security as the trail crosses a rock face above a precipice. After crossing a large slide area, the trail climbs on a stone staircase, then crosses two streams on wooden bridges. Be careful; at least two trekkers have fallen on this portion of the trail. All the bridges built under the trail renovation programme are identical in design, though many handrails have now been removed and burned for firewood. There is an extensive collection of bamboo huts and a cave formed by a large, overhanging rock that porters use for shelter. A few minutes beyond the cave is a hotel complex and a campsite. The *Tourist Lodge* and its unnamed neighbour are probably the best bets in this very jungly village. There are a few other establishments on the left side of the trail past the campsite. You can also continue to the *Holiday Inn*, the last house in Puiyan, about 15 minutes up the trail.

An old trail goes directly from Khari Khola to Surkhe and avoids the long climb through Puiyan, but it is in disrepair and is subject to rockfalls. There is no food or accommodation on this route and the local people don't use it. There are conflicting reports about the future of this trail. Some people say it is 'cancelled' and others say that it will be improved. This discussion has been going on for as long as I can remember.

Day 8: Puiyan to Phakding

The trail climbs for about an hour after Puiyan to a ridge at 2800 metres then up to another ridge. You can easily recognise Lukla airstrip from here by the multitude of

Everest Region – Flora & Fauna

Trees The chir pine and blue pine are the only two species of pine found in Nepal, so it makes it easy to identify them. The **chir pine** (also known as the long-leafed pine) is a tall, straight conifer that appears on sunny slopes in the subtropical zone. It has long, often bright green, needles in bundles of three, and medium-sized, oval cones.

The **blue pine** is generally found higher than the chir pine, growing at altitudes up to 4000 metres. Blue pines have shorter needles that are bluish green and come in bundles of five. Look for the long, dangling cones that distinguish this pine from the other.

Junipers are found in a dwarfed form in the subalpine domain at altitudes over 4000 metres. Their distinctive foliage should be unmistakable. Junipers in tree form are found around Thami. Look for the fleshy, berry-like fruit in both of these varieties. **Hemlock** and **silver fir** are also well represented in this area. See the 'Around Annapurna – Flora & Fauna' section for help in identifying these trees.

Silver fir

Birds The **golden eagle** is the most common of the resident Aquila eagles. This soaring bird can be distinguished from the griffon and lammergeier, not only by its smaller size, but by its broad wings indented at the base and by its wide-open 'V' profile in flight. These tawny brown birds are often seen in their juvenile plumage, which shows white markings in the wings and base of the tail. Look for hunting pairs in the upper Khumbu region.

Another smaller, but noticeable raptor is the **Eurasian kestrel**, a long-winged, long-tailed falcon that often hovers. The male has a cinnamon-coloured back that contrasts with the grey, black-banded tail, and is mostly pale from the front. Also look for the **goshawk**, the largest of the Accipiter species, which can be seen poaching snow pigeons in this region.

The bold, playful flocks of black birds often seen are from the crow family, the **red-billed** and **yellow-billed choughs**. These birds can usually be seen quite closely without the aid of binoculars due to their fearlessness. The yellow-billed species often pesters trekkers and mountaineers while eating and is so unafraid of humans that it can be virtually snatched from the sky.

Another species observed in large, muted flocks is the **snow pigeon**. Its sooty back provides camouflage while it forages in fallow fields, but the white undersides are exposed when it takes flight. The pheasants are probably the most spectacular birds seen on the ground in the Himalaya. The males tend to be regal in bright, rich colours, while the females tend to be drab-coloured and

large hotels. You might also be able to spot the remains of one of the two planes that crashed there. The trail descends to **Surkhe** (Buwa) at 2293 metres, on a small tributary of the Dudh Kosi. The trail stays above the village, circling it like an expressway. There are a few tea shops near the bridge, but these cater mostly to the porters that serve the Namche market. Beware of Friday and Saturday nights in Surkhe and the nearby villages. The porters to and from the Namche market start to travel at first light, and if there is a full moon, this can be at 2 am, causing an uproar in every hotel.

From Surkhe the trail climbs for about 15 minutes to a junction where a stone staircase leads off to the right. This is the trail to Lukla and it requires about an hour of steep climbing to reach the airstrip. It is not necessary to go to Lukla at this point unless you want to may even seem to be a different species to the undiscerning eye. The religious sanctuary around the Tengpoche Monastery in the Khumbu area creates ample opportunities to observe pheasant species such as the blood pheasant and the impeyan pheasant, the national bird of Nepal. The male **impeyan pheasant** (or Himalayan monal) which appears almost black in poor light, gleams radiantly when bathed in sunlight to reveal an iridescent, multi-coloured plumage. You cannot mistake this bird for anything else; it is frequently seen digging for tubers in the stark winter fields of Khumbu. The **blood pheasant**, on the other hand, is a finely streaked bird with a red and green tinge. Look for the reddish legs in both sexes.

It is also possible to spot the **crimson-horned pheasant** in this same region, considered by some to be the most beautiful of the family, but this bird is more secretive and prefers the cover of forests.

Look for **Tibetan snow cocks** above the tree line on scree slopes or among dwarf juniper. These otherwise grey birds have white underparts with black streaks and are often heard before seen, though they are quite visible in the Gorak Shep area. Also, look for the large (hawk-sized) **raven** that, while on the ground, 'croaks' as it hops and swaggers. This bird prefers the high, dry trans-Himalayan areas.

Mammals Contrary to what one might think, the Himalaya is mostly devoid of deer species. This is not necessarily because of hunting or environmental degradation, but because most of Nepal's deer species prefer the lowland jungles. The muntjak, or **barking deer**, a small reddish mammal with short antlers found up to 2400 metres in temperate forests, has a sharp, single-note alarm call, or 'bark', and is often heard rather than seen.

An even smaller, more unusual 'deer' (about 50 cm tall at the shoulders) is the **musk deer**, a beast taxonomically stranded between deer and antelopes. The male is not only hornless, but has oversized canine teeth that protrude from the mouth. The musk gland, also of the males, is found in the abdomen and due to its value has accelerated the demise of the species. This diminutive deer is very secretive and prefers forest cover near the tree line. Look for this species in the area from Phortse to Tengpoche.

The **Himalayan tahr** is another creature that's difficult to classify, though its niche is that of a 'mountain-goat'. Except during the winter rutting season, these animals are found in two different kinds of herds. The females, young, and inferior males form one group, and the older, more dominant males form the other. The dominant males also are sometimes seen alone and have long flowing ruff and coats and short, curved horns. Tahr are quite visible in Gokyo and the high trail from Khumjung through Phortse to Pangboche. ∎

Himalayan tahr

make a reservation for a flight back to Kathmandu, though you will usually be put on a waiting list at this end. To get to Lukla climb the stone steps and follow the trail up a gully, then onto a ridge. The trail passes several small valleys through a forest that has been severely denuded by woodcutters to a stream. Cross the stream on a wooden bridge near two houses and climb to the ridge. The trail switchbacks through rocks to the foot of the airstrip. You can head up either side of the runway; there are trails just outside the barbed-wire fence. Both routes pass the litter of propellers, wheels, wings and other pieces of crashed planes. Since you don't know whether planes are coming, it's not a good idea to walk up the runway itself.

The Khumbu trail goes north up the steep canyon on a route that a Sherpa contractor blasted out of the rock. The trail crosses the large stream that comes from Lukla, then climbs steeply up some wobbly stone steps past several caves to another stream where there is a small bhatti. It's then a short walk uphill through a jumble of boulders to a series of mani walls, then to two brightly painted houses at the beginning of **Mushe** (Nangbug). More mani stones and walls are along this part of the trail. Mushe blends almost imperceptibly into Chaunrikharka (Dungde), a large village at 2680 metres.

The region from Khari Khola to Jorsale is called Pharak. The Sherpas in this area have slightly different traditions from their neighbours in Solu and Khumbu and have better agricultural opportunities due to the gentler climate in the Dudh Kosi Valley. Pharak villagers raise large crops of corn (maize) and potatoes in summer. They grow wheat, turnips, cauliflower and cabbage in winter and raise herds of cows and yak crossbreeds, as well as sheep and goats.

The major hotel in **Chaunrikharka** is the wooden building on the right of the trail just after the short steep climb from Mushe. The house just before the stone kani (carved arch) over the trail to the north of the hotel (which isn't much of a hotel) also offers food and accommodation. A shop of sorts is further on, around the corner near the first large chorten. There are three more chortens and some wonderful mani walls, then the trail passes through fields to Chablung (Lomdza).

Here the trail from Lukla joins the route and the character of the trek changes abruptly. When flights operate, more than 100 trekkers fly into Lukla every day. If you have walked from Jiri, you will immediately recognise those who have stepped right off the plane – they are cleaner than you and don't smell. From here on, hotels are more frequent, crowded and expensive. Between 1990 and 1993 more than 25 new hotels were built between here and Namche Bazaar.

For the rest of the day, follow the route described in Day 1 of the later Lukla to Everest Base Camp trek to reach Phakding.

Day 9: Phakding to Namche
This is described as Day 2 of the Lukla to

Everest Base Camp trek. You will enjoy the climb to Namche more than those who flew to Lukla because you'll be in good physical condition and have a better understanding of your surroundings.

Lukla to Everest Base Camp

Day 1: Lukla to Phakding
After a long wait at the Kathmandu airport and an exciting landing at Lukla, you'll emerge from the plane to a throng of sherpas, porters and trekking company representatives clamouring for your attention. Nearby will be a group of trekkers clutching their boarding passes waiting to board your plane for the return flight to Kathmandu. Behind a barbed-wire fence will be the mournful faces of those who did not get a space on this flight.

If you are trekking with a group, your sirdar should magically appear and hustle you off for tea while the sherpas organise things for the trek. Sensible trekking companies do not make the final preparations for the trek until they actually see the trekkers get off the plane. If you are on your own, you can retire to one of Lukla's numerous hotels to plan your next move.

The trail from Lukla, elevation 2800 metres, leads north from the airstrip past hotels, *carrom* game parlours, airline offices and shops to the edge of the Lukla plateau. The trail drops steeply for a bit, then descends gently past the Chaunrikharka school to the intersection of the Jiri trail at Chablung.

At **Chablung**, the trail crosses a stream and continues past a few hotels then heads north through a brief stretch of forest. The trail descends steeply to the Kusum Kangru Khola, crossing it on a wooden bridge. A hotel is near the bridge. The peak at the head of the valley is Kusum Kangru (6367 metres), the most difficult of the trekking peaks.

Soon you will probably meet your first

yaks, wonderful shaggy beasts that create lumbering mobile roadblocks on the trail. Technically, what you will meet are mostly *dzopkyos*, male crossbreeds of yaks and cows, but yak is easier to remember and pronounce. Though yaks are uncomfortable at low elevations, Sherpas use them to transport trekking gear between Lukla and Everest base camp. They are relatively tame and well controlled, but beware of waving horns or an out-of-control-yak roaring down a steep hill. Yaks are all-purpose animals. In addition to their role as load carriers, their wool is woven into blankets and ropes, dung is burned as fuel and female yaks give high-quality milk. Being relatives of the cow, the slaughter of yaks is prohibited in Nepal, but when one of these sure-footed animals 'falls off the trail', the tasty meat makes its way into yak steaks and yakburgers in hotels throughout Khumbu. Since 1992 the yaks have been joined by teams of mules that carry loads for both trekkers and the Namche market. Yaks, mules, porters, Sherpas, trekkers and government officials all crowd the trail, often causing severe traffic jams.

Beyond the Kusum Kangru bridge, the trail climbs a bit, then contours around a ridge to **Ghat** (Lhawa), at 2550 metres, on the banks of the Dudh Kosi. Part of this village and much of the old trail was washed away by floods. A new trail climbs through the village to the *Lama Lodge*. People sleep on the funny platforms that you can see in the fields in order to chase bears away from the crops. Cross a ridge and climb a bit above the river, passing several scattered houses, then descend a steep stone staircase to the *Alpine Club Lodge* and camping place. The trail climbs again, then crosses a stream just before the *N D Lodge* and the *Namaste Lodge,* in Phakding. There are many hotels here on both sides of the river at 2800 metres.

In September 1977 an avalanche from Ama Dablam fell into a lake near the base of the peak. This created a wave of water 10 metres high that raced down the Dudh Kosi and washed away large parts of the trail, seven bridges and part of the village of Jorsale, killing three villagers. The drama

was repeated in 1985 when a glacial lake above Thami broke loose. The trail is continually undergoing repair and improvement. In 1993 another glacial lake was still building up near Chhukung, above Dingboche. When the moraine that created this lake breaks there will be yet another flood here, so be prepared for frequent changes in this part of the route.

At Phakding, the first signs of this devastation become apparent. Beyond the *Riverside Lodge* cross the suspension bridge to the *Sunrise Lodge* and two campsites. Below the campsite near the river are the stone cottages of the defunct *Khumbu Alpine Camp* where you can stay in a reasonably comfortable hotel room for about US$10 a night.

Day 2: Phakding to Namche Bazaar
Upper Phakding is just above the Khumbu Alpine Camp and has several bhattis and group campsites. From Phakding the trail continues north up the Dudh Kosi Valley, staying 100 metres or so above the river on its west bank. The trail crosses a small stream where a tiny hotel sits on the opposite side of the wooden bridge. Take the route straight up the hill and do not follow the old level trail that leads to the right. Climb through fields past a few hotels then past a waterfall to **Benkar** at 2700 metres. There are several hotels here just behind the huge mani stone in the centre of the trail. Past Benkar the trail crosses the river on another wooden bridge.

The trail follows a pleasant route alongside the river then climbs to the village of **Chomoa**, the site of an agricultural project that was set up to serve the *Hotel Everest View*, and the *Hatago Lodge*, a creation of eccentric Mr Hagayuki who lived here for almost 10 years without a visa before being deported. He was one of the most colourful of Nepal's many strange characters. All along this part of the trail, villages are interspersed with magnificent forests of rhododendron, magnolia and giant firs. In both the early autumn and late spring, the flowers on this portion of the trek make it a beautiful walk. On the cliffs above the river

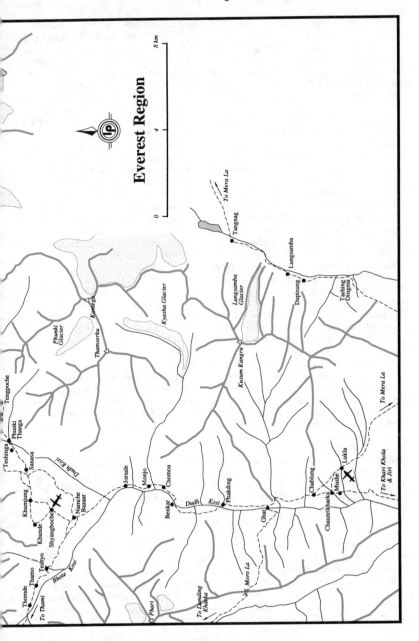

it is possible to see musk deer and Himalayan tahr. If you sit quietly beside the Dudh Kosi you may see water rats swimming in the fast current. When I first heard of these, I assumed they must have been related to the legendary yeti, but they actually do exist in the river here and further upstream towards Thami.

From the lodge at Chomoa, the trail climbs a bit to another hotel (there are more than 100 inns and hotels in Khumbu) and a campsite, then descends steeply into a big valley below Thamserku peak. The trail crosses the stream and climbs out of the valley to **Monjo**. The *Monjo Hotel* (which once had a sign proclaiming itself to be the Monjo Sheraton) is up a little rise at the northern end of the settlement of only three or four houses.

At Monjo the trek enters the Sagarmatha (Everest) National Park. There is an entrance station where rangers check your entrance permit. If you're in the mood for a bit of environmental activism, ask the rangers how much of the money you just paid is allocated for park development, in particular the construction and maintenance of public toilet facilities. The answer, of course, will be 'none'. The staff at the entrance station cannot control the situation, but perhaps if enough people make a fuss, the national park administration will take notice. There are no public toilet facilities in the park except at Tengpoche. Trekking groups dig pits, but the number of available sites is running out fast. Many hotels have toilets, but keep them locked so that only their customers can use them. Porters, as is their habit, hide behind the nearest rock. Many campsites in the Khumbu are disgusting – and a few well-maintained public loos would make a major contribution to the quality of life for both locals and trekkers. You could also pose the same question at the visitors' centre above Namche Bazaar.

Beyond the entrance station, the trail makes a steep rocky descent to a large farm. From this point there are two routes up the next part of the Dudh Kosi Valley. The easiest turns left at the cluster of buildings at the bottom of the hill, crosses the Dudh Kosi

and follows the west bank. A short distance up the river is **Jorsale** (Thumbug) at 2850 metres. Several hotels are packed together along the main street of Jorsale, and you usually have to detour around cows and crowds of porters hanging around the village. The trail follows the river for a while, then recrosses the Dudh Kosi and makes a steep climb to join the trail near the new Namche bridge.

The Jorsale trail involves two bridge crossings, so it may get washed away. If this happens, follow a high trail that stays on the east bank of the river, climbing over a ridge above the Dudh Kosi. Go straight ahead at the trail junction; there is a climb of several hundred metres, a steep descent and another steep climb, all through forests.

Both routes join above the confluence of two rivers – the Bhote Kosi from the west and the Dudh Kosi from the east. The trail crosses the Dudh Kosi on a new suspension bridge high above the river. After a long climb, the trail reaches a ridge where it joins the old (1970s) route. There is a welcome tea shop above the trail junction. It's called the *Everest View*, not to be confused with the Japanese Hotel Everest View which is near Khumjung.

Up the forested valley there is a view of Mt Everest peeking over the ridge of Nuptse. Because clouds usually obscure the peaks in the afternoon, Everest will probably not be visible when you reach this point. Leaving the tea shop the trail climbs less steeply, but still steadily, through forests to more tea shops and a national park forest nursery. Just beyond the nursery is a small spring and a hydraulic ram system that – when it works – pumps water to the national park and army offices on the hill. When the trail turns into a stream, take the right, upper trail to reach the main street of Namche. The left-hand trail leads to the lower pastures of the village.

Namche Bazaar (Nauche), at 3440 metres, is the administrative centre for the Khumbu region and has a police checkpost, the headquarters for Sagarmatha National Park, a bank (you can sometimes change money here), several shops selling items of every

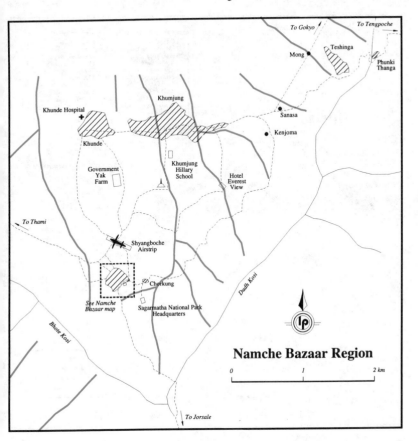

Namche Bazaar Region

0   1   2 km

description and a proliferation of hotels and restaurants. There is even a small bakery and several hotels with hot showers among the 100-odd houses of this prosperous village. You can stock up here on food, film, postcards and souvenirs. You can also buy or rent any trekking or climbing gear that you need. Several trekkers have reported that post cards they sent from the Namche post office actually reached their destinations. On the hill is a dental clinic sponsored by the American Himalayan Foundation that is staffed by two Canadian-trained dental therapists.

It is probably futile trying to keep up-to-date on the latest hotel developments in Namche. The flow of tourist money into Khumbu has encouraged excessive hotel construction in Namche. At any time there are several hotels in various stages of construction, renovation and expansion, so it's difficult to keep track of which one is currently the best. Not counting the small bhattis catering to porters and the homes that offer food and accommodation but do not have hotel signs, there are at least 11 major hotels here. The most popular is Lakpa Dorje's *Trekkers Inn*, which churns out yak steaks by the hundred. One of the largest is Passang

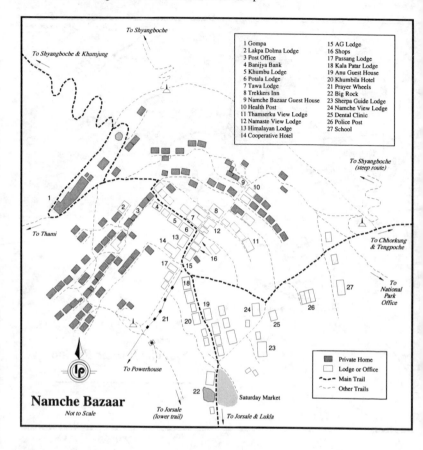

Namche Bazaar

Not to Scale

1 Gompa
2 Lakpa Dolma Lodge
3 Post Office
4 Banijya Bank
5 Khumbu Lodge
6 Potala Lodge
7 Tawa Lodge
8 Trekkers Inn
9 Namche Bazaar Guest House
10 Health Post
11 Thamserku View Lodge
12 Namaste View Lodge
13 Himalayan Lodge
14 Cooperative Hotel
15 AG Lodge
16 Shops
17 Passang Lodge
18 Kala Patar Lodge
19 Anu Guest House
20 Khumbila Hotel
21 Prayer Wheels
22 Big Rock
23 Sherpa Guide Lodge
24 Namche View Lodge
25 Dental Clinic
26 Police Post
27 School

To Shyangboche
To Shyangboche & Khumjung
To Shyangboche & Khumjung
To Shyangboche (steep route)
To Thami
To Chhorkung & Tengpoche
To National Park Office
To Powerhouse
To Jorsale (lower trail)
To Jorsale & Lukla
Saturday Market

Private Home
Lodge or Office
Main Trail
Other Trails

Kami's *Khumbu Lodge*, which offers private rooms including the 'Jimmy Carter slept here' suite. Private rooms are also available in *Namche Hotel* (also called the *Cooperative Hotel*) which is the large low building in the centre of town. Sit in the sun at the *Tawa Lodge* and watch the village activity as you eat freshly baked cinnamon rolls. *Namche Bazaar Guest House* also has a camp ground and features Friday night slide shows. Other popular hotels are the *Thamserku*, *Kala Pattar* and the *Sherpa Hotel*. The owners of the *Khumbila Hotel*, which is near the entrance to the village, have a sister who

married a Japanese, so this hotel is a bit up-market with private rooms and other amenities. It is also the village disco.

A UNESCO-sponsored project introduced electricity to Namche in October 1983. The hydroelectric plant is below Namche and uses the small stream that runs through the village. Each house has two 40-watt lights; some hotels have electric stoves that they can use during the day. All the wiring is underground. Despite technical problems caused by overloading the system, the electricity is working surprisingly well and Namche exudes a certain amount of charm in the evening. The lights go off at 10 pm. There are 125 houses with electricity, including the national park and government offices on the hill and the houses of Chhorkung, above Namche. Four hotels in Namche also have electric stoves. The electricity project is part of an effort to conserve energy and reduce environmental degradation in Khumbu. The large area fenced in by stones above Namche is a forest plantation that is part of the same effort. Note, however, that the electricity supply in Namche could change when the Thamo hydroelectric project comes on line in 1994 or 1995.

There is a lot of trekking equipment available for rent in Namche. If you discover that your jacket or sleeping bag is not warm enough, you can rent one here. There are three competing clocks in Namche. The bank, police and army all sound the hour day and night by striking an empty oxygen cylinder.

Historically, Sherpas were herders and traders. Namche Bazaar was the staging point for expeditions over the Nangpa La into Tibet with loads of manufactured goods from India. On the return trip they brought wool, yaks and salt. Today, Sherpas raise barley, potatoes and a few vegetables in the barren fields of Khumbu, but their economy has always relied on trading. As you walk through Khumbu you will see women excavating potatoes from the deep pits in which they store them during winter to keep them from freezing. Trekking has provided the people of Khumbu with the income to remain here despite the limited indigenous food supply.

Each Saturday there is an important weekly *haat* or market. Lowland people come to Namche to sell corn, rice, eggs, vegetables and other items not grown in Khumbu. During the trekking season, butchers usually slaughter two or more buffaloes each week, so meat is available on Saturdays and Sundays.

Porters carry their loads to Namche Bazaar from villages six to 10 days away (the buffaloes walk themselves) and sell their wares directly. It is an important social event,

as well as the focus for the region's trade. Sherpas from all the neighbouring villages come to purchase food and socialise, and the bazaar becomes a crowded rumpus of Sherpas, government officials, porters and sightseers. It is totally a cash market, in which Sherpas exchange money they have received from trekking or mountaineering parties for the goods they require. The market starts early and is usually finished by noon.

The fun-loving Sherpas often tell the Rais and other people who carry goods to the market that the money comes from Mt Everest, and it is not uncommon to find an unsuspecting lowland porter shivering with cold as he accompanies a trekking party to Everest base camp in search of the free money that tumbles from the highest peak on earth.

Day 3: Acclimatisation Day in Namche

Acclimatisation is important before proceeding higher. This is the first of two specific 'acclimatisation days' that everyone should build into their trek schedule. You can spend the day by taking a day hike to Thami, by visiting Khunde or Khumjung, or by relaxing and exploring Namche Bazaar.

One formality that you must complete before you spend the day gorging yourself on apple pie or getting sloshed on rakshi is registration with the police. The police checkpost is on the hill to the west of Namche near the school. The police officials endorse your trekking permit and enter the details into a register. Sometimes there is a form to fill in and often police require that trekkers sign the register. If so, you will have to go personally to the police checkpost, but often a trekking guide can take your permit and undertake the formalities for you. Bring both your trekking permit and national park entrance ticket for police to examine.

Above the police checkpost, at the top of the hill, is the Sagarmatha National Park headquarters. The visitors' centre here is well worth a visit. It has displays about the people, forests, wildlife, mountaineering and the impact of tourism.

Sagarmatha National Park – Rules & Requirements

At the entrance station to Sagarmatha National Park (Monjo), the rangers check your trekking permit. The rules printed on the back of the entrance ticket are:

Children below 12 years of age shall pay half the entry fee. This permit is nontransferable and good for one entry only. You enter the park on your own risk. His Majesty's Government shall bear no liability for damage, loss, injury or death. Trekking is an acceptable challenge, but please do not:

- litter (dispose it properly)
- remove anything from the park
- disturb wildlife
- carry arms and explosives
- scale any mountain without proper permission
- scale any sacred peaks of any elevation

Please keep all the time to the main trek routes. Please be self sufficient in your fuel supply before entering the park. Buying fuel wood from local people or removing any wood materials from the forest is illegal. This will apply to your guides, cooks and porters also.

Park personnel are entitled to arrest any person in charge of having violated park regulations or search his belongings.

For further information visit Park headquarter or ask any park personnel.

National Parks Family Wishes Your Trip Pleasant.

If you have a video camera, the national park administration assumes that you are involved in commercial film-making and charges you US$100 for a filming permit. If you refuse to pay for the permit, they will keep your camera here and return it when you leave the park.

Local people are not required to use firewood to cook food for trekkers. If you are staying in hotels and wish to minimise your impact, you should patronise only those few hotels that cook exclusively on electricity, gas or kerosene. Hotels do this in the Annapurna region, but because there are no firm rules here, many hotels in Khumbu still rely on huge piles of firewood. Theoretically the national park rules will eventually prohibit this.

It is not difficult to buy kerosene to use as a fuel, but it's almost impossible to find petrol or cooking gas. Kerosene is usually available in Namche at the Saturday market in 16-litre tins that are carried by porters from the roadhead south of Okhaldunga. The price is very negotiable depending on supply and demand. Lesser quantities are available from shopkeepers in Namche throughout the week. If you plan to use kerosene, bring along a filter. Dirt and water can mess up stoves, and both are present in most of the locally available kerosene.

Lukla General Store operates a kerosene depot out of the Yeti Lodge near the RNAC check-in counter in Lukla. It supplies kerosene and stocks stoves, jerry cans, lanterns and repair parts – available for either sale or rent. It maintains a smaller supply in Namche Bazaar, but Lukla is the main source of kerosene in Khumbu. Kerosene is a nasty porter load. It sloshes around and throws people off balance; and plastic jerry cans and tins always leak and cause chemical burns and irritate the skin of the porters. The Lukla kerosene depot transports kerosene to Lukla by plane and helicopter and has been quite successful in maintaining a reliable supply. The price is high because of the exorbitant cost of the flights. In 1993 the cost was Rs 35 per litre in Lukla and Rs 40 per litre at the Namche depot compared to the official rate of Rs 9.75 per litre in Kathmandu. The price is not unreasonable, however, as it costs Rs 3 to Rs 4 per litre per day to carry kerosene from Jiri by porter. When trekking with a group, you or your sherpas will at some stage need to make a side trip to Lukla to arrange a kerosene supply. ∎

The name of the region above Namche, but below the national park headquarters, is **Chhorkung**. This settlement has grown a lot, and now has several hotels and camp-sites. By far the largest is the *Hotel Sherwi Khangba* which has its own chorten.

Some of Namche's strangest visitors are the runners in the Everest Marathon, an annual event in late November that follows a route from Gorak Shep to Tengpoche, then to Namche and a loop out to Thamo before returning to the finishing line in Namche. Runners complete the 42-km (26-mile) run in a respectable 4½ to five hours, but remember that they made a slow ascent in order to acclimatise.

Day 4: Namche Bazaar to Tengpoche

There is a direct, reasonably level, route from Namche Bazaar to Tengpoche that starts from Chhorkung, winds around the hill to the tea and souvenir shops of Kenjoma and joins the trail from Khumjung. A more varied trip is via a slightly longer route visiting Khumjung, the largest village in Khumbu, and Khunde, its smaller neighbour. From Namche Bazaar it is a steep one-hour climb to the Shyangboche airstrip (3720 metres), which serves the Hotel Everest View. In the early morning you might see the spectacular landing (or the more spectacular take off) of a Pilatus Porter STOL aircraft at Shyangboche. Expensive seats on the six-passenger plane to Kathmandu are sometimes available at short notice. Ask about seats either at the airstrip or the Hotel Everest View.

There are a few tea shops near the airstrip, but there is a water problem here, so it isn't a good place to stay for the night. From the airstrip it is a 20-minute walk to the hotel, which provides excellent views of Everest and Ama Dablam. The hotel was closed for many years, but was refurbished in 1990. You can get a cup of coffee or tea or an extravagant meal here. Breakfast is US$7, lunch US$12 and dinner US$16, plus tax. Rooms are US$135 per person per night with an extra charge for oxygen or a pressurised room. Just outside the door of the posh hotel is a bhatti that offers cheaper food and lodging.

A trail descends from the hotel to **Khumjung** village (3790 metres) or you can walk from the airstrip directly to Khumjung. To take the direct trail from the airport, head for the chorten at the top of the hill and follow the trail down through the forest. In the morning, just follow the schoolchildren

from Namche to Khumjung, at the foot of the sacred peak of Khumbila (5761 metres).

The Khumjung Gompa possesses what is said to be the skull of a yeti or abominable snowman. Sir Edmund Hillary, village headman Khunjo Chumbi, Desmond Doig and Marlin Perkins took this relic to the USA in 1960 to be examined by scientists. The scientists said the scalp was made from the skin of a serow, a member of the antelope family, but the yeti legend still continues.

Also in Khumjung is the original Hillary school which has succeeded in providing an excellent primary education for many of the children of Khumbu. In 1983 the Himalayan Trust expanded the school to include a high school. Sherpa children no longer have to go to boarding school at Salleri, a week away, to complete their education. It is only a short detour from Khumjung to Khunde, the site of the Khunde Hospital, built in 1966 and still maintained by the Himalayan Trust. The *Nima Lodge* is below the gompa in Khumjung and there are several other lodges in lower Khumjung.

From Khumjung the trail goes westwards down the valley, continuously passing picturesque mani walls and chortens. After a short descent it meets the main Namche Bazaar to Tengpoche trail. Beyond a few mani stones is another group of tea stalls. This settlement, called **Sanasa** by the locals and 'schlockmeister junction' by trek leaders, is inhabited primarily by Tibetans. There is always an extensive display of Tibetan (and made-in-Kathmandu) souvenirs to tempt you. Bargaining is very much in order. The trail descends gradually to Teshinga, then steeply to Phunki Thanga, a small settlement with three small hotels and several water-driven prayer wheels on the banks of the Dudh Kosi at 3250 metres.

It is a two-hour climb to Tengpoche. From Phunki Thanga the trail climbs steeply at first, then makes a gradual ascent through forests and around mani stones as it follows the side of a hill up to the saddle on which Tengpoche Monastery sits at 3867 metres, in a clearing surrounded by dwarf firs and rhododendrons. The view from this spot, seen to best advantage in the morning, is rightly deemed to be one of the most magnificent in the world. Kwangde (6187 metres), Tawachee (6542 metres), Everest (8848 metres), Nuptse (7879 metres), Lhotse (8501 metres), Ama Dablam (6856 metres), Kantega (6779 metres) and Thamserku (6608 metres) provide an inspiring panorama of Himalayan giants. Kantega means 'horse saddle' and from Tengpoche it's clear how this peak got its name.

The following sign used to appear near the monastery guesthouse:

I am happy to welcome you to Tengpoche. This is the religious centre of the whole 'Sherpa-land', in fact the entire Solu-Khumbu area.

A very modest rest house has been built on the far end of the meadow facing Chomolungma (Mt Everest).

It has been erected with the funds collected from friends and visitors who have come to this sacred and beautiful place. If you wish, you may contribute to our meagre funds to enable us to make it more comfortable when you come again, for we hope you will. Anything you wish to give will be gratefully accepted.

While you are a guest at Tengpoche, whether you stay in the rest house or in your own tents, I wish to request you to observe the few rules in observance of the Divine Dharma. Please do not kill or cause to kill any living creature in the area of this holy place. This includes domestic fowls and animals, as also wild game.

Please remember that this holy place is devoted to the worship of the Perfect One, and that nothing should be done within these sacred precincts which will offend or cause to hurt those who live here in humility and serenity. May you journey in peace and walk in delight, and may the blessings of the Perfect One be always with you.

Nawang Tenzing Zang-Po
The Reincarnate of Tengpoche

The sign has long since disappeared and has been replaced by a fancy carved sign directing visitors to the New Zealand-built *Tengpoche Trekkers Lodge*, a part of the Sagarmatha National Park development. No longer is it necessary to endure the simple lodging offered by the monks; now you can sit around a stove burning charcoal (from Puiyan, outside the national park) and write comments in the guest book either praising or damning the lodge concept.

In addition to the national park lodge, there are only two other facilities at Tengpoche. The gompa-owned *Tengpoche Guest House*, north of the monastery grounds, has dormitory accommodation. The *Tashi Delek Lodge* across the field from the gompa is small and usually full, but Passang Thongdup is a personable and helpful hotelier. There is another unnamed hotel near the Namaste, but it caters primarily to porters.

If you have visited Tengpoche in years past and remember the raucous evenings at the Monastery Lodge, you'll be disappointed; it is no more. The gompa charges a fee for each tent erected at Tengpoche and a monk comes around with a receipt book to be sure that you pay. It is one of the few sources of revenue for the monastery, which supports about 50 or 60 monks, so it isn't reasonable to argue about this charge. Several trekking companies donate money to the monastery each year and in return receive the use of certain camping sites. The monks won't let you camp in these places. The small *Lhotse Lodge* is 15 minutes' walk north of Tengpoche.

There is also a camping place and two hotels at Devuche, about a 20-minute walk from Tengpoche. Ang Kanchi's lodge is more homely than the large green-roofed *Sherpa Guide Lodge*. These may be better choices when Tengpoche is filled to capacity.

Tengpoche (many older maps spell it as Thyangboche, but the preferred, phonetic spelling is Tengpoche) was founded by Lama Gulu, a monk from Khumjung, on the instructions of the abbot of Rongbuk Monastery. Construction of the main temple building was completed in 1919. An earthquake destroyed the gompa in 1934, killing Lama Gulu. The temple was rebuilt a few years later and the remains of the founding lama were buried inside the gompa. On 19 January 1989 a fire devastated the monastery. Many items of the monastery's extensive collection of books, paintings and religious relics were saved, but the entire gompa building was destroyed. The Sherpa people of Khumbu, with help from many international organisations, have raised funds for the reconstruction of the gompa building. Construction began in April 1990 and the new gompa was rededicated in September 1993. The statues in the gompa are of Pawa Chenrizig (Avalokitesvara) and Guru Rimpoche (Padmasambhava). The chapel is dominated by a statue of Sakyamuni (Buddha) that is almost four metres tall.

Day 5: Acclimatisation Day in Tengpoche

You will do much better in the high country if you spend another day acclimatising. You can make a day hike to Pangboche, climb up the hill behind Tengpoche for good mountain views or explore the monastery itself.

Tengpoche is the largest and most active monastery in Khumbu, but it is not the oldest. Sherpas believe that Buddhism was introduced into Khumbu towards the end of the 17th century by Lama Sange Dorje, the fifth of the reincarnate lamas of the Rong-phu (or Rongbuk) Monastery in Tibet, to the north of Mt Everest. According to legend, Lama Sange Dorje flew over the Himalaya and landed on rocks at Pangboche and Tengpoche, leaving his footprints. He is thought to have been responsible for the founding of the first gompas in Khumbu, at Pangboche and Thami.

The gompas of Khumjung and Namche Bazaar are of a later date. None of these were monasteries. Their priests were married lamas and there was no monastic community with a formal organisation and discipline. The first monasteries were established as offshoots of the Nyingmapa (Red Hat) sect monastery of Rong-phu in Tibet at Tengpoche and Thami (at about the same time), and young monks were sent there to study. Tengpoche's charter bears the seal of the abbot of Rong-phu. A nunnery was later founded at Devuche, just north of Tengpoche. Trakshindo was established in 1946 by a lama from Tengpoche.

A library and cultural centre behind the gompa was designed by the abbot to cater to both Tibetan scholars and trekkers. The plan

is to develop an extensive library of books on religion, culture and history in several languages. A school building adjoining the gompa provides facilities for about 30 young monks to pursue their religious education. Technically, only the abbot of the monastery is called a lama; the Sherpa word for a monk is *tawa*.

Day 6: Tengpoche to Pheriche

From Tengpoche it's a short, steep and muddy descent to Devuche through a forest of birches, conifers and rhododendrons. Because of the ban on hunting at Tengpoche, you can often see almost tame blood pheasants and Nepal's national bird, the Himalayan monal or impeyan pheasant which lives only at high altitudes. Only the male is colourful, with a reddish tail, shiny blue back and a metallic green tinge and pure white under its wings. It appears almost iridescent when seen in sunlight. Another common bird in this region is the snow pigeon, which swoops in great flocks above the villages of Khumjung, Namche and Pangboche. The crow-like birds that scavenge any food that you might drop (I have even seen them fly away with a full packet of biscuits that they have stolen) are red-billed choughs and occasionally ravens. The Sherpas call both birds *goraks*. Near Gorak Shep you are likely to see Tibetan snow cocks racing happily down the hillside. High above you may see goshawks, Himalayan griffons, golden eagles and lammergeiers circling on the updraughts from the mountains. In the early morning and just before dusk you may see musk deer, especially in the forests below Tengpoche, leaping like kangaroos.

Descend on a muddy trail to **Devuche**. The few houses and the gompa of this tiny village are off in the trees to the west, and the nunnery (which is not at all enthusiastic about visitors) is up the hill to the east. From Devuche the level trail passes many mani walls in a deep rhododendron forest. Watch the leaves curl up in the cold and open in the morning when the sun strikes them. After crossing the Imja Khola on a steel bridge, swaying a terrifying distance above the river at a spot where the river rushes through a narrow cleft, the route climbs past some magnificently carved mani stones to **Pangboche** at 3860 metres. Just before the village are two chortens, a kani and a resting place. Just east of here is a monument where you can see the footprint of the patron saint Lama Sange Dorje preserved in stone.

Pangboche is the highest year-round settlement in the valley. The Pangboche Gompa is the oldest in Khumbu and once had relics that were said to be the skull and hand of a yeti. These items were stolen in 1991, so another chapter of the yeti legend continues unsolved. Pangboche is actually two villages, an upper and a lower village. On the way to the Everest base camp the lower route is best, but on the return trip, use the upper trail and visit the gompa, 120 metres above the lower village. There are three hotels in lower Pangboche, one at each end of the village and one in the centre – good choices for lunch.

From Pangboche the route enters alpine meadows above the tree line. Most of the vegetation is scrub juniper and tundra. During the summer the hillside is covered with wildflowers, including edelweiss. At Shomare there is a tea shop, then the trail passes several yak herders' goths as it ascends on a shelf above the river to Orsho where there is a small hotel. Beyond Orsho the trail divides. The lower, more important-looking trail, leads to Dingboche while the trail to Pheriche goes up to the left, through the front yards of a few herders' huts, over a stone wall and climbs a small ridge before descending to the Khumbu Khola, crossing it on a wooden bridge. From the bridge it is a 10-minute walk, usually in the wind, to Pheriche at 4240 metres. Pheriche is windier, so it feels colder than most places in Khumbu. Be sure that you carry your warmest clothing on this day.

A trekkers' aid post operates at Pheriche, supported by the Himalayan Rescue Association (HRA) and Tokyo Medical College. A Western physician is usually in attendance during the trekking season. This establishment and the doctors who operate it specialize in the study and treatment of altitude sickness and strive to educate trekkers in the dangers of too fast an ascent to high altitudes. The doctors give lectures every day, usually at 3.30 pm. The aid post also lends books and sells HRA emblems, T-shirts and mani stones to raise money. Visit the clinic if you have even the slightest problem with altitude. Even though the doctors are volunteers, the HRA has considerable expenses, so they charge for consultations and treatment.

Pheriche is a labyrinth of walls and pastures. There are five hotels, including the *National Park Lodge* which is an on-off affair depending on who has the contract to operate it. The biggest hotel is Nima Tsering's *Himalayan Hotel*, a two-storey place with a tin roof. Other hotels are semi-permanent buildings which have evolved from mud huts with a tarp on the roof into more substantial structures that are forever expanding.

Be careful when you sit down in these crowded places – that comfortable-looking cushion in the corner is likely to be a baby wrapped up in blankets. The *Snow View Hotel* has a mountaineering equipment shop. The usual jumble of new and used climbing equipment is for sale and there is often an unlikely collection of expedition food available, such as Bulgarian stews, Russian borscht, French snails or American granola bars – depending on which country recently had an Everest expedition.

Day 7: Acclimatisation Day in Pheriche

The most important key to acclimatisation to high altitudes is a slow ascent. Therefore it is imperative that you spend an additional night at Pheriche to aid the acclimatisation process. This is the second of the mandatory acclimatisation days on this trek.

You can spend the day in many ways. You may wish to declare a rest day and relax in camp or you may wish to do some strenuous exploring. It is a short hike to the small Nangkartshang Gompa, a climb of about 400

Yetis

The yeti is a large human-like mammal, though taller than humans, that walks with a lumbering gait. It often stands upright, but usually moves on all fours. Its body is covered with thick black or brown fur and its feet are big. Its diet consists of fruit, vegetables and small mammals. It lives in caves and forests near the snow line in Nepal and Tibet, is very elusive and probably hibernates during the winter like a bear. It has a high piercing yell and its body gives off a garlic-like smell. Its hair covers its eyes, it has no tail and the female has long pendulous breasts. No yeti has been photographed at close range, but it has been seen by several people. Its tracks and spoor have been seen and photographed. It has a close relative that lives in the forests of north-western USA.

The word yeti is derived from the Tibetan *yeh*, 'snow valley' and *teh*, 'man'. The concept of an elusive man-like animal that lives in the high country is reflected in the various names that have been applied by people from many different cultures. Tibetans call it *ye-teh*, *mah-teh* or *mehton kangmi*, a name that translates as 'abominable snowman'. In the USA it is known as *Sasquatch* or *bigfoot*.

Before you dismiss all this as fiction, consider some of the sources.

The first recorded sighting of a yeti by a Westerner was in 1889 when Major L A Wassell saw footprints in north-eastern Sikkim. Since that time yeti footprints have been found by many mountaineering expeditions in Nepal and Tibet. The most famous footprint was the one found by Eric Shipton during the Everest reconnaissance in 1951. Both Lord Hunt and H W Tilman found yeti tracks on the Zemu Glacier in Sikkim in 1937. The late Tenzing Norgay once saw a yeti. Tim McCartney-Snape and Greg Mortimer found unexplained tracks near the summit of Everest in 1984. Don Whillans saw a yeti on Everest in 1970 and Reinhold Messner claims to have encountered a yeti in Tibet in 1986.

Several expeditions have set out to find the yeti, including three expeditions in the 1950s sponsored by the late Tom Slick, a Texas millionaire. The Himalayan Scientific & Mountaineering Expedition during 1960-61 included yeti hunting as part of its objective. It was this expedition that arranged for Sir Edmund Hillary to carry a yeti skull to the USA for examination and study.

Of course, all this evidence is inconclusive, and the mountaineering and scientific communities include a large number of nonbelievers. In *High in the Thin Cold Air* Hillary expresses his scepticism of Sherpa sightings of yetis. 'We found it quite impossible to divorce the yeti from the supernatural. To a Sherpa, the ability of a yeti to make himself invisible at will is just as important of a part of his description as his probable shape and size...'

Be on the lookout for yetis in the high country of Nepal and Tibet, particularly in Khumbu, Gokyo and the upper Hongu. In 1992 the people of Mustang reported a herd of yetis in Tibet, just north of Mustang and produced yeti hair that was collected by Peter Matthiessen. In 1993 two Tibetans told me that they had seen yetis near Mt Kailas, so this may be another place to search for them. If you do spot one, or want more information, contact the Bigfoot Information Centre in the USA, ☎ 1-800 BIGFOOT. ■

metres above the village. From this vantage point there is a good view to the east of Makalu; at 8475 metres it is the fifth-highest mountain in the world.

A more strenuous trip is to climb the hill to Dingboche, then hike up the Imja Khola Valley past Bibre to **Chhukung**, a small summer settlement at 4730 metres. The views from Chhukung and further up the valley on the moraines towards Island Peak (6189 metres) are tremendous. The great southern face of Lhotse towers above to the north, while Amphu Lapcha (a 5780-metre pass) and the immense fluted ice

walls that flank it dominate the horizon to the south.

To the south-west, the eastern face of Ama Dablam provides an unusual view of this picturesque peak. This hike is one of the highlights of the trek. It is a fast trip back down the valley to Pheriche for the night. There are hotels in both Chhukung and Dingboche that can provide lunch.

Day 8: Pheriche to Lobuje

The trail ascends the broad, gently sloping valley from Pheriche to **Phalang Karpo** at 4340 metres. In many places the trail crosses small streams on boulders. Look back down the valley from Phalang Karpo to see how much elevation you have gained. The views of Tawachee and Cholatse (6440 metres) are particularly good from this portion of the trail as it passes through country reported to be the habitat of the snow leopard and yeti. Ama Dablam is seen from a different aspect here and is hardly recognisable. The true top of Kantega is visible far to the left of the prominent saddle seen from Tengpoche. Beyond Phalang Karpo the trail climbs steeply onto the terminal moraine of the Khumbu Glacier then contours down to a stream, crossing it on a bridge just before the village of **Duglha** (4620 metres). There is a tea shop near the stream and two others a bit higher that specialize in lunch.

From Duglha the trail climbs higher on the moraine to a row of stone monuments in memory of six Sherpas who died in an avalanche during the 1970 Japanese skiing expedition on Everest. There are several other monuments to climbers who have perished since then. The collection now includes more than 18 memorials, mostly for Sherpas. The trail then drops a bit and follows the western side of the valley to Lobuje, a summer village that boasts several hotels at 4930 metres. The New Zealand National Park advisers built a lodge at Lobuje that has 24 bed spaces and is run on contract by Karma Sherpa. The *Above the Clouds Lodge* accommodates 18 and the *Kala Pattar* and *Sherpa* hotels provide a few more beds. The sherpas and porters that accompany trekking groups further crowd the hotels when they come in for tea or rakshi (which can have a dramatic effect at this elevation).

Everything is expensive in Lobuje. Prices are at least double those in Namche, but there is still a lot of variety thanks to expeditions that have jettisoned their supplies. Among the goodies that were available in 1993 were Becks beer at Rs 120 a can and imported Snickers bars for Rs 80. If you are travelling with a group, the sherpas will race ahead to stake out a good campsite and get the use of one of the two herders' huts as a kitchen. You can almost always rely on finding food and accommodation (though it may be crowded) at Lobuje, but you will certainly need a warm sleeping bag – there is usually no bedding available and only a limited supply of mattresses. The toilet facilities here are minimal and the mess that this has caused is truly horrible. In contrast, the sunset on Nuptse, seen from Lobuje, is a memorable sight.

Day 9: Lobuje to Gorak Shep

The first section of the trail from Lobuje follows the western side of the broad Khumbu Valley and ascends gently through meadows beside the glacial moraine. A pyramid-shaped Italian research station that looks like an invading spaceship is in the first side valley beyond Lobuje. Fortunately, you cannot see it from the trail. The station is open from March until mid-November and has communications facilities that could be used to contact Kathmandu in an emergency.

The ascent becomes steeper and rougher as it crosses several side moraines, although the trail is usually well defined. In places, however, an active glacier is under the moraine, so the trail is constantly changing. Route-finding techniques here include looking for stone cairns as markers and watching for traces of yak dung – a sure sign of the correct trail.

After rounding a bend in the trail, the conical peak of Pumori (7145 metres) comes into view. On the lower slopes of this mountain a ridge extending to the south terminates in a small peak. This peak, Kala Pattar, meaning 'black rock', is 5545 metres high and provides the best vantage point for viewing Mt Everest. Kala Pattar is actually a Hindi name. Legend has it that the late Dawa Tenzing accidentally named the peak when he accompanied the first foreigner, Jimmy Roberts, to the top. Roberts and Dawa Tenzing communicated in Hindi, not Nepali. You can easily make the ascent of Kala Pattar from Gorak Shep in the afternoon or the following morning.

The trail makes a short descent onto the sandy flat expanse of Gorak Shep (5160 metres). This was the base camp for the 1952 Swiss Everest expedition. In 1953 the British Everest expedition called this 'lake camp'. Gorak Shep has a small lake that is usually frozen and several monuments to climbers who have died during various Everest expeditions. The carved stone in memory of Jake Breitenbach of the 1963 US expedition and the monument for Indian ambassador H Dayal, who died during a visit to base camp after the 1965 Indian expedition, are northeast of the lake.

Most people usually reach Gorak Shep by lunch time, and spend the rest of the day resting, but if you are not tired by the altitude, you can climb Kala Pattar or go to the base camp in the afternoon. There are two herders' huts at Gorak Shep near the lake, but they are small and dirty and are only emergency shelter. The *Yeti Tea Shop*, run by Ang Lamu Sherpani, has a few bunks in its one-room building. Ang Lamu often shuts up shop during the coldest months from December to February and returns to Khumjung, so it is best to inquire at Lobuje before counting on this facility during winter. It should be possible to find food and shelter here at most other times during the trekking season. The best plan of all is to start early in the morning and go from Lobuje to Kala Pattar via Gorak Shep and return to Lobuje for the night, avoiding the necessity of staying at Gorak Shep.

Day 10: Gorak Shep to Lobuje

It is impossible to explain the discomfort of high altitude to someone who hasn't actually experienced it. Most people have an uncomfortable, often sleepless, night at both Gorak Shep and Lobuje, despite the extra time taken for acclimatisation. By descending 300 metres to Lobuje, or better yet, to Pheriche, most people experience an immediate improvement, so it is really not worth spending an additional night at 5160 metres.

Mornings are usually sparkling clear and the climb of Kala Pattar is one of the most rewarding parts of the trip. It is a steep ascent

up the grassy slopes west of Gorak Shep to a shelf at the foot of Pumori. Even from this low vantage point the entire Everest south face is visible as well as the Lho La (the pass between Nepal and Tibet, from which George Leigh Mallory looked into Nepal in 1921 and named the Western Cwm), Changtse (the northern peak of Everest) and most of the West Ridge route climbed by Unsoeld & Hornbein in 1963. Those familiar with the accounts of expeditions to the Tibetan side of Everest will be able to spot the North Ridge and the first and second steps, prominent obstacles during the attempts on the mountain in the 1920s and '30s. Continuing to the top of Kala Pattar, more of the peak of Everest itself comes into view, and a short walk north from the summit of Kala Pattar on the ridge towards Pumori will allow an unobstructed view all the way to the South Col.

The walk to base camp is about a six-hour round trip, possibly more unless an expedition in progress has kept the ever-changing trail in good condition. The route follows the Khumbu Glacier, sometimes on the moraine and sometimes on the glacier itself. The walk is especially intriguing for the views of the 15-metre-high seracs of ice, a feature peculiar to Himalayan glaciers.

Everest base camp is not actually a specific site. Various expeditions have selected different locations for a semipermanent camp during their assault on the mountain. Some of the sites that expeditions have used as base camps are identifiable from debris on the glacier at 5360 metres or more. The trip to base camp, while fascinating, is not as spectacular as the ascent of Kala Pattar because there is no view of Everest itself from base camp.

It is difficult to go to both base camp and Kala Pattar in a single day. If you wish to do both, use the afternoon of the day at Gorak Shep for one trip and the next morning for the other. The exhaustion and lethargy caused by the altitude limits many people to only one of the possible options. The descent to Lobuje is easy, but seems endless because of the many uphill climbs from Gorak Shep.

The night, however, will be much more comfortable than the previous one.

Day 11: Lobuje to Dingboche
To go to Dingboche, retrace your steps back down to Duglha, then go straight up the hill from the bridge to reach an upper trail, staying high above the valley floor, past the yak pastures at Dusa to a chorten at the head of the Imja Valley. From here the views are great – you can easily recognise Island Peak because its name is an apt description. Makalu is the greenish-grey peak visible in the distance over the pass to the right of Island Peak. From the chorten descend to Dingboche at 4410 metres, following the trail as it traverses east into the valley. The high pastures in this region are sometimes referred to as 'summer villages'. Sherpas with homes lower in the valley own small stone huts in the higher regions and occupy them in summer while their herds of yaks graze in the surrounding pastures. A few crops, especially barley, are also grown in these high fields. Dingboche is a more pleasant place than Pheriche, and the mountain views are outstanding, so many tourist facilities have recently been developed here. There are four large hotels, including Sona Hishi's *Sonam Friendship Lodge* that – according to Bob Peirce – plays Vivaldi as wake-up music. Dingboche, incidentally, is the only place in Khumbu where barley is grown. There are several real hotels in Dingboche and others in houses that have hotel signboards. There are also two hotels in Chhukung, several hours up the valley.

Day 12: Dingboche to Tengpoche
The route from Dingboche descends the Imja Khola Valley, then crosses the Khumbu Khola on a wooden bridge and climbs to rejoin the upward trail at some stone huts near Orsho. Following the trail downhill, it is easy to make a detour and visit the upper part of Pangboche and the village gompa, then continue to Tengpoche for the night. If you want to avoid the crowds below, you can choose from four hotels in upper Pangboche.

While ascents at high altitudes must be slow, you may safely descend as fast as you wish.

Day 13: Tengpoche to Namche Bazaar
The route descends to Phunki Thanga, then ascends the ridge towards Namche Bazaar. The direct route to Namche turns south just above Sanasa, passes Kenjoma and traverses along the side of the ridge. This avoids a lot of climbing, but it's a long walk in and out of side valleys. An alternative route through Khumjung allows a visit to either the Hotel Everest View or Sherpa villages before the steep descent to Namche, but involves climbing an extra 200 metres. In Namche Bazaar you will have a last opportunity to buy (mostly) fake Tibetan jewellery from a dozen Tibetan merchants who spread their wares beside every campsite and alongside the trail at the oddest places.

Day 14: Namche Bazaar to Lukla
It's a long walk from Namche to Lukla, but you are probably in good shape by now. If not, break the trip into two days with a night at Chomoa or Phakding.

From Namche, the steep descent back to the Dudh Kosi at Jorsale is a bit rough on the knees, but the warmer climate offers a good opportunity to finally shed down-filled jackets and woollen jumpers. Don't lose your national park permit or pack it away; you must check out of the park at Jorsale and show the permit to prove that you duly paid for the use of the national park facilities. You must be at the airport at Lukla the night before your flight to reconfirm reservations if you have these – your seats will vanish if you do not reconfirm reservations. The trail from Jorsale to Lukla follows the upward route as far as Chablung, then turns off above the village of Chaunrikharka towards Lukla.

There are signs beyond the stream at Chablung pointing you in the direction of Lukla. The broad trail leading uphill to the left climbs steadily past a few bhattis and the school, then through scrub forests above the school and houses of Chaunrikharka. After a steep final climb there is a collection of houses and bhattis in Tamang Tole, a new

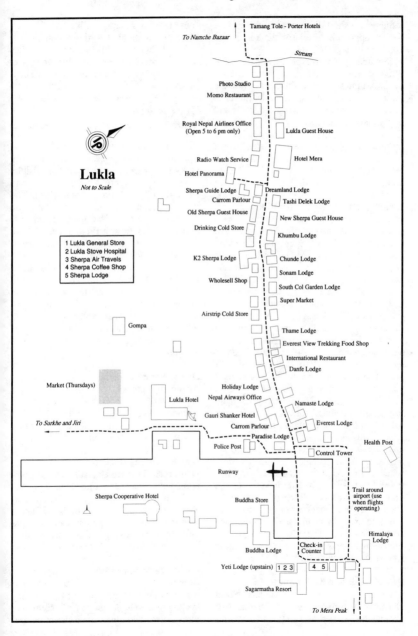

settlement a short distance from the airport. As you approach the airstrip the houses and hotels rapidly proliferate.

Situated high above the river on a shelf at 2800 metres, Lukla is another classic paradox in determining altitude because the runway is on a slope and there is a difference of almost 60 metres between the lower and upper ends of the runway.

Lukla has a good choice of hotels. The up-market *Sherpa Cooperative Hotel* halfway down the airstrip offers rooms for about US$10 a night. The hotel's Tibetan-style dining room is the centre of Lukla's social life and is also the source of all the rumours about flight operations. *Sagarmatha Resort* near the airport check-in building is the newest, fanciest and most expensive at US$25 per night. *Buddha Lodge* and *Paradise Lodge*, both near the airport, also have private rooms, hot showers and a reasonably efficient short-order kitchen. Most other hotels offer dormitories and less extensive (but cheaper) menus.

The RNAC office is open for an hour in the evening – usually from 5 to 6 pm, but sometimes from 6 to 7 pm. There is usually a sign announcing the office hours. You can reconfirm flights only during this period. If you are not present the night before the flight you probably will lose your seat. The radio message telling the RNAC staff how many flights are scheduled for the following day usually doesn't come until after the office closes. This adds an atmosphere of mystery and intrigue to the proceedings. In fact, the airline does not prepare the actual flight schedule for each day until about 7 pm when they know where each plane ended up for the night. Check-in begins early and can be chaotic. If your innkeeper or trekking agent offers to check you in for the flight, take advantage of this. There isn't much to do at Lukla other than wait for planes or talk about when the plane will come.

Day 15: Lukla to Kathmandu
The trek to Hile (see the Eastern Nepal chapter) becomes attractive because it avoids the pile-up at Lukla and explores some unusual country unlike any that you have seen on the first portion of the trek.

The flight from Lukla to Kathmandu takes 35 minutes and is a jarring return to the noise, pollution, confusion and rush of a large city.

To Gokyo

The trek to Gokyo offers an alternative to the traditional trek to Everest base camp. From Gokyo, more of Everest itself is visible, though from a slightly greater distance than from Kala Pattar above Gorak Shep. The mountains are more spectacular, the Ngozumpa Glacier is the largest in the Nepal Himalaya and from a ridge above Gokyo, four 8000-metre peaks (Cho Oyu, Everest, Lhotse and Makalu) are visible at once. The view of the tremendous ice ridge between Cho Oyu (8153 metres) and Gyachung Kang (7922 metres) is one of the most dramatic panoramas in Khumbu. There are many options for additional exploration and high altitude walking, including the crossing of Cho La, a 5420-metre-high pass into Khumbu.

Day 1: Namche Bazaar
Acclimatisation is essential for this trek. It is easy to get too high too fast and succumb to altitude sickness. Only after a minimum of three days in the Namche-Khumjung region is it safe to begin this trek.

Day 2: Namche Bazaar
Don't rush. The Himalayan Rescue Association doctors have determined that you must acclimatise before you begin the Gokyo trek. There are lots of things to do here. Take a hike to Thami, visit Khumjung or eat apple pie in Namche. Hiking will help acclimatisation more than the apple pie, however.

Day 3: Namche to Phortse Thanga
Climb the hill to Khumjung and descend to the west of the village down the broad valley leading to the Dudh Kosi. The Gokyo route turns north, climbing above the more fre-

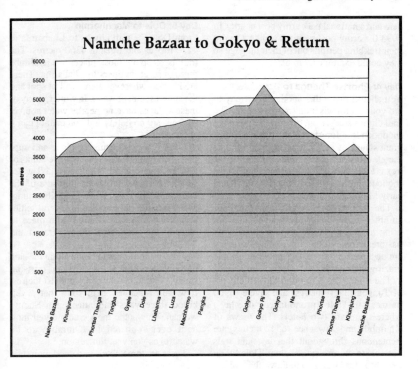

Namche Bazaar to Gokyo & Return

quented route to Tengpoche and Everest base camp.

There is a choice of routes in the beginning: the yak trail which climbs gently, but traverses a long distance around the ridge; or the steep staircase-like trail made of rocks embedded in a narrow cleft in a large boulder. The Sherpas claim that the steeper trail is better – for exercise. The two trails soon join and continue towards a large chorten on the ridge top at 3973 metres. This ridge descends from Khumbila (5761 metres), the abode of the patron god of the Khumbu region. Khumbila (or more correctly Khumbu Yul Lha) translates as 'Khumbu area god'. On thangkas and other monastery paintings this god is depicted as a white-faced figure riding on a white horse. Numbur, the mountain that towers over Junbesi and the Solu region, is the protector

god of that area and has the Sherpa name Shorong Yul Lha ('Solu area god').

Near the chorten are three teahouses at the settlement of **Mong** (Mohang). This is said to be the birthplace of the saint Lama Sange Dorje, the reincarnate lama of Rongbuk Monastery in Tibet who introduced Buddhism to Khumbu. From the ridge at Mong, the trail descends in a series of steep switchbacks down a sandy slope to the Dudh Kosi. There is an excellent camping spot at Phortse Thanga, near the river *(thanga* means 'riverside') at 3500 metres, just before the bridge that provides access to Phortse, an isolated village of about 60 houses. It is possible to go much further in a single day from Khumjung – as far as Tongba or Gyele – but it doesn't serve much purpose and it can be dangerous because of the rapid increase in elevation. There are two hotels here and a national park army post nearby. In 1993 the army post required trekkers to dig their trekking permits out of their luggage so they could examine them here.

Day 4: Phortse Thanga to Dole

You should make this another short day to aid your acclimatisation to the altitude. The trail climbs steeply out of the valley through rhododendron forests which give way to fragrant stands of juniper and large conifers as the elevation increases. This portion of the trek is especially beautiful in spring when the rhododendrons are blooming (late April and early May at this elevation).

The trail passes through many kharkas, summer settlements used when sherpas bring herds of yaks to graze in these high pastures. Some of the villages in this valley are occupied as late as December by people grazing their herds.

The route passes through the settlements of Tongba (3950 metres) and Gyele (3960 metres) to Dole (pronounced 'doe-lay') where there are two hotels. The views of Khumbila and Tawachee (6542 metres) are tremendous throughout the day, and it is possible to climb a ridge behind Dole for an even broader view up and down the valley.

Day 5: Dole to Machhermo

From Dole the trail climbs to Lhabarma at 4220 metres and Luza at 4360 metres. The trail is steep in most places as it climbs through scrub junipers to Lhabarma. There are kharkas wherever there is a flat spot and the slightest hint of water. In winter, many of these villages have no nearby water source, so there are no hotels and you cannot camp at them.

Luza is a good camping place and supports two hotels because it is on the banks of a large stream and has a year-round water supply. All the kharkas on this side of the valley are owned by people from Khumjung. Many families have houses in several settlements and move their herds from place to place as the grass becomes overgrazed and the snows melt.

The trail continues to climb along the side of the valley, high above the river, crossing sandy spurs to Machhermo at 4410 metres. It was in Machhermo in 1974 that a yeti killed three yaks and attacked a Sherpa woman. This is the most credible yeti incident ever reported in Khumbu, so be watchful as you visit this region.

There are three hotels and good mountain views in Machhermo.

Yaks

We tend to oversimplify the many manifestations of the yak into this single word, yet it is only the full-blooded, long-haired bull of the species *Bos grunniens* that truly has the name yak. The female is called a *nak* by Sherpas and *dri* by Tibetans.

Yaks and naks are crossbred with local cows or Tibetan bulls, which the Sherpas call *lang* and Nepalese call *khirkoo*. A nak-lang or yak-cow crossbreed is a *dzopkyo* if it's a male, and a *dzum* if it is female.

A dzum is prized for its butterfat-rich milk which Sherpas use to make cheese and butter. The male crossbreed, the infertile dzopkyo, is (relatively) docile and is used to transport loads and as a plough animal. Most of the 'yaks' seen along the trails of Khumbu are in fact dzopkyos. There are numerous other names for crosses between cattle and naks and for second-generation crossbreeds, but the yak, nak, dzum and dzopkyo are sufficiently confusing for this lesson in yak husbandry. ■

Day 6: Machhermo to Gokyo

Beyond Machhermo the trail climbs a ridge for an excellent view both down the valley to Kantega and up towards Cho Oyu (8153 metres). Beyond the ridge, the valley widens as the trail passes through Pangka (one hotel here) at 4390 metres, then descends to the river bank before beginning the climb on to the terminal moraine of the Ngozumpa Glacier.

It is a steep climb up the moraine, switchbacking alongside the stream to the first small lake at 4650 metres, where a family of Brahminy ducks has resided for many years. The trail now becomes almost level as it follows the valley past a second lake, known as Longponga, at 4690 metres and finally up a boulder-strewn path to Gokyo at 4750 metres. Gokyo is a kharka of seven houses and walled pastures on the shores of a large lake. The setting is reminiscent of an abandoned summer resort. There are five hotels at Gokyo; the *Gokyo Resort*, originally built by the 1991 Australian ballooning expedition, boasts a sun room.

Day 7: Gokyo

The views in the Gokyo region are tremendous. For the best view, climb Gokyo Ri, the small peak above the lake. This peak of 5350 metres is sometimes called Kala Pattar (not to be confused with the Kala Pattar above Gorak Shep, though the views are similar). It is a two-hour climb to the top of the peak, providing a panoramic view of Cho Oyu, Gyachung Kang, Everest, Lhotse, Makalu, Cholatse and Tawachee.

Those with more time and energy can make a trip up the valley to another lake, marked with the name Ngozumpa on the maps, or even beyond to a fifth lake. There are several small peaks in this region that offer vantage points for the surrounding peaks and views of the Nangpa La, the old trade route into Tibet.

Day 8: Gokyo to Phortse

You can descend to Phortse in a single long day, or you can spend the night at Thare or Konar on the way to make the day less strenuous. Rather than retrace the upward route, follow the eastern side of the valley on the downward route to gain different views of Khumbila and to enjoy somewhat warmer weather, because the sun stays on these slopes longer in the late afternoon.

If you have mountaineering experience and are well equipped, you can make a challenging side trip across the Cho La to the Khumbu Valley. About halfway between the first and second lakes a trail leads off across the moraine to the east. This is the route to the 5420-metre Cho La (or Chhugyuma Pass) into the Everest region. The pass is not difficult, but it is steep and involves a glacier crossing on the eastern side. Allow three days from Gokyo to Pheriche on this high altitude route. An ice axe, crampons and a rope are often necessary for negotiating the small icefall at the foot of the glacier on the other side of the pass, although in ideal conditions there are no technical problems and there is a trail of sorts in the rocks beside the icefall.

The western approach to the pass varies in difficulty depending on the amount of snow. It can vary from a rough scramble up a scree (gravel) slope to an impossibly technical ice climb. The best conditions are when there is snow soft enough for kicking steps up the slope. The pass is not possible for yaks and sometimes not suitable for heavily laden porters, but you can send the porters and yaks around the mountain via Phortse and they can meet you in Lobuje or Pheriche three days later. If you plan to cross the pass, spend a night at Chhugyuma and the following night at Dzongla on the other side. There is no teahouse or shelter in Chhugyuma or Dzongla.

The route to Phortse retraces the upward journey back to Pangka, then turns east and climbs to **Na** (4400 metres), the only year-round settlement in the valley, across the terminal moraine of the Ngozumpa Glacier. There are two scruffy tea shops here, but nothing resembling the quality of the hotels in the rest of Gokyo. The descent from Na along the eastern side of the Dudh Kosi Valley is straightforward, with a few ups and downs where landslides and streams have carved side valleys. The trail enters Phortse at its upper end. There are camping places in the potato fields of this large village. The *Khumbu Lodge* is near the top of Phortse village and the *Namaste Lodge* is lower down.

Day 9: Phortse to Namche Bazaar

A slippery trail descends from Phortse to the bridge at Phortse Thanga and rejoins the original route from Khumjung. It is easy to reach Namche Bazaar, or even go beyond to Jorsale, for the night.

An alternative route from Phortse leads up a steep, exposed trail with spectacular views to upper Pangboche, where it joins the trail to the Everest region. There is also a trail that descends steeply from Phortse to the Imja Khola and climbs through forests to Tengpoche.

To Thami

Thami lies at an elevation of 3800 metres near the foot of a large valley to the west of Namche Bazaar. The village is the departure point for crossing Tesi Lapcha, the 5755-metre-high pass into the Rolwaling Valley. Only experienced, well-equipped and well-informed parties should attempt Tesi Lapcha because frequent rockfalls near the pass present a very dangerous complication.

The trail to Thami starts above the village of Namche Bazaar and leads west past a large array of prayer flags and mani stones. The carved mani stones all the way to Thami are some of the most complex and picturesque in Nepal. Contouring around the hill on a wide and almost level trail, the route passes through Gonglha and Drama before reaching the large village of Thamo. Just before Thomde, a trail leads uphill to the monastery at **Mende**. A few Westerners are studying here under the tutelage of an English-speaking lama.

At **Thomde** are the remains of a dam and office buildings for a hydroelectric project

that was destroyed during the 1985 flood. The hydroelectric scheme is being rebuilt upstream and will some day generate electricity from the Bhote Kosi to provide lights for all the homes of Khumbu.

From Thamo a steep new trail climbs along the side of the valley, then makes a sharp descent to a good suspension bridge. The paintings on the rock cliff before the bridge are of Guru Rimpoche and Green Tara. Cross the bridge to Thami at 3800 metres, a total trek of about three hours from Namche Bazaar. There is also a lower, old trail that makes a short climb followed by a descent to the river, crossing on a wooden bridge. You can see the new Austrian-sponsored hydroelectric project near the river before you make a steep ascent beside a stream to Thami. The new, higher trail is better.

Thami is in a large valley with good views of the snow peaks of Teng Kangpoche (6500 metres) and Kwangde (6187 metres) to the south. To the north of the village is a police checkpost that doesn't allow trekkers to travel further north on the trade route between Nepal and Tibet. From here the trail leads to Nangpa La, the 5741-metre pass crossed by trains of yaks carrying goods between the two countries. Once a major crossing point for Tibetan refugees, the Nangpa La is now used primarily by Sherpas for the trade of yaks and wool.

About 150 metres above Thami is the Thami Gompa, a picturesque monastery set amongst the many homes of lamas and lay people. It's perched on the side of a hill overlooking the valley. This is the site for the spring celebration of the Mani Rimdu festival, held about the middle of May each year. During Mani Rimdu many Sherpas set up temporary hotels near the gompa and offer *momos* (meat-filled dumplings), *thukpa* (noodles) and endless quantities of tea, chhang and rakshi.

If you are in good shape and well acclimatised, it is possible to make the trip to Thami and back to Namche Bazaar in a single day, but it's more worthwhile to spend a night in Thami to see the peaks in the clear morning. This side trip provides a good acclimatisation day before proceeding to higher elevations. There is a hotel in Thami and another in Thamo.

Escape via Lamidanda

Occasionally the pile-up of people at Lukla becomes unmanageable. Imagine 350 people vying for seats on planes that carry 15 passengers. Many people, having completed a great trek, make themselves miserable by fighting for seats out of Lukla. It's a helpless feeling to be in a place where no amount of influence or money can make the planes come, but you did come to a developing country. If you expect things to operate on time (or sometimes to operate at all), you should head for the mountains of Switzerland.

Unbelievable things happen when people flip out at Lukla. I've seen the station manager chased around the airport by a tourist brandishing an ice axe. I've seen chanting mobs outside the airline office. I've seen rock fights on the airstrip. Twice I've seen planeloads of police arrive in Lukla to get things under control; and I've heard endless tales of woe from people who had to be at work the following day (they weren't). If it gets like this – usually in late October and early November, and occasionally at other unpredictable times – the only way to maintain your composure is to be sure your name is somewhere on the reservation list. Assign one of your sherpas (or better yet, your innkeeper or the Lukla representative of your trekking company) to ensure that other names are not slipped in ahead of yours, then retire to a kettle or two of chhang to consider your alternatives.

You can wait. It might be a day (I've seen 14 flights to Lukla in a single day) or as long as two weeks. You can walk to Jiri. At a normal pace, it's six days to Jiri where you can get a bus to Kathmandu. If you walk 10 to 12 hours a day (you save days in Nepal by walking a longer time each day, not by

walking faster) you could reach Jiri in four days, perhaps even three. You can walk to the airstrip at Phaphlu, two long days (or three comfortable days) from Lukla. It is an appealing walk, but it's uncertain that it will hasten your return to Kathmandu because there are only six flights a week and seats are in heavy demand for government officials stationed in nearby Salleri.

You can walk from Phaphlu south to Janakpur in six days. The 10-day trek to Dhankuta described in this book is also a route to escape from Lukla. Another alternative is described here. You can walk to Lamidanda, an airstrip five days to the south. The important thing is not to make yourself, and everyone else, miserable by fighting and bemoaning your fate. Instead, do something positive. You can always go back to Namche Bazaar for a few days and wait for things to clear up, or you can climb the ridge behind Lukla, where there are some wonderful high meadows and a good view of Kariolung peak.

The Lamidanda escape route works in either direction. You can walk to Khumbu after a flight to Lamidanda. Although I have called it a five-day trek, it can be done (if the porters agree) in four days. The opposite direction, however, will certainly require five days because of the long initial climb to Aiselukharka. (See the Dharan to Makalu map in the Eastern Nepal chapter.)

Day 1: Lukla to Bupsa
A trail leads off the end of the Lukla airstrip and descends to join the trail to Jiri. The descent continues on the Jiri trail to Surkhe, then the trail climbs to Puiyan, crosses the pass and descends again to Bupsa. See Days 7 and 8 of the Everest trek description.

Day 2: Bupsa to Wobsa Khani
The trail descends steeply to Khari Khola (2070 metres). If you did not walk from Kathmandu, this will be your first view of Nepal's Middle Hills and their extensive terracing. A bazaar is held in Khari Khola on Wednesdays if you need to stock up on provisions. Between here and the next bazaar at

Aiselukharka only dal bhat is available. The trail climbs out of Khari Khola at a higher level than the Jiri route, then turns south about 20 minutes beyond the village. The path climbs over a ridge, then contours south, high above the village of Jubing. The route passes through scrub forests and a few cultivated fields to Jube at 2100 metres, then through forests of rhododendron and oak. The trail descends, crosses the Thana Khola, then climbs steeply out of a side valley. There are a few houses and herders' huts, and for the most part the trail is reasonably level (for Nepal). The Rai village of Wobsa Khani is about two hours beyond the Thana Khola at an elevation of 1800 metres. Below Wobsa is Tamba Khani ('copper mine') where you can see the smelter and buildings of the mine that gave the town its name.

Day 3: Wobsa Khani to Lokhim
Porters carry oranges and rice from here to the market at Namche Bazaar. Except for those porters, few locals or trekkers use this trail, so there are no trekkers' hotels and few bhattis along the route. From Wobsa Khani the trail stays fairly level as the valley becomes wider, then it descends a bit to Waku, a Chhetri village at 1500 metres. The trail descends further through forests to Suntale at 1100 metres and drops steeply to the Hinku Khola, crossing it on an old suspension bridge at 980 metres. This is the same river (also called the Inukhu) that is crossed on Day 3 of the trek to Hile.

After a steep climb on a series of steps cut into the rock, the trail reaches a ridge at 1290 metres and descends a bit to the Rai and Chhetri village of Khorde. The trail descends further through trees to the Hongu Khola, crossing it on a temporary log bridge at 900 metres. The remains of an impressive cantilever bridge are here; it looks as if this bridge collapsed years ago. There is some trade up the Hongu from this point, and people who live in villages as far away as Bung travel down the valley to Aiselukharka on bazaar days. Climbing steeply past the herders' huts of **Utha**, the trail reaches a ridge at 1590 metres. It may be necessary to camp in Utha,

because it's another 1½ hours from Utha to Lokhim. Lokhim, a huge Rai village with beautiful stands of bamboo, is in a large side valley at an elevation of 1800 metres. This being Rai country, it is usual to encounter dhamis (shamans) walking the remote trails, or at least to hear the echoes of their drums in the distance.

Day 4: Lokhim to Ilim
Lokhim is a large village, almost 45 minutes' walk from beginning to end. From the eastern end of the village the trail climbs through Chuwa towards the pass at Deorali (2400 metres). The Schneider *Dudh Kosi* map covers this part of the trek, but does not show this section of trail. The trail contours around the Chuwu Khola Valley before it ascends steeply towards Deorali. A tea shop, the first since Khari Khola, is at the pass. Descending from the pass, the route travels through Harise, a Sherpa village at 2300 metres, then descends a steep stone staircase to **Aiselukharka**, a large town strung out along a ridge at 2100 metres. Aiselukharka has shops and government offices and a very large bazaar on Saturdays. The trail descends the ridge south to Ilim at 1450 metres.

Day 5: Ilim to Lamidanda
It is a steep descent through tropical country to the Ra Khola. A bridge is upstream at 800 metres, or you can wade the river. This is a region of intense rice cultivation. The trail follows a complex and intricate route through a network of dikes and irrigation canals alongside rice paddies. It makes a steep ascent up the Pipal Danda, then contours around the valley between 1200 and 1400 metres. The route is through terraced fields and has little shade – it will probably be very hot. Finally, the trail passes a school and follows a ridge out towards the airport. The Schneider map does not show either this trail or Lamidanda. Near the terminal building at 1200 metres there is a hotel that serves outstanding chicken curry. From Lamidanda there are flights several times a week to both Kathmandu and Biratnagar.

Local people say that it's a two-day walk

to Bhojpur and a one-day walk to Okhaldunga from here. Those timings are probably accurate. Once, however, the Lamidanda people terrified a trekking group by all agreeing that it required at least 12 days to walk to Lukla (where none of the villagers had ever been). There is nothing to see or do in the Brahmin village of Lamidanda, except wait for a plane. There is a Buddhist shrine about a day's walk away that might provide some diversion if you get stuck here for a long time. Lamidanda is the air-traffic control point for this part of Nepal, so the radio is in constant use here (unlike Lukla) and it is easy to find out about flights.

Barahbise to Jiri

It takes a bit of the continuity out of the Everest trek when you drive all the way to Jiri. The following route from Barahbise to Shivalaya avoids the Jiri road entirely, passing through country that trekkers rarely visit. Few people, including locals, follow the route I have described here, so villagers will probably not be able to point you in the right direction. A guide (or a basic knowledge of Nepali) is almost essential for this trek. There are so many trails leading in every direction that it is impossible to document all the junctions and alternatives. This description is only a suggestion. You can modify it in many ways once you are on the trail. There are some bhattis on this route, but none from Biguti to Mali, so you will be more comfortable if you carry food on this trek.

Day 1: Barahbise to Khartali
Barahbise is a 10-minute drive beyond Lamosangu on the east bank of the Bhote Kosi. Just south of Barahbise, a small branch of the Sun Kosi joins the Bhote Kosi ('river from Tibet') to form a much larger river, the Sun Kosi. This river flows south, then east across Nepal to join the Arun River near Biratnagar.

Barahbise is a crowded bazaar at 820 metres, inhabited mostly by Newars and Chhetris. The route begins on an unpretentious set of stone steps between two shops and begins a climb that will eventually be more than 2400 metres of uphill walking. Passing through a few scattered Gurung villages, the route soon enters country inhabited mostly by Tamangs. Most of the route is in open cultivated country with a few pipal trees, surrounded by stone chautaaras, providing welcome shade on hot days. The trail climbs steeply to Parati, a small village at 1300 metres. Beyond Parati the trail becomes less steep, and even has a few level stretches, as it continues through heavily cultivated country to the large Tamang village of Khartali at 1680 metres.

Day 2: Khartali to Thulo Tingsang
Beyond Khartali the trail continues to traverse eastward along the ridge, high above the Sun Kosi. Most of the travellers on this trail are porters carrying rice, wood and slate for roofing down to Barahbise. The trail climbs a ridge to a small bhatti and a rushing stream at 2290 metres. After the ridge, the trail enters deep rhododendron forests and makes some short climbs and descents as it weaves in and out of wooded side valleys. Below the trail and across the valley there are houses splashed across the hillside, but above the trail there is mostly forest. Rounding a ridge, the trail offers a view of the large, spread-out village of **Dolangsa**, a Sherpa village with clean whitewashed houses, each surrounded by fields of corn, potatoes, wheat and barley. From the ridge, the trail enters another side canyon (watch for stinging nettles) and crosses a stream on a bridge hewn from a huge tree – a reminder of what the forests of this region must have been like before a rising population forced the cutting of large amounts for firewood. A short distance beyond the bridge, take the left trail which makes a steep uphill climb to the Sherpa village of Dolangsa, at 2380 metres. There is no hotel here, but you can probably find accommodation in a private home. High above the village is a gompa.

Beyond Dolangsa the trail climbs through rhododendron forests past a few kharkas used during summer as pastures for herds of cattle. The pastures are uninhabited during the trekking season and make excellent campsites if you have a tent. The trail then begins a steep climb to the pass, crossing the Tingsang La at 3320 metres. The pass affords good views in every direction. On a clear day Gauri Shankar (7145 metres) dominates the horizon and peaks are visible from Chhoba-Bhamare (6108 metres), a rock spire in the west, all the way to Pigpherago (6730 metres) and Numbur (6959 metres) in the east. A short distance below the pass is Thulo Tingsang, a large kharka at 3260 metres. The views from this camp are as good as from the pass. During summer, many people live in this high pasture and there is even a small shop and hotel. In the winter, people remove the roofs from the stone huts and carry their household effects to lower permanent settlements. During the trekking season there is no food or accommodation here.

Day 3: Thulo Tingsang to Amatal
From Thulo Tingsang ('big Tingsang') the trail descends through conifer and rhododendron forests to Sano Tingsang ('small Tingsang'), another kharka at 3000 metres. The trail continues a gradual descent (a very pleasant walk – most descents in Nepal are steep and rough) through forests and past small kharkas to a stream at 2230 metres. A small paper factory is here and you'll see frames with Nepalese paper drying in the sun. A few minutes below is another stream crossed by a covered bridge at an elevation of 2100 metres. From this point a rough, steep trail climbs 400 metres to Bigu at 2500 metres. Bigu is a Sherpa village with a large gompa and a nunnery. It is a strenuous side trip that involves a steep descent to rejoin the main trail. The direct route continues down the river valley through Tamang, Chhetri and Kami (blacksmith caste) villages with slate-paved courtyards, to Amatal at 1680 metres.

Day 4: Amatal to Saunepani
It is a long but pleasant walk along the lower reaches of the Sangawa Khola to its confluence with the Tamba Kosi. Stay on the south

bank of the river, passing through Kopai and a few other small villages. Much of the route is in pine forest. Villagers have cut off the lower branches of most trees for firewood – a traditional method of avoiding total deforestation. The trail ascends and descends over ridges and spurs and finally makes a steep descent to the Sangawa Khola, crossing it at 1220 metres. The route follows the north bank of the river, making a few ups and downs, but generally staying level and passing a few side streams, two of which flow from beautiful tropical waterfalls. Not only is the trail level, but the route is almost totally uninhabited during the afternoon's walk – two very unusual things in Nepal. Finally the route reaches the Tamba Kosi (here called the Bhote Kosi) at the village of Saunepani (Sigaati) at 1000 metres. The village has a few houses and a small shop.

Day 5: Saunepani to Serukapti
Walk south for about an hour along the west bank of the Tamba Kosi. This trail, if followed in the opposite direction, leads to the Rolwaling Valley after a week of walking. The trail is level as it follows the river south to Biguti, across the Tamba Kosi on the east bank at 950 metres. A small shop is on the west bank and a wonderful old chain-link suspension bridge spans the river. These bridges are becoming rare in Nepal, being replaced by new cement and steel cable bridges, so the swinging bridge high above the river offers an exhilarating and unusual river crossing. About five minutes south of the bridge on the west bank is a new trading centre, **Gumbu Khola**. The ground floor of every house here is either a shop or hotel. If you are looking for an excuse to delay crossing the chain bridge, reinforce your courage with a glass of rakshi from this village.

Once you are on the east side of the river at Biguti, turn north and cross a small stream, then climb the ridge to the north-east. The trail climbs a bit and turns east as it passes through the Tamang villages of Jaku (1460 metres) and Yarsa. Unlike the brief walk along the Tamba Kosi, which is a main trade thoroughfare, the trail is now on a rarely used route that climbs through forests and small villages towards the head of the valley. Because this is an out-of-the-way trail, there are places where it is steep and narrow. Route-finding is also a problem. Ask for the trail to Serukapti when you reach a dead end in someone's front yard. The trail becomes better and more defined as it passes through Sarsepti, a large Tamang village at 1760 metres, then continues to climb through beautiful forests of oak and rhododendron with an abundance of ferns and orchids. After more climbing, you will reach the Sherpa village of Serukapti at 2300 metres.

Day 6: Serukapti to Mali

From Serukapti the trail continues up into forests. A trail junction is about 15 minutes beyond the village. The lower (right-hand) trail goes to Jiri and the upper (left-hand) trail crosses Hanumante Danda and bypasses Jiri. Since one of the purposes of all this uphill climbing is to avoid the motor road, there is no good reason at this point to go to Jiri, so continue up the valley to a large kharka, a beautiful high altitude meadow surrounded by big trees, at 2300 metres. Climbing through a forest of large moss-covered pines, the trail finally emerges at the top of the ridge at 2900 metres, high above Jiri. There are many trails here. One trail descends to a cheese factory and then climbs back to the ridge above Mali. The most direct trail runs along the ridge to the east for a while, then drops slowly below the ridge top, making another easy descent past a few slate mines before reaching the Patashe Danda and descending on a broad trail (stay on the ridge) to Mali, a Sherpa village at 2200 metres. Here the route joins the trail from Jiri and continues to Shivalaya and Bhandar.

Annapurna Region

Central Nepal is dominated by the Annapurna Himal and the village of Pokhara. There are three major trekking routes in central Nepal: to Jomsom, to Annapurna Sanctuary, and a circuit of the Annapurna Himal itself. Pokhara is also a good starting place for short treks of one to four days, including the 'Royal' trek, which I have described in this chapter. Mustang is also geographically a part of the Annapurna region, but because treks to Mustang are subject to special restrictions, I have described it in the separate chapter on restricted area treks.

About two-thirds of the trekkers in Nepal visit the Annapurna region. The area is easily accessible, hotels in the hills are plentiful, and treks here offer good scenery of both high mountains and lowland villages.

INFORMATION
Annapurna Conservation Area Project (ACAP)

ACAP was established in 1986 under the guidance of the King Mahendra Trust for Nature Conservation. The project encompasses the entire Annapurna range, more than 7600 sq km. In an innovative approach to environmental protection, it was declared a 'conservation area' instead of a national park. A large number of people live within the protected region, but traditional national park practices dictate that few, if any, people reside within park boundaries. In an effort to avoid any conflicts of interest, ACAP has sought the involvement of local people and has emphasized environmental education.

Projects include the training of lodge owners, with an emphasis on sanitation, deforestation and cultural pride. They have trained trekking lodge operators and encouraged hoteliers to charge a fair price for food and accommodation. ACAP encourages the use of kerosene for cooking throughout the region, and requires its use above Chhomrong in the Annapurna Sanctuary and

on the route between Ghandruk and Ghorapani. ACAP is supported by a 'conservation fee' of Rs 650 that is collected from all trekkers who obtain trekking permits for the Annapurna region.

ACAP has encouraged the construction of toilets throughout the area; use them no matter how disgusting they are. ACAP has also made provision for the supply of kero-

---

A Request from ACAP

Please assist in our efforts to maintain the natural and cultural equilibrium along the trekking route by following our 'minimum impact' code during your Himalayan sojourns:

- Avoid the use of non-biodegradable items, especially plastic mineral water bottles. Iodine drops are available at any ACAP office of drug store.

- Dispose of your trash responsibly. Use ACAP recycling and compost bins wherever available; take your used batteries home to your country; and incinerate all other wastes.

- Use ACAP toilets en route. If your trekking agency carries its own portable toilet tent, make sure the pit is covered on departure. Please encourage your porters to use toilet facilities as well.

- Insist on using kerosene for cooking and heating purposes. This should apply for your porters as well. If possible, avoid lodges and tea shops that use wood for fuel, and only take hot showers with solar-heated water.

- Trek gently. Do not trample or collect the flora of the region. It is illegal to hunt in the area or buy items made from endangered species. Please do not remove any religious artefacts from the area.

- Respect the culture by wearing modest clothing, asking permission before taking photographs, avoiding public displays of affection, behaving appropriately while at religious sites, and respecting local customs in your dress and behaviour.

- Encourage young Nepalese to be proud of their culture. ∎

Village woman, Annapurna Region (RI'A)

Annapurna Region
Top: Annapurna South (SB)
Middle: Dhaulagiri (GB)
Bottom: Last light on Machhapuchhare (RI'A)

Annapurna Region

A Ngadi village (SA)
B Marpha village (SA)
C Trail signs, Tatopani (SA)
D Muktinath (SA)
E Looking toward the Annapurnas (TW)

Annapurna Region
Top: Terracing near Pokhara (TW)
Bottom: Moonrise over Manaslu Himal (TW)

sene in those parts of the conservation area where the use of firewood by both trekking groups and hotels is prohibited.

In Pokhara, visit ACAP's Trekkers Information & Environmental Centre next to the Hotel Lakeside. In addition to providing information, the centre sells iodine, solar battery chargers and other products that can help you to protect the environment while you are trekking. There is also a 'trekkers meeting board' and a battery drop-off centre.

Books
The Moated Mountain (Hurt & Blackett, London, 1955), by Showell Styles, is a very readable book about an expedition to Baudha peak. Styles makes poignant cultural observations as he treks to the mountain.

Annapurna (Jonathan Cape, London, 1952), by Maurice Herzog, is a mountaineering classic that describes the first conquest of an 8000-metre peak. There is a good description of the Annapurna region, including Manang, and a visit to the Rana court of Kathmandu in 1950.

Annapurna South Face (Cassell, London, 1971), by Christian Bonnington, describes the beginning of a new standard of mountaineering in Nepal and provides an excellent description of the problems of organising an expedition.

Maps
ACAP has produced a contour map of the entire Annapurna region with detailed advice on the back. These maps are available in bookshops in Kathmandu and Pokhara for Rs 300 each.

There are no detailed, topographic maps of this region similar to the Schneider maps of Everest and Langtang, though one is in the works. Cartoconsult (Austria) has produced an expensive (Rs 400) 1:250,000 colour map titled *Annapurna Satellite Image Trekking Map* that shows the major trek routes. The US army maps that cover the region are NH 44-16 *Pokhara*, and NH 45-13 *Jongkha Dzong*.

There are many locally produced maps available in Nepal, some printed and some

blueprints; most are titled *Around Annapurna*. The best of the lot is the 1:150:000 Mandala map. The 1:320,000 map and trail description produced by Nepa Maps has numerous mistakes and missing landmarks.

ACCOMMODATION
Pokhara
All treks in the Annapurna region either start or end at Pokhara, the main city in central Nepal. The trek to Jomsom begins in Pokhara and the Around Annapurna trek ends there. The town is known for its lake, Phewa Tal, and its large collection of inexpensive hotels and restaurants along the lakeside. A spectacular panorama of Nepal's central Himalaya, the Annapurnas, Machhapuchhare and Manaslu, dominates the skyline.

Accommodation in Pokhara includes the fashionable and peaceful *Fish Tail Lodge* (☎ 20071), located on the lake. The Western-style *New Hotel Crystal* (☎ 20035/6), and the Tibetan *Mount Annapurna Hotel* (☎ 20037/27) are across from the airport. The hotels *Tragopan* (☎ 21708) and *Dragon* (☎ 20391, 20052) are a short distance south of the airport. The range of hotels along the lakeside is enormous. The *Base Camp Lodge* (☎ 20903), *Kantipur* (☎ 20886), *Baba Lodge, New Pokhara Lodge* (☎ 20875) and air-conditioned *Pumori Hotel* (☎ 21462) are all at the eastern end of the lake. There are dozens of other cheaper hotels to the west along the shore of Phewa Tal. There is also a government camp ground near the lake, at 900 metres elevation. If you are calling from Kathmandu, the telephone dialling code for Pokhara is 061.

Among the lakeside restaurants, try *Baba Lodge*, the *Hungry Eye*, *Billy Bunter*, *Le Bistro*, *Lhasa Tibetan* and *Beam Beam*.

Gorkha
Gorkha is an alternative starting point for the trek around Annapurna. If you find yourself benighted here try the fancy *Hotel Gorkha Bisauni* about half a km from the bus stop or the *Hotel Thakali* at the bus stop itself. A few

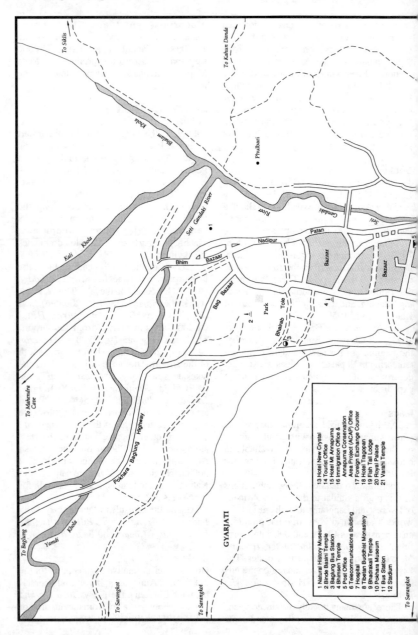

GYARJATI

1 Natural History Museum
2 Binde Basini Temple
3 Baglung Bus Station
4 Bhimsen Temple
5 Post Office
6 Telecommunications Building
7 Hospital
8 Tibetan Buddhist Monastery
9 Bhadrakali Temple
10 Pokhara Museum
11 Bus Station
12 Stadium
13 Hotel New Crystal
14 Tourist Office
15 Hotel Mt Annapurna
16 Immigration Office &
Annapurna Conservation
Area Project (ACAP) Office
17 Foreign Exchange Counter
18 Hotel Tragopan
19 Fish Tail Lodge
20 Royal Palace
21 Varahi Temple

To Siklis
To Kahun Danda
Bhalam Khola
Kali Khola
Seti Gandaki River
Phulbari
Seti River
Gandaki River
Patan
Nadipur
Bazaar
Bazaar
Bhim Bazaar
Bag Bazaar
Park
Bhairab Tole
Pokhara - Baglung Highway
To Mahendra Cave
To Baglung
Yamdi Khola
To Sarangkot
To Sarangkot

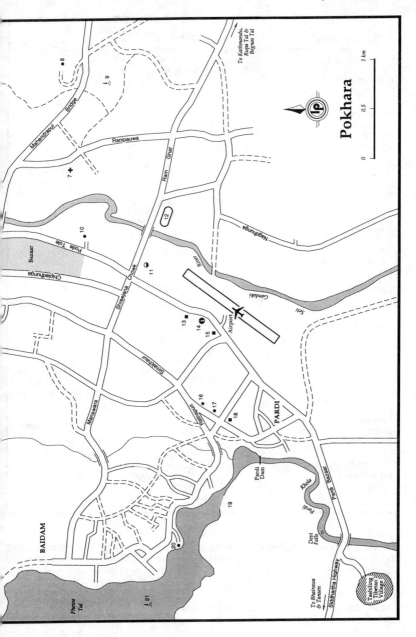

Pokhara

THE ACAP MENU

ACAP has published a series of menus that are used by all lodges in the Annapurna Sanctuary region. The following is the menu for villages close to the road such as Dhampus.

All prices are in rupees.

Hot Drinks

black tea	3
milk tea	4
hot lemon	5
lemon tea	5
milk coffee	10
hot chocolate	10
hot milk	10
mint tea	5

Breads

plain chapatti	7
chapatti & honey/jam	10
Tibetan bread	12
Tibetan bread & jam	10
corn bread	12
corn bread & jam	15
plain pancake	12
pancake & jam	15

Noodles

fried noodles	30
egg fried noodles	35

Soup

vegetable soup	20
garlic soup	20
egg soup	20
onion soup	20
pumpkin soup	25
noodle soup	25
potato soup	25

Porridge

oat porridge	25
muesli with milk	30

Potatoes

mashed potatoes	30
boiled potatoes	25
fried potatoes	30
potato chips	35
popcorn	20

Eggs

boiled egg	10
fried egg	12
omelette	12
vegetable omelette	15
onion omelette	15

Rice

rice, dal & vegetable	35
vegetable fried rice	35
egg & vegetable fried rice	40
plain rice	20
rice pudding	30
chocolate pudding	30

Lodging

bed single	40
bed double	60
dormitory bed	25
kitchen charge	75
hot shower	25
tent (per person)	20

Individual lodges add their own specialities, if any, to this basic menu. Prices increase the further into the hills you trek. As an example of how fast the costs increase, here are the prices for black tea and dal bhat in various places.

	tea	dal bhat
Dhampus	3	40
Landrung	5	40
Chhomrong	5	50
Bamboo Lodge	10	60
Himalayan Hotel	20	60
Annapurna Base Camp	25	75

km before Gorkha is the up-market *Gorkha Hill Resort*, situated on a ridge with good mountain views.

Trekking Lodges

There are numerous trekkers' hotels throughout the region; most are adequate and some are outstanding. You can assume that you will be able to find a room and food wherever you go on the main routes in the Annapurna region. During the busy October and November season most lodges are crammed beyond their capacity. During the high season it might be prudent to bring a mattress in case everything is full and you are forced to sleep on a floor. Bedding is often available, but you should not rely on this at high elevations, especially on a trek to Thorung La or Annapurna Sanctuary.

Up-market facilities in the Annapurna region include the *Lakshmi Lodge* (☎ 410740, Kathmandu) in Birethanti and the *Ker & Downey* lodge system in Dhampus, Ghandruk and Birethanti (☎ 416-751, 410355, fax 410407 in Kathmandu). You can pre-book a trek with either of these operations.

GETTING THERE & AWAY
Air
To/From Pokhara Pokhara is a 30-minute flight from Kathmandu (US$61). Most domestic airlines operate a Pokhara-based network that serves Jomsom, Manang, Baglung and sometimes Dolpo and Jumla with early-morning flights. All the domestic airlines serve Pokhara.

To/From Jomsom Jomsom is in the upper Kali Gandaki Valley and is served by frequent flights from both Kathmandu (US$83) and Pokhara (US$50). Don't fly to Jomsom; if your time is limited, walk up the spectacular Kali Gandaki Valley to Jomsom, trek up to Muktinath, then fly from Jomsom back to Pokhara.

Flights between Jomsom and Kathmandu are notoriously unreliable because the wind in Jomsom makes flying impossible after 10 or 11 am. Kathmandu is often fogbound until 10 am during the winter, and this delays flight departures. Everest Air schedules two flights per week from Kathmandu to Pokhara; RNAC has eliminated its direct flight from Kathmandu and operates flights to Jomsom only from Pokhara.

Pokhara to Jomsom flights are far more reliable because there is no fog problem in Pokhara. Though the morning check-in at Pokhara airport is particularly chaotic, it's usually easier to get to Jomsom from Pokhara than from Kathmandu. RNAC operates one daily 'tourist flight' from Jomsom to Pokhara on which even local people must pay the full tourist fare, and a second, regular flight that carries Nepalese at a subsidised fare. Because local people often cannot afford the fares on tourist flights, there is less competition for seats on these flights.

Everest Air and Nepal Airways also operate daily flights from Pokhara to Jomsom. If you get stuck while trying to fly out of Jomsom it is possible – though not particularly pleasant – to walk to Pokhara in four days or less.

To/From Manang At the upper end of the Marsyangdi Valley is Manang, just across the pass from Jomsom. There is a severe risk of altitude sickness if you fly to Manang and try to cross the Thorung La pass. You should view Manang as an emergency airport; it is not a sensible starting point for an Annapurna trek. RNAC is the only airline that serves Manang. The flight from Pokhara to Manang costs US$50.

Bus
To/From Pokhara There is frequent service by both day and night buses to Pokhara. Fares are Rs 74 to Rs 85, or Rs 200 for a more comfortable 'tourist bus'. The Pokhara road was rebuilt in 1992 by Chinese and British projects, so road conditions were reasonably good during the spring of 1993. A major flood in July 1993 washed out many bridges and caused extensive damage, so it takes five to six hours for the 200-km trip. The special tourist buses that operate between Kathmandu and Pokhara, including the famous 'Swiss Bus', are more expensive, but more comfortable and usually faster than public buses.

To/From Baglung A new road has been constructed between Pokhara and Baglung, a village on the Kali Gandaki. This road was completed in 1994, so the actual trailhead for the Jomsom trek is shifting to Birethanti, about 42 km from Pokhara. Another trailhead that the new road makes possible is the town of Maldhunga, 68 km from Pokhara, at the foot of the hill below Baglung.

CLIMATE

The climate in the Pokhara area is unique because there is no formidable barrier directly to the south to obstruct the spring and monsoon rain clouds. Consequently, it is subject to abnormally high rainfall, almost double that of Kathmandu. One effect of the rain is that it limits cultivation to under 2000 metres. Red laterite soils are typical of such areas, where most minerals are leached out of the soil except for iron and aluminium oxide.

Another effect of the rain is the extensive glacier system on the Annapurna massif and frequent snowfall, particularly in the region of Ghandruk, Chhomrong and the Annapurna Sanctuary. ■

Five buses per day operate on the Chinese-built road between Pokhara and Baglung. Buses depart from a separate Baglung bus terminal near Bhairab Tole in the north-western part of Pokhara. Most people know this as the Kusma bus station. Naya Pool is at Km 42, at the foot of the hill below Khare; if you get off here it's only a 20-minute trek upstream to Birethanti. If you are trekking to Jomsom and want to avoid the climb to Ghorapani and head directly to Tatopani, continue on to the trailhead at Maldhunga. The master plan is to extend the road all the way to Jomsom, through Lo Manthang and into Tibet, but the people of Jomsom have announced that they don't need, or don't want, a road. Now that the road to Baglung exists, there's little point in walking the first few days of the old trek route through Naudanda, Khare, Lumle and Chandrakot.

To/From Dumre Dumre is 135 km from Kathmandu and is the starting place for the trek around Annapurna. There is no service that specifically serves Dumre, so you should take a Pokhara bus and jump ship at Km 135.

To/From Besi Sahar A 43-km road links Dumre to Besi Sahar (also called Lamjung), the headquarters of the Lamjung district. The road is not paved, it fords several streams, and is poorly – if ever – maintained. The trip is reasonable, though bumpy, in late autumn when the weather is dry. The road is rutted and often impassable when it rains, especially during, or just after, the monsoon. When the road is impassable, and sometimes when the bus driver is tired, you will get dumped at Bhote Odar or earlier.

There is a daily minibus from Dumre to Besi Sahar, a four to five-hour trip when the road is dry, and another bus that takes the unusual route from Narayanghat in the Terai to Besi Sahar for a fare of Rs 48. When it is muddy you can ride in a tractor or 4WD truck. A bumpy, dusty ride in one of these decrepit, breakdown-prone ex-army trucks costs Rs 100 to Rs 200, plus an extra charge for luggage; trucks leave from Dumre only when they have a full load of passengers and baggage. The road dries out in early November allowing larger Indian Tata trucks to get through, so there is a better selection of vehicles later in the trekking season.

To/From Gorkha An alternative starting point for the trek around Annapurna is Gorkha. The 24-km-long Gorkha road starts from Anbu Khairieni, seven km from Mugling and provides access to a route that avoids the dusty Besi Sahar road, joining the trek in the Marsyangdi Valley near Tar-kughat. Gorkha is served by two buses daily; the cost is Rs 50 for the seven-hour ride. There is no night bus service.

SPECIAL RULES
Fees & Permits
No matter where you trek in the Annapurna region you come under ACAP's jurisdiction and must pay the Rs 650 conservation charge in addition to the normal trekking permit fee.

Fuel
If you are trekking with an organised group you will need kerosene for cooking. Envi-

ronmentally aware trekkers use kerosene wherever they trek whether it is required or not. Kerosene makes a cumbersome and difficult porter load. The use of kerosene is made easier by kerosene depots in the most heavily trekked parts of the Annapurna region. Kerosene costs Rs 9.75 per litre in Kathmandu. In 1993 the location of depots and the price for a litre of kerosene were:

Naya Pool	Rs 10
Tikedungha	Rs 12
Ghandruk	Rs 12.50
Chhomrong	Rs 18
Kagbeni	Rs 27

Short Treks from Pokhara

Most of the treks that I have described in this book are long treks that travel long distances. One of the attractions of the Pokhara region is the opportunity to make a short trek ranging from a few hours to several days. If you don't have time, or don't think you are ready for one of the longer treks, you can cobble together an interesting trek from parts of longer treks. Try one of the following.

ANNAPURNA PANORAMA
Days 1-3: Pokhara to Ghorapani
Start from Birethanti and trek to Tikedungha and Ghorapani, following days 1 to 3 of the Jomsom trek.

Days 4-5: Ghorapani to Landrung
Follow the Ghorapani to Ghandruk description at the end of the Annapurna Sanctuary trek, then descend to the Modi Khola and climb to Landrung.

Days 6-7: Landrung to Pokhara
Follow the first 1½ days of the Annapurna Sanctuary description in reverse, overnighting in Pothana or Dhampus.

GHANDRUK LOOP
Days 1-2: Pokhara to Ghandruk
Follow the Annapurna Sanctuary description to Landrung, then drop to the river and climb a steep staircase to Ghandruk.

Day 3: Ghandruk to Birethanti
Follow the clearly defined trail down the west side of the Modi Khola to Birethanti. Walk out to the road the following morning and catch transport back to Pokhara.

TATOPANI LOOP
Days 1-2: Pokhara to Ghandruk
Same as the first two days of the Ghandruk Loop.

Days 3-4: Ghandruk to Ghorapani
Follow the Ghorapani to Ghandruk description in reverse. It will probably take you two days because the trail is generally uphill.

Day 5: Ghorapani to Tatopani
Make a long steep descent to Tatopani. See Day 4 of the Jomsom trek for details.

Days 6-7: Tatopani to Baglung
Follow the Baglung to Tatopani description in reverse. Spend the night at the roadhead at Maldhunga and take a truck or bus back to Pokhara the following day.

Jomsom Trek

The trek to Jomsom is the classic teahouse trek and boasts some of the best trekking hotels in Nepal. You can trek to Jomsom and back in 14 days, and you will share the trail with trains of burros and ponies travelling to Mustang and other areas in the far north of Nepal. This is a major trade and trekking route, so there are facilities for trekkers almost every hour all along the trek. Many of these are surprisingly well-equipped hotels operated by Thakalis, people who inhabit the valley between Annapurna and Dhaulagiri.

From the Kali Gandaki Valley, you can

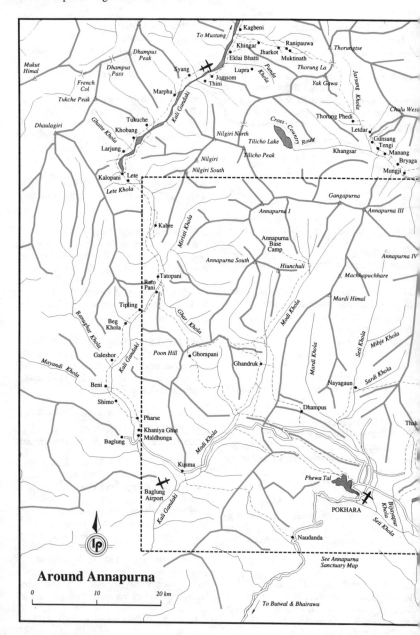

Around Annapurna

0   10   20 km

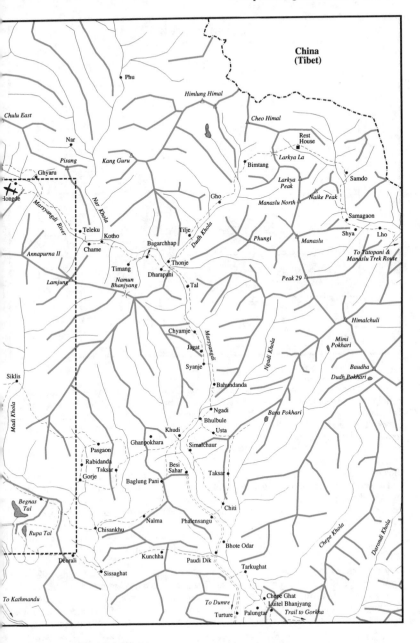

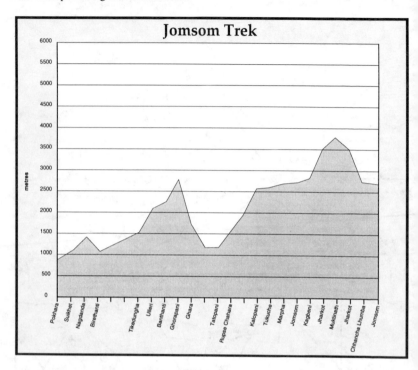

Jomsom Trek

make excursions to either the 1950 French Annapurna base camp or the base camp for Dhaulagiri, though there are no hotels on either of these side trips. The views of the mountains are spectacular, and the route actually crosses to the other side of the main Himalayan range for some unusual views of the northern flanks.

The entire route remains below 3000 metres, though the trek is still strenuous enough to be stimulating (see the Route Profile for the trek around Annapurna). This is a good trek if you wish to avoid high altitudes.

Day 1: Pokhara to Birethanti
From the lakeside or the airport in Pokhara, you can take a taxi (for about Rs 40) to the Baglung/Kusma bus station at the northern end of Pokhara. You can also walk through

the Pokhara bazaar, but it is a long uphill walk on a paved road full of noisy traffic. There are buses throughout the day to Kusma and Baglung; you should buy a ticket as far as Naya Pool.

The road passes the Tibetan camp, where there is a carpet factory, a monastery and a few hotels, then continues to Hyangja at 1070 metres. In the morning, there is a good view up the valley to Machhapuchhare. The road then emerges into the broad Yamdi Khola Valley at Suikhet, then goes on to Phedi and the foot of the Dhampus hill and switchbacks up to Naudanda.

Driving By road from Phedi, the road zigzags up the ridge and then winds down into the Modi Khola Valley. Naya Pool is a small collection of roadside shacks just beyond Km 42. Here you can leave the road,

Jomsom Trek – Flora & Fauna

Trees The **schima** and **chestnut** are the two dominant species of the wet subtropical forest (1000 to 2000 metres) and are easily distinguished from each other. The schima is called *chilanune* ('itchy') in Nepali due to the irritant nature of the bark. It is a medium-sized tree of the tea family with evergreen leathery leaves and white fragrant flowers that appear in late spring. Look for its small round, woody fruit in the fall. The chestnut is a larger tree and is a member of the oak or beech family. Its leaves are large and elliptical with serrated edges. This species has small white flowers on spikes and a distinctive prickly seed capsule that often litters the trail.

The **evergreen oaks** are found in the temperate zones, from 1700 to 3000 metres. They either form their own extensive forests, or cohabit with conifers and rhododendrons. Unless acorns are present they may be difficult to identify because the several varieties of oaks come in an assortment of sizes and leaf types. One common species of oak, the brown oak *(khasru* in Nepali), has young leaves that are spiny, like holly, while older leaves have smooth-edged margins. Oaks also tend to appear in many unusual shapes due to the extensive pruning by hill tribes for fuel and fodder.

There are more than 30 species of **rhododendrons** (in both shrub and tree form) in the temperate and subalpine zones of Nepal. Rhododendrons are readily recognised when they burst into magnificent blooms in spring and summer. The main tree variety, and national flower *(lali gurans* in Nepali) has flowers that are funnel-shaped and clustered at the ends of the branches in a wide variety of colours such as white, pink, mauve and red. When no flower is present, look for tapering leaves that can be silvery or rust-coloured on the undersides and for the loose, pale salmon-coloured bark.

Lammergeier

Birds In the skies the raptors, or birds of prey, are the birds most likely to catch one's eye. Of particular note are the large, soaring raptors that ride the thermals effortlessly for hours, such as the **Himalayan griffon** and **lammergeier**. These huge, graceful vultures are often mistaken for eagles, but are much more common than eagles and substantially larger with long, broad wings. The former is striking with white under-wing coverts that contrast with the black flight feathers, a stubby tail, and a wing span of about two metres. Although the lammergeier has a wing span of nearly three metres, its body is slighter and its plumage gold and brown-coloured. Look for the long, wedge-shaped tail, which differentiates it from anything else of this size. Both of these birds can be seen frequently across the high Himalaya.

Mammals The two species of monkey found in Nepal are the **rhesus macaque** and **common langur**, both protected due to religious ramifications. There should be little confusion distinguishing these two monkeys from each other. The former is small and stout with a pink face, brown fur and short tail, while the langur is large and lanky with a black face, greyish-white coat and long tail. The common langur is also found at higher altitudes than the

Common langur

rhesus, up to the tree line at 3700 metres. Occasionally, while on all fours in the shadows of a tree, this monkey can be mistaken for a leopard. Both of these species range from the Terai to the temperate forests across the Himalaya.

There are several smaller carnivores found in the Himalaya, which include the *Mustelids*, or weasels and martens. They feed on various smaller mammals, birds, eggs and even insects. The **yellow-throated marten** is found in the subtropical and temperate forests and displays great agility when cavorting amongst treetops, where it is most visible. The **Himalayan weasel** inhabits the realm above the tree line, where it can be seen stalking prey and following scent trails, occasionally stopping to stand on its hind legs for a look around. ∎

drop down the embankment to the trail and start walking. Go behind a ridge and walk about 20 minutes upstream on a level trail to a suspension bridge. On the far side of the bridge is Birethanti, a large and prosperous town with a winding street paved with large stones. Birethanti boasts many well-stocked shops, hotels, sidewalk cafes, a bank, a bakery and a police checkpost. The *Lakshmi Lodge* is expensive, but is also interesting and comfortable; one trekker described it as a real throwback to the days of the raj. You can probably negotiate a special rate if you show up without a booking. A trail up the Modi Khola to Ghandruk begins at Birethanti, behind the first house of the village.

Walking If you are walking, add an extra day to the trek. From Phedi, go uphill on a broad trail that climbs gently (for Nepal) to **Naudanda**, on the top of the ridge at 1430 metres. Naudanda is a large village with a police checkpost, school and several inns varying from tiny bhattis (tea shops) to well-developed, Western-style hotels. The correct name of this village is Nagdanda, but local people and most maps call it Naudanda.

The police checkpost here is insistent about looking at trekking permits. If you are on a day hike out of Pokhara without a trekking permit, this may be as far as you get. Climb from Naudanda to Kaski, then further to **Khare**, a large strung-out village situated at the head of the Yamdi Khola Valley at 1710 metres.

The Jomsom route descends from Khare on a muddy trail through deep forests, down a set of wide, stone stairs below the large buildings and fields of a British agricultural project, and continues to the village of **Lumle** (1585 metres). There are several hotels, and even a medical hall, among the slate-roofed houses of the village. The trail follows Lumle's flagstone-paved main street, exiting the village only a bit lower in elevation than when it entered it. If you find yourself heading steeply downhill, ask for directions; the downhill trail leads to the Baglung road, not to Jomsom.

Beyond Lumle, you leave the road and walk along the side of the ridge, finally rounding a bend and descending to **Chandrakot**, which is perched on the end of a ridge at an elevation of 1550 metres. The views of Annapurna South and Machhapuchhare, the 'fish tail' mountain, are excellent from this point, except that from this angle it looks more like the Matterhorn than a fish tail. To see the mountain in its proper perspective you must go into the Annapurna Sanctuary, several days to the north – but that's another trek. There are several hotels here with English signboards and menus – it's a good place for lunch.

From Chandrakot, the trail descends a steep, dusty (muddy when wet) trail that switchbacks down to the Modi Khola. Passing a few houses near the river, the route crosses a suspension bridge to Birethanti at 1065 metres.

Day 2: Birethanti to Tikedungha

The hotels in Birethanti are excellent, but if you spend a night here, it is a long, 1700-metre climb the next day to Ghorapani. It is more comfortable to break the climb into two stages by continuing to Hille or Tikedungha for the night. (If you are coming from Jomsom and are doing the trail in reverse, then Ghorapani to Birethanti is an easy, though long and knee-cracking, descent and Birethanti makes a good stopping place.) The trail follows the main street of Birethanti, going through bamboo forests and past a large waterfall and swimming hole. A small tea shop here provides cold drinks after your swim. The trail stays on the north bank of the Bhurungdi Khola to Baajgara – so don't cross the large, inviting-looking suspension bridge.

Beyond a pasture used by pony caravans, the trail reaches Sudami, then climbs steadily up the side of the valley, reaching **Hille** at 1495 metres. There are several hotels alongside the wide stone trail here and others in Tikedungha, about 15 minutes (and 30 metres) above Hille. There is a large campsite just beyond Tikedungha near two suspension bridges. If you started from

Birethanti, this will be a short day. If you arrive here early, you can easily trek on up the endless stone staircase to Ulleri.

Day 3: Tikedungha to Ghorapani

The trail crosses a stream on a suspension bridge near the campsite at Tikedungha, then drops and crosses the Bhurungdi Khola itself on a large bridge at 1410 metres. The trail climbs very steeply on a stone staircase; there are no tourist hotels from the bridge to Ulleri, just a few bhattis that have only tea. As you climb, the tops of Annapurna South (7273 metres) and Hiunchuli begin to emerge from behind the hills. The climb continues steeply to the large Magar village of **Ulleri** at 2070 metres. There are hotels in the centre of the village, and others above the village where the trail climbs gently through pastures and cultivated fields. The fields soon give way to deep forests as the trail climbs to **Banthanti**, a settlement of hotels in a forest clearing at 2250 metres.

Beyond Banthanti, there are magnificent oak and rhododendron forests. The trail crosses two sparkling clear streams, a small ridge and another stream before making a short, final climb to **Nangathanti**, a hotel complex in a forest clearing at 2460 metres. *Thanti* is a Magar word meaning 'rest house' or 'dharamsala'. In the winter the trail can be covered with snow, and in many places it is sloppy mud, so all sorts of short detours are necessary in this section.

Ghorapani is about an hour past Nangathanti, at 2775 metres. There are several hotels in Ghorapani, but most people continue to the pass and village of **Deorali** (which means 'pass'), at 2834 metres, about 10 minutes beyond Ghorapani. There is a large collection of hotels, shops and camping places and the requisite police checkpost at Deorali.

There is a big map on a signboard in the village that shows the location of 11 lodges; the *Annapurna Hotel* and the *Snow View Hotel* are among the largest. The *Super View* is said to be the best. All the hotel keepers have standardised their prices, so it's a waste of time to look for the cheapest food and accommodation. It is worth staying at the

pass to see the spectacular panorama of Dhaulagiri I, Tukuche, Nilgiri, Annapurna I, Annapurna South, Hiunchuli and Glacier Dome. An early-morning excursion to Poon Hill (3193 metres), about an hour's climb, provides an even better, unobstructed view of the high Himalaya.

Ghorapani means 'horse water', and it is no doubt a welcome watering stop for the teams of horses, mules and ponies that carry loads between Pokhara and Jomsom. The exotic horse caravans, with melodious bells that echo over great distances, and wondrous plumes and headdresses on the lead horses, are reminiscent of ancient Tibet. Herded by Tibetan men who shout up and down the trail, they lend a unique touch to the Jomsom trek. The ponies also grind the trail into dust and slippery mud with their tiny sharp hooves and careen downhill, frightening trekkers into jumping into the bushes, but the colourful photographic possibilities and the harmonious tinkle of bells almost make it worth the trouble.

Some people, almost overcome by the ammoniatic stench of horse urine on the trail, suggest a different derivation of the name Ghorapani. On a typical day, you will encounter 200 to 300 pack animals, travelling in large trains and ranging in size from huge mules to tiny burros no bigger than a large dog.

Day 4: Ghorapani to Tatopani

From the pass at Deorali, the trail makes a muddy, steep descent through rhododendron and magnolia forests, interspersed with a few shepherds' goths, bhattis and pastures, to **Chitre** at 2390 metres. The *New Annapurna* is the dominant lodge here. There are several trail junctions along this part of the trip. The correct trail almost invariably leads downhill. The country opens up into a region of extensive terracing. At one point the trail crosses a huge landslide. Observe the way the slick mica soil has slid off the underlying rock.

The trail descends towards **Sikha** (1980 metres), a large and prosperous Magar village with many shops and hotels. *Shanti*

& *Someone's Bar and Grill* (the name of Shanti's partner keeps changing) is near the top of the village, above the British army training centre. From Sikha, the trail makes a gentle descent across another slide area to Ghara at 1705 metres, then climbs to the top of a rocky spur where there are some bhattis. The trail makes a steep descent of about 500 metres to the Ghar Khola, crossing it on a suspension bridge near Ghar Khola village. The trail then makes a short climb above the Kali Gandaki and crosses the river on a large suspension bridge at 1180 metres. The peak in the background is Nilgiri South (6839 metres). On the opposite side of the river, the trail turns north; it is a short distance upstream to Tatopani.

Tatopani means 'hot water' in Nepali; the village gains its name from the hot springs near the river below the village. There are two cement pools on the banks of the river. Don't pollute these pools by using soap in them.

Tatopani is the epitome of the Thakali inn system; the extensive choice of hotels and garden restaurants rivals Thamel in Kathmandu and the lakeside in Pokhara. The town is supplied with electricity, but some hotels have installed bio-gas (which the Nepalese call *gobar*) generators to produce fuel for cooking. It is intriguing to see these facilities in daily use and shows good progress in the alternative energy field. Many people who are making only a short trek come here from Pokhara and spend their time relaxing in the hot springs and enjoying the hospitality of this small village.

A monsoon flood in the late 1980s washed away a number of lodges and bathing pools, and the remainder of the village sits precariously on a shelf above the river. Most of the lodges have garden restaurants and specialize in exotics like steaks, Italian and Mexican food. The *Tatopani Guest House* is just south of the village. The *Kamala Lodge, Namaste Lodge* and *Hotel Snow Leopard* are all at the northern end of town. The food at *Dhaulagiri Lodge* gets rave reviews. Tatopani's other facilities include a bank, blacksmith, tailor, shoemaker, bookshops and jeweller. This is

citrus fruit country, so you can stock up on small mandarin oranges.

From the mid-70s until 1985 the Kali Gandaki Valley was the focus of the US Resource Conservation & Utilisation Project (RCUP) and a vast amount of money was spent here on an integrated approach to rural development. The primary legacy of this effort is a collection of Western-style buildings, both offices and residences, that you will encounter on your journey up the valley. When you see a facility that looks totally out of place in Tatopani, Kalopani, Ghasa, Marpha and Jharkot, it's probably an RCUP leftover.

Day 5: Tatopani to Kalopani

Register with the Tatopani police checkpost and head up the Kali Gandaki Gorge, said to be the deepest in the world. The rationale for this is that between the top of Annapurna I and the top of Dhaulagiri I (both above 8000 metres and only 38 km apart) the terrain drops to below 2200 metres. From Tatopani, the route ascends gently, passing through a small tunnel carved out of the rocky hillside, to **Dana** at 1400 metres. Dana consists of three separate settlements of buildings with elaborately carved windows and balconies. The hotels in Dana are near the post office at the southern end of the village. Most of the people of Dana are Magars, though there are also a few Brahmins and Thakalis. The large peak across the valley is Annapurna South (7273 metres); the large village high on the hillside across the valley is Nerchang.

From Dana, a bridge provides access to a trail on the eastern side of the Kali Gandaki. After several days of rough climbing in bamboo jungle above the Miristi Khola, this trail reaches the base camp used by Herzog's Annapurna expedition in 1950. At the time of this first ascent, Annapurna was the highest mountain ever climbed. The base camp is also accessible by an equally difficult trail from Lete. Maurice Herzog's book *Annapurna* provides essential background reading for the trek up the Kali Gandaki. There are no hotels on this difficult side trip.

Above Dana, the trail continues to the

hamlet of **Rupse Chahara** ('beautiful waterfall') at 1550 metres, which not surprisingly is situated at the foot of a high waterfall. The falls tumble into a series of cataracts near the village after passing through some water-driven mills. Stop a moment and look at the wooden turbine that powers the rotating stone; these home-made mills are found throughout Nepal and are a very unusual design.

The next stretch of trail is through the steepest and narrowest part of the canyon; the way is cut through solid rock. This portion of the trail is subject to frequent landslides and from year to year the preferred route moves from one side of the river to the other, depending on which side has the less severe landslide. Beyond Rupse Chahara, the trail on the west bank descends to the river where the water rushes through a steep rocky canyon, then climbs across a landslide to join a rough rocky trail near Kabre, at 1800 metres. The route climbs along a spectacular stretch of narrow, cliffhanging trail, then descends to the river at 1935 metres.

The east-bank trail was the favoured route during the '80s and may be repaired by the time you read this. It crosses the river just beyond Rupse Chahara, then climbs on the east bank to Kopchepani, pops over a ridge and descends again to the riverbank. The trail on this side was also blasted out of the rock face and has a short section that is a three-sided tunnel. Beyond the steepest part of the gorge, the trail descends to the river, then crosses to the western side of the Kali Gandaki on a suspension bridge at 1935 metres.

Either route ends with a short climb to **Ghasa**, which has three settlements, at 2000 metres. This is the first Thakali village on the trek and the southernmost limit of Tibetan Buddhism in the valley. The *Eagle's Nest Guest House* at the southern end of the village is said to be the best in town and has a trailside garden. Other good facilities are in middle Ghasa; these include the *Lekahli* and the *Mustang* guesthouses. There are fine kanis in upper Ghasa and there is a large locally supported reforestation project

behind the school. Here the vegetation changes from subtropical trees and shrubs, including stinging nettles and cannabis, to mountain types such as pine and birch. You might spot grey langur monkeys in this area.

The trail crosses a ridge, descends to a stream, then ascends steeply through forests past the few houses of Kaiku before dropping into a side valley and a long suspension bridge over the Lete Khola. There are a few bhattis near the bridge, and the *Namaste Lodge* with its solar-powered electricity sits halfway up the opposite slope. The trail then climbs through **Lete** itself, which is a spread-out town with three clusters of buildings at 2470 metres. It's a long walk through town on a trail that varies from flagstone paving to a muddy wallow through piles of nettle-infested rocks. There are several bhattis and three other hotels, including the *Lete Guest House* near the police checkpost at the northern end of the town.

It is a steep 20-minute walk from Lete to Kalopani, elevation 2560 metres, another town that is prospering from the influx of trekkers. There is an enclosed camp ground among the whitewashed houses of this long village. Hotels include the Westernised *Kalopani Guest House*, the *Thak Lodge*, the *See You Lodge*, and the *Annapurna Coffee Shop*. The *Kalopani Lodge* in upper Kalopani has Western toilets and solar-heated showers. There is a 360° panorama of peaks here: Dhaulagiri, the three Nilgiris, Fang and Annapurna I.

Day 6: Kalopani to Jomsom

Beyond Kalopani, the trail goes upstream a short distance, then crosses to the eastern bank on a wooden bridge where the river races through a narrow cleft. The east-bank trail climbs over a wooded ridge past some small lodges and bhattis, then descends to a new suspension bridge over the Kali Gandaki. Here there are two trails to choose from.

West-Bank Trail By crossing the suspension bridge, you can take the west-bank trail that climbs to Sukung, then descends through fir, juniper and cypress forests to the riverbank.

A short walk across gravel bars, crossing several meandering branches of the Kali Gandaki on temporary bridges, leads you to **Larjung** (2560 metres), an architecturally exotic town with narrow alleyways and tunnels connecting houses which are built around enclosed courtyards. This is a complex and picturesque system that provides protection from the winds of the Kali Gandaki Gorge. At the southern end of Larjung are two hotels, neither of them particularly good. Pass an RCUP building and the school, then trek a short distance to **Khobang** at 2560 metres. There are a few small hotels here; you can make a side trip to the Kanti Gompa on a hill just above Khobang. There are good views of Dhaulagiri (8167 metres) and Nilgiri (7061 metres) along this part of the trail. On the roof of one of the houses of Khobang you may be able to see the remains of the hovercraft in which Michel Peissel travelled up the Kali Gandaki in 1972. Beyond Khobang the trail is mostly on gravel bars alongside the river to Tukuche.

A trail to the Dhaulagiri icefall begins just south of Larjung and climbs the south bank of the Ghatte Khola. Herzog's expedition explored this route in 1950 and abandoned it because it was too dangerous. In 1969, an avalanche killed seven members of the US Dhaulagiri expedition in this area. If you have a tent, you could take a side trip to a meadow near the foot of the icefall at an elevation of about 4000 metres. It's a long, long climb on very steep grassy slopes, so it is wise to make an additional camp at Tal, a lake above the village of Naurkot at approximately 3100 metres. From this camp you can make a day trip to the icefall area.

East-Bank Trail The east-bank route crosses the bridge and heads north, staying above the gravel riverbanks to Dhumpu. The trail climbs over a forested ridge, then heads down again and makes a long but easy traverse along the gravel bars alongside the riverbed, then crosses the river back to the west side on a series of temporary bridges just before Tukuche.

Here in its upper reaches, people call the Kali Gandaki the Thak Khola, thus the name Thakali for those who live in this region.

The Kali Gandaki/Thak Khola Valley has been a major trade route for centuries. Until 1959, traders exchanged salt collected from salt lakes in Tibet for rice and barley from the Middle Hills of Nepal. They also traded wool, livestock and butter for sugar, tea, spices, tobacco and manufactured goods from India, but the salt-for-grain trade dominated the economy. This trade has diminished, not only because of the political and economic changes in Tibet, but also because Indian salt is now available throughout Nepal at a much lower price than Tibetan salt.

Indian salt, from the sea, contains iodine. Many people in Nepal once suffered from goitres because of the total absence of iodine in their diet. Indian aid programmes distributed sea salt in a successful programme to prevent goitres, but the Tibetan salt trade suffered because of the artificially low prices of Indian salt. The Thakali people of the Kali Gandaki Valley had a monopoly on the salt trade of this region. They are now turning to agriculture, tourism and other forms of trade for their livelihood.

At 2590 metres, **Tukuche** was once the most important Thakali village. Tukuche (*tuk*, 'grain' and *che*, 'flat place') was the meeting place where traders coming with salt and wool from Tibet and the upper Thak Khola Valley bartered with traders carrying grain from the south. The hotels in Tukuche are in beautiful old Thakali homes with carved wooden windows, doorways and balconies. The *Himali*, *Tukche*, *Laxmi* and *Sunil* lodges are all along the stone-paved main street and some offer garden restaurants. At the northern end of town the *Yak Hotel* advertises a 'real yak on display inside' – it's worth a look.

Tourism has not totally offset the economic effect of the loss of the grain trade, so many people have moved from Tukuche to Pokhara, Kathmandu and the Terai. A walk along the back streets of the village, particularly close to the river, will reveal many abandoned and crumbling buildings behind the prosperous facade of the main street. There are few mani walls or religious monuments along the Kali Gandaki, although there are large gompas in Tukuche, Khobang and Marpha and a monastery in Shyang.

A dramatic change in the vegetation, from pine and conifer forests to dry, desert-like country, takes place during this stretch of trail. The flow of air between the peaks of Annapurna and Dhaulagiri creates strong winds that howl up the valley. The breezes blow gently from the north during the early hours of the day, then shift to powerful gusts from the south throughout the late morning and afternoon. From here to Jomsom, these strong winds will be blowing dust and sand at your back after about 11 am.

As the trail proceeds north, it passes the large stone buildings and orchards of an agricultural project set up in 1966 to introduce new types of produce into the region. The motivating force behind this project has always been Passang Khambache Sherpa who accompanied David Snellgrove during his studies throughout Nepal. It may be possible to purchase fresh fruits, vegetables and almonds here. Local apple cider and fruit preserves are available in Marpha and Tukuche, and there is also, of course, excellent apple, apricot and peach rakshi. Try the bottled Tukuche Brandy and then try to pronounce the official name of this establishment: His Majesty's Government of Nepal National Temperate Horticulture Research Station.

Between the agricultural project and Marpha is *Om's Home Marpha*, a very clean hotel that has excellent food, and a range of accommodation from dorms to rooms with private baths. The village of **Marpha** is huddled behind a ridge for protection from the wind and dust. This large Thakali village, at 2665 metres, exhibits the typical Thak Khola architecture of flat roofs and narrow paved alleys and passageways. The very limited rainfall in this region makes these flat roofs practical; they also serve as a drying place for grains and vegetables.

In Marpha, the Thakali inn system has reached its highest level of development. Hotels have private rooms, menus, room service and indoor toilets. In this clean and pleasant village, there is an extensive drainage system that flows under the flagstone-paved street and there is even a

library (open 5 to 7 pm) and impressive kanis at both ends of town.

There are 16 hotels in Marpha and a surprising number of souvenir shops. Near the southern end of town are the *Hungry Eye Restaurant* and the *Paradise Guest House & Lunch Box*. Central Marpha hotels include *Dhaulagiri Lodge* and *Baba's Lodge*. Both have elaborately carved windows, comfortable inner courtyards and good toilet facilities, and the *Miami* has a solar-heated shower. A plastic signboard advertises *Bhakti Guest House;* the proprietor, Bhakti Hirachan, is a good source of information and assistance.

Marpha is a better choice than Jomsom for a night stop because the hotels are better and there is less wind. It's a bit far, but not unreasonable to reach Muktinath in a single day from Marpha, though it would be more interesting to take an extra day and break the trip up with a stop at Kagbeni.

Across the river, about half an hour from Marpha, is the village of Chaira, a Tibetan settlement with a carpet factory. Traders from Chaira often sit along the trail near Marpha selling their wares. Pause a minute along this part of the trail and look at the scenery – high snow peaks, brown and yellow cliffs, splashes of bright green irrigated fields and flat-roofed mud houses clustered here and there.

From Marpha, the trail continues along the side of the valley, climbing imperceptibly, to **Shyang** where there are no hotels. The route passes a few houses and trailside vendors selling trinkets before reaching Jomsom (more correctly Dzongsam or 'new fort'). Jomsom is the administrative headquarters for the region and straddles the Kali Gandaki at an elevation of 2713 metres. The major inhabitants are government officials, army, and merchants engaged in the distribution of goods brought in by plane and pony caravans. From Jomsom, you can make an easy side trip to the gompa at Thini, about an hour from Jomsom on the east bank of the Kali Gandaki.

Jomsom has three distinct parts. You enter the town from the south, near the airport where there are large hotels, restaurants and the RNAC office (open only from 2 to 4 pm). The *Lali Guras*, the *Trekkers Inn* and the *Alka Marco Polo* are all hotels near the airport. Each has a central courtyard surrounded by rooms and meals are often served at a *kodatsu*, a Japanese-style table covered with a blanket to warm your legs with the heat from a charcoal brazier.

The up-market *Om's Home* has rooms with private tiled baths and electric hot-water heaters at prices starting from Rs 200. Also near the airport is the mandatory police checkpost and a tourist office. The tourist office is primarily concerned with controlling tourists headed for Mustang. If you have trekked from Manang, it is important to obtain a police endorsement on your trekking permit, because all police posts to the south will want to see it. The arrival of the morning flight from Pokhara is the highlight of the day in Jomsom. In addition to most of the townspeople, there is also a collection of fruit and vegetable vendors in front of the airport in the morning.

North of the airport, on the western side of the Kali Gandaki, are shops, bhattis and the telegraph office. There is a large army camp that houses the High Altitude Mountain Warfare Wing of the Nepalese army. You can often see the army practising rock climbing on the cliffs above Jomsom. The section of town across the new suspension bridge on the east bank of the river is the main part of Jomsom, with dwellings, bhattis, the *Nilgiri Lodge*, a bank, a German bakery and a post office. The power lines, electric lights and the military people jogging in the mornings are a bit incongruous in this remote location.

Day 7: Jomsom to Muktinath

Follow the narrow main street past several hotels to the school and a statue of King Birendra at the northern end of town. The trail follows the broad river valley, sometimes above the river, but mostly along the rocky bank of the river itself as it passes beneath vertical rock cliffs. The trail passes a stream and a side trail that leads to Lupra, a Thakali village and a Bon-po gompa. Pass a walled tree plantation and climb over a small ridge to Chhancha Lhumba, better known as **Eklai Bhatti** ('alone hotel'), at 2730 metres. Here, the *Kagbeni Lodge* offers a chance to get out of the wind and shop for 'all kinds of Tibetan something'. The direct route to Muktinath leads straight up the hill behind the *Munal Guest House*.

Unless you are in a tremendous rush, you should take a side trip to Kagbeni. From Eklai Bhatti, the trail follows the river to **Kagbeni** at 2810 metres, a green oasis at the junction of the Jhong Khola and the Kali Gandaki. Kagbeni looks like a town out of the medieval past, with closely packed mud houses, dark tunnels and alleys, imposing chortens and a large, ochre-coloured gompa perched above the town. Many people still dress in typical Tibetan clothing, though the children have, even in this faraway village, learned to beg, rather insistently, for sweets.

The *New Annapurna Lodge*, near a water-pipe-infested chorten in the centre of Kagbeni, has inexpensive dormitory accommodation and a sun terrace where you can eat apple pie and drink Mustang coffee. Other popular establishments are the *Red House Lodge*, the *Annapurna* and the *Mukti-*

nath View, which has a yak head over the doorway.

Kagbeni is the northernmost village in this valley that foreigners may visit on a normal trekking permit. The police checkpost at the northern end of the village fastidiously prevents tourists from proceeding towards Lo Manthang, the walled city of Mustang, without the proper documentation. If you have a Mustang permit, turn to the section on the Mustang trek, otherwise start trekking up to Muktinath.

The trail to Muktinath starts at the southern end of Kagbeni, behind the *Nilgiri View Hotel*. It makes a steep climb up the Jhong Khola Valley, passing the defunct windmills that once provided electric power for Kagbeni, and joins the direct trail to Muktinath below Khingar. Along the way you will see hundreds of small piles of rocks erected by pilgrims to honour their departed ancestors.

The direct route to Muktinath climbs from Eklai Bhatti along a windswept slope to a plateau above the Kali Gandaki, then turns east up the Jhong Khola Valley. The trail ascends to Khingar through country that is arid and desert-like, in the same geographical and climatic zone as Tibet. The striking yellows of the bare hillsides contrast dramatically with the blue sky, white peaks, and splashes of green where streams allow cultivation. The views of Dhaulagiri and Nilgiri are tremendous.

The walk from Khingar at 3200 metres to Jharkot is a delightful walk amongst meadows, streams and poplar and fruit trees. There are often flocks of cranes in the area. The trail here is high above the Jhong Khola as it climbs to **Jharkot**, an impressive fortress-like village at 3500 metres. Just above the village is a trail leading to the *Jharkot Hotel* and the *Himali Hotel*, which offers solar-heated rooms. The village itself, with its picturesque kani, is well worth exploring. There are some peach trees nearby; local people grind the peach seeds to make oil. Across the valley you can see the ruins of Dzong, the ancient capital of this region, and the smaller villages of Purang and Changur.

Climb over some walls, trek past the village mule stables and up a steep barren hillside. The first part of Muktinath that you reach is **Ranipauwa** at 3710 metres, the site of a large rest house for pilgrims, and a host of hotels, bhattis and camping places. This area is often crowded with both pilgrims and foreign tourists. The *North Pole Lodge* and *Mona Lisa* are good, but the *Shree Muktinath Hotel & Lovely Restaurant* is reported to have the best food in town. More mediocre choices include the *Hotel Pole Star,* the *Nilgiri View* and the *Lali Guras Lodge*. The *Muktinath Guest House* charges Rs 25 for a room with twin beds and hot bucket baths. The young couple who run the hotel serve good food (and good apple rakshi). It's wise to avoid the smaller, local-style hotels that cater to Hindu pilgrims. There is a police checkpost and a poorly maintained government camp ground in the middle of the settlement.

There is a municipal hot shower in Ranipauwa that heats water with the excess electricity from the local hydroelectric project. A five-minute shower costs Rs 20; the money goes to the school. Beware of exposed wiring.

The Tibetan traders here are unrelenting in their efforts to convince you to buy their wares. One item that is unique in this region is the *saligram*. These are black stones that, when broken open, reveal the fossilised remains of prehistoric ammonites, formed about 130 million years ago. You might find some yourself between here and Jomsom, though you can always buy them, at inflated prices, from the traders – and then curse yourself all the way back to Pokhara for carrying a backpack full of rocks. The gold specks that appear on many saligram are pyrite (fool's gold). Hindu pilgrims also purchase these ammonites because they represent the god Vishnu.

The most colourful pilgrims to Muktinath are the ascetic *sadhus*, whom you must have seen many times between Pokhara and here. They travel in various stages of undress, smear themselves with ash and often carry a three-pronged spear called a *trisul*. A rupee or two donation to these holy men is not out of place. They are Shaivite mystics on a pilgrimage that, more often than not, began in the heat of southern India.

The temple and the religious shrines of Muktinath are about 90 metres in elevation above Ranipauwa. There are no hotels, and the temple committee does not allow camping here. Muktinath is an important pilgrimage place for both Hindus and Buddhists. Situated in a grove of trees, the holy shrines at Muktinath include a Buddhist gompa and the pagoda-style temple of **Vishnu Mandir**, containing an image of Vishnu. Around the temple is a wall from which 108 waterspouts, cast in the shape of cows' heads, pour forth sacred water. Even more sacred is the water that issues from a rock inside the ancient Tibetan-style **Jwala Mai** temple a short distance below the pagoda. Inside this gompa, behind a tattered curtain, are small natural gas jets that produce a perpetual holy flame alongside a spring that is the source of the sacred water. This auspicious combination of earth, fire and water is responsible for the religious importance of Muktinath. It is often possible to see Tibetan women, with elaborate turquoise-embedded headdresses, engaged in devotions at these shrines.

The most charming description of Muktinath is the one on the signboard erected by the Ministry of Tourism at Jomsom:

Muktinath is beautiful, calm and quiet,
great and mysterious for pilgrims,
decorated with god and goddess.
Although you are kindly requested not to snap them.

Days 8-9: Muktinath to Jomsom

It's an easy walk back to Jomsom, though it becomes tedious if there is a strong wind. This is not the time to decide that you are going to cross Thorung La and trek around Annapurna. If you have come this direction from Pokhara you probably do not have the warm clothing and boots necessary for crossing the pass. It is also a long hard climb of 1300 metres from Muktinath to the pass.

Day 10: Jomsom to Kathmandu

From Jomsom it's easiest to fly to Pokhara first and then travel on to Kathmandu. In the early morning, Jomsom airport is the social centre of the town with tourists and locals alike vying for the limited number of seats.

BAGLUNG TO TATOPANI

You can avoid the long climb over the Ghorapani hill on the Jomsom trek by travelling by bus to the trailhead below Baglung and following the Kali Gandaki Valley to Tatopani. This can be a particularly attractive prospect if you have trekked around Annapurna and decide you don't want to cope with the 1650-metre climb from Tatopani to Ghorapani. The Baglung trek has no significant climbs and takes only a day and a half of walking, so it's reasonable to plan on two days for the trip between Pokhara and Tatopani in either direction.

The road travels 68 km from Pokhara to Maldhunga at the foot of the hill below Baglung. The trip takes less than three hours by bus.

Day 1: Pokhara to Beni

If possible, find transport by bus or private vehicle along the Baglung road to Maldhunga. The road is level from Pokhara, then climbs from Phedi to Naudanda and Khare. The road descends from the ridge into the Modi Khola Valley, dropping to Naya Pool, the jumping-off place for Birethanti. The road follows the Modi Khola south to Patichaur, then crosses the river and starts climbing up the side of the ridge to **Kusma** at Km 58. Kusma is perched at the end of the ridge between the Kali Gandaki and the Modi Khola. There are some trekkers' hotels here left over from the time when the road ended at Kusma. The road drops into the Kali Gandaki Valley passing Armadi, then reaches **Maldhunga** (Km 68) at the foot of the Baglung hill, elevation 720 metres. The road contines across the Kali Gandaki up the ridge to Baglung bazaar. If you are headed for Tatopani, get off at the bridge and head into the shanty town of Maldhunga, where there isn't a single reasonable hotel among the tin-roofed bamboo shacks. The *Lucky Hotel* is the best of the tin-roofed bamboo facilities here. With luck you will arrive in time to begin trekking; it is about four hours to Beni from here.

Leaving the squalor of Maldhunga, pass through **Khaniya Ghat** which has two tea shops and on to the tiny village of Kanyas where there is a large Nepalese paper factory. Follow the east side of the Kali Gandaki to **Pharse** at 760 metres where several tea shops huddle under the cables of a suspension bridge. You can continue to follow the mule trail on the east bank of the river or you can cross the bridge and trek to Beni without the company of mules. The west-bank trail passes through heavily farmed country and the villages of Belbot Dodane, Saremre, Shimo, Lamoghara and Chaunebagar, then crosses a ridge over the Myagdi Khola and enters Beni. The east-bank trail crosses the Kali Gandaki and rejoins the other trail in Beni at the southern end of town near a large police installation.

Beni, situated on a plateau above the river at 820 metres, is a large village with a long main street that has interesting facilities such as photo studios and barbers as well as the usual shops and bhattis. The trail to Dhorpatan and Dolpo starts at the southern end of Beni. Most of the mule trains follow this route up the Myagdi Khola towards Dhorpatan; few mules follow the route to Tatopani, so the trek now becomes more pleasant. The *Gauchan Guest House* caters to trekkers and is located below the Beni plateau at the north end of the village. If you arrive here early, continue an hour on to Galeshor, which is a more pleasant place to stay.

Day 2: Beni to Tatopani
Follow the west bank of the river for about an hour to **Galeshor,** situated above the Rahughat Khola at 870 metres. There are two hotels and several shops along the stone-paved streets of the village. In late November each year there's a large fair (mela) in Galeshor. Cross a suspension bridge over the Rahughat Khola, past the *Riverside Guest*

House to Ranipauwa. The Kali Gandaki now starts to close in and the rolling terraced hills disappear.

The route crosses several landslides before reaching **Baisari** at 960 metres where there are five hotels. The route is mostly in forests as the trail makes numerous ups and downs and crosses more landslides. After crossing the Beg Khola on a suspension bridge you will find yourself in a three-sided tunnel blasted out of the side of the cliff. The next stretch of trail is a particularly dramatic construction along the steep valley. It is this stretch that keeps the mule trains to Jomsom on the Ghorapani route instead of using this trail. There are numerous ups and downs, but they are all less than 100 metres, so the trekking, while tedious, is not exhausting. Trek out of the tunnel and through forests and corn fields to two small lodges in the village to Tipling.

At Tipling the route crosses to the east bank of the Kali Gandaki on an old suspension bridge to the Magar village of Dorsale. Beyond Moharbir the trail climbs broad stone steps inside another three-sided cliffhanging tunnel. The route gets a bit complex as it uses footholds cut into a large boulder to cross a landslide, then drops to Birkati on the banks of the river.

Climb another set of stone stairs to another vertigo-inducing cliffhanging trail, then descend a ridge to the Brahmin village of **Rato Pani** and the *Hema Guest House* at 1150 metres. Trek on another 20 minutes to meet the trail that descends from Ghorapani, then cross a stream and finally the high suspension bridge over the Kali Gandaki into Tatopani.

Annapurna Sanctuary

The route to Annapurna Sanctuary (Annapurna Deuthali in Nepali), the site of the Annapurna south face base camp, is a spectacular short trek. Though it has some steep climbs, the trek is not difficult. The major problem with this trek is that it can

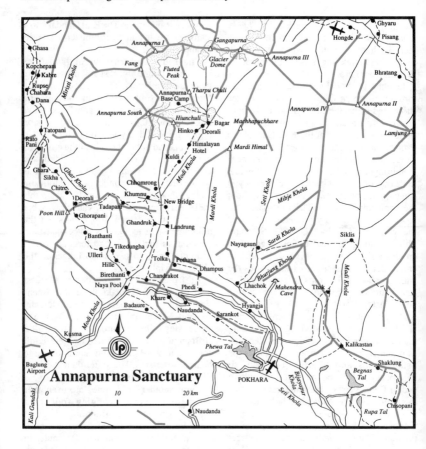

Annapurna Sanctuary

0   10   20 km

become impassable because of snow and avalanches in winter and early spring. It is the only major trekking route in Nepal that has significant avalanche danger, so you must inquire locally whether the trail is safe. Some trekkers have died because of avalanches, and others have been stranded in the sanctuary for days. The sanctuary trek traverses a variety of terrain, from lowland villages and rice terraces to glaciers, and offers outstanding high mountain views. This trek is a fine opportunity to surround yourself with Himalayan peaks in a short time, without having to contend with the altitude and flight problems of the Everest region.

You can make the trek, from Pokhara to Annapurna base camp and back, in as few as 10 or 11 days, but it is best to allow two weeks to fully appreciate the high altitude scenery. A diversion to Ghorapani on the return route provides a view of Dhaulagiri from Poon Hill. There are frequent tea shops along the entire trek, sometimes five or 10 minutes apart, and you will rarely walk for as long as an hour without finding some source of refreshment. The hotels extend all the way into the Annapurna Sanctuary, except in winter when the hotelkeepers retreat to their homes in Chhomrong.

Day 1: Pokhara to Tolka

The most direct approach to the Annapurna Sanctuary is via the trail from Dhampus to Chhomrong that uses a 'new bridge', built in about 1985. Take a taxi, jeep or bus from Pokhara to Phedi, then continue a few hundred metres along the road to a trail that climbs from a taxi stand and a small cluster of hotels steeply up the hill to the right.

Starting at an elevation of 1080 metres, in a forest that is so overgrazed that it looks like a manicured municipal park, the trail climbs steeply past some scattered houses to the ridge at **Dhampus**, at 1580 metres. At Dhampus, you are rewarded with great views of the mountains that continue to improve as

you ascend along the ridge. There are a few hotels at this end of Dhampus, but it is a large village strung out along the ridge over several km and you will pass several other hotels, including the up-market *Dhaulagiri View Hotel*, during the next half hour of walking.

Dhampus is the centre of the theft racket in central Nepal. Thieves often cut the tents of trekkers and remove valuable items during the night, so it is not a good idea to camp alone here. Trekking groups circle their tents like an old-time wagon train and post a guard with a lighted lantern throughout the night. If you stay in a hotel, be sure that you know who is sharing the room with you and lock the door whenever you go out – even for a moment. The thieves do watch everyone, in order to decide who has something worth taking or is likely to be careless.

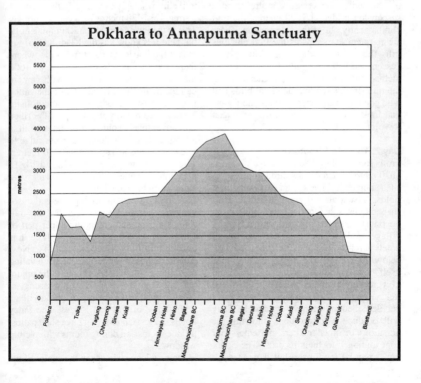

They will wait patiently all night to make their move if necessary.

The trail climbs through Dhampus, past a police checkpost, then gradually ascends a forested trail paved with stones. There is a short steep climb to **Pothana**, a bunch of hotels that grew up around a new water pipe, at 1870 metres. Just before Pothana is an inconspicuous trail junction; this is a trail that leads to the 'Australian Camp' and a route back to the Baglung road at Khare.

The trail climbs through forests to a clearing on top of the hill at 2010 metres, where there are views of Annapurna South and Hiunchuli. From there make a steep descent, through forests alive with birds, ferns and orchids, into a huge side canyon of the Modi Khola. The trail descends past several teahouses at **Bichok** (also known as Bheri Kharka), then descends further to the head of the canyon. After crossing a stream on a suspension bridge at 1690 metres, the trail climbs gently out of the side canyon. There are frequent tea shops as the trail emerges into the main Modi Khola Valley and descends to Tolka, a small settlement at 1710 metres, with several lodges scattered along the trail. In this region, men hunt birds and wild goats with ancient muzzle-loading guns that look like leftovers from the American Revolution.

Day 2: Tolka to Chhomrong

From Tolka, the trail descends to a stream at 1620 metres, then climbs through forests to a tea shop on a ridge. It's an easy walk, past fields, a school and some unusual oval-shaped houses, before the trail drops a bit to the flagstone streets of **Landrung**, a Gurung village at 1550 metres. There are many hotels here; the best ones are either above or below the village. The hotels in the village itself are in old houses, so they are small and a bit crummy compared to other hotels on the trek. Along the trail you will probably meet people collecting money for schools. They will produce a ledger book showing the donations of other trekkers and enter your contribution into their records. The donations may be legitimate, but it is an adult version of the creative forms of begging that tourists have encouraged.

Descend through the paved courtyards of Landrung to the small *Himalaya Hotel*, below the village at 1480 metres. The trail to the sanctuary leads to the right, just behind the hotel. There may be an orange sign pointing the way north.

The downhill trail leads to the river and then climbs to Ghandruk. You can see Ghandruk village high above you on the opposite side of the river.

The narrow trail to the sanctuary turns north up the Modi Khola Valley passing alongside rice terraces then through forests, to the rustic *Namaste Lodge*. A short walk up the river bed leads to **Naya Pool** (New Bridge), also known as Shiuli, at 1340 metres. There are several substantial hotels on both sides of the suspension bridge. The trail climbs steeply to Samrung, then crosses a stream at 1430 metres on a cement bridge. This is the lower part of the Khumnu Khola, but here it is known as the Kladi Khola.

A stiff climb leads to **Jhinu Danda**, where there are two hotels on a ridge at 1600 metres. There is a hot spring with cement bathing pools about 15 minutes up the valley from here; ask the lodge owner about them. You can see houses on the top of the ridge far above; this is your next destination. It is a long, steep climb along a treeless ridge to a few tea shops at **Taglung** at 2050 metres. The trek now joins the Ghandruk to Chhomrong route, so the trail is wider and better from here to Chhomrong.

A short distance from Taglung is the isolated *Himalayan View Lodge*, then the trail rounds a bend and enters the upper part of Chhomrong. This Gurung village has evolved into two separate parts. New Chhomrong is the upper part, at an elevation of 2040 metres, with resort hotels, the school and a helicopter pad; Old Chhomrong, at 1950 metres, is the main part of the village with shops, offices and lodges. The fancy hotels in New Chhomrong have slate patios, private rooms and dining rooms with picture windows.

Down a long staircase in the centre of the

village is a kerosene depot, the ACAP office and several shops. *Captain's Lodge* is Chhomrong's most popular inn, though the captain himself has a strong personality. The *Chhomrong Guest House* is also near the centre of town. All the hotels have provision shops at which you can stock up on food for the trip into the sanctuary. Some hotels also rent equipment like gaiters, gloves, sleeping bags and down jackets; check to be sure you have warm clothing before you head into the sanctuary. The ACAP regulations prohibit the use of firewood beyond Ghandruk, so all trekkers and hotels must cook with gas or kerosene. If you are camping, you can buy kerosene and rent Indian pressure stoves and plastic jerry cans here. Stoves cost about Rs 50 per day and jerry cans from Rs 1 to Rs 3 depending on the size. In 1993 kerosene cost Rs 18 per litre in Chhomrong; the operator of the depot can give advice on the quantity that you will need. If you are staying in hotels, the hotelier will take care of the kerosene problem.

The houses and hotels in old Chhomrong once had electric lights thanks to Mr Hayashi, popularly known as Bijuli Japani, the 'electric Japanese' who installed a small hydroelectric plant and equipped the houses with miniature light bulbs. By 1993 the system had broken down; ACAP plans to build a new generating facility. The hotels and lodges in this area have formed a committee to fix prices in all lodges. They have prepared printed menus for each locale – with increasing prices the further you go from Chhomrong. This is a positive move because trekkers used to bargain and stay in the cheapest hotel. Now everyone quotes the same rate, so you can choose a hotel according to quality, not price. The prices increase dramatically from here on, and the menu gets limited because of the kerosene restriction, though hotelkeepers are very resourceful at producing things like apple rolls over a roaring kerosene stove.

This is the highest permanent settlement in the valley, but herders take sheep and goats to upper pastures in the sanctuary during the summer. There is a tremendous view of Annapurna South, which seems to tower above the village, and there are good views of Machhapuchhare *(machha, 'fish', and puchhare, 'tail')* across the valley. It is from this point onwards that the reason for the name of this peak becomes apparent. In 1957, Wilfred Noyce and David Cox climbed Machhapuchhare to within 50 metres of its summit. After this attempt, the government prohibited further climbing on the mountain, so technically the peak remains unclimbed. A lower peak to the south, Mardi Himal (5587 metres), is open to trekking parties.

Day 3: Chhomrong to Bamboo Lodge
Leaving Chhomrong, the trail descends on a stone staircase and crosses the Chhomrong Khola on a swaying suspension bridge, then climbs out of the side valley. Climbing high above the Modi Khola on its west bank, the trail passes through the tiny settlement of Tilche in forests of bamboo, rhododendron and oak. Climbing further on a rocky trail (beware of the stinging nettles) you reach three hotels at **Sinuwa**, at 2250 metres.

The trail continues in rhododendron forests, climbing to **Kuldi**, at 2350 metres. This was once a British sheep-breeding project; now the stone houses are occupied by ACAP. In winter, it's common to find snow anywhere from this point on. From Kuldi, the trail descends a long, steep stone staircase into deep bamboo and rhododendron forests. It is then a short distance on a muddy trail to Bamboo Lodge (2190 metres), a collection of four hotels, none of which is built of bamboo. In early autumn and late spring, this part of the trail is crawling with leeches.

Day 4: Bamboo Lodge to Himalayan Hotel
The trail climbs steeply through stands of bamboo, then through rhododendron forest up the side of the canyon, occasionally dropping slightly to cross tributary streams, but ascending continuously. When there is snow this stretch of trail is particularly difficult, because the bamboo lying on the trail, hidden

beneath the snow, provides an excellent start to a slide downhill. Local people hack down the dense bamboo forests beyond Kuldi to make mats for floors and roofs, and for dokos, the baskets that porters carry.

At **Doban** (2430 metres), about two hours beyond Kuldi, there is also a good hotel. Beyond Doban the trail traverses several avalanche chutes, to upper Doban and the *Annapurna Approach Lodge*, at 2470 metres. ACAP is trying to consolidate these lodges into a new location called 'New Doban'; this may have been accomplished by the time you trek here. The trail is muddy and traverses high above the river, but it is no problem for those who suffer vertigo, because thick stands of bamboo block the view of the rushing river and waterfall. The trail then crosses a landslide and another avalanche track, to the *Himalayan Hotel* at 2680 metres. Just before the hotel you can see the debris left from an avalanche that killed a Sherpa kitchen crew in the spring of 1989. If you arrive here early, it is worth trekking on to Deorali to make the following day easier.

Day 5: Himalayan Hotel to Machhapuchhare Base Camp

From the Himalayan Hotel it's about an hour's walk, first on a rocky trail through forests then up a steep ravine, to **Hinko** at 2960 metres. This is called Hinko Cave because a huge overhanging rock provides some protection against rain and avalanches. There is a funny hotel built into the cave that can accommodate 12 or 13 people in a cold,

damp dormitory. This hotel is reported to charge high prices and run out of food when things get crowded. Deorali is a much better choice for a meal or overnight.

The trail crosses a ravine and a major avalanche track just beyond Hinko, then climbs through large boulders. About half an hour beyond Hinko is (yet another) **Deorali**, at 3000 metres, where two hotels offer an alternative to the crowded conditions at Hinko. Above Deorali, the valley widens and becomes less steep and you can see the 'gates' to the sanctuary. Avalanches from Hiunchuli and Annapurna South, peaks which are above, but not visible from this point, come crashing into the valley with frightening speed and frequency.

As the trail continues into the sanctuary, it crosses two wide avalanche tracks on a narrow trail that huddles up against the cliffs. The trail then descends to meet the Modi Khola and follows the river to **Bagar**, two lodges at 3110 metres. ACAP has given instructions to move these lodges to Deorali by 1994, so don't count on finding these facilities. The normal trail follows the left side of the valley, but when an avalanche has blocked the trail it may be necessary to take an alternate route. There is a trail that crosses the river, climbs along the eastern side of the river and then recrosses on a log bridge just before Bagar. The local people will know when to take this diversion. The normal trail will probably be open in October and November and late spring.

From Bagar, climb across more avalanche paths, cross a moraine and a stream, then

---

Wildflowers & Trees

In the Annapurna Sanctuary region there is a wide variety of wildflowers that linger in bloom long after the monsoon thanks to the high rainfall characteristic of this area. Look for **luculia**, (a pink mallow that is often mistaken for rhododendron), a variety of **impatiens** and composites (asters, daisies, etc) and the **pleone orchids** blooming in trees. Along the wet rock walls between Ghorapani and Ghandruk, near Banthanti, the profusion of mauve **primulas** cannot be missed.

In upper approaches to the sanctuary, the leafless **birch** trees of winter are also readily recognisable. These trees usually denote the upper limit of the tree line and are easy to identify with their reddish or whitish bark that tends to peel in sheets. ■

climb towards a two-storey building. This is a German meteorological project office. There is a hotel here, and two others five minutes beyond in an area known as Machhapuchhare base camp, elevation 3480 metres. These hotels, the *Fish Tail* and the *Gurung Co-op*, may or may not be open, depending on whether the innkeeper – and the supplies – have been able to reach the hotel through the avalanche area. Most of the inns in the sanctuary close during the winter. All are operated by people from Ghandruk or Chhomrong, so you can easily find out in advance which, if any, are open.

The mountain views are stupendous; the panorama includes Hiunchuli, Annapurna I (8091 metres), Annapurna III (7555 metres), Gangapurna (7454 metres) and Machhapuchhare (6997 metres).

Day 6: Machhapuchhare Base Camp to Annapurna Base Camp

It's about a two-hour climb to Annapurna base camp, elevation 3900 metres. Start early; clouds often come in before noon and can make the trail hard to find. The route passes a few roofless shepherds' huts alongside a moraine to four hotels situated on a knoll. In the high trekking season these hotels are ridiculously crowded. The *Snow Land* and *Paradise Hotel* are the up-market establishments with high altitude apple pie and pizza. The area is cold and windy and is often snowbound. When I was here one April the snow reached the roofs of the hotels.

There are tremendous views of the near-vertical south face of Annapurna that towers above the sanctuary to the north-west. This face was climbed in 1970 by an expedition led by Chris Bonington, and still remains as one of the most spectacular ascents of an 8000-metre peak.

Several peaks that are accessible from the sanctuary are on the trekking peak list. Tharpu Chuli (formerly Tent Peak, 5663 metres) offers a commanding 360° view of the entire sanctuary. Its higher neighbour, Fluted Peak (Singu Chuli, 6501 metres), offers a mountaineering challenge. Hiunchuli (6441 metres) to the south is also

open to trekking parties. All three of these peaks are significant mountaineering challenges and require skill, equipment and planning. A less challenging but worthwhile objective is Rakshi peak, a ridge south of Tent Peak.

There are few birds in the sanctuary, but there are tahr, Himalayan weasels and pika.

Day 7: Annapurna Base Camp to Deorali

It's much easier going down. You should have no problem reaching Deorali in a single day from Annapurna base camp.

Day 8: Deorali to Doban

Retrace your steps from the upward journey through Himalayan Hotel to Doban or beyond.

Day 9: Doban to Chhomrong

Trek back down to apple pie country.

Day 10: Chhomrong to Ghandruk

You can return to Pokhara by a variety of routes, the fastest being back to Ghandruk and down the Modi Khola to Birethanti where you can find transport back to Pokhara. A more interesting alternative is to trek to Ghorapani. From Ghorapani you can either head north to Jomsom and Muktinath or head back to Pokhara via Birethanti or Baglung. These alternatives are described after Day 11 of the Annapurna Sanctuary trek.

To reach Ghandruk from Chhomrong, follow the route back to Taglung, at the junction of the trail from Landrung and New Bridge. Stay on the wide main trail, walking west above the prosperous-looking houses and potato and wheat fields of Taglung, then descend gently through forests to a single tea shop, the *Hilcross Lodge* at 2020 metres. From here, the trail drops steeply on switchbacks to **Khumnu** (also called Kimrong) village, situated above the Khumnu Khola at 1720 metres. There are hotels in the village, and a very funky tea shop near the bridge.

At Khumnu, cross the suspension bridge and stay on the main trail as it climbs out of the Khumnu Valley. The trail makes a steep climb to some teahouses at **Uri**, situated on a pass at 2220 metres. The trail then descends through huge boulders to a small creek and descends gently into the maze of trails around Ghandruk, at 1940 metres.

Day 11: Ghandruk to Birethanti
At the foot of Ghandruk village turn south on a set of stone stairs and descend steeply towards the Modi Khola. Follow the route south through sparsely inhabited country to the *Ker & Downey Sanctuary Lodge*, then continue on a level trail into Birethanti. The following morning it's a 20-minute walk downstream to Naya Pool where you should have no problem getting a bus or truck to Pokhara.

KHUMNU TO GHORAPANI
To reach Ghorapani from Khumnu, cross the river on a suspension bridge and then walk about 20 metres upstream to the site of the defunct old bridge. A faint, hard-to-find trail leads steeply uphill. Don't risk getting on the wrong trail; ask the people in the teahouse near the bridge for directions. The trail becomes more distinct as it switchbacks up through wheat fields to the Brahmin village of **Melanche** at 2050 metres. Above Melanche, the trail becomes less steep as it climbs steadily through rhododendron forests to **Tadapani** at 2540 metres. Here the route joins the main Ghorapani to Ghandruk trail. It's a long trek to make in a single day; you will be happier if you break it into two days and spend the night at Tadapani.

GHORAPANI TO GHANDRUK
It is a long, though not difficult, day (except when the trail is snow-covered) from Ghorapani to Ghandruk because the trail heads generally downhill. If you are trekking from Ghandruk to Ghorapani, it's a long hard day. Few local people use this trail, but it is becoming an increasingly important trekking route, and there has been overwhelming and uncontrolled development of the area in the past 10 years. Villagers have chopped down large parts of what was once an unbroken forest of rhododendron to build hotels.

In 1993 ACAP, in collaboration with local village development committees, wisely banned the use of firewood between Ghorapani and Ghandruk, so all lodges should be using bottled gas or kerosene for cooking. Unfortunately the ban does not yet apply to Ghorapani.

From the Ghorapani pass, known as Deorali, the trail climbs south on a muddy path through deep forests. It finally emerges on a grassy knoll which offers good mountain views, including a view of Machhapuchhare (not visible from the Ghorapani pass), and a panorama all the way south to the plains of India. It is a similar view to that from Poon Hill. Keep climbing along the ridge in pine and rhododendron forests to a crest at 3030 metres, then descend to two inns at a second pass, also called Deorali, at 2960 metres.

There is a trail junction here with a route that leads down to Chitre and Tatopani. The Ghandruk trail descends to the *Lali Guras Lodge* in a rhododendron forest, then follows a dry stream bed. A ridge hides the mountains as the trail makes a steep, sometimes treacherous, descent on a narrow path alongside the stream, which becomes larger as the descent continues. The stream has some clear pools alongside the trail (remember the Nepalese disapproval of skinny-dipping) and finally becomes a series of waterfalls over a jumble of boulders and logs that were washed down when this harmless-looking stream ran amok during the monsoon rains.

The steep descent becomes more gentle as the route reaches **Banthanti**, six hotels in the shadow of a huge rock face. The tables and benches outside the lodges here present a scene reminiscent of a ski lodge – especially when there is snow. (This is not the same Banthanti that is between Ulleri and Ghorapani.) Follow the stream down to a bridge, where a tiny trail leads off to a rock quarry; porters carry slabs of slate from here to make roofs for homes in Ghandruk and Melanche.

The trail starts climbing, leaving the moist, high mountain forests and entering a field of cane, making some ups and downs

Ghandruk village

past the *Tranquillity Lodge*, to a vantage point that offers a brief view of the mountains. The trail then descends steeply to a stream before climbing again through forests to Tadapani, a clutter of hotels with a dramatic view at 2540 metres. Not content with the view from ground level, one hotel has built a stone lookout tower. Tadapani means 'far water'. The village water supply is a long distance below the village. Before the water pipe was constructed it took porters more than half an hour to fetch a load of water.

From Tadapani, there is a trail to the left that descends through forests, then through terraced fields, to the Khumnu Khola. This direct route to the Annapurna Sanctuary is described, in reverse, in the previous Khumnu to Ghorapani section.

The Ghandruk trail descends steeply from Tadapani, through forests to a clearing with two hotels. (This is yet another spot called Deorali!) A short, steep descent among rocks leads to a stream crossing, then the descent

continues gently past other streams, finally leading out on a ridge towards Ghandruk.

The trail reaches the edge of Ghandruk near the tin-roofed handicraft factory, then descends on stone steps into the maze of the village itself. The first hotels that you come across from this direction are the *Himalayan Hotel* and the *Gorkha Lodge*. Both are very heavy advertisers along the trail – you can't miss them. There are other hotels at the southern end of the village where the trail to Landrung begins.

Ghandruk, a huge Gurung village at 1940 metres, is the second-largest Gurung village in Nepal (the largest is Siklis), and is a confusing cluster of closely-spaced, slate-roofed houses. There are neatly terraced fields situated both above and below the town. Older maps spell the village name 'Ghandrung', but Ghandruk is the currently accepted spelling. Ghandruk is the Nepali name, but the village's real Gurung name is Kond.

It is wonderfully easy to get lost in the

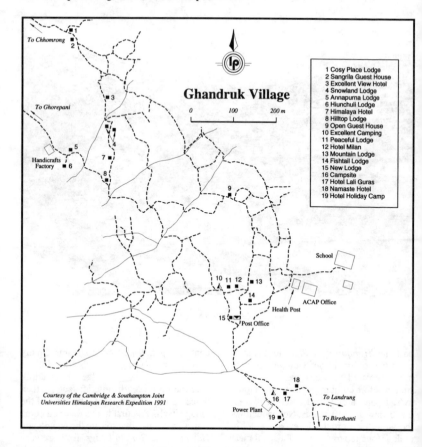

Ghandruk Village

0   100   200 m

1 Cosy Place Lodge
2 Sangrila Guest House
3 Excellent View Hotel
4 Snowland Lodge
5 Annapurna Lodge
6 Hiunchuli Lodge
7 Himalaya Hotel
8 Hilltop Lodge
9 Open Guest House
10 Excellent Camping
11 Peaceful Lodge
12 Hotel Milan
13 Mountain Lodge
14 Fishtail Lodge
15 New Lodge
16 Campsite
17 Hotel Lali Guras
18 Namaste Hotel
19 Hotel Holiday Camp

To Chhomrong

To Ghorepani

Handicrafts Factory

School

ACAP Office

Health Post

Post Office

Power Plant

To Landrung

To Birethanti

*Courtesy of the Cambridge & Southampton Joint
Universities Himalayan Research Expedition 1991*

network of narrow alleyways while trying to trek through the village. As you enter Ghandruk, either from above or below, you will find a set of signs that describe the town's many facilities. The largest hotels are near the top of the village; the rest of the inns are at the bottom of Ghandruk, not among the houses of the village itself.

Ghandruk has an extensive water supply with tanks, pipes and taps throughout the village. There is a large handicraft factory at the top of Ghandruk, near the Himalayan Hotel. The views of Annapurna South (Annapurna Dakshin in Nepali) from here

are outstanding. Machhapuchhare, seen from here in its 'fish tail' aspect, peeps over a forested ridge. ACAP has a visitors' centre and an office in Ghandruk and provides information about its activities.

Around Annapurna Trek

It takes a minimum of 18 days to trek around the entire Annapurna massif, visiting the Tibet-like country on the northern slopes of the Himalaya and the dramatic Kali Gandaki

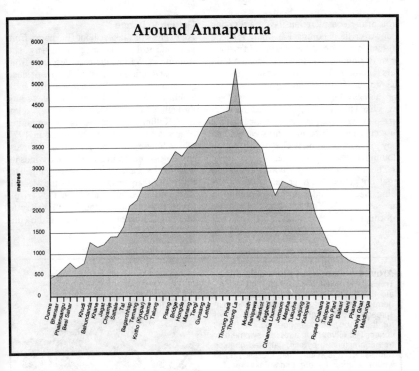

Around Annapurna

Gorge. Nepal opened Manang to trekkers in April 1977, although a few expeditions and scientific parties visited the region in the 1950s.

The last seven days of this trek are the reverse of the popular trek from Pokhara to Jomsom; you will have to read the Muktinath to Pokhara section earlier in this chapter. There are tea shops and hotels about every hour all along the route from Dumre to Pokhara, except on the Thorung La pass between Thorung Phedi and Muktinath.

It is easiest and safest to cross Thorung La, 5416 metres, from east to west, as shown in this route description.The reason is that if you travel from west to east, there are no camping spots or water sources on the west side of the pass from a meadow above Muktinath, at 4100 metres, to a spot two to three hours beyond the pass on the Manang side, at 4510 metres. This means that you have to make a 1300-metre climb, plus at least a 900-metre descent, in a single day. This is an impossible feat for many people, especially those who have not yet acclimatised to high elevation. The trails are less steep on the Manang side of the pass and, in the event of a problem, rescue facilities are better in Manang.

From Manang to Muktinath, the pass is not difficult, but it is still a long trek at high elevation. You should be aware that you might have to return to Dumre if it is impossible or dangerous to cross Thorung La because of snow or altitude sickness. There are years when the weather allows it to stay open, but Thorung La is usually snowbound and closed from mid-December to mid-April.

Clothing and equipment for porters must

be a prime consideration if you are taking them over the Thorung La. Many lowland porters from Dumre have suffered frostbite or snow blindness on this pass because trekkers (and/or their sherpas) have not provided the proper footwear, clothing and sunglasses for the pass. Porters from near-tropical villages like Dumre have no idea what to expect on a snow-covered pass, or they hope that the pass crossing will be in warm weather, and they join a trekking party clad only in cotton clothing. If you employ porters for a crossing of Thorung La, you incur both a moral and legal obligation for their safety and well-being. See the Guides & Porters section in the Facts for the Trekker chapter for more information.

Getting to Dumre

An express bus takes about five hours from Kathmandu to Dumre. Leaving the Kathmandu Valley, the road descends from the Chandragiri Pass on a wild series of steep switchbacks along the narrow Indian-built Tribhuvan Rajmarg. It then continues south through cultivated fields to Naubise, 26 km from Kathmandu. Naubise is the beginning of the Prithvi Rajmarg, completed in 1971 with Chinese aid. The Tribhuvan Rajmarg continues south from this point and winds its way to the Indian border at Birganj. The Prithvi Rajmarg heads east along the Mahesh Khola to its confluence with the Trisuli River. It then follows the Trisuli Valley to Mugling, elevation 220 metres, at the con-

---

Around Annapurna – Flora & Fauna

Trees Two conifer species of the high temperate forest are hemlock and silver fir. The **hemlock** is a graceful pyramidal tree with outspread sweeping branches. Be on the lookout for the short, delicate needles and small cones. The **silver fir** is a robust, symmetrical tree characterised by stiff, flattened needles with silvery undersides that are situated in whorls around its branches. This species should be readily recognised for its Christmas tree-like appearance. The erect, dark purple cones oozing with resin are also keys to identification.

Hemlock

Birds There are many small birds found along the water courses of the Himalaya that are quite striking despite their size. The thrushes are especially well represented. Perhaps one of the more common species is the **white-capped river chat**, a handsome red-and-black bird with a white crown and nape. Another species typically sighted is the **plumbeous redstart**, a slaty blue bird with a red tail. The female, though, is completely different, appearing drab grey with a white rump and black tail. The latter is sometimes confused with the **little forktail**, another thrush found near water. The other forktails are larger with long black-and-white tail feathers and seem clad in tuxedos. The **whistling thrush** may appear as a plain black bird in the shadows, but actually is dark blue with pearly white specks. The long lilting song of this bird carries over the din of the rushing torrents delightfully at dawn and dusk.

Other birds that make their niche near the water are the kingfishers. On the bigger rivers look for the **large pied kingfisher** which is black and white with a large crest, while higher up along smaller streams look for the iridescent turquoise of the **white-breasted kingfisher** and the smaller **Eurasian kingfisher**.

Still another species of the waterways to look for is the **brown dipper**, a plump, chocolate-coloured bird that appears to do deep knee-bends on the stones at the water's edge. This bird jumps into the torrents and forages on the stream bottoms. Look for the **white-breasted dipper** west of the Kali Gandaki river. ∎

Langtang & Helambu
Top: Langtang village (RI'A)
Bottom: Gosainkund Lake (SA)

Langtang & Helambu
Top Left: Kyanjin Gompa (SA)
Bottom Left: Tharepati (TW)
Right: Porter (RI'A)

fluence of the Trisuli and Marsyangdi rivers, 110 km from Kathmandu. The large river thus formed flows south to become the Narayani River, one of the major tributaries of the Ganges. Most rafting in Nepal is done on this part of the river, finally emerging in the Terai and entering Royal Chitwan National Park. A road follows the Narayani Valley south from Mugling to join the east-west Mahendra Rajmarg at Narayanghat in the Terai.

Beyond Mugling, the road follows the Marsyangdi River, passing the huge Marsyangdi power project, actually crossing the dam in front of the powerhouse, and passing the junction of the road to Gorkha. Dumre is 25 km beyond Mugling at an elevation of 440 metres. This village was settled in the 1970s by Newars from the nearby town of Bandipur after the completion of the road from Kathmandu to Pokhara. Dumre exists because it used to be at the beginning of trails that led both to Gorkha, a day's walk away, and to the Marsyangdi Valley and Manang. Most of the village consists of warehouses, shops and bhattis that serve the porters who carry loads from the roadhead to remote villages. In Dumre there are also a few hotels, including the *Annapurna* and the *Dhaulagiri* that cater to trekkers.

Day 1: Dumre to Besi Sahar

The hotel facilities along the road above Dumre are mediocre because most trekkers bypass them and drive to Besi Sahar. The following is a brief description of the Besi Sahar route in case you have to walk, and to provide you with some clues as to your progress if you are bouncing around in a bus or truck. The road fords the Chudi Khola at Dumre, then passes through terraced rice fields and small villages inhabited by Newars, Brahmins and Chhetris, to Bhansar at 530 metres. It then follows the west bank of the Marsyangdi upstream through a region dotted with gigantic banyan and pipal trees.

A short distance on, from the town of **Chambas** at 500 metres, there are good views of the high Himalaya, especially Baudha (6674 metres) and Himalchuli (7893

metres). The road passes through the upper part of Turture at 530 metres; most of this large village is below the road. Across the river you can see Palangtar, the site of Gorkha's defunct Palangtar airport. (Gorkha is the major town in the central hills and is the site of the ancient palace of King Prithvi Narayan Shah, the founder of modern Nepal; the airport is no longer served by any flights because the new road to Gorkha has made flying unnecessary.)

The road stays on the west bank of the river through fairly level country, passing through Baisjan Ghar. The road fords a stream and climbs past Paudi Dik to **Bhote Odar** at 550 metres. Some buses and trucks end their trip here. There is a police checkpost in Bhote Odar and the *Star Hotel* offers accommodation. The road climbs over a ridge, passing Udipur at 730 metres and descends to the Thakali bazaar of **Phalensangu**, situated below the road at 670 metres.

At Phalensangu, there is a bridge perched high above a narrow wooded gorge. If you cross the Marsyangdi on this bridge, you can make a side trip to Bara Pokhari. This is a high altitude lake (elevation 3100 metres) that offers outstanding views of Manaslu, Himalchuli and Baudha. The trip involves a long, steep climb, but you can make a trek to Bara Pokhari in as few as three days, leaving the main trail at Phalensangu and rejoining the trail to Manang below Usta on Day 2.

The bridge at Phalensangu also provides access to an alternative route that avoids the motor road. From the east side of the bridge at Phalensangu, a trail climbs to Chiti, then follows the river valley north. The trail passes through sal forests and rice terraces to Chaur at an elevation of 760 metres, then enters a sugar cane-growing region. From **Chaur** (also called Simbachaur), the trail stays near the river, crosses the Bhachok Khola, and climbs through Baragaon, elevation 910 metres, and over a ridge before descending to Bhulbule, where it rejoins the main route to Manang.

From Phalensangu, the road makes a few small ascents and descents and fords a lot of small streams before reaching Besi Sahar, situated on a plateau at 820 metres. There are several bhattis and two trekkers hotels at the bus stop at the southern end of the town. If you are planning to spend the night in Besi Sahar, stop here and patronise the *Hotel S'Annapurna* or the *Hotel Tukche Peak*, which advertises that it is able to supply porters. There are also several bhattis here; one of them offers '24 hours service in a running sour'.

The road continues about 500 metres to the disagreeable bazaar of Besi Sahar, a km-long collection of shops and noisy bhattis. There is a police checkpost, radio and watch-repair facilities, shops selling Chinese and Japanese goods, a bank and a telephone office.

One way to avoid the Besi Sahar road is to start the trek from Gorkha. It is a three-day walk from Gorkha to Tarkughat, a fair-sized bazaar on the east bank of the Marsyangdi at 490 metres elevation. You can stay on the eastern side of the river and join the normal trek route at Phalensangu or Bhulbule.

Above and to the west of Besi Sahar is Gaonsahar, elevation 1370 metres, where there are the remains of an old fortress and palace. From the 15th to 18th centuries, this region was a collection of independent kingdoms that continually waged war on each other. In 1782 the kingdom of Gorkha absorbed Lamjung, the principality that was ruled from Gaonsahar palace.

The trail to Manang has been renovated, graded and widened to allow horse and mule caravans to transport supplies to these remote villages – though you may not believe this as you walk the rough trails. The mules travel from Besi Sahar to Manang village, though they only travel as far as Chame when there is snow in the higher regions of the Manang Valley.

Day 2: Besi Sahar to Bahundanda

After a long walk through the Besi Sahar bazaar, the trail drops to a stream, then climbs a rough rock staircase to Denauti. After traversing some fields, the trail makes a steep descent of about 150 metres on slip-pery marble rocks into the Marsyangdi Gorge. Rock-hop across the Bhalam Khola and climb to a shack that has the effrontery to call itself the *Hotel Bhalam*. A wonderful bamboo bridge spans the Marsyangdi here – but you don't have to cross it. It is a long walk with several ups and downs, across rice paddies and subtropical forests to Shera Bazaar, a collection of bamboo bhattis in a grove of shady trees.

Continue on to **Khudi** at 790 metres elevation, a mixture of tin and thatch-roofed houses, hotels and shops clustered around the anchors of a long, sagging suspension bridge. The old bridge is precarious, but there is a new one about 10 minutes upstream next to a collection of government offices. Khudi is the first Gurung village on the trek. Most of the people in the wide river valley below Khudi are Brahmins and Chhetris, although there are a few Gurung villages in the side valleys and slopes above the river. The trail passes the Khudi school and a forest nursery and continues northward up the Marsyangdi Valley. Himalchuli and Ngadi Chuli (also known as Manaslu II and formerly known as Peak 29), at 7879 metres, dominate the horizon.

At **Bhulbule**, elevation 830 metres, the trail crosses the Marsyangdi River on a long, decrepit suspension bridge. The *Thorung La Guest House* is on the west side of the bridge and the *Hotel Arjun*, which looks like a Spanish hacienda, is just across the bridge on the right. The other major hotel here is the *Hotel Manang & Lodge* which offers 'variable dishes with worm hospitality'. There are shops, bhattis and even a tailor, all near the bridge. The trail now travels up the east bank of the river, past a majestic waterfall 60 metres high that is surrounded by a tropical tree called a pandanus, or screw pine. The path then wanders through small villages scattered amongst extensive rice terraces with continuing views of Manaslu (8156 metres) and Ngadi Chuli. There are a few trail junctions between Bhulbule and Lampata; in each case take the trail to the left. The right-hand trails lead on to ridges above the Marsyangdi. The Ministry of Tourism has erected orange signs saying 'Manang' at the confusing trail junctions along the route, so it is almost impossible to get lost.

The mountain views disappear as you near the small settlement of **Ngadi**. This used to be only a winter settlement before trekkers proliferated, but now there are several hotels run by Manangis near a defunct bridge. The *Ngadi Hilton* is at the southern end of town, the *Himalayan Lodge* offers 'clean and friendly service' and the *Kamala Lodge* is decorated with photos of Hindi film stars. There are also shops, porter hotels and a campsite. A short distance beyond the tourist Ngadi is a Tibetan settlement and porter stop on the east side of a long suspension bridge that crosses the Ngadi Khola at 880 metres.

It is fascinating to see the extensive public works programme in the hills of Nepal. To build this bridge, porters had to carry the steel cables and towers for several days. There are thousands of bridges throughout the country in unbelievably remote locations that have required huge expenditures of time and money for their construction. It is all too easy to see only the undeveloped aspect of Nepal and ignore the extensive expenditure of labour and money over the last 40 years that has developed an extensive network of trails and bridges. There is an excellent campsite just after the bridge.

On the hills above the Ngadi Khola is the village of Usta, where the trail from Bara Pokhari rejoins the route to Manang.

The trail moves gently upwards through scrub forests for about a half hour, then climbs to some bhattis and cold drink stalls opposite the rice terraces of **Lampata**. The trail winds around to the *Hotel Manaslu,* then makes a short steep climb to Bahundanda, an attractive village situated at 1310 metres in a saddle on a long ridge. The school nestles in a grove of bamboo, and there are a few shops, bhattis and several hotels near the town square. The *Hotel Bluebird & Vegetarian Restaurant* is north of the square and the *Hotel Mountain View* is on the ridge to the west. Bahundanda ('hill of the Brahmins') is the northernmost Brahmin settlement in the Marsyangdi Valley. If you are camping, try

the school; they have built an excellent campsite with decent toilet facilities. They expect a donation to the school in addition to a camping fee. There is, of course, also a police checkpost here.

Day 3: Bahundanda to Chyamje

Descend on a steep, slippery trail past amphitheatre-shaped rice terraces. The flocks of birds in the rice fields are slaty-headed parakeets. Contour across terraces and eventually drop to a log bridge across a stream at the foot of a waterfall. Climb to a tea shop at **Lili Danda** where you can get directions to a small hot spring nearby. The trail then traverses high above the river to the pleasant village of **Hani Gaon** at 1180 metres. About five minutes beyond is the *Hotel Annapurna & Syange Fall Restaurant* which advertises itself as 'the nature yoga for better health' and offers 'good services for massage'. This is the last of the rolling Middle Hills. Soon the valley narrows and the trail drops to cross the Marsyangdi on a long suspension bridge at 1190 metres and reaches **Syange**.

There are shops and three hotels, in order of preference, the *New Thakuri Guest House,* the *Karma* and the *Sonam,* along the stone streets of Syange on the west bank of the river. One of the best trekking camps on the trip is located under the eastern end of the bridge. Beyond Syange, the trail stays near the river for a while, then climbs quite high on an exposed trail carved into near-vertical cliffs, which are forested with rhododendron and pine and garnished with healthy crops of stinging nettles and marijuana.

Because of the steep terrain, the villages in this region are small and infrequent. When Tilman visited Manang in 1950, this portion of the trail did not exist. Instead, the route followed a series of wooden galleries tied to the face of the rock cliffs alongside the river. There is a small hotel at Shree Chour, then there is a steep 200-metre climb to a trail blasted out of the rock face. The next stretch of trail rates 10 on the vertigo scale, but the trail is wide; if you are nervous you can hug the rock wall.

It's a short descent past a small waterfall to **Jagat** at 1250 metres, inhabited, as are most villages in this region, by people of Tibetan heritage. Jagat means 'toll station'; this was once the site of a tax-collecting post for the Tibetan salt trade of the Marsyangdi Valley. The stone village has a medieval atmosphere and the shops and hotels are small and not very clean. There are three rough lodges near a bunch of bamboo shacks at the southern end of town; the mediocre *Manaslu Lodge* is at the northern end.

From Jagat, the trail descends almost to the river then climbs through forests past two bhattis to a waterfall, then slides gently into Chyamje at 1430 metres. Pass through a turnstyle into the *Tibetan Hotel* which has bins of roasted soybeans, *chiuraa* (beaten rice) and popcorn, and is a good place to load up on trail snacks. The design feature of Chamje hotels is an outdoor gazebo. You can get out of the rain or sun here, at the *Potala Guest House* and another small establishment a short distance below. Just across the suspension bridge on the west side of the river there is a place to camp.

Day 4: Chyamje to Bagarchhap

Cross the Kali Gandaki and follow the trail along the river embankment on rocks and exposed wire. These wire cages filled with rocks are called *gabions*. They are used extensively throughout Nepal to stabilise riverbanks and road-cuttings. The trail passes under an overhanging rock, then climbs a rocky trail and a steep stone staircase to a bhatti at Sattale, at 1430 metres elevation.

The path climbs past fields, then through stands of bamboo and rhododendron to an exposed trail that traverses high above the steep riverbank. The trail makes a short descent to **Tal Besi**, three bhattis at 1580 metres, then a steep climb beside the Marsyangdi which has become an underground waterfall beneath huge boulders. The trail crests a ridge and the valley suddenly opens into a large plateau. In this dramatic setting, at the foot of a large waterfall, is the village of **Tal** at 1675 metres. There are many

shops and hotels in Tal, arranged so they look like an old American pony express outpost. The *Hotel Good Luck* is in the centre of the town; the *Tibetan Hotel* is at the northern end. Don't get your hopes up when you spot the sign on the *Manaslu Guest House* offering 'Fosters on tap'.

The Buddhist influence is apparent from the small white chorten on a nearby hill; the trek has now entered the Manang district.

Tal is the southernmost village in Manang and is in a region called Gyasumdo, one of three distinct divisions within Manang. Gyasumdo was once highly dependent on trade with Tibet. Since the disruption of this trade in 1959, herding and agriculture have assumed greater importance. Corn, barley, wheat, buckwheat and potatoes are grown in Gyasumdo, which has enough warm weather and rainfall to produce two crops a year. The people of Gyasumdo used to hunt musk deer, and the sale of musk was once an important source of income and trade. Although they are Buddhists, the people throughout Manang slaughter animals and hunt in the nearby hills, unlike other Buddhists who have strict taboos against the taking of life.

The trail crosses the broad, flat valley that was once a lake *(tal* means 'lake'), through fields of corn, barley and potatoes, then crosses a small stream on a wooden bridge near two tea shops. There is a short climb, then the trail makes its way along a cliff and along the riverbed to Shirental. A short distance beyond is a wooden cantilever bridge across the Marsyangdi at 1850 metres. This bridge is so long that it must be pushing the limits of cantilever bridge design.

This portion of the trail was constructed in the 1980s to replace a steep trail on the eastern side of the river. Climb past several bhattis in the new settlement of Ningala. Trek past corn fields and clumps of bamboo, then descend along a cliff to a stream. Climb over a ridge that is topped by a bhatti, then descend to a long, high suspension bridge that leads to **Karte**. Don't expect too much from the town's only hotel, the *Dorchester*. There is only a bit more cliff walking before dropping to a suspension bridge that leads back to the west side of the Marsyangdi. Just after the bridge is a tiny, dirty hot spring that flows from a fissure near the trail; you need a cup to collect the hot water.

The trail climbs from the bridge to an unpainted stone kani that marks the entrance to **Dharapani**, elevation 1920 metres. All the old villages from here to Kagbeni have entrance chortens at both ends of the village; the kanis get more elaborate and picturesque as the Tibetan influence becomes stronger in each successive village.

There are two parts to this village. In lower Dharapani you will find the *Bishnu Hotel, Robin Guest House* and *Alina's Guest House*. Trek about 10 minutes beyond to the *Tibetan Hotel*, the funkier *Dharapani Hotel & Lodge* and a police checkpost built under an over-hanging rock at 2050 metres.

There's a long suspension bridge across the Marsyangdi that leads to Thonje, an important village at the junction of the Marsyangdi and the Dudh Khola. It's not necessary to go to Thonje en route to Manang. There is a police checkpost in Thonje that controls the route up the valley that leads to the Larkya La. If you have trekked around Manaslu, you will emerge here and can either continue to trek around Annapurna or trek south to Besi Sahar and Dumre. The building with the huge tin roof in Thonje is the regional high school.

Beyond Dharapani, the trail passes a school and climbs over a spur before descending to Bagarchhap. The trail contin-ues into the east-west Manang Valley in a forest of blue pine, spruce, hemlock, maple and oak. The jay-like bird that you see is the nutcracker; it eats the seeds from the blue pine cones.

Bagarchhap, at 2160 metres, is the first village on the trek with typical Tibetan archi-tecture: closely spaced stone houses, with flat roofs piled high with firewood. The village is in a transition zone between the dry upper Marsyangdi and the wet regions of the lower valley, so there are also many sloping wooden shingle roofs. Higher in the Marsyangdi and Kali Gandaki valleys, where there is little rainfall, the shingle roofs disappear, the houses are packed even closer together, and all have flat roofs.

The well-maintained, whitewashed Diki Gompa in Bagarchhap contains many Tibetan Buddhist paintings and statues. The *Pearly Gates* hotel offers 'heavenly food and lodging', and there is a well-stocked shop nearby. The trail now travels west up the Manang Valley with the high Himalayan peaks to the south; there are occasional glimpses of Lamjung Himal and Annapurna II (7937 metres) through the trees. To the east, some of the peaks of Manaslu Himal provide a dramatic backdrop at the foot of the tree-filled valley.

Day 5: Bagarchhap to Chame

Much of the Manang Valley is virgin forest of pine and fir, but construction of new houses and hotels, and the constant require-ments for firewood are causing people to cut down many of these fine trees. On the trail to Manang there is much evidence of this cutting. People have stacked huge piles of firewood alongside the path and have hauled great timbers to home sites.

The trail climbs along the mule track through forests to **Dhanakyu** (also called Syal Khola, 'the river of jackals', and some-times Temang Phedi, 'lower Temang'), a settlement at 2290 metres with several hotels run by people from Bagarchhap. On the hill to the south of this village a trail leads to upper Temang, at 2600 metres, and climbs over Namun Bhanjyang (5784 metres) en route to Ghanpokhara in the south. This was the old route to Manang; few people, other than herders, use it now. Namun Bhanjyang is a difficult pass because there is often snow, and there is no food or shelter for four days.

Climbing further, the trail continues to be rough and rocky. Suddenly a broad level stretch of trail appears. There is a fine wooden bridge near a waterfall, and out-standing stonework supports the trail. Climbing further, the route reaches **Tyanja**, also called Lattemarang, at an elevation of 2360 metres. There are four or five small but comfortable hotels here. There is a tiny hot spring across the river, but it is hard to get to.

The track stays near the Marsyangdi in forests of oak and maple, climbing and descending amongst river-worn boulders, then crosses a large stream before reaching Kotho. Nearby is **Kyupar** (2590 metres), situated in a meadow surrounded by huge pine and spruce trees. This is a police checkpost that controls access to the Nar-Phu Valley to the north. That remote valley, populated by only 850 people, is one of the three regions of Manang. It has a heritage and traditions different from that of other parts of the district. The restricted area regulations prohibit foreigners from the entire Nar-Phu Valley.

The next village is Chame (2630 metres), the administrative headquarters for the Manang district. There is electricity here, and also a wireless station, a school, many shops, a health post, post office, police checkpost and a bank among the closely spaced stone dwellings. The incongruity of a shotgun-toting guard in front of the bank is almost worth a picture. There are many hotels in Chame, and also beyond the village on the other side of the river; the *Kamala Lodge* is the most popular trekkers' hotel. Across the river there are two small hot springs, but they're not big enough for swimming. Throughout the day there are views of Lamjung Himal (6986 metres), Annapurna II (7937 metres) and Annapurna IV (7525 metres).

Day 6: Chame to Pisang

From Chame, the trail crosses a side stream, and then the Marsyangdi itself on a large suspension bridge, passes by a few houses, the *Kesang Lodge* and *Chhiring Lodge* on the northern side of the river, and proceeds through fields of barley to Teleku at 2775 metres. The large *New Tibetan Lodge* is downstream from the bridge on the way to the hot spring.

After climbing past a huge apple orchard surrounded by a stone wall (apples and peaches are available everywhere in the region during the autumn), the trail descends to a bridge at 2840 metres. The village just across this bridge, **Bratang**, used to be a Khampa settlement, though it is now largely abandoned. The Khampas had installed a

gate on the bridge, thus controlling the traffic up and down the Manang Valley; you can still see the remnants of the gate. In Bratang, there is a small, stone memorial to a Japanese climber who died in an avalanche while trekking across the Thorung La – a grisly reminder to wait several days after any heavy snowstorm before trying to cross the pass.

Don't cross the bridge to Bratang; stay on the northern side of the river and follow a new trail that was blasted out of the side of the cliff.

The valley is steep and narrow here, and the trail goes through deep forests. When the trail crosses to the south side of the river on a long suspension bridge at 3040 metres, there is the first view of the dramatic Paungda Danda rock face, a tremendous curved slab of rock rising more than 1500 metres from the river. There are also views of Annapurna II to the south and Pisang peak to the north-east. Climbing over a ridge marked with a stone cairn and prayer flags, the trail continues the steep ascent to the upper Marsyangdi Valley.

The lower portion of Pisang, a cluster of houses and a long mani wall near the bridge, is at an elevation of 3190 metres. Note the wooden canals for water to drive the two mills in this village. There are many hotels bunched together at the bridge here, including the *Annapurna Lodge*, the *Ghalung Gurung* and the *Himali Hotel*. The main village of Pisang is across the bridge and 100 metres uphill, but there are no hotels in that part of the village. There are excellent camping places in the forest on the south bank of the river.

Day 7: Pisang to Manang

The trek is now in the region known as Nyesyang, the upper portion of the Manang district, which has about 5000 inhabitants in six major villages. The region is much drier than the Gyasumdo region in the lower reaches of the Marsyangdi Valley. There is only a small amount of rainfall here during the monsoon because the Annapurna range to the south alters the climate significantly from that of the rest of Nepal south of the

Himalaya. The people of Nyesyang raise wheat, barley, buckwheat, potatoes and beans, but the cold, almost arid, climate limits them to a single crop annually. They keep herds of yaks, goats, cows and horses. Horses are an important means of transport in the relatively flat upper portion of Manang Valley. People often ride them, or use horses as pack animals to altitudes as high as 5416 metres, over the Thorung La between Manang and Jomsom.

Many people in Nyesyang villages speak fluent English and dress in trendy Western clothing they have bought during overseas trading excursions. This presents an incongruous picture as they herd yaks and plough the fields of these remote villages. Their exposure to the West also makes them shrewd and eager businesspeople, so the traders and shops of Manang are all expensive. There are few bargains to be had here. If you travelled to Kathmandu from Hong Kong or Bangkok, perhaps you were aware of the Tibetan-looking people all dressed in identical jackets or jogging suits and carrying identical luggage; these people were Manangis returning from a shopping expedition.

A short distance beyond Pisang, the trail climbs a steep ridge that extends across the valley. At the top of this spur is an excellent view of Manang Valley, with Tilicho peak (7132 metres) at its head and a view back to Pisang peak, one of the trekking peaks. After a short descent from the ridge, the trail reaches the broad, forested valley floor. Most of the valley is used as grazing land for sheep, goats, horses and yaks. Across the river, high on the opposite bank, is the village of Ghyaru.

There is an alternate high route from upper Pisang along the north bank of the river that passes through **Ghyaru** and **Ngawal** and rejoins the main trail at Mungji. The trail is steep and takes about 1½ hours longer than the direct route along the south bank, but provides spectacular views of the Annapurna range to the south, and is a worthwhile side trip. There is an interesting gompa in Ghyaru and a gompa in Ngawal that was built in

1990. The people of Ghyaru are happy to welcome trekkers and there are a few hotels that offer basic facilities. This is also the start of the climbing routes to Pisang peak, Chulu East and Chulu West, all of which are visible from the trail. You can also make a diversion to Ser Gompa, located on a plateau high above the river on the northern side.

The southern trail avoids all this climbing and follows the valley past Manang's airstrip at **Hongde**, elevation 3325 metres. The last police checkpost in the valley is at the airport. A few bhattis and hotels have grown up around Hongde; the largest is the *Marsyandi Hotel*. Several curio shops nearby sell 'real Tibetan things' made in India, Hong Kong and Kathmandu.

There are scheduled flights from Hongde to Pokhara, and occasional direct flights to Kathmandu. They are usually booked by rich Manangis en route to and from trading excursions, so there is little chance of obtaining a seat except in an emergency.

Half an hour beyond the airport is the huge Sabje Khola Valley, with Annapurna III and IV at the head. Just south of the trail, in this spectacular setting, is a mountaineering school which was built in 1979 with a grant from the Yugoslav Mountaineering Federation. It's now operated by the Nepal Mountaineering Association in cooperation with the Union of International Alpine Associations (UIAA). It offers a six-week course for climbers from Nepal and neighbouring countries during August each year.

The trail crosses the Marsyangdi again on a big wooden bridge near Mungji at 3360 metres, then traverses to **Bryaga** at 3475 metres. The largest part of this Tibetan-style village of about 200 houses hides behind a large rock outcrop. The houses are stacked one atop another, each with an open veranda formed by a neighbour's rooftop. The gompa, perched on a high crag overlooking the village, is the largest in the district and has an outstanding display of statues, thangkas (ornate Tibetan paintings) and manuscripts estimated to be 400 to 500 years old. Take a torch (flashlight) and visit the gallery that runs behind the main altar. The kanis over the trail that mark the entrance and exit from Bryaga are particularly impressive.

There is a good place to camp in the meadow below the village. Bryaga was one of the last villages to join the trekking bandwagon. For years there were no hotels here, but now there are several establishments, including the large *New Yak Hotel* near the trail. There are also hotels half an hour away in Manang. Be careful when you enter the village of Bryaga, especially at night; the dogs are vicious. In the spring there are archery contests in Bryaga and Manang. It's a colourful spectacle with lots of drums and dancing, but be a bit careful of standing close to the target after the booze starts flowing.

The country here is very arid, dominated by weird cliffs of yellow rock, eroded into dramatic pillars alongside the trail, and by the towering heights of the Himalaya across the valley to the south. It is only a short walk, past mani walls and across a stream where several mills grind wheat and barley, to the plateau of Manang village at 3535 metres. The *Annapurna Himal Hotel* adjoins the entrance kani to Manang village, and has Tibetan gloves, hats and sweaters for sale, as well as food and lodging. The walls are decorated with pictures from Chinese and Hindi film magazines. There are other hotels before the main part of Manang; the *Karma Hotel*, in the centre of the village, is the most popular facility. Manang has electricity and the villagers have a very Western outlook; hot showers and videos are the speciality here, and many Manangi youths travel up and down the valley by mountain bike.

The Himalayan Rescue Association operates an aid post here, with a doctor in attendance throughout the trekking season. The HRA post occupies a new building to the right of the trail as you enter the village and provides daily lectures on altitude sickness, usually at 3 pm. The doctors are available for consultation and treatment. Their services are not free; ask to see the schedule of charges before you request a diagnosis. There are shops where you can stock up on medical supplies, food, clothing and equipment for the pass crossing. If you or your porters do not have warm socks, hats and gloves, this is the time and place to buy them.

Day 8: Manang

You should spend the day in Manang village and the vicinity to acclimatise to the higher elevations you will encounter towards Thorung La. There are many opportunities for both easy and strenuous day excursions from Manang. It is possible to climb the ridge to the north of the village for excellent views of Annapurna IV, Annapurna II and Tarke Kang (formerly known as Glacier Dome, 7193 metres); or to descend from the village to the glacial lake at the foot of the huge icefall that drops from the northern slopes of Gangapurna (7454 metres).

From the village of **Khangsar**, the last settlement in the valley en route to Tilicho Lake, there are splendid views of the 'Great Barrier', a name given by Herzog to the high ridge between Roc Noir and Nilgiri North. Another choice would be a walk to visit the **Bhojo Gompa**, the red edifice perched on the ridge between Bryaga and Manang, and the most active monastery in the region. The village gompa at the western end of the village is also worth visiting.

Before the first trekkers came to Manang in 1977, the region saw few outsiders. The only traders were the people of Manang themselves, and the population was intolerant of outsiders. There was little need for inns and other facilities. In 1950, Maurice Herzog came to Manang village in a futile search for food for his party, only to return nearly starving to his camp at Tilicho Lake. With the advent of tourism, however, there has been extensive hotel construction, and the Manangis warmly welcome tourists – particularly those with lots of rupees. The resourceful Manangbhot people have been quick to adapt to this new source of income, selling semiprecious stones (from Tibet, they claim, but more likely from Bangkok), foodstuffs, Tibetan jewellery and other items of interest to tourists. An alternative to a day hike is a bargaining session with these skilful traders.

The village itself is a compact collection of 500 flat-roofed houses separated by narrow alleyways. To reach a doorway you must ascend a steep log notched with steps. The setting of the village is most dramatic, with the summits of Annapurna and Gangapurna less than eight km away, and a huge icefall rumbling and crashing on the flanks of the peaks.

Day 9: Manang to Letdar

The trek now begins an ascent of almost 2000 metres to Thorung La. From Manang village, the trail crosses a stream, climbs to Tengi, 120 metres above Manang, then continues to climb out of the Marsyangdi Valley, turning north-west up the valley of the Jarsang Khola. The trail follows this valley north, passing a few goths as it steadily gains elevation. You have left the large trees below; here the vegetation consists of scrub juniper and alpine grasses.

The trail passes the small village of **Gunsang**, a cluster of flat mud roofs just below the trail at 3960 metres. The *Marsyandi Hotel & Lodge*, alongside the trail, specializes in Tibetan bread and chhang. The route then passes through meadows, where horses and yaks graze, and sparse forests of juniper, rose and barberry. After crossing a large stream that flows from Chulu West and Gundang, the trail passes an ancient mani wall in a pleasant meadow at 4000 metres.

Beyond here is **Yak Kharka**, also known as Koche, where the new *Gangapurna Hotel* operated by Maya Gurung (who specializes in yeast rolls) offers an alternative to staying at Letdar. Villagers from Manang collect firewood from the slopes above, which also support herds of blue sheep. An hour further, at 4250 metres, is a rapidly deteriorating two-storey house – the stone walls are falling down and the biscuit-tin roof is both rusting and blowing away. This is Letdar, the next-to-last shelter before the pass. The *Pema Hotel*, first on the left, is said to be the best; second is *Jimmy's Home* and least popular is the *Lathair Guest House*.

Day 10: Letdar to Thorung Phedi

From Letdar (some spell it Lathar), the trail continues to climb along the east bank of the Jarsang Khola, then descends and crosses the stream on a wooden bridge at 4310 metres. Make a short ascent on a good trail to a tea shop. The route then follows a narrow trail across a high, unstable, scree slope, then descends to Thorung Phedi, a dirty rock-strewn meadow surrounded by vertical cliffs at 4420 metres. If you are staying in hotels, climb to a shelf about 10 minutes above the river to a police checkpost and Thorung Phedi's only hotel. If you are camping, either stay here by the river or at the main campsite on a shelf about 10 minutes beyond the hotel.

Local traders ride horses from Manang to Muktinath in a single day, but the large elevation gain, the need for acclimatisation, and the high altitudes all make it imperative to take at least two days to do the trip on foot. The *Thorung Phedi Hotel* can be very, very crowded, especially if there is snow. There are two buildings; one for dining and one for sleeping. Forget about sitting around a pleasant fire here. When it's crowded, you buy a meal coupon from a faceless person behind a window and are handed a cup of tea (Rs 6) or a plate of dal bhat (Rs 45) through another window. A hundred people or more cram into the hotel each night, except when snow has blocked the pass for a few days – at those times, several hundred impatient and irritable trekkers pack themselves into every corner of the hotel.

Nights are even more miserable because of the 3 am departure that many people schedule. It really isn't necessary to start that early. In fact it can be dangerous because it is quite cold until the sun rises and this can lead to hypothermia and frostbite. A reasonable departure time is just before daybreak, at 4 or 5 am. The hotel operator at Thorung Phedi has a horse that you can ride over the pass for an exorbitant price (last quotation was Rs 1500) if you are not well. Blue sheep, and even snow leopards, sometimes magically appear in this valley; the crow-like birds are choughs and the large birds that circle overhead are lammergeiers and Himalayan griffons, not eagles. Be sure to boil or treat water here; the sanitation in Thorung Phedi and Letdar is terrible, and giardiasis is rampant.

Day 11: Thorung Phedi to Muktinath

Phedi, which means 'foot of the hill' is a common Nepali name for any settlement at the bottom of a long climb. The trail becomes steep immediately after leaving Thorung Phedi, switchbacking up moraines and following rocky ridges as it ascends to the pass. Local people have used this trail for hundreds of years to bring herds of sheep and yaks in and out of Manang. Thus the trail, while often steep, is well defined and easy to follow.

The only complications to the crossing are the high elevation and the chance of snow. The pass is usally snowbound in late December and during January. Snow can also block the pass at any time of year if there is an unseasonable storm. When there is deep new snow, the crossing becomes difficult – often impossible. It then becomes necessary to retreat back to Dumre, or to wait until the snow has consolidated and local people have forged a trail. The only shelters between here and Muktinath are the tiny facilities at 4100 metres, far down the other side of the pass. An overnight stop in the snow, unless well planned in advance, can be treacherous and deadly, especially for porters.

The trail climbs and climbs, traversing in and out of many canyons formed by interminable moraines. It is a reasonably good trail unless there is snow, in which case the route may traverse scree slopes and ascend through steep snow. It takes from four to six hours from Thorung Phedi to the pass, but the many false summits make the climb seem to go on forever.

Thorung La, with its traditional chorten, prayer flags and stone cairn, is at an elevation of 5416 metres. The views from the trail, and from the pass itself, are outstanding high Himalayan scenes. You can see the long ridge of high mountains, that Herzog called the 'Great Barrier', which separates the drier, Tibet-like region of Manang from the rest of Nepal. You can also see (to the south) the Annapurnas, Gangapurna and Yak Gawa (6484 metres), a heavily glaciated peak; the barren Kali Gandaki Valley far below to the west; and the rock peak of Thorungtse (6482 metres) to the north.

The descent is steep and rough on the knees – a loss of more than 1600 metres in less than three hours. The descent often begins in snow, which soon gives way to switchbacks down another series of moraines. Sometimes the correct route is not obvious; just remember that you are headed downhill and that Muktinath is on the left side of the valley. During the descent there are excellent views of Dhaulagiri (8167 metres) standing alone in the distance across the valley. Eventually the moraines yield to grassy slopes and the final descent to Muktinath is a pleasant walk along the upper part of the Jhong Khola Valley.

There is a hotel at **Muktinath Phedi** (4100 metres), where the grassy slopes begin. It's run by a Tibetan man from Jharkot, and offers drinks, food and even souvenirs. It is better to rely on this hotel only for refreshment, not for accommodation, though you could stay here if you were crossing the pass in the opposite direction. It is also possible to camp here if the tiny stream nearby is flowing. If, for some reason, you are following this route in reverse, Muktinath Phedi is about an hour and a half from Muktinath.

The trail crosses meadows, drops into a ravine that is the start of the Jhong Khola, climbs out of the ravine and enters Muktinath at 3800 metres, near the temple. There is no accommodation here, but it is only a five to 10-minute walk to Ranipauwa where there is a large choice of accommodation and a police checkpost. See the description of Muktinath on Day 7 of the Jomsom trek for suggestions on where to stay in Rainipauwa.

Days 12-18: Muktinath to Pokhara

The route to Pokhara follows the Jomsom trek described earlier, but you must read this part in reverse. Kagbeni is worth a visit, as is the Dhaulagiri icefall above Larjung, so schedule an extra three days for side trips. The winds in the Kali Gandaki are powerful and can drive sand and dust into your face. A scarf and sunglasses provide good protection as you trek down the valley.

When you reach Tatopani you have a

choice of routes. You can either follow the old trail up to Ghorapani and back down to Birethanti, or you can take a more level route that follows the Kali Gandaki to Baglung. You can also make a side trip to Ghandruk, Landrung or the Annapurna Sanctuary. All these possibilities have already been described.

The Royal Trek

This is an easy, short trek that starts near Pokhara and offers good mountain views. It gained its name because Prince Charles and an entourage of 90 guests, camp followers and staff trekked here. The trek has also seen the likes of such luminaries as Mick Jagger. The route is not a popular one, so you will see few other trekkers, but this also means that the hotel facilities are mediocre.

Day 1: Pokhara to Kalikastan
It is about five km (a 20-minute drive by taxi) to the Bijayapur army camp just east of the Bijayapur Khola. A broad trail starts in rice fields, then ascends through the village of Rakhigaun to a chautaara, a resting place under a large pipal tree.

These trees, planted centuries ago, have broad leaves and branches that extend outwards for a long distance in mushroom fashion, offering welcome shade to travellers. It was under a banyan tree (also called a Bodi tree) that Buddha attained enlightenment in India, over 2000 years ago. You can differentiate the banyan from the pipal tree (a related species) by the long roots that droop down from the limbs, a peculiarity of the banyan. Around these shade trees, people have built walls and chautaaras (stone benches) for porters to rest their loads upon as they pause during the hot, steep climbs. Many people build a chautaara in the name of a deceased relative.

The trail climbs gently along a ridge top through Brahmin and Chhetri villages towards Kalikastan at 1370 metres. The children along this part of the trail are

particularly persistent about asking for money, balloons or pens. Depending on the time that you start walking, you can camp either before or after the village of Kalikastan. Both campsites are on ridge tops with good mountain views, including Machhapuchhare and Annapurna.

Day 2: Kalikastan to Shaklung
The trail continues along the forested ridge top through Thulokot to Mathi Thana, where there are a few tea shops. There is a short climb, then the trek reaches Naudanda. Continue along the ridge to a school at Lipini village, then make a steep but short climb through forests to the Gurung village of Shaklung at 1730 metres.

Day 3: Shaklung to Chisopani
The Himalayan skyline continues to change as the route comes abreast of Annapurna II, Lamjung Himal, Manaslu and Himalchuli. From Shaklung, the trail drops steeply down the south side of the hill to a large tree, a chautaara, several tea shops and a police checkpost. This is a trail junction; trails lead from here west to Begnas Tal and east to the Marsyangdi Khola. The Royal trek route climbs towards Chisopani, winding around the back of the hill to the village. A short distance above Chisopani village is a high knoll where there is a small temple. This is Chisopani Danda (danda means 'ridgetop') where there is a camp with splendid mountain views.

Day 4: Chisopani to Pokhara
From Chisopani Danda, descend along the ridge for an hour or so, then descend steeply on the stone steps, into a small valley and a stream that feeds Rupa Tal. Continue for a short distance through the rice fields, then make a final ascent to the ridge that separates Begnas Tal and Rupa Tal, on a wide path that you will share with many local people. From the ridge, descend into the Pokhara Valley, joining the road at the crowded, dirty and noisy Begnas Bazaar. Take a taxi or a bus for the 12 km, 30-minute drive back to Pokhara.

Langtang & Helambu

The region north of Kathmandu offers a multitude of trekking destinations, all accessible without flights. The three major areas are Langtang, Gosainkund and Helambu, which can be combined in many different ways to make treks from seven to 16 days long.

Langtang is a narrow valley that lies just south of the Tibetan border. It is sandwiched between the main Himalayan range to the north and a slightly lower range of snowy peaks to the south. Langtang Lirung (7246 metres) dominates the valley to the north; Gang Chhenpo (6388 metres) and Naya Kangri (5846 metres) lie to the south; and Dorje Lakpa (6966 metres) protects the east end of the valley. The area was designated Nepal's first Himalayan national park in 1971.

This high and isolated region is inhabited by Tamangs whose religious practices, language and dress are much more similar to those of Tibet than to the traditions of their cousins in the Middle Hills. A visit to the Langtang Valley offers an opportunity to explore villages, to climb small peaks and to visit glaciers at a comfortably low elevation. According to legend, a lama following a runaway yak discovered the valley. Hence the name – *lang* is Tibetan for 'yak' and *teng* (more correctly *dhang*) means 'to follow'. Yaks still live in the valley, but they now share it with trekkers who make a seven to 11-day round trip from Kathmandu. Because there are good opportunities for moderate climbing excursions here, you should allow a few extra days for exploration of the extensive glacier system.

You can vary the trek to Langtang by returning to Kathmandu via the holy lakes of Gosainkund at 4300 metres, or you can make a short trek from Dhunche to Gosainkund. Thousands of Hindu pilgrims visit the lakes during a full moon festival in August. The lake is also sacred to Buddhists.

Helambu, about 75 km north of Kathmandu, is an area inhabited by Sherpas. You can include Helambu in a Langtang trek, either via Gosainkund or across the 5106-metre Ganja La. In winter, both of the high routes from Langtang are usually snow-covered and dangerous, difficult or impossible. The Helambu trek is popular because it is short, stays below 3500 metres and is feasible all winter. It is an easy trek to organise because transport from Kathmandu to Sundarijal, the starting point of the trek, is readily available and inexpensive.

The language, culture and dress of the Helambu Sherpas are very different from the Solu Khumbu Sherpas. The accessibility of Helambu has created an influx of tourists who have encouraged begging, the sale of 'genuine antiques' aged over the family fireplace, and several incidents of thievery. It takes eight days to trek from Kathmandu to Helambu and back, or 12 to 14 days to include both Langtang and Helambu in a single trek without any backtracking.

INFORMATION
Maps
The best maps of Langtang and Helambu are the German *Helambu-Langtang* 1:100,000 map (1987) and the more detailed 1:50,000 east and west sheets titled *Langtang Himal* (1990). The Mandala *Helambu-Langtang, Gosainkund* 1:100,000 map is a Nepalese version of the more expensive German map. The Hotel Langtang View in Dhunche has produced a good trekking map with route profiles and up-to-date information on tea stalls and other facilities.

The US Army Map Service maps of the region are sheets 45-1, *Kathmandu*; 45-13, *Jongka Dzong*; and 45-2 *Mount Everest*. All are based on the Survey of India maps that were published in the early 1960s, so all show the trails as they existed then – not now. Beware especially of the area from Dhunche to Langtang village as shown on any of these maps.

GETTING THERE & AWAY
Air
Langtang The airstrip is about an hour beyond Kyanjin Gompa, but has no scheduled service. Charter flights are irregular, and are only in six-passenger Pilatus Porter aircraft or charter helicopters, so don't count on finding a seat back to Kathmandu unless you have made prior arrangements. The airstrip is notorious for becoming snowbound in December, January and February.

Bus
Dhunche The starting place for Langtang treks is Dhunche (pronounced 'doon-chay'), 112 km from Kathmandu. Buses to Dhunche leave from the bus terminal north of Kathmandu. The first bus leaves at 7 am, costs Rs 64 and takes all day to reach Dhunche. You can also take a bus to Trisuli Bazaar and walk to Dhunche, but the trail is steep and has nothing to offer except physical exertion. It is better to take a bus all the way to Dhunche and let the bus do all the initial climbing.

The bus from Dhunche to Kathmandu leaves at 7.30 am. Make reservations the day before at the Thakali Hotel in Dhunche.

Sundarijal At 1350 metres, Sundarijal is the best place to start a Helambu trek. You can get to Sundarijal by minibus, or even a taxi, on an unpaved road seven km from Boudhanath. You can also begin the trek from Boudhanath, taking a few hours to walk to Sundarijal along the level roadway.

Panchkal This is an alternate starting point for a trek to Helambu. Panchkal (the name of the settlement where the trail meets the road is actually Lamidanda) is on the road to the Tibetan border. Take a bus to Barahbise or Lamosangu, bang on the roof of the bus just after the army camp and jump off.

The Helambu road joins the Kathmandu to Kodari road at Lamidanda, near Panchkal; here you can catch one of the rickety local buses that ply between Barahbise and Kathmandu.

Indrawati Valley You can finish the Helambu trek by flagging down a jeep, truck or bus from the road in the Indrawati Valley. Minibuses are available in Sipa Ghat or Malemchi, and seats are negotiable on vehicles even further up the valley.

SPECIAL RULES
Fuel
Use of firewood is prohibited throughout the Langtang National Park, so you must carry stoves and fuel if you are not using teahouses.

The Rs 650 national park entrance fee is conscientiously collected. There are entrance stations and park checkposts throughout the region that hassle endlessly about permits. The road to Dhunche passes through a portion of the park, so you must pay the park fee even if you only drive to Dhunche.

Langtang Trek

This section suggests a five-day approach to the heart of the Langtang Valley. From Langtang village or Kyanjin Gompa there are several alternatives for returning to Kathmandu. It is possible to make the trek back to Dhunche in only three days from Langtang village because much of it is downhill. If you have basic mountaineering skills, you can cross the high route over the Ganja La into Helambu. A third alternative is to trek back to Syabru from Langtang, then cross into Helambu via Gosainkund.

Day 1: Kathmandu to Dhunche via Trisuli Bazaar
It is about a four-hour drive (six hours by local bus) on a paved highway that twists and climbs over ridges to the Trisuli Valley. Passing Balaju and Nagarjun, the road leaves the Kathmandu Valley at Kakani (2145 metres), where there are excellent views of Annapurna II, Manaslu and Ganesh Himal, and descends into the broad Trisuli Valley. The bus usually makes a tea stop at

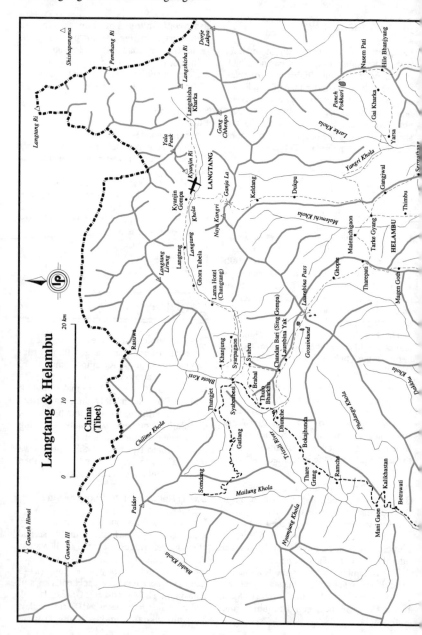

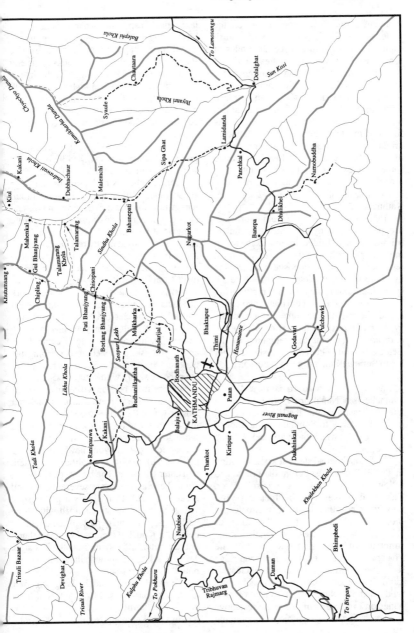

Ranipauwa, the only large village on the route, at Km 27. This region is the radish capital of Nepal; you can see huge piles of long freshly washed radishes *(mula* in Nepali) alongside the road awaiting transport to the markets of Kathmandu.

After a long descent through terraced fields, the road crosses the Tadi Khola at Km 60, then climbs onto a plateau and passes fields of mustard, corn and rice planted in bright red soil. There is a police checkpost two km before Trisuli where the police sometimes examine trekking permits. The road then passes an army camp and rolls into Trisuli Bazaar at 548 metres, 72 km from Kathmandu.

Trisuli is the site of a dam and hydroelectric project built by the Indian Technical Mission. A large bridge dominates the town; most shops are before the bridge, and most restaurants are on the opposite side, near the hydroelectric plant. Hotel facilities here are spartan and the restaurants are pretty grim. Try the *Ranjit Lodge* for dal bhat. If you must spend the night here, take a look at the *Pratistha Lodge* near the power plant or the *Shakyar Lodge* near the beginning of the Betrawati road. Otherwise, continue eight km to Betrawati for a slightly better selection of hotels.

The unpaved road to **Betrawati** and Dhunche is a Nepal army project. It took almost 10 years to build the 105-km road that goes all the way to Somdang at the foot of Ganesh Himal, where there are lead and zinc mines.

The Dhunche road starts at a petrol station in Trisuli Bazaar just before the bridge and follows the east bank of the Trisuli River. The road passes two bridges carrying massive pipes that feed the hydroelectric project and climbs slightly to the village of Betrawati at 620 metres. Betrawati is at the junction of the Trisuli River and the Phalangu Khola, at the foot of a steep ridge that rises towards Langtang and Gosainkund. It's 42 km of steep switchbacks on a wild road to Dhunche; at some points it hangs on to a steep cliff 1000 metres above the river. The road is subject to continual landslides – especially when it rains – so a bus trip to Dhunche can be an adventure.

At Betrawati the road crosses the Phalangu Khola, then switchbacks at the end of the ridge for 15 km, through Brahmin and Chhetri villages to **Kalikhastan** at 1390 metres. This is the entrance to Langtang National Park; the police examine trekking permits here. The villages now become more spread out, and as the elevation increases the intense cultivation of the lowland rice-growing country gives way to herding, and small fields of corn, millet and vegetables. The road reaches its high point on the ridge at 1980 metres, then makes a long contour, with a few ups and downs through oak and rhododendron forests, passing above Ramche at Km 33, and then through Thare at Km 37. The road finally reaches Dhunche, the administrative headquarters of the region, at 1950 metres, three to four hours' drive from Betrawati.

Just before Dhunche is the national park headquarters, where park personnel collect the park fee and charge US$100 for a filming permit if you tell them you have a video camera. There is a small visitors' centre here, and if you ask, a bronchure describing the park may be available. Keep the receipt for the park fee safely with your trekking permit – everyone from here on will want to see this document. Drive 50 metres further to another barrier where the driver records the vehicle information, and then a few hundred metres more to an army checkpost – your first chance to show off your newly purchased national park receipt. Formalities completed, you enter Dhunche. The bus stop is in upper Dhunche where there are several hotels and a camp ground. Dhunche is a picturesque village with narrow streets lined with stone buildings. The main part of Dhunche is below the road, but there are no hotels there; you are better off staying near the bus stop. There is a large army installation in a compound above the road.

The *Hotel Thakali* and the *Langtang View* are the up-market establishments, but there are several other less fancy operations nearby. The Langtang National Park administration has prepared a fixed menu and price list and requires lodges throughout the park to follow it, so choose a hotel based on looks and service because the prices are (or should be) the same. The camping charge is a larcenous Rs 50 per tent and Rs 100 for use of a kitchen shelter. Hotel rooms are only Rs 20, so if you have a tent, save it for the next day or hike 1½ hours on to Thulo Bharkhu. If you have your own vehicle, it is preferable to drive the few km to Thulo Bharkhu and camp there.

You can also continue driving 15 km to **Syabrubesi**, an interesting village on the banks of the Bhote Kosi at 1420 metres. From Syabrubesi you can begin the trek to Langtang and save a day of walking, joining the route described here on the third day of this trek near the *Landslide Lodge* at 1550 metres.

Day 2: Dhunche to Syabru

From the bus stop at Dhunche, take a short cut down a ravine next to the Hotel Thakali through the main part of the village. The short cut saves a long walk on a big switchback and rejoins the road at the bottom of the village. Follow the road downhill, past a government agriculture station and a small army post, to a left-hand switchback. Nearby is the start of the direct (steep) trail to Chandan Bari and Sing Gompa; follow this trail eastward up the Trisuli Valley if you are going directly to Gosainkund.

To go to Langtang, stay on the road and cross a new cement bridge over the Trisuli River, which is much smaller here in its upper reaches. Take a moment to reflect on the power of Himalayan streams as you pass the remnants of a twisted steel bridge that once spanned the stream. Alongside the first

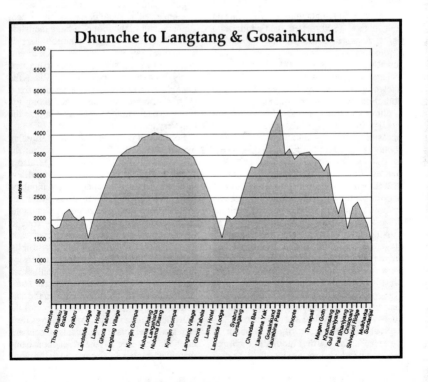

Dhunche to Langtang & Gosainkund

waterfall beyond the bridge is an alternative trail to Sing Gompa – straight up an almost vertical cleft in the rock beside the stream.

The Trisuli River flows from Gosainkund where, according to legend, Shiva released the waters of the holy lakes with his trident *(trisul)*. The trail north, up the main valley, was once a major trade route with Tibet and is still used by a fair amount of traffic. The route to Tibet via the border town of Rasuwa and the Tibetan village of Kyirong may eventually be opened for trekking if the present trend of allowing cross-border trekking continues. The upper part of the river is named Bhote Kosi ('river from Tibet'), as are most of the rivers that cross the Himalaya into Nepal. When a Nepalese river joins it, the Bhote Kosi assumes the name of its smaller tributary. Thus the larger fork of the Trisuli River becomes the Bhote Kosi above Dhunche.

The route to Langtang follows the road up to a ridge at 1800 metres, then continues a short distance to the Tamang village of **Thulo Bharkhu** at 1860 metres, which has a few rough hotels. About 100 metres from the village, the road crosses a small stream with a few water-driven mills. Leave the road here and climb steeply to the schoolhouse, then continue up a stone staircase. The walk eventually becomes a delightful – and occasionally level – hike through pine and rhododendron forests to Dau Danda, which is a single tea shop in the forest at 1980 metres. At the Tamang village of **Brabal** (2200 metres) there is a wooden bhatti (tea shop) near the trail. Most of the village and its potato and corn fields is hidden behind a ridge.

After a short climb, the trail reaches a ridge crest at 2300 metres, where the trek finally enters the Langtang Valley. There are views northward of snow peaks in Tibet, west to Ganesh Himal and east to Naya Kangri, the 5846-metre peak above Ganja La. A short, steep descent through bamboo forests leads to Syabru at 2100 metres.

Syabru is a pleasant village of about 70 houses, many with elaborately carved wooden windows, strung out along a ridge.

There are numerous hotels at the upper end of the village where the trail enters it. There is no need to suggest a hotel here; a bevy of very aggressive English-speaking Tamang women will accost you as you enter the village to extol the virtues of their establishments. Before you settle in for the night, consider the implications of the sign at the campsite before the village that advertises 'no dogs here'. There are good places to camp before Syabru and also in corn and millet fields far below the village.

Day 3: Syabru to Lama Hotel

The trail to Langtang descends along the ridge on Syabru's main street, then drops to the Ghopcha Khola, first through terraced fields, then through forests of oak, maple, alder and finally bamboo. The trail crosses the stream on a stone and cement bridge, then begins a climb across a ridge dotted with a few bhattis. The route descends on a steep, slippery path to the foot of a huge landslide at 1550 metres. A trail junction here is marked with signs painted on a rock directing you either to Langtang or back to the road at Syabrubesi. Just beyond the slide, the *Landslide Lodge* provides a chance for a short rest, before climbing back along the southern banks of the Langtang Khola as the trail very quickly gains elevation.

For the rest of this day and the following morning, there are few settlements, but the forest abounds with birds. There is also a variety of wildlife in these forests: yellow-throated martin, wild boar, langur monkey, red panda and Himalayan black bear. The trail climbs to *Bamboo Lodge*, a jungly hotel at 1850 metres that is not quite as exotic as its name implies. This region specializes in the sale of colourful woollen socks and belts. The ascent continues to a steel suspension bridge at 2000 metres; there is a small bhatti on the south (shady) side, and the *Hotel Bridge Side* on the opposite bank in the sun.

The route crosses to the north bank of the Langtang Khola, then climbs alongside a series of waterfalls. The forest is sparser and drier on this side of the river, consisting mainly of scrub oak, as opposed to the damp forest of large pines on the shady southern bank. Climb steeply to a landslide and the *Langtang View & Lodge* at **Rimche**, 2250 metres. The *Namaste Tibetan Lodge* is a bit higher at 2330 metres, and the *Tibetan Lodge* is 10 minutes beyond. There is a trail junction here that connects to a high route back to Syarpagaon and Syabrubesi; this was the old trail to Langtang before the bridge was built across the Langtang Khola. You have now finished most of the day's climbing; descend gently to the settlement of Changtang, popularly known as Lama Hotel, at 2380 metres. There are at least five hotels here, including the *Lama Hotel* itself, and a few camping spots. The next accommodation is about 1½ hours beyond at *Riverside Lodge*.

Day 4: Lama Hotel to Langtang Village

The day starts with a gentle climb, but it soon becomes steeper, climbing high above the Langtang Khola. In places it is so steep that the trail is on logs anchored to the valley wall. Tantalising glimpses of Langtang Lirung, 7246 metres, appear through the trees. The settlement of **Gumnachok** consists of *Riverside Lodge*, on the banks of the river, and another *Riverside Lodge*, in a clearing known as Chhunama, 15 minutes beyond. The trail crosses a stream on a log bridge, then climbs through meadows to **Ghora Tabela** at 3000 metres. Once a Tibetan resettlement project, this is now a Nepalese army and national park post and has no permanent inhabitants.

The national park lodge is operated on contract and is now named *Lovely Lodge*. There is another police checkpost where they check, yet again, to be sure that you paid the national park entrance fee. If you somehow slipped past the station at Dhunche, they will collect the fee – and possibly a fine – here. The trail ascends gradually, as the valley becomes wider and wider, past yak pastures, *Thangshyap Lodge*, some mani stones and scattered Tamang villages to the *Langtang Gompa Hotel*. You can see the village gompa just above the hotel; if you want to visit the

temple, ask the hotel for information and assistance. The trail then descends into a valley to cross a stream and climbs past several water-driven mills and prayer wheels to the large settlement of Langtang at 3500 metres.

This village is the headquarters for Langtang National Park; the park buildings are those with green metal roofs below the village. The best hotel is the *Village View Lodge* at the entrance to the town; most other hotels in Langtang are rooms in private homes, which are heated and scented by yak-dung fires. The park administration allows an increase in hotel prices at Langtang village and above, so everything suddenly becomes more costly. The houses of Langtang and the neighbouring communities have Tibetan-style flat roofs and are surrounded by stone walls enclosing fields of buckwheat, potatoes, wheat, turnips and barley. The villagers keep herds of yaks and cattle here and in pastures above the village.

It is easy to go beyond Langtang, but not a good idea from the point of view of acclimatisation. You may not have noticed it because the trail has climbed gently, but you have ascended more than a thousand metres today. Trekkers have fallen ill, and some have died in this region because of altitude problems. Don't go beyond Langtang village if you have come from Lama Hotel, and descend immediately if you have a severe headache or vomiting.

Day 5: Langtang to Kyanjin Gompa

The trail winds through the village and climbs onto a ridge dominated by a large square chorten and a long row of mani walls. It then climbs gradually past the small village of Muna to Singdum, where there is a small lodge. Continuing through yak pastures as the valley becomes broader, the path crosses a wooden cantilever bridge, then climbs a moraine where you can finally see Kyanjin Gompa. It is a short descent to lodges, a cheese factory and an almost defunct gompa. The Swiss Association for Technical Assistance started the cheese factory in 1955. It

Langtang & Helambu – Flora & Fauna

Trees The **larch** of the Langtang area and western Nepal is an unusual conifer in that it is deciduous. When this species displays its yellow colours in the fall it will not be mistaken for anything else.

Wildflowers In order to really experience the wildflowers in their profusion, one must endure the monsoon rains or trek to the remote rain shadow areas of the west during summer. There are, however, some species that bloom during many parts of the year, like the sky-blue **gentians** of the dry subalpine and alpine regions, and the lavender primulas, or **primroses**, of moist areas. The varieties of **epiphytic orchids** which adorn the wet forests also flower at various times of the year.

Gentians

Birds In Langtang watch for hawks or **buzzards**, medium-sized raptors with broad wings and rounded tails, often fanned. Though there are only three species to look for, their highly variable plumage makes identification difficult. These birds are highly visible during winter and are likely to be seen in pairs, mostly below 3000 metres.

A much smaller, but very distinctive bird seen on the open ground, is the **hoopoe** with orange plumage and black wings with broad white stripes. This species also features a retractable crest that is flared when it alights and a long, slender decurved bill that is used for probing the ground.

In order to identify the birds of the forest, one will need a keen eye and some tenacity. The ability to recognise birds by their calls will greatly facilitate identification in this habitat. This becomes especially advantageous when one is dealing with species that for the most part remain hidden when they call, and/or are nocturnal. In particular are the usually drab-coloured **cuckoos** that call most often in spring and summer, the plump green, fruit-eating **barbets**, and at nightfall the various **owls** and owlets and the **nightjars**, which are similar to the North American nighthawks.

The **laughing thrushes** are another group that usually betray their presence with characteristic calls before they are spotted. These diverse, animated birds are more easily seen as they often congregate in large, raucous foraging parties. Related to these species are the **black-capped sibias**, gregarious bronze and black birds typical of the oak forests with a persistent ringing call. Look also for the **red-billed** and **yellow-billed magpies**, as they follow each other through the trees with long trailing, white- tipped tails.

Two more species of the forest canopy which stand out are the **minivets**. The male is bright red with black, and the female yellow on black, which is quite striking when they burst into flight together. The **slaty-headed parakeet**, the only parakeet to venture into the hills, has a long yellow-tipped tail and is quite vocal in its feeding flocks. ■

now produces about 7000 kg of cheese annually, all of it hauled by porters to the dairy in Kathmandu. It is easy to reach Kyanjin Gompa, elevation 3800 metres, before lunch, allowing time to acclimatise and explore the surroundings. The best place in town is the *Hotel Yala Peak*. The National Park Lodge, with its fancy solar heating, has been leased by a local person and has gone to seed – probably because of the park's price controls.

Days 6-7: Langtang Valley

Spend the first day hiking up the moraine north of Kyanjin Gompa to an elevation of 4300 metres or more. From the moraine, there is a spectacular view of Langtang Lirung and the foot of one of its major glaciers.

There are two good viewpoints in the area that you can climb. The peak to the north of Kyanjin Gompa is Kyanjin Ri (4773 metres) – about a two-hour climb. Do not head directly up the ridge behind the gompa; there is a trail of sorts that starts on the opposite side of a stream beyond the national park lodge. The views are superb.

A longer excursion is to Tsergo Ri ('Tserko' on the German map) at 4984 metres, a four-hour climb from Kyanjin Gompa. Both of these peaks are visible from Kyanjin Gompa and prayer flags mark their tops.

There are also two possible climbing projects: 5500-metre Yala peak (not to be confused with Yala Kharka on Tsergo Ri), and 5749-metre Tsergo peak (which is different from Tsergo Ri). Both are two-day expeditions that involve glacier climbing and a high camp on a saddle above the trail near Nubama Dhang.

It's also worthwhile taking an extra day or two to continue further up the Langtang Valley to **Langshisha Kharka** for views of Langshisha Ri (6310 metres), Gang Chhenpo (6388 metres), Urkeinmang (6151 metres), and Penthang Karpo Ri (6830 metres). There are no hotels beyond Kyanjin Gompa, but you can make a day trip and return to Kyanjin Gompa for the night. If you have a tent and food you can camp at Langshisha Kharka at 4080 metres or another of the summer pastures high in the valley.

Kyanjin Gompa to Kathmandu
You can return to Kathmandu by the same route, or you might be lucky enough to find a plane at the Langtang airstrip above Kyanjin Gompa at 3960 metres.

Alternative routes to Kathmandu are either over Ganja La or via Gosainkund when conditions are suitable on these high altitude routes.

Across Ganja La

The route from Kyanjin Gompa in Langtang to Tarke Gyang in Helambu requires crossing the 5106-metre high Ganja La. This pass is difficult and dangerous when covered by snow, so for a safe crossing, local inquiries about its condition, good equipment and some mountaineering experience are necessary. You can assume the pass will be open from April to November, though unusual weather can alter its condition at any time. A guide who knows the trail, plus a tent, food and fuel are essential for crossing the Ganja La.

Days 1-6: Kathmandu to Kyanjin Gompa
For the first five days, follow the Langtang trek route described in the preceding section. An extra day in Langtang Valley for acclimatisation is essential before beginning the ascent to Ganja La.

Day 7: Kyanjin Gompa to Ngegang
This is a short day from Kyanjin Gompa, but Ngegang is the last good place to camp before beginning the final climb to the pass, and you should minimise the elevation gain to aid acclimatisation. Crossing the Langtang Khola below Kyanjin Gompa, the trail makes a steep climb along the ridge on the south side of the valley through a forest of rhododendron and juniper. Finally becoming more gentle, the trail reaches the yak pasture of Ngegang at about 4000 metres. There are stone huts here and on the other side of the pass, but they have no roofs during the winter, so a tent is very handy on this trek. During the monsoon, herders carry bamboo mats to provide roofs for the huts here, and live the entire summer in high meadows with herds of yaks and goats.

Day 8: Ngegang to Keldang
The trail continues south, following streams and moraines, and climbing steeply towards the pass. As the trail climbs higher, and comes under the shadow of the 5800-metre peaks to the south, you will find more and more snow. Turning south-west, the trail makes the final steep ascent to the pass at 5200 metres. The last 100 metres of the climb is a tricky balancing act on a snow slope above some steep rocks.

The pass itself is flanked by pinnacles that mountaineers call gendarmes and topped by prayer flags and a large cairn of rocks. The views to the north, of Langtang Lirung and the snow peaks in Tibet, including 8013-metre-high Shisha Pangma, are outstanding from the pass. On a clear day there are also views of many ranges of hills to the south. West of the pass is 5846-metre-high Naya Kangri, previously named Ganja La Chuli. This is one of the trekking peaks that you can climb with a permit from the Nepal Mountaineering Association. A base camp in this region provides a good starting point for this reasonably easy climb.

The descent from the pass is steep and dangerous, as it follows a loose scree slope for about 200 metres before emerging onto a snow slope. Somehow, the descent from Ganja La, like most mountain descents, seems more treacherous than the ascent, no matter which direction one crosses the pass. However, Ganja La is one of the steeper and more difficult of the major passes in Nepal. After the initial steep drop, the trail descends gradually in a huge basin surrounded by glaciated peaks.

The route descends through the basin along an indistinct trail, marked occasionally by rock cairns, to a small stream at 4400 metres. If you are travelling in the reverse direction, from Helambu to Langtang, it will require a full day to reach this point from Keldang, and you should schedule two days from Keldang to the pass.

From this campsite, the trail enters the steep Yangri Khola Valley and drops quickly down a rough scree slope to the stream. Following the stream for some distance through grassy meadows, the trail reaches a few goths (again without roofs) at Keldang, about 4270 metres elevation.

Day 9: Keldang to Dukpu
This is a long and tiring day as the trail descends along a ridge, making many ups and downs. In winter, there is no water from Keldang to the bottom of the ridge, near Phedi, so you should plan food accordingly for this stretch of the trail. In October and November, there is usually no water problem because the monsoon rains leave an ample ground water supply in several small springs.

The route heads down the valley, but stays high above the river, finally meeting the ridge itself, then follows the ridge line to the small summer settlement of Dukpu at 4080 metres.

Day 10: Dukpu to Tarke Gyang
From Dukpu, the trail descends further along the ridge, then makes a 180-metre climb to a pass at 4020 metres. The pass offers a commanding view of the Himalaya, from Dorje Lakpa east almost to Everest, and a panorama of the first part of the Everest trek from Lamosangu to Khumbu. From the pass, the trail descends through pine and rhododendron forests past tiny herders' settlements to a ridge high above Tarke Gyang. It then drops steeply to Gekye Gompa at 3020 metres, a small monastic community, and the first permanent settlement since Kyanjin Gompa. The trail continues its steep plunge to the large Sherpa village of Tarke Gyang at 2560 metres.

Days 11-13: Tarke Gyang to Kathmandu
For the return to Kathmandu, use one of the routes described below. You can travel in either direction, following days 5, 6 and 7 of the Helambu circuit or days 4, 3, 2 and 1.

Helambu Circuit

This is the description of a seven-day trek that makes a circuit of the Helambu region. The easiest starting point for this trek is Sundarijal because of its proximity to Kathmandu. You can make the trek in either direction, because it closes a loop from Pati Bhanjyang, the first night stop of the trek. The preferred route is clockwise as I have described here; first visiting the high ridge to the west of Helambu Valley, then heading to Tarke Gyang and descending the Malemchi Khola before climbing back to Pati Bhanjyang. There are all kinds of other possible variations, including a direct route to

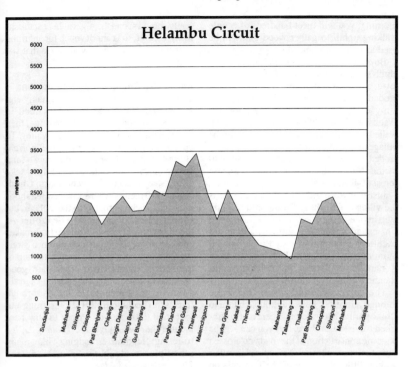

Helambu Circuit

Tarke Gyang from Pati Bhanjyang, then down the ridge through Sermathang, ending at Panchkal.

The Helambu trek is an easy trek to organise. Transport to and from Sundarijal, the starting point of the trek, is fast and cheap, and the trek is at a low elevation, so you do not usually need any fancy warm clothing. There are fewer trekkers here than either the Everest or Annapurna regions and good hotels are abundant and uncrowded.

Day 1: Kathmandu to Pati Bhanjyang

At Sundarijal (1350 metres), there is a large water project that supplies much of Kathmandu's drinking water via an immense pipe. Just before Sundarijal there is a Dutch training project for Himalayan rescue dogs. The unpaved road from Boudhanath turns into a trail near a small hydroelectric plant

and starts up concrete steps alongside the water pipe. Beyond Sundarijal the trail climbs continuously through forests (still following the water pipe) to a medieval-looking reservoir, dam and waterworks. Crossing the dam, the trail leaves the water supply system and climbs steeply to a road at 1550 metres. Cross the road and continue the climb to the top of the Shivapuri ridge.

The road is an unfinished (in 1993) project that will eventually lead from Budhanil-kantha to Chisopani and beyond, on the north side of the Shivapuri ridge. The first village on the trail is the sprawling Tamang settlement of **Mulkharka**, at 1895 metres. There are a few small tea shops here, where you can sit and enjoy a spectacular panoramic view of the Kathmandu Valley and watch planes taking off from Tribhuvan Airport. If you start the trek early in the morning, you will meet hundreds of people walking uphill to gather wood that will be used as fuel in Kathmandu.

Beyond Mulkharka, the trail continues to climb steadily. Portions of the trail are almost level, but much of the climb is steep in deeply eroded chasms. After passing through an army camp, the trail enters the Shivapuri Watershed & Wildlife Reserve, a 112-sq-km walled area. You can see the remnants of the village of Chaurabas as you climb on a heavily eroded trail to the top of the ridge at 2440 metres. Most of the Shivapuri ridge is a dense forest of pine, oak and rhododendron trees.

Just below the ridge on the north side is the village of **Borlang Bhanjyang**. A night stop in one of the hotels in this village, or in Chisopani (45 minutes further), will afford excellent mountain views the following morning. The sunrise on the Himalaya, from Annapurna to Everest, is particularly outstanding from this point.

The route continues down the ridge through a forest of oak and rhododendron to **Chisopani** at 2300 metres. There is an unfinished tourist resort here, and you can see the ongoing construction of the road you crossed early the same morning. Chisopani is a rather grubby little place, more like a truck stop (without the trucks!) than a Himalayan village. Take care of your possessions here, theft can be problem. The *Himalayan Guest House* and the *Gauri Shankar Guest House* are both in Chisopani.

The trail continues to drop from Chisopani on a good, sometimes level, trail that crosses meadows and fields. The final descent to Pati Bhanjyang is on a trail that has eroded into a steep slippery slide.

Pati Bhanjyang is on a saddle at the bottom of the ridge at 1770 metres. This is a Brahmin and Chhetri village with a few shops and hotels and a police checkpost, though the police here are usually not interested in trekking permits. There is a big hotel here, the *New Shivapuri Lodge*, plus the *Pati Lodge* and the *Himal Lodge*. On the Kathmandu edge of the village, the old lady who runs the down-market *Sewa Sadan Lodge* insisted in a very friendly way that I

really should spend the night at her establishment. I didn't, so I cannot vouch for anything except the cardamom-flavoured tea that she prepared.

Day 2: Pati Bhanjyang to Khutumsang

The trail heads north out of Pati Bhanjyang. If you want to do the Helambu circuit in reverse, turn right and climb the ridge, then descend into the Malemchi Khola Valley. To go to Langtang, or to make the normal Helambu circuit, bear left and follow a long stretch of level trail to the foot of a hill. Make a very steep ascent on switchbacks to **Chipling** at 2170 metres. There are a few tea shops in shacks at the entrance to the village, but Chipling does not have much else to offer. At the upper end of the village, the trail makes another steep, 200-metre climb on a stone staircase to a pass at 2470 metres, the top of the Jhogin Danda ridge. There are good mountain views along this stretch of trail. From the ridge the trail descends through forests to **Thodang Betini**, a long strung-out village at 2100 metres. Places to stay here include the *Tasi Lodge*, the *Thotung Lodge* (offering 'fooding & lodging' like many other places along this route) and the *Thotong Sherpa Lodge*.

Continuing along the forested ridge, the trail descends to a large chorten overlooking the Tamang village of **Gul Bhanjyang** at 2130 metres. This is a delightful, classic hill village with a pleasant main street, several shops and a number of places to stay including the *Shree Ganesh Lodge* on the Kathmandu side of the village, the *Gosai Kunda Lodge, Gol Phubhanjyang Lodge* and the *Deepak Lodge*.

The trail climbs the ridge from Gul Bhanjyang to another pass at 2620 metres. From a grassy meadow you can look back over Gul Bhanjyang to the big chorten you walked by early on. The meadow makes a good camping spot and there's also the *Dragon Lodge*. The trail then descends to Khutumsang at 2470 metres, in a saddle atop the ridge.

This village has completely adapted itself to trekkers; almost every house in town is a hotel or shop. You can stay at the *Helambu View Lodge, Shree Sherpa Lodge, Karna Lama Lodge, Gosainkunda Lodge, Dimlana Lodge, Dame Sherpa Lodge* or *Dolma Lodge*. The national park office is at the far side of the village. Pay Rs 650 if you started at Sundarijal; show your receipt again if you are headed in the opposite direction.

Day 3: Khutumsang to Tharepati

The trek proceeds due north up the Yurin Danda ridge and affords views of the peaks above Langtang and of the Gosainkund peaks. The trail climbs above Khutumsang on a steep, eroded trail, mostly through fir and rhododendron forests where there are no permanent settlements, although there are a few small shepherds' huts. There are two bhattis at the settlement of **Pambu**, then the route climbs to a large cairn at the top of the Panghu Danda (3285 metres). This is herding country, and there are many goths along the way; in season you may be able to buy milk or curd from the herders.

The trail descends to **Magen Goth** at 3150 metres. There is a hotel here and a fancy-looking army checkpost – again they check your national park entry ticket. Continuing to climb, steeply at first, then more gradually, the trail makes some ups and downs passing through forests, across flower-strewn meadows and crossing streams.

It finally reaches Tharepati, which consists of a few goths and hotels at 3490 metres. The very prettily situated *Himaliya Lodge* is on the Khutumsang side of the pass and costs Rs 20. The *Sumche Lodge* is just below the pass while the *Top Lodge* is right at the top. It can get very chilly here at night.

The trail to Gosainkund turns north-west from this point while the trail that completes the Helambu circuit turns east and drops steeply down from the Top Lodge. The region is now truly alpine, with meadows and shrubs typical of high elevations. If you are continuing on the Helambu circuit it is worth walking for half an hour or so up along the Gosainkund route for the fine views. The site of the 1992 Thai Airbus crash is far up the ridge to the north-west.

It was north of this section of trail that James Scott, an Australian medical student, was lost in 1991.

In late December 1991 James Scott, a young Australian medical student, left Phedi to cross the Laurebina Pass to the Gosainkund lakes. When snow started to fall, visibility became limited, the trail indistinct and he and his partner disagreed on the best course of action. Eventually his partner decided to press on alone to try and find a way over the pass while James opted to make his way back to Phedi. In the bad conditions he wandered off the track and followed a creek down until he became trapped below the ridge line which the trail follows from Tharepati through Ghopte to Phedi. Uncertain of his location, and with movement made difficult by the snow and his weakening condition, he soon gave up hope of walking out and waited to be rescued. Remarkably he was rescued, but not for 43 days by which time he was nearly dead from starvation. A huge search effort involving numerous people at ground level and in the air eventually spotted him from a helicopter.

James was very lucky to be found and the whole story reads like an object lesson of what not to do, but in similar conditions many trekkers could quickly find themselves in an equally difficult situation. His mistakes included making a difficult trek at a tricky time of year – he was attempting to cross a 4600-metre pass late in the season when snowfalls can be sudden and dangerous. He was not trekking with a familiar and reliable partner – the friend he had set out with had turned back due to an injury and he had only met his new partner a couple of days before he was lost. Close friends with more of a commitment to each other would have been less liable to have split up at a dangerous time. He became lost by following a creek, an easy trap for the unwary – Nepalese trails generally follow ridges, following a creek will usually bring you to a waterfall or some other dead end. When he was lost his problem was compounded by having only limited food supplies, the famous single bar of chocolate – although he had originally set out from Kathmandu intending to make the easier Helambu circuit where there are frequent villages so emergency rations are not necessary at all.

James was lost between Ghopte and Talu and trekking maps of the region indicate the two settlements are only about 2½ km apart. Trekkers in Nepal soon realise that distance is of less importance than altitude and the 1000 metres between Talu at 2500 metres and Ghopte at 3500 metres is probably more important than the distance. The tale of his ordeal, told by James Scott and by his sister, Joanne Robertson who was in Kathmandu during the search effort, is told in in the *Himalayas* (Lothian Books, Melbourne, 1993).

Day 4: Tharepati to Tarke Gyang

Turn east from the northern end of the settlement and descend steeply down a ravine. The vegetation changes to large firs, then to oaks and rhododendrons, as you rapidly lose all the altitude you gained during the last two days. Crossing a stream on a suspension bridge, the trail makes a short final climb to reach the prosperous Sherpa village of **Malemchigaon** at 2530 metres.

The Sherpas of Helambu are very different from their cousins in Solu Khumbu. Instead of the Tibetan-style black dress and colourful apron, the Sherpa women of Helambu wear a dress of red printed cotton. Their language is also quite distinct from the Sherpa language of Solu Khumbu, being grammatically different. In addition, Helambu Sherpas speak much more rapidly than other Sherpas. Helambu women have a reputation for being very beautiful, and many Helambu Sherpa girls were once employed in aristocratic Rana households in Kathmandu during the Rana regime. Many of their benefactors gave gifts of land to these girls, so many Helambu families now own large tracts of farmland in the river valley far below.

Malemchigaon has a very glossy gompa with a line of prayer flags at the front and brightly painted walls and statues. If it's locked up, inquire at one of the nearby lodges about the key. You can stay at the *Tashi Dhalek Lodge* right by the gompa, the *Sun Lodge* or the *Green View Lodge* on the Tharepati side of the village or the comfortable-looking *Yangrima Lodge* overlooking the village from the top end. Electricity supply lines snake down the hill from Malemchigaon, connecting it with Tarke Gyang up the other side of the valley.

From Malemchigaon, the trail continues to descend to the *River Side Lodge* and the Malemchi Khola which is crossed on a sturdy suspension bridge at 1890 metres. Once across the river the trail immediately begins the ascent up the other side of the valley towards Tarke Gyang. Sometimes hoteliers from Tarke Gyang come all the way down to the river to try to induce you to

patronise their establishments. It is a long climb to this picturesque village at 2600 metres, situated on a shelf high above the river.

Tarke Gyang is the largest village in Helambu and the destination for most trekkers in this region. The stone houses of Tarke Gyang are close together with narrow alleyways separating them. Inside, the homes are large, clean and often elaborately furnished with elegant brassware and traditional Tibetan carpets on highly polished wooden floors. The village has a huge brass prayer wheel.

The people of Helambu do a lot of trading in India during the winter. Many of the people are quite well-to-do, and own cultivated fields in the lower Malemchi Khola Valley. A special racket among the people of Helambu is the sale of antiques, usually manufactured in Kathmandu and aged over smoky fires in the homes of Tarke Gyang. Beware of any such bargain here. It is illegal to export any item over 100 years old from Nepal, so it is better to purchase well-made handicrafts in Kathmandu or Patan, rather than try to beat the system by purchasing a phoney antique in the hills.

The *Mount View Hotel* on the Malemchigaon edge of the village has beds for Rs 20. Right by the village's large gompa is the *Lama Lodge* while the *Tara Lodge* and the *Helambu Lodge* are further back in the village. At the far side of the village the trail crosses a stream past a water-driven prayer wheel and then a long mani wall beside the entrance to the rambling *Tarkeghyang Guest House*. Trekking groups often camp in the garden here.

Tarke Gyang is a good place to take a rest day and there's the option of making a half-day climb to the peak (3771 metres) directly north of the village. From the chorten on the summit there are superb views of the mountains to the north. This ascent is the first part of the route to the Ganja La pass which leads to the Langtang region.

From Tarke Gyang, there is a choice of trails back to Kathmandu. A description of the alternative route along the ridge through

Sermathang and down to the Kodari road follows the Day 7 description.

Day 5: Tarke Gyang to Kiul

The circuit route back to Sundarijal leaves Tarke Gyang past the guesthouse and mani wall (walk to the left), then drops off the west side of the ridge in a rhododendron forest, along a broad, well-travelled path. The trail passes several chortens, mani walls and kanis. Passing through the Sherpa villages of **Kakani** at 2070 metres and **Thimbu** at 1580 metres, the trail enters the hot rice-growing country of the Malemchi and Indrawati valleys, and leaves the highland ethnic groups for the Brahmin, Chhetri and Newar people who inhabit the lower regions.

The steep descent continues to Kiul (1280 metres), strung out on terraces above the Malemchi Khola. The trail is now in semi-tropical banana-and-monkey country at an elevation below that of Kathmandu.

Day 6: Kiul to Pati Bhanjyang

From Kiul, the trail follows the river, descending slightly, then crosses the river on a suspension bridge (do not take the first bridge the trail reaches, take the second one a bit further downstream) at 1190 metres. A short distance beyond the bridge, the trail reaches Mahenkal (1130 metres) and joins the road. As the road descends the valley, it passes through the village of Gheltum, the site of an imposing two-storey schoolhouse and a post office. You can follow a trail that cuts across some large road switchbacks as you descend into **Talamarang**, a pleasant village on the banks of the river at 940 metres. There are some small shops here, and you can probably find a jeep or truck here if you decide to get a ride back to Kathmandu.

Crossing the Talamarang Khola on a long, rather precarious suspension bridge, the trail leaves the road and proceeds west along the south bank of the stream through rice terraces and fields. The trail then deteriorates into a boulder-strewn route up the river valley. The same monsoon flood that destroyed the road at Talamarang also destroyed this portion of the trail, and

washed many fertile fields downstream in the process. After following the stream for a long distance, you begin a steep climb towards the top of the ridge on a wide, well-constructed trail. From the uninhabited valley floor, the trail soon enters a densely populated region, passing through the village of Batache en route to the top of the ridge, which it reaches near the village of Thakani at 1890 metres. Following the ridge through meadows and terraced fields, the trail crosses over to its south side and descends to Pati Bhanjyang at 1770 metres, completing the circuit through Helambu.

Day 7: Pati Bhanjyang to Kathmandu

Retrace the route back to Sundarijal, as described on the first day of the trek. From Sundarijal it is easy to find cheap transport back to Kathmandu.

TARKE GYANG TO KATHMANDU

There is an excellent alternative route from Tarke Gyang to the road at Panchkal that gets you back to Kathmandu in three easy days. The trail heads south along the ridge through Sermathang, down to the river at Malemchi, and along the road to Panchkal. The first part of the trail, along the ridge through forests and Sherpa villages, is quite delightful. Although the later part of the route, on the dusty road along the Indrawati River, is boring you can probably get a ride in one of the jeeps or trucks that ply this stretch of road. There is a regular minibus service from Sipa Ghat. The route meets the Chinese road at Panchkal and from there it's a three-hour ride back to Kathmandu by bus. You might want to stop at Dhulikhel, before Kathmandu Valley.

Day 1: Tarke Gyang to Sermathang

From Tarke Gyang the trail leaves the village near the big guesthouse and follows the electricity supply line around the hillside to Parachin. The trail makes a sweep around the wide valley end between Parachin and the pretty village of **Gangjwal** at around 2500 metres. At the end of the village the *Dolma Lodge* sells cold beer and soft drinks and from its position on the edge of the ridge has views right across to Sermathang.

The trail drops down from the edge of the ridge but then continues at around the same altitude along the side of the ridge crossing a number of streams and waterfalls and picking its way over the debris from a huge landslide. Finally it passes a gompa at the edge of the large village of Sermathang (2620 metres). There is a Langtang National Park office in the village where you must pay the park entrance fee if you are coming from the opposite direction.

Sermathang has a number of places to stay including the *Mountain View Lodge*, the *Tara Lodge* and the very comfortable-looking *Yangri Lodge* and *Hotel Snowfall*. If you are staying at lodges you might want to make a short day of it and stop here as there are not so many accommodation possibilities further down the ridge before Malemchi.

Day 2: Sermathang to Malemchi
From Sermathang the trail follows the ridge all the way down to Malemchi, making a drop of 1790 metres. After passing a large gompa at the southern end of the village the trail undulates along the west side of the ridge passing chorten after chorten before dropping down to Kakani at around 1900 metres. Don't confuse this Kakani with the one just south of Tarke Gyang which you pass through on Day 5 of the regular Helambu circuit route.

A chorten marks the saddle at the northern end of Kakani and there is a gompa at the top of the hill overlooking the village but at this point you are in the transition zone from the Buddhist regions to the Hindu lowlands. The fairly primitive-looking *View Lodge* and a couple of tea shops can be found near the chorten.

From Kakani the trail drops steeply past a small village and down to the attractive larger village of **Dubhachaur** at 1500 metres. A very Australian-looking eucalyptus tree makes a shady lunch stop in the village. From here the trail continues to descend even more steeply right down the ridge to the junction of the Indrawati River

and the Malemchi Khola. A suspension bridge takes you over the Malemchi Khola, just before the junction, and after a short walk along the riverbank a larger and grander suspension bridge crosses the Indrawati into Malemchi at 830 metres. A plaque on the bridge proclaims that it was made by John Henderson & Co Ltd, Engineers of Aberdeen, Scotland.

Malemchi has a collection of shops and teahouses and numerous lodges including the *Indrawati, Helambu, Shanti* and the quite luxurious-looking *Lama Lodge*.

Day 3: Malemchi to Kathmandu
Transport (including buses) runs reasonably frequently along the road (known as the Helambu Highway) from Malemchi via Bahunepati and Sipa Ghat to Panchkal on the Kodari road.

Gosainkund

You can make the trek through Gosainkund in either direction combined with a trek to Helambu or Langtang. It is also a worthwhile seven or eight-day trek in its own right. There are lodges all along the route except during the winter (late December to early March). There is a strict ban on the use of firewood in Gosainkund, so if you are camping, be sure to bring kerosene for fuel. The route I have described here is from Dhunche or Syabru to Tharepati. From Tharepati, you can either continue to Helambu or go directly back to Kathmandu. You can also make the trek in the opposite direction, starting from Sundarijal or Helambu.

Day 1: Syabru or Dhunche to Sing Gompa
From Dhunche From Dhunche, at 1950 metres, follow the road to the first switchback. There is a sign marking a level trail that follows the south bank of the Trisuli River through fields and pastures to a few houses. Cross the river on a wooden bridge just

before the valley narrows and becomes steeper. The trail follows the north side of the river for a short while, then begins the steep climb towards the ridge. After the initial climb, the trail levels a bit, passes through a village, then continues up to the ridge. Climb through a forest of firs and rhododendrons for about an hour to a small clearing, then another hour to a very basic teahouse where there are views back down the valley. The trail continues to climb to the ridge and a trail junction. Turn right and continue up past an army camp, then up through scrub and oaks to Sing Gompa, near the top of the ridge in an area of dead trees. Do not take the inviting-looking trail that descends steeply to an apple farm.

From Syabru There are at least three routes from Syabru to Gosainkund. Two of these bypass Sing Gompa and head directly to two tea shops at Chalang Pati. The route I have described here is a more circuitous trail via Sing Gompa. This trail is easier to follow and breaks the climb into more manageable segments. The direct route from Chalang Pati to Syabru is a good choice if you are coming down from Gosainkund because the trail is easy to see from above, but it's a bad choice if you are headed uphill because it's not an obvious route. A guide who knows the way will be very helpful, perhaps essential, if you plan to climb up this route, otherwise you will probably follow a lot of useless yak trails.

Once you evade the pushy Syabru hoteliers, climb past the gompa, school and army post, and switchback up the steep hill above the village. There are a few houses and potato fields, but always take the upper, steep trail and you will eventually find yourself at two pleasant tea shops in the settlement of **Dursagang** at 2550 metres. The trail continues less steeply, now mostly in forests, past an old chorten to the top of the ridge and two shoddy tea shops at 3000 metres.

This is also a trail junction; the right-hand trail leads downhill to Brabal and the Dhunche road, and the left trail is a short cut to Chalang Pati. The Sing Gompa trail

climbs, then cuts across the ridge top, staying fairly level in forests as it crosses the head of a valley. Take the uphill trail at each junction and cross another forested ridge. There is a view of Dhunche far below in the valley. The trail continues across the head of a second valley, then reaches a final ridge at 3260 metres. Sing Gompa is about 100 metres along the trail to the left.

Sing Gompa is the main attraction at Chandan Bari, elevation 3250 metres, which also has several hotels and a small cheese factory. The gompa, which houses a statue of the Green Tara, is not well cared for; the caretaker will unlock it for you for a small fee. The hillside near Chandan Bari is bare and scorched through a combination of logging, fire and wind storms.

Day 2: Sing Gompa to Gosainkund
The trail climbs steeply up the ridge, at several points on top of the ridge itself. The ridge is a transition zone between rich, moist mountain forests on the northern slopes and dry scrub vegetation on the slopes that face south. The trail crosses behind the ridge and stays in deep forests for a while, then emerges onto a saddle at **Chalang Pati** (3380 metres) where the *Chalang Pati Hotel* offers a welcome cup of tea. When you start walking again, you will see a sign in Nepali. It says that you are now entering the Gosainkund protected area where the killing of animals, lighting of wood fires, and grazing of goats is prohibited.

As the trail ascends, there are outstanding views across Langtang Valley to Langtang Lirung. There are a few goths along the way to the tea shops at Laurebina, elevation 3930, known locally as **Laurebina Yak**. There are three hotels here; one advertises 'astounding mountain views' as you eat 'breakfast on top of the world'. The views here are truly magnificent – you can see the Annapurnas, Manaslu (8156 metres), Ganesh Himal (7406 metres), some unnamed peaks in Tibet and finally Langtang Lirung.

The trail ascends, now in alpine country, up the ridge to a pair of small stone pillars that say 'Welcome to Gosainkund' – but you still have a lot more climbing to do. Continue to the ridge at 4100 metres and climb further for a view of the first of the lakes, **Saraswati Kund**, in a valley several hundred metres below. The trail leaves the ridge and follows a trail high above the Trisuli Valley. This is not a trail for acrophobics; fortunately it is on the sunny side of the hill, so the snow here melts quickly. The trail is spooky and dangerous if it is snow-covered. Indeed, if there has been a lot of snow, it may not be possible to cross into Gosainkund. People have perished floundering in the deep snow in this region, so return to Dhunche if conditions are not good.

After the trail crosses a spur, the second lake in the chain, **Bhairav Kund**, comes into view. The trail climbs gently but continuously to a ridge and drops about 20 metres to the third and largest lake, Gosainkund, at an elevation of 4380 metres. There are two small hotels, a shrine and several small stone shelters for pilgrims on the north-western side of the lake. Hundreds of people come here to worship and bathe in the lake during the full moon festival each August.

Gosainkund lake has a black rock in the middle, said to be the head of Shiva. There is also a legend about a white rock under the water that is the remnants of an ancient shrine of Shiva. According to legend, Shiva himself created this high altitude lake, when he pierced a glacier with his trident to obtain water to quench his thirst after consuming some poison. It is also said that the water from this lake disappears underground via a subterranean channel and surfaces in Kumbeshwar pool, next to the five-storey Shiva Temple in Patan, more than 60 km away.

Day 3: Gosainkund to Ghopte
The trail passes the northern side of Gosainkund lake and climbs further through rugged country towards Laurebina Pass. The trail is rough and crosses moraines, but it is well marked with rock cairns. Passing three more small lakes, the trail finally reaches the pass at 4610 metres. There is a small hillock above the trail that offers good views in both directions.

From the pass, the trail descends alongside a stream through alpine country to a single hut at 4100 metres. Here, at **Bhera Goth**, there is a choice of trails. The upper trail is a new direct route to Tharepati. It is very dangerous when there is any snow at all on the trail, and there is no accommodation or food between here and Tharepati. Get advice from other trekkers or from the man who lives at Bhera Goth before you take this trail. The lower, safer trail descends along the middle of the valley to Phedi (3500 metres), which comprises two funky hotels (the *Taj Mel* is one) by a stream and a wooden bridge.

Across the valley, you can see a ridge with a steep trail across its face at an angle of almost 45°. Yes, this is where you are going. The route continues across the head of the valley on an extremely rough trail, across moraines and past two goths that have minimal hotel facilities – just tea and Pepsi – to the bottom of the 160-metre climb to the ridge. The ascent is just as steep as it looks, but it is not as exposed (and therefore not as frightening) as it looked from across the valley.

I climbed this trail in the snow, following steps that the trek cook had cut with his kitchen knife. Another sherpa led the way tossing gravel onto the snow and into the steps to provide a footing on the hard and slippery surface. As I sat at the top of the ridge taking photographs, I was thinking how to describe this particular stretch of trail. Was it dangerous or impassable in winter? My musing was interrupted by a sadhu in bare feet and loincloth who carried only a blanket, a brass bowl and an iron trisul. He was on his way to Gosainkund for a day and would return two days hence. Off he went down the trail, followed in quick succession by a Nepalese in gumboots striding along listening to a football match on a radio – the only item he was carrying. These apparitions add a bit of perspective to the trail. Just be careful, go slowly and travel with reliable companions.

From this infamous ridge, the trail descends through forests, climbing in and out of ravines across the head of the valley.

Giant cliffs tower far above, forming the top of the Thare Danda. On one of the ridges there are some prayer flags; just beyond these flags is the settlement of Ghopte at 3430 metres. There are two tea shops here and a cave that offers some shelter. This is a long and rough day of trekking. The hotels of Tharepati are visible on the far ridge; at night you can see the lights of Trisuli Bazaar far below and the glow of Kathmandu to the south-east.

Day 4: Ghopte to Tharepati
Descending from the ridge at Ghopte, the trail continues up ravines and across the boulders of old moraines below the wreckage of a plane that crashed in 1992, then makes a final ascent to Tharepati, on the ridge at 3490 metres. There are several hotels below the ridge, and two more on the ridge itself. Take a moment to climb the hill to the east of the ridge for views of Dorje Lakpa, Shisha Pangama (8013 metres) and peaks all the way to Khumbu. Here, the trail joins the Helambu circuit (see Day 3 of the circuit description earlier in this chapter). You can travel two hours downhill to Malemchigaon and on to Tarke Gyang, or go directly down the ridge to Kathmandu via Pati Bhanjyang.

The 'new' high trail from Bhera Goth rejoins the trail here. If you are walking from Sundarijal to Gosainkund, be sure to ask the people of Tharepati if this trail is safe. The dangerous snow-covered parts of this high trail are on the north-west slopes, and not visible from here.

If you want to return directly to Kathmandu, the days work out as follows:

Day 5: Tharepati to Khutumsang
See Day 3 of the earlier Helambu circuit description.

Day 6: Khutumsang to Chisopani
You might be able to get all the way to Kathmandu from Khutumsang, but the view of the Himalaya from Chisopani is spectacular enough to justify a night here. Beware of thieves in Chisopani, especially if you are camping in tents.

Day 7: Chisopani to Kathmandu
Follow Day 1 of the Helambu circuit in reverse, back to Borlang Bhanjyang, then down the Shivapuri ridge to the road at Sundarijal. Here you can get a taxi or bus back to Kathmandu.

Jugal Himal

To the north-east of Kathmandu lies a chain of peaks called Jugal Himal, which includes Dorje Lakpa (6966 metres), Madiya (6257 metres) and Phurbi Chhyachu (6637 metres). From the south it is an easily accessible region, although it requires a long uphill climb. Just above Dolalghat on the Kodari road there is a jeep road to the large bazaar of Chautaara (1410 metres). A trail from Chautaara descends to the Balephi Khola, then follows a ridge to Bhairav Kund, a holy lake at 3500 metres.

You can return from there to Tatopani on the Kodari road or make a circuit around the head of the Balephi Khola Valley to Panch Pokhari ('five lakes') at 3600 metres. From Panch Pokhari, trails lead to Tarke Gyang in Helambu or back down the ridge to Panchkal on the Kodari road. This is a remote and unfrequented region, despite its proximity to Kathmandu. Treks in this area involve a lot of climbing on narrow trails. There are few villages and no hotels on this route and water is very scarce on the ridge.

Day 1: Kathmandu to Chautaara and Syaule
Chautaara is a large village with a police post and many well-stocked shops. There is a large clinic here operated by Save the Children, UK. The main trail climbs through pleasant hill villages to Syaule.

Day 2: Syaule to Kamikharka Danda
From Syaule the trail rises steadily to the village of **Okrin Danda** at 2300 metres. Continue steeply up toward the forested Kamikharka Danda ridge. One hour beyond Okrin Danda is an unusual double mani wall

where there are fine campsites; there may be water here in the autumn, but there is no water during the spring. From this point the route ascends steeply through forests full of woodcutters to the ridge crest. Camp in a grassy area surrounded by forest. The water supply is 30 minutes' walk down the western slopes of the ridge.

Day 3: Kamikharka Danda to Chyochyo Danda

The route along the Khamikharka Danda is an excellent trail through beautiful oak and rhododendron forest with magnificent views. Water is scarce for much of the way.

The trail follows the ridge crest, rising to a large chorten at 3160 metres, then traverses pasture across the western slopes of Chyochyo Danda where there are many summer pasture shelters. After another descent the trail passes a ruined stone house and a well-used campsite with a good spring a short distance down the western slope. This is the first free water on the ridge and is an excellent camp in pleasant forest.

Day 4: Chyochyo Danda to Hile Bhanjyang

The trail ascends steeply and steadily across stony, grassy pastures to cross the ridge near some cairns at 3750 metres. From the ridge the route descends through forest, crossing gullies with water to reach another crest at Chang Samarphu. The final descent to Hile Bhanjyang is steep. In spring this can be in deep snow with difficult icy sections in the gullies. At Hile Bhanjyang there is a campsite with water at 3800 metres.

Day 5: Hile Bhanjyang to Nasem Pati

The trail climbs steeply to a hillock at 3980 metres, then traverses open ground along a flagstone trail to another crest. The views are wonderful in clear weather. There is a stone house above Nasem Pati (3800 metres) and well-trodden trails that lead off the ridge crest to both east and west. There is no running water here in the spring. Under good walking conditions Days 4 and 5 could be combined into one day of about six hours' walking.

Day 6: Nasem Pati to Panch Pokhari

It's about a four-hour climb on a well-defined trail to Panch Pokhari, five holy lakes at 4050 metres. There are two metal-roofed huts, a sheet metal-enclosed shrine to Shiva and a pile of cast-iron tridents. During the June/July full moon thousands of Nepalese come here to worship. You should not wash in the holy stream near the temples.

There is often snow on this ridge, making the trek more difficult. You can make a day trip to Panch Pokhari from Nasem Pati and avoid camping in the snow.

Day 7: Panch Pokhari to Gai Kharka

Return to Nasem Pati and descend west on a good trail past several ravines with water but no camping to a good campsite at Gai Kharka (2530 metres).

Day 8: Gai Kharka to Yarsa

The descent continues through forest on a sometimes steep and rough track crossing two major water courses. Pass a few substantial villages then descend a small and very steep trail directly to the bridge below Hutanbrang. Follow the Larke Khola downstream to the first of the two bridges below Yangri village where there is a pleasant campsite on the east bank at 1360 metres.

Day 9: Yarsa to Laghang Gompa

The trail crosses bridges over the Larke and Yangri kholas, and passes through Yangri village climbing rapidly to the west and north. There are lateral trails everywhere. At the stream crossing below and southwest of Dalegaon there is a beautiful lunch or camping site with fine water and big shade trees.

From here the trail continues, often steeply, up through country dotted with villages and fields, scrub hillsides and pleasant forest. The large village between Dalegaon and Gangkharka is called **Gangdwang**. From Gangkharka a large trail leads into the

Eastern Nepal

Top Left: Nepali inscription on a Rai memorial (SA)

Top Right: Icefall on Kyabru (SA)

Bottom: Terracing in Eastern Nepal (SA)

Western Nepal
Top: Chorten at Ringmo village, Phoksumdo Lake (SA)
Middle: Taking a break from trekking (SA)
Bottom: Danphe Lagna, en route to Rara Lake (SA)

next side valley where camping is possible. From here the trail climbs relentlessly 900 metres to Laghang Gompa. This is a beautiful forested area and a lovely quiet campsite at an elevation of 2800 metres.

Day 10: Laghang Gompa to Tarke Gyang

It takes just over three hours from Laghang Gompa to Tarke Gyang. The trail climbs through beautiful forest, then enters an area of small pastures, stone houses, scrub growth and cow trails. Be sure to backtrack if you find yourself headed south on the ridge trail to Sermathang. The trail down to Tarke Gyang is very steep, rough and eroded.

Days 11-13: Tarke Gyang to Kathmandu

You can finish this trek via Tharepati, Khutumsang, Pati Bhanjyang and Sundarijal in another four days. You can also connect to the ridge route south via Sermathang or extend the trek to Gosainkund and Langtang.

The easiest way back to Kathmandu is to follow the Tarke Gyang to Panchkal route described earlier. This would make Day 11 from Tarke Gyang to Sermathang; Day 12 from Sermathang to Malemchi; and Day 13 from Malemchi to Kathmandu.

Eastern Nepal

Trekking goals in eastern Nepal include Makalu base camp, an eastern approach to Everest, and the area near Kanchenjunga. There is endless variety in this part of the country. Most ethnic groups are represented and many villages, such as Dhankuta, Khandbari and Bhojpur, are large, prosperous and clean. The area has hot, rice-growing districts and also encompasses the cooler tea-growing region of Ilam. The heavily populated Middle Hills are gouged by the mighty Arun River which has cut through at an elevation of less than 400 metres. The Arun is flanked by the major mountain massifs of Kanchenjunga and Makalu.

Treks here tend to be more expensive, since you and your gear must travel to eastern Nepal by bus or plane. The treks are also longer because it requires two weeks to travel from Dharan to the high mountains. Flying to STOL airstrips at Tumlingtar and Taplejung can shorten the time, but increases the expense. Inhabitants of this part of Nepal have not seen many Westerners in their villages. If you travel in eastern Nepal, you should take great care to avoid the mistakes that trekkers have made in the more popular regions; mistakes which have contributed to theft, over-reliance on the whims of tourists to support the economy, and to problems of garbage, pollution, begging by both adults and children and unnecessary hotel construction.

Kanchenjunga, at 8586 metres, is the world's third-highest mountain. The peak is on the border of Nepal and Sikkim (India) and has several distinct summits. It is visible from Darjeeling, so many expeditions explored this region and tried to climb the mountain during the British rule in India. A British team led by Charles Evans made the first ascent of Kanchenjunga in 1953. They trekked from the south of Nepal and climbed the south face of the peak.

One of the most spectacular peaks in the region is Jannu, at 7710 metres. The Nepal-ese renamed this peak Khumbakarna in 1984 when a committee Nepalised the names of many peaks. Jannu was also called 'Mystery Peak' and 'Peak of Terror' by early expeditions. A French team made the first ascent of Jannu in 1962.

INFORMATION
Books
Eastern Nepal has not received the attention that has been lavished on the Everest and Annapurna areas, so information about this part of the country is sparse.

The Arun (Houghton Mifflin Company, Boston, 1979), by Edward W Cronin Jr, is a natural history of the Arun River Valley.

Round Kanchenjunga (Ratna Pustak Bhandar, Kathmandu, 1979), by Douglas W Freshfield, is a reprint of the most definitive book about the Kanchenjunga region. Originally published in 1903, it describes a circuit of the mountain in 1899.

The Kanchenjunga Adventure (Victor Gollancz, London, 1930), by F S Smythe, is another account of the early exploration of eastern Nepal.

The Kulunge Rai (Ratna Pustak Bhandar, Kathmandu, 1979) by Charles McDougal, is an anthropological study of the Rais in the Hongu Valley, especially the village of Bung.

Maps
The British colonial names of several peaks near Kanchenjunga were changed during the Nepalising process. Tent Peak (7365 metres) became Kirat Chuli, the Twins (7350 metres) became Givigela Chula, White Wave (6960 metres) is now Andesh Chuli, Wedge Peak (6750 metres) was renamed Chang Himal and Pyramid Peak (7168 metres) became Pathi Bhara. Most of the literature about Kanchenjunga refers to Jannu and uses other Anglicised names, so I have used these names throughout the text. Newer maps that

are published in Kathmandu all use the Nepali names.

US Army Map Service sheets NG 45-3 *Kanchenjunga*, and NG 45-2 *Mount Everest* cover eastern Nepal, as do Mandala Maps' *Kanchenjunga* and *Arun Valley*.

ACCOMMODATION

Because eastern Nepal is not swarming with trekkers, there is not the abundance of trekking hotels that there is in central Nepal. The region is, however, well served by local bhattis (tea shops) that cater to the unbelievably large number of porters carrying goods to remote villages. The facilities tend to be primitive and unsanitary, and the food dreadful, but if you can handle this, you can make your way through much of eastern Nepal using local accommodation.

GETTING THERE & AWAY

Air

Biratnagar This airport is the centre of RNAC's eastern Nepal hub. There are morning flights from Biratnagar to Taplejung (US$50), Tumlingtar (US$33) and Lamidanda. Biratnagar airport is a fancy facility built in the 1980s by a South Korean contractor when there was a vague plan to promote Biratnagar as Nepal's second international airport, but it is now dirty and run-down. The airport is quite a distance from the city and the most reliable transport into town is by rickshaw.

Unlike Lukla, the flights to Biratnagar are regular because there is rarely a weather problem. There are instrument-landing facilities and a paved runway, so airlines can use larger planes that have enough capacity to meet the demand for flights. A flight to Kathmandu takes 50 minutes and costs US$77. In clear weather, it provides an excellent overview of the entire trek and good views of the Himalaya from Kanchenjunga to Langtang. All of Nepal's domestic airlines serve Biratnagar, most with daily flights, so air travel is easy to arrange.

Taplejung This is the focal point for Kanchenjunga treks. At present it is accessi-

---

Bazaars

One of the unique cultural institutions of eastern Nepal is the weekly market or *haat bazaar*. Almost every village from the Dudh Kosi eastward to the border of Sikkim is within a day's walk of a large weekly market. In each place the haat bazaar is held on a specific day of the week in a space that the village has set aside for the market. The schedule is coordinated throughout the region so that traders can sell their wares. Itinerant bangle sellers, tailors, barbers, cloth vendors, fortune-tellers, and con artists travel throughout the week, often with a retinue of porters, between various eastern Nepal bazaars selling their wares. Local people bring their own goods, usually meat, grain or baskets woven from bamboo. Shopkeepers, hoteliers and village entrepreneurs set up stalls to sell food and, most importantly, drink. People from far-away villages dress in their best clothes and start early in the morning. They often return home after dark in a festive mood burdened with newly purchased goods.

The following list of eastern Nepal bazaar days is far from exhaustive:

Aiselukharka	Saturday
Barahbise (near Tumlingtar)	Monday
Bung	Monday
Chainpur	Wednesday
Hile	Thursday
Jiri	Saturday
Kenja	Sunday
Khandbari	Saturday
Khari Khola	Wednesday
Lukla	Thursday
Namche Bazaar	Saturday
Siswa Bazaar	Wednesday
Sotang (south of Bung)	Friday ■

---

ble only by air, but there is a road nearing completion that will provide more reliable access to the region. There is a weekly direct flight from Taplejung to Kathmandu (US$110) and several services each week to Biratnagar. The airport is in Suketar, a village high on a hill about a 1½ hour walk above Taplejung; reservations are controlled from the city office, not at the airport.

Tumlingtar This airport is on a flat plateau

in the Arun Valley and provides an access to, and from, treks to Makalu, and an early bail-out from the Lukla to Hile trek. The runway is long and will accommodate 44-seat Avro aircraft, so seats to Tumlingtar may be available when all other destinations are fully booked. For some strange reason, the airfare from Kathmandu to Tumlingtar is one of the lowest in Nepal (US$44).

Bhojpur On a ridge above the west bank of the Arun River is Bhojpur. It is a possible emergency airstrip if you are walking from Khumbu to Hile. Flights to Kathmandu cost US$77.

Lukla Read about Lukla in the Mt Everest Region chapter. Avoid this airport if you can.

Bus
Biratnagar Night buses from Kathmandu to Biratnagar cost Rs 225 for the 540-km, 13-hour journey. Day buses are cheaper at Rs 180.

Biratnagar is Nepal's second-largest city and the kingdom's industrial centre. The largest factories here process jute into carpets, bags and rope. There are also many smaller factories making matches, cigarettes, tinned fruit, jam and other items. For trekkers, Biratnagar is strictly a transit point because the hotels are abominable. If possible, move on immediately to Dharan, Hile or Basantpur.

A good road connects Biratnagar and Dharan, passing through villages and cultivated fields for most of the distance between the two cities. Originally this was all jungle and fine sal forest, but over the years logging and development have drastically reduced the extent of the forest. There is little to remind one now of the extensive malarial jungle that once blanketed this region – although there are still glimpses of this jungle in Royal Chitwan National Park and the Terai of western Nepal.

Biratnagar is a typical Terai town, with noisy bazaars, inhabited mainly by people from the plains. There is nothing of interest for the trekker in Biratnagar and the chaos of

rickshaws and trucks makes it pointless to spend much time there as a tourist. The 45-km drive from Biratnagar to Dharan takes about an hour.

Dharan This town is north of Biratnagar at the foot of the hills. A road connects Dharan with Hile and Basantpur, starting places for treks to Kanchenjunga and the Arun Valley. Dharan is 540 km from Kathmandu and is served by night buses for Rs 225, and day buses for Rs 180. The night bus takes about 14 hours. You can also reach Dharan from Biratnagar and from Itahari on the east-west Mahendra Highway. Much of Dharan's bazaar was severely damaged by an earthquake in 1988.

You can return to Kathmandu by night bus directly from Dharan to Kathmandu. A more costly but less tedious route is by bus to Biratnagar, then a flight back to Kathmandu.

Hile This is the starting point for treks up the Arun Valley. Many buses from Dharan or Biratnagar go only as far as the large village of Dhankuta, about 10 km before Hile. To avoid this walk, be sure you get a bus that goes on to Hile or Basantpur. There's a direct bus from Hile to Kathmandu, departing at 1 pm and arriving in Kathmandu the following morning, 604 km later, at a cost of Rs 253. You can also get to Dhankuta or Hile on a local bus from Dharan; it costs Rs 35 to Rs 40 for the three-hour, 50-km trip. There is a good hotel in Dhankuta and there are several comfortable Tibetan-operated hotels in Hile.

Basantpur About two hours' drive beyond Dhankuta on a rough gravel road is Basantpur, a starting point for treks to Kanchenjunga. The bus service to Basantpur is irregular, but there are usually several buses each day from Dharan. If you have trouble, hire your own vehicle or try for a ride in a truck from Dhankuta or Dharan.

Ilam Another possible starting point for Kanchenjunga treks is Ilam. There is no direct bus service; take the bus from Kathmandu to Kakarbhitta and get off in

Arun Power Project

There is a huge hydroelectric project planned on the Arun River. A road up the Arun Valley is also planned, and several dams and generating stations will eventually be built near Num in the upper part of the valley.

The Arun Project is an expensive and highly controversial development that will change eastern Nepal in many ways. Many aspects of the project are described in the following article by Binod Bhattarai which appeared in the March-April 1993 issue of *Himal Magazine* and is reprinted here with their permission.

The possibility of generating power in the upper Arun basin was first identified by the Japanese in 1985. The project's detailed design and even its tender documents were prepared by a consortium of Western consulting companies, the Joint Venture Arun 3. Since the mid-1980s, World Bank, government officials and commission agents stalled all progress on alternative projects. For this reason alone there is now heavy load shedding in Nepal; this load shedding is expected to continue well into the 2000s.

The original plan was for a 268 megawatt project. When there were no takers, it was upgraded to 402 MW, costing US$1.2 billion, with the idea that prospects of sale of power to India would make the project more attractive. But when everyone baulked at the price, rather than look to other projects, the World Bank pulled 'Baby Arun' out of its bag. Now the project will generate only 201 MW, and the quoted figure is down to US$764 million. To put things in perspective, Nepal's total annual revenue comes to about US$300 million.

Where will the money come from? US$355 million and DM235 million have been committed, according to official information, by donors who include the World Bank, the Asian Development Bank, the Kredittanslt fuer Wiederaufbau, and the Overseas Economic Cooperation Fund. The Japanese would also like to construct the powerhouse and provide electrical equipment. The Finns have agreed to provide diesel generators for the power required during construction.

One reason the bureaucrats are so bent on Arun 3 is that, as one official claimed, '89 percent of the financing is through grants'. This however, is not proven, especially because high-profile donors include the OECD, the ADB and the World Bank, all of which provide loans, albeit some of them soft.

The project will use helicopters to ferry construction material including cement and equipment. Hile and Tumlingtar will be transformed in 'air support' bases and helipads will also be constructed at the dam site, powerhouse and the permanent and temporary camps of contractors. The cost of the helicopter services is expected to be about US$50 million. (For comparison, the United Nations Transitional Authority in Cambodia (UNTAC) will reportedly spend US$47 million for an armada of helicopters, including heavy lift Russian MI-7s, for two years of continuous support.)

The Nepalese government is committed to proceeding with Arun 3 and the National Planning Commission is staunchly behind the project. Neither government officials nor NPC members found it worth their while to attend a public hearing on Arun 3 organised by some Kathmandu NGOs on 12 February. Ironically, when it was learnt subsequently that the World Bank requires a public hearing for 'Category A' Projects such as the Arun, some officials were quick to claim that that requirement had already been fulfilled.

Hundreds of thousands of dollars were spent on an environmental impact study of the road up to the project site, but this report is now waste paper. Because, to make 'Baby Arun' cheaper and more palatable, the planners decided to take the low road, a route along the steep valley bottom. Meanwhile, no environmental impact study has been carried out for the project as a whole.

The projected per-kilowatt cost of power generation for Arun 3 is US$3800, which experts say is more than twice the cost of power from projects of up to the 60 MW range (about US$1500 per KW). Arun's power would cost four times the cost per KW expected from the first phase (1000MW) of the controversial Tehri Dam in Garhwal, claims Rajendra Dahal, a journalist who has followed Arun 3 for more than four years.

Load shedding, which averages 10 hours every alternate day, is not likely to improve regardless of Arun 3. Over time, this will blow the fuse of tolerance of the middle and lower-middle classes, and when that happens, Arun 3 will be of no help to the government.

Are Nepalese officials and the World Bank free to blunder into projects that will mire the country in economic quicksand, just because activism is weak in Nepal? The day when Nepalese activists are able to organise villagers to challenge faraway bureaucratic decisions is still remote.

Says Dahal, 'The World Bank and the bureaucracy love to keep the information close to their chest. We will ultimately bring out all the information on Arun 3, and the alternatives that are being neglected'.

Like journalists, Kathmandu's engineers and economists too have begun to speak out. A group calling itself the Alliance for Energy has begun to ask questions about Arun 3, and promises to be insistent. ∎

Charali, just east of Birtamod, then take a six-hour local bus ride on the winding road to Ilam. The road to Taplejung passes through Ilam; when this road is completed, this will be the best way into the Kanchenjunga region.

To India An alternative to the return to Kathmandu is to take a bus from Itahari to Kakarbhitta, cross into India and take a taxi to Siliguri. From Siliguri, it is about a three-hour drive by taxi (or a seven-hour ride on the famous 'toy train') to Darjeeling, a pleasant Indian hill station.

Solu Khumbu to Hile

This section describes an alternative to the Jiri to Everest base camp trek. Though I have shown it as a route from Solu Khumbu (the Mt Everest region) to Hile, you can also use it as an approach route to the Everest region. Tilman, the first foreign visitor to Everest base camp, used this route in 1950 and described it in some detail in *Nepal Himalaya*.

By walking from Jiri to Everest, and then walking via the route described here to Hile, you can make a rewarding 32-day trek. Walking to Hile avoids the flight complications at Lukla and lends a sense of continuity to the trek that you will not feel if you fly back from Lukla.

Though it's possible to make this walk as a teahouse trek, the facilities do not resemble those of the Everest region. The first six days, from Lukla to Phedi, are through country that sees few travellers, so the hotels are small and the stocks of beer, coke and other goodies are meagre. In the Inkhuwa and Arun valleys the hotels cater primarily to locals, and the food is limited to dal bhat and biscuits.

Special Rules

Amazingly, this is one of the few treks in Nepal that, so far, has no extra fees or rules associated with it.

Day 1: Lukla to Puiyan

Instead of flying from Lukla, take a leisurely stroll down the 550-metre-long runway, continue down to Surkhe, then climb back up to Puiyan at 2730 metres. If you are travelling from Namche Bazaar it is not necessary to go to Lukla; you can walk from Jorsale to Chaunrikharka, then from Chaunrikharka to Puiyan.

Day 2: Puiyan to Pangum

The trail follows the same route as the Lamosangu to Namche Bazaar trail as far as Bupsa, then heads into new trekking country. The beginning of this trail is not obvious. Ask people for the trail to Pangum (pronounced 'Pankoma' locally); *kun baarto Pankoma jaanchha?*

From the hotel complex on the ridge in Bupsa, head up the ridge on an eroded trail to an inconspicuous trail junction that leads off the south side of the ridge. If you cannot find this trail, continue up the ridge to the large white house at the top of Kharte, then climb over a fence and turn south-east up the broad Khari Khola Valley. There are some ups and downs as the trail gradually gains elevation up the forested valley, passing isolated Sherpa houses and small streams. Though the trail is not steep, it gains a lot of elevation, so it is a laborious climb to the village of Pangum, at 2850 metres. Here is yet another Hillary school (there are 12 such schools in the region), a gompa and a paper factory. The Nepalese paper produced here is used for all official government transactions and is carried to Kathmandu in huge loads by porters. We call it rice paper, but actually it contains no rice; it is made from the inner bark of the daphne bush, known in Nepali as *lokta*. As you enter the town, stay on the largest trail, bearing left, to reach the *Himalayan Trekest Lodge* (sic) at the foot of Pangum.

Day 3: Pangum to Najingdingma

From Pangum, it is a short climb to the 3173-metre **Pangum La** (also called the Satu La), the pass between the watersheds of the Dudh Kosi and the Inukhu Khola. From the

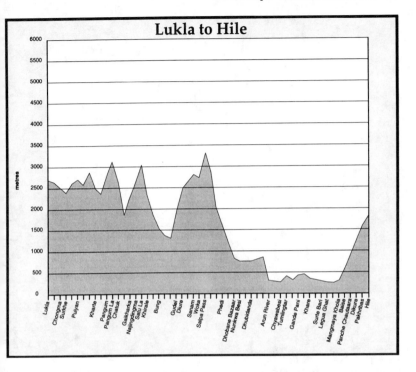

Lukla to Hile

pass, there is a great view, not only of the Khumbu Himalaya, but also of the peaks at the head of the Inukhu (also called Hinku) Valley, including Mera Peak, one of the easiest but least accessible of Nepal's trekking peaks. The trail contours to the north and descends gradually through a burned rhododendron forest to **Chatuk**, a small Sherpa settlement on a ridge. This unpretentious village has a multitude of names; it is also known as Shibuche and as Basme. At the top of the village is a small gompa; keep descending to the *Namaste Hotel* and a well-stocked shop. Stay on the ridge, descending past houses and fields to the foot of the village. Here the trail drops almost vertically down a steep rocky face with a few trees clinging to it to the river at 1855 metres. The trail crosses an exciting bridge suspended high above the river on steel cables. A Hima-

layan Trust team built this bridge in 1971 and replaced it again with a spectacular new 62-metre-long structure in 1993. When I asked one of the volunteers about the fantastic engineering that must be required for the construction of a bridge in such a remote location, he replied: 'We don't engineer them, we just build 'em'.

The trail ascends the side of the wild, sparsely inhabited Inukhu Valley to the extensive potato fields of the Sherpa hamlet of **Gaikharka** ('cow pasture'), at about 2300 metres. Although the only permanent settlements in this valley are those of Sherpas, the neighbouring Rais graze their cattle here. Gurungs who live far to the south also graze large herds of sheep during the summer. There are no hotels in Gaikharka, so climb an hour further to Najingdingma where several very basic hotels adjoin a large

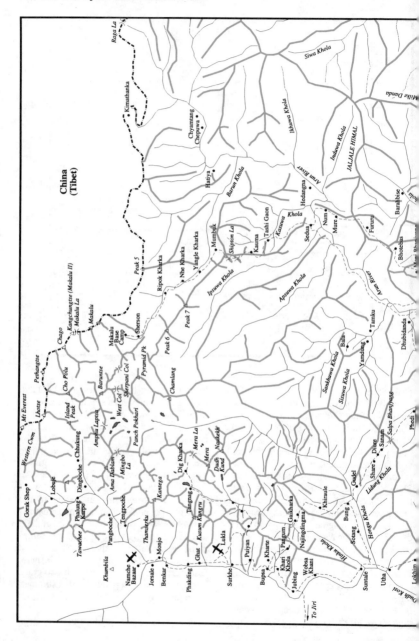

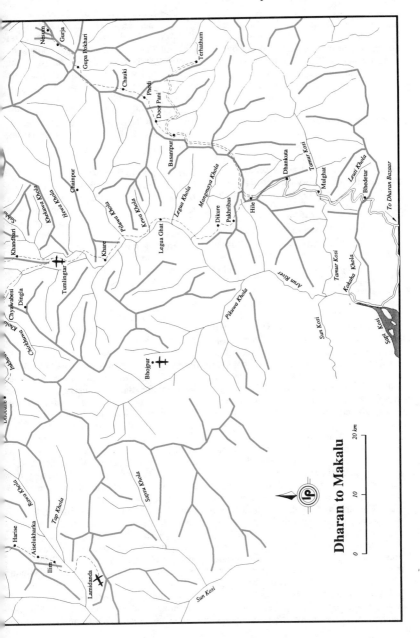

Dharan to Makalu

meadow at 2650 metres. When I first came here in 1971 this was an empty pasture with no permanent residents and Chatuk on the opposite side of the valley had only a few houses. The migration of people into the Inukhu Valley is a good illustration of the pressures of population growth in Nepal.

Day 4: Najingdingma to Bung

The route crosses pastures, then makes a steep ascent in forests towards Sipki (or Surkie) Pass, a steep notch at 3085 metres. Beyond the pass, the trail descends a short distance through forests that were devastated by a fire in April, 1992. The entire upper Hongu valley burned for six weeks as a result, they say, of a fire that started in Najingdingma. Near a tin-roofed rest house there is a trail junction. Turn right (south) to reach Bung. The trail that heads straight downhill leads to villages in the upper Hongu valley; the trail that leads uphill to the north goes to Panch Pokhari and eventually reaches Mera Peak. As you descend, the valley suddenly opens up above the Sherpa village of **Khiraule**, about 2400 metres. Far below you can see Boksom Gompa surrounded by a large circle of trees. It is particularly sacred, but has fallen into disuse and disrepair. There are many crisscrossing trails here used by the people of Bung when they collect wood, so it is easy to get lost; aim south and a bit east to the ridge above the gompa.

The trek is now in the great Hongu Valley, one of the most fertile regions of Nepal. Much of the rice for the Namche Bazaar market comes from this area and is carried across three ridges to Khumbu. Except for some Sherpas living at higher elevations, and some Chhetris and Brahmins downstream near Sotang, the Hongu Valley population is exclusively Rai.

The trail descends a ridge crest to the large village of Bung, spread out over the hillside from about 1900 to 1400 metres elevation. The most direct route through the village follows a ravine downhill, but soon gets lost wandering among the houses, fields and bamboo groves in the lower part of this Rai village. There are two hotels in lower Bung; the *Solu Khumbu Lodge* and the better *Sagarmatha Lodge* are both in Sherpa-style houses that look out of place among all the typical Rai houses. The people of Bung are a bit unhappy about trekking groups camping in the village, so it's best to continue downhill and camp in fields below the village near the river. You are almost certain to hear the drum of a *dhami*, a local shaman, in the Hongu Valley.

Day 5: Bung to Sanam

From Bung, there is a steep descent through bamboo forests to the Hongu Khola, which is crossed by a large suspension bridge at 1316 metres, followed by an equally steep climb to **Gudel**, another large Rai village, at 2000 metres. It was this long, useless descent and ascent that H W Tilman, travelling in the opposite direction, described poetically in his book *Nepal Himalaya*:

For dreadfulness, naught can excel
The prospect of Bung from Gudel;
And words die away on the tongue
When we look back on Gudel from Bung.

There are some rudimentary tea shops and the *Alp Lodge* near the Gudel school; if you are camping, the schoolmaster will allow you to camp here – for a fee. The first stretch from Gudel is steep, much of it on a stone staircase. Eventually the ascent along the side of the Lidung Khola, a tributary valley of the Hongu, becomes more gradual. It is a long and tiring climb, past a major wood-cutting operation that is devastating the rhododendron forests, to **Share**. Here there are several Sherpa houses, a gompa and shop. The climb becomes more gentle as it passes through fields to a small schoolhouse and a waterfall. It then climbs on to **Diure** at 2470 metres where there is a good campsite near a house that doubles as a hotel. Descend to a stream, then climb a bit more to Sanam at 2850 metres.

Rai villages in the valley have a maximum elevation of about 2400 metres. Sherpas exploit different resources than Rais, so there is little economic competition between the two groups. Sanam is a compact settlement of houses arranged in a single row. It is primarily dependent on herds of cattle, and milk, yoghurt and excellent cottage cheese (ask for *serkum*) is sometimes available. The *Sherpa Hotel* is reported to have good cheese, but is not good for sleeping. The *Gumpa Lodge* and *Salpa View Lodge* are said to be better.

Day 6: Sanam to Phedi

The route now climbs through a totally uninhabited area. The trail drops slightly to the floor of the canyon that it has been ascending, crosses the Lidung Khola, which at this point is only a stream, and makes a final steep climb to the Salpa Bhanjyang, the 3349-metre pass between the Hongu and Arun watersheds. It is a long climb; the total distance from the Hongu Khola is 2033 metres. The pass is often snowed in during winter; if you trek here between December and February, ask the people in Sanam if the route is open.

This area is covered by thick hemlock and fir forest that abounds with bird and animal life, including Himalayan bear, barking deer and the lesser panda, a smaller, red-coloured relative of its more famous namesake. A large chorten marks the pass and is the final influence of Sherpa culture on the route. The first available water is about an hour beyond the pass, making the lunch stop on this day quite late.

It is possible, by following the ridge to the south of Salpa Bhanjyang, to take an alternate route to the one described here. This route passes through Bhojpur, a large hill bazaar, famous for its excellent *kukhris*, the curved Nepali knives. There are flights from Bhojpur to both Kathmandu and Biratnagar, or you can keep walking to the Arun, crossing it near Sati Ghat, and rejoin the trail described here on Day 10. This is the route that Tilman followed in 1949 when he became the first trekker to visit Khumbu.

Descend from the pass through rhododendron forests to a meadow at 2880 metres. Here are two rough hotels that cater to porters carrying goods between Gudel and Dingla. If you are trekking up from Phedi, this is a good place to stop en route to the pass. Descend past a small dirty lake and shepherd's goths onto a rocky spur that separates the Inkhuwa Khola and the Sanu Khola. On this portion of the trail there is ample evidence of forest fires which occur in the dry season each spring. They are caused by fires in villages, careless smokers, lightning and shepherds burning the underbrush to allow new grass to grow.

Follow the trail through birch and rhododendron forests until it reaches a large stone overlooking the Inkhuwa Khola Valley. The trail then drops almost vertically through bamboo forests into the Rai village of Phedi. There are many opportunities to get lost on the ridge; stay as high as possible and keep going east. Several shepherds' trails lead down from the ridge to the north and south. You should stay on the ridge itself; the trail to Phedi starts its steep descent from the eastern end of the ridge. In the settlement of **Thulo Fokte** there is a teahouse, and 15 minutes below in Jau Bhari ('barley field') there are two trekkers' hotels. Descend on a rock staircase to Phedi at 1680 metres.

The best camp is below the village, near a shop and paper factory on the banks of the Inkhuwa Khola. You can also stay in the village at the *Sherpa Lodge*. This is one of the longest days and the longest downhill walk of the trek. The rakshi in Phedi is terrible, but is preferable to a bottle of the rotgut pineapple wine or Everest Special Madira that is portered in from Dharan.

Day 7: Phedi to Dhubidanda

The trek has now emerged into the fertile rice-growing Arun River Valley. The route follows the Inkhuwa Khola, a tributary of the Arun, crossing and recrossing the stream on a series of bamboo bridges. Some of these are substantial and some very flimsy, but all are picturesque. The Survey of India maps and all those derived from it show this river as the Irkhuwa, but after years of investigation I finally confirmed that the correct name is Inkhuwa. After the continuous ups and downs of the last week, this is a particularly relaxing day. The trail loses elevation almost imperceptibly, yet by the end of the day you will have lost almost 900 metres. There are many pools large enough for swimming, and the water temperature – especially in comparison with streams higher up – is comfortable.

A few hours below Phedi is **Dhobane Bazaar**, which has shops and some very ethnic restaurants. There is even a tailor shop that can outfit you with a new set of clothes while you wait. Continue through Nunkwa Besi, then cross a ridge to reach a cantilever bridge over a side stream just before Gote Bazaar. There is a good camping place on the banks of the Inkhuwa Khola near the village of Dhubidanda, at an elevation of about 760 metres.

The predominant ethnic groups in this part of the Arun basin are the Rais, Chhetris and Brahmins. Before the Gurkha conquest, about 200 years ago, the population of the Middle Hills region between the Dudh Kosi and Arun was almost entirely Rais. Following the conquest, when the Rais were defeated by the Gurkha army, considerable numbers of Hindus settled here, especially in the more fertile regions.

Day 8: Dhubidanda to Chyawabesi

The trail makes a final crossing of the Inkhuwa Khola. Bridges get washed away frequently here, so you may cross the river on a fancy new suspension bridge or perhaps a wobbly bamboo affair. The trail soon begins to climb over a spur separating the Arun River from the Inkhuwa Khola. The primary trail in this region climbs much higher, via the large village of Dingla at the top of the ridge. If you have a guide who knows the way or can ask local people, you can avoid this long, unnecessary climb and follow a circuitous course through the fields and back yards of the lower village of **Chalise**. The route is difficult to find as it crosses fields, doubles back on itself and traverses small irrigation canals and rice terraces. Ask people for the trail to Majwa or Tumlingtar. As you cross the ridge, you can

finally see the mighty Arun River to the north. This river, which has its headwaters in Tibet, is one of the major rivers flowing into the Ganges in India.

The trek now turns south and descends to a small tributary of the Arun, the Chirkhuwa Khola, where there is a small shop and a fine swimming hole overlooked by a huge and noisy band of rhesus monkeys. This village, called **Balawa Besi**, makes an excellent spot to stop for lunch, though it is usually hot.

A short distance on, the route crosses the Arun River, here at an elevation of only 300 metres, on a large suspension bridge. There used to be a dugout canoe ferry here, but in 1984 the bridge replaced this exciting ride. From the bridge at Kartike Ghat, the trail follows the eastern side of the river southward for about a half hour to a good camp at Chyawabesi, at 280 metres elevation. Along the Arun Valley there are frequent bhattis, so finding food is no longer a problem, though both the quality and sanitation are marginal.

Day 9: Chyawabesi to Khare

The trail follows the Arun as it flows south, sometimes climbing high above the river and sometimes traversing the sandy riverbed. The climate, even during the winter, is hot and tropical. Houses sit atop stilts for ventilation and the people are darker-skinned than those seen so far on the trek. You will probably want to change your schedule to do most of the walking in the very early morning to avoid the heat. Many of the settlements along the bottom of the Arun Valley are inhabited only during the planting and harvesting seasons by people who own fertile farmlands in the valley, but live higher up in the hills.

It is a short climb to a huge plateau that provides almost six km of completely level trail to **Tumlingtar**, a small village with an airport served by regular flights. Many of the inhabitants of Tumlingtar are of the Kuhmale (potter) caste, and earn their livelihood from the manufacture of earthenware pots from the red clay of this region. There is very little water on the plateau, so you must continue a long distance in the morning before lunch.

There are several hotels near the airport. For more ethnic fare, a cup of tea, some oranges or bananas, stop at the big shop under the banyan tree at the southern end of Tumlingtar. Unless you are walking in the very early morning, you will need some refreshment to help you keep moving under the hot sun.

The trek gets more pleasant immediately after the short descent from the plateau when the trail crosses the Sabha Khola, a tributary of the Arun. There is an excellent lunch spot beside a fine swimming hole in the warmest and most delightful stream along the entire trek route. You can swim or wade across the river, though the riverbed is rocky and slippery. The afternoon is short, involving a climb of only 100 metres to a few bhattis at Gande Pani, then a descent to Khare, a tropical village on the banks of the Arun. There are two bamboo trekkers' hotels at the southern end of town and a number of open-air facilities for porters.

Day 10: Khare to Mangmaya Khola

The trail continues south along the east bank of the Arun. There are many porters on the trail from here to Hile. These men and boys carry goods from warehouses in Hile, Dhankuta and Dharan to the bazaars of Khandbari, Bhojpur, Dingla and Chainpur. On the return to Hile porters carry big loads of *rudaraksha*, the holy seeds that are used for yogi beads from a source near Dingla. They often walk at night with small kerosene lamps tied to their dokos (the bamboo baskets in which they carry their loads).

In another of his classic anecdotes, Tilman imagined these porters nose-to-doko along the trail. Each porter carries a T-shaped stick that he places under his doko whenever (and wherever) he wishes to rest, usually when he is standing in the middle of the trail. Tilman imagined the entire trail backing up, as each porter waited until the man ahead of him finished his rest, thus halting a long line of porters. It presents a ludicrous picture, but a picture not totally removed from reality on this part of the trail. Beware especially of quick stops. The porters can shove their sticks under their load and make an abrupt stop with amazing speed and agility. You risk a collision if you follow too closely.

An excursion into the villages here will often uncover such appealing items as papayas *(mewa* in Nepali), peanuts *(badam)* and pineapples *(bhui katahar)*. You may also find fish from the Arun river for sale. This region is also famous for its wonderful oranges *(suntala)*.

The trail continues south, climbing more than 100 metres above the river on a ledge, then descends to the Piluwa Khola. The trail along this part of the Arun varies depending on water levels. At the Piluwa Khola there is a bridge upstream, but it's far away. If the water is low, everyone wades this warm, side stream of the Arun. Continue across the sandy riverbank to **Surte Bari**, two settlements with tea shops about an hour apart. Sometimes the trail climbs above the river and sometimes it is on the riverbank, passing scattered bhattis before reaching a schoolhouse at Chanawa. At **Legua Ghat** a long suspension bridge leads across the Arun to Bhojpur. There are hotels here that offer soft drinks and beer and are attempting to prepare food that will appeal to trekkers.

The trail passes under a cable that supports a river-gauging station just before a small village named Sati Ghat, the site of a dugout canoe ferry. Herds of goats and sheep have devoured much of the vegetation along this part of the river. These animals, more than humans, are responsible for the extensive deforestation in Nepal, because they prevent any new saplings from growing into trees. After a short distance the trail comes to a large pipal tree and chautaara overlooking a huge side valley of the Arun. At the foot of this valley flows the Mangmaya Khola; the grassy banks of this stream, beyond the village of Mangmaya at 200 metres elevation, afford an excellent campsite.

Day 11: Mangmaya Khola to Hile

The trail crosses the broad valley, then climbs through hot tropical forests to the village of **Dhele**, which has two tea shops facing a small village square, at approximately 700 metres elevation. The upper portion of this town has several large shops. The trail continues to climb through villages inhabited by Limbus, relatives of the Rais, to Baise, at 1250 metres. It's a long hot climb to Panche Chautaara, a settlement at 960 metres that supports several porters' hotels and a huge family of pigs. The trail finally gains the ridge near **Dikure** where there's a fine view of Makalu (8475 metres) and Chamlang (7317 metres) almost 150 km away.

The route continues to gradually ascend the waterless ridge to **Pakhribas** at 1640 metres. Continue through the village and keep climbing to an English medium school and the British Agricultural Project. This fantastic development presents a real contrast to the small gardens that surround every home throughout the trek. At Pakhribas, there are huge rows of vegetables, all neatly labelled with signs; there are walls, roads and irrigation canals, all paved with stone and cement. There are buildings of every description carefully labelled according to their function. Princess Diana choppered up to visit the Pakhribas project during her 1993 visit to Nepal.

The trail then climbs a ridge crest past many bhattis to the roadhead at Hile. This is a pleasant roadside town situated high on a hill at 1850 metres; the elevation and cool breezes provide a welcome relief from the heat of the Arun Valley. Many of the people who inhabit this village are Tibetans who have resettled here. They came from Tibet and other parts of eastern Nepal, particularly from the village of Walunchung Gola, when the Chinese occupation disrupted trade with Tibet in 1959. There is often some genuine Tibetan jewellery for sale here, and many Chinese goods are available at prices below those in Kathmandu. The village is also famous for its ample supply of *tongba* (a fermented millet drink) available at the *Hotel Milan*, *Doma Hotel* or the *Gajut*, all of which have little curtained-off cabins so you can get sloshed in private. The *Hotel Himali* is

reported to have good food. There is telephone service and electricity in Hile; the weekly bazaar day is Thursday.

Day 12: Hile to Kathmandu via Biratnagar

The road descends a spur to **Dhankuta**, at 1220 metres. There is one direct bus daily from Hile to Kathmandu. Fewer buses come to Hile than travel to Dhankuta, 10 km below. If you get bored with waiting, walk to Dhankuta to find a bus. From Dhankuta, there are hourly buses to Dharan (about a 1½ hour ride to cover the 50 km) or you might find direct service to Biratnagar. Take whatever is available; bus service is frequent in this region, especially once you reach Dharan.

The road does not pass through Dhankuta itself, but the town is worth a visit. It is a Rai, Newar and Limbu town – large, attractive and clean, with whitewashed houses and winding streets paved with stone. This is the largest town on the entire trek route. There is a police station flanked by polished brass cannon, a hospital, a cold-storage facility, bank, bakery, telegraph office and hundreds of shops.

The road descends from Dhankuta and crosses the Tamur Kosi at Mulghat. The Tamur Kosi flows west to join the Arun at the same point where the Sun Kosi joins it after its long trip eastward across Nepal. Together these rivers form the Saat Kosi ('seven rivers') that flows to the Ganges containing the waters of the Sun Kosi, Bhote Kosi, Tamba Kosi, Dudh Kosi, Arun Kosi, Likhu Kosi and Tamur Kosi.

The road turns south, following a side valley of the Tamur Kosi until it reaches the Churia Hills, the last range of hills before the plains. In India this range is called the Siwalik Hills. The road climbs to **Bhedetar**, a pass at 1460 metres. From some places on this ridge, there are views of Kanchenjunga (8598 metres) and its prominent neighbour Jannu (7710 metres), on the eastern border of Nepal.

The view from the pass is a most dramatic sight – to the south are nothing but plains.

After weeks in the hills, it is unusual to see country that is absolutely flat as far as the eye can see. The road descends to Dharan at 370 metres. Dharan used to be the major trading centre serving the eastern hills region, and was the site of a British Gurkha recruiting centre, but its role has changed with the opening of the Dhankuta road and the closure of the British camp. Although Dharan is located in the plains, most of the population consists of hill people who have resettled here. Dharan is also a major centre of Communist Party influence, so strikes and demonstrations are common.

Kanchenjunga Treks

Nepal opened the Kanchenjunga area to trekkers in 1988, though people have trekked in the area in connection with mountaineering expeditions since the turn of the century. Kanchenjunga is a long way from Kathmandu, and the nearest roads and airports are a long way from the mountain. You can trek either to the north or south Kanchenjunga base camp, but it takes luck, determination and a lot of time to visit both sides of the peak. The northern side is particularly remote; it takes almost two weeks of walking to get to the base camp at Pang Pema.

Kanchenjunga is on the border of Nepal and the Indian state of Sikkim, so a circuit of the mountain is politically impossible. The next best alternative is to visit both the north and south sides of the mountain from the Nepal side; you need to be equipped for a high pass crossing and have a minimum of four weeks. If for any reason you cannot cross the pass, then it's a long way around.

Since the region was opened, few groups have made successful crossings of either the Lapsang La or Mirgin La. Bad weather and snow is often to blame, but more often it is simply a lack of time. Many trekkers have wallowed around in the lowlands near Taplejung because they miscalculated the time required to reach the high country.

Unless you have at least four weeks, and preferably five, you should plan to visit either the north or south base camp, not both. If you can get to Taplejung by either road or air, the trek can be shortened by four days, making it a bit more reasonable.

The lowland portion of this region is culturally intriguing, but there are few good mountain views. The two treks that I have described here will probably need to be extended by a few days because of porter problems, weather, or the need for a rest day.

The Kanchenjunga region is the home of the Limbus. Relatives of the Rais, Limbus dominate the region east of the Arun River and few live elsewhere. Limbu men wear a distinctive tall *topi*, a Nepalese cap that is much more colourful than that worn by other Nepalese.

A noteworthy contribution of Limbu culture is the drink tongba. A wooden pot is filled with fermented millet seeds and boiling water added. You sip the dangerously potent mixture through a special bamboo straw, with tiny filters to keep the seeds out of the drink, as the hotelier merrily adds more hot water. It is often served in a large plastic mug, but ethnically correct hotels serve it in a special wooden tongba pot, which has brass rings, and a wooden cap with a hole for the straw. Tongba goes down easily, as you might do yourself when you arise after a lengthy tongba session. Watch for this speciality anywhere north of Dharan.

Accommodation

There are a few teahouses in the lowlands, but in the high country you must have food and a tent. If you are planning to take porters across the Lapsang La or Mirgin La, you will need to provide shoes, clothing and snow goggles for them.

Special Rules

The immigration office will issue trekking permits for the Kanchenjunga region only to groups, not to individual trekkers. The Kanchenjunga region remains technically restricted, but you can trek here if you arrange your trek through a trekking

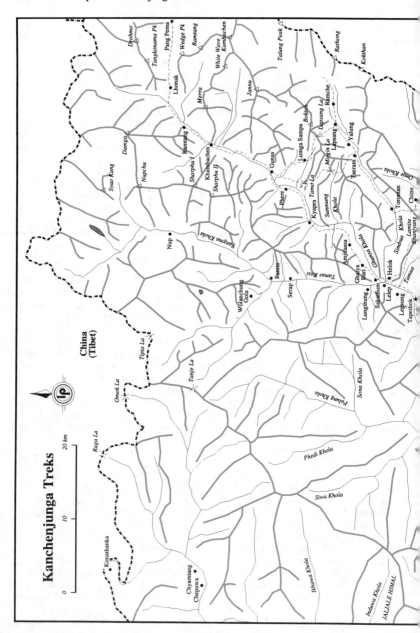

Kanchenjunga Treks

China
(Tibet)

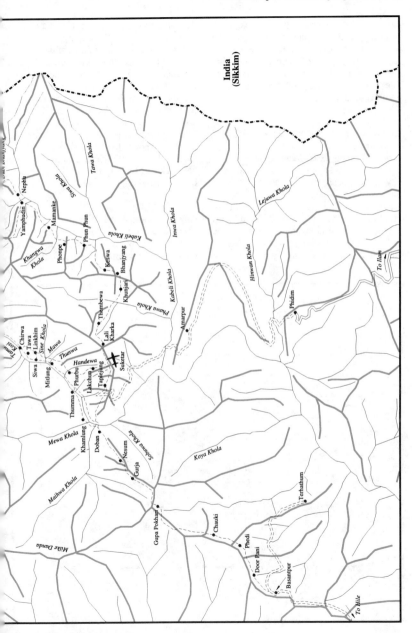

company and get a special US$10 per week trekking permit. Yamphudin, a village on the route to the south side of Kanchenjunga, is listed on both sides of the printed trekking permit form. It is included first as a village that is permitted, and on the reverse side as a village in the 'restricted area'.

BASANTPUR TO KANCHENJUNGA NORTH
Day 1: Biratnagar to Basantpur

If you are travelling by air, fly to the Terai city of Biratnagar, at an elevation of only 70 metres. Try to get a morning flight to Biratnagar. The flight takes about 50 minutes, so if you have arranged for vehicles to meet you in Biratnagar, there may be time to drive to the trailhead at Basantpur before dark. If you are travelling by bus, take the direct night bus to Dharan or Hile, then transfer to a local bus to Basantpur.

From Dharan, the road climbs over the Siwalik Hills to Dhankuta, then to Hile, a Tibetan settlement at 1850 metres. The paved road ends here, but an unpaved road wends its way to Basantpur, a large bazaar at 2200 metres on a ridge above the Tanmaya Khola, with a view of the entire Kanchenjunga massif. There are lots of shops and local-style hotels here, but it's a dirty, noisy roadhead town. It's more pleasant to walk about a km up the trail and camp in a meadow beyond the village.

Day 2: Basantpur to Chauki

The trek starts with a slow ascent on a wide trail through mossy rhododendron forests, with super views off both sides to the Arun

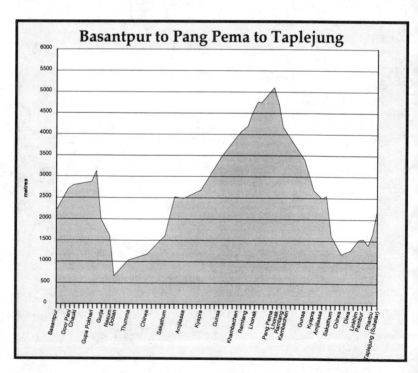

Kosi and Tamur Kosi drainages and north to Makalu. This is a major trade route to Chainpur and the Arun Valley, as well as to Taplejung and the upper Tamur Valley, so you will travel in the company of droves of porters. At **Tude Deoral** the Chainpur trail turns off, so the horde of porters diminishes a bit as you approach Door Pani at 2780 metres. It's uphill to a tea shop at Panch Pokhari, then the trail drops gently to Tinjuri Danda and climbs through Phedi to a good campsite at Chauki, elevation 2700 metres.

Day 3: Chauki to Gupa Pokhari

Most of the day's hike is along the ridge of the Milke Danda, through pretty, grassy meadows with views of Chamlang, Mera, Makalu and Kanchenjunga. After some ups and downs through Manglebare, Srimani and Balukop, the trek reaches two small lakes at Lamo Pokhari. It's generally downhill past the bamboo huts at Koranghatar to more lakes at Gupa Pokhari, elevation 2930 metres.

Gupa Pokhari has several lodges and lots of places to buy food, biscuits, beer, rum and chhang. The shopkeepers are Tibetans who say they settled here two generations ago. Industrious women weave scarves and carpets alongside the trail. A large pond behind the village has a Buddhist shrine, and prayer flags in the trees surrounding it. The murky waters of the lakes are heavily polluted; boil or chemically treat the water here. The area is subject to violent windstorms.

Day 4: Gupa Pokhari to Nesum

The route leaves the Milke Danda and heads out onto a ridge above the Tamur Kosi. The trail wanders uphill along the ridge through rhododendron forests to Akhar Deorali at 3200 metres, then makes some ups and downs en route to Buje Deorali, down to a kharka, up again to Mul Pokhari, then down through hazel and chestnut forests to **Gurja** at 2000 metres. Keep going down through cultivated country to Chatrapati, and then to Nesum at 1620 metres. There is a hotel in Chatrapati and two bhattis in Gurja.

Day 5: Nesum to Thumma

Make a long, zigzagging descent past scattered houses and the village of Banjoghjara to the Maihwa Khola. Deal with formalities at the police checkpost and cross the suspension bridge into the village of **Doban** at 640 metres.

The trail now meets the Tamur Kosi. There are trails up both sides of the river. Both are lousy, and subject to landslides; it seems to make little difference which side of the river you start out on. There are frequent bridges across the Tamur Kosi in various stages of technological advancement and repair. Inquire locally and change your route to suit the current situation, though you need to end up on the east bank by the time you reach Siwa.

At Doban, you can cross the Tamur Kosi and climb almost 1200 metres up to Taplejung. It is a long ascent and the village is not particularly lively, so there is no point in making a side trip unless you are trying to confirm flight reservations. Once the road is completed from Ilam to Taplejung it will be possible to drive to this point to begin the trek.

The population of the Tamur Valley is primarily Limbu, with a few Chhetris in the lower regions and Sherpas at higher elevations. Doban is a small, grubby Newar bazaar town with shops selling soap, toothpaste, cloth, thread, sandals, beer and rum. Many Tibetans live in flimsy bamboo shelters alongside the bazaar, and sell tongba and weave woollen scarves and aprons. Characteristic of misplaced priorities in completing development projects, there are electric lines and power poles here – but no electricity.

If you cross the Tamur Kosi on the suspension bridge at Doban and follow the east-bank trail, you will travel up the Tamur in tropical forests, sometimes climbing above the river and sometimes on the riverbank itself. Thumma is on the west side of the river about two hours beyond Doban. If you stay on the west bank you will pass through Khamlung, then reach Thumma about two hours beyond Doban where you can cross to the east side on a reasonably safe suspension bridge.

Day 6: Thumma to Chirwa

From Thumma, stay on the east bank as the trail undulates along the riverside through rocky fields and across landslides to the Chhetri bazaar of Mitlung, elevation 800 metres, then climb over a ridge to Sisnu. In 1990, most people crossed the river on a bamboo bridge here and followed the west bank for about 45 minutes before crossing back to the east side. This diversion may not be necessary if the trail on the east side is in good condition. Pass the settlements of **Siwa**, Tawa and Porke. At Porke there is a flimsy bamboo and wire bridge which, fortunately, you do not have to cross. The valley narrows and the trail becomes worse as it climbs across landslides and boulder-strewn river deposits to Chirwa, a pleasant bazaar with a few bhattis and shops at 1190 metres. Take a look at the village water-supply system. It's an elaborate setup of bamboo chutes, pipes and channels that Rube Goldberg or Heath Robinson would have been proud of – if it has not yet been replaced with plastic pipe.

Day 7: Chirwa to Sakathum

Continue up the Tamur across big boulders, passing below the Chhetri village of **Tapethok**. Beyond Tapethok, there is a bridge across the Tamur that leads to the Sherpa settlements of Lepsung, Lelep and Lungthung. Lelep and the route up the Tamur Kosi to Walunchung Gola are specifically listed as restricted areas on the back of your trekking permit.

The trail makes more ups and downs, traverses a landslide, then crosses the Tamua Khola on a suspension bridge below the village of **Helok**. There is a tongba and tea shop near the junction where the trail to the Limbu village of Helok leaves the main Tamur Kosi route. To bypass Helok, climb over a spur and descend to the Simbua Khola, crossing it on a new suspension bridge. This river comes from the Yalung Glacier on the south side of Kanchenjunga; if you trek to the south base camp, you will reach the headwaters of this river.

A short climb over another ridge brings

you into the steep and narrow Gunsa Khola Valley. Cross the Gunsa Khola on a rickety bridge and camp by the banks of the river near the Tibetan village of Sakathum at 1640 metres. There is a helipad, tea shop and vegetable garden here. If it's clear, you will have your first good close-up views of Jannu up the Gunsa Khola Valley.

Day 8: Sakathum to Amjilassa

The hike is along a steep, narrow trail up the north bank of the Gunsa Khola. Climb steeply for 100 metres, then drop back to the river and follow the riverbed for about a km. The trail then begins a sustained climb on stone steps to a waterfall and the settlement of Ghaiya Bari. The ascent becomes gentler, following an exhilarating, exposed, and potentially dangerous trail through arid country to a crest at 2530 metres, then descends a bit to the Tibetan settlement of Amjilassa at 2490 metres.

Day 9: Amjilassa to Kyapra

Ascend for 100 metres, then level off and round a bend of the river into lush bamboo, oak and rhododendron forests, with views of Nango Ma and the south-west part of the Kanchenjunga massif. The trail makes many short climbs and descents and passes several waterfalls and pastures. Beyond a large waterfall in the Gunsa Khola itself, start a steep climb to a campsite at Kyapra, called Chapla or Gyabla by the Tibetan inhabitants, at 2730 metres.

The Mandala map shows that the trail crosses the Gunsa Khola at Kyapra; it does not. Kyapra is on the north bank and you stay on the north side of the river all the way to the bridge at Gunsa.

Day 10: Kyapra to Gunsa

Descend steeply into a side ravine, then follow along the river through a fir and rhododendron forest. It takes all morning to trek past Killa and on to the yak pastures and potato fields of **Phere**. Both are Tibetan villages with pleasant gompas and friendly monks; you may find a better supply of food, especially potatoes, in Phere than Gunsa.

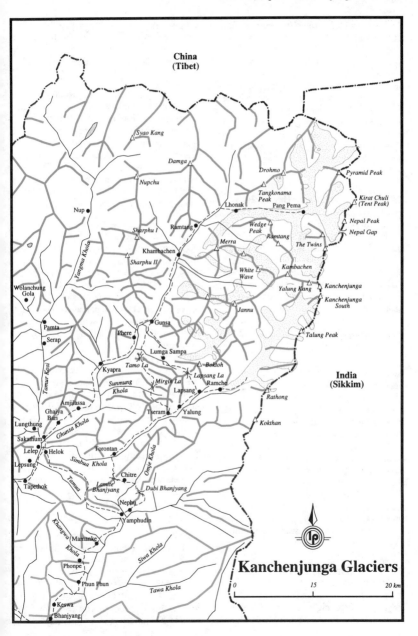

Kanchenjunga Glaciers

China
(Tibet)

Syao Kang

Damga

Nupchu

Nup

Sharphu I

Ramtang

Khambachen

Sharphu II

Drohmo

Tangkonama
Peak

Lhonak

Pang Pema

Pyramid Peak

Kirat Chuli
(Tent Peak)

Nepal Peak

Wedge
Peak

Ramtang

The Twins

Nepal Gap

Merra

White
Wave

Kambachen

Yalung Kang

Kanchenjunga

Kanchenjunga
South

Jannu

Wolanchung
Gola

Yangma Khola

Pamta

Serap

Gunsa

Phere

Talung Peak

Lumga Sampa

Tamu La

Boktoh

Kyapra

Sunmung
Khola

Mirgin La

Lapsang La

Ramche

India
(Sikkim)

Lapsang

Tamur Kosi

Amjilassa

Ghaiya
Bari

Tseram

Yalung

Rathong

Lungthung

Ghunsa Khola

Sakathum

Kokthan

Lelep

Helok

Torontan

Lepsung

Simbua Khola

Chitre

Tamua

Lamite
Bhanjyang

Omje Khola

Dubi Bhanjyang

Tapethok

Nephu

Yamphudin

Khangwa
Khola

Mamanke

Siwa Khola

Phonpe

Phun Phun

Tawa Khola

Keswa

Bhanjyang

0   15   20 km

The valley widens as you trek through fields and larch forests to a bridge across the Gunsa Khola.

The prayer-flag bedecked houses of Gunsa (which means 'winter settlement') are on the south side of the river at 3430 metres. The police checkpost in Gunsa takes itself very seriously; be sure your permit is in order before you pay them a visit. The high route to the south Kanchenjunga base camp via the Lapsang La begins here. Gunsa is slowly developing into a trekking village and has a teahouse and a few shops.

Day 11: Acclimatisation Day at Gunsa

The trek is now getting into high country; since you have been traipsing about in the lowlands for almost two weeks, you need to spend some time to allow your body to acclimatise to high altitude. You can use the day to reconnoitre the route over the Lapsang La by trekking to a small lake at the foot of the Yamatari Glacier, south of Gunsa. The people of Gunsa move their yaks over the Mirgin La to the high country south of Kanchenjunga in the summer, and take them down to Phere in the winter.

Day 12: Gunsa to Khambachen

The trail makes a gradual ascent along the south bank of the Gunsa Khola, then crosses a boulder-strewn flood plain and crosses back to Rambuk Kharka on the north side of the river. Once on the opposite side, the trail passes a waterfall then makes a short, steep ascent to a very unstable scree slope. It's a dangerous 250-metre passage across the slide, with loose footing, a steep fall to the river and lots of tumbling football-sized rocks. Beyond the slide, the trail drops to the single locked hut at Lakep, then traverses to Khambachen, a Tibetan settlement of about a dozen houses at 4040 metres.

Day 13: Acclimatisation Day in Khambachen

It's again time to stop and acclimatise. There are views of the high peaks near Kanchenjunga: Khabur, Phole, Nango Ma and Jannu.

Climb a ridge above the village for more views, or take a day hike to the Jannu base camp. You might come across blue sheep grazing in the valley or on the slopes above.

Day 14: Khambachen to Lhonak

The trail climbs gradually through open rocky fields to Ramtang at 4240 metres, then across moraines north-west of the Kanchenjunga Glacier. Lhonak, at 4790 metres, is near a dry lake bed on an open sandy plain; water is scarce here. There are no houses, but you can camp among the large boulders here to get out of the wind. Terrific mountain views abound in all directions.

Day 15: Lhonak to Pang Pema

You cannot see the main Kanchenjunga peak from Lhonak; for a view of this peak you must go on to the base camp at Pang Pema, elevation 5140 metres. You could make a day trip from Lhonak, but clouds often obscure the peak after about 9 am, and you could find yourself in Pang Pema without a view. It's really worth camping in Pang Pema in hopes of a cloudless vista just before sunset or in the early morning.

From Lhonak, the trail ascends gradually across the plain, then gets a bit steeper as it follows the moraine. You can drop off the moraine and follow the bottom of the valley to avoid the steeper section. The views are dramatic, but you cannot see Kanchenjunga or Wedge Peak until you are near Pang Pema. The spectacular main peak of Kanchenjunga, and a panorama of other peaks that make up one of the largest mountain masses in the world, tower over the single roofless hut at Pang Pema.

Day 16: Pang Pema to Khambachen

Take a morning hike up the ridge north of Pang Pema. A climb of 200 to 300 metres provides a vantage point with views of Kanchenjunga, Wedge Peak, the Twins, Pyramid Peak and Tent Peak. As usual, the descent goes faster, so you can easily get back to Khambachen in a single day.

Day 17: Khambachen to Gunsa

Day 18: Gunsa to Amjilassa

Day 19: Amjilassa to Chirwa

Descend to Helok. If you are headed for the south side of Kanchenjunga, start climbing the stone stairs in Helok to the ridge. A local guide will probably save you a lot of energy on this route, because the trails here are used primarily by woodcutters and herders, not by trekkers.

The Mandala map shows a trail from Helok up the Simbua Khola towards Tseram. This trail, where it exists at all, is strictly for monkeys. There is a way through, but it is not a trail, it's a steep, slippery climb through thick bamboo forests up the side of the Deorali Danda. I came down this once; it was great fun, but it's not a sensible route. Everyone seems to agree that it's more practical to take an extra day and follow the woodcutters trail up the ridge from Helok to Yamphudin, then climb to the Lamite Bhanjyang from the south and re-enter the Simbua Valley.

If your destination is Taplejung, retrace your steps through the lower part of Helok and meander back down the Tamur Kosi to Chirwa.

Day 20: Chirwa to Linkhim

It's a straight shot down the Tamur Kosi to Taplejung. You can avoid the steep climb from Doban by contouring up the side of the valley. From Chirwa, start uphill, passing through **Diwa** village. Climb over a landslide and keep going up steeply, staying above Tawa. The trail drops into a large side canyon, then climbs back to the ridge before reaching Linkhim.

Day 21: Linkhim to Suketar

Trek in and out of side canyons through the small Limbu villages of Helate, Pumbur and Phurbu to a ridge overlooking a monstrous slide area. Climb above the slide area to the Sherpa villages of Bung Kulung and **Lakchun** and you can get directly to the airport without going in to Taplejung.

Day 22: Fly to Kathmandu

TAPLEJUNG TO KANCHENJUNGA SOUTH

There are lots of ways to make this trek, but the way I have described here is the easiest – if you can arrange a flight in to Taplejung. Take a look at the route profile for this trek; there is an incredible amount of up-and-down climbing. When I trekked this route, I calculated that we climbed – and descended – more than 15,000 metres during two weeks of walking. Be sure you are ready for this kind of effort before you set out; there are no escape routes if you get sick, tired or bored.

If you cannot get a flight to Taplejung, consider driving to **Phidim**, two days' walk to the south. The road is complete to this point and there is a bus or truck service from Ilam. From Phidim, you can bypass Taplejung and head over some ridges to the Kabeli Khola and Yamphudin. Be sure that Phidim is included on your trekking permit if you plan to use this option.

Day 1: Taplejung to Thembewa

A flight to Taplejung takes half an hour from Biratnagar and 1½ hours from Kathmandu. To avoid clouds and wind, Taplejung flights operate early in the morning, so you can probably accomplish a few hours of walking on the day you fly in. The airport is on the top of a ridge in **Suketar** village, far above Taplejung. Unless you need to confirm a flight back to Kathmandu or load up on supplies, it's not worth the long walk into Taplejung and the tedious, steep climb back up to Suketar.

If the road is in operation, you will probably spend a night in a hotel in Taplejung, then start the trek to the south base camp with a climb up the ridge to the airport.

From Suketar, elevation 2300 metres, the trail climbs gradually along a rhododendron-covered ridge. The trail crosses the ridge and contours past the Deorali Khola and four more streams to a pass at 2570 metres. Descend through forests to Lali Kharka, two houses at 2220 metres, then through fields to

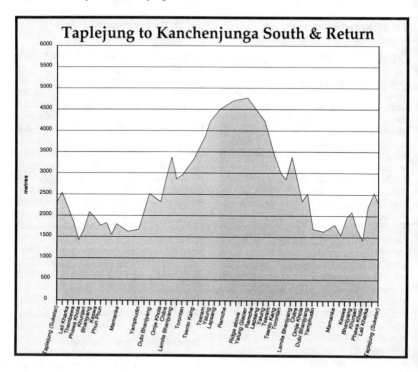

Taplejung to Kanchenjunga South & Return

the substantial Limbu village of Thembewa at 1880 metres.

Day 2: Thembewa to Keswa

From Thembewa, the trail ascends a bit to a ridge, then drops steeply through Shimu and Pokara villages to a suspension bridge across the Phawa Khola at 1430 metres. There is a good swimming hole here and a possible campsite near the river. Climb steeply to **Khunjari**, a Limbu village at 1700 metres. Turn left just beyond the school and climb through wheat fields to a saddle. From here, the trail makes a long, looping traverse to **Bhanjyang**, a Gurung settlement with several bhattis, on a pass at 2120 metres. From Bhanjyang there are views of Kanchenjunga and Kyabru.

The trek has now entered the Kabeli Khola Valley, but you will spend the next two days climbing up and down, in and out of ravines and over ridges, only to end up in Yamphudin at the bottom of the valley. Turn left from Bhanjyang and head north just below the top of the ridge, descending to the scattered village of Keswa at 1960 metres.

Day 3: Keswa to Mamanke

Pass below waterfalls and cross several streams and a landslide to reach the village of Phun Phun, which is shown on some maps with the fanciful spelling *Fun Fun*. Cross a saddle, with a stately pipal tree offering a rest in the shade, and traverse to Yangpang, then head generally upwards through forests past a large waterfall. Descend through a series of side valleys to two shops on a ridge at 1850 metres, then drop a bit to **Phonpe** village at 1780 metres. Descend steeply through rice terraces into a side canyon, crossing a stream on a long suspension bridge at 1540 metres, then climb back to Mamanke, a prosperous Limbu village with bhattis, shops and a large school at 1810 metres.

Day 4: Mamanke to Yamphudin

Climb to a ridge and then descend gradually to the Tenguwa Khola. Forego the decrepit bridge; cross the stream by jumping from stone to stone. Switchback steeply up to another ridge marked by a chorten and prayer flags, then descend across rubble and rock slides and cross another stream. This portion of the valley is steep, and portions of the trail are on cliffs high above the river as it makes its way down to the Kabeli Khola at 1640 metres. There is a lot of flood damage here, so it becomes a rock-hopping exercise, over boulders, tree roots and intersecting stream channels as you head upstream. Stay on the west side of the Kabeli Khola, climbing gently to Yamphudin (1690 metres) at the junction of the Omje Khola and the Kabeli Khola.

Yamphudin is a mixed community of Sherpas, Limbus, Rais and Gurungs. Among the corn and rice fields of the village there is a police post, a school, and some shops with minimal supplies. The 1989 monsoon produced floods that washed away portions of the village and many of its fields. A goat trail leads from Yamphudin up the ridge to the west, to Helok and the Tamur Kosi Valley. See Day 19 of the Basantpur to Kanchenjunga North route description for more information about this rough and difficult trail.

Day 5: Yamphudin to Omje Khola

Beyond Yamphudin, you should plan to carry your own food and shelter. The only facility from here on is a teahouse in upper Omje Khola which is only open when the proprietor is in the mood.

Cross the Omje Khola on a couple of bamboo poles and follow the Kabeli Khola upstream for a short distance, ignoring the suspension bridge. After you pass behind a ridge out of sight of Yamphudin, cross a small stream and take a trail that heads

straight uphill. Zigzag up through fields of corn and barley to Darachuk, and keep climbing past meadows to Dubi Bhanjyang, a pass at 2540 metres. Descend through ferns and big trees to the Omje Khola at 2340 metres and follow the stream uphill for a short distance. Cross the stream on a log bridge, and go a bit further upstream to a campsite.

It's a bit depressing to make the long climb over the Dubi Bhanjyang only to end up on the banks of the same stream that you camped beside last night. Unfortunately, there is no trail that follows the stream bed; besides, the Nepalese do not fret about steep trails as much as we do. This is a pretty short day, but the next part of the trek is steep and has few campsites. If you are a small party you might keep going on to Chitre, but there isn't space there for a large camp.

Day 6: Omje Khola to Torontan

From the stream, the trail makes a steep climb through bamboo to a kharka at Chitre (2920 metres) and continues up to a notch. After a short descent, the ascent is less strenuous to a clearing, and then the trail passes through a forest of pines and rhododendrons to a pond at Lamite Bhanjyang, 3410 metres elevation. This is not a good place to camp. There is a water shortage in the spring and it is muddy in the autumn. On a clear day this ridge provides views of Jannu and of the Taplejung road far to the south.

From the ridge, you can see a trail across a huge landslide scar; a better route is to stay on the ridge and follow it east along its top until you are well beyond the landslide, then follow a steep set of switchbacks leading downhill. Once the initial steep descent is finished, the trail becomes more gentle. The trail is generally level and wide, though it is muddy in the autumn and there are a few short, steep descents. It passes through damp, orchid-filled forests, crossing streams and isolated clearings used by herders and woodcutters.

The trail emerges into the open just above the Simbua Khola. A 1987 flood washed away large parts of the trail. Stay above the white silty river and follow it upstream, on a series of ascents and descents, to a temporary bridge built of stones and logs. There are campsites near the river, and also in a clearing beyond Torontan, near a few caves at 2990 metres.

Day 7: Torontan to Tseram

The hike starts in forests of several varieties of rhododendron, then crosses landslides to Tsento Kang, a goth at 3360 metres. The deeply forested valley is dotted with clearings, meadows and streams as it rises to another goth at Watha.

An hour beyond is a Buddhist shrine decorated with rock cairns, prayer flags and iron, three-pronged trisuls. The shrine is in a cave that has a streak of dark stone along it, which is thought to be the image of a snake. This shrine marks the boundary of a sacred part of the valley, beyond which the killing of animals is prohibited. Peaks begin to appear in the distance as you climb further. There is a short stretch along the gravel bottom of the stream bed, then a climb to Tseram, a large, flat meadow with a single house at 3870 metres. The settlements in this valley are goths used by yak and cow herders from Gunsa who cross the Mirgin La to graze their animals during the summer.

Day 8: Tseram to Ramche

Climb through forests to a slide area; the junction of the trail to the Mirgin La is nearby, but the trail is hard to find. Stumble across a stream on a loose, rocky path and climb to some mani walls and a stone house near the tree line at 4040 metres. The peaks of Rathong and Kabru loom at the head of the valley; it's hard to believe they are both less than 6700 metres high. The trail climbs into the valley alongside the moraine of the Yalung Glacier. The valley opens up as you approach Yalung, a pasture full of yaks at 4260 metres.

Climb alongside the moraine through scrub junipers up a stream to a lake at **Lapsang**, 4430 metres. Here you can see the start of the route to the Lapsang La headed off over the moraines in a valley to the north.

Keep climbing to another lake and a big meadow at Ramche, elevation 4620 metres. There are two well-built stone houses here; one of them thinks it is a hotel, but the owner spends so much time away that it rarely fulfils its ambitions. The view is dominated by the spectacular Rathong peak, elevation 6678 metres, situated on the Nepal-India border to the east. Herds of blue sheep live on the cliffs above.

Day 9: Day Trip to Yalung Glacier

Make a day trip to the Yalung Glacier. Follow a stream alongside the moraine for a long distance, then bear right to climb onto the moraine itself. From a chorten at 4800 metres elevation there is a fine view of the Kanchenjunga south face. A short distance beyond the chorten is a view of Jannu. This is a good place to turn around. To go further, you must climb down the rough moraine onto the Yalung Glacier and pick your way through the boulder-strewn glacier towards Kanchenjunga. It's a one or two-day project to reach the base camp itself.

Day 10: Ramche to Tseram

Day 11: Tseram to Lamite Bhanjyang

Day 12: Lamite Bhanjyang to Yamphudin

Day 13: Yamphudin to Phonpe

Day 14: Phonpe to Khunjari

Day 15: Khunjari to Suketar

There are a few tea shops at the airport that have rooms for rent. If you are camping, set up your tents near the airfield and hope for clear weather for the flight in the morning. The hotel specializes in tongba, so you will have something to amuse you if the plane does not come. In the autumn of 1993 some enterprising village youths were scamming tourists for an unofficial departure tax and donations for the 'Taplejung Youth League for Aids'.

Day 16: Fly to Kathmandu

Fly to Biratnagar or, if you are lucky, directly to Kathmandu.

KANCHENJUNGA NORTH SIDE TO SOUTH SIDE

There are two routes between Gunsa and the Simbua Khola. The higher Lapsang La, elevation 5110 metres, is often snow-covered and may be difficult and dangerous for both trekkers and porters. This is a very remote area where help is a long way off, and evacuation is almost impossible. You will need to make a choice whether to cross the Lapsang La, or the lower and safer Mirgin La, or retreat down the Tamur Kosi Valley. Either of the high routes takes three days, with high camps on either side of the pass. The most critical factor on the high passes is snow. There is no regular traffic on these routes; if there is snow, you will have to break the trail yourself without any rock cairns or other landmarks to guide you.

The Mirgin La route actually crosses five passes: the Tamo La, 3900 metres; an unnamed, 4115-metre-high pass; the Mirgin La, 4663 metres; Sinion La, 4660 metres; and a final, unnamed pass of 4724 metres elevation. It then makes a long, steep 1000-metre descent to the Simbua Khola. The route enters the Simbua Khola Valley above Tseram, at 3900 metres, and you can probably make it on to Ramche the same day.

The Lapsang La route starts at Gunsa and climbs across the foot of the Yamatari Glacier to a goth at Lumga Sampa. Cross the Lapsang La and make your way down through the large boulders of a moraine to a camp below the glacier. Descend further into the valley and meet the Simbua Khola trail at Lapsang, elevation 4430 metres. Then it's a short distance up the valley to Ramche at 4620 metres.

Makalu Base Camp

You can make an outstanding trek in eastern Nepal from either Hile or Tumlingtar by walking north up the Arun River to Sedua and Num, then crossing Shipton La (4127 metres) into the upper Barun Khola Valley for a close look at Makalu (8475 metres) and Chamlang (7290 metres). The trek to Makalu base camp visits one of the most remote and unfrequented areas of Nepal. The Barun Valley is part of a huge international protected area under an agreement between Nepal and China.

The dam project on the upper reaches of the Arun River will change the character of this region forever. The plans include the construction of a road from Dharan to Num, a tunnel under the ridge below Num and several dams and powerhouses along some magnificent regions of the Arun Valley.

Some groups have attempted an even wilder trek by crossing Sherpani Col and West Col into the upper Hongu basin. This trek has proved itself difficult and potentially very dangerous. It's better to travel from Lukla if you want to go into the upper Hongu basin and the Panch Pokhari ('five lakes'), situated there.

MAKALU BARUN NATIONAL PARK

The Makalu Barun National Park was established in 1992 as Nepal's eighth national park. The 2330-sq-km park is bordered by the Arun River in the east and the Sagarmatha National Park on the west. To the south the park is bordered by an 830-sq-km conservation area.

Special Rules

The Makalu Barun National Park is subject to all the rules relating to national parks, including the Rs 650 entrance fee, fees for video cameras and restrictions on firewood use. In 1993 there was no official entrance station, so no fees were collected. This will probably have changed by the time you trek here. The present park office is in Khandbari, but it is likely that an entrance station will be established in Sedua.

Day 1: Kathmandu to Khandbari

It is a one-hour flight by Twin Otter (45 minutes by Avro) from Kathmandu to

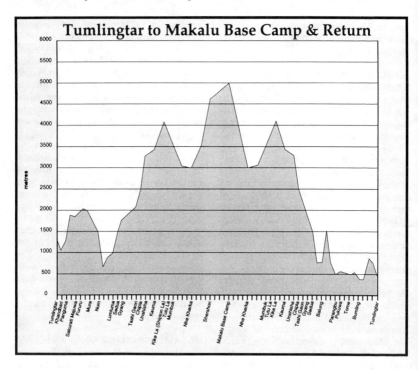

Tumlingtar, situated on a plateau just above the Arun River at an elevation of 460 metres. Have lunch at one of the airport hotels – *Hotel Makalu* or the *Kanchenjunga* – both of which have refrigerators full of cold drinks. In Kuhmalgaon, 100 metres north of the airport, are the *Hotel Manakamana* and the Nepal Airways office. Kuhmalgaon is named after the potter caste (Kuhmale) who make their living here manufacturing earthenware items from the red clay of this plateau. If you are camping, follow the signs that read 'way to if you need place for camping'.

The extensive plateau of Tumlingtar has several settlements, each surrounded by fields of rice and corn. Be prepared to dodge bicycles that schoolchildren race recklessly down the narrow paths. Tumlingtar is on a major trade route that is scheduled to be converted into a road in connection with the

Arun hydroelectric project. Until the road is built you will encounter many porters and local people on the first day of the trek. From the Tumlingtar airstrip, walk east through the village to the main trail that begins a long ascent up the ridge between the Arun river and the Sabha Khola. Beginning in rice terraces, the path soon becomes a ridge walk with teahouses and tree-shaded chautaaras. There are views of the huge massif of Chhamlang in the distance.

The climb continues to the outskirts of Khandbari at 1040 metres. The police checkpost is on a hill to the south of town near the microwave antenna. They expect a visit from all passing trekkers. Continue past shops to a large village square paved with flagstones that is the site of the Saturday market. Nearby are the Makalu-Barun project office, the *Arati Hotel* and the *Barun*

Hotel & Bar that offers 'modern toilets and showers'. Continue north up the shop-lined street to the bank, school, many small hotels and restaurants, carrom parlours and government offices. If you are camping, continue trekking for an hour to a good campsite near Mani Bhanjyang.

Day 2: Khandbari to Fururu

The trail finally emerges between shops onto a ridge, continuing a short distance to the settlement of **Mani Bhanjyang** at 1100 metres. The *Padma Hotel & Lodge* offers accommodation, or you can camp in a grassy meadow alongside the village. Here the electric lines end and the countryside becomes much more rural. Make a gentle climb through terraced fields and past a paper factory to Panguma at 1300 metres. Continue through fields, bamboo groves and big rocks to Sheka at 1350 metres. Keep climbing to the Tamang village of **Bhotebas**, a few tea stalls and a trekkers' hotel at 1740 metres. Beyond the village the cultivated fields disappear as the trail climbs through trees to a pass at 1850 metres that offers a spectacular view of Chamlang, Makalu and Jaljale Himal. Descend a bit to the next ridge, then follow the crest as it makes some ups and downs through a rhododendron forest to Chichela, a tea shop and a few houses inhabited by Gurungs at 1830 metres. Follow along the ridge to the small settlements of Kuwa Pani at 1910 metres and Sakurati Majuwa at 1860 metres. Just past a mani wall the trail leads up to a campsite. The lower trail heads to the village of Fururu, situated below the ridge at 1900 metres. There were no hotels of any kind there in 1993.

Day 3: Fururu to Num

If you went down to Fururu, scramble back to the ridge at 1960 metres and trek through forests of huge rhododendrons just below the ridge line to a mani wall and dirty pond. A lot of the forest here has been burned to make fields to support the ever-growing population of nearby villages. Continue along the ridge past a small stream to a single Sherpa house and tea shop. This is **Mure**, a spread-

out village at 1980 metres that is inhabited by both Sherpas and Rais.

Below Mure the trail passes many tracts of burned trees where more fields are under development. The route cuts across the ridge, then makes a tedious descent on a rocky eroded trail to some stone steps and a final walk to Num at 1490 metres. Num is situated on the ridge above an S-shaped bend in the Arun River; it is planned that the intake pipes for the Arun power plant will be in tunnels through this ridge. There is a primary school and a few shops and hotels in the town square. The hotels cater mostly to locals, but they do offer the first soft drinks and beer since Khandbari. On the opposite side of the Arun is the village of Sedua; behind Sedua the peaks that flank Shipton La should be visible.

Day 4: Num to Sedua

The trail descends steeply from Num through the corn fields of Lumbang. Below the village the trail drops very steeply through jungle to a suspension bridge over the Arun River at 660 metres. From the bridge the trail climbs steeply to a primitive tea shop at 820 metres, then through corn and buckwheat fields. The country is particularly rocky; tiny terraces planted with corn and barley dot the slope as you make a long, steep, rough climb to Sedua at 1460 metres. There are two tea shops and a school on a saddle that separates the Arun Valley from the side valley of the Kasuwa Khola. Continue over the ridge, then a short distance to a camp near a stream.

Day 5: Sedua to Tashi Gaon

The trek makes a gradual climb high above the Kasuwa Khola to Gyang at 1770 metres. Climbing past the school at Gyang, it is a gentle walk through terraced fields and forested areas to Hindrungma village, and on to Rupisa. The route crosses meadows and several streams, then climbs to the Sherpa village of Tashi Gaon, the last permanent settlement in the valley. It's a long climb from the bottom of the village past houses and fields to the village's only hotel at the top of town at 2070 metres. It may be possible to continue on to a campsite about an hour beyond Tashi Gaon in the autumn, but in the spring there is no camping place because the small fields in this hamlet are all planted with barley and potatoes.

Day 6: Tashi Gaon to Kauma

This is a tough day, with an elevation gain of almost 1400 metres on a steep trail. Climb over the ridge behind the hotel and ascend through forests to a stream and onto a ridge where there is a small campsite. The trail levels out, then climbs to a shepherd's hut called Chipla atop another ridge. Climb past two small streams, then switchback up the ridge in forests to a kharka at 2900 metres and up to a saddle and Unshisha, a tiny meadow at approximately 3300 metres elevation. Here the trail joins the ridge that separates the Iswa and Kasuwa drainages. The slope gets steeper and becomes a series of moss-covered stone stairs to Dhara Kharka, a meadow atop the ridge. Continue through the sparse forests along the ridge over a hillock and descend a bit to Kauma at 3470 metres. On the Kasuwa Khola side there are primitive bivouac caves – which are good emergency accommodation for porters.

I have trekked to Makalu twice and this is as far as I have gotten. In the spring of 1993 Kauma was buried under three metres of snow, and expedition porters returning from Makalu base camp reported deep snow on the entire route above Kauma. In March, 1991 I turned back at Tashi Gaon after sloshing around in clouds and rain – without a single mountain view – for three weeks. Bruce Klepinger of Ibex Expeditions in Eugene, Oregon, kindly provided the following description of the route above Kauma. Bruce trekked here in 1992 in perfect spring weather, then was skunked at the same time as me during April, 1993.

Day 7: Kauma to Mumbuk

Climb on steep switchbacks for a while, then less steeply through rhododendron forests to the top of the ridge where there is a large mani wall adorned with prayer flags. There is a superb view of Chamlang (7290 metres), Peak 6 (6739) and Peak 7 (6105 metres), which together form the headwaters of the Iswa Khola and Makalu (8475 metres) in the distance. Far to the east is the outline of Kanchenjunga.

Shipton La is actually two passes: the Kike La and the Tutu La. Follow the ridge for a while, then ascend a stone staircase. After a few false summits the trail veers left off the crest to a small lake. Climb gently up a shallow rocky gully to the Kike La at 4127 metres. From the pass descend to another lake, then ascend steeply through large boulders to the Tutu La. Descend about 150 metres into sparse rhododendron forests to a level area. The final descent is through a forest of firs and rhododendrons to Mumbuk, a forest camp at 3570 metres. Mumbuk is on a grassy slope about 100 metres above a small stream, with views of snow peaks through the trees.

Day 8: Mumbuk to Nhe Kharka

From Mumbuk, descend a steep gully with a stream for about 500 metres, then bear left along the flank of the Barun Valley, still in fir forests. The trail is ill defined, rocky and sloppy mud in places as it leads up the glacial valley, getting closer to the Barun Khola; there are good views of Peak 6. Cross a 200-metre-long slide area, then follow the river to a kharka. The trees are now birch and scrub rhododendron and the valley widens as you reach Yangle Kharka. Climb from Yangle Kharka, finally crossing to the north side of the Barun Khola to Nhe Kharka, located on a large open grassy plain at an elevation of 3000 metres. There is a small gompa at the side of the valley that offers great mountain views in all directions. To get there, cross from the south bank on two log bridges over a rocky chasm.

Day 9: Nhe Kharka to Sherson

Beyond Nhe Kharka follow the north bank of the Barun Khola for a while, then cross a small wooden bridge before the river turns northward. The Barun Valley makes a huge

S-shaped curve and the walls rise almost vertically 1500 to 2000 metres above the river, but the trail climbs gently as you approach Ripok Kharka. Still on the north side of the Barun, the trail turns westward and leaves the rhododendron forests for alpine tundra. Above Ripok Kharka the route crosses a rocky crest with a few goths, then ascends alongside a moraine formed by the Barun Glacier. There are excellent views of Pyramid Peak (7168 metres), Peak 4 (6720 metres), Chamlang, Peak 3 (6477 metres) and Peak 5 (6404 metres), but Makalu is not yet visible.

As you pass a ridge the glacier turns slightly north. You enter an alluvial valley and Makalu pops into view just before Sherson at 4615 metres elevation. Sherson is somewhat sheltered, but still is a very cold spot. It took a strong group seven to eight hours to trek from Nhe Kharka to Sherson.

This is a potentially dangerous day because the altitude gain (more than 1500 metres) exceeds the recommended daily maximum at these elevations. There is little choice, however, because there is no suitable camp between Nhe Kharka and Sherson. Be very wary of altitude problems when you camp here.

Day 10: Sherson to Makalu Base Camp

From Sherson, stay to the right in a gully on the east side of the valley. It's a gradual climb to a minor pass about 100 metres above Makalu base camp. You then descend to a stream, cross on boulders to the base camp on the west bank of the river. Here there are terrific views of the south face of Makalu. The large buttress of the south face rises across from base camp. An ascent of this buttress yields views of Peak 6, 7 and Baruntse (7220 metres); Everest and Lhotse complete the panorama. There are no huts, no shelters and no vegetation at the base camp, which is at an elevation of about 5000 metres.

Day 11: Makalu Base Camp to Nhe Kharka

Retrace your steps down the Barun Valley.

Day 12: Nhe Kharka to Mumbuk

Continue descending to the trees of Mumbuk.

Day 13: Mumbuk to Kauma

Trek across the Shipton La and descend to Kauma.

Day 14: Kauma to Tashi Gaon

Make a long steep descent back to civilisation. The hotel at Tashi Gaon usually has a good stock of beer and Kukhri rum to help you recover from the high altitude.

Day 15: Tashi Gaon to Balung

You can return to Tumlingtar the same way you came, but for variety I recommend a direct route down the Arun River. Be prepared. It's hot along the bottom of the Arun Valley no matter what the season. Descend the Kasuwa Khola Valley back to Sedua, then turn south down the west bank of the Arun River. From Sedua, follow a trail that descends gently to Mulgaon, then drop steeply on a rocky trail through fields of corn and barley to the Ipsuwa Khola, crossing it on a suspension bridge at 760 metres elevation.

The trek has now entered the hot bottom lands of the Arun Valley. Most of the settlements in this area are temporary settlements used by Rai and Chhetri farmers who live in villages high on the hillside above. They live in rough bamboo and wooden huts when they tend their crops. The trail for the next several days is generally level (for a trail in Nepal), climbing only a few hundred metres as it crosses side valleys. The trail makes some ups and downs through rocky fields to a camp in Balung at 760 metres.

Day 16: Balung to Pukuwa

Continue through temporary farming settlements to the spread-out Rai village of **Walung** at 880 metres. The trail descends to the Apsawa Khola crossing it on a suspension bridge at 600 metres, then climbs steeply to Chhayang, a pleasant Rai village with an extensive bamboo-pipe water supply at 800 metres elevation.

The trail crosses a stream at 590 metres and makes some ups and downs to Parangbu, a delightful camping spot among rice fields on the banks of the Arun River at 520 metres. Continue in forests past several small streams to Pukuwa, then descend to a camp under an old suspension bridge on the banks of the Pukuwa Khola at 550 metres.

Day 17: Pukuwa to Bumling

The trail now follows a route through forests and follows some spectacular high and exposed narrow tracks as it climbs over rocky ridges. There is a mine across the Arun, near the village of Yaphu. The route eventually enters a region of intense valley bottom cultivation, crosses a huge landslide and some more scrub jungle before descending to Tome at 520 metres.

Below Tome the Arun Valley becomes wider and more U shaped. The trail climbs over another ridge on a steep, narrow stairway of rock steps. From the top of the ridge at 530 metres, the trail descends to a delightful camp on the banks of the Sankhuwa Khola at an elevation of 370 metres, across from the Chhetri village of Bumling. Even in the winter, this part of the trek is through country that tends to be hot even in the winter; there is a great swimming hole under the suspension bridge that crosses the Sankhuwa Khola.

Day 18: Bumling to Tumlingtar

The trail traverses the fields of lower Bumling, then climbs over a ridge and descends to the Inkhuwa Khola, crossing it on a rickety wooden cantilever bridge. The trail follows the river downstream to its confluence with the Arun, then follows the Arun downstream, crossing it on a large suspension bridge at 300 metres.

Now following the east bank of the Arun, the route passes through **Chyawabesi** before making a short climb back to the Tumlingtar plateau. It is a few km of completely level walking to the airstrip.

Day 20: Tumlingtar to Kathmandu
Fly to Kathmandu.

Mustang

A Tangbe village (SA)
B Chorten near Charang (SA)
C Kali Gandaki river (SA)

D Sign in Kagbeni (SA)
E Champa Lakhang in
  Lo Manthang (SA)

Restricted Areas
Top: Start of trek near Dhading (SA)
Middle: Taklakot village (SA)
Bottom: North face of Mt Kailas (SA)

Western Nepal

Many people describe western Nepal as 'unexplored', but Westerners have a bad habit of assuming that what is unknown to them is unknown to everyone. Western Nepal has a large population of both Hindus and Buddhists, and the countryside is criss-crossed by trails in all directions. It is remote and unknown from the Western viewpoint because of its relative inaccessibility and its distance from Kathmandu. Regular flights to Jumla and several other airstrips in the west reduce this remoteness somewhat, but add considerably to the cost and to the logistical problems.

Another factor that discourages trekkers in western Nepal is that many of the culturally and scenically exotic regions are in restricted areas with high permit fees. Many of the trails in the west continue to the northern side of the Himalayan ranges of Nampa, Saipal and Kanjiroba, making it easy for trekkers to zip up trails along river valleys and into Tibet – a practice that both the Nepalese and Chinese would like to discourage. Some of these treks, including Shey Gompa to the north of Phoksumdo Lake and Humla to the north-west of Jumla are described in the Restricted Areas chapter.

The history and anthropology of western Nepal is complex and fascinating. The region is predominantly Hindu. Tibetans make up only a small part of the population, yet they have had a significant influence on the area through trading. Most of the homes are Tibetan style. Their flat roofs covered with packed earth are well suited to the semi-arid conditions of the region behind Dhaulagiri. In many villages the houses are packed closely together one atop another, climbing up the hillside and sharing common roofs. There are few stairs inside the dwellings. Instead, people climb from one level to another on carved log ladders outside the house. This is the only place in Nepal where Hindus live in such obviously Tibetan-style houses.

Cultural roots extend north into Tibet and west to Kumaon in India. Until Jumla was conquered by the army of Bahadur Shah in 1788, the people of western Nepal had very little reliance on Kathmandu. The Chhetris of western Nepal are categorised into three groups: Thakuris, who are the aristocracy; normal Chhetris as found throughout Nepal; and Matwali Chhetris, 'those who drink liquor'. The status of Matwali Chhetris is fascinating because many Tibetan immigrants long ago masqueraded as Chhetris. For many generations they have evolved their own form of religion that is a peculiar combination of Hinduism and Buddhism.

INFORMATION
Books
Karnali under Stress (University of Chicago, Chicago, 1990), by Barry C Bishop, is a study of the geography and trading patterns of western Nepal.

Stones of Silence (Viking Press, New York, 1980), by George B Schaller, is a naturalist's view of travels in Dolpo.

The Snow Leopard (Harper Collins, New Delhi, 1989), by Peter Matthiessen, is a personal account of the same trip to Dolpo that George Schaller made.

Dolpo – The World Behind the Himalayas (Sharda Prakashan Griha, Kathmandu, 1978), by Karna Sakya, is an early account of a Nepalese naturalist's trip to Dolpo.

Maps
US Army Map Service sheets 44-11 *Jumla*, 44-12 *Mustang* and 44-16 *Pokhara*, and Mandala Maps' *Jomsom to Jumla & Surkhet*, *Dhaulagiri Himal* and *Api, Nampa & Saipal* cover western Nepal. The US army Mustang sheet 44-12, edition 1-AMS, contains a large amount of fantasy. Phoksumdo Lake, Shey Gompa and many other features on this map are totally misplaced more than 12 km to the south of where they actually are. A 1:30,000

map titled *Dolpa* by Paolo Gondoni details much of Dolpo; it is published by Nepa Maps and is available in Kathmandu.

Elevations are difficult to confirm in this region. All the available maps were derived from the Survey of India maps which had little ground control in remote western Nepal. Most elevations I have indicated are based on altimeter readings related to the known elevations of Jumla and Dolpo airports, and to the Royal Geographical Society's *Kanjiroba Himal* map of 1967.

Language & Place Names

The people of western Nepal speak their own version of Nepali. When local people speak among themselves, Kathmandu Nepalese can barely understand them. They employ peculiar mannerisms in their speech. One porter told me that the hike to the next village was an easy one by saying that the trail was *sasto*, which translates as 'inexpensive'. He also said that one trail was *ek bhat* shorter than another; this translates as 'one rice' or 'one meal' – a charming way to say half a day. This charm, of course, can lead to complications.

West Nepal lingo also pervades place names. The name for a river is *gaad*, a high meadow is a *patan*, a pasture or camping place is a *chaur* and a pass is a *lagna*.

Food

Despite the extensive rice cultivation near Jumla, there is a chronic food shortage in this region. Much of the problem is because no self-respecting Nepalese government official will eat the locally grown red rice. White rice must be carried from villages at lower elevations to Jumla by foot or by air. Most of the Nepalgunj to Jumla shuttle flights are cargo flights that carry rice and other staples, so it is difficult to purchase enough food for a trek in Jumla Bazaar. It is better to carry all your food from Kathmandu – if you can get it onto the plane.

Merchants fly white rice to Jumla and then transport it to more remote regions using trains of horses, mules, sheep and goats. The goat 'trucks' of western Nepal are fascinat-ing. Traders equip herds of 100 or more sheep and goats with tiny woollen panniers that carry 10 kg of rice, then herd the animals through the countryside devouring grass as they travel. Hundreds of kg of rice and sugar are delivered throughout western Nepal in this manner.

Porters

There are a few porters available in Jumla, but they are expensive, they don't speak English, and they are not particularly eager to leave their homes. That being said, I was lucky enough in Jumla to hire two teams of excellent porters who, unlike porters in other parts of Nepal, were willing to carry loads long distances each day.

Cultural Considerations

The people throughout the region are Thakuris, a Chhetri caste that has the highest social, political and ritual status. Westerners, who are considered low caste by high-caste Hindus, are traditionally not welcome in Thakuri homes. For this reason hotels are scarce and cater mainly to locals. Consequently, do not plan a trek in the Jumla region as a teahouse trek.

Trekking Season

Most of western Nepal is either outside of the monsoon's influence or else in the rain shadow of Dhaulagiri Himal. Summers tend to be dry and there are few leeches. The best time for trekking is from late August to September when the wildflowers are in bloom. Winters are cold and there is a considerable amount of snow – so much, in fact, that there is some potential for skiing in parts of western Nepal. The trekking season, therefore, is from late spring and throughout the summer until late October. One problem with summer treks in the west is the inordinate number of flies that gather on food and inside tents.

GETTING THERE & AWAY
Airports

Jumla Everest Air operates two flights per week from Kathmandu to Jumla, but seats are very difficult to get. The day before the reservation chart is opened, Jumli people camp in front of the airline office to be first in line to get seats. The most reliable, though expensive, way to get to Jumla is to fly via Nepalgunj (US$99 plus US$44), or there is the twice-weekly Nepal Airways flight from Pokhara to Jumla.

The flight from Nepalgunj to Jumla (US$44) takes 35 minutes, climbing from the plains over many sets of hills, into the huge Tila Valley. Jumla airport is one of the best of Nepal's remote airstrips – 900 metres long and an easy approach – so flights operate more regularly than at places such as Lukla. Upon arrival at Jumla airstrip you must register with the police. An official sits in the security check booth and writes down the names of all passengers, both Nepalese and foreign, who arrive by air.

Jumla Bazaar is a 10-minute walk from the airport. There are shops, pharmacies, a bank, camps for both army and police, and a few restaurants along the stone-paved main street. Accommodation is available at the *Rara Hotel* near the airport and also at the *Himalaya Trekking Hotel* in the western part of the bazaar, near the police post. Jumla has electricity, and one house sports a television satellite dish. The hotels are basic, food is limited to dal bhat and potatoes, and many goods are in short supply or are totally unavailable. There is a very limited supply of canned goods, jam and other packaged items, but you probably will not find speciality foods such as muesli.

Jumla, on the banks of the Tila Khola at 2370 metres, is one of the highest rice-growing areas in the world. The entire Tila Valley is covered with paddy fields growing a unique red rice that is more tasty than white rice, but is scorned by most local people.

Dolpo Dolpo airport is in Juphal village, on a hill about three hours' walk from Dunai. There are regular scheduled flights and also lots of charter flights that carry food into the region. Flying in is difficult because of heavy passenger and cargo traffic, but flying out is often easy, even without advance planning,

because the cargo charters carry passengers on the return trip. There is no direct service from Kathmandu to Dolpo. All Dolpo flights originate in Nepalgunj except for a weekly Pokhara to Dolpo flight. Only RNAC operates flights to Dolpo (US$72 from Nepalgunj).

Chaurjhari This airport is three days south of Dunai on the Bheri River. A good new trail from Chaurjhari to Dunai involves almost no climbing. It is an alternative to Dolpo airport when winds or snow delay flights.

Bajura Named after the Bajura district, the airport is actually in the village of Kolti. It is two days' hard walking south of Simikot and could be used in an emergency if Simikot is snowed in. RNAC operates several flights a week between Nepalgunj and Bajura.

Simikot Perhaps the most remote airstrip in Nepal, Simikot is the jumping-off place for treks to Humla, the restricted area trek to Mt Kailas and, if it is opened, Mugu. Sometimes snowed in during the winter, Simikot is served by RNAC, Everest Air and Nepal Airways, all of which operate flights from Nepalgunj (US$88). There is no direct service between Simikot and Kathmandu.

Nepalgunj This town is in the Terai near the Indian border. Both RNAC and Nepal Airways operate a western Nepal hub from here with frequent flights to Jumla (US$44), Dolpo (US$77), Simikot (US$88) and many other destinations (some fascinating and others dreary) in western Nepal.

The daily 1½-hour Nepalgunj RNAC flight is reasonably reliable because it operates in the afternoons when there is less demand for aeroplanes. Necon operates Avro flights to Nepalgunj via Pokhara (US$67 from Pokhara) and both Nepal Airways and Everest Air have a regular service (US$99).

Night buses from Kathmandu to Nepalgunj cost Rs 225 for the 16-hour, 530-km trip. Day buses are cheaper (Rs 180), but take longer.

Nepalgunj is not an exciting place, but

because it is the largest city in a region that has a considerable number of development projects, it boasts some moderately good hotels. The *Sneha* and the *Batika* are both on the main road, three km from the main bazaar, three km from the Indian border and about 10 km from the airport. Costs are in the Rs 1000 range for a room with an air cooler and Rs 2500 for a double room with air-con. Another possibility is the *Rapti Hotel*, near the hospital. In the bazaar, at Birendra Chowk, the *Shanti Sakya* and *Punjabi* hotels offer low end accommodation. The Punjabi is said to have excellent Indian food, otherwise the fare is basic dal bhat. You can also stay at a rough hotel adjoining the airport.

Transport from Nepalgunj airport is difficult. It's a half-hour ride in a horse-drawn *tonga* or one hour by rickshaw. If you call before you leave Kathmandu, the Sneha Hotel (☎ 081-20119) will send a jeep to collect you for Rs 500.

Jumla, Dolpo and Simikot flights are scheduled at dawn. Transport from Nepalgunj to the airport is difficult to arrange, so be sure you have a firm commitment the night before. There are no taxis, only horse-drawn tongas and bicycle rickshaws in Nepalgunj. Allow more than one hour for the trip to the airport by rickshaw, about 45 minutes by tonga and half an hour by jeep.

Beware of baggage charges on Jumla and Dolpo flights. The free allowance is a miserly 15 kg. The rate for excess baggage from Nepalgunj to Jumla is Rs 24 per kg. Many cargo charter flights are operated by businesspeople sending rice and other goods, so if you are having trouble sending all your gear, you may be able to freight it on one of these flights.

Trailheads

Surkhet A night bus service goes to Surkhet (renamed Birendranagar), a roadhead in the hills north of Nepalgunj. It costs Rs 265 for the 600-km, 15-hour trip. It takes eight or nine days to walk from Surkhet to Jumla with porters, and there are no trekkers' hotels along the way. Local traders in Jumla bring most of their goods by horse or mule caravan from Surkhet.

Sallyan This roadhead south of Chaurjhari is a four to five-day walk from Dunai. There is no direct bus service from Kathmandu. Take a bus to Tulsipur or Nepalgunj, then a local bus to Sallyan. Porters from Sallyan and other villages in this region will probably refuse to go beyond Dunai.

Pokhara The trek from Pokhara to Dunai takes 13 days, or you can make a long trek from Pokhara all the way to Jumla via Dolpo.

SPECIAL RULES

There are two national parks in western Nepal, Rara Lake and Shey Phoksumdo, for which you must pay the normal park entrance fee of Rs 650. The Dolpo trek requires a special US$10 per week trekking permit, but this is easy to obtain. Parts of western Nepal, including Shey Gompa and the trek from Simikot towards the Tibetan border, are governed by the restricted area regulations. I have described the rules for these treks in the Restricted Areas chapter.

Jumla to Rara Lake

Rara Lake (2980 metres) is the focal point of Rara Lake National Park and is a good destination for a trek in western Nepal. The route is very much 'off the beaten track' and affords glimpses of cultures and scenery very different from that in the rest of Nepal. Rara is a clear, high altitude lake ringed with pine, spruce and juniper forests and snowcapped Himalayan peaks. In winter there is often snow on the ridges surrounding the lake. Except for the army assigned to the park, nobody lives at the lake because the government resettled all the people of Rara and Chapra villages when the area was declared a national park.

The trek to Rara is somewhat strenuous and tends to be expensive because both food

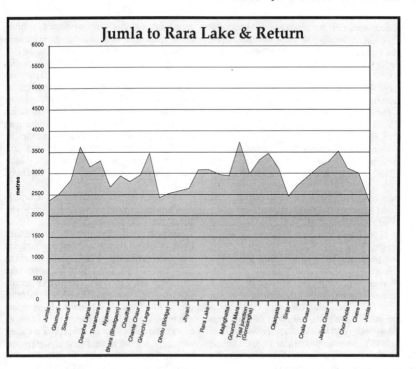

Jumla to Rara Lake & Return

metres

Jumla, Ghumurti, Sisnamul, Danphe Lagna, Tharamara, Nyawre, Bhara (Bhadgaon), Chauha, Chante Chaur, Ghurchi Lagna, Dhotu (Bridge), Jhyari, Rara Lake, Mahghatta, Ghurchi Mara, Trail Junction (Gorosingha), Okarpata, Sirja, Chala Chaur, Jajala Chaur, Chor Khola, Chere, Jumla

and labour are scarce and overpriced in this part of Nepal. If you are looking for wilderness solitude, and can overcome the logistical complications of the region, this trek is a good choice.

Day 1: Jumla to Danphe Lagna
There are two routes to Danphe Lagna. If there is snow, take the longer, lower route.

High Trail Follow the main street of Jumla north up the Jugad Khola Valley past the red-roofed hospital. The wide, level trail leads past college buildings to a settlement known as Campus. As the trail slowly gains elevation it passes a collection of very Western-style houses. These are the residences of teachers and administrators of the Karnali Technical Institute, a vocational school at **Ghumurti**, a short distance above.

The school is a collection of more than 40 buildings at 2550 metres. It is operated by the United Mission to Nepal and has about 150 students studying agriculture, engineering and health.

After a long climb past the school, the trail passes through Sisnamul, at 2830 metres, then enters a forest of big trees that soon gives way to meadows. **Chere**, at 3010 metres, is a large horse and sheep pasture with a few open herders' huts. Beyond Chere the trail becomes steeper and climbs through meadows to a pass on a route that is impassable in heavy snow. From the pass at 3600 metres there are views of Patrasi Himal (6860 metres) and Jagdula Himal (5785 metres) to the east. The trail descends gently in forests of spruce, birch and rhododendron to Danphe Lagna at 3130 metres. A single house stands in an attractive meadow beside a clear stream. It is often possible to spot the Himalayan monal (or impeyan pheasant), the colourful national bird of Nepal, in the nearby forests.

Low Trail From Jumla the lower trail to Rara follows the north bank of the Tila Khola, then turns north up the Chaudhabise Khola. The Jumla Valley disappears behind a ridge as the trail follows the river, keeping fairly level, passing through fields and pine forests. The trek heads in the direction of Uthugaon (2530 metres), then begins an ascent up the Dusni Khola Valley, beginning gently, but becoming steeper as the climb continues. A good campsite is near the school, across the river from the village.

From Uthugaon the trail begins an ascent up the Dusni Khola Valley, beginning gently, but becoming steep as the climb continues. The canyon becomes very narrow with vertical cliffs on both sides as the trail ascends through a deep forest of pines, spruces and firs. The large Chhetri town of **Padmora** is the last village in the valley, at 2900 metres. The climb continues in forests over the pass at 3400 metres and down to Danphe Lagna on the opposite side. This route takes half a day longer than the high trail.

Day 2: Danphe Lagna to Chautha

The trail descends gently alongside the stream to two bhattis at Tharamara (3280 metres). The descent becomes steep, through forests of fir, birch, walnut and bamboo, to a single house at Hiran Duski (2840 metres). After a short level stretch the trail zigzags down to the Sinja Khola, crossing it on a log bridge at 2680 metres. Follow the river downstream to some tea shops at **Nyawre** (2660 metres), then through potato and wheat fields near the riverbed. A new, big trail which climbs steeply up the ridge is longer and more difficult than the riverbed route.

The trail leaves the river and starts a serious climb, passing through marijuana fields below Bumra village, then over a ridge into a side valley, dropping to cross a stream near some water-driven mills. A steep, nasty

set of switchbacks leads to **Kabra**, a ludicrous hotel and dirty health post crammed under a huge overhanging rock. The health post specializes in natural Ayurvedic medicines. The rock is a source of *silaji*, a mineral that has such amazing properties that it is carried from here to Jumla, then flown to Nepalgunj and exported to India. This stone is said to have tremendous medicinal and therapeutic uses. I bought some in Kathmandu and the literature claimed that '...there is hardly any curable disease which cannot be controlled or cured with the aid of Silaji'.

The steep climb continues for a while, then levels out before Bhara, also known as Bhadgaon (2920 metres). This is a classic Tibetan-style village surrounded by splendid fields of wheat. Beyond this large village the trail turns into a big valley then descends to the Chaura Khola. Just across this stream are two shops and a school in the tiny village of Chautha (2770 metres). The *Bhandari Hotel* offers rough accommodation. If you are camping, try the fields before the village, or else continue an hour or more up the valley and make a camp in the forest alongside the stream. The trail that exits the village to the south follows the Sinja Khola to Sinja. The Rara Lake trail heads north up the Chaura Khola. Local folklore says that this is the halfway point between Jumla and Rara Lake.

Day 3: Chautha to Dhotu

A rocky trail follows the stream uphill, crossing the stream as the wooded valley becomes narrower. About half an hour beyond Chautha the valley widens, and there is a single house and some fields at Chante Chaur (2940 metres). The climb continues to **Bhulbule**, the Rara Lake National Park entrance station at 3130 metres. Pay Rs 650 here and have a cup of tea at a bhatti five minutes beyond the entrance station. Above Bhulbule the trail emerges into an immense treeless meadow, and climbs gently but steadily to an assortment of chortens, cairns and prayer flags atop the Ghurchi Lagna, a 3450-metre-high pass. From the pass there

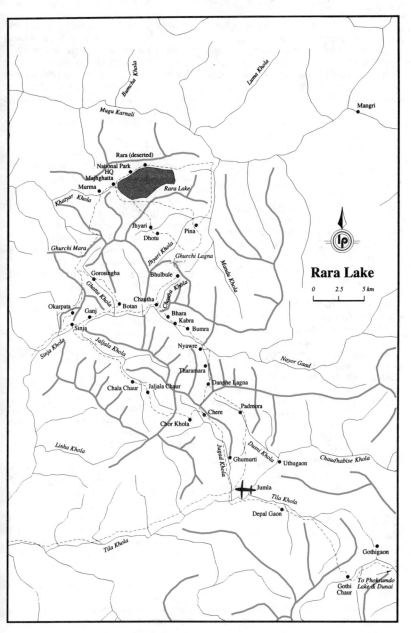

Rara Lake

0   2.5   5 km

are views of the Mugu Karnali River and snow peaks bordering Tibet.

The trail continues to follow the trade route to Mugu through the Mandu Khola Valley. From the pass the route descends gently on a broad path to a hut, then drops precipitously down a rough trail through spruce forests. The trail levels out around 2900 metres elevation, 45 minutes below the pass. Here there is a trail junction. It may still be marked with a wooden post with 'Rara' painted in red. The inconspicuous trail to the left (west) is a new direct route to Rara Lake. The broad trail that goes straight on leads to the village of Pina (2400 metres), and then on to Mugu. Follow the new trail that stays more or less level through pine forests, then descends to the Jhyari Khola at 2400 metres. Another stretch of easy walking leads to the small settlement of Dhotu, an army camp and helipad. Stay level and left; do not descend and cross the river.

Day 4: Dhotu to Rara Lake
Cross a stream and make a steep climb to the squalid Thakuri village of Jhyari at 2630 metres, in a picturesque grove of giant cedars. Continue climbing through cedar forests to a huge meadow atop a 3050-metre-high ridge with a great view of Rara Lake. Don't follow any of the trails that lead along the top of the ridge; descend a short distance to the lake. There are no camping spots along the southern shore. The national park headquarters and camp ground are on the northern side of the lake. It will take two hours or more to walk around the lake to the camp ground. The ban on the use of firewood is strictly enforced, so cook on kerosene stoves.

Day 5: Rara Lake
Rara Lake (3062 metres) is the largest lake in Nepal. It is almost 13 km around the lake, and a day devoted to making this circuit is well spent. Designated a national park in 1975, the region offers a remoteness and wilderness experience unlike any other in Nepal. There are a few park wardens' houses, and the remnants of the now deserted vil-

lages of Rara and Chapra on the northern side of the lake, but otherwise it is an isolated region where birds, flowers and wildlife thrive. Among the mammals in the region are Himalayan bear, Himalayan tahr, serow, goral, musk deer, red panda and both rhesus and langur monkeys. The 170-metre-deep lake has otters and fish and is an important resting place for migrating water fowl.

Day 6: Rara Lake to Gorosingha
Although you can return to Jumla via the same route, it is more rewarding to make a circuit via a different trail. From the bridge at the western end of Rara Lake the trail follows the Khatyar Khola (called the Nisa Khola in its upper reaches) to a small hotel in the settlement of **Majhghatta**, about 15 minutes from the bridge. A trail ascends from here to the village of Murma. You do not have to go through Murma on the way back to Jumla. Take a lower trail that descends gradually to the river, cross the river on a log bridge, and then cross another stream beside a decrepit mill that grinds away merrily. A small trail leads straight up the hill, climbing first through an area reforested with pine, then through spruce and rhododendron forests.

The ascent gets less steep through forests of pine and birch, then across meadows to a ridge at 3660 metres. There are views of Rara Lake far below as the trail skirts the head of a huge valley to the crest of the Ghurchi Mara at 3710 metres. If the weather is clear, there is an excellent view of the western Himalaya from the top of this ridge. The trail drops into the Ghatta Khola Valley, then heads towards Gorosingha, which the local people call 'the poster', referring to the army post there. Watch for an inconspicuous trail junction at 3000 metres, about an hour below the pass, just before the main trail reaches the Ghatta Khola. This is yet another short route to Sinja.

Day 7: Gorosingha to Sinja
There are two choices, the long route and the short, steep route.

The Long Way This route heads down the Ghatta Khola Valley, then follows the Sinja Khola downstream to the village of Sinja. There are several excellent camping places along the Ghatta Khola, both above and below Gorosingha. After working your way down the Ghatta Khola past Botan you will meet the Sinja Khola. It is a short walk down the fertile valley, on a newly renovated trail, through a heavily populated region to Sinja itself.

The Short (Steep) Way Don't descend into the valley towards Gorosingha. Stay high on the side of the treeless Ghatta Khola Valley. From above, the army 'poster' at Gorosingha looks like a classic Hollywood western ranch in a beautiful grassy vale. The trail descends to a stream, then climbs a big gully to a ridge at 3450 metres. It's easy to get lost between here and Sinja, so you'll be much better off with a local guide, if you can find one. From the ridge, follow the left trail and stay as high as possible on the ridge, looping in and out of side valleys and descending gradually to the village of **Okarpata** at 3070 metres. This is a big village of whitewashed, flat-roofed houses, with huge fields of wheat and barley and extensive apple orchards. The trail descends to a stream and then goes steeply down the ridge on a rough rocky trail to the Brahmin and Chhetri village of Sinja, on the banks of the Sinja Khola at 2440 metres.

From the 12th to 14th centuries, western Nepal was ruled by a Malla Dynasty that was different from the Malla rulers in Kathmandu. Sinja was the capital of the western Malla kingdom. The ruins of the palace can be seen across the river. The large temple at the top of a promontory is the Bhagwati Than, a temple dedicated to Bhagwati, the goddess of justice who rides atop a tiger. The big buildings across the river from the village are government offices and a school.

Day 8: Sinja to Jaljala Chaur

It is very difficult to reach Jumla in a single day from Sinja, so it's best to break the trek with a night in the high meadows near the ridge. From Sinja, the trail crosses the Sinja Khola on a wooden cantilever bridge, then begins a long trip up the Jaljala Khola. After passing a few small villages and the trail to the temple, the trail crosses back and forth across the river on a series of quaint log bridges. Most of the trek is through forests of pine, birch and oak, though there are a few scattered houses and fields of barley and corn. From Chala Chaur, a meadow with a few herders' huts at 2900 metres, the trail makes a steep climb to Jaljala Chaur, a gigantic meadow full of horses at 3270 metres.

Day 9: Jaljala Chaur to Jumla

Keep climbing through forests to yet another meadow, just below the ridge at 3510 metres, then descend to a few houses at Chor Khola (3090 metres). Cross a stream and contour across the head of the valley, staying high, eventually crossing another ridge to rejoin the upward 'high trail' at **Chere** (3010 metres). The final descent to Jumla is the reverse of Day 1, through Sisnamul, past the school at Ghumurti, then from Campus village to Jumla Bazaar.

Jumla to Dolpo

Dolpo is a remote region of Nepal that has been bypassed by development and, until recently, by tourism. Although a few anthropologists and geographers had explored the region, the entire district was closed to trekkers until 1989 when the southern part of Dolpo was opened to organised trekking groups. In 1990 individual trekkers were allowed into the region if they obtained a special US$10 per week trekking permit and did a bit of a bureaucratic run-around. There are no teahouses along the route to Dolpo. I met a couple of trekkers who had trekked here and bought food in villages, but they had a rough time. You would be far better off in Dolpo with a fully equipped trek.

You can reach Dolpo from Jumla (six days), Dhorpatan (10 to 12 days), Surkhet (nine days), Sallyan (five days) and Jomsom

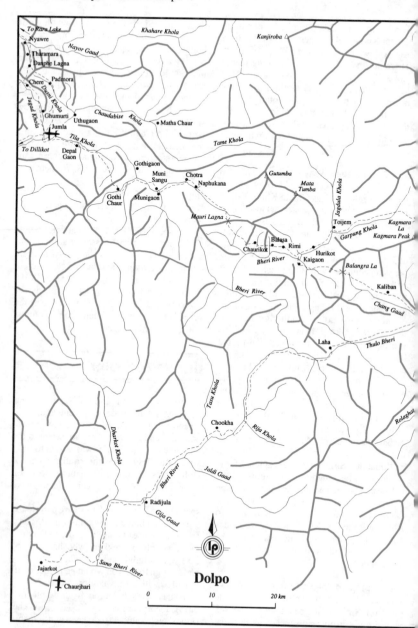

Dolpo

0   10   20 km

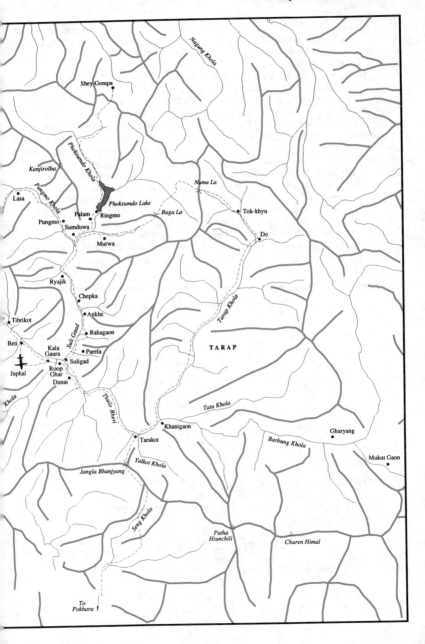

(11 days, but not allowed). The Dolpo airport in Juphal is half a day from the district headquarters in Dunai. Another airstrip is in Chaurjhari, three days from Dunai.

Peter Matthiesen's *The Snow Leopard* and Snellgrove's *Himalayan Pilgrimage* have contributed to the mystique and attraction of Dolpo. Both writers visited Shey Gompa to the north of Phoksumdo Lake. See the separate section on Shey in the Restricted Areas chapter.

There are Tibetan-style 'inner Dolpo' villages in Tarap and at Phoksumdo Lake, but most of the southern part of Dolpo is a region of Hindu influence.

This section describes the trek from Jumla to Dunai, side trips to Phoksumdo Lake and Tarap, and an alternate high route over the Kagmara La to the Dolpo district. There's also an outline of a trek from Pokhara to

Dolpo. All these trips could be combined into one long trek of 25 to 30 days, from Pokhara to Jumla via Dolpo.

JUMLA TO DUNAI
Day 1: Jumla to Gothi Chaur

It's best to fly into Jumla and then spend the rest of the day hiring porters, buying last-minute provisions and sorting loads. If you fly into Jumla and start walking the same day, you will probably have to alter the stopping places I have suggested, because it takes a full day to reach Gothi Chaur.

From Jumla (2370 metres) the trail leads past the airport to the eastern end of the runway, past several water-driven mills, then drops to the confluence of the Tila Khola and the Chaudhabise Khola (also known locally as the Juwa Nadi) at 2330 metres. Cross both rivers on cantilever bridges that look like

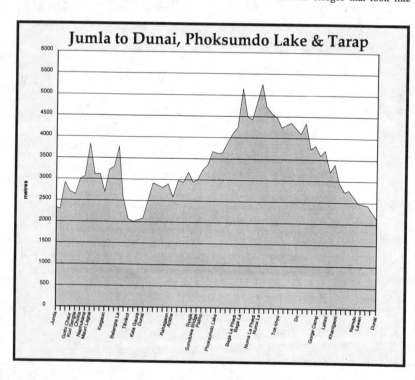

Jumla to Dunai, Phoksumdo Lake & Tarap

they are held together by giant clothes pegs. A major logging operation is on the upper reaches of the Chaudhabise. Loggers upstream dump logs into the river. They float down to this point where they are snared and cut into timbers for use in Jumla and neighbouring villages. Unlike most rivers in Nepal, which are filled with silt, the Tila and the Chaudhabise are clear because they are not glacier fed.

The trail climbs gently in a fertile valley of rice terraces along the southern side of the Tila to Depal Gaon. It crisscrosses irrigation canals to Jharjwala, then leaves the Tila Khola and climbs a ridge to the small villages of Bhajkati, Dugri Lagnu and finally Dochal Ghara at 2530 metres. Do not follow the steep trail that leads uphill here. Instead, take the lower trail that follows a stream through a forest of maple and walnut to a meadow at 2830 metres. In season the wildflowers include cinquefoils, louseworts, scrophs, terrestrial orchids, forget-me-nots, geraniums, asters, mints, buttercups, impatiens, edelweiss, primulas and gentians.

Beyond the meadow the trail climbs to a rock cairn at Pattyata Pass (2830 metres), then descends into a magnificent alpine amphitheatre that looks totally uninhabited from this point. Hidden behind a ridge is a huge government sheep-breeding research project, but there are no villages in this isolated valley. The trail descends past the project buildings at Gothi Chaur, to a stream at the bottom of the valley. There are some 13th century Malla Dynasty stone carvings at the spring here.

Day 2: Gothi Chaur to Naphukana

Another trail junction is at Gothi Chaur. Do not take the trail that leads uphill out of the Gothi Chaur Valley. Instead, walk downstream through forests to a series of mills at **Kuri Sangta** (2660 metres). A good campsite is a short distance beyond where the Kuri Sangta Khola joins the Tila Khola.

The route has now re-entered the Tila Valley and over the next day you will follow the river to its source. Here the Tila is known as the Bapila Khola. The largish villages of

Gothigaon and Khudigaon are visible high on the opposite side of the river. The trail crosses to the northern side of the Tila and passes corn and potato fields, then climbs through fields of buckwheat and barley and attractive meadows full of grazing horses and cows.

The river forks at Munigaon, a village with a complex mixture of Chhetri, Thakali and Tibetan inhabitants. There are several houses and a rudimentary hotel at the trail junction, **Muni Sangu**. Look both above and behind the houses for some peculiar carved wooden faces. You will see these effigies throughout Dolpo. They are called *dok-pa* and are supposed to offer protection from evil. The cops at the Muni Sangu police checkpost will probably want to see your trekking permit.

The route follows the left fork of the Tila Khola which has again changed its name and is now the Churta Khola. The valley narrows and enters a forest of live oaks, spruce, poplar and maples. The trail stays on the southern side of the river, so don't cross any of the several bridges that you pass. A short distance beyond Changrikot (a series of four houses built into the hillside on the opposite side of the river at an elevation of 2900 metres) the trail finally crosses the river and climbs to the grey stone houses of **Chotra** at 3010 metres. The inhabitants of Chotra are Khampas, people from eastern Tibet who are traditionally Buddhists. The village has the typical Tibetan mani walls and a kani arching over the trail. Despite their background, these villagers long ago adopted Hindu names, dress and traditions in an effort to integrate themselves into mainstream Nepalese society.

Anthropologists categorise these people as Matwali Chhetris and trace their heritage to Kumaon in India. Their religious practices have very little to do with Hinduism. Their rites are conducted by shamans known as *dhamis* or *jhankris* and their major deity is the god Mastha. There are shrines to Mastha in Tibrikot and Rahagaon.

A short distance beyond is the Tibetan settlement of Naphukana at 3080 metres.

The large gompa above the village is Urgen Sanga Chorling where Tulku Tsewang Dorji Lama was recently installed as rimpoche (reincarnate lama). The villagers of Naphukana keep large herds of yaks and horses. There are campsites near the village, but better camping places are an hour further on, in a meadow at 3200 metres.

Day 3: Naphukana to Balasa

The trail becomes steeper as it climbs past the rocky fields of Rapati Chaur in forests of oak and birch trees tangled with Spanish moss. After crossing a side stream, the trail crosses the Churta/Bapila/Tila Khola and starts a serious climb through birch, oak and rhododendron forests to the Mauri Lagna ('honey pass'). When trekking in spring, the final approach to the pass is through meadows alive with blue lilies and stands of blooming azaleas and rhododendrons. In winter the trail is hidden under deep snow. From the pass (3820 metres) there are views of the snow peaks of Gutumba (5608 metres) and Mata Tumba (5767 metres) to the north and Bhalu Himal (5460 metres) to the east.

From the pass the trail descends a bit, then makes a long traverse across a potentially dangerous area. A Tibetan porter told me a tale of 20 yaks tumbling down this slope in an avalanche a few winters ago. At the end of the traverse, marked by cairns of stones, the trail starts a steep descent into a forest of pines and oaks, passing a few herders' huts before reaching a stream at 3110 metres. Staying in forests, the trail makes a few ups and downs, then climbs again to a ridge at 3140 metres. Here the trail turns into the Bheri Valley, keeping high on the side of the ridge, making short excursions in and out of side valleys past scattered houses and fields of corn and potatoes en route to **Chaurikot** at 3060 metres. There is no possible camp and no hotel – or even a shop – in this large Khampa village, but the children are already trained in the ritual of asking for pens.

I met a man in Chaurikot who was 67 years old and insisted that his grandfather's grandfather settled here from Kham in eastern Tibet. He had the unlikely name of Pemba (a Tibetan first name) Budhathoki (a pure Hindu surname) and, like many men in this part of Nepal, wore an Afghan-style turban. Many Matwali Chhetris, like Pemba, are in fact descendants of people of Tibetan ancestry whose names and traditions encompass both Hindu and Tibetan traditions.

From Chaurikot the trail drops to a stream at 2940 metres then climbs right back up again to an inviting-looking notch on the ridge at 3080 metres. This would be an excellent camp except that there is no water. About 30 minutes beyond the ridge is the settlement of Balasa. There are several possible campsites alongside the trail in the fields of Balasa, or further on in the fields of Jyakot or Rimi. You can see Kagmara peak on the horizon and Balangra La, the next obstacle on the route to Dolpo.

Day 4: Balasa to a Forest Camp

The trail descends to a stream, then climbs to the ridge in a forest of walnut trees. Walnuts will be constant companions throughout the rest of the trek to Dolpo. Although the local people occasionally eat them, their primary value is as a source of cooking oil. The trail contours past the corn and potato fields and apple orchards of Jyakot then descends to Rimi at 2890 metres, where the amusing faces of more dok-pa peek from the tops of houses. The trail descends, steeply in places, through walnut groves to the closely spaced stone houses of Majagaon, then down a rocky trail to the Bheri River. A police checkpost and a large school and hostel complex dominate the bank of the Bheri River at 2610 metres.

Just across the bridge is the village of **Kaigaon**, which boasts a veterinary station for cattle, a bhatti and the first real shop since Jumla. Stock up on the items for sale here – biscuits and cigarettes and, if you are lucky, beer.

The shopkeeper here told me a peculiar story about religious practices in Kaigaon, Chaurikot and Hurikot. The Hindu Chhetri people in these villages practice Tibetan Buddhism, hence the prayer flags that festoon the houses. The complication is that they also celebrate Hindu festivals, including Dasain, during which each house sacrifices an animal. It's all very complex and strange, especially when combined with Pemba Budhathoki's tale of the Chaurikot Khampa heritage.

Kaigaon is the departure point for a crossing of the Kagmara La. See the brief description of this crossing later in this chapter.

From Kaigaon the route climbs through pastures, then into a forest of birch and wild rose. Near the top of the ridge the climb rates the maximum scale for steepness. There are no stone steps, so you must either walk sideways in a crab-like fashion or walk uphill on your toes. It's so steep that your heel cannot reach the ground unless you are double jointed. The trail crests at an elevation of 3230 metres, then levels out in a forest of rhododendron and oaks, the home of a band of black langur monkeys. A trail heads south from the pass and this is a route to Jajarkot and Chaurjhari. The Dolpo trail continues east, and descends gently along the side of a large valley to a few small campsites in forests of pines draped with Spanish moss.

Day 5: Forest Camp to Tibrikot

The trail makes many ups and downs as it contours out onto a ridge. Soon the downs become shorter and the ups longer, ending in a long climb to a false summit at 3660 metres. There is yet another false summit before the Balangra La itself, marked with cairns and prayer flags at 3760 metres. If it's clear, you'll see Dhaulagiri Himal to the east. You will also probably see herds of yaks grazing high on the grassy slopes above the pass.

There are two trails off the pass. The old trail heads straight down into forests while a new trail contours around the ridge to the left. Both end at a government yak farm complex in a forest at 3160 metres. One trekker commented on the profusion of health facilities for animals along this trek, in contrast with the total lack of health care for people. Keep this in mind as you put together your medical supplies for a Dolpo trip.

From the yak farm, the trail heads out onto

a ridge high above the Chang Gaad. There are a few campsites along the route and there's even a bhatti at Ghora Khola. Stay on the upper trail and beware of any steep drop towards the river. Beyond Bungtari, cross a stream and climb to **Kaliban**. Drop to a stream in a large side valley, then climb again to Dagin at 2930 metres. After passing Para and a few other small villages, the route reaches a treeless, waterless, uninhabited ridge, then makes a miserable 500-metre descent on a clutter of loose rocks to a stream just below Tibrikot at 2100 metres.

Day 6: Tibrikot to Dunai

From the stream, the trail climbs slightly to Tibrikot, a picturesque village on a promontory overlooking the Thulo Bheri ('big Bheri') Valley. This is an old fortress town and the police checkpost commands a view up and down the river. The houses have carved wooden windows and a large shrine and temple is dedicated to the goddess Tripura Sundari Devi. From the shrine, the trail descends past extensive rice terraces to a new, long suspension bridge at 2050 metres.

For the next day, you will follow the large, fast-flowing, dark grey Thulo Bheri river, through arid country on the new trail that follows the Bheri all the way from Chaurjhari. Because of heavy silting the Thulo Bheri is unfit to drink, so settlements in the valley occur only where there is a side stream. Passing the tiny settlement of Su Pani, the route passes over a low ridge and drops to Beti, several houses beside a small stream.

The trail to Dolpo airport, above Juphal village, starts from Beti. If you want to confirm a flight, take the upper route that goes to the airport and rejoins the river trail at Kala Gaura. The lower trail passes far below the airport. The stream leading from Juphal village creates a green oasis atmosphere in contrast to the barrenness of the valley. After more desolate country you will reach a few tea shops at Kala Gaura where the airport trail rejoins the route. The trail climbs a little over two ridges, then drops to a large side stream and three small bhattis at **Roop Ghar**. This is an excellent place to camp if you want to avoid staying in Dunai village. You can see the start of the trail to Phoksumdo Lake high on the opposite river bank.

From Roop Ghar the trail remains level, passing the national park and army offices that are on the opposite side of the river at the confluence of the Phoksumdo Khola and the Thulo Bheri. The Survey of India maps, and all others that have been derived from it, show the river named as the Suli Gaad, but most local people refer to it as the Phoksumdo Khola.

A few twists and turns of the trail lead to a view of Dunai and a large new hospital complex across the river. The trail enters the village through a fancy gate near the health post, then passes through the old bazaar along a stone pavement. There are a few hotels and shops in this part of the town, but these cater mostly to porters and traders. The larger facilities are at the eastern end of the village, past government offices, the police post and a statue of King Mahendra. No signs instruct you to visit the police post but, as this is the district headquarters, it's a good idea to seek out an official to fulfil bureaucratic formalities and gather the latest news on areas that are recently opened or closed to foreigners.

At the eastern end of the village is the *Phoksumdo Hotel* and the fancy new *Blue Sheep Trekkers Inn*, which has three private bedrooms and a separate restaurant facility. The large complex with turrets across the river is the district jail.

DUNAI TO JUPHAL (DOLPO AIRPORT)

Dolpo flights are always early in the morning. This is because high winds in the Thulo Bheri Valley begin around 10 am, making later flights impossible. It takes at least three hours to walk from Dunai to Juphal, so the only reasonable solution is to spend a night at the airport.

From Dunai, follow the river trail downstream to Roop Ghar and on to the small hotels at Kala Gaura (2090 metres). Take the uphill trail and climb through meadows past a few houses. Stay high and avoid the lower trail that leads to the large village of Dangi Bhara, eventually reaching a large school just before the airport at 2500 metres. The airport is surrounded by a tangle of barbed wire. There are no sensible campsites here but it is possible to camp below the airfield – or perhaps on the runway itself – if the airline people agree. Be sure you arrange an early wake-up call.

You should reconfirm your seats the day before the flight at the airline office in Juphal village, not at the airport. There are some basic shops in a complex of flat-roofed, mud buildings beside the airport. The *Parbat Hotel* has food and funky accommodation, and will also allow you to camp on their rooftop.

Take a walk down the runway, one of the most unusual airports in Nepal. The 490-metre runway is the minimum length required for Twin Otter landings at this elevation. To make matters even more frightening, the airport is on a slope and has a depression in the middle, which makes a take off reminiscent of a roller coaster ride. Also, there is a huge rock just at the end. Fares are high at US$77 for a 35-minute flight to Nepalgunj. Weight limits are strictly enforced and excess baggage is expensive. In 1990, the airline staff were enforcing a 10 kg free baggage allowance and leaving extra baggage behind. There is a lot of cargo traffic in and out of Dolpo. If you were a crate of apples you could fly at a subsidised rate of Rs 1.50 per kg.

Across the Kagmara La

A high route to Dolpo leads across the 5115-metre-high Kagmara La. It is not a difficult pass crossing, but you may have trouble finding porters willing to make the trip. The pass is snowbound, and potentially dangerous or impassable, from November to early

Dolpo – Flora & Fauna

Mammals The **blue sheep** and **Himalayan tahr** are neither true sheep nor mountain goats, respectively. The tahr is considered a primitive member of the goat/antelope family, while the blue sheep is lost, in an evolutionary sense, somewhere between sheep and goats. Both of these ungulates can be found in the same locale, generally high above the tree line. The tahr, though, prefers habitats in the vicinity of precipitous cliffs, while the blue sheep likes scree slopes and plateaus of the high desert. The blue sheep has horns like a sheep, except that they are not as long, curved or swept back. This beast is referred to as 'blue' due to the slaty blue and grey colour of its winter coat. Look for these animals in the rain shadow areas of not only Dolpo, where

Blue sheep

they are common, but also Manang and Mustang. The tahr, though known to the Dolpo area, is more readily seen in Khumbu and the Annapurna Sanctuary.

The **jackal**, found up to 3700 metres, is another carnivore that one may come across, at least audibly. This member of the dog family, often a timid scavenger, has a sustained macabre howl that is heard after dark. The **wolf**, a larger canine than the latter, has a thick coat and bushy tail and is known to roam up to 6000 metres. Its movements generally follow those of wandering game and grazing herds, but will also prey on domestic livestock, particularly from the high summer settlements.

The **spotted leopard** is found up to the tree line and the **snow leopard** usually beyond, more often in the trans-Himalayan areas. Deforestation has severely encroached on the habitat of both the spotted leopard and its prey species. This, compounded by its secretive habits, makes the likelihood of seeing a spotted leopard quite remote. If one happens to come across one of these cats, it's difficult to say whether human or beast will be the more surprised.

The snow leopard, which has distinctly paler colouration than the latter, is often placed in another genus due to its different skull shape, broad paws and long, thick tail. Since it competes for virtually the same space as the wolf, when the two encounter, one is usually displaced. As wolves have a tendency to be more sociable and hunt in packs, they will outnumber the cat, which generally must depart. One's best chances of sighting a snow leopard are better in the sparsely populated Dolpo and other remote areas of western Nepal, but don't count on it. Realistically, the odds of seeing a snow leopard are about the same as catching a glimpse of a yeti. ∎

May. A reasonable crossing takes four days from Kaigaon to Sumduwa. Kagmara translates as 'crow killer'; the high pass on the eastern edge of Dolpo is Cheelmara, 'eagle killer'.

Day 1: Kaigaon to Toijem

From the school at Kaigaon, stay on the west bank of the Bheri River, passing Hurikot, to a sign proclaiming the entrance to Shey Phoksumdo National Park. The trail stays high above the river to the confluence where the Jagdula and Garpung rivers join to form the Bheri. Drop to the Jagdula Khola, crossing it on stones, and camp near the army post at Toijem (2920 metres).

Day 2: Toijem to Kagmara Phedi

Follow the trail up the western side of the Garpung Khola to about 3650 metres, then cross to the eastern side and continue upstream. The valley narrows and the river becomes a series of waterfalls as the trail climbs to a moraine at 3900 metres. Make a high camp in boulders at an elevation of about 4000 metres. The panoramic views of the peaks are sensational. Wildflowers are of the more hardy alpine species, including blue poppy, buttercup, mint, gentian and puffball. Among the birds you may sight are snow pigeons, redstarts, ravens and griffons. This is also an excellent place to sight blue sheep.

Day 3: Kagmara Phedi to Lasa

Start early and climb alongside the Kagmara Glacier to the Kagmara La at 5115 metres, then descend about 900 metres alongside a stream to a camp on pastures in the Pungmo Khola Valley. On this side of the pass there are sweeping scree slopes and massive rock formations in stacked layers which contrast with the vertical uplifts and thrusts of the southern side. Descend to a shepherd's camp called Lasa.

Day 4: Lasa to Sumduwa

The trail stays high above the stream, which eventually becomes the Pungmo Khola (incorrectly named the Dorjam Khola on the Survey of India maps). The route enters birch and juniper forests which give way to blue pine as the trail crosses the river on a wooden bridge. There are views up side valleys of Kanjirolba peak in the stretch before the barley fields of Pungmo, a fortress-like village. Continue downstream to the national park headquarters at Sumduwa.

The following day, follow the trail up the Phoksumdo Khola to Phoksumdo Lake.

To Phoksumdo Lake

The trek to Phoksumdo Lake is steep and difficult. If you have the slightest fear of heights, don't even think about this trek. The trail is narrow and the small number of camping places imposes a fairly strict schedule. There are no hotel facilities of any kind along the entire route, though there are vague plans to build a new trail following the river from its confluence with the Thulo Bheri to Sumduwa.

The lake is within Shey Phoksumdo National Park, established in 1981. The national park literature uses the spelling Phoksundo, but local informants believe that the correct transliteration is *Phok*, *sum* (three), *do* (stones), relating to the three arms of the lake. The park is said to abound in wildlife, though the most spectacular inhabitants, snow leopards and herds of blue sheep, are found primarily in the restricted regions of the park near Shey Gompa. The lake and trail are snowbound from mid-November to mid-May. Almost all the inhabitants of Ringmo village move to lower elevations at this time.

National park restrictions prohibit the use of firewood, so you must carry kerosene in addition to food. This requires some advance planning because there is no reliable kerosene supply in either Dunai or Jumla. Promoters in Dunai are talking of opening a kerosene depot which would simplify logistics for the trek.

Day 1: Dunai to Rahagaon

From the King Mahendra statue in Dunai, cross the new suspension bridge and turn west, following the trail past the hospital. The trail soon begins climbing up the side of the treeless Thulo Bheri Valley. The rocky trail crests a ridge and enters the Phoksumdo River Valley, finally reaching another ridge marked by cairns at 2500 metres. There is a view of Kagmara peak up the valley. The trek enters a large side canyon, making a long gentle descent past scattered houses and walnut groves to a stream at 2810 metres. High above the stream is the village of Parela. The trail below the stream leads to **Dhera**, a winter settlement where people from higher villages keep herds of cows and goats. The camping opportunities here are very limited and the area is notorious for swarms of flies – worse in spring than in the autumn. This region produces a lotus-like plant called *chuk* that is used to make vinegar and medicines. It is dried and flown from Dolpo to Nepalgunj and exported to India.

From the stream the trail climbs to Rahagaon, a Thakuri village at 2910 metres.

In the fall it may be possible to camp in the village corn fields. In spring the only choice is the flat rooftops. There is no water sourse inside the village of Rahagaon, so you must carry water from a stream about 15 minutes beyond the village. Above the village is a gompa dedicated to the local god Mastha.

Day 2: Rahagaon to Ryajik

The trail passes through the lower part of Rahagaon, then turns and descends to the village water supply. The route is now high above the Phoksumdo Khola. The trail turns into another side canyon and descends through deep dark forests to a large stream, then climbs to the entrance station for Shey Phoksumdo National Park at Ankhe. After paying the required entrance fee of Rs 650 you may be subjected to a baggage inspection – ostensibly for drugs and stolen art objects. It's a very peculiar formality in this remote locale. The three villages on the trail have a strange name connection: Parela *(parela* means eyelash), Rahagaon *(raha* means eyebrow) and Ankhe *(ankha* is eye).

There is no camp ground or accommodation at the entrance, so if you want to stay nearby, proceed another 45 to 60 minutes to several good camps by the river. Climb to the ridge and stumble down a rocky trail to the river bank at 2650 metres. There is a single house at **Chepka**. Nothing is available here, but the Tibetan house owner has vague plans to build a campsite, toilet and shop, probably another addition to his already sprawling house. You can find another good campsite beside a huge rock in a walnut grove about 20 minutes beyond Chepka.

The trail makes some small ups and downs along the forested riverbed, then ascends steeply to about 2900 metres. A small dangerous trail traverses under a huge cliff. Instead, it's far better to take the main trail that climbs another 90 metres over the top of the cliff, then descends under a huge overhanging rock. The ups and downs begin to be a bit tedious, but there are several streams along the way that offer a chance to cool off.

The trail leaves the forests and traverses a grassy slope high above the river. Near a point where a stream enters from the west, the Phoksumdo Khola Valley turns eastwards and becomes even steeper and narrower. The trail descends steeply through forests to a cliff, then makes a dizzying drop on a wobbly stone staircase to the river bank. You can almost look down between your toes to see the fast-flowing river below. One slip and you are on your way back to Nepalgunj.

After reaching the river at 2950 metres, the trail becomes a collection of rocks and sticks that form a dyke along the river bank. It's hard to imagine how people bring yaks and cows along this trail, but they do. Up, down, up, down; the trail continues upstream to a bridge near Ryajik village. A good camp is here and another is about five minutes further on.

Day 3: Ryajik to Phoksumdo Lake

The trail continues its ups and downs along the valley floor to the confluence of the Phoksumdo and the Pungmo kholas. Cross to the western side of the Phoksumdo Khola on a wooden bridge. You can climb to the park headquarters at Sumduwa or take a lower trail that heads upstream. This is a major trail junction. The route to Kagmara La leads up the Pungmo Khola; the trail to Do and Tarap leads up the east bank of the Phoksumdo Khola; and the trail to Phoksumdo Lake and Shey Gompa follows the west bank of the river. The village name reflects this. In Tibetan *sum* means 'three' and *duwa* is 'trail'.

Follow the trail up the western side of the river through forests to another bridge. Stay on the western side. There is a trail up the eastern side of the river, but it goes to the village of Murwa and eventually to Tarap, not to Phoksumdo Lake. The Phoksumdo trail climbs though a forest of big cedars to a good campsite and then on to **Palam** (3230 metres), a winter settlement used by the people of Ringmo village. The houses here are almost buried in the sandy soil. The route climbs steadily through open country to an elevation of 3370 metres, then starts up a steep set of switchbacks to a ridge at 3660 metres. From the ridge there are distant views of Phoksumdo Lake and a close view of a spectacular 330-metre-high waterfall, the highest in Nepal. This is the source of the river that you have been following for several days. The trail makes a steep descent in birch forests to the upper reaches of the Phoksumdo Khola, then climbs gently to Ringmo village, a picturesque settlement with lots of mud-plastered chortens and mani walls.

Just below Ringmo, cross a bridge and follow a trail north to the ranger station at Phoksumdo Lake. Continue to the shores of the lake near the point where the Phoksumdo Khola flows out of the lake. The national park camp ground is south-east of the lake. Park rules prohibit camping in other places, except perhaps on rooftops in Ringmo. Phoksumdo Lake is 4.8 km long, 1.8 km wide and is said to be 650 metres deep. A trail along its western side leads to Shey Gompa. However, access to this route is restricted to those with a special US$700 permit, so you may not be allowed to go beyond the first wooden bridge on this trail. The lake is known for its aquamarine colour – a greenish blue similar to a special Tibetan turquoise. The large snow peak above the ridge on the western side of the lake is Kanchen Ruwa (6612 metres), also known as Kanjirolba.

A trail leads from the lakeside through juniper trees to an ancient ramshackle gompa that overlooks the lake. In addition to the main temple, said to have been built 60 generations ago, there are four houses, each containing a private room for worship. These establishments are some of the few remaining facilities in Nepal dedicated to the ancient shamanistic Bon-po religion, the antecedent of Tibetan Buddhism. The insides of the temples contain dusty Buddhist paintings and statues, but the trappings also reflect the animistic elements of the Bon-po religion, so some of the chapels are reminiscent of an ancient witch's cavern. Bon-po tradition dictates walking around mani walls to the right and uses the swastika symbol with the arms to the right, both exactly the opposite of Buddhist practice.

Do & Tarap

The following itinerary was prepared by Lewis Underwood who trekked here in 1992 during a period when trekkers were allowed into Tarap. (Several trekkers were allowed through the region in 1989 and early 1990, but by May 1990 both Tarap and the Baga La were closed and I had to return from Ringmo to Dunai.) Permission to trek between Phoksumdo Lake and Tarap is subject to the current interpretation of the rules; sometimes people are allowed to trek and sometimes permission is refused. Check with the national park and immigration authorities for the current interpretation.

The route crosses two high passes. You would do well to have a guide who knows the route. Do not attempt the crossing if there is a lot of snow.

Day 1: Ringmo to Baga La Phedi
From Ringmo village, follow a trail through forests of blue pine and juniper to a ridge and continue eastwards. There are two routes. One stays high and the other descends to the river and follows the main trail from Murwa. The upper trail is more direct, but hard to find without a knowledgeable guide. The route continues up the valley to a waterfall and a campsite.

Day 2: Baga La Phedi to Numa La Phedi
It is an even, steady three-hour climb through rock formations that look like crumbling fortresses to the Baga La at 5090 metres. The initial descent from the pass is gradual, but the trail soon drops abruptly to the Poyun Chu, a stream at 4370 metres, then ascends again to a camp near the foot of the Numa La.

Be careful of the route between the two passes. The larger trail leads to Saldang and Shey Gompa; the Baga La route is a smaller side trail. Because the Nepal authorities are insistent about restricting access to Shey, it is this trail that is the incentive to keep the Baga La route closed.

Day 3: Numa La Phedi to Tok-khyu

Continue through arid country with wonderful eroded pillars tinged with green to the Numa La, marked with mani stones at 5360 metres. If it is clear there are views of the Dhaulagiri massif, north of high desert country towards Tibet and down into the Tarap Valley. The trail descends steeply past a massive mani wall to meadows for camping at 4190 metres near Tok-khyu, the uppermost village of the Tarap region.

Day 4: Tok-khyu to Do

It's an easy three-km walk down the Tarap Valley through barley fields and scattered settlements. It is worth visiting all the gompas, even though they are not very active. The men of the area wind red yarn into their hair forming buns in the same manner as the Khampas of Tibet. The women wear ornate but cumbersome silver headgear. The houses are smoky from the desert shrubs they burn in the hearth in lieu of firewood. This is a short day because of a shortage of campsites in the lower Tarap Valley.

Do is the largest settlement in Tarap. Of special interest on the ridge above Do is the Ri Bhunpa Gompa and the chorten within a chorten. The Bon-po gompa in the village of Shipchhok and Doro to the east towards Tsharka are also unusual destinations that are worth exploring. There are also many possibilities to climb a ridge for a greater view of the valley, snow peaks and – if you are lucky – blue sheep. Strong winds blow up the valley from midday until dusk.

Day 5: Do to Gorge Camp

It is a long, difficult two-day journey down the Tarap Chu to Khanigaon. The morning is an easy, almost level walk down and around bends in the canyon. The wildflowers have disappeared, mostly because of a proliferation of domestic animals, especially sheep and goats. Be sure to look for the white-breasted dippers, only found in western Nepal, along the river, and throughout the trek watch for blue sheep high on the ridges.

After the third bridge the river goes into a gorge, ending the easy walking. A total of seven river crossings in about as many hours brings you to a flat expanse ideal for camping next to the river at 3560 metres elevation. There are large rose shrubs, yellow poppies, magenta-blooming legumes and bicoloured impatiens along the route. Crag martins fly above the gorge and wall creepers probe fissures in rock faces chasing insects.

Day 6: Gorge Camp to Khanigaon

The trail continues to be steep, narrow and dangerous. This is an even longer day than the previous one, mostly due to the improvisation required because of washed-out bridges. The harrowing detour trails, mostly makeshift and clinging to cliffs, require ropes in many places, especially for porters. You would do well to find a local guide familiar with the area who can help you find the route. This is definitely not for anyone frightened of heights.

What forest remains – mostly spruce fir, juniper and cypress – is high on cliffs and inaccessible to humans. The valley finally widens out and the route becomes easier. Camp near a checkpost below the village of Khanigaon.

Day 7: Khanigaon to Namdo

Climb high above the river, eventually descending to the Thulo Bheri (known here as the Barbung Khola), crossing it just before Namdo, a village on the river below the fortress village of Tarakot. It is possible to get all the way to Dunai on this day, but it is a long walk; it's better to break the journey into two days.

Day 8: Namdo to Dunai

Follow the Thulo Bheri downstream along the south bank to **Lawan**, cross to the north bank and walk several hours to reach Dunai.

Pokhara to Dunai

This is a long, remote, difficult trek with very few facilities along the way. The route is described in detail by George Schaller in *Stones of Silence* and by Peter Matthiesen in *The Snow Leopard*. There are no hotels beyond Beni, so you will be most comfortable if you take porters and food. With porters the trek takes 12 or 13 days. A rough itinerary follows.

Day 1: Pokhara to Beni
Drive to Maldhunga, then trek up the Kali Gandaki to Beni, the last large village on the route to Dunai.

Day 2: Beni to Dabang

Day 3: Dabang to Dhara Khola
Camp at 1830 metres.

Day 4: Dhara Khola to a Forest Camp
Camp at 2900 metres.

Day 5: Forest Camp to Dhorpatan
Cross the Jalja La at 3350 metres and descend to Dhorpatan (2300 metres). There is a defunct airport at Dhorpatan, but there is no scheduled service and nobody can remember when the last charter flight landed.

Day 6: Dhorpatan to a Forest Camp
Cross a pass at 4080 metres and descend to a camp in the forest.

Day 7: Forest Camp to Yamarkhar
Descend to the Ghustung Khola at 2800 metres, then climb to Yamarkhar at 2550 metres.

Day 8: Yamarkhar to Jagir
Continue up the ridge to a camp at Jagir (3350 metres).

Day 9: Jagir to Seng Khola
Cross the Nautala La at 3970 metres and descend into the Seng Khola Valley, camping at an elevation of 3600 metres.

Day 10: Seng Khola to Saure Khola
Climb a rock staircase leading to a pass at 4650 metres and descend to the Saure Khola. Camp at 4100 metres.

Day 11: Saure Khola to Tarakot
Cross the Jangla Bhanjyang (4500 metres) and descend through spruce and pine forests, then terraced fields, to Tarakot (2800 metres).

Day 12: Tarakot to Dunai
Follow the Thulo Bheri to Dunai.

Restricted Areas

In October 1991 the Home Ministry announced the opening of the restricted areas in Nepal, a move which was partly a political decision to remove a regulation that was inconsistent with the principals of Nepal's new democratic constitution. Once the announcement was made, most of the attention was directed at upper Mustang, previously the most inaccessible and firmly controlled area in Nepal. It took several months for the Ministry of Tourism to develop regulations and procedures for the newly opened areas, but by late March 1992 the first foreign trekking groups were allowed into upper Mustang.

Other trekking areas opened in 1991 were inner Dolpo and Nupri, the region north of Manaslu. The entire region of Dolpo, Mustang and Nupri was first explored by the Tibetan scholar David Snellgrove, and is described in his book *Himalayan Pilgrimage*.

The regulations for the restricted areas were designed primarily to protect the environment and culture of remote regions and to provide security, both for the safety of trekkers and the protection of Nepal's northern border with China. Unfortunately, the emphasis has shifted to the financial aspects of the permit process. It appears that the high

---

Terms & Conditions for Restricted Areas

The company that arranges your trek must agree to abide by the terms and conditions outlined below. The company must agree to be prosecuted as per the laws of the Kingdom of Nepal if they flaunt these terms and conditions.

The terms and conditions under which a trekking company may operate a trek in upper Mustang state:

1. You can operate only groups.

2. You will be responsible for arranging the entire trek from the start to the end of the trek.

3. Unless His Majesty's Government makes other provisions, you must compulsorily take a liaison officer with you in the newly opened areas.

4. You will be responsible for organising the security of the trekking group and, if need be, seek the help of the local police. If you thus need the police's help, you will arrange to meet their personal expenses.

5. You will arrange for medical care and other needs of the trekkers during the trek.

6. You must compulsorily provide solar fuel, electricity, gas, kerosene or a similar alternative fuel to cook food for the trekkers and all others accompanying them. Fuel wood cannot be used.

7. Tin cans, bottles etc necessary for the trek should not be thrown away at random. They should be buried/destroyed at designated sites.

8. You will arrange to ensure that the group travels only on authorised routes and does not break-up into separate groups.

9. You will not allow distribution of money or gifts or charity to local residents and students. If trekkers wish to do so, small parcels can be donated through the Chief District Officer (CDO).

10. Do not take foreigners into religious or cultural sites that are restricted to foreigners.

11. You will not perpetrate or allow any acts that destroy religion, culture or the environment.

12. You will insure all Nepalese staff on the trek. Moreover, you will insure or deposit a sum for emergency rescues.

13. Trekking parties to Lo Manthang of the Mustang area must submit to the Tourist Information Service, Jomsom, a copy of the goods and equipment taken with them. Upon returning, you should give them garbage to be dumped at the dumping site, get clearance and submit the same to the Ministry of Tourism.

14. You will provide the liaison officer with food, lodging, trip expenses and Rs 200 (two hundred rupees) per day for the duration of the trek. You will also compulsorily provide the officer necessary items like a sleeping bag, jacket, clothes, boots etc for the duration of the trek.

15. Permission to trek in the Lo Manthang region of Mustang area must be obtained within 21 days of recommendation by the Ministry of Tourism.

16. You must insure the liaison officer for Rs 200,000.

17. You will arrange for the necessary medicines and medical care of the liaison officer. ■

Environmental Officer's Role

The liaison (environmental) officer is given the following instructions titled 'The Job, Duty & Authority of the Environmental Officer':

1. You will implement and follow the rules.

2. You will only trek on the designated routes and dates.

3. You will register the names of all trekkers in the police posts on the trail.

4. You will submit a report of the trek.

5. You will search for illegal trekkers and hand them over to the concerned officials.

6. During the trek, you will not allow trekkers to distribute money or goods to local residents and students.

7. During the course of the trek, if a trekker flaunts the terms and conditions or does not follow the rules, you will abort his trek and, if necessary, seek the help of the local police to send him back.

8. You will help to ensure the cleanliness of the environment in the trekking areas. You will ensure that empty bottles and cans used by the group are properly destroyed or returned to the point of origin.

9. You will make suggestions for promotion of trekking tourism.

10. If the trekking agency taking the group does not follow the terms and conditions or prevailing laws, you can abort the trek and if the agency does not obey, you will recommend to the Ministry of Tourism and the Department of Immigration for prosecution of the agency.

11. Trekking parties to Lo Manthang of the Mustang area must submit to the Tourist Information Service, Jomsom, a copy of the goods and equipment taken with them. Upon returning, you should give them garbage to be dumped at the dumping site, get clearance and submit the same to the Ministry of Tourism. ■

of applications, guarantees and letters, a process that requires about two weeks and can be started only 21 days before the arrival of the group. You may not trek alone; there must be at least two trekkers in each group. For some areas there is a limit to the number of trekkers per season. There is no system of advance reservation, and no clear indication of what will happen if the quota is reached the day before you make an application.

Each group is assigned an 'environmental officer' who will accompany it during the trek. Despite the fancy name, what you will get is a Nepalese policeman who you must equip, insure and take on the trek. The liaison officer is supposed to handle all the formalities with police and government offices en route.

Mustang Trek

In common usage, the name Mustang refers to the arid Tibet-like region at the northern end of the Kali Gandaki (known to its inhabitants as Lo). Mustang is probably a Nepalese mispronunciation of the name of the capital of Lo, the city of Manthang. The name is pronounced 'Moo-stang' and has nothing to do with either the automobile or horse with a similar name. Officially, Mustang is the name of the district along the Kali Gandaki from the Tibetan border south to Ghasa. The capital of the Mustang district is Jomsom; the region of Tibetan influence north of Kagbeni is generally referred to as upper Mustang.

Upper Mustang consists of two distinct regions: the southern region, with five villages inhabited by people related to the Manangis; and the northern region (the ancient kingdom of Lo) where the language, culture and traditions are almost purely Tibetan. The capital of Lo is named Manthang, which translates from the Tibetan as 'plain of aspiration'. Many texts refer to the capital as Lo Manthang, but this is not strictly correct. Other texts spell the name of the kingdom as Lho, but this is a translitera-

permit fees will become institutionalised and the need for additional revenue will overshadow efforts to limit the number of tourists.

PERMITS & FORMALITIES

A trek to a restricted area must be arranged as a fully equipped organised trek through a registered trekking agency using tents, sherpa staff, cooks and porters. The trekking agency arranges the permit through a series

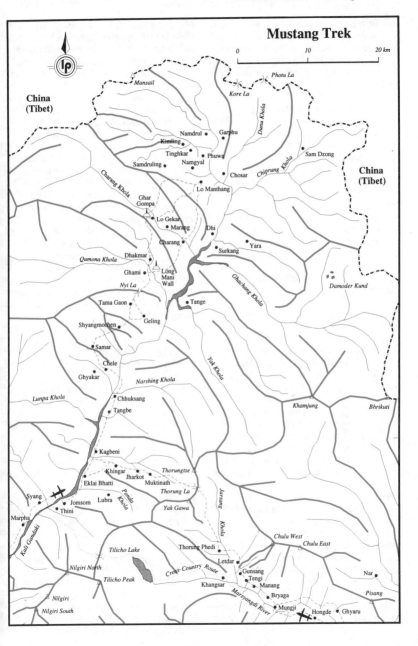

Mustang Trek

0   10   20 km

China
(Tibet)

Mansail

Photu La

Kore La

Dunu Khola

China
(Tibet)

Namdrul   Garphu

Kimling

Tinghkar   Phuwa

Samdruling   Namgyal

Chosar   Chiprung Khola   Sam Dzong

Charang Khola

Lo Manthang

Ghar Gompa

Lo Gekar

Marang   Dhi

Charang   Surkang   Yara

Dhakmar   Ghachang Khola

Qumona Khola

Ghami   Long Mani Wall

Nyi La   Damoder Kund

Tama Gaon   Tange

Geling

Shyangmochen

Samar

Chele   Narshing Khola

Ghyakar   Yak Khola

Lunpa Khola

Chhuksang   Khamjung   Bhrikuti

Tangbe

Kagbeni

Khingar   Thorungtse

Jharkot   Jarsang Khola

Eklai Bhatti   Muktinath

Syang   Thorung La   Chulu West   Chulu East

Jomsom   Lubra   Thorung Phedi   Marpha   Pandu Khola

Thini   Yak Gawa

Marpha   Kali Gandaki   Letdar   Nar

Gunsang

Tilicho Lake   Tengi

Nilgiri North   Cross-Country Route   Khangsar   Manang

Tilicho Peak   Bryaga   Pisang

Nilgiri   Mungji   Hongde   Ghyaru

Nilgiri South   Marsyangdi River

314 Restricted Areas – Mustang Trek

tion of the Tibetan word for 'south' and is also incorrect. Thus the portion of the upper Mustang district north of Samar is Lo and its capital is Manthang. The king of Lo is the Lo Gyelbu, though I will use the Nepalese term *raja* here. To avoid total confusion with existing maps and texts, I will also refer to the capital of Lo as 'Lo Manthang'.

There are many complex issues relating to the development of upper Mustang and the procedures under which trekkers are allowed to visit the area. I have not attempted to address these in detail here. Change and development will come to Lo regardless of the degree of protection that is exerted. Despite their isolation, the people of Lo are worldly, well travelled and resourceful. They are essentially Tibetans and are skilful traders, travellers and merchants. One hopes that they can retain their traditions under an influx of tourists, but they are by no means a primitive tribe that must be protected from outside influence.

History

Mustang has a long, rich and complex history that makes it one of the most interesting places in Nepal. The early history of Lo is shrouded in legend, myth and mystery, but there are records of events in Lo as early as the 8th century. It is quite likely that the Tibetan poet Milarepa, who lived from 1040 to 1123, visited Lo. Upper Mustang was once part of Ngari, a name for far western Tibet. Ngari was not a true political entity, but rather a loose collection of feudal domains that also included parts of Dolpo. By the 14th century, much of Ngari, as well as most of what today is western Nepal, was part of the Malla Empire governed from the capital at Sinja, near Jumla.

It is generally believed that Ame Pal (A-ma-dpal in Tibetan) was the founder king of Lo in 1380. The ancestry of the present Mustang raja can be traced 25 generations back to Ame Pal. Ame Pal, or perhaps his father, conquered a large part of the territory in the upper Kali Gandaki and was responsible for the development of the city of Lo

Manthang and many gompas. To the west, the Malla Empire declined and split into numerous petty hill states. By the 18th century, Jumla had consolidated and reasserted its power. In an effort to develop their domain as a trading centre and to obtain Tibetan goods, the rulers of Jumla turned their attention eastward. In the mid-18th century they assumed control over Lo, from which they extracted an annual tribute.

When he ascended the throne in 1762, Prithvi Narayan Shah began to consolidate what is present-day Nepal. At the time of his death, the kingdom extended from Gorkha eastward to the borders of Sikkim. His descendants directed their efforts westward and by 1789, Jumla had been annexed. The Gorkha armies never actually entered Lo; they recognised the rule of the Mustang raja. Although Mustang became part of Nepal, the raja retained his title and Lo retained a certain amount of autonomy.

Lo maintained its status as a separate principality until 1951. After the Rana rulers were overthrown and King Tribhuvan reestablished the rule of the Shah monarchs on 15 February, 1951, Lo was more closely consolidated into Nepal. The raja was given the honorary rank of colonel in the Nepalese army.

During the 1960s, after the Dalai Lama had fled to India and Chinese armies established control over Tibet, Mustang was a centre for guerrilla operations against the Chinese. The soldiers were the Khampas, Tibet's most fearsome warriors who were backed by the CIA (some Khampas were secretly trained in the USA). At the height of the fighting there were at least 6000 Khampas in Mustang and neighbouring border areas. The CIA's support ended in the early 1970s when the USA, under Kissinger and Nixon, initiated new and better relations with the Chinese. The government of Nepal was pressed to take action against the guerrillas and, making use of internal divisions within the Khampa leadership, a bit of treachery, and the Dalai Lama's taped advice for his citizens to lay down their arms, it managed to disband the resistance without committing to action the 10,000 Nepalese troops that had been sent to the area.

Though Mustang was closed, the government allowed a few researchers into the area. Toni Hagen included Mustang in his survey of the entire kingdom of Nepal, and the Italian scholar Giuseppi Tucci visited in the autumn of 1952. Professor David Snellgrove travelled to the region in 1956 but did not visit Lo Manthang. Longtime Nepal resident Barbara Adams travelled to Mustang during the autumn of 1963. The most complete description of the area is *Mustang, the Forbidden Kingdom*, written by Michel Peissel who spent several months in the area in the spring of 1964. Dr Harka Bahadur Gurung also visited and wrote about upper Mustang in October 1973. A number of groups legally travelled to upper Mustang during the 1980s by obtaining permits to climb Bhrikuti peak (6364 metres) south-east of Lo Manthang. Other than a few special royal guests, the first legal trekkers were allowed into Mustang in March 1992 upon payment of a high fee for a special trekking permit.

Geography

Mustang has been described as a thumb-like part of Nepal extending into Tibet. Yet, on the map, it is hardly a bump in Nepal's northern border. This is not the result of an inaccurate description by early writers; the map changed. In 1960 there was a controversy between Nepal and China over the ownership of Mt Everest. This resulted in extended negotiations and the Chinese-Nepalese Boundary Treaty of 1963 that completely redefined Nepal's northern frontier. Nepal gained a considerable amount of territory to the east and west of the old boundaries in Mustang, so the protrusion of Mustang into Tibet became much less pronounced. To make matters more confusing, most official maps were not updated until about 1985.

The trek to Lo is through an almost treeless barren landscape. Strong winds usually howl across the area in the afternoon, generally subsiding at night. Being in the rain shadow of the Himalaya, Lo has much less

rain than the rest of Nepal. During the monsoon the skies are cloudy and there is some rain. In the winter there is usually snow; sometimes as much as 30 or 40 cm accumulates on the ground.

In Lo itself the countryside is similar to the Tibetan plateau with its endless expanses of yellow and grey rolling hills eroded by wind. There is more rain in the lower part of upper Mustang and the hills tend to be great red fluted cliffs of tiny round stones cemented together by mud. Villages are several hours apart and appear in the distance almost as mirages; during the summer season, after the crops are planted, they are green oases in the desert-like landscape.

People & Culture

The people of upper Mustang call themselves Lobas. To be strictly correct, this word would be spelled 'Lopa,' meaning 'Lo people,' in the same way as Sherpa means 'east people' and Khampa, 'Kham people'. The people of Lo, probably because of regional dialect, pronounce the word with a definite 'b' sound instead of the 'p' sound that the Sherpas and Khampas use. I will follow Lo tradition and spell the word as it is pronounced: 'Loba', however, most anthropological texts disagree with this.

House and temple construction throughout the region uses some stone but mostly sun-baked bricks of mud. Astonishing edifices, such as the city wall and the four-storey palace in Lo Manthang, are built in this manner. It is said that there were once large forests in Lo, but now wood for construction is hauled all the way from Jomsom or pruned from poplar trees that are carefully planted in every village.

Religion

The form of Tibetan Buddhism practised in Mustang is primarily that of the Sakyapa sect. This sect was established at Sakya Monastery in Tibet and dates from 1073. The Sakyapa sect is more worldly and practical in outlook and is less concerned with metaphysics than the more predominant Nyingmapa and Gelugpa sects. Sakya Monastery is unique for the horizontal grey, white and yellow stripes on its red walls, an identifying feature of Sakyapa structures. Most chortens and gompas in Lo are painted in these colours that reflect the surrounding hills.

Information
Books & Articles *Mustang – a Lost Tibetan Kingdom* (Collins & Harvill Press, London, 1968), by Michel Peissel, is the first contemporary description of the Lo Manthang region of Mustang, north of Jomsom.

Mustang – A Trekking Guide (Tiwari's Pilgrims Book House, Kathmandu, 1993), by Bob Gibbons & Sian Pritchard-Jones, is a description of a trek to Mustang via the route to Muktinath along the east side of the Mustang Khola.

Other books include *The Mollas of Mustang* (Library of Tibetan Works & Archives, Dharamsala, 1984) by David P Jackson; *Mustang Bhot in Fragments* (Himal Books, Kathmandu, 1992) by Manjushree Thapa; and *Journey to Mustang* (Ratna Pustak Bhandar, Kathmandu, 1977) by Giuseppe Tucci.

Maps US Army Map Service maps NH44-12, NH44-16, NH45-9 and NH45-13 cover upper Mustang. Sheet NH45-9, which covers the top right corner of Lo has not been reprinted and is virtually unobtainable. The maps are based on surveys made in 1925 and 1926 and are very inaccurate near the northern border of Nepal. They improperly locate several peaks and do not show Tilicho Lake.

The 1989 series *Western Region* map (1:250,000) and *Mustang District* map (1:125,000) produced by the Nepal Ministry of Works & Transport show the current border and are quite accurate, though they do not name the peaks.

Currently, the best available map of the area is Paolo Gondoni's 1:125,000 scale map entitled *Mustang* (Nepa Maps, Kathmandu).

The National Remote Sensing Centre maps with the same keys as the US army series also cover Mustang. These are satellite photos and obviously show geographical features properly, though the features are difficult to interpret. Note also that many annotations in the 1986 edition are not correct; among other errors, Charang is shown in the wrong place.

Mandala Trekking Map series *Jomsom to Mustang* (1:125,000) is a blueprinted map available in Kathmandu.

Trekking Season Because of the cold and snow, most of the population departs from Lo on trading expeditions during the winter. The trekking season, therefore, is from late March until early November. The trek does not go to extremely high elevations, but the cold, dust and unrelenting afternoon winds can make the trek less pleasant than other treks in Nepal.

Because of the wind and the lack of water, you must always camp in a village, but these are not conveniently spaced, so some days are too short and others too long. There is little opportunity to vary the itinerary as there is on most Nepal treks.

Horses If possible, you should replace your porters with horses from upper Mustang at Jomsom or Kagbeni. Horses carry 40 to 50 kg and cost about Rs 200 per day. Porters demand Rs 200 or 250 per day, so horses are economically competitive with porters. Using horses is also more reliable and environmentally friendly than taking a group of lowland porters into the cold and wind of Mustang where they will be culturally isolated. By hiring horses from Mustang, you are benefiting the local economy in a culturally sensitive manner. A major advantage of using Mustang horses is that you also gain the services of a local horseman who can serve as a guide and expediter.

Getting There & Away
The trek I have described here begins and ends in Kagbeni, about two hours' walk north of Jomsom. There are daily flights to Jomsom from Pokhara; flights are in the early morning, so you must spend a night in Pokhara en route to Jomsom. The cost of a trip to Mustang escalates severely if you fly

in either direction. The airfare from Pokhara to Jomsom is reasonable (US$50) considering you save five days of walking, but you still must calculate the expense of moving your gear to Jomsom. Your food, stoves, tents and kerosene, all of which is required by law for a trek to Mustang, must be carried from Pokhara. Once you add the cost of five or six days' porterage plus the salary of camp staff both to and from Jomsom, the trek becomes quite expensive. If you have time, it is very worthwhile to walk from Pokhara, visit Lo Manthang, trek back to Jomsom and fly or walk back to Pokhara. If you do plan to fly, be aware that Jomsom can occasionally be as bad as the notorious Lukla airstrip in terms of flight delays.

Alternate Routes Some trek groups have trekked back via villages on the east side of the Kali Gandaki. These villages are isolated and not frequented by travellers of any kind. Most do not have even basic facilities for porters and are not used to coping with the demands of tourists. Villages are far apart and there is no shelter, except possibly caves, between them.

Special Rules
Group Size The rules require that you trek as a member of a group. You will be much happier if you travel as part of a small group. Campsites are small and a typical trek group of 16 foreigners plus their staff and liaison officer can overpower a village. I would recommend a maximum group size of 10.

Permits Trekking permits cost US$700 for 10 days; this is defined as 10 *days*, not nights, starting and ending at Kagbeni. Extra days are US$70 each.

ACAP administers trekking in upper Mustang. According to the plan, ACAP also is responsible for channelling a portion of the Mustang trek royalties into development projects in Mustang. Mustang is currently the only restricted area for which the permit fee goes into a special fund.

If you are trekking from Pokhara to Jomsom, you should get an additional

normal US$5 per week trekking permit; the US$70 per day permit is required only from Kagbeni northwards. Because of possible delays in Jomsom flights, the entry date on the permit is supposed to have a three-day leeway, though some bureaucrats are not aware of this. Once you start from Kagbeni, you must return within the period of your trek permit, but you need not start on a precise date.

Registration In Jomsom, you must register with the police post and also with the tourist information office across from Om's Home, just north of the airport. The tourist office will check your permit, equipment, stoves, food and fuel. You should have several lists of group members and equipment available for this purpose. The physical presence of all group members is required at both the police post and the tourist office. Allow at least an hour in both Kagbeni and Jomsom for formalities.

At the conclusion of the trek, you are required to register again with the tourist office and hand over all your rubbish to them for disposal. If the tourist office is satisfied that you have followed all the rules, they will give your liaison officer a letter stating so. This letter is important; any trekking company that does not follow the rules risks being barred from operating treks in to restricted areas.

Your liaison officer can register the group with the other checkposts on the trek.

Fuel There is usually no kerosene available in Jomsom and it is never available in upper Mustang. Kerosene is not allowed on flights, though you may carry empty stoves. There is an ACAP fuel depot in Kagbeni that supplies kerosene at Rs 27 per litre. Otherwise you must carry kerosene from Pokhara.

THE ROUTE TO LO MANTHANG
Day 1: Kagbeni to Chele
Kagbeni's electricity is supplied by a wind-powered system that seems to be permanently broken, so the town is usually without lights. The large *Nilgiri View Lodge*

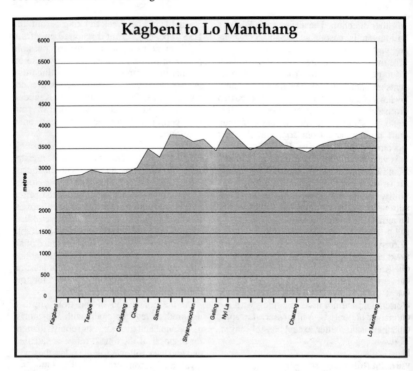

at the southern entrance to the town is at the trail junction for the route to Muktinath. Other hotels are situated throughout the town, with the *Red House, Muktinath View* and *Annapurna* lodges clustered around the town's main square at an elevation of 2780 metres. The ACAP office that administers Mustang is in Kagbeni. The narrow alleyways and tunnels, irrigation canals, green fields of wheat and barley and large red gompa of Kagbeni are a taste of scenes to come in upper Mustang.

At the police checkpost at the north end of the village, there is a sign saying 'Restricted Area, tourists please do not go beyond this point'. If you have the correct permit for upper Mustang, your liaison officer will complete formalities here and you are free to enter this long-forbidden region of Nepal.

There is a trail up the east bank of the Kali Gandaki that climbs over many ridges as it heads north. In the dry season, it is possible to trek the entire route up the river along the sand and gravel of the riverbed. This will require at least two, and perhaps many, fords of the several channels of the meandering Kali Gandaki. When Lo people bring their horses to Kagbeni, they travel straight down the centre of the river valley, jumping onto the backs of their horses whenever it is necessary cross the river. The best solution is to get local advice and then stick to either the high trail or the riverbank route depending on river conditions. It's hard to get back to the high trail if you reach a dead end along the river.

You can see Gompa Kang and some caves on the west bank of the river. Unlike most gompas in upper Mustang, Gompa Kang is of the Nyingmapa sect. The village of

Tangbe is situated alongside the east-bank trail above the river at an elevation of 2990 metres. Here are the first of the trio of black, white and red chortens that typify upper Mustang. The town is a labyrinth of narrow alleys among whitewashed houses, fields of buckwheat, barley and wheat and apple orchards. Nilgiri peak, which dominates the southern skyline at Kagbeni, continues to loom at the foot of the valley.

Chhuksang village is about 1½ hours beyond Tangbe at the confluence of the Narshing Khola and the Kali Gandaki at 2920 metres. There are three separate parts of this village and some broken castle walls on the surrounding cliffs. Up the Narshing Khola is the gompa and village of Tetang and a small salt mine.

Across the river from Chhuksang are some spectacular red organ-pipe eroded cliffs above the mouths of inaccessible caves. The five villages in this area, Chele, Ghyakar, Chhuksang, Tangbe and Tetang, are a culturally unified group of people who call themselves Gurungs and are more closely related to the Manangis than to the Thakalis or Lobas. Note that these five villages are not the Thakali *panchgaon* ('five villages'); those villages are lower on the Kali Gandaki and include Marpha, Jomsom-Thini, Syang, Chivang and Chherok.

Continue north to a huge red chunk of conglomerate that has fallen from the cliffs above forming a tunnel through which the Kali Gandaki flows. A steel bridge spans the river just in front of the tunnel. North of here, the Kali Gandaki becomes impassable for those on foot, though the Lobas sometimes travel this route on horseback through a steep narrow canyon that is dangerous because of falling rocks. There are many caves high on the fluted red cliffs here.

The trek now leaves the Kali Gandaki Valley and climbs steeply up a rocky gully to Chele at 3030 metres. This is a small village that boasts upper Mustang's first hotel, the *Nilgiri,* and a shop among the extensive fields of wheat and barley that blanket the hillside.

The culture changes from the Manangi culture of the five 'Gurung' villages to the Tibetan culture of Lo. Most Lo houses have sheep horns above their doorways and you will see many twigs in the shape of a cross with threads in five colours woven in a diamond-shaped pattern. These are called *zor* and are supposed to capture evil spirits that threaten the population. Being now in a region of Tibetan influence, many people also keep ferocious Tibetan mastiff dogs. Most are chained to houses and their threats are confined to low-pitched barks, but do not treat these animals lightly. If you are surprised by one of these animals on the loose, you can usually keep it at bay by threatening to throw a rock at it. Make a discreet retreat until the owner appears – or until another villager actually does throw a well-aimed stone.

The trading patterns also change in Lo. Despite the ever-changing political situation, Chinese goods still make their way into Lo. There is more packaged Chinese food available than Nepalese or Indian food. Several houses have Chinese wood stoves, porcelain and other articles. Much of the material and decoration for the gompas also comes from Tibet.

Day 2: Chele to Geling

The climb from Chele is up a steep spur to a cairn at 3080 metres. Here there is a view of the village of Ghyakar across a huge canyon. A long wall of packed earth encircles Ghyakar and its fields. The climb continues – a long, steep, treeless, waterless slog – along the side of the spectacular steep canyon to a pass and cairn at 3480 metres. Here the trail makes a long gradual descent to some chortens on a ridge, then descends further on a pleasant trail to **Samar**, situated in a grove of poplar trees at 3290 metres. This is a major stopping place for horse caravans; there are many stables available for hire and there is a hotel catering to locals. The Annapurna Himal, still dominated by Nilgiri, is visible far to the south.

The trail climbs above Samar to a ridge, then descends into a large gorge past a chorten painted in red, black, yellow and white – all pigments made from local rocks. The trail goes into another valley filled with juniper trees, crosses a stream and climbs up to a ridge at 3800 metres and drops to **Bhena**. The route skirts a gorge, climbs slightly to Yamda, then climbs over yet another pass, follows a ridge, then descends to **Shyangmochen**, a tiny settlement with a few tea shops at 3650 metres.

The trail climbs gently from Shyangmochen to a pass at 3700 metres and enters another huge east-west valley. There is a trail junction here. The left trail is the direct route to the Nyi La, bypassing Geling. Take the right fork and descend to Geling with its poplar trees and extensive fields of barley at 3440 metres.

Day 3: Geling to Charang

From Geling, the trail climbs gently through fields up the centre of the valley, passing above the settlement of **Tama Gaon** and its imposing chorten. It rejoins the direct trail and then becomes an unrelenting climb across the head of the valley to the Nyi La at 3840 metres. This pass is the southern boundary of Lo itself. The descent from the Nyi La is gentle. About a half hour from the pass is a trail junction; the right trail is the direct route to Charang; the left trail leads to Ghami.

The Charang trail descends below the blue, grey and red cliffs across the valley to a steel bridge across the Tangmar Chu river, then climbs past what is perhaps the longest and most spectacular stretch of mani wall in Nepal. Climbing over another pass at 3770 metres, the route makes a long gentle descent to Charang at 3490 metres.

Charang is a maze of fields, willow trees and houses separated by stone walls at the top of the large Charang Chu canyon. The huge five-storey white *dzong* (Tibetan-style fortress) and red gompa are perched on the edge of the Kali Gandaki Gorge at the eastern end of the village. The gompa houses a collection of statues and thangkas as well as many large paintings of seated Buddhas. Near the gompa is the house of Maya Bista

which, if you have the nerve to get past the ferocious mastiff at the door, doubles as a hotel and restaurant; there is a camp ground nearby. The village has its own electricity supply; you cross under the pipes of the hydro plant just beyond the village.

Day 4: Charang to Lo Manthang

The trail descends about 125 metres from Charang, crosses the Charang Chu and climbs steeply up a rocky trail to a cairn on a ridge opposite the village at 3530 metres, then enters the Tholung Valley. The trail turns north and climbs gently to a large isolated chorten that marks the boundary between Charang and Lo. Still climbing, the trail crosses a stream, then becomes a grand wide thoroughfare travelling across a desert-like landscape painted in every hue of grey and yellow. Finally, from a ridge at 3850 metres, there is a view of the walled city of Lo.

A short descent leads onto the 'plain of aspiration' at 3780 metres. The trail then crosses a stream and climbs up onto the plateau of Lo Manthang itself at 3730 metres, crossing an irrigation canal at the southern wall of the city. The only entrance to the city is at the north-eastern corner, so circumambulate the wall to the gate where you are sure to find a group of adults and children playing, spinning wool and gossiping.

The whitewashed wall around Lo Manthang resembles a misshapen 'L' with a short vertical arm oriented north- south and a very fat, almost square horizontal arm. The closely packed houses of the city itself, the palace and temples are in the bottom portion; the vertical part of the 'L' houses the monastic community and two gompas, and this portion of the city wall is painted red.

The school, health post, police checkpost and several important chortens are located outside the walls to the north of the gate and east of the monastic part of the city. Peissel described the gates as being closed at night, but now they remain permanently open. The city contains about 150 houses plus numerous lama residences. The only agricultural

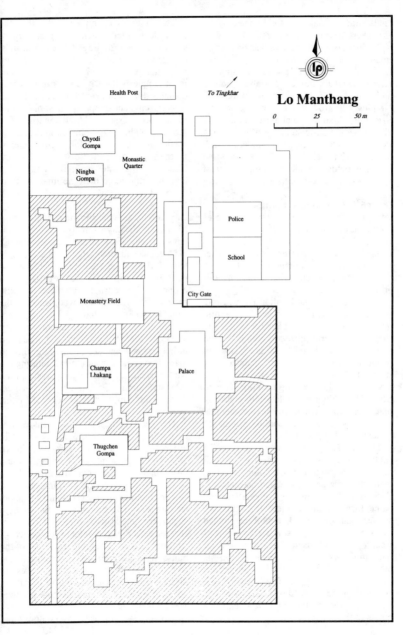

Health Post

To Tingkhar

Lo Manthang

0   25   50 m

Chyodi
Gompa

Monastic
Quarter

Ningba
Gompa

Police

School

Monastery Field

City Gate

Champa
Lhakang

Palace

Thugchen
Gompa

land inside the walls is a field owned by the monastery near the city centre.

The wall of Lo Manthang was once more imposing than it is now. In the mid-1980s the raja sold much of the land surrounding the city; as a result, numerous stables, houses and stone-walled fields now adjoin the wall. Nothing will grow in this arid land without irrigation. A small canal flows around the city providing sustenance for a few willow trees and another canal flows under the wall and through the city itself. The surrounding irrigated fields provide one crop a year of wheat, barley, peas or mustard.

Days 5 & 6: In Lo Manthang
Temples There are four major temples within the city walls. Each of these buildings is locked. The villagers feel it necessary to control access to the temples; the caretaker and the key are available only at certain times, and usually only after a bit of negotiation.

The tall **Champa Lhakang** *(lha kang* translates as 'god house') is said to date from the 1420s and is accessible only on the 2nd storey. The central courtyard with its carved wooden pillars has fallen into disrepair. Inside the temple is a huge painted clay statue of Maitreya, the future Buddha, sitting on a pedestal that occupies the entire ground floor. The walls are painted with elaborate mandalas almost two metres in diameter that are in marginally better condition than the paintings in Thugchen Gompa.

The red **Thugchen Gompa** is near the centre of the city, a massive assembly hall supported by huge wooden columns dating from the same period as Champa Lhakang. Tucci observed that the same artists had painted frescoes in both temples. There are statues of the deities Sakyamuni surrounded by Avalokitesvara, Vaisravana (the god of wealth) and Padmasambhava. One wall of the temple is completely destroyed; on the other walls are intricate frescoes in various stages of deterioration. The entrance hall contains huge scowling statues of four Lokapala, the protectors of the cardinal points of the compass.

The other two temples are within the monastic quarter which is the domain of several large growling Tibetan mastiffs. Secure the services of a monk before you even attempt to enter this part of the city. The main temple is the **Chyodi Gompa** which contains dozens of beautifully crafted small bronze, brass and copper statues, many said to have been cast in Lo Manthang itself. The monks prohibit taking photographs of these statues in an apparent effort to limit interest in them among collectors of stolen art. Nearby is the older assembly hall which contains little more than the images of the three Sakyapa lamas.

City Life Despite the apparent squalor of Lo Manthang, the city is prosperous and maintains a strong sense of community. Though the people call themselves Lobas (people from Lo) they are very much Tibetan and practice a sophisticated culture and economy. Before trade with Tibet was disrupted, all of the salt and wool trade on the Kali Gandaki passed through Lo Manthang, and this brought a sizeable amount of money to the city. Wealth is now primarily measured in land, horses and social standing, though many Lobas travel south to India during the winter where they are major players in the sale and distribution of acrylic sweaters manufactured in the Punjabi city of Ludhiana.

The door of most houses opens onto a two-storey open central courtyard. The ground floor is used for storage of food, horse trappings, a pile of dung for fuel and farm implements. A wooden staircase leads to the 1st storey which typically has a balcony overlooking the courtyard and doors leading off to living rooms and the kitchen. A notched log leads to the roof which is surrounded by huge stacks of juniper twigs and firewood and is an important part of the house, used for relaxing or working in the sun. Adorning the roofs of most houses are the horns of sheep and yak and, on the palace, horns of extinct Sikkim stags that are over 100 years old.

Virtually every house has an indoor toilet

on the upper floor that drops into a ground-floor chamber. Ashes from the hearth are dumped into the toilet to eliminate smell, and the resulting product is a nutritive, not unpleasant fertiliser. The stoves used in Lo are of a special design. Stoves are a three-armed affair with a 30-cm-high burning chamber that gets roaring like a volcano when fed with yak dung and goat droppings. People rarely burn the wood on the roof for cooking; it is there largely as a show of wealth and for ceremonial occasions.

Raja's Palace The raja's palace is an imposing four-storey building in the centre of the city. It is the home of the present raja, Jigme Parbal Bista, and the queen, or rani, who is from an aristocratic family of Lhasa. The raja is an active horseman and keeps a stable of the best horses in Lo. He also breeds Lhasa apso dogs and several monstrous Tibetan mastiffs that can be heard barking angrily in the 2nd storey of the palace. Though his duties are largely ceremonial, he is respected by the people and consulted about many issues by villagers throughout Lo.

The raja's family name was originally Tandul. It was changed in accordance with a recent tradition in which many people of Tibetan descent Nepalised their surnames. This practice is similar to the custom of the 'Matwali Chhetris' of Dolpo in which Khampas adopted Hindu surnames. It is also similar to the practice of many Manangis who call themselves Gurungs. Many Lobas use their original Tibetan name, but almost all have a second Nepali name that was assigned when they enrolled in school.

Places to Stay There are two houses that provide basic hotel facilities. One hotel is operated by Surendra Bista, and is above the post office in the square across from the palace. The second hotel is primarily a tea shop and drinking establishment, and is in an alley to the right of the entrance gate.

Around Lo Manthang There is a lot to do in Lo Manthang. After visiting the temples in the city, consider hiring a horse to visit some

of the other villages in the area. In 1992, horses with a saddle covered with a colourful Tibetan carpet were available for Rs 500 per day. The Rs 500 applies whether you use the horse for one hour or from dawn to dusk. Mount and dismount outside the city gate; only the raja may ride a horse within the city walls.

There are two valleys above Lo Manthang. In the western valley are **Tingkhar**, the site of the raja's summer palace, Kimling, Phuwa and **Namgyal Gompa** ('the monastery of victory'). Namgyal, situated in a spectacular setting atop a desolate ridge, is the newest and most active gompa in Lo.

The valley east of Lo Manthang contains **Chosar**, the site of the high school, and Garphu and Nyphu gompas. This is the main trading route to Lhasa, a route that Tucci describes as '...used over the centuries by pilgrims and apostles, robbers and invaders'. The ruins of numerous forts along the trail lend credence to this observation.

Note Usually, the police in Lo Manthang do not allow trekkers to go north of Lo Manthang village. This restriction may or may not still apply when you trek here. Check carefully about this rule before you plan a trek to Mustang.

Day 7: Lo Manthang to Ghami

There is an opportunity to vary the return route, visiting two villages that you did not see on the trek northwards. From Lo Manthang the trail to Charang heads south; to reach Lo Gekar, turn west along an indistinct trail that passes the irrigated fields of the city.

The trail to Lo Gekar is not a main trading route and the area is crisscrossed with herders' trails, so a local guide is particularly useful here. The trail climbs steadily to a pass marked by a cairn, offering a last glimpse of Lo Manthang. The trail contours across the head of a valley and crosses another ridge, then drops into another large desolate valley. After descending to the valley floor, the route heads to the west, up the centre of the valley to its head. Cross a ridge at 4070 metres and traverse across the heads of two more valleys to an indistinct pass. Cross the pass to some meadows and a stream. The trail then makes a long rocky descent down a ravine to the settlement of **Lo Gekar** (which means 'pure virtue of Lo'), then reaches a grassy valley where **Ghar Gompa** is situated in a grove of large trees alongside a stream.

Ghar Gompa means 'house temple' and is so-named because the structure is built like a house with small separate rooms. The gompa is decorated with paintings and statues and several large prayer wheels. The primary deities are placed on a brass altar inside a dark alcove; on one wall of the alcove there is a self-emanating statue. The real treasure of Ghar Gompa is the hundreds of painted carved stones displayed on the walls in wooden frames. Snellgrove learned that the lama of Syang, the village south of Jomsom, presented many of the gompa's decorations and that he often stayed there.

In Lo Manthang, I was told an interesting legend that relates Ghar Gompa to Samye Monastery, which is in Tibet, near the Lhasa airport. During Samye's construction, it is said, demons destroyed the monastery several times. Construction was stopped and Ghar Gompa was built to appease the demons, after which the construction of Samye proceeded without incident. This story corroborates a legend that the great saint Padmasambhava visited Ghar Gompa and hid some texts for later discovery by the right teachers. Since Padmasambhava is also recognised as a founder of Samye, which was built between 775 and 787, this suggests that Ghar Gompa is one of the oldest active gompas in Nepal.

There is no village nearby, but there are a series of quarters for monks and pilgrims near the gompa that provide protection from the wind. The gompa is supplied with electricity via a long transmission line from Marang village. You can see Marang, and below that Charang, in the valley below.

Climb to a ridge, then across a valley to a cairn and a pass 200 metres above Ghar Gompa. The route crosses some alpine meadows to a crest, then drops down a steep eroded gully to the upper part of the village of **Dhakmar**, whose name means 'red crag'. A large stream meanders through this village, making this a particularly pretty valley. Most of the surrounding hills are pastel shades of grey and yellow, but a huge, red, fluted cliff provides a dramatic contrast. The trail descends alongside the stone walls and fields of the extensive village, then climbs to a ridge. It is a short descent to Ghami at 3460 metres.

Ghami is a large village of whitewashed houses situated above hectares and hectares of fields. About half of the fields are barren because of problems with the irrigation system. Ghami has a police post and the *Raju Hotel* operated by a grand nephew of the Lo raja. In the winter of 1991, there were a number of rabid dogs in this village. The villagers solved the problem by killing every dog in the locality. The gompa here is being restored using local money and the villagers and lamas are not happy at all about allowing tourists to visit the gompa. They are fearful of theft of religious objects, and their fears are not unfounded, as several old and important thangkas were stolen from the gompa at Geling in early 1992. A small red nunnery dominates a crag at the far end of the village.

Day 8: Ghami to Samar
From Ghami, follow the direct route to the Nyi La, climbing to a cairn on a ridge and then contouring upwards to meet the trail from Charang. Continue to the pass and descend steeply into the Geling Valley. Follow the trail that bypasses Geling to an isolated teahouse and descends gently to the three houses of **Tama Gaon**. A steep set of switchbacks leads to a stream, then the trail climbs to a huge painted chorten before rejoining the Geling trail near the ridge, just below a chorten. The remainder of the day is on already-travelled trails back to Samar.

Day 9: Samar to Kagbeni
Retrace the upward trail back to the Kali Gandaki and downstream to Kagbeni – hopefully before your permit expires.

Alternative Routes from Lo Manthang to Kagbeni
To return to Kagbeni there is another route

down the eastern side of the Mustang Khola Valley through Tange and Tetang to Muktinath. If you attempt this route, be prepared for at least one long 10-hour (30+ km) day. There is no water and no vegetation between the few villages on this rarely travelled route.

Around Manaslu

This trek was officially opened to tourists in 1991, but mountaineering expeditions have long had access to the area. In 1950 a party led by H W Tilman trekked from Thonje to Bimtang and Colonel Jimmy Roberts crossed the Larkya La looking for an interesting mountain to climb. Manaslu (8156 metres) was attempted by Japanese expeditions every year from 1952 until 1956, when the first ascent was made. Having become known as a 'Japanese mountain', much of the information about the area was available only in Japanese. The Japanese continued to dominate the climbing scene on Manaslu until 1971.

A few trekkers, including the peripatetic Hugh Swift, managed to obtain trekking permits for the region, but otherwise this trek has always been the domain of the mountaineering expedition.

The book *Honey Hunters of Nepal* (Thames & Hudson Ltd, London, 1988) by Eric Valli & Dianne Summers, makes good background reading for this area.

Getting There & Away
Trailheads You can begin this trek from Gorkha, Trisuli Bazaar or Dhading. All these routes converge at Arughat, two days from Gorkha, three days from Trisuli and one long day from the road above Dhading. A road from Dhading to Arughat is under construction.

Gorkha Gorkha is the traditional starting point for treks up the Buri Gandaki. The bus ride from Kathmandu to Gorkha follows the Pokhara road as far as Abu Khaireni, then

climbs 24 km to Gorkha. Gorkha is served by buses from Narayanghat, Pokhara and Kathmandu. The cost is Rs 39 from Pokhara and Rs 50 from Kathmandu.

Dhading Dhading provides an excellent starting point for the Manaslu trek and saves a day of walking compared to the trek from Gorkha.

There is no direct bus service to Dhading. You need to take a local bus to Pokhara and get off at Malekhu. Cross the Trisuli river on a footbridge and take another bus for the remainder of the trip.

Trisuli Bazaar Trisuli Bazaar is an alternative starting point for the Around Manaslu trek. Arughat is a four-day walk from Trisuli along the old route from Kathmandu to Pokhara.

Buses to Trisuli leave from the bus terminal on the Ring Rd north of Kathmandu. The first bus leaves at 7 am, costs Rs 32 and takes about five hours to reach Trisuli.

Special Rules
The rules for this trek are the same as those for Mustang and inner Dolpo: you must trek with a fully organised group; take a liaison (or 'environmental') officer; pack out all cans, bottles and 'plastic paper'; use only kerosene for cooking and pay a special fee.

For the Manaslu trek the fee is lower than Mustang – US$90 per week during October and November and only US$75 per week during the remainder of the year. The 1993 quota was 400 trekkers per year for this route.

THE ROUTE AROUND MANASLU
Though the Larkya La is not a difficult pass, the trek is harder than most in Nepal. In many places the walls of the Buri Gandaki Valley are perpendicular, so you cannot walk along the bottom of the valley. There is a huge amount of wasted climbing involved during the first part of the trek as you climb up and down over ridges or onto shelves to bypass cliffs. The trail is rough and steep and it often literally hangs on a bluff high above the river.

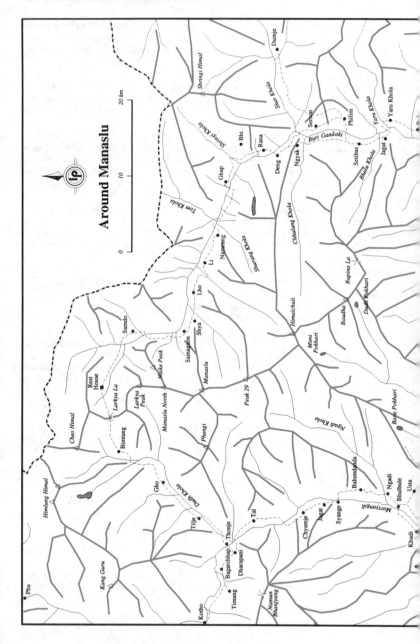

Around Manaslu

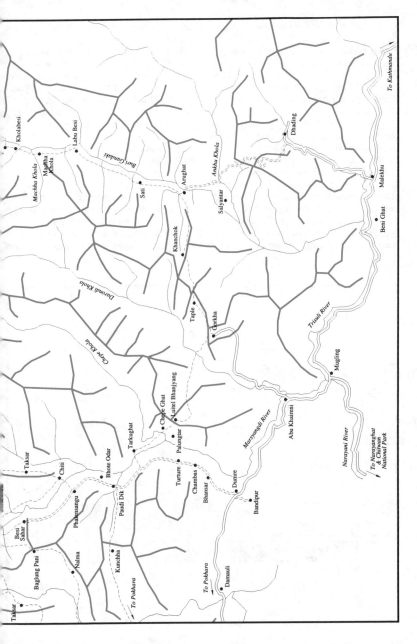

Don't read any further if you have the slightest tendency towards acrophobia. The trek is remote and has no rescue facilities or opportunities to bail out if you are tired. There is only one facility that might conceivably be called a trekkers' hotel, and in 1992 there was not a single English signboard between Arughat and Tilje.

The trek is geographically spectacular and culturally fascinating. The Tibetans of the upper Buri Gandaki, a region known as Nupri ('the western mountains'), are direct descendants of Tibetan immigrants. Their speech, dress and customs are almost exclusively Tibetan. There is still continuous trade between Nupri and Tibet; Chinese cigarettes, for example, are found more frequently than Nepalese cigarettes. The mountain views in Nupri are sensational, and the Larkya La is one of the most dramatic Himalayan pass crossings.

Because much of this trek is in a region of strong Tibetan influence, most places have Tibetan names in addition to their better known Nepali monickers. Where possible, I have included the Tibetan name in brackets, but have used the more common Nepali name throughout the text.

Day 1: Kathmandu to Dhading to Kafalpani
It is about a two-hour drive from Kathmandu to Malekhu (485 metres) on the Pokhara road. A bridge over the Trisuli River is under construction, but you can cross the river by foot on a suspension bridge. There was once a ferry here that could carry vehicles, but it disappeared during the July 1993 monsoon

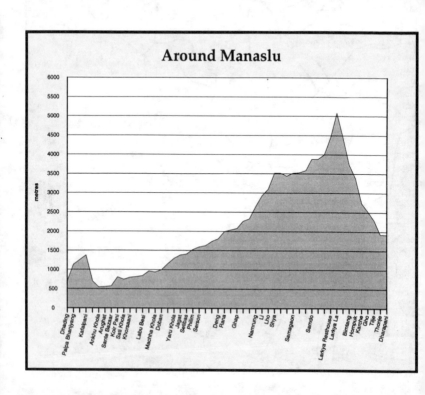

floods. Buses now wait on the opposite side to take you the 17 km to Dhading Besi.

The road follows a stream as it climbs through dense sal forests past the village of Bungchung in a steep valley. Finally the valley opens up as Dhading village comes into view at 670 metres elevation. The snow peaks of Ganesh Himal are visible to the north. The road beyond Dhading is suitable only for jeeps; if you are travelling by bus decamp at Dhading and start climbing along the trail that follows a more direct route than the road.

If you have your own jeep, turn left at the entrance to the village and follow a road upwards. This road will eventually reach Arughat in the Buri Gandaki Valley. At present it climbs all the way to the top of the ridge between Dhading and the Buri Gandaki Valley, saving a lot of uphill walking. I started trekking from Palpa Bhanjyang, 11 km by road from Dhading Besi, at 1120 metres. I followed the road for a while, cutting switchbacks. The road heads north over another ridge, but the trail continues level through Nigalpani; there are views of Annapurna II and Manaslu along the route. The trail crests the ridge at Kafalpani (1350 metres). The major peak groups visible here, west to east, are the Annapurnas, Manaslu (8156 metres), Shringi Himal (7187 metres) and Ganesh Himal (7406 metres).

Day 2: Kafalpani to Arughat

From the ridge the trek descends gently to **Chainpur**, a village with a few tea shops on a saddle. The trail descends steeply to a stream at 680 metres, then traverses rice fields before dropping to a long suspension bridge across the Ankhu Khola at 580 metres. The trail then climbs to **Salyantar**, situated on a flat plateau between the Buri Gandaki and the Ankhu Khola. After a few km of flat walking, the trail enters the valley of the Buri Gandaki.

The trail is flat through forests to Doren and then to Arughat. The village of Arughat is in two parts, on opposite sides of the Buri Gandaki. The route first enters the eastern part of Arughat, a large, prosperous clean

bazaar with hotels and shops selling cloth, food and hardware. There is a trail junction here. Turn west across the bridge over the Buri Gandaki to continue the trek. The trail joining from the east is the route from Trisuli Bazaar.

From the trail junction descend a set of stone steps to where the village blacksmiths, or Kamis, ply their trade just beside the eastern end of a big steel suspension bridge. On the west side of the bridge, follow the stone paved street north through the bazaar to a police checkpost. Here the trail to Gorkha leads west and the route around Manaslu turns north.

Pass the stone buildings of the hydroelectric power plant and walk through fields of rice and millet to a camp north of Arughat near Maltar.

Day 3: Arughat to Sati Khola

Continue past forests full of monkeys to Sante Bazaar, a few thatched houses and a shady pipal tree at 630 metres with a view of Shringi Himal up the valley. The Buri Gandaki Valley now becomes steeper and the trek more difficult as the trail crosses the Arket Khola and climbs through fields and over a rock outcrop. Descend to a high cascading waterfall, then make a long steep slog up a ridge to **Koir Pani**, a small Magar and Gurung village at 820 metres. The trail then descends to Sati and a few minutes beyond to a good camp by the Sati Khola at 710 metres. There is a good swimming hole here and a small waterfall up the Sati Khola just above the trail. A much larger waterfall, with a 60-metre drop, is visible by climbing upstream. This valley is said to have beehives where honey is harvested in a manner similar to that described in the book *Honey Hunters of Nepal.*

The Gurungs of the Buri Gandaki are primarily farmers, though there are many remnants of a hunting society. You are likely to encounter men with locally made rifles or to hear shots in the woods as the hunt for a deer concludes.

The focus of the region's trade is Gorkha, though many people have never ventured beyond Arughat. Few Gurungs of this region make it into the British army Gurkha regiments. The women often dress elegantly and have extensive collections of jewellery, bangles and saris. The men tend to dress in more simple, locally made clothing, often using cloth woven from nettle fibre. Most men wear a quaint, heavy, brown woollen cape called a *bokkhu*. This versatile garment is usually worn as a coat, but can be used as a hooded raincoat, sleeping bag, tent or even a cloak to protect the wearer from bees during a honey hunting expedition.

Day 4: Sati Khola to Labu Besi

The trail crosses the bridge and climbs up onto a ridge above huge rapids on the Buri Gandaki before continuing up to **Khorsaani** and a big Gurung house at 820 metres. The trail gets a bit precarious here as it passes over a big rock and crosses a stream on a single log perched high above it. The rocky trail then weaves its way up and down through large stands of nettles, past two tropical waterfalls and back down to the banks of the Buri Gandaki where a farmer has scratched out a few rice terraces. Trek up again on a steep rocky trail clinging to the side of a cliff, down and past a few more rice terraces, then up and around to the Gurung village of Labu Besi at 880 metres.

Day 5: Labu Besi to Doban

The path climbs behind a rocky outcrop to a dilapidated school. Here the valley opens and the Buri Gandaki meanders among wide gravel bars. The narrow exposed trail drops to a high cascading waterfall and wooden bridge, then over another ridge before dropping to the sandy riverbed at 860 metres. It's just a short walk along the rounded stones of the riverbed before climbing about 110 metres over a side ridge to avoid a spot where the river changed course and erased the riverside trail. Down again to the river, up over another ridge, then traverse above the river to the village of **Machha Khola**, situated above a stream with the same name. You can drop into the village or take the elevated bypass route to a suspension bridge, several

tea shops and a camp by the stream at 900 metres. The Buri Gandaki is spanned here by a cable ropeway, and passengers cross in a small cable car called a *ghirling*. Many local people have their own personal pullery systems that they connect to the cable and use to zip across the river.

The trail makes some minor ups and downs and crosses a stream in a rocky ravine en route to Kholabesi. There are two houses, a rudimentary shop, a tea stall and an outside covered restaurant here. Climb over a small ridge, then make a very steep climb and descent to a single house. After more ups and downs there is a small trailside hot spring, then the route reaches **Tatopani**. There is no village at Tatopani, just a stone structure and a single spout of hot water.

From the hot spring the trail climbs over another ridge, then crosses the Buri Gandaki on a suspension bridge in a state of moderate decay. Now on the eastern side of the river, the trail climbs on a wide, well-crafted staircase over a ridge to Doban, which boasts a small shop. A long suspension bridge carries the trail over the Doban Khola; the trail reaches the bridge via an interesting cloverleaf approach.

Day 6: Doban to Jagat

The next stretch of trail is about as rough as trekking can get, although hopefully by the time you trek here the trail will have been rebuilt. The route climbs on a rugged rocky trail to two tea shops at Duman. After crossing under a big landslide you will find yourself boulder-hopping, climbing up and down ravines and notched trees, hanging on roots and dodging nettles as you struggle to reach a big field. There is more scrambling up and down gravel slopes and teetering rocks, then up another tree as the river roars below you, dropping steeply in a clutter of huge rocks. Eventually you will cross a ridge. Here the river valley widens, and the trail descends to the Buri Gandaki which is now meandering serenely among gravel bars. The village of **Yaru Khola**, at 1330 metres, is a single large house and a good campsite near the river. An old man is trying to eke out a living selling cigarettes, roasted soybeans and beer.

Cross a 93-metre-long suspension bridge over the Yaru Khola and ascend a wide set of stone stairs, then drop to the river and then climb more big stone stairs to **Thado Bharyang**, two houses and a shop next to a bridge. The bridges and trail in this region were constructed as part of a CARE project in 1983. The magnificent stone trail that this project built is a marked contrast to the dreadful trail below Yaru Khola.

Cross the Buri Gandaki, climb over a ridge, trek along the river for a while, then climb up to the compact village of Jagat at 1410 metres. Jagat has a beautiful flag-stone village square in front of a rudimentary trekkers' hotel. In the village is a shop, a police post and a customs office that assesses duty on goods brought from Tibet. There is a good camp by the Bhalu Khola below Jagat.

Day 7: Jagat to Serson

Either rock-hop across the Bhalu Khola or go upstream and cross the suspension bridge. Climb over a rocky ridge to **Salleri**, a settlement of 10 houses and herders' huts. There are good views of Shringi Himal as you continue up along the side of a cliff. The trail descends to Setibas (Tara) at 1430 metres where a decrepit stone kani and several mani walls indicate that the trek is now entering a region of Tibetan influence, though the people are still Gurungs. The valley widens a bit as the trail continues up to the stone houses of **Ghatta Khola**. Cross the rock-strewn stream where several mills (*ghatta* in Nepali) spin merrily away.

The trail continues upstream to a long suspension bridge that looks just like the Golden Gate bridge in San Francisco. The best route around Manaslu crosses the bridge and follows a new trail on the eastern side of the river. The old (west bank) trail goes up to Pangsing, then climbs to **Ngyak** (Nyak), a Gurung village perched high above the river, then descends and climbs over another ridge before rejoining the new trail. From a distance, Nyak does not seem interesting

enough to visit; I have not met anyone who has been there.

Cross the bridge and climb up to **Philim** (Dodang) at 1550 metres. This is a large Gurung village with fields of corn and millet. The trail that climbs through the village and heads up over a ridge leads to Ganesh Himal base camp. The valley behind Ganesh Himal is called Tsum and it is still off limits to foreigners. The people of Tsum are Tibetan and their valley is towards Tibet across two passes at the head of the Shar Khola ('east river') valley. The Manaslu trail turns north just above the lowest houses in the village and stays fairly level as it traverses millet fields to Serson.

Day 8: Serson to Deng

Beyond Serson the route enters a steep uninhabited gorge. The trail descends through grassy slopes dotted with tall pine trees. Cross the Buri Gandaki on a wooden cantilever bridge where the river is at its narrowest. The trail now hangs on a cliff, climbing over ridges and descending to the river. If you have the courage to take your eyes off your feet you can see the Shar Khola joining the Buri Gandaki on the opposite bank. The trail then makes its way up the western side and the valley finally widens, offering a pleasant walk through bamboo forests to the Deng Khola and the tiny village of Deng. You have now traversed across the main Himalayan range. The trail follows the Buri Gandaki Valley as it turns from north-south to east-west. This region is known as Kutang and is inhabited primarily by Gurungs who practise Buddhism.

Day 9: Deng to Ghap

A short distance beyond Deng the trail recrosses the Buri Gandaki onto what is now the north bank near Rana. There is a rudimentary shop at **Rana** (elevation 2000 metres), near the bridge. Several villagers also have stashes of provisions in their homes; a bit of inquiry will produce almost anything that you might need. Japanese-influenced maps call this village Lana, but the locals insist that the correct name is Rana.

From the bridge the trail climbs a bit to join a trail from Bhi, then heads west up the Buri Gandaki Valley. It's level for a bit, then the route climbs on steps past a waterfall. Cross the stream on a crooked wooden bridge, then drop to another stream that flows in a steep narrow canyon. Contour up and out of the canyon for a view of the Buri Gandaki looking like a tranquil lake above a bunch of rocks that form a dam. The trail darts in and out of two ravines, then continues to climb high above the river before dropping into the Shringi Khola Valley. There are a few houses above steep cliffs on the opposite side of the river that are accessible via a bridge that crosses the Buri Gandaki here.

Cross the Shringi Khola on a funky suspension bridge, then climb steeply and traverse above the Buri Gandaki where it flows between vertical rock walls. The trail makes more ups and downs in forests, passing an occasional house or mani wall, then turns a corner and contours to Ghap (Tsak). The trail passes through a kani (arch-shaped chorten) with intricate, well-preserved paintings on the inside, then through corn and wheat fields below Ghap's half dozen stone houses.

The mani wall in Ghap has particularly elegant carvings said to have been made by a family of stone carvers from Bhi, high on the hillside above. Many of the carvings depict the Buddha in various meditative poses and others are of the Tibetan saint Milarepa who is said to have travelled and meditated in this valley. The stone in this region is quite hard, so the carvings do not have the deep relief that is typical of mani walls throughout other parts of Nepal and Tibet. The trail from Ghap crosses the Buri Gandaki to the south side on a 26-metre-long blue steel trestle bridge at 2100 metres.

There is an alternative route from Deng to Ghap that stays on the south bank of the river, passing through the village of Prok before rejoining the trail here.

Day 10: Ghap to Namrung
Pass more mani stones on the south side of the river, cut across fields and head into the woods. Pass a few houses and three streams in a forest of big firs alive with birds, including the *danphe* or impeyan pheasant, Nepal's colourful national bird. On the north side of the river is the Tom (Tum) Khola which flows in a deep gorge from Tibet, almost doubling the flow of the Buri Gandaki. The trail climbs alongside the river past two long mani walls to a waterfall. There is a lot of trading between villages in this region and villages higher in the Buri Gandaki valley and also with Tibet. Most of this trade is by caravans of horses, yaks and yak crossbreeds that stomp the trail into muddy bogs. There are some interesting rock-hopping exercises along this stretch of trail if you want to keep your feet dry. You'll need to climb over a large rock to avoid one big mud hole, then continue up through deep fir and rhododendron forests.

In the middle of the forest is a wooden bridge that spans the Buri Gandaki. The river has cut through the rock and thunders through a steep narrow crevice below the bridge. The bridge crossing is made more exciting by the lack of handrails. The trail climbs on the northern side to a big rock cave, then crosses the river again on another wooden bridge under the watchful eyes of a tribe of grey langur monkeys. Back on the south bank the trail makes a long serious climb through bamboo and rhododendron forests, finally entering Namrung (Namdru) through a stone archway at 2660 metres. This village has lovely stone houses and a police checkpost that controls access to the upper part of the valley. This is a border police station which takes its work seriously. Your liaison officer will see that the police stamp your trekking permit and take care of the rest of the formalities. The trail drops past a small dilapidated schoolhouse to a stream. There are excellent camps in the forests to the right of the trail. There is another part of Namrung across a bridge.

Day 11: Namrung to Shya
Beyond Namrung the trek enters the Nupri region. The people of Nupri are all descen-

dants of Tibetan immigrants and most dress in *chubas*, the Tibetan-style wraparound cloak. Climb past a mani wall and the many fields and houses of **Barcham** (Bartsam), then up through a forest of firs, rhododendron and oak to a promontory. The trail passes through a stone arch and enters the closely packed houses and wheat fields of **Li** at 2900 metres. There is a gompa on the side of the trail and another above the village.

The stone houses of Li exhibit the unusual architecture of this region. They are grouped together like apartments into units of five or six that share a common roof and courtyard. Most roofs are made of heavy wood shingles. Unlike the shingle roofs in other regions of Nepal, these are not piled with rocks to keep them from blowing away. The people say that there are rarely strong winds in this valley.

The trail leaves the village through a kani, then makes a long sweep into a wooded canyon. Cross the Hinan Khola on a double-span cantilever bridge, then huff and puff back up to another kani and the closely packed houses of Sho. By this time you will have been hassled by children asking for *shim shim*. This is Tibetan for sweets or candy and the demands increase from here until you leave the Buri Gandaki Valley.

The views now start to get spectacular. Manaslu, Manaslu North (7154 metres) and Naike peak appear at the head of the valley. The villages on the opposite side of the river are Shonju and, further to the west, Tong. The trail crosses a small ravine to a big prayer wheel in the middle of the trail, then climbs through more fields to the small settlement of **Shrip**. The strange-looking platforms in the fields are watchtowers where people sit all night to scare bears away from the crops. The trail then climbs past a small stream crowded with dirty kids in tiny chubas collecting water to **Lho** (Lö) at 3100 metres. Lho is a big village with a gompa, a rough stone archway at the entrance and a Tibetan-style chorten and huge mani wall at the western end. There's a spectacular view of Manaslu from the kani above Lho.

Drop down to the Damonan Khola, cross-ing it on a two-span bridge near some mills and the trail starts to ascend again. It follows the north fork of the stream up for a long distance through damp forests on ground that is either muddy or icy, depending on the season. (Don't take the left-hand trail that follows the south fork and ends up at Pung-gyen Gompa, the Pungen Glacier and the Manaslu east face base camp.) Finally the trail emerges onto a plateau at Shya (3520 metres) with a wide vista of Himalchuli, Ngadi Chuli (the Survey of India called this Peak 29) and Manaslu.

There is a chorten and a building housing a huge prayer wheel here. When I was here the prayer wheel was being built and I had the opportunity to see inside the wheel – its entire two-metre height was crammed with paper covered with prayers. The paper was carried from Kathmandu – or Tibet – and must have been many, many porter loads.

Shya is shocking because of the total deforestation in this area. Some time during the last 20 years there was a fire in this forest. This inspired the locals to hack down all the remaining trees, burned or not, to build houses – and the prayer wheel. The acres of blackened stumps creates a scene that is one of almost total desolation.

Day 12: Shya to Sama Gompa

Cross the ridge out of the stream valley to the Buri Gandaki side, trek in and out of a side canyon, then descend onto a rock-strewn moraine. Clamber across the boulders and emerge onto a ridge overlooking the extensive pastures and fields of **Samagaon** (Rö). Sama Gompa is visible in the distance nestled against a wooded moraine at the far end of the valley. Walk across fields of wheat and buckwheat past a chorten to a large yellow kani with bright, well-preserved paintings inside. The extensive village of Samagaon is nestled in the valley at an elevation of 3530 metres beyond the kani. Descend to a large collection of mani stones and walk through the village. Many houses have courtyards that overlook the trail, so you become immersed in the domestic affairs of the village during the trek through.

Weaving is a big occupation in Samagaon, and you will see many women working looms as you make your way through hoards of persistent 'shim shim' and 'give me pen' kids. Follow the stream that runs through the village and you will eventually pass through a kani and find yourself headed for the gompa. Climb up to the many buildings and residences of the gompa and on to a camp in a large field beyond. When I stayed here we were terrified of the howling winds that we could hear in the distance, though there was no wind in the camp. It took us until the following day to discover that what we thought was howling wind was only the roar of the Buri Gandaki echoing off the sides of the valley.

If you have a day to spare, climb the ridge to the south of Samagaon to the Pung-gyen Gompa, which is hidden behind the ridge in front of Manaslu. The Japanese call this Honsansho Gompa. It was destroyed by an avalanche during the winter of 1953 after the first Japanese expedition to Manaslu, killing 18 inhabitants, mostly nuns. The villagers believe that the god residing on Manaslu destroyed the gompa to show his wrath for the trespassers and refused to let the second Japanese expedition to Manaslu climb the mountain in 1954.

Day 13: Sama Gompa to Samdo
Descend to the Buri Gandaki, which has now turned north again, and follow it to a bridge over a side stream. There is a trail to the left that leads to the Manaslu base camp. The Larkya La trail passes several mani walls as the valley begins to widen. It's an easy trail on a shelf above the river past juniper and birch forests and the stone huts of **Kermo Kharka**, then it gets rougher as it reaches a ridge where yak trains have ground the trail into mush. Drop off the shelf, cross the river on a wooden bridge and climb steeply onto a promontory between two forks of the river. From a stone arch you can see a large white kani. It looks close, but it will take you a long time before you finally pass through the kani to find Samdo nestled behind a ridge at 3860 metres. There is a mani wall near the small

stone-roofed primary school and the closely packed stone houses of the village extend off to the east. Somewhere in the village a police checkpost lurks, but the police often head for warmer climes during the colder months of the trekking season. A major Tibetan trade route heads east through the village and over the Lajyang La at 5098 metres into Tibet, a day's walk from here.

Day 14: Samdo to Larkya Rest House
Descend on a wide gentle trail from Samdo past many fields to a big old mani wall and stone archway. Drop to the river, which is now very small and narrow, and cross it on a wooden bridge at 3850 metres. The Survey of India map shows the village of Larkya Bazaar located here; however, this village seems to have been a myth since there is not a house to be seen.

There is a fine old mani wall that marks the start of the climb to Larkya La. Climb gently through tundra and juniper opposite the huge Larkya Glacier that drops from Manaslu. After more than an hour of climbing, the trail becomes indistinct. Stay high on the ridge to the right and you will find a trail that crosses the top of two large ravines. The trail gets steeper and climbs the side of a ridge to about 4000 metres where there is a viewpoint at the edge of a huge gorge. You can see a single stone house in the distance and a row of abandoned houses, perhaps the remains of the mythical Larkya Bazaar (Babuk), far below. Before the political situation made it impossible, Sherpas from Namche Bazaar used to bring their yaks on a long trip via Tibet, then into Nupri, to trade.

Climb in and out of the gorge and contour to the only shelter on the route to the pass, a rest house at 4480 metres. The stone house is large enough for porters and a kitchen, but there is a real scarcity of flat places to pitch a tent. If you find yourself on a slope, place your clothing under your mattress on the downhill side to make a primitive hammock to keep you from falling out of bed all night.

Day 15: Larkya Rest House to Bimtang
The route starts up the ridge in front of the

rest house, eventually becoming a long gentle climb beside a moraine. Cross a small ridge, descend a bit to a lake, and keep climbing the ridge until you reach the top of the moraine at 4700 metres. The trail becomes rougher and indistinct as it crosses the moraine to the south of steep grassy slopes. There are a few cairns to mark the route, but if there is snow you will have a real route-finding problem. Stay on the moraine to a ridge with two cairns; you should be able to see the prayer flags on the pass from here. Descend to four frozen lakes, then make the final steep climb to the pass at 5100 metres.

I crossed the pass with a party of people from Samdo who were headed off to spend the winter in Tal, two days away in the Marsyangdi Valley. The group consisted of five Tibetan men, an old Tibetan woman, four yaks, a horse and a dog. At the pass they placed new prayer flags and celebrated by offering a ceremonial cup of chhang to everyone they could find.

It should take three to four hours from the rest house to the pass. It is best to make an early start in order to cross the pass safely. It can be extremely cold and windy during the climb and porters have perished on the Larkya La in snowstorms. The views are tremendous. The peaks to the west of the pass are Himlung Himal (7126 metres) Cheo Himal (6820 metres) Gyaji Kung, Kang Guru (6981 metres) and Annapurna II (7937 metres).

The descent follows along the top of a moraine to the west, then drops steeply and traverses scree slopes. It makes a long set of steep, rough, switchbacks, crosses the moraine and then descends more gently. There is a final long, steep, slippery descent on loose gravel to another grassy moraine at 4450 metres – a drop of 650 metres in little more than an hour. The trail becomes better and easier, descending along the grassy moraine to a small meadow and spring at 4080 metres. The trail turns a corner, the valley becomes larger, and the trail heads down to a large meadow, a mani wall, and a small rest house. This is Bimtang, a Tibetan name meaning 'plain of sand', elevation 3720 metres. The Survey of India maps this

place as Bimtakothi; Snellgrove suggests that the ending *kothi*, meaning 'settlement', seems to be the gratuitous addition of some Nepalese informant.

The ruins of a much larger building, said to have been two storeys high, are a mute testimony to Bimtang's earlier prominence as a major trading post. Tilman reports that during the season more than 3000 animal loads of goods were traded here. Bimtang was also a Khampa guerrilla staging area during the 1970s. This is a huge valley surrounded by high peaks – we heard many avalanches during the night.

Day 16: Bimtang to Gho
The trail drops from the Bimtang meadow and crosses a glacial stream, the headwaters of the Dudh Khola, on a wooden bridge. Climb over the side of the moraine and descend into a pine and rhododendron forest to **Hompuk** at 3430 metres.

The walking improves as the trail descends, switchbacking down to a fork of the Dudh Khola, then follows the river through forests to a goth at 3030 metres. The going stays easy to a stream at 2700 metres and the fenced fields of **Karche**. The trail crosses a landslide, then goes across fields before making a steep climb over a ridge decorated with prayer flags while the river loops around in a pronounced S shape below. The trail comes off the ridge in a big sweeping arc down to the riverbank at 2580 metres near a few houses and fields on the opposite side. A short distance beyond is the settlement of Gho, at 2560 metres, which boasts a real tea shop where our porters gorged themselves on the first dal bhat they had eaten in days. At the foot of the valley you can see part of Lamjung peak above the Marsyangdi Valley.

Day 17: Gho to Dharapani
Continue through fields, over a clear stream, past houses and more fields interspersed with rhododendron and oak forests. Do not cross a suspension bridge that crosses the

Dudh Khola; stay on the north bank as you trek into **Tilje** (Tiljet). The first building you reach is the school. Climb over a small ridge to the stone-paved village street and wind among the closely spaced houses of this large Gurung village to the communal water tap and the primitive *Hotel Samden* at 2300 metres. Leave the village through a stone arch, cross the Dudh Khola and trek along the river embankment.

As the trail descends through scrub forests the wall of the Marsyangdi Valley looms larger, and finally the houses of Dharapani become visible. Cross a wooden bridge back to the northern side of the Dudh Khola at 1930 metres and climb up through a chorten-shaped arch, past a mani wall to the *Himlung Hotel* in the centre of **Thonje** (Thangjet). You will need to allow time here for your sirdar and liaison officer to contact the police to show off the garbage they collected and obtain a 'clearance certificate' stating that you have fulfilled all the regulations related to restricted areas. The police post is on the paved village street.

To get to Dharapani turn left just beyond the hotel, pass the large tin-roofed high school and cross a long suspension bridge over the Marsyangdi. You end up at upper Dharapani, elevation 1920 metres. You would do well to stay here, perhaps on the grounds of the *Dharapani Hotel & Lodge,* to allow completion of the lengthy formalities, or you might trek south 10 minutes to Dharapani where the signboards advertise 'comfortable laundries'.

The remainder of the trek follows the first days of the Around Annapurna trek in reverse. By now you should be in good shape, and the trail is generally downhill, so you should be able to make a fast trek back to the roadhead.

Day 18: Dharapani to Syange
Trek south through the steepest part of the Marsyangdi Gorge.

Day 19: Syange to Bhulbule
Follow the Marsyangdi south into rice terrace country.

Day 20: Bhulbule to Besi Sahar
Trek to Besi Sahar and arrange transport back to Kathmandu.

Shey Gompa

The northern part of Dolpo is usually called Inner Dolpo and has always had an aura of mysticism about it, largely because of the metaphysical discussions of the region in Peter Matthiesen's book *The Snow Leopard.* Shey was closed to foreigners until 1992. One story cites the reason for closure as the large-scale theft of statues from monasteries several years ago.

The description of this trek was provided by Sushil Upadhyay who made an extended trek in this region, crossing from Phoksumdo Lake to Shey Gompa, then over some horrific passes to Kagbeni in the Kali Gandaki Valley. Despite the mysticism surrounding Shey and the 'crystal mountain', this is not a popular trek by any means. The harsh terrain, the physical conditioning necessary and the exorbitant fees for visiting this region have deterred most people.

Getting There & Away
The 'restricted' part of this trek starts from Ringmo village at the southern end of Phoksumdo Lake. To visit Shey you need to trek from Dolpo airport in Juphal or make a longer trek from Jumla. See the Western Nepal chapter for information on how to get to Phoksumdo Lake. The trek from Shey to Kagbeni is not open to foreigners, but you can make a loop trip by travelling north from Phoksumdo Lake to Shey and then returning via another route to join the Tarap trail between the Baga La and Numa La.

Special Rules
The permit for Shey is as expensive as Mustang – US\$700 for 10 days and US\$70 per day thereafter. It becomes especially expensive because the trek only takes five or six days to complete.

Day 1: Phoksumdo Lake to Phoksumdo Khola

From Phoksumdo Lake, the trail skirts the lip of the lake as it contours on a rocky ledge along the western bank. A precarious trail suspended on a gangway of wood supported on pegs driven into crevices in the rocks signals the remoteness of the area you are about to enter. Beyond a stream, the trail makes a steep climb onto a hillock overlooking the lake. It descends and continues above the lake on an up-and-down trail to a pine forest, then makes a steep descent to the westernmost edge of the lake. Where the Phoksumdo Khola enters the lake, there is a lush meadow that opens up into a long valley. Continue through the valley, crisscrossing the Phoksumdo Khola and avoiding thorn bushes. The valley has steep sides with tundra and occasional boggy marsh underfoot. Camp at a grassy knoll on the bank of the river.

Day 2: Phoksumdo Khola to Snowfields Camp

Continue along the level path through a glacial valley that now heads due north. At the confluence of the Phoksumdo Khola and another mountain stream there is an old wooden bridge. Here you should take the barely discernible path to the north-east up the valley. There is no trail, as such, so you need to climb over rocks and boulders and ford the stream that rushes down the steep incline of the valley. A long climb brings you to a sheep meadow where the trail veers up a steep ravine. A hard climb to the top brings you to yet another valley where you can see the Kang La, the pass leading to Shey Gompa. If you are in good shape and the porters agree, you might make it on to Shey on the same day, or you can camp before the pass in the place that Peter Matthiessen christened 'Snowfields Camp'.

Day 3: Snowfields Camp to Shey Gompa

Climb up the steep hill littered with slate towards the pass. The climb is physically demanding, especially when you slip and slide on the slate dump. From the top of the Kang La at 5400 metres elevation, you can look down upon a large valley which is bisected by a gushing river. Descend steeply to the valley floor and make a long meandering trek along the banks of the river, crossing and recrossing it several times. Notice the mud caves on the banks of the river and the hills overlooking the river. A red chorten heralds the gate to Shey Gompa. Continue along the path to a large meadow where hairy yaks and hundreds of sheep can be found grazing. There are a few nomads' huts. Cross the river for the final time across a quaint wooden log bridge and climb up to the Shey Gompa compound at approximately 4500 metres.

The gompa itself is not large, and there are no artefacts or paintings of note in its premises, except for an ancient Tibetan scroll that describes the myth of the crystal mountain and Shey Gompa. The monk who accompanied our trekking group managed to get hold of this manuscript and read it from cover-to-cover. According to the book, in a crater in the mountain ranges that dominate Shey Gompa, there is a holy lake. Making nine circumambulations of this lake turns the water into milk. A sip of this milk, and the pilgrim can see Mt Kailas in the distance.

A caretaker lives in a hut adjacent to Shey Gompa. To the east of the gompa, notice the trail that leads to Saldang village, and eventually to Kagbeni via Charkabhot. To the west of the gompa, a narrow yak trail climbs up the valley floor to the remote village of Phijergaon.

Humla to Mt Kailas

In May 1993 the governments of Nepal and China reached an accord that allowed the first treks across the border between the two countries. While it had been a route for Nepalese pilgrims for years, foreign trekkers were never allowed to trek from Nepal into Tibet. It has always been possible, however, to bend or ignore the rules. Early British

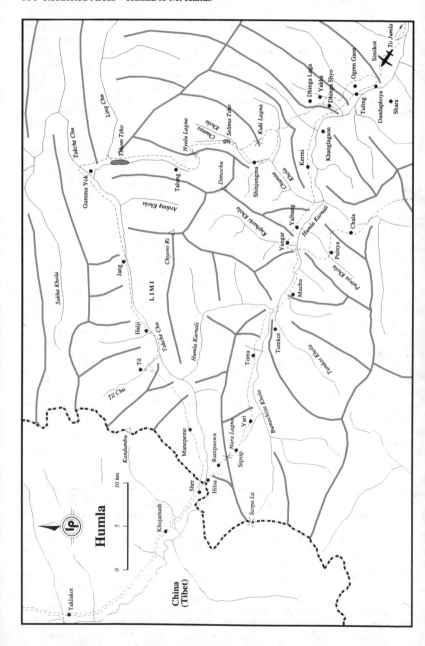

explorers visited Kailas in a variety of disguises, and numerous individual trekkers still manage to make their way from Tibet into Nepal each year.

Though the *raison d'être* for this trek is theoretically Mt Kailas in Tibet, the journey through Humla, Nepal's highest, northernmost and most remote district, is also culturally and scenically rewarding. The people of Limi in northern Humla are Bhotias whose roots are in Tibet and who still enjoy the freedom to graze their animals on the Tibetan plateau. The upper Humla Karnali Valley is also populated by Bhotias who trade extensively with Tibet in traditional ways that have totally vanished elsewhere. It is only near Simikot, the district headquarters, that you will encounter people of other ethnic groups, mostly Thakuris and Chhetris.

Because the area covered by this trek encompasses two countries and numerous ethnic groups and religions, most places have two or more names. I have used the most common local name and listed alternate names in parentheses.

A trip to Mt Kailas has always been regarded as a pilgrimage. It satisfies the romantic in us that the pilgrimage to Kailas is a difficult one. Whether you drive for seven days or walk for six days, it is still not possible to make a quick, easy visit to Kailas and Manasarovar. You cannot yet travel all the way to Kailas by helicopter or airplane. This is certainly as it should be.

History

Humla was once part of the great Malla Empire administered from Sinja near Jumla. Until 1787 this empire included Jumla and Purang (Taklakot) and extended as far west as Googay, the 'lost' villages of Toling (Zanda) and Tsaparang located in a remote Tibetan valley to the north of Nanda Devi, and Kamet Himal. Taklakot was once part of Nepal; on a map you can see the chunk taken out of the north-west corner of Nepal like a bite.

In Humla the traditional salt grain trade with Tibet continues much as it has for centuries. This trade has virtually ceased in the rest of Nepal because of the import of Indian salt and because China has eliminated many border trading posts in remote regions. The Chinese village of Purang, better known by its Nepalese name, Taklakot, is an important trading centre that is a short drive from both the Nepalese and Indian borders. Trade via Taklakot is an important factor in the economy of Humla, which is about a 15-day walk from Surkhet, the nearest Nepalese roadhead.

Taklakot is an extraordinary melting pot of Indian tourists, Chinese and Tibetan traders, Muslim traders from Kashgar, Nepalese entrepreneurs trading wool, salt and Indian goods, Chinese government officials and a huge army contingent. Plan on spending at least a day exploring this unusual frontier town.

Information

Books The following is a list of books which would provide good background reading for this area:

A Mountain in Tibet (London, André Deutsh Ltd, 1982) by Charles Allen
Himalayan Traders (John Murray, London, 1975) by Christoph Von Fürer-Haimendorf
Kailas – on Pilgrimage to the Sacred Mountain of Tibet (Thames & Hudson, London, 1989) by Russell Johnson & Kerry Moran
Kailas Manasarovar (Delhi, 1983) by Swami Pranavananda
The Sacred Mountain (East-West Publications, London, 1990) by John Snelling
Tibet – a travel survival kit (Lonely Planet Publications, Australia, 1992) by Robert Strauss
To the Navel of the World (Hamish Hamilton Ltd, London, 1987) by Peter Somerville-Large
Trekking in Nepal, West Tibet & Bhutan (Sierra Club Books, San Francisco, 1989) by Hugh Swift
Trekking in Tibet (The Mountaineers, Seattle, 1991) by Gary McCue
Vignettes of Nepal (Sajha Prakashan, Kathmandu, 1980) by Dr Harka Gurung

Maps Maps for this region include *Mid Western Region* 1:250,000, 1989 (HMG Suspension Bridge Division) and *Humla, Nepal* (1:250,000) sheet 44-7 from the National Remote Sensing Centre, 1986.

Food & Fuel It is important to remember that there is a shortage of food in Simikot, so you should arrange to send it ahead by plane or porter. You must use kerosene for cooking. Since this is usually not available in Simikot, and cannot be transported by plane, it requires advance planning. There is a reliable supply of kerosene in Taklakot, so you can arrange a porter caravan to bring Chinese kerosene from Taklakot and avoid the long haul from Surkhet.

Trekking Season This trek is possible only in the summer monsoon season from May to September. The entire region is snowbound in the winter; passes are closed and Taklakot itself is isolated until the snowplough arrives in late March.

Getting There & Away

Kathmandu to Nepalgunj There is no direct air service from Kathmandu to Simikot. You must first fly 1½ hours to Nepalgunj on the southern border of Nepal, spend the night, and take an early-morning flight to Simikot. See the Western Nepal chapter for suggestions on where to stay in Nepalgunj.

Nepalgunj to Simikot It takes about 50 minutes to fly the 218 km from Nepalgunj to Simikot, almost the entire breadth of Nepal, over a 3800-metre pass. Look for the 7031-metre Saipal Himal off the left side of the plane as you approach Simikot; you may also be able to spot Rara Lake some distance off to the right. Simikot (elevation 2910 metres) is on a ridge high above the Humla Karnali encircled by high snow-covered ridges.

The airstrip dominates the town, which is divided into four parts. South of the airport are government offices, a school, police headquarters, government guesthouse and a few shops. The main bazaar area, consisting of shops, a barber, bank and airline offices is just north of the runway. East and north-west of the bazaar are two large settlements consisting of flat-roofed houses, inhabited mostly by Chhetris.

Simikot is the headquarters of Nepal's most remote district, Humla, and the only major village for many days' walk. There is a continual stream of 'Humli' people from surrounding villages trading, buying supplies and dealing with various bureaucracies. To accommodate these travellers, there are several tea shops and restaurants and a few rooms for rent. Facilities are very much local style; there is nothing that even approaches the standard of the poorest trekkers' hotels in the Annapurna or Everest regions. Even though Simikot itself has been open to trekkers for years, in 1993 the only English signboards were those of airlines. Electricity is supplied by a huge bank of solar panels north-east of the airport; this system provides electricity to the town for about four hours a night.

Surkhet to Simikot If you want to walk to Simikot, start in Surkhet and walk for about 15 days.

When our Sherpa crew embarked on their trek from Surkhet carrying kerosene supplies for our trek, they promptly got themselves lost in the remote district of Kalikot, a good 10 days' walk from Simikot. The villagers had never seen a trekking crew before and believed them to be merchants out selling kerosene. Many locals, particularly high-caste Thakuris, boarded up their houses when the Sherpas inquired if they could buy some food. The more helpful ones said it would take a month to reach Simikot. When asked for directions, the reply was, 'follow the waves of the Karnali'. Knowing that we were scheduled to fly to Simikot very soon, the hardy crew decided to stay on the hill trails, instead, and literally walked day and night to reach Simikot after a 12-day ordeal.

Transport to Taklakot & Darchan (Tibet) If you are headed for Kailas, you should arrange in advance for a vehicle to transport you from the Nepalese border at Sher to Taklakot where Chinese immigration and customs formalities are centred. You will also want to arrange transport for the 100-km drive to Darchan at the foot of Mt Kailas. A travel agent in Kathmandu that specializes in Tibet should be able to assist you with this at the same time they arrange your Chinese visa.

The Tibetan plateau is harsh, windy and

barren. It makes little sense to walk huge distances in such inhospitable country.

Special Rules

The area is subject to the same regulations as other restricted areas. You must trek as part of an organised group with a liaison officer. The trekking permit fee for the trek from Simikot to the border and back is US$90 for the first week and US$15 per day thereafter. The permit becomes complicated because there is a break in the Nepal trek while you are in Tibet. When I trekked here the immigration office issued two trekking permits with dates 10 days apart, one for the trip to the border and the other for the return.

You need a Chinese visa if you plan to cross the border. This will be arranged at the same time you organise transport within China. The rules for individual travel in China if you enter via Taklakot are still unclear. You will also need a re-entry permit for Nepal in order to avoid excessive visa fees. Your liaison officer can stay behind in Nepal or Taklakot while you go to Mt Kailas, though you must continue to provide food, accommodation and salary.

SIMIKOT TO TAKLAKOT (TIBET)
Day 1: Simikot to Tuling

This is a short day. Hopefully, your flight has arrived in Simikot in the early morning and you are ready for a half day of trekking. Start climbing from the Simikot airstrip at 2960 metres past wheat and barley fields on a rocky trail bordered with cannabis and nettles. Trek past the stone houses of upper Simikot and the community water supply. It does not look far, but it's a long 300-metre pull to the top of a forested ridge overlooking

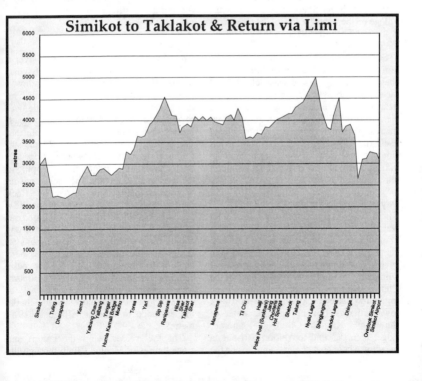

the town. The trek then makes a long, steep descent on a rocky switchbacking path, passing above the rooftops of **Dandaphoya**. The village on the opposite side of the river is Shara. Continue past a single house, then on to Tuling, also known as Majgaon, a compact Thakuri village at 2270 metres. There is a small campsite about a half hour beyond the village. At these lower elevations among unsanitary villages, flies are a real nuisance.

Day 2: Tuling to Kermi

The trail is reasonably level, and walnut and apricot trees provide welcome shade, as the trek passes through **Dharapani**. The two parts of this scattered village are separated by the Yakba Khola; there is a police checkpost in the upper part. It's a long, rough traverse across a scree slope to a stream. Below the trail a bridge over the Humla Karnali leads to Khanglagaon, a Thakuri village on the opposite side of the river. This is the last Thakuri village in the valley and the upper limit of rice cultivation.

Stay on the north side of the river as the trail snakes up and down to **Chachera**, a shepherds' camp near a waterfall at 2350 metres. Climb over a ridge past swarms of lizards sunning themselves as you approach Kermi, situated beside a stream at 2690 metres. The route bypasses Kermi village itself; the only camp nearby is below the left side of the trail about 10 minutes beyond the village. There is a hot spring about an hour's climb above Kermi.

Day 3: Kermi to Yangar

Climb over a ridge into a big valley with walled potato and buckwheat fields, then climb through a sparse pine forest to a rock cairn on a ridge at 2990 metres. Make switchbacks down to an extensive growth of wild marijuana and nettles on the bank of the Chumsa Khola. Cross the stream on a huge log, climb a steep rocky ridge and drop back towards the fast-flowing, light grey waters of the Humla Karnali. Climb over another ridge, then descend to **Yalbang Chaur**, a meadow where goat herders camp beside the

river at 2760 metres. In November there is an annual trade fair, or *mela*, at this site.

Above this sandy meadow the Humla Karnali Valley narrows and the sides become quite steep. Climb over two more ridges to **Yalbang** village at 2890 metres. The trail follows an irrigation canal to a huge rock just to the north of the village. Yalbang shares a hydroelectric power supply with its neighbour Yangar, a few km away. Take the lower, left-hand fork and contour up and around to a house and horse pasture on the ridge. Below, you can see a bridge over the Humla Karnali and a ridiculously steep trail on the opposite side that leads to Puiya (Poyun), the village where Yalbang people live during the summer. This is also a trade route to the once important Humli trading centre of Chala and on to Bajura south of Humla. Climb over another ridge at 2930 metres and descend gradually to the extensive fields surrounding the compact village of Yangar at 2850 metres.

Day 4: Yangar to Torea

An old route followed a steep trail over a 3500-metre-high ridge, the Illing La, beyond Yangar. Fortunately you can now follow a new, lower path that avoids the climb. The trail passes through the compact settlement of Yangar, in some places in tunnels beneath houses, then climbs behind a rock spur to a fast-flowing stream. Decline the old trail and follow the new route across a scree slope and out to the end of the ridge before dropping to the river at 2770 metres. The trail wends its way precariously close to the river on a track built up with rocks and wooden props and a few stretches where the path was blasted out of the cliff. After more than an hour of ups and downs you will reach a new suspension bridge at 2800 metres. Cross to the south bank of the Humla Karnali and a big rocky camp beside the river. Climb to a stream, rock-hop across it and ascend past apricot orchards to a totally defunct kani that marks the entrance to **Muchu** village at 2920 metres.

The trail passes below the gompa and stone houses of Muchu. Climb through the orchards and fields of the village to a ridge, then drop into a ravine and climb to a chorten on the opposite side. There are a few houses on the ridge and a border police post hidden just behind it. The ridge near the chorten offers a good view of the upper part of the valley and of Tumkot village (also known as Mota Gompa) and its large white gompa on the next ridge. Enjoy the next easy stretch of trail as it contours down to the Tumkot Khola, follows the rocky stream bed for a short distance, then crosses it on a log bridge. Don't climb the hill towards Tumkot; follow the trail around the foot of the ridge and cross the Bumachiya Khola on a wooden bridge at 2900 metres. The Humla Karnali disappears into a steep cleft to the north behind a high ridge that provides you with the opportunity to climb uphill for the next two days.

The first part of the climb from the Bumachiya Khola is quite steep. About half an hour up there is an obvious trail junction. Take the lower, left-hand trail. The upper trail, which eventually rejoins the lower trail, is a short cut for goats. The route enters a steep rock-filled gully; it's a long, slow slog up to a ridge at 3270 metres. The path levels out as it ascends to a cairn at 3310 metres, then descends gently through juniper trees and climbs again to Palbang, a single teahouse at 3380 metres. Palbang has a Nepali name, Torea, after the bright yellow mustard (tori) fields that surround it. There's a field above the teahouse that may be available for use as a camp.

Day 5: Torea to Sipsip

From Torea the trail ascends to a stream and a campsite deep in goat droppings, then contours up to a small cairn at 3660 metres where a few policemen maintain order from a tent. Rounding a ridge you can see the extensive fields of Yari. The trek follows an irrigation canal into the huge valley of the Jhyakthang Chu, marked by a mani wall at 3640 metres. Climb gently to Yari, a compact settlement of stone houses, a police post, customs office and a schoolhouse just below the trail at 3670 metres. The police post is the last in Nepal and maintains a register of the comings and goings of both locals and foreigners.

In upper Humla they grow two kinds of millet – finger millet (kodo) and common millet (chinu) – and two kinds of barley – 'naked' Tibetan barley (uwa) and regular 'bearded' barley (jau) – amaranth (marcia), wheat, buckwheat (phaphar), potatoes and radishes. In the lower portions of Humla they grow winter barley; in higher villages such as Yari, only one crop per year is possible.

Himalayan Barley

At elevations above 3000 metres barley becomes one of the most important grains. Although barley is cultivated widely at lower elevations, it is less important there because other grains are available. Above 3300 metres barley assumes a vital role because it is the only grain that thrives at high altitudes. The upward limit of barley cultivation in Nepal is around 4200 metres in Dolpo and in Dingboche. In the Tingri and Gyantse counties of Tibet it is found as high as 4700 metres.

After threshing, barley corns are dry roasted and ground into a meal called *sattu* or *tsampa*. The roasting is accomplished by sifting the corns in a basin of hot sand. Tsampa is eaten with tea, milk or yoghurt, sometimes with savoury dishes.

Another common use of barley is to produce the highlanders' beer called *chhang*. Barley, although coarser than wheat, is occasionally mixed with other grains to make bread. It is an extremely nutritious grain with a fairly high protein content, and is considered by Himalayan peoples to be a heat-producing food.

Tibetan-speaking ethnic groups classify the several thousand generic strains of barley into a threefold system. This system is based on the colour of the grain (red, white, black), the length of time the barley needs to ripen (90 to 130 days) and its morphology (bearded, naked, fat grain, slim grain). 'Naked' or 'beardless' Tibetan barley is called *uwa* in Nepali, and regular, 'bearded' barley is *jau*. ■

To the west of the village a trail leads to Sarpa La, a less-frequented route to Tibet. This is the way the Khampa leader Wangdi travelled in 1975 in an attempt to escape into India after the USA removed its support of the Tibetan resistance. He crossed into Tibet at an unmonitored and isolated corner and recrossed into Nepal via Tinkar Pass south of Taklakot where he was ambushed by the waiting Nepalese army.

From Yari the trade route climbs the broad valley to the source of the village's extensive irrigation system that is carried in a series of channels and wooden conduits. There's a flat spot and possible camp at an elevation of 4000 metres, but it's better to continue towards the pass to make the following day easier. There's a meadow and stream at 4160 metres and another meadow, Sipsip, near the foot of the pass at 4330 metres. Despite the remoteness of this location, there is a considerable amount of traffic. You will probably be travelling in the company of several contingents of traders, pilgrims and pack animals (goats, sheep, horses and yaks).

Day 6: Sipsip to Taklakot

The trail makes a steep, continuous ascent along the side of the ridge above Sipsip to a huge rock cairn atop the Nara Lagna at 4580 metres. I measured this pass with both a GPS and an altimeter (see the Getting Around chapter for details on these instruments) and found it to be well below the 4902-metre elevation shown on the Survey of India and US army maps. In 1979 Dr Harka Gurung correctly identified this discrepancy without the aid of any instruments. Snow usually closes the pass from November to April.

A short distance below the pass you will round a ridge for a view of the Tibetan plateau, the Humla Karnali and the green barley fields of Sher (also called Shera) far below. The descent is tolerable as far as Ranipauwa, a hotel in a tent at 4370 metres. Beyond Ranipauwa the trail consists of steep loose pebbles that either wear the bottoms off your boots or provide a natural ball-bearing surface that shoots your feet out from under you. You've done well if you make it down

this hill without a few slips and slides. The trail contours around a large canyon before making a final steep, dusty drop to the Humla Karnali at 3720 metres. It is a walk of only a few minutes along the river to **Hilsa** – a couple of tents and stone houses surrounded by barley fields.

A stone pillar that marks the Nepal/Tibet border is just across a rickety wooden bridge, perhaps one of the most informal border crossings in the world. Climb a short distance to **Sher** a Tibetan salt-trading post at 3860 metres where, if you have made prior arrangements and all goes well, you will find a jeep waiting for you to make the 1½-hour drive into Taklakot. All of China is on Beijing time, which is 2¼ hours later than Nepal time, so set your watch accordingly. Because the Ngari region of Tibet is so far west of Beijing this means that it's dark when you arise at 7 am and light until about 10 pm during the season for this trek in July and August.

Sher is where Humli people sell wood and rice from Nepal. The illegal trade in wood beams further helps to deplete Nepal's forest resources. The grain/salt trade is responsible for the thousands of goats you have seen on the trail, each carrying up to 10 kg. Humli people make as many as six or seven trips a year and traders from throughout western Nepal make a single trip each year exchanging one measure of rice for two measures of salt. Somehow this turns out to be a profitable trip, though it is baffling that it is so.

The Drive from Sher to Taklakot

From the Nepalese border at Sher the road makes a long descent to a stream and some mills, then follows the Humla Karnali to **Khojarnath** at 3790 metres. Khojarnath is the first large village in Tibet and boasts an important gompa of the Sakya sect. This gompa escaped most of the excesses of the Cultural Revolution, though the silver statues and other items described by early travellers have disappeared. The new statues are of Chenresig (Avalokitesvara), Jambyang (Manjushree) and Channadorje (Vajrapani). The monks, familiar with Indian

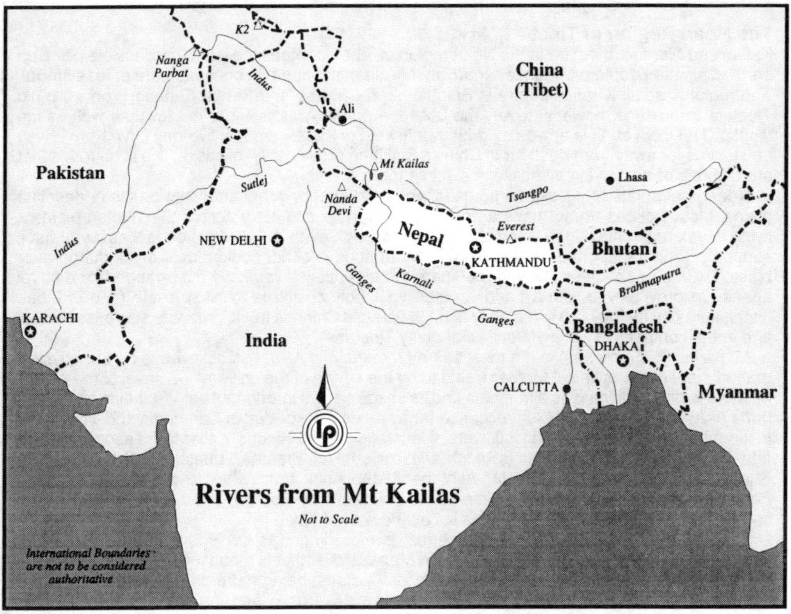

Rivers from Mt Kailas

Not to Scale

International Boundaries
are not to be considered
authoritative

pilgrims, explain these gods as the Buddhist manifestations of Ram, Laxman and Sita.

Also of interest in the gompa are the stuffed carcasses of a yak, Indian tiger, snow leopard *(chen* in Tibetan) and wolf *(changu)* hanging from the ceiling. These are also replacements dating from 1985.

The road climbs over a 4000-metre pass where 13 Humli porters were killed in July 1993 when a truck carrying two dozen Nepalese passengers on top of a load of salt turned over. The route then passes Kangtse which has a gompa on a nearby hill. Ford the Kangtse Chu and the Gejin Chu and drive on to Gejin and Kirang villages before reaching Taklakot at 3930 metres.

Taklakot

Taklakot, which the Chinese and Tibetans call Purang, is a large trading centre and is composed of many distinct settlements. The route from Sher enters from the south along a walled road lined with willow trees. This is the Chinese section of town where the bank, police (including immigration and public security), post office and tourist hotel are located. There are two decent restaurants in this part of Taklakot, both with English signboards saying 'dining room'. The northernmost one, apparently run by the army, is best. There are a few hole-in-the-wall shops along the road, but for any real purchases you must go to the bazaar near the Karnali River bridge, about a km away. Here you will find more restaurants, an amazing collection of snooker parlours, and Chinese-run shops trying to sell polyester clothing to Tibetans, Nepalese traders and Indian pilgrims. Nearer the road are at least two department stores that carry pots, pans, TVs and bolts of cloth.

On the opposite side of the Karnali is **Humla Bazaar**, a collection of Nepalese hotels, restaurants and small shops. For serious purchases of food and supplies, walk 15 minutes over the hill to **Darchula Bazaar**, an extensive collection of shops with mud

---

The Ngari Region of Tibet

Kailas and Manasarovar are in the Ngari region of Tibet, perhaps the most inaccessible place on earth. Chinese people pronounce 'Ngari' as 'Ali,' so this name has become more or less official. The region's administrative centre is Shiquanhe in Chinese and Senge Khabab ('lion town') in Tibetan. In practice, however, everyone uses the name 'Ali' to refer to the town as well as the district. The town of Ali is a two-day drive north-west of Kailas, a dusty five-day drive from Lhasa and just as far away from Kashgar in China's Sinkiang province. All of this driving is on roads that are capable of destroying a vehicle in a single trip.

Ngari is populated by Dokpas, nomads who herd sheep, goats and yaks on these desolate plains. Most Dokpas do not have a house; they wander endlessly across the Tibetan plateau, living in yak hair tents. Ngari is the last frontier of Tibet; even in Taklakot you feel as if you have suddenly been transported back in time. In Ngari, food is either cooked over a yak dung fire or blasted with a petrol-fuelled blowtorch. There are no buses; if you have not arranged for a travel agency to provide you with a Land Cruiser, your only choice is to hitch a ride (and in Tibet, hitchhikers pay for the ride) in the back of a 1950s-style Chinese truck, probably atop piles of wool and in the company of several families of dusty Tibetans.

Mt Kailas (6714 metres) is the most sacred mountain in Asia. It is believed to be the physical embodiment of the mythical Mt Meru, said to be the centre of the universe or 'navel of the world'. Mt Meru is often depicted as a mandala and its image occurs throughout both Buddhist and Hindu parts of Asia. Images of Mt Meru occur as far away as Angkor Wat in Cambodia and Borobadur in Indonesia. Mt Kailas is holy to followers of four religions. To Hindus, Kailas is the abode of Shiva and nearby lake Manasarovar is the *manas* or soul of Brahma. Tibetans call Kailas Kang Rimpoche; Jains worship it as Mt Ashtapada, the peak from which the religion's founder, Rishabanatha, achieved spiritual liberation. Followers of Bon-po, the ancient pre-Buddhist shamanistic religion of Tibet, revere Kailas as the soul of Tibet.

Lake Manasarovar, elevation 4510 metres, is more important to Hindus than to Buddhists. Hindu pilgrims make an 85-km circuit around Manasarovar that is made longer and more difficult by marshes and complicated stream crossings. Tibetans, being more pragmatic, often make a circuit of the lake in the winter when the streams are frozen and the route is shorter. Near Manasarovar is another large lake, Rakshas Tal, the 'Demon Lake,' that holds far less spiritual significance.

Another geographical factor that contributes to the mystical aspect of Kailas is that nearby are the headwaters of four major rivers of the Indian subcontinent, the Sutlej, Karnali (a major tributary of the Ganges), Brahmaputra and Indus. The mouths of these rivers are more than 2000 km apart, yet they all have their source within 100 km of Mt Kailas.■

---

walls and white canvas roofs. A large trade in Tibetan wool is conducted here; the wool is rolled into huge balls. There is one street for white wool and another street for black wool, also streets for Indian tinned food, cloth and necessities like rice, sugar and flour. The focus of trade is with the Darchula district of Nepal, several days' walk to the south, though many goods from India also appear here. Indians are not allowed the same freedom as Nepalese to trade in Tibet, so Darchula people dominate this market.

As you trek back from Darchula Bazaar you will see the remains of Simbiling Gompa on the hill overlooking Taklakot. In 1949 Swami Pranavananda described this gompa, housing 170 monks, as the biggest monas-

tery in the region. There is nothing left of Simbiling after the destruction and shelling of the Cultural Revolution except a forlorn mud relic. In the hills along the trail there are caves, one containing the Gokung Gompa, and others which are used as houses. Many caves have been equipped with doors and windows and are quite substantial dwellings. On the hill to the north-west of Taklakot is a huge army base, said to extend far into the mountain in a series of caves. You will meet hundreds of People's Liberation Army (PLA) soldiers in their baggy green uniforms throughout Taklakot in shops, restaurants and snooker parlours.

To the north of the snooker parlour street are Tibetan stalls selling goats, yaks, wool

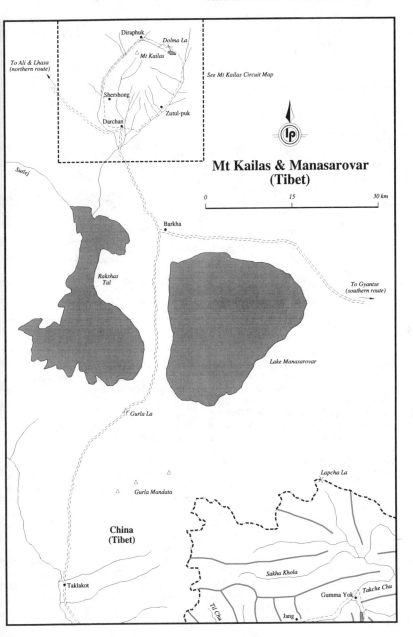

To Ali & Lhasa
(northern route)

Diraphuk

Dolma La

Mt Kailas

See Mt Kailas Circuit Map

Shershong

Zutul-puk

Darchan

**Mt Kailas & Manasarovar
(Tibet)**

0   15   30 km

Sutlej

Barkha

To Gyantse
(southern route)

Rakshas
Tal

Lake Manasarovar

Gurla La

Gurla Mandata

Lapcha La

China
(Tibet)

Taklakot

Sakha Khola

Til Chu

Jang

Gumma Yok

Takche Chu

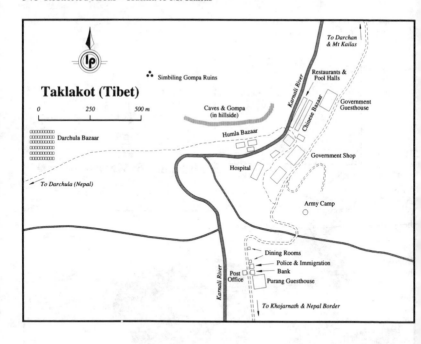

and other items of strictly local interest. Sheep are slaughtered by tying their long snout tightly shut so they suffocate. This somehow absolves the Tibetans of having taken a life. When our sherpas went shopping for meat, a Tibetan astonished them by grabbing a yak-hair rope and lassoing a nearby sheep without rising from his seat. The deal was not consummated, however, since we only wanted a bit of meat, not an entire sheep.

In Taklakot, transactions are conducted in Chinese yuan as well as both Indian and Nepalese rupees. There is an unofficial rate of about eight Nepalese rupees to the yuan, which the Nepalese call a *sukur*. To our embarrassment, we discovered that the local bank had never heard of travellers' cheques.

The region around Taklakot is dotted with traditional Tibetan settlements that make up a sizeable population. On the full moon day in August 1993, a festival was held that included lama dancing in front of a huge picture of Chairman Mao. This fair attracted hundreds of people, many dressed in polyester track suits, but also numerous people in traditional Tibetan dress.

The Drive from Taklakot to Darchan

It is about 100 km from Taklakot to Darchan. From Taklakot the road climbs past many Tibetan-style settlements to the Gurla La at 4590 metres and on to Darchan at 4560 metres, 2½ hours from Taklakot. Much of the road is an ad hoc route made by drivers who created one where they saw fit, with only the straight line of telephone poles defining the way. At one point more than 15 parallel lines of vehicle tracks scar the plateau. This drive is best done in the morning; by afternoon the melting snows of Gurla Mandata (7728 metres) have caused streams to rise so high that fording them may be impossible. Watch for huge jack rabbits and wild asses *(kiang)* along the route.

Darchan

Only the top of Kailas is visible from Darchan; you must climb a ridge for a better view. Darchan guesthouse is pretty rough. There is a kitchen where you may be able to get a bowl of noodles, though it takes considerable investigation to find out how and when. Occasionally there is a shop open which sells beer, (sometimes) a few canned goods, miscellaneous useless items, souvenir stickers and enamelled Kailas pins. When we were here they had a late evening performance of Chinese and Hindi videos in a tent within the guesthouse compound. The Dolma Lhakhang Gompa and some basic Tibetan hotels, shops and camps are above the guesthouse compound.

Warning Beware of trekking according to the itinerary described in the Mt Kailas Circuit section and camping at 5200 metres elevation unless you have spent at least *two nights* at Darchan to acclimatise.

MT KAILAS CIRCUIT

Day 1: Darchan to Damding Donkhang

Trek west from the guesthouse compound high above the Barkha plain to a cairn and prayer flags at 4730 metres. This is the first of four *chaktsal-gang* ('prostration stations') on the kora and offers an excellent view of the peak.

Turn north up the valley of the Lha Chu, descending to **Darbochhe**, a tall pole adorned with prayer flags at 4750 metres. The prayer flags are replaced annually during a festival on Buddha's birthday, the full moon day in May. Nearby is **Chortenkangni.** It is considered an auspicious act to pass through the small archway formed by the two legs of this chorten. The trail continues across the plain to Shershong.

An hour past Shershong is a bridge leading to Chhuku Gompa high on the hillside above. All the monasteries on the Kailas circuit were destroyed during the Cultural Revolution. Chhuku Gompa was the first to be rebuilt and contains a few treasures that

---

Pilgrims to Mt Kailas

The circumambulation of Mt Kailas is an important pilgrimage for Hindus, Buddhists and Jains. Hindus perform a *parikrama,* Buddhists call it a *kora.* You are welcome to do either of these, or simply make a trek around the peak. Tibetan Buddhists believe that a single kora washes away the sins of one life and 108 circuits secure nirvana in this life. Devout Tibetans often make the 52-km circuit in a single day. Indian pilgrims make the circuit in three days, but this also is rushed, particularly since the circuit, though mostly level, involves the crossing of a 5630-metre pass. A four-day trek is far more enjoyable and rewarding.

An agreement between China and India allows 350 Indians per year to make the pilgrimage to Manasarovar and Kailas. The trip is so important to Hindus that the trips are oversubscribed and the quota is filled by lottery. They trek for nine days through India in order to reach Taklakot.

Hindu and Buddhist pilgrims make a clockwise circuit of the peak. Bon-po tradition is to circumambulate in the opposite direction. As you circle Kailas via the traditional route, you will meet followers of Bon-po making a kora in the opposite direction. When I was at Kailas there was a large contingent of Bon-po pilgrims from faraway Kham and Nakchu. We were astounded at the huge number of adherents to what has been described as an 'ancient pre-Buddhist' religion making the counterclockwise circuit.

The most pious of the pilgrims are those who prostrate themselves around Kailas, lying flat on the ground, then rising, walking to the point that their hands touched and repeating the process. It's an awesome spectacle to meet a group of pilgrims performing this feat.

There is also an 'inner kora' that passes two lakes to the south of Kailas. Tradition dictates that only those who have made 13 circumambulations of Kailas may follow this inner route. This tradition is so important to Tibetans that we were required to assure our hosts that we would not violate the sanctity of this route before they allowed us to proceed to Darchan. ■

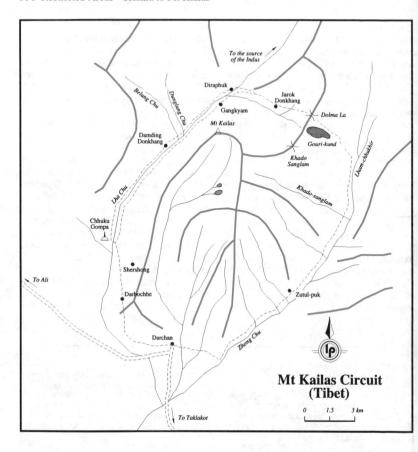

Mt Kailas Circuit (Tibet)

0   1.5   3 km

were rescued from the original gompas. The normal pilgrims' route stays on the east bank of the Lha Chu, but for better views of Kailas, and generally better campsites, cross the bridge and follow the west bank. The west-bank trail treks across scree slopes to a camp near Damding Donkhang at 4890 metres that offers a good view of the west face of Kailas.

Day 2: Damding Donkhang to Jarok Donkhang

Cross the side streams Belung Chu and Dunglung Chu on log bridges as the north

face of Kailas comes into view. On the opposite side of the Lha Chu you can see a stone guesthouse and camp. Several groups of nomads tend herds of goats and yaks nearby. Pass their tents carefully; like most Tibetans they keep ferocious Tibetan mastiff dogs. As you reach the gompa and frugal guesthouse at **Diraphuk** you are rewarded with a fine view of the north face of Kailas. This is the first night stop for Indian pilgrims.

Cross a bridge across the Lha Chu. If you were to trek up the valley of the Lha Chu you would eventually reach the true source of the Indus. The kora route now makes a serious climb onto a moraine, eventually meeting the trail from the east bank. The trail climbs more gently to a meadow full of fat marmots *(phiya)* at 5210 metres. This is a good camp that will make the pass-crossing easier than it would be if you camped at Diraphuk. It's dangerous to camp higher because of acclimatisation problems. The snow-covered pass to the right, the Khado-sanglam, is protected by a lion-faced *dakini* goddess. Pilgrims may cross this difficult pass only on their auspicious 13th circuit of the mountain.

Day 3: Jarok Donkhang to Zutul-puk

Climb past piles of clothing at **Shiva-tsal**, elevation 5330 metres. Tibetans leave an article of clothing or a drop of blood here as part of leaving their past life behind them. Continue past thousands of small rock cairns to a large cairn at 5390 metres and beyond to a stone hut and camp. The trail leads across a boulder field and up to the **Dolma La** at 5630 metres. A big boulder on the pass representing the goddess Dolma (better known by her Sanskrit name Tara) is festooned with prayer flags and streamers. It is traditional to leave, and take, something as part of the collection of coins, prayer flags, teeth and other offerings attached to the rock. This is the physical and spiritual high point of the kora. Money is pasted to the rock with butter and pilgrims make the requisite three circumambulations of the rock. This must be the world's largest collection of prayer flags. If you meet Tibetan pilgrims here you will probably be invited to join them for a picnic in celebration of completing the hardest part of the kora.

The trail is rocky at first, then begins a series of switchbacks as it passes lake Gourikund at 5450 metres. Devout Hindu pilgrims are supposed to break the ice and bathe in its waters. More switchbacks lead down to the valley and a stone guesthouse alongside the Lham-chhukhir at 5150 metres. There is a footprint of Buddha, called a *shapje,* nearby. Even though the trail is better and less marshy on the other side, stay on the west side of the river; it becomes too large below to cross back. The trek makes a long, gentle,

uninteresting descent of the valley. When crossing the stream of the Khado-sanglam you reach the third prostration station; look upstream for the only view of the east face of Kailas.

The Zutul-puk Gompa, a guesthouse, and camp are further down the valley at 4790 metres. *Zutul* means miracle and *puk* means cave. This gompa is named after a cave in which the saint Milarepa stayed, meditating and eating only nettles. Among the miracles he performed were adjusting the height of this cave to make it more comfortable. His footprint still remains on the roof. Here the river is known as the Zhong Chu.

Day 4: Zutul-puk to Darchan

Cross a bridge over a side stream from Kailas, then contour up as the river descends towards the plain. Make a dramatic exit from the river valley onto the plain at the last prostration station (elevation 4610 metres). Rakshas Tal glistens in the distance as you pass mani walls decorated with carved yak skulls. Trek a further 1½ hours to Darchan along the edge of the plain.

TAKLAKOT TO SIMIKOT VIA LIMI

This is a longer, harder route than the direct route to Simikot via Yari. Limi is a remote valley in the north of Humla inhabited by Bhotias. The people of Limi are sophisticated and well-to-do. They trade *pashmina* wool, which retails for about US$400 per kg, in India and export wooden utensils to both Tibet and India. Limi is isolated from the rest of Nepal by snow from November to April, so the primary focus of Limi's trade is through Taklakot. For this reason the trails to Tibet are far better maintained than the trails from Limi to Simikot. The last few days of this trek are tough going over high passes on rough trails. Don't attempt this route unless you are fit and well equipped – and have permission (which is not always given readily).

Day 1: Taklakot to Manepeme

The drive from Taklakot to Sher is about 1½ hours, so theoretically you will arrive in

Tibetan spinning a prayer wheel

Sher in time to do some trekking. However, with the time change and customs and immigration formalities, we ended up here at night and had to camp at Sher in a continual upriver wind. Set your watch back 2¼ hours to Nepal time and enjoy reasonable time again.

The Limi trail starts climbing from the salt-trading post where the road ends. If you plan to follow this route, do not descend to the Humla Karnali at Hilsa. By the time you trek there, Nepal may have built an immigration post in Hilsa, so you might have to go down to the river and then climb back into Tibet in order to start walking to Limi. Plan your departure from Sher carefully; it's about four hours from Sher to Manepeme and there is no possible camping place in between.

From the end of the road at 3800 metres, the trail starts steeply up across a barren slope, crossing unannounced into Nepalese territory. A pole with tattered prayer flags marks a ridge at 4120 metres and the end of the first steep climb. The trail contours along the side of the ridge high above the Humla

Karnali, making minor ups and downs to a ridge with a stone chorten at 4110 metres. Follow some switchbacks down, then cut across a slope dotted with scrub juniper. A well-maintained trail crosses a rock slide, then climbs above a recent landslide. Take the upper, new trail over the top of the landslide and drop down to meet the original trail on the opposite side. Manepeme is behind a ridge in a large side canyon near a stream at 3970 metres. It is not an ideal camp because the only flat spaces are deep in goat droppings, as are most campsites on this trek – though Manepeme is perhaps the worst case. Manepeme is named after a huge stone above the campsite that is carved (now rather faint) with the mantra *om mani padme hum*.

Day 2: Manepeme to Til Chu
From Manepeme the trail weaves in and out of ravines along the side of the valley, climbing gradually towards the foot of a rock cliff. Ascend along the foot of the cliff, climbing to a ridge at 4070 metres. The Humla Karnali turns south and flows through a steep gorge towards Muchu. The Limi trail now follows a tributary, the Takchi Chu.

The trail then drops into a gully and climbs onto another ridge at 4040 metres. The trail beyond here looks horrific – winding up a steep rock face onto what looks like a pinnacle. It's not as bad as it looks, just a long slow series of switchbacks that climb on a well-maintained trail over a ridge at 4120 metres. Look for blue sheep *(naur)* on the cliffs above. The trail descends from the ridge to Lamka, a stream and some tiny camping places (along with the requisite goat droppings) at 4000 metres.

Climb steeply again from Lamka to the Lamka Lagna at 4300 metres where there is a first view of the Limi Valley and the green fields of Halji in the distance. The trail descends to a tiny stream, then continues down and across a slope. Climb over two rocky ridges and make a short descent to two chortens that mark the end of the ridge above the Til Chu. The houses across the valley are Til Gompa; the lowest fields of Til village are also visible below. The main trail descends gently to the stone houses of Til, the first village since Sher, situated about an hour up the Til Chu at 3700 metres. To avoid Til, follow a steep trail downhill to join a lower trail that crosses the Til Chu and descends to a super campsite at its confluence with the Takchi Chu, elevation 3580 metres. Just east of this camp is a large pit lined with stones. This is a snow leopard trap and there is one near each village in the Limi Valley. When a cat has killed local livestock, villagers stake a goat in the pit. The theory is that when a snow leopard jumps in, the overhanging rock walls prevent its escape.

Day 3: Til Chu to Jang

Beyond the campsite the trail climbs a stone staircase over a rock spur, then drops back down to the Takchi Chu, crossing it on a wooden bridge at 3590 metres. The trail follows the river along its sandy bank to another bridge that leads back to the north side of the river at 3710 metres. It's a short walk past barley fields into **Halji** at 3670 metres. The trail bypasses the village, staying near the river in a pleasant plantation of willow trees. The unpainted stone houses of Halji are surrounded by extensive barley and wheat fields just behind a ridge in a large valley. The houses surround a white gompa that has a single red wall painted with a white inscription of *om mani padme hum* similar to the gompa at Khojarnath. Inside the gompa are numerous recently made statues and paintings. Photography has been prohibited in the gompa since a recent theft in Khojarnath.

Cross a low ridge that protects Halji from wind, and climb steeply to a ridge at 3850 metres. From there the descent to the police post at **Sunkhani** (also known as Tayen, at 3830 metres) is a gentle one. There's a reasonably good campsite five minutes beyond Sunkhani and another 15 minutes beyond that. The valley has become very rocky as the trail makes ups and downs. A series of irrigated barley fields mark the beginning of Jang, also called Jyanga or Jyangba, an impressive stone village with a white gompa at 3930 metres.

The people of Limi make wooden bowls from pine, birch and maple trees that grow on the south side of the river. You will probably see piles of these bowls drying in the sun. Surprisingly, Limi dominates the entire supply of wooden bowls to Tibet. High-quality bowls are made from the burls of maple trees. The scarcity of these burls in Limi has required people to find alternate sources of supply from Kumaon in northern India, yet the bowls are still manufactured in Limi.

When we visited Jang they were in the midst of a six-day-long celebration in honour of the birth of a son to one of the families in the village. The parents (in this case represented by the grandfather since the father was off tending his flock of sheep) had to provide food and drink for the entire village – though they were compensated through the ample donations that were offered.

There's a terrific camp 45 minutes up the trail. Climb gently to two small white chortens and a snow leopard trap that mark the eastern end of Jang. The river cascades though a narrow defile as it makes a steep drop. At the top of this cascade the route enters the upper portion of the Takche Chu valley where the river meanders across broad meadows. Jump across a small stream, pass three more chortens and you will arrive at a small stone edifice beside two more chortens at 4070 metres. The stone wall encloses a small hot spring. You can camp in the meadows nearby and spend the afternoon ridding yourself of the dust of Tibet. The long rows of white stones in the meadow were placed to form a path for an important rimpoche from Dehra Dun in India who visited Limi in the summer of 1993.

Day 4: Jang to Talung

Continue the trek across meadows, hopping across a few side streams. A short climb takes you over a rocky ridge, but the trail is mostly level and pleasant. The trail reaches a point that overlooks the river valley and turns north. The geography here is a bit confusing; you trek north along the Takche Chu to the only bridge, then turn south again. The trail north leads to the Lapcha La, once an important trade route from Limi into Tibet – and one that offers a short cut to Manasarovar Lake. The Chinese emphasis on Taklakot as a trade centre has left this route generally unused, though there is a Nepalese police post nearby that controls access to the pass. Turn right before the police post and head down to the river and a wooden bridge at 4160 metres. The trail rounds a ridge and turns south through country similar to Tibet, with marmots and nettles. To the south you can see the white sand of a moraine that forms the lake of Tshom Tsho.

Below this plateau was **Gumma Yok** (elevation 4170 metres), once the most important village of Limi. The village was abandoned many years ago; you can see the remnants of a few buildings here and there.

Climb onto the fine white sand of the moraine and drop to the other side above the huge lake, Tshom Tsho. The best trail bears left across meadows to a bridge over the Ling Chu, though you can wade the stream near the point where it enters the lake if you get lost – or if your feet are hot. Traverse scree slopes above the eastern side of the lake. This huge U-shaped valley rises in a series of steps created by ancient glaciers. Ascend the first of these into a flat valley at 4320 metres. Yak and sheep herders from both Humla and Limi have semipermanent settlements with Tibetan-style yak-hair tents at many places in the valley. They are not used to visitors, but stop and see if you can buy a cup of hot milk *(dudh* in Nepali, *oma* in Tibetan), yoghurt *(dahi)*, fresh cottage cheese *(serkum)* or dried cheese *(churpi)*. Climb another short steep slope to the next valley, a pasture and tent camp called Talung, at 4380 metres. You can camp here or a half hour beyond, on the last 'step' in the valley at 4450 metres.

Day 5: Talung to Shinjungma
Climb to the next valley and cross the meadows to the foot of the pass. The last of the shepherds' tents are visible at the foot of the huge glaciated peak Dimochu that dominates the head of the valley. Now the hard

work begins as you head east into a rocky valley at the foot of the climb to the pass. Grind your way uphill for about two hours to a collection of cairns and upturned rocks. From here, on a clear day, you can see Mt Kailas. Continue to the pass, Nyalu Lagna, at 4990 metres, crossing it in a north-easterly direction.

Below the pass the trail makes a U-turn and heads south, descending along the moraine to an attractive high altitude lake, Selima Tsho at 4570 metres. Make a long, knee-cracking descent on the moraine that formed the lake, eventually crossing two streams and reaching the valley floor at 4140 metres. Head east across alpine meadows to a wooden bridge over a large stream that enters from the north-west. When I trekked in this valley the herders in a nearby camp had just made temporary repairs to the bridge, which looked like it was going to be washed away at any moment by the fast-flowing, mud-coloured stream.

You are now presented with a choice. There is a steep short cut over a 4900-metre ridge to the east called the Kuki Lagna, or you can do as our local guide recommended and trek around the edge of the ridge, avoiding the extra climbing. The lazy person's trail follows a rocky route into a birch and rhododendron forest starting around 4050 metres – the first real vegetation since you left the Humla Karnali on the upward trek. Saipal Himal (7025 metres) looms in the distance to the south. Descend through forests on a steep trail to a primitive camp near Shinjungma at 3850 metres. The Chumsa Khola is fast and muddy in the afternoon because of glacial runoff, so it's a lousy water supply. There are a few clear side streams and springs in the area that a local guide can find for you. On the west side of the valley is a terrific rock face that rivals Yosemite in the USA.

Day 6: Shinjungma to Dhinga Laga
Descend further along the wooded Chumsa Khola Valley to an inconspicuous trail junction at 3780 metres. The larger trail (which you do not take) continues down the valley,

eventually reaching the Humla Karnali far below near Kermi. It was at the foot of this valley that you probably had lunch in the marijuana fields on the third day out of Simikot.

To go to Simikot, take the smaller, left-hand trail and start uphill. The trail becomes more prominent as it rounds a ridge and ascends through pine, then birch, forests alongside the Takchi Chu. Keep climbing through a rocky meadow at 4110 metres, then further to a bridge at 4220 metres. The trail from Kuki Lagna rejoins the route here. It's another hour of steep climbing to the Landok Lagna, the last major pass on the trek, at 4550 metres elevation. I crossed this pass in a rainstorm and complete whiteout, so I have no idea what the views are like.

Be careful of the trail as you descend. A few minutes below the pass a cattle trail that looks like the main trail heads down a gully to the left. Don't follow this; stay to the right on an indistinct trail that follows the ridge. The trail moves towards the right side of the ridge, dropping to a tiny stream at 4140 metres. Continue down the ridge, dropping off the end to a larger stream at 3940 metres. The trail gets better as it winds its way through a forest of big juniper trees covered with moss. Follow the wide trail down to a stream and a mill, crossing it on a wooden bridge at 3710 metres.

There is no camp here, so keep climbing. Trek up hard through oak, birch and rhododendron forest, ferns and wildflowers to a notch in a ridge at 3860 metres. Head north along the eastern side of the ridge through burned forest, climbing gently to a side ridge at 3890 metres that leads into a high alpine bowl. Trek downhill to a trail junction. The trail straight ahead leads to the upper village of Dhinga – a summer settlement called Dhinga Laga. The right-hand trail leads steeply downhill to a meadow and small pond surrounded by a forest of blue pines

and a good campsite – if the local people agree to allow you to camp in the village grazing land.

Day 7: Dhinga Laga to Simikot

Lace your boots up tightly in preparation for a rough day. From the meadow camp, trek onto the ridge for a view of the huge valley of the Yakba Khola. Turn south on a good trail that heads towards Dhinga Shyo, the lower, winter settlement of Dhinga. Most people of Dhinga have houses in both settlements. About half an hour below the ridge, at an elevation of 3400 metres, there is another inconspicuous trail on the left that heads downhill. Local people assured us that this is the part of the 'main' trail to Limi, though this is hard to believe as you plummet down through forests, duck under tree limbs, tear your clothing on thorn bushes and dodge stinging nettles. A tough, hot exercise lands you at the Yakba Khola and a bridge at 2630 metres. You can see the village of Yakba at the foot of the valley some distance upstream.

Follow a narrow, nettle-lined trail downstream, then start uphill. Climb and climb to a few houses at 3010 metres, eventually cresting the ridge at 3100 metres. The going is easier now as you walk around the ridge through groves of walnut trees to a tiny stream – the first available potable water and an opportunity for lunch.

The trail passes north above the scattered settlements of Ogren Gaon, passing several streams as it makes its way along the rocky slope. You can see the Humla Karnali far below as you ascend to the final ridge of the trek at 3270 metres. It's only a few minutes' walk to the junction of the Humla Karnali trail, and a few more minutes after that to the top of the ridge overlooking Simikot. Descend on the loose gravel of the trail to the village water supply, then down a clutter of loose rocks to the airport at 2960 metres.

Other Trekking Areas

As scenic, interesting, culturally enriching and historic as the major treks may be, you should consider a trek to other regions. Although there are restrictions involved with the issuance of trekking permits, and some areas are still closed to foreigners, there are many places in Nepal that are both fascinating and accessible.

Many trekkers make the mistake of varying their route by attempting a 5500 to 6000-metre-high pass. Upon reaching the pass they discover that they, their equipment or other members of the party are totally unfit for the cold, high elevation and the technical problems that the pass presents. Often the problems force the party to turn back, severely altering their schedule. In the end, they fail to reach their primary goal. It is best to plan a high-pass crossing after achieving the major goal of the trek – usually on the return to Kathmandu.

You need not go to a particularly remote region to escape heavily travelled trails. The major trade and trekking routes are the shortest way to a particular destination, but if you allow another few days it is possible to follow less direct, often parallel, routes through villages that are not even on the maps, in areas with less Western contact than the major trails.

In 1984 I visited an area less than a day's walk from an important trekking route. The local people insisted that I was the first trekker who had ever been there. Other foreigners had visited the region, of course, as engineers, doctors and teachers, but no foreigner had come there before simply to trek. There must be thousands of similar places in Nepal. Even in the 1990s I have trekked to many places where there were few, if any, other trekkers. Some of those places are described in this book, although some are not. It seems contradictory to leave the congestion of an urban area only to be overpowered by crowds in Khumbu and Manang during the high trekking season in October, November and April. By choosing an unusual destination during the high season or by trekking to popular places in the low season, you can recapture some of the spirit of unhurried life in the hills that so entranced early trekkers to Nepal.

On remote or exotic treks a guide is helpful, and it is almost imperative to carry your own food and the means with which to cook it. In areas that neither trekkers nor local porters frequent there are no bhattis. Food is available, but the time and effort necessary to scrounge out food and accommodation in homes can make progress almost impossible.

KATHMANDU TO POKHARA

Before the Pokhara road was completed in 1971, the only way to reach Pokhara from Kathmandu was to fly or to walk. The trek from Kathmandu is an easy nine or 10-day trek from Trisuli Bazaar to Begnas Tal, just outside Pokhara. This is the easiest trek in Nepal and has few uphill climbs of any significance. Trekking westwards there are many alternatives. A northern route presents a trek close to the mountains – Manaslu (8156 metres), Himalchuli, Baudha (6674 metres) and a side trip to Bara Pokhari, a fine high altitude lake. The more direct southern route to Pokhara allows a visit to the ancient town of Gorkha with its large bazaar and fort. This route has the attraction of lower altitudes and avoids the extreme elevation gains and losses common to other treks in Nepal. The views of the Himalaya are good on this trek, but the route never actually gets into the high mountains.

A lot of the interest and remoteness of this trek has vanished because the new road to Gorkha has totally changed the trading habits and culture of the region. Local people hardly ever walk this route now, so the facilities for food and accommodation have degenerated. A few Westerners travel the southern routes, but many parts of the northern regions are both remote and untram-melled by trekkers.

GANESH HIMAL

Between Kathmandu and Pokhara are three major groups of peaks: Ganesh Himal, Manaslu and Himalchuli, and the large Annapurna Himal. You can drive to Dhunche on the same road that leads to the start of the Langtang trek, then either continue driving on the road to Somdang or walk towards Ganesh Himal.

ROLWALING

Rolwaling is the east-west valley below Gauri Shankar (7145 metres), just south of the Tibetan border. This is an isolated and culturally diverse area, but most treks conclude their visit to Rolwaling by crossing the Tesi Lapcha pass (5755 metres) into Khumbu. It is better to cross Tesi Lapcha from Khumbu into Rolwaling, not by visiting Rolwaling first. There are two reasons for this: well-equipped, willing porters are easier to get in Khumbu than in Rolwaling; and in case of altitude sickness there are better facilities for help if you make your retreat on the Khumbu side rather than making a retreat back to the isolated villages of Beding or Na in Rolwaling. A second way to visit this region would be to forego Tesi Lapcha and go as far as Na, then retrace the route back to Kathmandu.

Tesi Lapcha is particularly dangerous because of frequent rockfalls on its western side. The route through the icefall is becoming technically more and more difficult due to the movements of the glacier. The Rolwaling porters operate a Mafia-like system and will not allow outside porters to approach the pass from Rolwaling, forcing parties to accept people from Beding and Na as porters. The local porters either get frightened of the falling rocks and return without notice or demand exorbitant pay after the party is halfway up the pass. There are no facilities at all between Na and Thami. Tesi Lapcha is a true mountaineering project!

Rolwaling and Tesi Lapcha are technically closed to foreigners. However, if you obtain a climbing permit for Ramdung, one of the trekking peaks, the immigration office will issue you a trekking permit for Rolwaling.

TILICHO LAKE

There is another pass south of Thorung La between Manang and Jomsom. From Manang, the trail goes on to the village of Khangsar, then becomes a goat trail scrambling over moraines to Tilicho Lake (4120 metres) at the foot of Tilicho peak (7132 metres). Herzog's maps depicted Tilicho Lake as the 'great ice lake'. It is usually frozen (except when you decide to trust the ice and walk on it). From the lake, there are several alternative routes, including Meso Kanto Pass (5330 metres) and another pass a little further north. The trail is difficult and hard to find. One very experienced trekker described the trail as only a figment of someone's imagination – he claimed there was no trail at all. In 1985 a New Zealand trekking group was snowed in near Tilicho Lake. Four sherpas went for help, using the seats of bamboo stools for snowshoes, and were killed in an avalanche.

Thorung La is a good safe route between Manang and Jomsom. It's better to make a side trip to Tilicho Lake from Manang and not take all your equipment and porters on the Tilicho Lake trail. One complication of this trek is that the army does not want you wandering through the training exercises they run in the valley east of Jomsom. Inquire at Kathmandu and again in Manang before making plans to cross the Tilicho route. You might cross the pass only to have the army turn you back to Manang an hour before Jomsom.

MUGU

Mugu is a remote region east of Humla and north of Rara Lake. The area is inhabited by people of Tibetan ancestry, and is an old trade route to Tibet. Most of Mugu is closed to trekkers, including the route up the Humla Karnali to Mugugaon, however it is possible to trek north of Rara Lake, cross a pass to Darma and continue to Simikot.

NAR-PHU

The Nar-Phu Valley lies north of Kyupar village on the way to Manang. This valley, like most valleys that lead to the Tibetan border, is generally closed to foreigners. There have been exceptions, and some trekkers have been allowed if they were engaged in authorised studies. Other trekkers have been allowed upon presentation of a climbing permit for Chulu East. Perhaps it is also possible to visit the region if you agree to take a liaison officer, but this is not clearly specified.

MILKE DANDA

There is a long, high forested ridge that divides the Arun and Tamur valleys. You can start from Basantpur (see the Kanchenjunga North trek) and make a trek of several days up this ridge that offers views of Makalu to the west and Kanchenjunga to the east. The Milke Danda ridge eventually ends in some high peaks, so you must retrace your route back down, perhaps dropping off the west side through Chainpur and ending the trek at Tumlingtar. There are huge forests of rhododendrons along the ridge, making a spring trek an attractive prospect. You may forgo mountain views if you schedule a trek in April to see the rhododendrons in bloom; eastern Nepal in the springtime can often be rainy and cloudy.

AROUND DHAULAGIRI

There is a long, difficult trek around Dhaulagiri that starts from Beni on the Kali Gandaki. Follow the Mayangdi Khola westwards to Darbang and turn north on a tiny trail that leads through forests into the high country. Much of the route is on snow and glaciers as it crosses French Col (5240 metres), traverses the head of Hidden Valley, and crosses 5155-metre Dhampus Pass. The trek ends with a steep descent to Marpha and a return to Pokhara, either via the Kali Gandaki or over the Ghorapani ridge for a panoramic view of the entire Dhaulagiri massif.

Mountaineering in Nepal

Although this is a book about trekking, a short discussion of mountaineering in Nepal is appropriate. The first trekkers in Nepal were, of course, mountaineers who were either on their way to climb peaks or were exploring routes up unclimbed peaks. There was furious mountaineering activity in Nepal from 1950 to the 1960s and all the 8000-metre peaks were climbed during this time.

By the early 1970s the emphasis had shifted to impossible feats such as the south face of Annapurna and the south-west face of Everest, both climbed by expeditions led by Chris Bonington. The expeditions in the '60s and '70s were often well equipped and sometimes lavish due to sponsorship from governments, foundations, magazines, newspapers, film makers, TV producers and even private companies. Expeditions have become big business and climbers now approach the job with the appropriate degree of seriousness and dedication. It is not uncommon for expeditions to refuse trekkers admission into their base camps. The team members do not have the time or energy to entertain tourists and there have also been incidents of trekkers taking souvenirs from among the expensive and essential items that often lie around such camps.

There are three seasons for mountaineering in Nepal. The pre-monsoon season from April to early June was once the only season during which expeditions climbed major peaks. In the '50s all expeditions were in the 'lull before the storm' period that occurs between the end of the winter winds and the beginning of the monsoon snow. Cold and high winds drove back the Swiss expedition to Mt Everest in 1952 when they attempted to climb the mountain in the autumn. It was not until 1973 that an expedition successfully climbed Everest in autumn. Now the autumn or post-monsoon season of September and October is a period of many successful expeditions.

In 1979 the Ministry of Tourism established a season for winter mountaineering. It is bitterly cold at high elevations from November to February, but recent advances in equipment technology have allowed several teams to accomplish what was thought before to be impossible – a winter ascent of a Himalayan peak. Climbing during the monsoon, from June to August, is not practical from the Nepalese side, though the north face of Everest has been climbed during August.

Two organisations control climbing in Nepal. The Ministry of Tourism is responsible for major expeditions and the Nepal Mountaineering Association (NMA) issues permits for the peaks that are open to trekking groups. The type of climbing that appeals to most trekkers is encompassed by the regulations for small peaks.

TREKKING PEAKS

Since 1978 the NMA has had the authority to issue permission for small-scale attempts on 18 peaks. It is not necessary to go through a long application process, hire and equip a liaison officer or organise a huge assault on a major peak in order to try Himalayan mountaineering. The 18 'trekking peaks' provide a large range of difficulty and are situated throughout Nepal.

There is a minimum of formality, requiring only the payment of a fee and the preparation of a simple application. The fee is US$300 for peaks above 6100 metres and US$200 for peaks less than 6100 metres. The permit is valid for one month for a group of up to 10 people. An extra US$5 per person is payable if the group exceeds 10 climbers. Because the regulations for climbing a small peak also require an established liaison in Kathmandu (usually a trekking company), it is easiest to use a trekking agent to organise a climb rather than try to do the whole project yourself.

The designation 'trekking peak' is an unfortunate misnomer, because most of the peaks listed are significant mountaineering challenges. Few of the peaks are 'walk-ups', and some peaks, such as Kusum Kangru and Lobuje, can be technically demanding and dangerous. As you think about these 'small' peaks, remember that all of them are higher than any mountain in North America. Before you consider climbing a trekking peak, reread some books on Himalayan expeditions. The weather is often bad and may force you to sit in your tent for days at a time. Usually a well-equipped base camp is necessary, and the ascent of a peak requires one or more high camps that must be established and stocked. Most of the trekking peaks require a minimum of four days and it can take as much as three weeks for an ascent.

Bill O'Connor's excellent and comprehensive guidebook, *The Trekking Peaks of Nepal*, is usually available in Kathmandu and in bookshops overseas. The book includes photographs, maps, trekking information and climbing routes on the 18 trekking peaks.

To get a climbing permit, go to the NMA office (☎ 411525, 416278) in Kamal Pokhari. You must pay the peak fee in foreign currency cash or travellers' cheques. You must also employ a sirdar who is currently registered with the NMA, and if any Nepalese are to climb above base camp, you must insure them and supply them with climbing equipment. A climbing permit does not replace a trekking permit; you need both if you are climbing a trekking peak.

You can buy or rent climbing gear in Kathmandu, saving the expense of air freighting ironmongery around the world. Good mountain tents, stoves, sleeping bags, down clothing and most other expedition necessities are all available for rent. As with trekking gear, the items that might be in short supply are socks, clothing, cooking gas cylinders, large-size boots and freeze-dried food.

Peaks which can be climbed under the trekking peak regulations follow.

Everest Region

Island Peak (6189 metres) – now called Imja Tse; involves one steep and exposed 100-metre ice or snow climb, otherwise a non-technical snow climb

Kwangde (6187 metres) – north face (seen from Namche) is a difficult climb; southern side (from Lumding Kharka above Ghat) is a moderately technical climb (allow two to three weeks)

Kusum Kangru (6367 metres) – the most difficult of the trekking peaks

Lobuje East (6119 metres) – top is exposed and often covered with rotten snow; there's also an exposed knife ridge and some crevasses

Mehra peak (5820 metres) – now called Khongma Tse. This is a rock and ice climb that's not difficult from either the Imja Valley or Lobuje.

Mera peak (6476 metres) – easy snow climb from the Mera La, but sometimes crevasses complicate the route; no villages or food on the approach from Lukla; requires two weeks

Pokhalde (5806 metres) – short, steep snow climb from the Kongma La above Lobuje

Rowaling Region

Pharchamo (6187 metres) – steep snow climb on a route subject to avalanches; peak is just above Tesi Lapcha

Ramdung (5925 metres) – requires a long approach through Rolwaling Valley. A permit for Ramdung allows you to trek into the restricted area of Rolwaling, so many groups that get permits for this peak do not even attempt to climb it.

Manang Region

Chulu East (6584 metres) – ascent starts after a long approach from Manang; needs one or two high camps

Chulu West (6419 metres) – route circles Gusang peak to climb Chulu West from the north; requires at least two high camps

Pisang peak (6091 metres) – long snow slog above Pisang village, steep snow at the top. The mountaineering school at Manang uses Pisang peak for training climbs.

Langtang Region

Ganja La Chuli (5846 metres) – now Naya Kangri; involves a snow and rock climb from a base camp either north or south of Ganja La

Annapurna Region

Fluted Peak (6501 metres) – now Singu Chuli (named for the steep ice slopes that make it difficult to climb); this peak is reached from the Annapurna Sanctuary

Hiunchuli (6441 metres) – snow, ice and rock; not an easy climb

Mardi Himal (5587 metres) – five-day slog up the Mardi Khola to approach the peak, an outlier of Machhapuchhare

Tent Peak (5500 metres) – now Tharpu Chuli; climb involves glaciers and crevasses; most people climb the easier Rakshi peak to the south

Ganesh Himal

Paldor Peak (5928 metres) – 10-day trek to base camp from Trisuli Bazaar

MOUNTAINEERING EXPEDITIONS

The rules for mountaineering on major peaks require a minimum of six months advance application to the Ministry of Tourism, a liaison officer, a royalty of US$1000 to US$50,000 depending on the elevation of the peak, and endorsement from the government or the national alpine club of the country organising the expedition. There are 87 peaks open for foreign expeditions and another 17 peaks open for joint Nepalese-foreign expeditions. Some peaks, such as Everest, are booked many years in advance, while other peaks remain untouched for several seasons.

Further information is usually available through alpine clubs in your own country. Even the most budget-conscious expedition under these regulations would cost US$20,000 or more to cover salary, insurance and equipment for sherpas and a liaison officer, peak fees and other compulsory expenses. If you want an inexpensive climb in Nepal, it is far more reasonable to set your sights on one of the trekking peaks.

Eight of the world's 14 peaks over 8000 metres are in Nepal. Those outside Nepal include K2 (8611 metres), Nanga Parbat (8125 metres), Gasherbrum I (8068 metres), Gasherbrum II (8035 metres) and Broad Peak (8047 metres), all in Pakistan. The remaining 8000-metre peak is Shisha Pangma (8013 metres), which is in Tibet, just north of the Nepal/Tibet border.

The following sections summarise the important early climbs on the 8000-metre peaks of Nepal. For a comprehensive reference on these mountains, climbs and an exhaustive bibliography of books about the Himalaya, I recommend *Sivalaya* (Gastons-West Col Publications, England, 1978) by Louis Baume. Elizabeth Hawley kindly provided the up-to-date statistics on the number of ascents and deaths. Miss Hawley has lived in Nepal since the 1950s and, in addition to her duties running Sir Edmund Hillary's Himalayan Trust, has maintained an exhaustive record with details of every mountaineering expedition that has climbed on peaks in Nepal.

Everest

Mountaineering and trekking in Nepal has relied heavily on the progress and inspiration developed by various expeditions to Everest. Much of the attraction of Nepal in the early days resulted from the discovery that the highest peak in the world lay within the forbidden and isolated kingdom. Though it was named Mt Everest by the Survey of India in 1856 after Sir George Everest, retired Surveyor-General of India, the peak had been known by other names long before. The Nepalese call it Sagarmatha and the Sherpas call it Chomolungma. The Chinese now call it Qomolangma Feng.

The list of attempts and successes on Everest is one of the classics of mountaineering history. By 1989 there had been 274 ascents of Everest, including several by people who climbed it two or more times. In 1993 the record stood at 301 expeditions, 519 different people had reached the summit, and 125 climbers had been killed. The following section lists all the Everest expeditions until 1982. By 1983 both China and Nepal allowed several expeditions on the mountain at the same time, causing traffic jams, queues for the use of routes and fixed ropes, confusion, squabbling, crowded base camps and the inevitable trashing of the mountain. From 1983 onwards I have listed only the more spectacular or interesting expeditions. For a complete list of Everest ascents and an amazing set of statistics about climbs on the mountain, see the latest edition of *Everest* (Oxford University Press, London, 1989) by Walt Unsworth.

Early Attempts from Tibet The first expeditions to Everest were two British reconnaissance teams that approached the peak through Tibet from Darjeeling. They spent months mapping and exploring the Everest region and ran the first climbing school for Sherpas on the slopes leading to the North Col. On the second expedition George Leigh Mallory named the Western Cwm and declared that Everest was probably impossible to climb from the Nepalese side.

The first serious attempt to climb Everest was made in 1922. The expedition, as did all attempts until 1950, climbed the mountain from the north after a long approach march across the plains of Tibet. The highest point reached was 8320 metres. An avalanche killed seven Sherpas below the North Col.

In 1924 another team of British gentlemen in their tweed suits set off to climb Everest. They didn't have crampons and had a furious argument about whether the use of oxygen was 'sporting'. On this expedition Mallory and Andrew Irvine climbed high on the mountain and never returned. Nobody has ever found out whether they reached the top before they perished.

In 1933 another British expedition reached a height of 8570 metres, just 275 metres short of the summit. Frank Smythe's book *Camp Six* is an excellent personal account of this expedition. At the same time a British expedition flew over Everest in two Westland biplanes. This was a spectacular technical achievement at the time and produced many useful photographs.

A year later a strange man named Maurice Wilson flew alone in a small plane from the UK to India, then crossed Tibet to make a solo attempt on Everest. He carried little food, believing that fasting would give him strength; he eventually froze to death on the slopes below the North Col.

In 1935 Eric Shipton led a small expedition as far as the North Col. Tenzing Norgay accompanied this expedition as a porter. The following year another expedition reached a point only slightly above the North Col. In 1938 another famous name associated with Everest came to the fore when H W Tilman led a small expedition in which Eric Shipton reached almost 8300 metres.

In 1947 Earl Denman, a Canadian, disguised himself as a Tibetan monk, travelled to Everest and made a solo attempt. He quit below the North Col and returned immediately to Darjeeling.

Early Climbs from Nepal After the war Tibet was closed, but Nepal had begun to open its borders. In 1950 Tilman made a peripatetic trip all over Nepal, including a trek from Dharan to Namche Bazaar. This was the first party of Westerners to visit the Everest region. They made the first ascent of Kala Pattar and walked to the foot of the Khumbu Icefall. In 1951 K Becker-Larson, a Dane, followed the same route as the Tilman party, then crossed into Tibet, reaching the North Col before returning.

The British still considered Everest their mountain and the Royal Geographical Society and the Alpine Club teamed up to sponsor a serious programme to climb the mountain. Eric Shipton led a reconnaissance in 1951, reaching the Western Cwm at the top of the Khumbu Icefall and proving that Everest was climbable from the south. Nepal allowed only one expedition per year on Everest; in 1952 it was the turn of the Swiss. During this expedition Raymond Lambert and Tenzing Norgay reached a height of almost 8600 metres. Rushing to beat the British, the Swiss tried again in the autumn but cold and high winds drove them back from a point just above the South Col. In

1953 a huge British expedition, led by John Hunt, finally succeeded. Edmund Hillary and Tenzing Norgay reached the summit of Everest on 29 May 1953.

Climbs After the First Ascent In 1956 the Swiss finally succeeded and placed four climbers on the summit of Everest and also made the first ascent of Lhotse. The era of large expeditions continued and in 1960 the first Indian expedition reached a height of 8625 metres before bad weather forced them to retreat. While the Indians were attempting Everest from the Nepal side a Chinese expedition made the first ascent from the north. The climb was discredited at first because three members of the team reached the summit at night, but mountaineering history now acknowledges the ascent.

In 1962 Woodrow Wilson Sayre and three others obtained permission to climb Gyachung Kang, then crossed into Tibet and tried to climb Everest without permission. They reached a point above the North Col before returning. Their antics almost jeopardised the US Mt Everest expedition the following year. This large expedition, led by Norman Dyhrenfurth, was successful in placing six people on the summit, including two by the unclimbed west ridge. The traffic jam on Everest began two years later when Captain M S Kohli led an Indian team that placed nine climbers on the summit of Everest.

From 1966 to 1968 Nepal was closed to mountaineers. When climbing was again allowed the Japanese had become interested in Everest and in 1970 a 38-member team placed four climbers on the summit. This was the expedition that included the famous 'ski descent' of Everest. Six Sherpas were killed in the Khumbu Icefall.

Attention now turned to new routes on Everest, especially the south-west face. In 1971 Norman Dyhrenfurth led an ambitious expedition with climbers from 13 nations attempting both the south-west face and the west ridge, finally retreating from a height of 8488 metres on the face route. Further attempts on the south-west face were made

in 1972 by a European expedition and a British expedition led by Chris Bonington.

During the 1970s it seemed that there was an unlimited amount of money available for Everest expeditions. In 1973 a huge Italian expedition placed eight climbers on the summit and two members of a Japanese team made the first successful ascent in autumn. The following year saw an unsuccessful Spanish expedition and a disastrous French attempt on the west ridge that ended when an avalanche killed the leader and five sherpas.

The following year saw some spectacular successes, including the first ascent of Everest by a woman, Junko Tabei, who was a member of a Japanese expedition. A few days after the Japanese success, a Chinese team placed nine people, including one woman, on the summit. The large survey tripod they erected is still on the top of Everest. The south-west face was finally climbed by a British expedition funded by Barclays Bank and led by Chris Bonington.

Mountaineering continued through the 1970s with numerous successes. In 1978 Everest's largest challenge was overcome when Reinhold Messner and Peter Habler made the first ascent of the mountain without using oxygen. Climbers began attracting media attention and, in 1978, a gigantic German/French expedition placed 16 climbers on the summit via the South Col and made a live radio broadcast from the 'roof of the world'.

In 1980, after more than 40 years of closure, Tibet was once again accessible to mountaineers. A large and expensive Japanese expedition reached the summit by two different routes from Tibet. In 1980 Reinhold Messner made his second oxygen-less ascent of Everest, this time from the Tibetan side – and alone. Another precedent was set when a 1982 Canadian expedition made live TV transmissions from the mountain.

One of the more unusual accidents on Everest occurred during a 1982 Belgian expedition to the west ridge. One member fell into Tibet and was given up as dead; he eventually made his way back to Kathmandu by bus. The Everest traffic jams began in

1983 when three Japanese climbers reached the summit via the South Col on the same day that six Americans made the first ascent of the difficult Kangshung face from Tibet.

Nepal now allowed several expeditions on the mountain at the same time and sometimes allowed more than one expedition on the same route. In 1984 there were 14 expeditions, five from Tibet and the rest from Nepal. The first Indian woman and four other climbers reached the summit via the South Col. Five Bulgarians reached the summit via the west ridge; four climbers made a traverse and descended via the south-east ridge. Climbing from Tibet, Greg Mortimer and Tim McCartney-Snape were the first Australians to reach the summit of Everest.

New Records & Firsts By the mid-80s expeditions had to rely on more and more complex gimmicks to obtain funding for their activities. Everest also became a goal for older and less experienced climbers; the natural result of this was the evolution of guided climbs on the world's highest peak.

In 1985 there were 14 attempts on Everest, but only three were successful. A record 17 climbers from a Norwegian expedition reached the summit via the South Col. Throughout the rest of the 1980s there were many expeditions each year, but few were successful. In the spring of 1988 more than 250 climbers made up a joint Chinese-Nepalese-Japanese expedition that traversed the mountain in both directions. The teams met on the summit and made a prime time live TV broadcast. In autumn, three French teams, and American, Korean, Spanish, Czech and New Zealand teams all gathered at base camp. Latecomers were charged for the use of fixed ropes through the icefall. Four French climbers reached the summit and Jean-Marc Boivin jumped off by paraglider, landing at Camp Two 12 minutes later. During the year a total of 31 climbers reached the summit and nine people died.

In 1991 a group of four hot-air balloonists crossed from Gokyo, over the summit of Everest to Tibet in an hour and 20 minutes. The 1992 climbing season saw a queue of climbers waiting at the foot of the Hillary Step for their turn to reach the summit. A total of 17 expeditions were on the mountain, 13 from the Nepal side, with 58 climbers reaching the summit, 32 in a single day. On several occasions sherpa teams set up a route through the icefall and charged a toll for climbers who wished to use it. Several novice mountaineers reached the summit of Everest on guided climbs. The first Nepalese woman to climb Everest died on the descent, but she became a national hero.

Nepal has upped the fee for Everest and limited the number of expeditions on the mountain. Each expedition is limited to 10 climbers, though another two may climb if they pay an extra US$5000 each. Climbers who violated rules used to be banned from climbing in Nepal for 10 years; in the autumn of 1993 a British expedition that sent two unauthorised climbers to the summit was fined US$100,000 for the infringement.

Kanchenjunga

Kanchenjunga, at 8598 metres, is the third-highest peak in the world, second highest in Nepal. It was first climbed by a British team in 1956. The peak consists of four summits. The west summit, Yalung Kang is 8420 metres high and some people classify it as a separate 8000-metre peak. By the end of 1993, a total of 107 people had climbed Kanchenjunga on 59 expeditions and 26 climbers had died on the mountain.

The first Westerner to explore Kanchenjunga was J D Hooker, the British botanist, who visited the area twice in 1848 and 1849. Exploration of the Sikkim side of the peak continued with both British and pundit explorers mapping and photographing until 1899. In that year a party led by Douglas Freshfield made a circuit of Kanchenjunga and produced what is still one of the most authoritative maps of the region.

Exploration continued, mostly from the Sikkim side, with expeditions starting from Darjeeling in British India. One of the major contributors of information about the region was Dr A M Kellas who later died in Tibet during the approach march of the 1921

Everest expedition. German expeditions attacked the peak in 1929, 1930 and again in 1931, but none was successful. After the war Sikkim was closed but Nepal was open. In 1955 a team led by Dr Charles Evans approached the peak via the Yalung Glacier. Two teams climbed the peak, stopping just short of the summit to conform to an agreement with the Maharaja of Sikkim that the summit would remain inviolate.

The Japanese now took up the challenge and mounted expeditions in 1967, 1973 and 1974 during which they climbed Yalung Kang. A German expedition climbed Yalung Kang in 1975, and in 1977 an Indian army team mounted the second successful expedition to the main peak of Kanchenjunga.

Lhotse

Lhotse (8501 metres) was climbed by a Swiss expedition in 1956; its lower peak, Lhotse Shar, 8383 metres, is sometimes considered a separate 8000-metre peak. Lhotse, which means 'south peak', is part of the Everest massif, just to the south of Everest. The primary route on Lhotse is via Everest's South Col, but despite the activity on Everest, by 1955 Lhotse was the highest unclimbed peak in the world. Lhotse has had the least climbing activity of any 8000-metre peak in Nepal. The record in 1993 stood at 58 summiters, 42 expeditions and six deaths.

The first attempt on Lhotse was by an international team in 1955. One member of the party was Erwin Schneider; during this expedition he began work on the first of the series of high-quality 'Schneider maps' of the Everest region. The same Swiss that made the second ascent of Everest in 1956 made the first ascent of Lhotse from a camp just below the South Col.

Lhotse Shar was first climbed by an Austrian expedition in 1970. Various routes on main peak were attempted by Japanese, South Koreans, Germans, Poles and Italians before the summit was reached again by a German expedition in 1977.

Makalu

Makalu (8475 metres) was first climbed by

a French party in 1955. By 1993, 92 climbers had reached the summit on 99 expeditions; only nine climbers died in the attempt. The peak was first mapped and photographed from the Tibetan side by the 1921 British Everest reconnaissance. Hillary and Shipton photographed the peak during a side trip on the 1951 Everest reconnaissance. Hillary and others approached the peak a year later after the failure of their Cho Oyu expedition.

The first attempt on Makalu was in 1954 by a US team, mostly from California, that trekked all the way from the Indian border near Biratnagar. At the same time a British team approached the mountain, but this expedition had to be abandoned when Hillary became seriously ill and had to be evacuated.

In the autumn of 1954 a French team attempted the peak. In the following spring, a successful ascent was made by three teams of French climbers on successive days.

In 1960 a large scientific and mountaineering expedition wintered at the foot of Ama Dablam, occupying the Green and Silver Huts. In May 1961, members of the expedition trekked across the Mingbo La and other high passes to the foot of Makalu where they planned to climb the French route. Sickness stopped the expedition, which turned into a heroic struggle for survival.

The Japanese climbed Makalu in 1970, another French team climbed in 1971 and a Yugoslav expedition reached the summit in 1975. In 1976 Spanish and Czechoslovakian teams joined up near the summit.

Dhaulagiri

Dhaulagiri (8167 metres) was first climbed by the Swiss in 1960. Its name is derived from Sanskrit: *dhavala* means 'white' and *giri* is 'mountain'. The mountain was sighted by British surveyors in India in the early 1800s and was mapped by one of the secret Indian surveyors, the pundits, in 1873, but the region remained largely unknown until a Swiss aerial survey in 1949. In 1993, 177 climbers had summited on 115 expeditions, and 40 climbers had died.

The French Annapurna expedition in 1950

had permission to climb either Annapurna or Dhaulagiri but decided on Annapurna after a reconnaissance of Dhaulagiri. A Swiss party failed in 1953 as did an Argentinian group in 1954.

After four more expeditions had failed, eight members of a Swiss expedition reached the summit in 1960. The climb followed a circuitous route around the mountain from Tukche, over Dhampus Pass and French Col to approach the summit from the north-east col. The expedition was supplied by a Swiss Pilatus Porter aircraft, the yeti, which landed on the North-East Col at 5977 metres. Near the end of the expedition the plane crashed near Dhampus Pass and the pilots, including the legendary Emil Wick, walked down the mountain to Tukche.

Tragedy struck in 1969 when an avalanche killed seven members of a US expedition on the east Dhaulagiri glacier. The peak was climbed by the Japanese in 1970, the Americans in 1973 and the Italians in 1976. Captain Emil Wick airdropped supplies to the US expedition from a Pilatus Porter aircraft. Among the delicacies he dropped were two bottles of wine and a live chicken. The Sherpas would not allow the chicken to be killed on the mountain, so it became the expedition pet. It was carried, snow-blind and crippled with frostbitten feet, to Marpha where it finally ended up in the cooking pot.

Manaslu

Manaslu (8156 metres) was first climbed in 1956 by a Japanese expedition. Its name comes from the Sanskrit word *manasa* meaning 'intellect' or 'soul'. This is the same word that is the root of the name of the holy lake Manasarovar near Mt Kailas in Tibet. Just as the British considered Everest to be their mountain, Manaslu has always been a 'Japanese' mountain. The record on Manaslu in 1993 was 108 summiters, 90 expeditions and 44 deaths.

Tilman and Jimmy Roberts photographed Manaslu during a trek in 1950, but the first real survey of the peak was made by a Japanese expedition in 1952.

A Japanese team made the first serious attempt on the peak from the Buri Gandaki Valley in 1953. When another team followed in 1954 the villagers of Samagaon told them that the first team had been responsible for an avalanche which destroyed a monastery, and refused to let the 1954 expedition climb. The expedition set off to climb Ganesh Himal instead.

Despite a large donation for the rebuilding of the monastery, subsequent Japanese expeditions, including the first ascent in 1956, took place in an atmosphere of animosity and mistrust. The second successful Japanese expedition was in 1971.

There was a South Korean attempt in 1971, and in April 1972 an avalanche resulted in the death of five climbers and 10 Sherpas, ending the second South Korean expedition. Reinhold Messner made the fourth ascent of Manaslu as a member of a Tyrolean expedition that climbed the peak from the Marsyangdi Valley in 1972.

Cho Oyu

Cho Oyu (8153 metres) was first climbed by Austrians in 1954. It is about 30 km west of Everest at the head of the Gokyo Valley. The mountain was reconnoitred by the 1951 Everest reconnaissance and a British team led by Eric Shipton attempted the peak in 1952. The first ascent was made in 1954 via the north-west ridge using a route through Tibet from the Nangpa La, not a strictly legal route. An Indian expedition made the second ascent in 1958 and a German ski expedition made the third ascent in 1964. By 1992 a total of 100 expeditions had been made on Cho Oyu. Most of the Nepal-based expeditions had made the illegal approach through Tibet and the Chinese had dispatched police to try to collect peak permit fees from climbers who crossed the border. The approach to the mountain from both Nepal and Tibet is easy, and the ascent through Tibet is not particularly difficult. Cho Oyu is second only to Everest in the number of expeditions and successful ascents. In 1993 the record stood at 400 climbers reaching the summit, 152 expeditions and 14 deaths.

Annapurna

Annapurna (8091 metres) was first climbed by a French expedition in 1950. There are four summits called Annapurna; the entire massif forms a barrier on the northern side of the Pokhara Valley. The main summit of Annapurna is to the west of the Annapurna Sanctuary; Annapurna II is above Chame, about 24 km to the east. Fewer climbers have reached the summit of Annapurna than any other 8000-metre peaks in Nepal. Only 78 climbers on 93 expeditions had reached the summit by the end of 1993; 45 climbers had died on the mountain.

A French expedition led by Maurice Herzog explored the Kali Gandaki Valley in 1950. After deciding that Dhaulagiri was too difficult, they turned their attention to climbing Annapurna. Hampered by inaccurate maps they spent considerable time and effort finding a way to the foot of the mountain. They eventually ascended via the Miristi Khola to the north face, making the first ascent of an 8000-metre peak on June 3, just before the start of the monsoon. The summiters suffered frostbite on the descent and were finally evacuated back to the roadhead in India.

Annapurna was not climbed again until 1970 when a British army expedition followed essentially the same route as Herzog. At the same time Chris Bonington led a successful British expedition to the very steep and difficult south face.

Appendix – Personal Equipment Checklist

The following equipment checklist is based on the experience of many trekkers over the years. I use it myself when preparing to trek, to be sure that I don't forget some important item. Everything on the list is useful, and most of it necessary, on a long trek. You can omit many items if your trek does not exceed three weeks in duration or ascend above 4000 metres. All of this gear (except the sleeping bag) will pack into a duffel bag that weighs less than 15 kg.

Some gear will not be necessary on your particular trek. You might be lucky enough to trek during a warm spell and never need a down jacket. It might be so cold and rainy that you never wear short pants. These are, however, unusual situations, and it is still important to prepare yourself for both extremes. As you read the checklist, be sure to evaluate whether or not you need a particular item of equipment. Do not rush out to an equipment shop and buy everything on this list. It works for me and has worked for many other trekkers, but you may decide that many items in this list are unnecessary.

Footwear
    boots or running shoes
    camp shoes or thongs
    socks – polypropylene
    *boots
    *socks, high to wear with plus fours
    *socks, light cotton for under plus fours
    *down booties (optional)
Clothing
    down or fibre-filled jacket
    woollen shirt, jumper or polypropylene pile jacket
    hiking shorts or skirt
    poncho or umbrella
    sun hat
    underwear
    swimwear (optional)
    cotton or corduroy pants (optional)
    cotton T-shirts or blouses
    *down-filled pants or ski warm-up pants
    *nylon windbreaker

    *nylon wind pants
    *plus fours (knickers)
    *long underwear
    *woollen hat (or balaclava)
    *gloves
    *gaiters
Other Equipment
    backpack
    sleeping bag
    water bottle
    torch (flashlight), batteries & bulbs
Miscellaneous Items
    toilet articles
    toilet paper & matches
    sunblock (SPF 15-plus)
    towel
    laundry soap
    medical & first-aid kit
    pre-moistened towelettes
    sewing kit
    small knife
    bandanna
    *goggles or sunglasses
    *sunblock for lips
Optional Equipment
    camera & lenses
    lens cleansing equipment
    film (about 20 rolls)
    *altimeter
    *thermometer
    *compass
    *binoculars

* Add these items if you're trekking to higher altitudes.

If you have a porter, you will need a large duffel bag with a padlock, and some stuff bags. A small duffel bag or suitcase to leave your city clothes in is also useful.

Footwear
Boots or Running Shoes Proper footwear is the most important item you will bring. Your choice of footwear will depend on the length of the trek and whether or not you will be walking in snow. Tennis or running shoes are good trekking footwear, even for long treks, if there is no snow. However, boots

provide ankle protection and have stiffer soles. If you have done most of your previous hiking in boots, you may experience some discomfort in lighter and softer shoes. The trails are usually very rocky and rough. If the soles of your shoes are thin and soft, the rocks can bruise your feet and walking will be painful. There are several lightweight trekking shoes patterned after running shoes that have stiffer lug soles and are available in both low and high-top models.

Wherever there is snow (likely anywhere above 4000 metres), boots can become an absolute necessity. If you are travelling with porters, you have the luxury of carrying two sets of shoes and swapping them from time to time. If you are carrying everything yourself, you may have to settle for one or the other.

You should try out the shoes you plan to wear on the trek during several hikes (particularly up and down hills) before you come to Nepal. Be sure your shoes provide enough room for your toes. There are many long and steep descents during which short boots can painfully jam your toes (causing the loss of toenails).

Boots and camp shoes, both new and used, are available for both sale and rent in Kathmandu.

Camp Shoes Tennis shoes are comfortable to change into for the evening. They can also serve as trail shoes in an emergency. Rubber thongs or shower shoes make a comfortable change at camp during warm weather. You can buy these in Kathmandu and along most trails. They are called *chhapals* in Nepal. I always carry a pair of these in my backpack. I wear the thongs at lunch and in camp and put my shoes and socks in the sun to dry. I'm sure this has saved me a lot of foot troubles.

Socks Good socks are at a premium in Kathmandu, so bring these with you. There are some heavy scratchy Tibetan woollen socks available in Kathmandu and Namche Bazaar.

Thermal ski socks, a nylon-wool combination, or polypropylene hiking socks (which cost astronomical prices) are the best bet. You will wash your socks several times during a long trek and pure wool socks dry slowly. Synthetic socks dry in a few hours in the sun – often during a single lunch stop. Most people can wear these without an inner sock, but a thin cotton liner sock is usually necessary with heavy woollen rag socks. Try on a pair on your next local hike and see whether you need an inner sock. Three pairs should be enough unless you are a real procrastinator about washing clothes.

If you bring plus fours, you will need a pair of high woollen socks and two pairs of thin cotton or nylon inner socks. Most treks do not spend enough time at high altitudes to require more than one pair of high woollen socks.

Footwear – high altitude
Down Booties Many people consider these excess baggage, but they are great to have and not very heavy. If they have a thick sole, preferably with ensolite insulation, they can serve as camp shoes at high elevations. Down booties make a cold night seem a little warmer – somehow your feet seem to feel the cold more than anything else. They're also good for midnight trips outside into the cold.

Clothing
Down-Filled or Fibre-Filled Jacket Down clothing has the advantage of being light and compressible. It will stuff into a small space when packed, yet bulk up when you wear it. You should bring a good jacket on a trek. Most ski jackets are not warm enough and most so-called expedition parkas are too heavy and bulky. The secret is to choose one that will be warm enough even at the coldest expected temperatures, but also comfortable when it is warmer. Don't bring both a heavy and light down jacket; choose one that will serve both purposes. If your jacket has a hood, you can dispense with a woollen hat.

Your down jacket can serve many functions on the trek. It will become a pillow at night and will protect fragile items in your backpack or duffel bag. If you are extremely cold at high altitude, wear your down jacket to bed inside your sleeping bag. You probably won't need to wear down gear for walking as it rarely gets that cold even at 5000 metres. Most trekkers leave their down clothing in their duffel bag at lower elevations and only use it during the evening. At higher elevations, carry your jacket and put it on at rest or lunch stops.

Artificial fibre jackets (filled with Polargard, Thinsulate or Fibrefill) are a good substitute for down and are much less expensive. You can rent a jacket in Kathmandu, Pokhara or Namche Bazaar.

Woollen Shirt, Jumper or Polypropylene Pile Jacket Two light layers of clothing are better than a single heavy layer. One or two light jumpers or shirts are superior to a heavy woollen jacket. Most of the time you will need only a single light garment in the morning and will shed it as soon as you start walking. A long sleeved shirt or jumper will suffice to keep you warm until you start walking. A shirt has the advantage that you can open the front for ventilation without stopping to remove the entire garment.

Polypropylene 'pile' jackets and jumpers come in a variety of styles and thicknesses. Helly Hansen (Norway) and North Face and Patagonia (California) are major manufacturers of pile jackets. They are light, warm (even when wet) and easy to clean. They are a little cheaper, much lighter and dry a lot faster than woollen garments. It is usually possible to rent pile jackets in Kathmandu. Tibetan woollen jumpers are also for sale in Kathmandu, but they are bulky and scratchy.

Hiking Shorts or Skirts It will often be hot and humid, the trails steep and the wind calm. Long pants pull at the knees and are hot. For hiking at lower elevations, the sherpas usually switch to shorts. It's a good idea. Either 'cutoffs' or fancy hiking shorts with big pockets are fine, but only for men. Skimpy track shorts are culturally unacceptable throughout Nepal.

Villagers can be shocked by the sight of women in shorts, so it's better to wear a skirt. Many women who have worn skirts on treks are enthusiastic about them. The most obvious reason is the ease in relieving oneself along the trail. There are long stretches where there is little chance to drop out of sight, and a skirt solves the problem. Skirts are also useful when the only place to wash is in a stream crowded with trekkers, villagers and porters. A wrap-around skirt is easy to put on and take off in a tent. Long 'granny' skirts are not good because you will be walking through too much mud to make them practical.

Poncho or Umbrella There is really no way to keep dry while hiking in the rain, however, a poncho – a large, often hooded, tarp with a hole in the centre for your head – is a good solution. The weather is likely to be warm, even while raining, and a poncho has good air circulation. The condensation inside a waterproof jacket can make you even wetter than standing out in the rain. An inexpensive plastic poncho is often as good as more expensive coated nylon gear. The plastic one is completely waterproof at a fraction of the cost. Nylon ponchos are manufactured in Kathmandu.

The most practical way of keeping dry is an umbrella. This is an excellent substitute for a poncho (except on windy days), and can serve as a sunshade, a walking stick, an emergency toilet shelter and a dog deterrent. Umbrellas with bamboo handles are available in Kathmandu for about US$2, but are bulky and leak black dye over you when they get wet. Collapsible umbrellas are an excellent compromise, although they cannot serve as walking sticks. Imported collapsible umbrellas are available in shops on New Rd and in the supermarket in Kathmandu. An umbrella is necessary in October, April and May and optional for treks in other months.

Sun Hat A hat to keep the sun off your head is an important item, but its design is not critical. Obviously, a hat with a wide brim affords greater protection. Fix a strap that fits under your chin to the hat so it does not blow away in a wind gust. The Nepal Cap House in the shopping centre at the entrance to

Thamel has an amazing assortment of hats to choose from. There are outdoor hat stalls near the immigration office that also offer a selection of locally produced sun hats.

Swimwear Almost nobody older than eight goes without clothing in Nepal or India. You will upset sherpas, porters and an entire village if you skinny dip in a river, stream or hot spring, even to wash. There are many places to swim, although most are ridiculously cold – except along the Arun River in eastern Nepal, where there are some fine swimming holes. There are hot springs in Manang and in Tatopani (literally hot water) on the Jomsom trek. Either bring along swimwear or plan to swim in shorts or a skirt and be prepared to wear them till they dry.

Clothing – high altitude

Insulated Pants Most stores do not carry down-filled pants, but they are a real asset on a trek that goes above 4000 metres. You do not hike in down pants. Put them on over your hiking shorts or under a skirt when you stop for the night. Some down pants have snaps or a zipper down the inside seam of each leg. This feature allows you to use them as a half bag for an emergency bivouac and also lets you put them on without taking off your boots. As a half bag they add insulation to your sleeping bag when the nights become particularly cold.

Often you will arrive at your camp or hotel at 3 pm and will not dine until 6 pm, so unless you choose to do some exploring, there will be about three hours of sitting around before dinner. There is rarely a chance to sit by a fire to keep warm, even in hotels. In cold weather, down pants make these times much more comfortable. Ski warm-up pants are a good substitute, are much cheaper and are available at all ski shops. Down pants and sometimes ski warm-up pants are available for rent in trekking shops in Kathmandu and Namche.

Nylon Windbreaker Strong winds are rare in the places visited by most treks, but a windbreaker is helpful in light wind, light rain and drizzle, when a poncho is really not necessary. Be sure that your windbreaker breathes, otherwise perspiration cannot evaporate and you will become soaked. A windbreaker is more in the line of emergency gear. If there is a strong wind, you must have it, otherwise you will probably not use it. If you're rich, or spend a lot of time in the outdoors, a Gore-tex parka is a good investment.

Nylon Wind Pants Many people use these often. The temperature will often be approaching 30°C and most people prefer to hike in shorts except in the early morning when it is chilly. Wind pants provide the best of both worlds. Wear them over your shorts or under your skirt in the morning, then remove them to hike in lighter gear during the day. Most wind pants have special cuffs that allow you to remove them without taking off your shoes.

You can substitute ski warm-up pants, or even cotton jogging pants, for both wind pants and down-filled pants. The cost will be lower and there is hardly any sacrifice in versatility or comfort.

Plus Fours (Knee-Length Pants) The prime rule of selecting equipment for any hiking trip is to make each piece of gear serve at least two purposes. The great advantage of plus fours is that, combined with long woollen socks, they provide both short and long pants, simply by rolling the socks up or down.

If you are going to high elevations, you will truly be 'in the mountains' for several days. Here the weather can change quickly and sometimes dramatically. Although it will often be warm, it can cloud up and become cold and windy very fast – a potential problem if you happen to be wearing shorts. With plus fours you can wear the socks rolled up on cold mornings before the sun rises (which, since high peaks surround you, is about 10 am). As exercise and the heat of the sun warm you, roll the socks down to your ankles. Because of this versatility, plus fours are better than long pants. Plus fours may be available in Kathmandu, but are usually for sale, not for rent.

Long Underwear Long johns are a useful addition to your equipment. A complete set makes a good warm pair of pyjamas and is also useful during late-night emergency trips outside your tent or hotel. Unless the weather is especially horrible, you will not need them to walk in during the day. You can bring only the bottoms and use a woollen shirt for a pyjama top. Cotton underwear is OK, though wool is much warmer. If wool is too scratchy, duo-fold underwear (wool lined with cotton) is an excellent compromise.

Woollen Hat or Balaclava A balaclava is ideal because it can serve as a warm hat or you can roll it down to cover most of your face and neck. You may even need to wear it to bed on cold nights. Because much of your body heat is lost through your head, a warm hat helps keep your entire body warmer.

Gloves Warm ski gloves are suitable for a trek. You might consider taking along a pair of woollen mittens also, just in case your gloves get wet.

Gaiters If your trek visits high elevations, there is a chance of snow and also an opportunity to do some scrambling off the trails. A pair of high gaiters will help to keep your boots and socks cleaner and drier in rough conditions.

Equipment
Backpack A backpack should have a light internal frame to stiffen the bag and a padded waistband to keep it from bouncing around and to take some weight off your shoulders. There are many advantages to keeping your pack small. Its small size will prevent you from trying to carry too much during the day. It is a good piece of luggage to carry on a plane. A small backpack will fit inside your tent at night without crowding and will not be cumbersome when you duck through low doorways into houses and temples.

If you don't plan to take a porter, you will need a larger pack. This can be either a frame (Kelty type) pack or a large expedition backpack, although a soft pack is more versatile. If you do eventually hand your pack over to a porter, he will certainly stuff it into a bamboo basket called a *doko* and carry it with a tumpline called a *naamlo*. A frame pack is difficult for a porter to carry because he will refuse to use the shoulder straps. There is a wide assortment of day packs and backpacks available for rent in Kathmandu.

Sleeping Bag This is one item that you might consider bringing from home. Sleeping bags are readily available for rent in Kathmandu, but the dry-cleaning facilities in Nepal are pretty strange and bags lose their loft quickly during the process. The choice is usually between a clean (old and worn) bag, a dirty (warm) one or a new (expensive) sleeping bag. Most sleeping bags available in Kathmandu are mummy-style expedition bags that rent for less than US$2 a day. It is cold from November to March, even in the lowlands, so a warm sleeping bag is important at these times. A warm sleeping bag is a must at altitudes over 3300 metres, no matter what the season.

Water Bottle Because you must drink only treated or boiled water, bring a one-litre plastic water bottle that does not leak. During the day your bottle provides the only completely safe source of cold drinking water. If you use iodine, fill your water bottle from streams or water spouts, add the iodine and have cold safe water half an hour later.

Fill your water bottle with boiled water at night and take it to bed with you as a hot water bottle on cold nights – very luxurious. By morning the water will be cool for your use during the day. Many people require two litres of water during the day. If you are one of those, consider a second water bottle. Good water bottles are sometimes hard to find in Kathmandu, but you can always find (leaky) plastic Indian bottles or empty mineral water bottles that will do at a pinch.

Torch (Flashlight) Almost any torch will

do; a headlight is usually not necessary. You can get spare batteries almost anywhere in the hills of Nepal if you bring a torch that uses 'D' cells. Larger batteries also perform better in the cold than small penlight 'AA' cells, but of course they are heavier. Indian and Chinese torches and exotic torches left over from expeditions are available in Nepal.

Duffel Bag If you travel with porters, protect your gear with a duffel bag. Several companies make good duffel bags that have a zipper along the side for ease of entry. This is not an item to economise on; get a bag that is durable and has a strong zipper. A duffel 35 cm in diameter and about 75 cm long is large enough to carry your gear and will usually meet the weight limit of porters and domestic flights – typically 15 kg. Army surplus duffel bags are cheaper, but they are inconvenient because they only open from the end, although there is no zipper to jam or break.

If you have porters, they will carry most of your equipment. During the day, you will carry your camera, water bottle, extra clothing and a small first-aid kit in your backpack. Do not overload the backpack, especially on the first day of the trek.

It is impossible to describe how your duffel bag will look after a month on a trek. To find out how it is treated, load a duffel bag with your equipment, take it to the 2nd storey of a building and toss it out a window. Pick it up and shake the contents, then put it in the dirt and stomp on it a few times. Get the idea?

When it rains, your duffel bag will get wet. When it's raining, porters will leave their loads outside tea shops while they go inside to keep dry. You should pack your duffel bag in a way that important items stay dry during rainstorms. A waterproof duffel bag and waterproof nylon or plastic bags inside your bag are both necessary.

Use a small padlock that will fit through the zipper pull and fasten to a ring sewn to the bag. The lock will protect the contents from pilferage during the flight to and from Nepal and will help protect the contents on your trek. It also prevents kids, curious vil-

lagers and your porter from opening the bag and picking up something they think you won't miss. Duffel bags are hard to buy or rent in Kathmandu.

Extra Duffel Bag or Suitcase When starting a trek, you will leave your city clothes and other items in the storeroom of your hotel in Kathmandu. Bring a small suitcase or extra duffel bag with a lock to use for this purpose.

Stuff Bags It is unlikely that you will be able to find a completely waterproof duffel bag or backpack. Using coated nylon stuff bags helps you to separate your gear, thereby lending an element of organisation to the daily chaos in your tent or hotel. Stuff sacks also provide additional protection in case of rain. If you get stuff bags with drawstrings, the addition of spring-loaded clamps will save a lot of frustration trying to untie the knots you tied in too much haste in the morning. You can also use plastic bags, but these are much more fragile. A plastic bag inside each stuff sack is a good bet during the rainy season.

Sunglasses or Goggles The sun reflects brilliantly off snow, making good goggles or sunglasses with side protection essential. At high altitude they are so essential that you should have an extra pair in case of breakage or loss. A pair of regular sunglasses can serve as a spare if you rig a side shield. The lenses should be as dark as possible. At 5000 metres, the sun is intense and ultraviolet rays can severely damage unprotected eyes. Store your goggles in a metal case as, even in your backpack, it is easy to crush them.

Sunblock Because most treks are during autumn when the sun is low in the sky, sunburn is not a concern for most people. However, during April and May and at high altitudes, sunburn can be severe. Use a protective sunblock; those with more sensitive skin need a total sunblock such as zinc oxide cream. Beware of the hazard of snow glare at high altitude; you'll need a good sunblock. Sunblock is hard to find in Nepal.

To protect your lips at high altitude you need a total sunblock such as Labiosan.

Additional Items

There is not much to say about soap, scissors and the like, but a few ideas may help. If there are two people travelling, divide a lot of this material to save weight and bulk.

Laundry soap in bars is available in Kathmandu and along most trails. This avoids an explosion of liquid or powdered soap in your luggage.

Pre-moistened towelettes are great for a last-minute hand wash before dinner. You can avoid many stomach problems by washing frequently. If you bring a supply of these, check the way they are packaged. You can buy them in a plastic container and avoid leaving a trail of foil packets in your wake.

A pair of scissors on your pocket knife is useful. Also bring a sewing kit and some safety pins – lots of uses.

Be sure all your medicines and toiletries are in plastic bottles with screw on lids. If in doubt, reread the section on the treatment duffel bags receive.

The most visible sign of Western culture in the hills of Nepal is streams of toilet paper littering every campsite. Bring a cigarette lighter or matches so you can burn your used toilet paper.

You might also bring a small shovel or trowel to dig a toilet hole when you get caught in the woods with no toilet nearby.

Optional Equipment The equipment checklist suggests several items that you might bring on a trek. Do not carry all of them as you will overload your backpack.

Cameras People have brought cameras ranging from tiny Instamatics to heavy Hasselblads. While most trekkers do bring a camera, it is equally enjoyable to trek without one.

A trek is long and dusty. Be sure you have lens caps, lens tissue and a brush to clean the camera and lenses as frequently as possible.

Three lenses: a wide angle (28 mm or 35 mm), a standard lens (50 mm or 55 mm) and a telephoto lens (135 mm or 200 mm) are useful if you wish to take advantage of all the photographic opportunities during the trek, but lenses are heavy. Since you will probably carry them in your backpack day after day, you may want to limit your selection. If you must make a choice, you will find a telephoto (or zoom) lens is more useful than a wide angle, because it will allow you close-up pictures of mountains and portraits of shy people. Be sure to bring a polarising filter. Don't overburden yourself with lots of heavy camera equipment; an ostentatious display of expensive gear invites theft. Insure your camera equipment.

Glossary

ACAP – Annapurna Conservation Area Project, pronounced 'A-cap'

badam – peanut
Bahun – see Brahmin
baksheesh – a tip or donation
banyan – a species of fig tree, related to the pipal
bari – field where dry crops like wheat and corn are grown
bazaar – market area; a market town is called a bazaar
BCE – before Common Era, non-Christian representation of years BC
bhanjyang – pass or ridge top
bhat – cooked rice (correct transliteration is *bhaat)*
bhatti – tea shop or small restaurant in the hills
Bhote – Nepali for Tibet
Bhotia – Nepali for Tibetan
bodhi tree – or *bo* tree; a pipal tree under which the Buddha was sitting when he attained enlightenment
Bon-po – the ancient pre-Buddhist animistic religion of Tibet
Brahmin – the priest caste of Nepal, also called Bahun

cairn – pile of stones to mark a trail or pass
carrom – a game similar to snooker or pool that is played on a small wooden board using checkers instead of billiard balls
chang – north (Tibetan)
chappati – flat unleavened bread, also called *roti*
charpi – toilet
chaur – flat meadow or place for camping (western Nepali)
chautaara – rock wall built as a resting place for porters, almost always near a pipal or banyan tree
chhang – Tibetan-style beer made from rice, corn or millet, it is pronounced as 'chung'. Lowland people call it *jaand.*
chahara – waterfall

Chhetri – Hindu prince or warrior caste
Chitwan – district in the southern plains of Nepal where Royal Chitwan National Park is located
chiuraa – beaten rice
chowk – courtyard or square
Chomolungma – the Sherpa name for Mt Everest
chorten – round stone Buddhist monument, often containing relics
chu – river (Tibetan)
chuba – Tibetan woollen cloak
Churia – the southernmost range of hills in Nepal, bordering the Terai
col – mountain pass
crevasse – deep fissure in a glacier
cwm – in 1920, George Mallory used this Welsh word to name the high glaciated valley between Everest and Nuptse

dakshin – south
dahi – curd or yoghurt
dal – lentil soup, usually served with rice (correct transliteration is *daal)*
danda – hill (correct transliteration is *daanda)*
Dasain – the week-long autumn festival worshiping the goddess Kali
deorali – ridge top
dhami – shaman, sorcerer or medicine man
Dharma – Buddhist teachings
dhindo – paste of wheat, barley and corn; a common meal for hill porters
dhoka – door or gate
dingma – clearing (Tibetan)
Diwali – Indian name of the 'festival of lights' that follows Dasain (called Tihar in Nepal)
doko – woven bamboo basket carried by porters
dudh – milk
durbar – palace
dzong – fort or palace in Tibet
dzopkyo – male crossbreed between a yak and a cow

dzum – female crossbreed between a yak and a cow

gaad – river (western Nepali)
gandaki – river
gaon – village
ghar – house
ghat – place beside a river. A 'burning ghat' is used for cremations.
ghatta – mill, almost always water-driven
ghora – horse
gobar – cow dung. 'Gobar gas' generators are used in the hills to provide combustible gas for lighting and cooking.
gompa – a Tibetan Buddhist temple
gorak – Sherpa name for a raven or large crow
goth – cowshed or hut in a high pasture
GPS – Global Positioning System; a device that calculates position and elevation by reading and decoding signals from satellites
gunsa – winter settlement (Tibetan)
gurkha – Nepalese mercenaries who serve in the British and Indian armies
Gurkhali – British army name for the Nepali language
Gurung – people from the western hills, mostly around Pokhara
Guru Rimpoche – founder of Tibetan Buddhism 1250 years ago; also called Ogyan Rimpoche or Padmasambhava

haat – market or hill bazaar in eastern Nepal
himal – Sanskrit word for mountain
HRA – Himalayan Rescue Association
jaat – caste or ethnic group
jhankri – shaman, sorcerer or medicine man
jutho – ritual pollution. Once you have eaten food from a plate it is *jutho* and no Hindu may eat the remaining food

Kali – the most terrifying manifestation of the goddess Parvati
Kami – blacksmith caste
kani – an arch over a trail, usually decorated with paintings on the inside (correct transliteration is *kaani)*
kata – a white scarf presented by visitors to a Buddhist lama

Kham – a province in eastern Tibet, home of the Khampas
Khampa – the group of Tibetans best known as guerrilla warriors
khani – mine or quarry
kharka – commonly owned grazing land in the hills
khet – irrigated field for growing rice
khola – river or stream
khorsaani – hot chilli
Khumbu – region near Mt Everest inhabited by Sherpas
kora – Tibetan word for circumambulation of a religious shrine
kosi – one of the seven large rivers in Nepal
Kuhmale – the potter caste
kukhri – traditional curved knife of the Gurkhas
kund – holy lake

la – mountain pass (Tibetan)
lagna – ridge or pass (western Nepal; correct transliteration is *laagna)*
lama – Tibetan Buddhist teacher or priest
lamo – long
lekh – ridge or highlands
lha – god or deity (Tibetan)
lho – south (Tibetan)
Limbu – warrior caste (eastern Nepal)
Loba – people from Lo, the northern part of the Mustang district
Losar – Tibetan or Sherpa new year

maasu – meat
machha – fish
Magar – Tibetan-Burmese people related to the Gurungs
Mahabharata – epic war in Hindu mythology
Maitreya – a Buddha who will come in a future era
Malla – royal dynasty of the Kathmandu Valley. It is also the name of a totally unrelated ancient kingdom in western Nepal.
mandir – Nepali word for temple
mani stone – stone carved with the Tibetan Buddhist prayer *om mani padme hum* (the correct transliteration is *maani)*
mantra – prayer formula or chant
mathi – Nepali for up or upper

mela – country fair

mewa – papaya

Milarepa – Tibetan poet and saint (1040-1123)

mithai – candy or sweet

momo – steamed or fried dumplings

moraine – ridge of rocks that a glacier pushed up along its edges (a medial moraine) or at its foot (a terminal moraine)

Musalman – Nepali word for Muslim

naamlo – tumpline used to carry a load

nadi – small stream or river

naike – leader or chief, usually referring to the leader of a team of porters

nak – female yak

nala – stream; the correct transliteration is *naalaa*

namaste – Nepalese greeting, sometimes translated as 'I salute the God in you'

nanglo – round, flat-woven bamboo tray used for cleaning rice; commonly used as a tray for serving meals for trekkers

Newars – people of the Kathmandu Valley

NMA – Nepal Mountaineering Association, responsible for issuing permits for trekking peaks

nup – west (Tibetan) eg, Nuptse is the west peak of Everest

Nyingmapa – one of the three Red Hat sects of Tibetan Buddhism

om mani padme hum – sacred Buddhist mantra that roughly translates as 'hail to the jewel in the lotus'

paisa – one one-hundredth of a rupee, but used commonly as a word for money

panch – five

panchayat – the partyless parliamentary system of Nepal until 1990

pani – water

parbat – mountain

pashmina – blanket or shawl made from fine goat's wool

Pharak – Sherpa region south of Khumbu

phedi – foot of a hill

phul – egg

pipal – also known as the bo or bodhi tree, it is the female counterpart of the banyan tree

pokhari – large water tank or lake

prayer flag – long strips of cloth printed with prayers that are 'said' whenever the flag flaps in the wind

prayer wheel – cylindrical wheel inscribed with prayers and containing paper on which are written innumerable prayers. They can be hand-held or as much as three metres high.

puja – religious offering or prayer (pronounced 'pooja')

pundits – Indians who were sent into Nepal and Tibet by the Survey of India to secretly gather geographical information

Rai – major ethnic group of eastern Nepal

rajmarg – road or highway, literally 'king's road'

rakshi – distilled spirits made from grain

Rana – hereditary prime ministers who ruled Nepal from 1841 to 1951

rato – red

ri – peak or mountain (Tibetan)

rimpoche – reincarnate lama, usually the abbot of a gompa

RNAC – Royal Nepal Airways Corporation, the government-owned airline

roti – see chapatti

saat – seven

SAARC – South Asia Association for Regional Cooperation. This includes the seven countries of Bangladesh, Bhutan, India, Maldives, Nepal, Pakistan and Sri Lanka.

sadhu – wandering Hindu holy man

Sagarmatha – Nepali name for Mt Everest

sahib – term for a Westerner that dates from the time of the British Raj

Sakyamuni – another name for Gautama Buddha

sal – hardwood tree of the Terai and Himalayan foothills

saligram – black ammonite fossils of Jurassic period sea creatures, proof that the Himalaya was once under water

sangu – bridge

serac – large ice block on a glacier

shar – east (Tibetan)

Sherpa – literally 'people from the east', the Sherpas are Buddhist hill people who are most famed for their work with treks and mountaineering expeditions. With a small 's', sherpa means worker with a trek group.

Sherpani – female Sherpa

Shiva – most powerful Hindu god, the creator and destroyer

sirdar – boss or headman on a trekking or climbing expedition; the role is traditionally filled by a Sherpa

sisnu – stinging nettle

Siwalik – Indian name for the Churia Hills

solja – Tibetan tea flavoured with salt and butter

Solu Khumbu – the district immediately south of Mt Everest, inhabited mostly by Sherpas

sonam – good luck (Tibetan)

STOL – 'short-take-off-and-landing' aircraft

stupa – hemispherical Buddhist religious structure similar to a chorten

suntala – orange or tangerine

TAAN – Trekking Agents Association of Nepal

tahr – wild mountain goat

tal – lake; the correct transliteration is *taal*

Tamang – Tibeto-Burman ethnic group, most of whom live in the Middle Hills

tamba – copper

tarkari – vegetables

tato – hot

tawa – Tibetan Buddhist monk

tempo – three-wheeled taxi scooter

Terai – flat plains in the south of Nepal

Thakali – people of the Kali Gandaki Valley who specialize in running hotels

Thakuri – highest warrior caste from western Nepal

Thamel – the trekkers' and budget travellers' district of Kathmandu

thangka – Tibetan religious painting

thar – species or clan (similar to *jaat*)

Tharu – indigenous people of the Terai

thukpa – noodles, often served in a soup

thulo – big

Tihar – the 'festival of lights' that occurs a week after Dasain

tole – street or quarter of a town or village

tonga – two-wheeled horse drawn cart

tongba – a drink made from fermented millet seeds

topi – traditional Nepalese cap

trisul – trident weapon of Shiva

tsampa – barley flour, a staple food of Tibetans

tsho – lake (Tibetan)

Wai Wai – a brand of instant noodles good for a quick trekking meal. Another brand of noodles is Rara.

yak – main beast of burden and form of cattle above 3000 metres elevation

yarsa – fields for crops above the uppermost houses of a village. Its literal translation is *yar* 'summer', *sa* 'ground'

yeti – the abominable snowman

Index

TREKS

PLANET TALK
Lonely Planet's FREE quarterly newsletter

We love hearing from you and think you'd like to hear from us.

When...*is the right time to see reindeer in Finland?*
Where...*can you hear the best palm-wine music in Ghana?*
How...*do you get from Asunción to Areguá by steam train?*
What...*is the best way to see India?*

For the answer to these and many other questions read PLANET TALK.

Every issue is packed with up-to-date travel news and advice including:

- *a letter from Lonely Planet founders Tony and Maureen Wheeler*
- *travel diary from a Lonely Planet author - find out what it's really like out on the road*
- *feature article on an important and topical travel issue*
- *a selection of recent letters from our readers*
- *the latest travel news from all over the world*
- *details on Lonely Planet's new and forthcoming releases*

To join our mailing list contact any Lonely Planet office (address below).

LONELY PLANET PUBLICATIONS
Australia: PO Box 617, Hawthorn 3122, Victoria (tel: 03-819 1877)
USA: Embarcadero West, 155 Filbert St, Suite 251, Oakland, CA 94607 (tel: 510-893 8555)
TOLL FREE: (800) 275-8555
UK: 10 Barley Mow Passage, Chiswick, London W4 4PH (tel: 081-742 3161)
France: 71 bis rue du Cardinal Lemoine – 75005 Paris (tel: 46 34 00 58)

Also available: Lonely Planet T-shirts. 100% heavyweight cotton (S, M, L, XL)

Guides to the Indian Subcontinent

Bangladesh – a travel survival kit
This practical guide – the only English-language guide to Bangladesh – encourages travellers to take another look at this often-neglected but beautiful land.

India – a travel survival kit
Widely regarded as *the* guide to India, this award-winning book has all the information to help you make the most of the unforgettable experience that is India.

Karakoram Highway* the high road to China *– a travel survival kit
Travel in the footsteps of Alexander the Great and Marco Polo on the Karakoram Highway, following the ancient and fabled Silk Road. This comprehensive guide also covers villages and treks away from the highway.

Kashmir, Ladakh & Zanskar – a travel survival kit
Detailed information on three contrasting Himalayan regions in the Indian state of Jammu & Kashmir – the narrow valley of Zanskar, the isolated 'little Tibet' of Ladakh, and the stunningly beautiful Vale of Kashmir.

Nepal – a travel survival kit
Travel information on every road-accessible area in Nepal, including the Terai. This practical guidebook also includes introductions to trekking, white-water rafting and mountain biking.

Pakistan – a travel survival kit
Discover 'the unknown land of the Indus' with this informative guidebook – from bustling Karachi to ancient cities and tranquil mountain valleys.

Sri Lanka – a travel survival kit
Some parts of Sri Lanka are off limits to visitors, but this guidebook uses the restriction as an incentive to explore other areas more closely – making the most of friendly people, good food and pleasant places to stay – all at reasonable cost.

Tibet – a travel survival kit
The fabled mountain-land of Tibet was one of the last areas of the world to become accessible to travellers. This guide has full details on this remote and fascinating region, including the border crossing to Nepal.

Trekking in the Indian Himalaya
All the advice you'll need for planning and equipping a trek, including detailed route descriptions for some of the world's most exciting treks.

Also available:
Hindi/Urdu phrasebook, ***Nepal*** phrasebook and ***Sri Lanka*** phrasebook.

Lonely Planet Guidebooks

Lonely Planet guidebooks cover every accessible part of Asia as well as Australia, the Pacific, South America, Africa, the Middle East, Europe and parts of North America. There are five series: *travel survival kits*, covering a country for a range of budgets; *shoestring guides* with compact information for low-budget travel in a major region; *walking guides*; *city guides* and *phrasebooks*.

Australia & the Pacific
Australia
Bushwalking in Australia
Islands of Australia's Great Barrier Reef
Fiji
Melbourne city guide
Micronesia
New Caledonia
New Zealand
Tramping in New Zealand
Papua New Guinea
Bushwalking in Papua New Guinea
Papua New Guinea phrasebook
Rarotonga & the Cook Islands
Samoa
Solomon Islands
Sydney city guide
Tahiti & French Polynesia
Tonga
Vanuatu
Victoria

South-East Asia
Bali & Lombok
Bangkok city guide
Cambodia
Indonesia
Indonesia phrasebook
Laos
Malaysia, Singapore & Brunei
Myanmar (Burma)
Burmese phrasebook
Philippines
Pilipino phrasebook
Singapore city guide
South-East Asia on a shoestring
Thailand
Thai phrasebook
Vietnam
Vietnamese phrasebook

North-East Asia
China
Beijing city guide
Cantonese phrasebook
Mandarin Chinese phrasebook
Hong Kong, Macau & Canton
Japan
Japanese phrasebook
Korea
Korean phrasebook
Mongolia
North-East Asia on a shoestring
Seoul city guide
Taiwan
Tibet
Tibet phrasebook
Tokyo city guide

Middle East
Arab Gulf States
Egypt & the Sudan
Arabic (Egyptian) phrasebook
Iran
Israel
Jordan & Syria
Middle East
Turkish phrasebook
Trekking in Turkey
Yemen

Indian Ocean
Madagascar & Comoros
Maldives & Islands of the East Indian Ocean
Mauritius, Réunion & Seychelles

Mail Order

Lonely Planet guidebooks are distributed worldwide. They are also available by mail order from Lonely Planet, so if you have difficulty finding a title please write to us. US and Canadian residents should write to Embarcadero West, 155 Filbert St, Suite 251, Oakland CA 94607, USA; European residents should write to 10 Barley Mow Passage, Chiswick, London W4 4PH; and residents of other countries to PO Box 617, Hawthorn, Victoria 3122, Australia.

Indian Subcontinent
Bangladesh
India
Hindi/Urdu phrasebook
Trekking in the Indian Himalaya
Karakoram Highway
Kashmir, Ladakh & Zanskar
Nepal
Trekking in the Nepal Himalaya
Nepali phrasebook
Pakistan
Sri Lanka
Sri Lanka phrasebook

Africa
Africa on a shoestring
Central Africa
East Africa
Trekking in East Africa
Kenya
Swahili phrasebook
Morocco, Algeria & Tunisia
Arabic (Moroccan) phrasebook
South Africa, Lesotho & Swaziland
Zimbabwe, Botswana & Namibia
West Africa

Central America
Baja California
Central America on a shoestring
Costa Rica
La Ruta Maya
Mexico

North America
Alaska
Canada
Hawaii

Europe
Baltic States & Kaliningrad
Dublin city guide
Eastern Europe on a shoestring
Eastern Europe phrasebook
Finland
France
Greece
Hungary
Iceland, Greenland & the Faroe Islands
Ireland
Italy
Mediterranean Europe on a shoestring
Mediterranean Europe phrasebook
Poland
Scandinavian & Baltic Europe on a shoestring
Scandinavian Europe phrasebook
Switzerland
Trekking in Spain
Trekking in Greece
USSR
Russian phrasebook
Western Europe on a shoestring
Western Europe phrasebook

South America
Argentina, Uruguay & Paraguay
Bolivia
Brazil
Brazilian phrasebook
Chile & Easter Island
Colombia
Ecuador & the Galápagos Islands
Latin American Spanish phrasebook
Peru
Quechua phrasebook
South America on a shoestring
Trekking in the Patagonian Andes

The Lonely Planet Story

Lonely Planet published its first book in 1973 in response to the numerous 'How did you do it?' questions Maureen and Tony Wheeler were asked after driving, bussing, hitching, sailing and railing their way from England to Australia.

Written at a kitchen table and hand collated, trimmed and stapled, *Across Asia on the Cheap* became an instant local bestseller, inspiring thoughts of another book.

Eighteen months in South-East Asia resulted in their second guide, *South-East Asia on a shoestring*, which they put together in a backstreet Chinese hotel in Singapore in 1975. The 'yellow bible' as it quickly became known to backpackers around the world, soon became *the* guide to the region. It has sold well over half a million copies and is now in its 7th edition, still retaining its familiar yellow cover.

Today there are over 130 Lonely Planet titles in print – books that have that same adventurous approach to travel as those early guides; books that 'assume you know how to get your luggage off the carousel' as one reviewer put it.

Although Lonely Planet initially specialised in guides to Asia, they now cover most regions of the world, including the Pacific, South America, Africa, the Middle East and Europe. The list of *walking guides* and *phrasebooks* (for 'unusual' languages such as Quechua, Swahili, Nepali and Egyptian Arabic) is also growing rapidly.

The emphasis continues to be on travel for independent travellers. Tony and Maureen still travel for several months of each year and play an active part in the writing, updating and quality control of Lonely Planet's guides.

They have been joined by over 50 authors, 60 staff – mainly editors, cartographers & designers – at our office in Melbourne, Australia, at our US office in Oakland, California and at our European office in Paris; another five at our office in London handle sales for Britain, Europe and Africa. Travellers themselves also make a valuable contribution to the guides through the feedback we receive in thousands of letters each year.

The people at Lonely Planet strongly believe that travellers can make a positive contribution to the countries they visit, both through their appreciation of the countries' culture, wildlife and natural features, and through the money they spend. In addition, the company makes a direct contribution to the countries and regions it covers. Since 1986 a percentage of the income from each book has been donated to ventures such as famine relief in Africa; aid projects in India; agricultural projects in Central America; Greenpeace's efforts to halt French nuclear testing in the Pacific and Amnesty International. In 1993 $100,000 was donated to such causes.

Lonely Planet's basic travel philosophy is summed up in Tony Wheeler's comment, 'Don't worry about whether your trip will work out. Just go!'.